STIRLING MACOBOY'S

WHAT
FLOWER
IS THAT?

STIRLING MACOBOY'S

WHAT FLOWER IS THAT?

CHARTWELL
BOOKS, INC.

Published by

CHARTWELL BOOKS, INC.

A Division of **BOOK SALES, INC.**

114 Northfield Avenue

Edison, New Jersey 08837

© Copyright: Stirling Macoboy 2000

© Copyright design: Lansdowne Publishing Pty Ltd 2000

Produced and created by Lansdowne Publishing Pty Ltd

Project Coordinator: Kate Merrifield

Editor: Sue Wagner

Designer: Stephanie Doyle

Production Manager: Kristy Nelson

Set in Minion and Tiepolo on QuarkXPress

Printed in Singapore by Kyodo Printing Pte Ltd

CIP data available on application:

Book Sales Inc.

276 Fifth Avenue, Suite 206

New York, New York 10001

ISBN 0-7858-1187-7

Unless otherwise credited, all photographs are from Stirling Macoboy's photo library.

Photographs

Endpapers: *Cosmos sulphureus*

Half title page: *Tigridia pavonia*

Page 2: *Fuchsia* 'Flash'

Title page: *Lilium* 'Casablanca'

Page 5: *Portulaca grandiflora*

Page 6: *Cyclamen persicum*

Page 9: *Neomarica caerulea*

Page 419: *Gelsemium sempervirens*

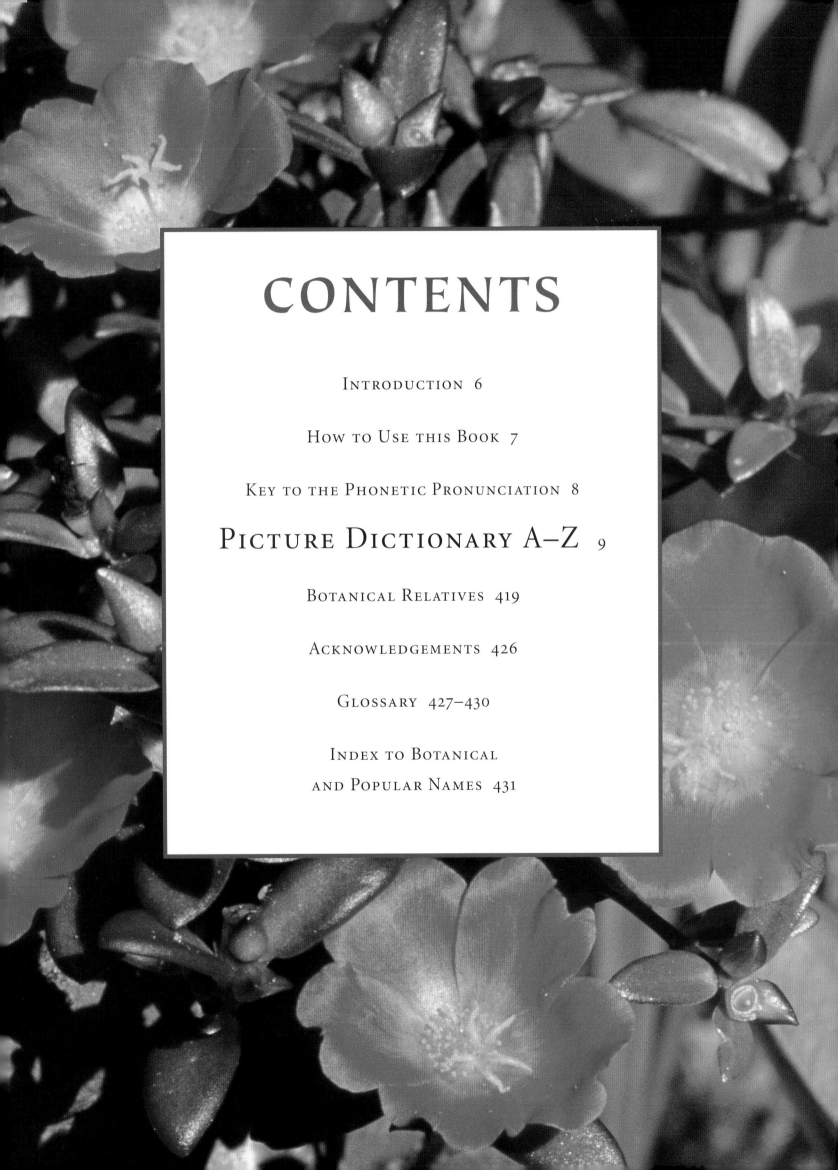

CONTENTS

INTRODUCTION

When *What Flower is That?* first came out way back in 1969, I little dreamed it would outlive the century. Yet to my surprise and delight, people are still asking for it – so here is a wholly new edition to take it into the new millennium.

Many new flowers have been added; actually most are not really new – they have been around for millennia, but haven't posed for my cameras before. But some *are* new, for gardeners never cease to create new cultivars in our favourite genera, and it seemed timely to bring my selection of these up to date. In many other cases, the flowers are the same familiar and much-loved faces, but presented in new and, I hope, better and more life-like portraits.

The text has also been completely revised, corrected and brought up to date – and here I must pay tribute to my collaborators, Roger Mann and Tony Rodd, though any errors that remain are of course mine. Tony's specialised knowledge has been invaluable in steering me through the maze of changes to the scientific names that have been made since the last edition was published in 1986, some of which were only put in place while the text was being prepared; and Roger's help has been invaluable in writing and reorganising the individual entries.

Sue Wagner, editor of so many of my titles over the years, went far beyond what would normally be expected of an editor on this project. For her expertise and tireless efforts I truly am most grateful. My thanks also to my assistant Colin Olson, who, in addition to assembling the photographs as well as numerous other such onerous tasks, also took some of the photographs for this edition.

As listing alphabetically by the Latin scientific name is really the simplest way to present a collection of plants as diverse as this – and I flatter myself that there are now very few garden-worthy genera that have escaped inclusion – this has meant that some old friends will be turning up in unfamiliar places. I've tried to cross-reference as comprehensively as may be; but if you have trouble finding a familiar flower, the index will lead you to its new address.

If you find changes of name vexatious, well so do I: but the botanists don't change a familiar name except for good and cogent reasons, and we gardeners must learn to live with them. We soon become used to the new name, and the beauty of the flower remains the same as it ever was.

What success this book has had is entirely due to the beauty of its subject; and I place this new edition before you in the knowledge that the flowers themselves will be its best ambassadors. May they long endure to speak their age-old message of peace and joy, whatever changes and troubles the new millennium brings.

STIRLING MACOBOY
Neutral Bay, New South Wales

HOW TO USE THIS BOOK

The flowers in this book are arranged in the alphabetical order of their botanical names – names which are used and recognized throughout the world in the scientific community. Some of these names may be hard to remember, as they are largely based on Latin and Ancient Greek, both dead languages. But it is precisely because they *are* dead languages, and thus not subject to day-by-day change, that Latin and Greek are used for scientific purposes. They are not in everyday use, but do have the advantage of being internationally understood, which popular names in any modern language are not.

Even in the botanic gardens of Japan and the USSR, you will find the plants labelled with their botanical names as well as any common name in local use.

If you already know the botanical name of a flower you want to look up, just turn through the alphabetically arranged pictorial section until you find the right heading, followed by the picture of the flower you seek.

If you don't know the botanical name, or what the flower looks like, turn to the index at the back of the book, where you'll find the more common English-language names listed, also alphabetically, with cross-references to the correct botanical name. Be warned, however: one popular name may apply to several different plants, and there are more popular names listed than there are plants in the book, because one plant may have many different popular names in many different countries.

The botanical names are also listed in the comprehensive index, together with all known synonyms. In the context of plants, a synonym (abbreviated to SYN) is a scientific name which is no longer accepted, but may still appear. All synonyms have been indexed, with cross-references to the correct generic name.

genus or generic name . . . . *CLARKIA*
pronunciation guide (see page X) . . . . (klah-kee-ə)
synonym . . . . (SYN Godetia)
common or popular names . . . . Rocky Mountain Garland, Godetia, Satinflower, Farewell-to-spring
family name species . . . . ONAGRACEAE
or specific name

Each main entry in the pictorial section is headed with the botanical name of the flower's *genus*, which corresponds to your family name, e.g. *Narcissus*. These generic names are printed in *italic* type everywhere in the book; in the headings they appear in *ITALIC CAPITALS*. Beneath the generic name, in parentheses, is a simple phonetic guide to its pronunciation; a key to this pronunciation guide is on page 8. Any synonym, or superseded generic name, is given in parentheses next.

Underneath the phonetic pronunciation you will find the popular names of the most prominent flowers in the genus – one or more of them, according to usage.

Beneath a horizontal line, and this time in CAPITALS, is the name of the botanical family to which the flower belongs. (In the case of *Narcissus* it is AMARYLLIDACEAE, the Amaryllids.) In botany,

the family is a larger group including many related genera with similar characteristics – for example, the family Amaryllidaceae includes many other bulbous plants, such as *Clivia, Crinum, Hippeastrum* and *Nerine.*

Within many dictionary entries, you will find reference to some of the most popular species of the genus in cultivation. *Specific* or *species* names correspond to our given or personal names. Specific names are also printed in italic type, but without an initial capital. Where several species are described, the generic name is abbreviated after its first usage to its initial *Italic* capital with a full stop, to save space.

Sometimes, the generic and specific names will be followed by a third name. This is either a varietal or a cultivar name, which further identifies the flower when two varieties have the same generic and specific names.

Varietal names are used when it is necessary to distinguish some small natural point of difference – a flower colour or leaf marking, or a particular habit of growth that reproduces constantly from seed. Varietal names are also printed in *italic* type.

Cultivar names fall in the same position when it is necessary to refer to some characteristic or sport of the flower that seems capable of cultivation only by means of cuttings (raised from seed it might revert to the original). Cultivar names are usually in a modern language instead of Latin or Greek. They are printed in roman type and enclosed in quotes. Sometimes they are identified by the abbreviation CV.

Another word you'll run across is *hybrid* or *hybrida*. This is used when each of a plant's parents is of a different species. Hybrids are often raised by nurseries to produce superior new strains, just as breeders of horses and cattle try to improve their stock. A hybrid is often indicated by X between the generic and specific names.

When the X appears before the generic name, the plant is a bigeneric hybrid or cross between two different genera. These are quite rare.

Individual generic entries give all sorts of additional information for the home gardener: the plant's type, e.g. annual, perennial, tree, bulb, shrub; its mature height and spread and speed of growth; its flowering time, country of origin, methods of propagation, soil requirements, minimum necessary winter temperature, ideal position or light intensity, natural pests and diseases, popular names, uses in medicine, commerce or history and many other things.

Under every photograph is a brief caption giving the illustrated flower's botanical name, and one or more of its popular names.

Later in the book you'll find a useful glossary of botanical terms, and an illustrated listing of genera included in the most poplar botanical families – yet another useful way of deciding just where a particular flower belongs by its family relationships.

Nothing, we hope, that would help you identify (at least partially) any flower that you're likely to see anywhere in the world has been overlooked.

And you'll never be stuck for an answer when somebody asks – *What Flower is That?*

Magnolia liliiflora

Magnolia stellata

Magnolia denudata

Pictures tell the story best. The three lovely flowers above share the Latin generic name *Magnolia*, but have individual specific names to describe their differing habits.

Magnolia liliiflora has lily-shaped flowers, and is one parent of the more popular hybrid *M.* X *soulangeana*. Slender petalled.

Magnolia stellata is called the Star Magnolia. A many-branched shrub, it generally has 14-petalled blooms only 7cm/3in wide.

Magnolia denudata, the Yulan, has 7 or 8 pure white petals; it is often sold under an earlier name, *M. heptapeta*.

KEY TO THE PHONETIC PRONUNCIATION

Each flower entry in this book is headed by that flower's generic name, followed immediately by a simple phonetic guide to its pronunciation. There are still many differences of opinion as to how these botanical names should be pronounced, but the phonetic guide below should help set you on the right track. The spelling will often differ from the normal spelling of the generic name, because English vowels, and some consonants, can be pronounced in many different ways. (Look at the vowel 'a' in fat, fate, father and fare, or the consonant 'c' in cat and ace.) In a phonetic guide, each letter or group of letters represents one specific sound, and that sound only. But because there are more sounds in English than there are letters in the English alphabet or its recognised diphthongs, we also use one extra symbol (∂) to represent the many indeterminate vowel sounds heard in words like alone, system, terrible, gallop and circus.

Beyond that, we have separated each syllable from the next by a hyphen, and printed the syllable to be stressed in bold type.

Each separate letter or letter combination is always pronounced according to the following.

a	. . . . fat	d	. . . . do, cod
ae	. . . . . . pay, fate, sleigh	f	. . . . reef, rough, phone
ah	. . . . . mark, father	g	. . . . gas, bag
ai	. . . . ice, high, buy, cycle	h	. . . . help, ahoy
∂	. . . . alone, system, terrible, gallop, circus	j	. . . . jaws, gem, rage
e	. . . . deaf, den	k	. . . . cat, sack
ee	. . . . . teach, see	l	. . . . limb, mill
e∂	. . . . . air, dared	m	. . . . . . more, rummy
i	. . . . fit, tiff, gym	n	. . . . ton, tonight
o	. . . . sot, toss	p	. . . . pal, lap
oh	. . . . . oath, both, crow	r	. . . . rot, trot
oi	. . . . . . boy, royal	s	. . . . sale, lace
oo	. . . . . prove, pool, glue	sh	. . . . . . shade, motion
or	. . . . . ought, more, roar	t	. . . . tone, note
ou	. . . . . cow, crouch, slough	th	. . . . . . thin, both, loathe
u	. . . . . . suck, son, rough	v	. . . . vat, cave
ur	. . . . . err, circus	w	. . . . win, twin
b	. . . . bat, tab	y	. . . . yellow
ch	. . . . . chip, patch	z	. . . . zip, toes, rose
		zh	. . . . . . measure, invasion

Remember, the sound of each phonetic letter or letter-group remains constant. As examples, here are five consecutive generic names and their phonetic pronunciations.

ARCTOTHECA (ark-**toth**-e-k∂)
ARGEMONE (ar-**gem**-o-nee)
ARISAEMA (ar-is-**ee**-m∂)
ARISTOLOCHIA (ar-is-to-**loh**-kee-∂)
ARPOPHYLLUM (ar-poh-**fil**-lum)

PICTURE DICTIONARY A-Z

Abelia triflora. Deciduous Abelia

Abelia grandiflora. Glossy Abelia

Abelia floribunda. Mexican Abelia

Abelmoschus moschatus. Musk Mallow

ABELIA
(a-**beel**-ee-∂)
Abelia
CAPRIFOLIACEAE

Panicles of fragrant bell-flowers cluster in summer at the tips of graceful, arching canes in *Abelia*. This useful shrub genus from Mexico and China grows fast to a height of 1–2m/3–6ft. Lightly toothed, glossy foliage, a fountain-like habit and persistent red calyces are among other decorative features. All species may be planted out in autumn or early spring in any leaf-rich soil; they prefer full sun. In really cold areas, they'll need the shelter of a wall or larger bushes to protect them from prevailing winds.

Popular species include: Mexican *A. floribunda* with tubular carmine blooms 5cm/2in long; *A. grandiflora* with pink-flushed bells only 1.5cm/½in long, and its variegated sport, 'Frances Mason'. Chinese *A. schumannii* has a denser habit, and 2.5cm/1in mauve-pink blooms. Himalayan *A. triflora* is especially fragrant. All normally deciduous, they'll remain evergreen in warmer climates. Propagate from summer cuttings at a temperature of 16°C/61°F. Prune to change habit in winter, trim lightly from time to time where a more compact shape is desired. Feed in spring.

Abelias belong to the Honeysuckle family, Caprifoliaceae, along with Weigela, Kolkwitzia and the Viburnums.

ABELMOSCHUS
(ae-bel-**mos**-k∂s)
Musk Mallow
MALVACEAE

In its native India *Abelmoschus moschatus* is widely grown for its fragrant seeds, which are used in perfumery; elsewhere it is admired for its cheerful red and white flowers. The plant is an annual and is sown in spring to bear its flowers in succession as long as the summer lasts. Older strains grew to a rather ungainly 2m/6ft tall, but now that dwarf cultivars of 60cm/2ft or less are available, we should see it more often. Rich soil and sunshine are preferred, and the longer and hotter the summer the better. *A. moschatus* is one of several similar species recently transferred from Hibiscus to a genus of their own; the inelegant name *Abelmoschus* is a latinisation of the Arabic *abu-l-mosk*, meaning 'father-of-musk', alluding to the seeds.

ABUTILON
(ab-**yew**-til-on)
(SYN Corynabutilon)
Chinese Bellflower, Chinese Lantern
MALVACEAE

Fast-growing, leggy shrubs to 2.5m/8ft, *Abutilons* are best trained up columns or against sunny walls so the beauty of their hanging flowers can be enjoyed all through the warm weather. They like rich, damp soil, and flower best in full sun. Pinch back often to encourage branching and improved flower yield. Heavy feeding makes them bolt, so give only a very dilute fertiliser to replace nutrient leached out of the soil.

Most commonly seen are the many cultivars grouped as *A. hybridum*. These include 'Emperor' and 'Vesuvius' with red blooms; pink 'Tunisia'; bright yellow 'Golden Fleece'; white 'Boule de Neige'; and the variegated form 'Souvenir de Bonn'.

Abutilon hybridum. Chinese Lantern

Abutilon megapotamicum. Big River Abutilon

Abutilon suntense. Chilean Bellflower

Acacia baileyana. Cootamundra Wattle

Acacia boormanii. Snowy River Wattle

Acacia cultriformis cultivar. Knife-leaf Acacia

Acacia podalyriifolia. Silver Wattle

Acacia pycnantha. Golden Wattle

Some 100 natural species are also grown. Among the most worthwhile is the sprawling Big River Abutilon, *A. megapotamicum,* from Brazil, particularly in its variegated form. This may be used as a dense groundcover in warmer areas, or trained as a wall shrub. Its hybrid *A. milleri* has larger leaves and more open, red-veined blooms. *A. pictum* has orange blooms veined in red.

The Chilean Bellflower, *A. suntense,* formerly *Corynabutilon suntense,* may reach 7.5m/25ft; its flat, 5-petalled flowers are mauvish in tone.

In cold climates, *Abutilons* are sometimes raised as indoor plants; they bloom best when rootbound.

ACACIA
(ə-**kae**-shə)
Wattle, Mimosa
Mimosaceae

So typically Australian that one of them (the Golden Wattle) is the nation's floral symbol, *Acacias* are by no means exclusive to that continent: Africa has many species, Asia and America quite a few. There are more than 1200 species worldwide.

Australia's *Acacias* are, however, notably the most decorative, bursting into fragrant masses of golden blossom at different times of the year according to species, but principally in winter and spring. *Acacia* flowers are very *un*typical members of the pea family, Mimosaceae. They have no petals, only stamens, but they do develop into the same long pods as other peas, with the seeds attached alternately to either shell.

Acacia blossom is generally sold as 'mimosa' in Europe and America, but the true *Mimosa* is a different, though related plant, illustrated elsewhere in this book. Few *Acacia* species grow into large trees, or live very long, but they grow fast and are often used to provide quick colour in the new garden, or give protection from sun along fields and roads. All prefer full sun and grow satisfactorily in poor soil.

Acacia saligna. Golden Wreath Wattle

Acalypha wilkesiana cultivar. Beefsteak Plant

Acaena novae-zelandiae. Bidi Bidi

ACAENA
(a-**kee**-n∂)
Bidi Bidi, New Zealand Burr
ROSACEAE

Unlike most other members of the rose family, *Acaena* has no petals to its flowers. In fact the very name comes from the ancient Greek *akanthos*, meaning a thorn. Not that they are spiny plants – they just look it. Each inflorescence consists of a number of petal-less flowers, arranged so that their colourful stamens point outward in all directions like a spiny dandelion puffball or surrealistic modern fountain. There are some 100 species of these dwarf, ground-covering plants, all looking exceedingly attractive planted between stones or spilling over flat, gravelly surfaces. They blanket the ground completely with tiny, compound, evergreen rose-like leaves, sending up their puffball flower clusters on slender stems. They are reasonably frost hardy, and better suited to cool temperate climates in open sunny positions, though illustrated *A. novae-zelandiae* looks best in semi-shade. Most species are from New Zealand; a few are South American in origin. Propagate from cuttings.

Acalypha hispida. Red Hot Cat's Tail

ACALYPHA
(a-**kal**-i-f∂)
Red Hot Cat's Tail, Beefsteak Plant, Fire Dragon Plant, Copper Leaf
EUPHORBIACEAE

Acalyphas are eye-catching plants for the warmer climate or glasshouse. The Red Hot Cat's Tail (*A. hispida*) is noted for woolly red flower spikes which droop to a length of 45cm/18in all over the plant, and are spectacular in a mature specimen. Warmth, high humidity and plenty of liquid fertiliser are advisable. Its cousin *A. wilkesiana*, a tall shrub with variegated red and pink leaves, might be mistaken for an overgrown Coleus. It is actually related to the Poinsettia. Of tropical origin, they grow quite satisfactorily in mild coastal areas with winter temperatures down to 2°C/36°F, though with some loss of leaves. They strike easily from cuttings in warm weather. Plant several of them in a large pot for maximum display; cut back to about 25cm/10in and fertilise in late winter to stimulate growth. They'll look good all year round in a sheltered courtyard or sunroom, or can be used as a hedge or background plant. Many colour varieties are available.

ACANTHUS
(a-kan-th∂s)
Oyster Plant, Bear's Breech

ACANTHACEAE

Immortalised by the Greeks in the carved capitals of their Corinthian columns, the *Acanthus* species are hardy perennials, grown mostly for their handsome foliage. Use them in temperate gardens as a striking feature. Plant in semi-shade or in a sheltered court-yard – but lay plenty of snail bait! All manner of pests seem to find them irresistible. Grow *Acanthus* from autumn divisions or from seed sown in spring at a temperature of 14ºC/57ºF. Germination takes about three weeks. Soil should be well drained, rich and neutral in acidity. The satiny leaves vary greatly in shape according to species, but are all elegantly lobed and broadly toothed. Early summer flowers of mauve and grey appear in spikes up to 2m/6ft tall, after which the plant dies back. Slow to establish, *Acanthus* spreads rapidly when settled in. Dead-head after blooming and water generously except when dormant.

ACHILLEA
(a-kil-lee-∂)
Milfoil, Yarrow, Sneezeweed

ASTERACEAE

Named for Achilles, a hero of the Greeks, who used the plant medicinally, the popular Yarrows are among the most trouble-free of perennials. They'll grow in any moderately fertile soil, so long as it is fast-draining. Propagate them from winter divisions, or from seed, which germinates in days.

Achilleas need only full sun and occasional water to help them produce masses of bloom in the summer border. Leaves of all species are lacy and finely divided; available flower colours include white, yellow, pink and red. The genus includes dainty dwarf plants and tall perennials ranging from 50–150cm/20–60in.

Plant at intervals of 36–60cm/1–2ft and water lightly. They are fairly drought resis-tant, and produce masses of dull, fern-like foliage with minimum water. Several bloom-ings can be expected each summer when you cut flower stems. *A. filipendulina* produces flat heads of tiny gold flowers. *A. millefolium* is deep pink, centred white. *A. ptarmica* (Sneezeweed) blooms greenish-white. Cut all species back almost to ground level in winter, and give complete fertiliser in spring.

Acanthus dioscoridis var. *parringii*. Oyster Plant

Achillea filipendulina. Goldplate, Fernleaf Yarrow

Acanthus spinosus. Mountain Thistle

Acanthus mollis. Oyster Plant

Achillea jaborneggii. Hybrid Achillea

Achillea ligustica. Yarrow

Achillea millefolium cultivar. Milfoil

Achillea tomentosa. Sneezeweed

Achimenes hybrid. Hot Water Plant

Acokanthera oblongifolia. Bushman's Poison

Actinodium cunninghamii. Swamp Daisy

ACHIMENES

(a-kə-**mee**-neez)

Hot Water Plant, Magic Flower

GESNERIACEAE

Related to African Violets and Gloxinias, *Achimenes* are found wild in Central America. Their name means 'cold-suffering', and a cold snap in the growing season may make them go dormant unless you give warm water, hence the popular name. Put the small scaly tubers in a sandy-acid soil mixture with plenty of leaf mould, and maintain a constant level of moisture until flowers appear. They like sun in the spring, but more sheltered conditions in summer. The many varieties (which include white, pink, blue, orange and red-spotted yellow flowers) are hybrids from original species, and have varying habits – upright, bushy or trailing – the latter particularly spectacular in hanging baskets.

Aconitum napellus. Monkshood, Wolfbane

ACOKANTHERA

(ak-o-**kan**-thur-ə)

Wintersweet, Bushman's Poison

APOCYNACEAE

This genus of decorative African shrubs was once valued principally as the source of arrow poison. But European settlers eagerly adopted them for garden use, particularly in coastal areas, for *Acokantheras* are tolerant of poor soil, wind and salt air. Plant in full sun as 3m/10ft specimens, or trim as a hedge; all they need is ample water in summer to turn on a year-round show. In the case of *A. oblongifolia*, the evergreen leaves glow with red-purple, and dense clusters of pale pink flowers appear all year. They are lightly fragrant, and are followed by 2.5cm/1in plum-coloured poisonous fruits in autumn and winter. Propagate from seeds, cuttings or, in the case of the variegated form, by grafting. *Acokantheras* should be pruned lightly after bloom, and are hardy down to –2°C/28°F.

ACONITUM

(ak-o-**nai**-təm)

Monkshood, Wolfbane, Aconite

RANUNCULACEAE

Steeped in medieval mysticism, as their popular names suggest, there really is something sinister about these European perennials – they are poisonous in every part, and were used in many potions of bygone days. Mostly they are tall-growing plants (up to 1.5m/5ft) with purple, blue or white helmet-shaped flowers in late summer. Plant them 40cm/16in apart in semi-shaded, rich soil – or a more sun-bathed position in cooler climates. They grow easily from divisions or seed – but the latter may take three years to bloom. Sow after spring at a temperature of 16°C/59°F. The deeply divided leaves are dark, satiny green, and the flowers develop in tall racemes, often branched, and keep

opening over a long period. *Aconitum napellus* blooms in violet-blue; *A. vulparia* may be mauve, pinkish or yellow. All Aconites die down in winter, and are a waste of space in warmer climates.

ACTINODIUM

(ak-tin-**oh**-dee-əm)

Swamp Daisy, Albany Daisy

MYRTACEAE

Papery pink and white daisy flowers nod on thin stems of *Actinodium*, the Swamp Daisy, a useful 1m/3ft shrub for acid coastal soils. Raise from cuttings, which strike easily in a damp mixture of peat and sand, then grow where they'll receive full sun all year but get wet feet during the cool winter-spring flowering period.

An erect, brittle plant with heath-like foliage, *A. cunninghamii* is altogether sparsely furnished when not in bloom. Though its spring flowers look like daisies (Asteraceae), they actually belong to the same family as eucalypts (Myrtaceae). The flower stems can be dried for arrangements, but the pale blooms are sometimes coloured by standing stems in a dye/water mixture. Short lived, *Actinodium* may be pruned after flowering.

ACTINOTUS

(ak-tin-**oh**-təs)

Flannel Flower

APIACEAE

The pale, furry Flannel Flower, *Actinotus helianthi*, has become a popular perennial in gardens of Australian native plants, and is grown in other warm, dryish places, such as southern California. It can also be used in cold-winter areas if treated as an annual, and is becoming popular as a cut flower. A sparse, erect-growing plant (to 50cm/20in), it bears much-divided foliage of soft greyish-green.

Actinotus helianthi. Flannel Flower

Adenandra uniflora. Enamel Flower

Adenium obesum. Impala Lily, Desert Rose

In spring and summer, furry flowering stems appear, topped by one or more star-shaped inflorescences up to 10cm/4in wide. These consist of a mass of pink-stamened, greenish florets, surrounded by green-tipped, flannel-textured bracts of dull white. They prefer full sun, good drainage and minimum disturbance. Plant *Actinotus* in sandy, acid soil with a little humus and gravel. Its needs are minimal once established.

ADENANDRA
(ad-en-**an**-drə)
Enamel Flower, China Flower

RUTACEAE

Included in the same family as Citrus and the Australian Boronias, this handsome handful of South African shrubs includes several popular evergreen species. Their foliage is minute, and very similar to that of the related Diosma. The flowers of illustrated *Adenandra uniflora* are about 2.5cm/1in across, borne singly at stem terminals. They are notably white and glossy, often bearing a deep pink streak in the centre of each petal; each anther is tipped with a tiny, curiously sticky gland. New stems are lightly

haired; dark leaves are paler on the reverse. Foliage is aromatic, the flowers mildly fragrant. All species are hardy down to –5ºC/23ºF, and do best in well-drained, gravelly soil. The plants do not grow large, and light watering is adequate. Propagate from cuttings in autumn.

ADENIUM
(ae-**den**-ee-əm)
Desert Rose, Desert Azalea, Impala Lily, Sabie Star

APOCYNACEAE

Named for the former British colony of Aden, part of its natural territory, the gorgeously flowering Desert Rose (*Adenium obesum*) resembles and is closely related to the Frangipani. A 2m/6ft tall, sparsely branched shrub in nature, with a swollen trunk base, it is more often seen in cultivation as a rather dwarfed pot plant. More drought resistant than Frangipani, it is propagated from dried-off branches struck in damp sand. *Adeniums* are evergreen in a warm climate, but it is useless to try them where there is frost. The leaves are glossy, oval, and widest at the tips. Flowers in

winter-spring are a brilliant scarlet-pink, centred with white and yellow, and borne in terminal clusters. They like a dry winter, and good drainage.

ADENOPHORA
(ad-en-**off**-or-ə)
Ladybells, Grand Bellflower

CAMPANULACEAE

No surprise to find these striking perennials included in the Campanula family – they look alike and are closely related, the difference being the presence of a nectar gland at the base of the style.

Illustrated *Adenophora liliifolia* blooms in late summer, sending up stems of mauve-blue bell-flowers 45cm/18in and more in height. They prefer a cool climate, full sun and a light but rich soil. Propagation by division is difficult, for they resent disturbance of the roots. Try ripe seed, sown in spring: it's slower but more reliable. Pleasantly fragrant.

Adenophora liliifolia. Ladybells

Aechmea fasciata. Urn Plant

ADONIS

(ə-**doh**-nis)

Pheasant's Eye, Red Morocco

RANUNCULACEAE

A favourite European and American annual not often seen in southern hemisphere gardens, the Pheasant's Eye (*Adonis aestivalis*) is closely related to Ranunculus, with feathery, dark green foliage and 4cm/2in flowers like scarlet buttercups. It enjoys light soil, moist and rich, and should be sown *in situ*, late autumn or early spring. Seeds take 2 weeks to germinate and young plants should be thinned to about 30cm/12in spacing; they grow to 40cm/16in. Fertilise

Adonis aestivalis. Pheasant's Eye

and water regularly, but don't expect flowers till early or midsummer. *Adonis* do well in light shade, and prefer coastal or hill areas where night temperatures drop below 18°C/65°F. They wilt badly in extreme heat and are best left as garden decoration, for the blooms shatter quickly when cut.

AECHMEA

(**ak**-mee-ə)

Vase Plant, Urn Plant

BROMELIACEAE

Fancy-dress members of the Pineapple family (or Bromeliads) from tropical America, *Aechmeas* are air-feeders, collecting nourishment from water and decaying matter in the upturned cups of their leaves. They can be grown wired onto pieces of driftwood (the roots covered in sphagnum moss); supported among clusters of large pebbles in open containers; even in open mixtures of leafmould and fibre with small additions of charcoal and sand. They are winter hardy provided they receive shelter from frost. Fertilise only once a year. A diluted solution of calcium carbonate in the leaf vase will produce flowers in about 6 weeks in warm weather.

A fine example of the 100-odd species is *Aechmea fasciata*, in which tiny mauve

blooms nestle among pink bracts, looking for all the world like a Victorian posy. Also popular is the Foster's Favourite group of cultivars, in which chains of coral berries hang among the wine-dark leaves.

Aechmea caudata. Urn Plant

Aechmea nidularioides. Vase Plant

Aeschynanthus 'Fireworks'. Lipstick Plant

Aeschynanthus speciosus. Lipstick Plant

AESCHYNANTHUS
(ees-kin-**an**-thus)
Lipstick Vine, Royal Red Bugler
GESNERIACEAE

Midsummer-flowering relatives of the African Violet, *Aeschynanthus* are succulent-leafed trailers from Southeast Asia. They are generally grown in baskets of moist, acid compost and hung in a warm, humid position in semi-shade. They need plenty of water in the warm-weather growing season. The flowers look like an orange-scarlet lipstick poking out of a dark red-green holder. Propagate in spring or late summer from hardened stem-tip cuttings.

A. *speciosus* has yellow-throated orange flowers; A. *lobbianus* has glossy light-green leaves, and yellow-lined red flowers; A. *marmoratus*, the Zebra Basket Vine, has handsome dark leaves veined with yellow, backed in purple, and brown-spotted green flowers; A. 'Fireworks' has light green leaves and red flowers with golden throats.

AETHIONEMA
(eth-ee-**on**-ə-mə)
Stonecress
BRASSICACEAE

Dainty members of the cress family, the 30-odd species of *Aethionema* are found naturally from the Mediterranean area to as far east as Iran. In cooler climates, they are great rock garden favourites, producing masses of tiny flowers like pink candytuft in late spring. They enjoy full sun with a cool root-run among stones which protect them equally from scorching summers and frosty winters. They like perfect drainage and a good but sandy soil, slightly on the alkaline side. Though they will rarely grow more than 20cm/8in high, they will easily spread twice as wide. The handsome, elongated leaves are evergreen and somewhat fleshy, and often of a distinctive greyish-green. Grow from seed or summer cuttings.

Aeonium arboreum. Pinwheel

AEONIUM
(ae-**oh**-nee-əm)
(SYN Sempervivum)
Canary Island Rose, Pinwheel
CRASSULACEAE

Over 30 species of succulent shrubs from North Africa and various Atlantic islands, the *Aeoniums* are excellent material for terraces, courtyards and dry, sunny positions. A poor-quality porous soil mixture grows them to perfection if you add plenty of sand and limestone chips. Propagation is easy from cuttings set into damp sand at the beginning of the growing season. The new plants will soon form a formal rosette of leaves (often on a long stalk) and produce tall spikes of starry yellow flowers in branched clusters. By no means frost hardy (they are mostly coastal plants), *Aeoniums* need a minimum winter temperature of 10°C/50°F and can take plenty of water in hot summers.
A. *canariense* is known as the Canary Island Rose or Velvet Rose, while illustrated A. *arboreum* is sometimes called the Pinwheel plant.

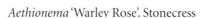
Aethionema 'Warley Rose'. Stonecress

Agapanthus praecox subsp. *orientalis.* Lily of the Nile

Agave americana. Century Plant

AGAPANTHUS
(ag-a-**pan**-thəs)
Lily of the Nile, African Lily
AMARYLLIDACEAE

An elderly gardening friend of mine enjoyed for years the incursions of small boys looking for lost tennis balls on his demesne. 'Beware the agapanthers', he would roar from the bushes, and then chuckle as the youngsters made off over the nearest fence. But the only thing these gentle summer flowers have in common with the black carnivores is Africa – their place of origin. *Agapanthus* are world favourites for their striking starbursts of blue or white midsummer blooms. Extremely tough, they enjoy full sun, and will grow in any soil with regular water. Common species grow to 1m/3ft, but there are dwarf forms too.

AGAPETES
(ag-ə-**pee**-tees)
(SYN Pentapterygium)
Flame Heath
ERICACEAE

The Flame Heath, *Agapetes serpens*, is a decorative shrub known for many years as Pentapterygium, and often sold under that name. Usually rather squat, it grows to 1.5m/5ft from a tuberous rootstock, sending out slender, weeping branches that are densely hairy and furnished with evergreen 1cm/½ in red-tipped leaves. The tubular flowers of vivid scarlet may appear any time from winter on, hanging loosely in pairs beneath the arching stems and sometimes bending them with their weight. *Agapetes* are propagated from tip-cuttings which strike

easily in summer and autumn in a sand/peat mixture, or at other times in a glasshouse with mist and bottom heat. Sometimes epiphytic in nature, these decorative shrubs demand perfect drainage. Most effective as a container plant or set in a large rockery, *Agapetes* enjoy leafy, acid soil, plenty of water, and a light feeding with manure in autumn. They revel in partly shaded conditions with high humidity. Tip-prune regularly to encourage a dense, compact shape.

AGAVE
(a-**gah**-vee)
Century Plant, Foxtail Plant
AGAVACEAE

The gigantic leaf-rosettes of these splendid succulents rank them among the most popular accent plants for modern gardens. They grow in poor soil, forming 2m/6ft clumps, and need plenty of water to look in top condition. *Agave attenuata* produces arching spikes of cream flowers up to 4.5m/14ft long. The closely related Century Plant (*A. americana*) may take a good 10 years before it decides to send up a 6m/20ft spike of greenish-yellow flowers. Then it will give up the ghost after leaving the legacy of a few suckers. While you cope with the suspense of waiting for the big flowering event, you will enjoy the dramatic appearance of its viciously spined leaves – blue-green or yellow-striped in the variety *A. americana* 'Marginata'. A little animal manure around an *Agave* works wonders.

Agapanthus praecox subsp. *orientalis.*
White form

Agapetes serpens. Flame Heath

Agave attenuata. Foxtail Plant

Ageratum houstonianum. Floss Flower

Ageratum houstonianum 'Spindrift'.
Pussy Foot

Agonis flexuosa. Willow Myrtle, Peppermint
Tree

Agrostemma githago 'Milas'. Corn Cockle

AGERATUM
(aj-er-**ah**-tǝm)
Floss Flower, Pussy Foot
ASTERACEAE

A member of the daisy family, in spite of its
appearance, *Ageratum houstonianum* is an
easy-to-manage annual with many uses
according to variety: tall-growing types to
60cm/2ft for bedding and cutting, dwarf
cultivars for edging and container work.
Their colourings, in many shades of blue,
mauve, and white, make a refreshing contrast
when used near many of the gaudier-
flowered annuals. One useful point: they can
be moved any time, even in full bloom, to
make a quick cover-up for bare patches.

Sow in boxes 8 weeks before the flowers
are needed, do not cover, and expect germination as quickly as 5 days, when the temperature is around 21ºC/70ºF. Plant
20–30cm/8–12in apart in a warm spot; feed
and water regularly. They'll bloom from
spring through into autumn in full sun or
part shade. There are dwarf varieties for
edging, and hybrids range in colour from
blue and glowing violet to pure white.

AGONIS
(ǝ-**goh**-nis)
Willow Myrtle
MYRTACEAE

I often see weeping willows planted in
gardens far too small for them and wonder
why the owners haven't thought to plant
Agonis flexuosa, the Willow Myrtle, instead. It
is every bit as graceful in its weeping
branches and narrow leaves, but only half the
size – to 8m/25 feet tall and wide at the most
– and it is evergreen, the leaves having a
pleasing pepperminty aroma. As a bonus, it
bears abundant small white flowers in
spring. Any sort of soil seems to suit it, but it
must have a warm-temperate climate like
that of its native Western Australia. Frost
cripples it and severe frost kills it.

AGROSTEMMA
(ag-roh-**stem**-mǝ)
Corn Cockle, Purple Cockle
CARYOPHYLLACEAE

The European Corn Cockle (*Agrostemma
githago*) is a wonderfully showy tall annual
with a many-branched, willowy habit.
Though it is very sturdy and can cope with
average wind and rain, it is best used at the
back of the annual border or in the shelter of
larger plants on which it can rely for protection. The original wild form habitually grows
in the wheat fields. Full sun suits them best.

Seed should be sown outdoors in
autumn or earliest spring in freshly turned
and raked soil. Young plants should be
thinned to about 25cm/10in spacing and
may need light staking or support in exposed
places. The finely branched 1m/3ft plants
have an overall greyish-green appearance,
with slender, willowy leaves. The flat, open
flowers, 7.5cm/3in across, come in many
shades of rose, cerise, lilac and white. They
bloom throughout summer, and cut well for
indoor decoration. But be careful – the seeds
are poisonous.

AJANIA
(a-**jah**-nee-ə)
Silver and Gold Chrysanthemum
ASTERACEAE

Chrysanthemum, as once known, has been split up by botanists into more manageable groups, for example *Argyranthemum* (Marguerites), *Leucanthemum* (Shasta Daisies) and *Tanacetum* (Pyrethrums and Tansies). *Ajania* is one of the more obscure genera resulting from this split, though it does include at least 30 species from northern Asia, one of which has become known as a garden plant in recent years. *A. pacifica*, as its name implies, grows near the shores of the Pacific in Siberia and Japan, and this origin gives a clue to its hardiness. A vigorous plant, it forms a mass of tough stems springing from knotty rhizomes to a height of about 45cm/18in. The bluntly toothed leaves are backed with felty hairs, which show above as a neat silver margin. The golden-yellow flowerheads, lacking ray florets, appear in profuse flat sprays held close above the leaves in autumn. Cut back to the ground after flowering; divide roots in spring; plant in a sunny spot.

Ajania pacifica. Silver and Gold Chrysanthemum

Ajuga reptans 'Purpurea'. Blue Bugle

AJUGA
(a-**joo**-gə)
Bugleweed, Blue Bugle
LAMIACEAE

Colourful dwarf perennials 10–30cm/4–12in tall, the many attractive species of *Ajuga* spread rapidly from runners, and are used to carpet the ground anywhere. They invariably look and grow better in shade. The Carpet or Blue Bugle, *A. reptans*, is the popular species, with neat rosettes of shining, elliptical leaves, which may be deep green, bronze, purple, dark red or variegated with white and yellow. Propagate all varieties from division at any time, separating new plants and shortening their leaves before replanting at about 20cm/8in spacing for rapid cover. They enjoy well-drained, humus-rich soil and need regular water. A sprinkling of complete fertiliser in early spring will ensure a heavy crop of warm-weather flowers. These appear in dense spikes and are generally a rich blue-violet, but paler blue, white, pink and purpled-red cultivars are sometimes sold. Remove spent flower heads and watch for fungus disease if drainage and air circulation are poor. Check this with a systemic fungicide.

Ajuga reptans. Blue Bugle

Akebia quinata. Five Leaf, Chocolate Vine

AKEBIA
(ak-**ee**-bee-ə)
Five Leaf, Chocolate Vine
LARDIZABALACEAE

A delicate evergreen vine, justly famed for its dainty 5-leaf clusters and delicately fragrant spring flowers in shades of purple and milk-coffee. Grow *Akebia quinata* in full sun or shade, but with strong support, and just let it go. It will twine around itself and everything else in sight, but can be cut back to the ground after flowering. It is a fast grower (to about 10m/30ft), and sometimes produces edible fruits in a mild climate. A second species, seen less often, is *A. trifoliata*, in which the leaflets develop in threes. This species has pale purple male flowers less than half the size of the darker female blooms. Propagate by layers in autumn or cuttings taken in summer and struck under glass.

ALBERTA
(al-**ber**-tə)
Natal Flame Tree
RUBIACEAE

A small South African tree, slow-growing and sometimes not much above shrub size, *Alberta magna* was named for the famous 13th century philosopher, Albertus Magnus. Botanically it is classed in the family Rubiaceae, which also includes other subtropical favourites such as Gardenia, Luculia and Rondeletia.

The foliage consists of glossy 15cm/6in leaves that are handsome all year, while the flower display (generally in winter or early spring) appears in terminal panicles. These consist of a number of scarlet, 5-petalled tubular blossoms which look quite stunning against the background of dark foliage. Each bloom is about 2.5cm/1in long, and is followed by a small fruit encased in two enlarged calyx lobes. *Alberta* can be grown from seed or cuttings.

Alberta magna. Natal Flame Tree

Alchemilla mollis. Lady's Mantle

Albizia julibrissin. Silk Tree

Alcea rosea double cultivar. Hollyhock

ALBIZIA
(al-**bit**-zee-ə)
Silk Tree, Cape Wattle, Siris
MIMOSACEAE

Sometimes mistaken for Wattles (see *Acacia*), the related Silk Trees or *Albizia* are a small genus found in Asia, Africa, Australia and Mexico. They're fast-growing, but short lived. Prettiest is the Persian Silk Tree, *A. julibrissin*, a favourite in the Middle East, Australia, France, California and other temperate climates. Short and spreading, it is decked in summer with large clusters of pink puffball flowers and is quite hardy down to −12°C/10°F. The Siris Tree, *A. lebbek*, 25m/80ft tall and popular throughout the tropics, bears deciduous bipinnate leaves like a Jacaranda, uninteresting panicles of green-ish wattle-flowers for a few days in late spring, and then a mass of rattling brown pods, the tree's main display.

ALCEA
(al-see-ə)
Hollyhock
MALVACEAE

The stately Hollyhock (*Alcea rosea*) enjoys full sun and shelter from wind damage – it's no coincidence that one sees them so often close to walls, where they can be tied for support as they shoot up to perhaps 2m/6ft. But they can be grown in the open with a heavy wire column or tall stake for support. Grown from seed sown *in situ*, and later thinned out to 45cm/18in spacings, they prefer a rich, heavy soil and lavish water during dry weather. A mulch of well-decayed manure will speed growth.

They are really biennial, and should be sown in autumn to bloom the following summer, but rust can be a problem. Spray with fungicide at the first sign of those tell-tale orange spots on the handsome, maple-shaped leaves. Caterpillars can be discouraged with a systemic insecticide – check with your local nursery. Modern Hollyhock strains are mostly double; they come in shades of pink, cerise, white and yellow. Dwarf varieties reaching only 60cm/2ft are sometimes available.

ALCHEMILLA
(al-ke-**mil**-lə)
Lady's Mantle
ROSACEAE

Old-fashioned Lady's Mantle (*Alchemilla mollis*) is a delightful herbaceous perennial for moist, well-drained soil. It can be raised from seed, sown in early spring and set out late summer for bloom in the following summer. Mature plants are generous in their production of new seedlings – or can be divided any time between autumn and spring. *Alchemilla* is bushy in habit, grows to about 40cm/16in, and produces masses of pale green, palmate leaves that have rounded lobes and lightly-toothed edges. These some-what resemble those of a Pelargonium and are covered in woolly hairs. The dainty yellow-green flowers are without petals and scarcely larger than a pin's head. They appear in dense trusses throughout summer, turn-ing the entire planting into a mass of gold. Plants should be kept continuously moist. Cut them back to about 3cm/1in above the ground when blooming is done.

Alkanna orientalis. Oriental Alkanet

ALKANNA
(al-**kan**-nə)
Dyers' Bugloss

BORAGINACEAE

The books tell us that *Alkanna tinctoria* is the original holder of the name Alkanet; but these days the much-better-known genus *Anchusa* claims it. Its other name, Dyers' Bugloss, saves confusion. It is a low-growing perennial from southern Europe, where it was used to make dyes. Synthetic dyes have long since superseded it, now, and its blue summer flowers are too small and sparse to win much admiration from gardeners.

The illustrated *A. orientalis*, from Greece and Turkey, is a much more attractive plant, I think. It is a small grey-leafed perennial, about 30cm/1ft high, studded with little golden stars in summer. Like its sibling, it prefers a temperate climate, perfect drainage and a sunny position.

ALLAMANDA
(al-lə-**man**-də)
Golden Trumpet, Bush Allamanda
APOCYNACEAE

Showy, trumpet-flowered plants from South America, *Allamandas* mostly climb and sprawl untidily, and are used in the tropics for informal fences. The most dazzling are *A. cathartica* and its cultivar 'Hendersonii', which have large golden trumpet flowers. Another vining type, *A. blanchetii* (often listed as *A. violacea*), with reddish-purple flowers, is commonly grafted on rooted cuttings of *A. cathartica*. One species, *A. schottii*, is content to remain as a shrub,

Allamanda cathartica. Golden Trumpet

Allamanda schottii. Bush Allamanda

and can make a spectacular specimen in sunny courtyards of temperate climes. Propagated from 8cm/3in tip-cuttings taken in spring, it grows into a compact bush in well-drained soil. Light watering is sufficient in colder weather, but step it up through the warmer months and alternate with liquid manure to produce dazzling clusters of 6cm/2in trumpet flowers. All *Allamandas* may drop a few leaves in cooler areas, where they can be used as greenhouse specimens. A minimum winter temperature of 10ºC/50ºF is said to be advisable, but I've found *A. schottii* can cope with less. Prune heavily in spring to improve shape.

Allamanda blanchetii. Purple Allamanda

Allium aflatunense 'Purple Sensation'.
Flowering Onion

ALLIUM
(al-lee-yəm)
Flowering Onion, Allium, Lily Leek
AMARYLLIDACEAE

Spectacularly flowering bulbs for pots or garden, easy-to-grow *Alliums* return year after year with colour for the border and flowers for the vase. They are closely related to the edible onions and garlic, and their hollow, tubular leaves exude a typical onion smell when bruised. The flowers, however, are very different from the kitchen species. Stunning *A. aflatunense* from central China may grow to 1.5m/5ft in height, producing one enormous, brilliant violet spherical flower mass per bulb. The dazzling Lily Leek, *A. moly,* flowers in an intense shade of yellow, each bulb sending up a 30cm/12in stem topped by a hemispherical umbel or flower cluster. The leaves are blue-green. *A. unifolium* is a Californian species, producing 10 to 30 mauve-pink blooms on each 30cm/1ft flower stem. It grows from a rhizome rather than a bulb.

All *Alliums* like full sun and shelter from strong winds.

Allium cristophii. Star of Persia

Allium moly. Lily Leek

Allium karataviense. Turkish Leek

Allium insubricum. Pink Nodding Onion

Alloxylon flammeum. Tree Waratah

ALLOXYLON

(al-**lok**-si-lon)

(SYN Oreocallis, Embothrium)

Tree Waratah, Red Silky Oak

PROTEACEAE

Much of the world seems unaware of Australia's gorgeous *Alloxylon flammeum*, once known as *Oreocallis wickhamii*. A tree-sized relative of Chile's famous Embothrium (which see) it is rarely seen in cultivation and has certainly not achieved the popularity it deserves.

Planted among other trees, it grows tall and narrow to around 15m/50ft; but when used alone it adopts a more spreading habit, rarely exceeding 8m/26ft. A tree of the moist eastern forests, it likes deep, rich soil and plenty of water at all times. The flower display has brought it a number of popular names, including Fire Tree, Red Silky Oak and Tree Waratah, the latter seeming most appropriate, for the inflorescence does resemble that of the Waratah (*Telopea speciosissima*). It is a bright-red, flat-topped mass of tubular florets that form a head about 15cm/6in across, borne at the ends of branchlets in late spring. Flowers in 7–8 years from seed.

ALOCASIA

(al-oh-**kae**-shə)

Spoon Lily, Elephant's Ears, Cunjevoi

ARACEAE

Arum relatives from Borneo, Sri Lanka and other tropical parts of Southeast Asia, the exotic *Alocasias* are grown principally for their spectacular foliage. Though popular all over the world, they are rarely successful outside conservatories except in warm-winter temperate climates.

Alocasia macrorrhiza. Spoon Lily   *TONY RODD*

Alocasias grow from tubers, or sections of tuber, planted in early spring in a rich, peaty compost and gradually potted up into progressively larger containers as they develop. That, of course, is assuming you're planning an indoor display, which will be limited by the available temperature range. With most species, 16ºC/60ºF is the winter minimum.

In the warmer climate, where outdoor cultivation is possible, *Alocasias* do best sheltered from direct sun. Feed them regularly with diluted fertiliser, preferably organic, and water heavily, but check the drainage, as they can easily damp off.

Species include *A. amazonica*, metallic blue-green leaves, to 60cm/2ft, dramatically veined white, yellowish spathe, and *A. plumbea* or Elephant's Ears (syn *A. indica* 'Metallica'), often seen outdoors in temperate areas where it develops masses of long-stemmed purplish stems and spreads from runners. Many fragrant butterscotch-toned aroid flowers appear in summer. *A. macrorrhiza* or Spoon Lily develops giant arrow-shaped leaves up to 2m/6ft in height. The boat-shaped flowers are highly perfumed.

ALOË
(a-**loh**-ae)
Aloe, Aalwyn
LILIACEAE

Splendid ornamentals for dry, frost-free areas, the *Aloës* include more than 200 species, mostly with thick, succulent spiky leaves attractively blotched, banded or spotted with grey. The plants vary wildly in size, from 60cm/2ft all the way to 20m/60ft (a tree species, *A. bainesii*). When not in bloom, they are often mistaken for the American Agaves (which see), but they belong to a different botanical family, and are all native to Africa. Both genera have toothed leaf margins, but unlike Agaves, *Aloës* bloom every year and do not die back after flowering. They make good balcony or courtyard plants in large pots of well-drained sandy soil, infrequently watered. *Aloës* rarely bloom indoors, but in full sun produce tall candelabra spikes of tubular flowers in scarlet, pink, orange and yellow. They tolerate drought and salt air, but are attacked by mealy bug, best destroyed with regular applications of a recommended insecticide.

Aloë speciosa. Aloe

Aloë ferox. Bitter Aloe

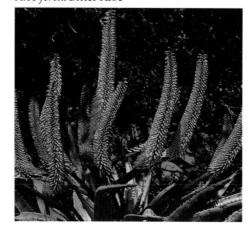

Aloysia triphylla. Lemon-scented Verbena

ALOYSIA
(al-oh-**wis**-ee-ə)
(SYN Lippia, Verbena)
**Lemon Verbena, Lemon Plant,
Lemon-scented Verbena**
VERBENACEAE

The dainty, overpoweringly fragrant Lemon Verbena (*Aloysia triphylla*) seems rooted in botanical confusion. First in the matter of its name – is it Verbena, Lippia or Aloysia? Each name is bound to be used by some of our readers, but I'll plump for the last, although in doing so I tumble headlong into further confusion. Just who was it named for? *Aloysia* is a latinised version of the feminine Louisa – and some authorities insist it was named for Maria Aloysia, Queen of Spain. Others say Maria Louisa, Duchess of Parma and Napoleon's widow. In this case I'd pick the first, for the plant is a native of South America, once part of the Spanish Empire. *Aloysia's* minute mauve and white summer flowers are quite uninteresting, but its mint-like leaves are overpoweringly lemon fragrant when crushed. Growing 2.5m/8ft in height, it is a straggly, untidy plant, hardy down to –3ºC/27ºF. Raise it from soft-tip cuttings in spring or mild winters – plant in well-drained sandy soil. Probably we wouldn't grow it if it didn't smell so delicious!

Aloë striata. Coral Aloe

Alpinia purpurata. Red Ginger

Alpinia zerumbet. Shell Ginger

Alstroemeria aurea. Flower of the Incas

Alstroemeria 'Striped Bird'. Chilean Lily

Althaea armeniaca. Mallow

ALPINIA
(al-**pin**-ee-ə)
Ornamental Gingers
ZINGIBERACEAE

Very showy flowers, much used for making garlands in their tropical homelands, *Alpinias* are likely to bloom only in a warm, moist position. *A. zerumbet*, Shell Ginger, has dense foliage and long clusters of red-tipped, satiny pink buds which open singly to reveal showy red and yellow flowers. A tall plant, (2–3m/6–10ft) it needs part shade, plenty of water and good soil to bloom well, which it does after several years. Red Ginger, *A. purpurata*, is native to the Pacific. The actual flowers are white and inconspicuous among the profusion of bright red bracts at the end of long stems. *A. calcarata*, found in India and southern China, is an altogether daintier plant, with showy spikes of white blossom, tinted red and rosy purple.

ALSTROEMERIA
(al-stroh-**meer**-ee-ə)
**Chilean Lily, Flower of the Incas,
New Zealand Christmas Bell**
ALSTROEMERIACEAE

These widely spreading perennials are seen at their best naturalized under trees, or on sloping banks of sandy soil. They are planted from root divisions in autumn, and enjoy plenty of water until the leaves yellow.

Orange is the basic colour of *Alstroemeria aurea* (often listed as *A. aurantiaca*), but hybrids are now available in shades of white, pink, yellow and brick red; they're popular cut flowers. *A. psittacina* is known in Australia as the New Zealand Christmas Bell despite the fact that it comes from Brazil. Less tolerant of cold than *A. aurea*, its green and red flowers last well when cut. Plant where they can be left undisturbed for years.

ALTHAEA
(al-**thee**-ə)
Mallow
MALVACEAE

Althaea was once the botanical name of the tall-growing biennial Hollyhock, but now that lovely plant has lost its lisp and become Alcea again (following a primary rule of nomenclature, that the earliest recorded name holds sway, and Alcea is a very old name indeed). But now we're dealing with the real *Althaeas*, a similarly flowered group of perennials found throughout Asia Minor and beyond, as far as Siberia.

Like the Hollyhock, *Althaea armeniaca* produces handsome, slightly furry leaves divided into 3 or 5 segments and frequently coarsely toothed. It may be propagated from seed or, more generally, by division of the rhizome, which should be done in autumn. In spring, the plants grow fast to above a metre in height, and produce 5–7cm/2–3in pink flowers at the leaf axils. Not common outside European gardens.

ALYOGYNE
(al-ee-**oj**-e-nee)
(SYN Hibiscus)
Blue Hibiscus
MALVACEAE

A stunning Hibiscus lookalike from south west Australia, *Alyogyne huegelii* is also widely grown in California and other temperate areas. Able to withstand a light frost and flourish in a range of soils, it's easily propagated from seed, or from cuttings taken any time and struck in a fast-draining mixture of peat and sand. *Alyogyne* is a rather scraggy bush, growing fast to a height of about 2m/6ft, and of open, spreading habit. Its rough stems are lightly clothed with 8cm/3in leaves, generally 5-lobed and hairy, with each lobe deeply toothed. The showy

Alyogyne huegelii. Blue Hibiscus

Alyssum murale. Yellow Tuft

warm-weather blooms are up to 15cm/6in in diameter, their shiny, overlapping petals twisted like the blades of a ship's propeller. They last for several days before closing. Somewhat brittle, *Alyogyne* needs protection from strong winds and does best in a warm, dry climate. Rainfall normally satisfies the plant's water needs.

ALYSSUM
(a-**liss**-∂m)
Madwort, Yellow Tuft
BRASSICACEAE

That old-fashioned cottage garden annual Sweet Alice, or *Alyssum maritimum,* has been re-christened *Lobularia maritima,* and the gorgeously golden-flowered perennial *Alyssum saxatile* or Yellow Alice will be found as *Aurinia saxatile.* Both are described under their respective names. That still leaves some 150 species of small perennials and sub-shrubs, mostly native to the Mediterranean area, with a few outliers from the Caucasus and Siberia. Ideal for the sunny rock garden or in well-drained gravelly soil, they are mainly plants for the specialist collector. Clothed mostly in small silvery leaves, they bear lavish heads of tiny golden blooms in

Amaranthus caudatus. Love-lies-bleeding

Amaranthus tricolor cultivars 'Joseph's Coat' and 'Flaming Fountain'

spring. Grow from seed or propagate from 7.5cm/3in cuttings struck in a semi-shaded place in early summer. *Alyssum* species are prone to attack by downy mildew.

AMARANTHUS
(am-a-**ran**-th∂s)
Love-lies-bleeding, Prince's Feather, Molten Fire, Joseph's Coat
AMARANTHACEAE

Over 60 species of heat-loving annuals grown principally for their dazzling foliage. They are easily raised from seed, which germinates at a temperature of 21–24ºC/70–75ºF. Prepare soil for planting with plenty of manure and packaged fertiliser. Set seedlings out at 40cm/16in spacings and water regularly. They will take up to 14 weeks to reach display size – 1.2m/4ft.
Amaranthus species vary widely. The most commonly cultivated are: *A. caudatus* (Love-lies-bleeding), with large green or red heart-shaped leaves and drooping red tassels that cascade to the ground; Prince's Feather (*A. hypochondriacus*) has purple-bronze leaves, small plumes of fuzzy red flowers; Flaming Fountain (*A. salicifolius*) has willow-

like leaves that change from green to a dazzling orange. Most eye-catching of all is *A. tricolor,* with heart-shaped scarlet leaves tipped yellow and green. All *Amaranthus* need protection from snails when young, and regular spraying against caterpillars.

AMARYLLIS
(am-∂-**ril**-lis)
Belladonna Lily, Naked Lady
AMARYLLIDACEAE

Alas for Amaryllis, the Greek beauty whose name was once immortalised in a very large genus of bulbs indeed! One by one her species have been stolen away, renamed by heartless taxonomists until she has but one namesake left. *Amaryllis belladonna,* the beautiful lady, sends up bare flower stems from the earth at summer's end, to break into a riot of gorgeous pink lily-blooms with an equally gorgeous perfume.

Plant out in summer with the neck of each bulb just at ground level and the naked flower stalks shoot up to 30cm/12in almost overnight, the musk-pink flowers lasting for weeks. Strap-like leaves appear later, and last through winter. There are also white and deeper pink varieties. Belladonnas need good drainage and plenty of water during the winter months.

Amaryllis belladonna. Naked Lady, Belladonna Lily

AMELANCHIER
(am-el-**an**-chee-∂r)
Service-berry, Shadbush, Snowy Mespilus
ROSACEAE

The chief services that the trees and shrubs of this mainly American genus perform for gardeners are lavish displays of snow-white flowers in spring and bright autumn colour. The small black berries are sometimes used for making jam, but I haven't tried it myself: these are plants of cold climates and my mild winters don't suit them. The species all look

Amelanchier lamarckii. Shadbush

Ammobium alatum. Winged Everlasting
TONY RODD

Amorphophallus bulbifer. Krubi, Snake Lily

rather alike in flower and leaf, the chief distinction from the gardener's point of view being their size. *Amelanchier canadensis* makes a medium-sized tree, to about 12m/40ft; the illustrated *A. lamarckii* is a tall shrub or small tree about half that size; and *A. ovalis* is a shrub about 2.5m/8ft tall and wide. None is at all fussy about soil or position.

AMHERSTIA
(am-**her**-stee-∂)
Pride of Burma
CAESALPINIACEAE

The gorgeous *Amherstia nobilis* has been hailed as the world's most beautiful flowering tree. Simple, light, lacy, it grows to 13m/40ft in the wild. The graceful leaves have six or eight pairs of leaflets and new growth is flaccid and often shaded with bronze, red and purple. The flower clusters hang like inverted candelabra. Individual blossoms remind some people of orchids, others of hummingbirds. They are pale pink, spotted and marked in red and white, with a splash of golden yellow on the large upper petal. *Amherstias* are generally propagated by cuttings and have flowered in Hawaii, Florida, the Philippines, the Caribbean and South America. Even England under glass.

Amherstia nobilis. Pride of Burma

AMMOBIUM
(am-**moh**-bee-∂m)
Winged Everlasting
ASTERACEAE

A rather untidy-growing native of eastern Australia, the Winged Everlasting is more commonly seen in annual displays overseas than in its native land. It loves full sun and sandy soil, and can be grown from seed sown directly outdoors or raised in flats for later transplanting. Seedlings should be set out 30cm/12in apart for mutual support as they grow. They produce a rather angular series of winged stems with only occasional true leaves.

The name *Ammobium alatum* means 'winged sand dweller'. Both stems and foliage are silvery-green and the 1m/3ft stems are topped from spring through summer with crackling white paper daisies, yellow-centred. For winter decoration, cut the stems before flowers are fully open, and hang them to dry in a shaded, airy place. When desiccated, arrange in a vase *without* water and they'll last for months.

AMORPHOPHALLUS
(a-**mor**-fo-fal-∂s)
Snake Lily, Krubi
ARACEAE

Modesty forbids our repeating what early botanists thought *this* flower looked like – but *Amorphophallus* really is a conversation opener! In early summer, a sturdy flower stem pushes up from a rather large tuber – it is patterned like a snakeskin in dark green, silver and pink. Reaching around 30cm/1ft in height, this stem unfurls into something like an Arum lily. In illustrated *A. bulbifer* the spathe is tinted soft apricot, shading to green, while the spadix or flower spike is pink and yellow. (Note surrounding foliage is *Houttuynia cordata*.)After bloom, the inflorescence withers, and a second snake-

patterned stem arises to 1m/3ft in height. This opens into the most complicated single leaf, carrying plump bulbils from which new plants can be started. *Amorphophallus* species need plenty of moisture in hot weather, drying off in cold. They are all subtropical, and do best in dappled shade.

AMSONIA
(am-**soh**-nee-∂)
Blue Star
APOCYNACEAE

Related to Allamanda and Plumeria (though you'd never know it), *Amsonias* include about 20 herbaceous perennial plants found naturally in Japan, southern Europe and North America. Not spectacular, they are grown for their delicate bluish flowers and ability to flourish in shade. There, in any average garden soil, they'll form a dense clump in cooler climates, producing their delicate sprays of blossom in spring and early summer. The plant's stems are more blue than green, the foliage slender and of little substance – and of course they exude the typical white and unpleasantly sticky sap of all the milkweeds when picked. Since the plants die down, they can be considered

Amsonia tabernaemontana. Blue Star

Anagallis arvensis. Scarlet Pimpernel

Ananas bracteatus. Red Pineapple

Anacyclus depressus. Mount Atlas Daisy

perfectly frost hardy, and generally reach 1m/3ft in height during their summer growth. Flowers of *A. tabernaemontana* are light blue, those of *A. ciliata* and *A. orientalis* purple. All were named for Charles Amson, an 18th-century medico.

ANACYCLUS
(a-na-**kick**-ləs)
Mount Atlas Daisy
ASTERACEAE

A delightful prostrate daisy from Morocco's Atlas Mountains, the decorative *Anacyclus depressus* is grown by alpine plant enthusiasts in many cooler-climate areas. Soft grey fern-like foliage hugs the ground over a spread of 30cm/1ft, but is rarely more than a few centimetres in height. *Anacyclus* is frost hardy, does best in a perfectly drained, gritty soil, and may rot if drainage is suspect. It revels in full, baking sunlight. All through the summer, tiny crimson buds open regularly, transforming themselves into golden-centred, snowy white daisy flowers. Propagate from fresh seed sown in autumn, or cuttings of side shoots taken in spring. Water is needed only in drought conditions.

ANAGALLIS
(an-a-**gal**-əs)
Scarlet Pimpernel, Shepherd's Clock, Poor Man's Weatherglass, Pimpernel
PRIMULACEAE

Though often classed as a weed, the charming Pimpernels (*Anagallis* species) are grown by many plant collectors for their brilliant flowers of blue, scarlet or lilac. Their continued popularity over centuries is surely proven by such ancient names as Poor Man's Weatherglass and Shepherd's Clock, though their significance has faded with the years. Most suitable for small rockery work or edging of large containers, Pimpernels are sown direct in early spring. Soil composition is no worry so long as it drains well. Blooming for months from midsummer on, the fiery *Anagallis arvensis* rarely tops 5cm/2in in height; its leaves are less than 2cm/1in long, its dashing flowers the size of forget-me-nots. And yes, this *is* the Scarlet Pimpernel that lent Baroness Orczy's hero his name. *A. monellii* is the blue variety.

ANANAS
(an-ə-**n**-as)
Pineapple
BROMELIACEAE

The best known member of the Bromeliad family is the edible Pineapple, *Ananas comosus,* though conversely it is the least grown by plant enthusiasts. This may be because the pine is so subtropical in its needs – a winter minimum of 10°C/50°F is a must! But if heat can be provided, there is a wide range of spectacular forms to be raised for the beauty of their floral display.

Most often seen is the Striped Wild Pineapple, *A. bracteatus,* which features 1.5m/5ft leaves banded in cream and flushed pink. Small violet blooms appear in a dense head, each enclosed by a red bract. After

flowering, these form into a brilliant compound fruit. Technically, the Pineapple is a syncarp, in which many small fruit grow to be part of the whole. *A. comosus* var. *variegatus* is similar, but with more noticeable and spectacular flowers. *Ananas* like a sandy compost with leafmould and charcoal for home cultivation, and moderate water at all times. Propagate from suckers.

ANAPHALIS
(an-**af**-a-lis)
Pearl or Pearly Everlasting
ASTERACEAE

Bearing a strong resemblance to southern-hemisphere Everlasting Daisies (see Chrysocephalum, Bracteantha, Rhodanthe and Helichrysum), the 100-odd species of *Anaphalis* are found on all continents north of the equator. They are perennial members of the daisy family, greatly valued in the mixed border for their heads of small, silvery daisy flowers, and can be cut and dried for long-lasting arrangements.

Easy to grow, they can be propagated in many different ways: from spring cuttings; from divisions of the plant taken in autumn or early spring; and from seed, which can be

Anaphalis margaritacea. Pearly Everlasting

Anchusa azurea 'Dropmore'. Summer Forget-me-not

Andromeda polifolia. Bog Rosemary

Androsace foliosa. Rock Jasmine

sown under cover in winter and will germinate in about 2 weeks at a temperature of 13–18°C/44–64°F. The young plants are set out in spring at spacings of 45cm/18in and spread quickly into a mass of long, pointed leaves, generally a woolly grey-green on their reverse side. The flowers appear in many branched umbels, and are bright yellow and surrounded by a mass of papery white bracts. They prefer an alkaline soil with only moderate water and are quite drought resistant. Divide and replant every 3 or 4 years. Prune back hard in winter.

ANCHUSA
(an-**choo**-s∂)
Alkanet, Summer Forget-me-not
BORAGINACEAE

Summer Forget-me-nots (*Anchusa azurea* and *A. capensis*) are just like over-sized versions of the smaller Forget-me-not (Myosotis) but with one grand difference. The flowers are a clear, true blue. Seed can be sown in trays or directly into the garden when the daily temperature is around 20°C/68°F and will germinate in 2 to 3 weeks. Plant in clumps at 30cm/12in spacings in poor soil. Full sun is the rule except in very hot areas, where semi-shade helps maintain the flowers' brilliance. *Anchusa* makes a wide, basal rosette of pointed, hairy leaves, from which 45cm/18in flower stalks appear in late spring. Cut these back after blooming for a new flush of growth. Feed sparingly, water generously. There are good named varieties, including dwarf strains and the deeper blue cultivar 'Dropmore'.

ANDROMEDA
(an-**drom**-∂-da)
Bog Rosemary
ERICACEAE

Like its namesake, the Andromeda who was rescued from a sea monster, this delightful little plant is a real survivor. Once upon a time, *Andromeda polifolia* was one of a large genus of decorative shrubs. The others have been rooted out of the group one by one and are now reclassified as Cassiope, Enkianthus, Leucothoë and Zenobia, among other names. And *A. polifolia* is now one of only 2 members of the genus. It grows naturally in peat bogs of sub-arctic regions of the northern hemisphere, rarely exceeding 30cm/12in in height. It prefers full sun and naturally enough, an acid, poorly drained soil. It can be propagated from seed, divisions of rooted runners or cuttings, and is a suitable small shrub for the base of large rockeries. Leaves are small and linear, while the pretty heath-type flowers of palest pink appear for a short time only in late spring.

ANDROSACE
(an-**dross**-a-see)
Rock Jasmine
PRIMULACEAE

Most charming and unreliable of alpine plants, the genus *Androsace* includes some 100 or so dwarf perennial plants related to the primroses, though this is often far from obvious. They are all native to northern parts of the northern hemisphere, and are not often seen south of the equator except in

mountain gardens. Their principal needs are a well-drained soil containing plenty of grit, sand and leafmould; lots of moisture when the weather's dry in warmer months; and a position sheltered from sun for at least part of the day. In the lee of feature rocks is ideal. Mostly spreading from stolons or runners, *Androsace* species may be propagated from divisions, summer cuttings or ripe summer seed. Illustrated *A. foliosa* is from the Himalayas – its flowers open pink, but fade. It loves lime, so try limestone chips as a mulch.

ANEMONE
(an-**em**-o-nee)
Windflower, Lily-of-the-Field, Wind Poppy
RANUNCULACEAE

This spectacular genus is commonly represented in gardens only by the garish spring-flowering *Anemone coronaria* or Wind Poppy. It is mostly treated as an annual and bracketed with Ranunculus, which belongs to the same family.

The showiest *Anemone* varieties for the perennial border are a hybrid group of Japanese and Chinese species which are mostly autumn blooming. These are generally taller plants and include as one parent either the pink-flowered *A. hupehensis* or the white-blooming *A. vitifolia* (Grape Leaf Anemone). These hybrids are planted out from divisions at spacings of 30–60cm/1–2ft in colder weather, and enjoy sheltered semi-shade. They resent disturbance and will make little growth the first year, but once established, they will spread into a dense clump with flowering stems 75–100cm/30–36in tall.

Anemone coronaria 'St Brigid'. Wind Poppy

Anemone hupehensis var. japonica. Japanese Windflower

Anemone blanda. Wood Anemone

Anemone multifida. Windflower

Anemopaegma chamberlaynii. Yellow Trumpet Vine

Entire stems should be cut as they fade and the whole plant taken back to ground level when blooming has finished. A good ration of complete fertiliser in early spring, followed by light cultivation, will start the blooming cycle again. White-flowered A. hybrida 'Alba' (formerly A. japonica) is the tallest, sometimes reaching 1m/3ft. Delicate pink A. 'Lorelei' is a little shorter. Both have handsome leaves, mid-green and slightly hairy. A. lesseri has white-centred crimson flowers and foliage divided like a buttercup's. A smaller plant, rarely reaching 45cm/18in, it is particularly effective in shaded rock gardens and blooms early in summer. All can be multiplied from root cuttings or from seed sown outdoors in late autumn/fall for spring germination.

The European Wood Anemone (A. blanda), a dainty, spring-flowering species often used under trees, grows from root divisions. The delicate flowers may be pink, white or powder blue. It rarely passes 20cm/8in in height and the individual flowers are only 2.5cm/1in in diameter. But what they lack in size they make up for in splendid profusion.

ANEMOPAEGMA
(an-em-oh-**peg**-mə)
Yellow Trumpet Vine
BIGNONIACEAE

Sometimes mistaken for the Cat's Claw Vine (see Macfadyena), this Brazilian beauty has little real resemblance if you look closely. Though both have yellow flowers, Anemopaegma has larger leaves and climbs by means of tendrils rather than Macfadyena's distinctive hooks.

Anemopaegma is really only suited to subtropical or warmer climates, where it climbs rampantly, given adequate support. Each evergreen, compound leaf consists of 3 to 5 leaflets – the showy golden flowers are borne in racemes which appear from the leaf axils. Propagation is easy from cuttings taken in late summer and struck over heat. Plenty of water in the warmer months is a necessity, and rich soil is a great help.

ANGELONIA
(an-jel-**oh**-nee-ə)
Granny's Bonnets, Angelon
SCROPHULARIACEAE

Not often seen away from subtropical climate zones, the charming Angelonia is closely related to the Snapdragon (Antirrhinum), and is used there as its equivalent. There are some 25 species found

Angelonia salicariifolia. Granny's Bonnets

in scattered areas from Brazil to Mexico, and because of their fragrance and use as a cut flower, they have spread to warm-climate gardens all over the world. I first noticed them in Ra'iatea, near Tahiti. Flowers are blue, white, cyclamen or purple according to species, and all produce tall spikes of showy bloom up to 60cm/2ft in height. They are often used as annuals, sown in spring to bloom the following autumn/fall, particularly in cooler areas where the winter might kill them off. They need a rich but fast-draining soil, and plentiful water in warm weather. In really hot gardens, midday shade will prevent flop. Leaves are 2.5–7.5cm/1–3in long and lightly toothed.

ANGOPHORA
(an-**gof**-or-ə)
Apple Gum
MYRTACEAE

The *Angophoras* or Apple Gums are a small Australian genus greatly resembling the Eucalypts but with opposite leaves. Popular in other dry areas such as California and South Africa, they are native to the fast-draining sandstone of eastern Australia. They have elegant orange or pinkish bark which peels unevenly from the trunk, and two forms of leaf – pale green, heart-shaped juvenile foliage and long, drooping adult leaves up to 12.5cm/5in long. The summer flowers (invariably cream) are very largely a mass of stamens but, unlike the Eucalypts, they also have small petals. The fruits are like gumnuts but ribbed.

Species commonly planted are the tall and graceful *A. costata* or Smoothbarked Apple Gum, and the smaller *A. hispida* (syn *A. cordifolia*) or Dwarf Apple Gum, which has a rugged, spreading appearance and rarely exceeds 4m/13ft in height.

ANGRAECUM
(an-**grae**-kum)
Angurek, Comet Orchid
ORCHIDACEAE

Like so many of the world's exotic plants, lovely *Angraecum superbum* hails from Malagasy, and its very large genus is from tropical Africa and Sri Lanka. Most of them thrive with the same treatment – a loose compost of fibre and bark chips in a (preferably) hanging container to which they can attach their long aerial roots. The plant does not spread via pseudo bulbs as other orchids do, but just grows taller and taller, producing flower racemes from the axils. Almost all species bloom in white with a touch of green. The botanical name is an adaptation of *Angurek* – a Malay word meaning 'air plant'.

ANIGOZANTHOS
(an-i-go-**zan**-thos)
Kangaroo Paw, Cat's Paw
HAEMODORACEAE

These startling West Australian perennials become more popular every year. None of the many cultivars likes a cold winter or humidity in summer, and they are irresistible to slugs and snails. Species *Anigozanthos manglesii* (the floral emblem of Western

Angraecum superbum. Angurek

Anigozanthos flavidus. Kangaroo Paw

Angophora hispida. Dwarf Apple Gum

Anigozanthos 'Regal Claw'. Hybrid Kangaroo Paw

Australia) is also particularly prone to attacks of ink disease, a fungus that withers and blackens the foliage. It is best to cut away all affected leaves and drench with fungicide. *A. flavidus* is easiest to grow, and can reach 2m/6ft. It has attractive cultivars, including a fine deep red, and a brilliant pink and green. Individual Kangaroo-paw flowers split almost to the base, revealing starry throats of many exotic tones, lime and turquoise among them. The plants enjoy sandy soil, manure, and lots of water. They flower in spring, last for months, and fade gradually, and can be used in dried arrangements.

ANISODONTEA
(an-ais-oh-**don**-tee-ə)
(SYN Malvastrum)
Cape Mallow
MALVACEAE

The Cape Mallow, *Anisodontea capensis*, a small, bushy perennial, has been enjoying a modest burst of popularity lately, though sometimes under its old name *Malvastrum capense*. With a summer-long display of mauve-pink flowers, it makes an attractive change from scarlet geraniums in bedding-out schemes. Like the geranium, it comes from South Africa, and is happiest in a frost-free climate. In cold ones it is either sown in the greenhouse in late winter or grown from cuttings, the young plants being planted out in a sunny, well-drained bed when all danger of frost is over. Where it survives the winter, a springtime trim will ensure bushiness and abundant summer bloom.

Anigozanthos manglesii. Green Kangaroo Paw

ANOMATHECA
(an-oh-mə-**theek**-ə)
Painted Petals, Flame Freesia
IRIDACEAE

The showy South African Flame Freesia is not nearly as widely known or grown as its popular namesake, despite its delightful sprays of two-tone red flowers, freely produced in spring.

Anomatheca laxa (formerly *Lapeirousia laxa*) grows readily from seed sown as soon as it is ripe in late summer. Germination takes about a month, but after this slow start, clumps of iris-like leaves quickly grow and a token flowering can be expected in the first spring. By the second season, the plants, which die back in summer, will have reached their full height of 60cm/2ft, and flowering will be profuse over about 6 weeks. Grow in pots where winters are bitterly cold.

Anisodontea capensis. Cape Mallow

ANSELLIA
(an-**sell**-ee-ə)
Leopard Orchid
ORCHIDACEAE

This small genus of orchids, African in origin, consists of 2 species with a handful of varieties; they are most often seen in the open gardens of tropical homes. Elsewhere, they may need the protection of glass, particularly in winter, for they have a minimum temperature need of 15ºC/59ºF. The flowers of all species are of simple orchid form, with five petals and a lip or labellum: the background shade is pale yellow, tending to green in some varieties, cream in others – the whole is spotted with purplish brown in varying degrees. Being naturally epiphytic, *Ansellias* grow best in a loose mixture of fibre, broken pot shards, sphagnum moss and compost-rich loam. Make sure the drainage is perfect, and water lavishly when in active growth. They prefer high humidity.

Anomatheca laxa. Flame Freesia

Ansellia argentea. Leopard Orchid

ANTHEMIS

(an-them-is)

**Golden Marguerite, Dog Fennel,
Ox-eye Chamomile**

ASTERACEAE

Most brilliant of the summer-flowering daisies, the golden Ox-eye Chamomile (*Anthemis tinctoria*) shines blindingly right through warmer weather, and makes a dazzling display in the summer border. The dense, fern-like foliage, highly aromatic when crushed, is a source of chamomile tea. The 5cm/2in flowers on 30cm/12in stems pick well, and have been the source of a yellow dye. Plant them in well-drained soil about 30cm/12in apart, fertilise lightly and give occasional water. The flower display will be prolonged by cutting back the spent stems. Though perennial, the plants are not long lasting, and should be renewed every second year from cuttings or seed sown in winter under cover at a temperature of 21ºC/70ºF. Also grown are dwarf *A. punctata* subsp. *cupaniana*, with white summer flowers, and *A. sancti-johannis*, with its lobed, greyish leaves and bright orange daisy blooms.

Anthemis tinctoria. Dyer's Chamomile, Golden Marguerite

ANTHERICUM

(an-ther-i-kəm)

St Bernard's Lily, Spider Plant

LILIACEAE

The word *antherikos* was used by Ancient Greeks to describe a wheat stalk, and it is easy to see how it came to be adapted for the name of this lovely flower genus – just look at the budding flower stalks in our picture! So *Anthericum* the flower has been called, in a fair adaptation. They are bulbous perennials with the fleshy, succulent roots of a dry-country plant. They are, in fact, found in Asia Minor, southwestern Europe and northern Africa. Not really frost hardy, they do best with a deep winter mulch. They can be raised from seed or divisions in a light soil, which should be both rich in nutrient and well drained. The long, strap-like leaves are joined in summer by erect stems of starry white flowers. These vary from 45–100cm/18–40in in height, according to species. Keep them moist in summer.

ANTHURIUM

(an-thoo-ree-əm)

**Flamingo Flower, Palette Flower, Obake,
Little Boy Flower**

ARACEAE

Forty years and more ago, before Waikiki land prices went through the roof and the gardens of old Hawaii began to shrink, there were unbelievable experiences for the foreign tourist. I used to love to wander through the demesne of the exclusive Royal Hawaiian Hotel where vivid, waxy *Anthuriums* were used as ground cover! Coming from a

Anthericum liliago 'Major'. St Bernard's Lily

country where these gorgeous tropical flowers were rarely seen outside exhibitions of exotics, such profligacy seemed unbelievable. Now, those gardens have mostly given away to parking lots and fast-food stores, and the ghosts of the *Anthuriums* live on only in extravagant arrangements in the lobby.

Anthuriums are often grown and shown with orchids, although they are not related in any way. They form a splendid genus of more than 700 species within the arum family, and like a rich, moisture-retaining compost, perfect drainage and high humidity all through the warm weather.

Anthurium andraeanum 'Rhodochlorum'. Obake, Ghost Anthurium

Anthurium andraeanum 'Album'. Little Boy Flower

The teeming jungles of Central America are their home, and they must have a winter minimum of not less than 15ºC/59ºF to give any sort of spectacular result. Fortunately, this can be maintained near the window of a centrally-heated, sunny room. Best results, of course, will be obtained in a greenhouse, with the heavily humid atmosphere beloved of all jungle plants.

Propagation of all species is possible by division of older plants. This, and the necessary repotting, is best done in early spring. As with all Aroids, the spadix or column of the *Anthurium* consists of a myriad tiny flowers. The decorative shield or spathe is merely a specially developed protective leaf. *Anthurium* flowers last for months.

ANTHYLLIS
(an-**thill**-is)
Kidney Vetch
FABACEAE

A dainty mounded shrub from Corsica and southern Europe, *Anthyllis hermanniae* is useful in the well-drained rock garden where it lights up with a profuse display of tiny stemless yellow flowers in summer. It is not fully frost hardy, but will usually recover from frost damage except in the most severe

Anthyllis hermanniae. Kidney Vetch

Anthurium scherzerianum. Flamingo Flower

winters. Growing best in a cool temperate climate, it enjoys full sun and a sandy, well-drained soil that's not *too* rich in nutrient. *Anthyllis* grows from seed or cuttings and needs water only during very dry spells. The tiny trifoliate leaves are deciduous and drop to reveal spiny stems in winter. It is, of course, one of the pea family. Related perennial *A. montana*, the Mountain Vetch, bears masses of white-tipped pink or red flowers, and grows to about 30cm/12in.

ANTIGONON
(an-**tig**-o-n∂n)
Coral Vine, Chain of Love, Corallita, Bride's Tears, Queen's Wreath
POLYGONACEAE

The charming old-fashioned Coral Vine will take as much heat as you can give it, and is rarely seen at its best in cooler coastal gardens. Its botanical name is *Antigonon leptopus*, and it is characterised by the light, lacy habit of both flowers and leaves. This makes it ideally suited for planting on arbors or pergolas, where it can shade without cutting out too much of the light or view.

Grow them from seed or nursery-bought plants, and trim back at the onset of winter.

Antigonon leptopus. Chain of Love

A leaf-rich soil in a sunny, well-drained position seems to suit them best. Feed heavily in early spring, increase water as the warm weather advances and you'll be rewarded throughout summer and autumn with long stems of tiny heart-shaped flowers in a vivid electric pink. There's also a white cultivar.

ANTIRRHINUM
(an-ti-**rhai**-n∂m)
Snapdragon
SCROPHULARIACEAE

Seed of Snapdragon (*Antirrhinum majus*) is so fine it cannot be covered after sowing, for light is needed to germinate it. It is mostly sown indoors, kept in a bright, warm place until the tiny seedlings appear in 10–14 days. These should later be pricked out to wider spacing in compost-rich seed-raising mix, and finally set out in the garden after about 6 weeks. Dwarf cultivars are spaced at 20cm/8in; intermediates at 30cm/12in; tall strains as much as 40cm/16in apart. Snapdragons are really woody perennials, though universally grown as annuals. They need well-drained soil with plenty of manure and fertiliser, and quality is improved with a sprinkling of lime or dolomite before planting. Full sunlight is preferred except in very hot areas. Seed is best sown in early autumn at a temperature of around 20ºC/70ºF. Flowers take about 16 weeks to develop and you have a choice between pinching out early buds to force branching or leaving them be, for taller, earlier flower spikes.

In addition to the long-flowered, 'dragon-mouth' type of *Antirrhinum*, hybridists have now given us open, cup-shaped cultivars, but where is the charm of a Snapdragon minus its snapping mouth? Happily, modern strains are fairly resistant to the disease 'rust', but if it does appear, spray thoroughly with a suitable fungicide.

Antirrhinum majus. Snapdragon

Antirrhinum majus 'Cheerio'. Snapdragon

Aphelandra tetragona. Red Aphelandra

APETAHIA
(a-pe-**tah**-hee-ə)
Tiare Apetahi, One-sided Flower

CAMPANULACEAE

Arguably one of the rarest flowers in the world, *Apetahia raiatiensis* is certainly unique in the limitation of its natural range. It grows only in hidden places at the top of Temehani, a mountain on the sacred Polynesian island of Ra'iatea (the ancient Hawaiki), and has resisted all attempts to grow it elsewhere on the same island or on any other island, though French botanists are hopeful of establishing it on Huahine. It is the only species of the campanula family which opens its plump green buds at dawn with an audible pop! They split right down one side as they become 5-petalled half-flowers, very fragrant. Because Mount Temehani was sacred to the old gods, so, the Raiateans believe, is the flower.

Apetahia raiatiensis. One-sided Flower

APHELANDRA
(af-el-**an**-drə)
Zebra Plant, Golden Spike
ACANTHACEAE

One of the more spectacular South American shrub genera, *Aphelandras* are familiar as indoor plants, for a minimum winter temperature of 10°C/50°F is a must if they are to survive. But in warm climates with rich porous soil they turn on a magnificent summer show outdoors. *Aphelandras* are members of the Acanthus family, with typical spear-shaped leaves and terminal

Aphelandra squarrosa 'Louisae'. Zebra Plant

spikes of showy, tubular flowers. Given the right climatic conditions, they are easy to grow from cuttings; they self-seed readily in tropical gardens. All species need dilute fertiliser and plenty of water while in active growth; taper off the supply after bloom, when the entire flower head will drop away. To avoid legginess, prune hard after flowering in earliest spring.

A. *squarrosa* 'Louisae' has deep yellow flowers, red stems, white-striped leaves and grows to 30cm/12in. A. *aurantiaca* has orange-scarlet flowers and grows to 1m/3ft. A. *tetragona* can reach 1.2m/4ft.

Aponogeton distachyos. Water Hawthorn

APONOGETON

(a-pon-o-**gee**-tən)

Water Hawthorn, Cape Pondweed

APONOGETONACEAE

Found in Africa, Malagasy, Southeast Asia and Australia, all believed to be parts of a one-time super continent, the genus *Aponogeton* includes 40-odd decorative water plants with floating oval leaves and submerged tuberous roots. The most widely seen is *Aponogeton distachyos,* from South Africa. In its common form, it bears white flowers on forked stalks throughout warm weather. These have purplish anthers and the sharp scent of hawthorn blossoms. Plant the tuber in a small pot of loam and support it so it is barely covered with water. Later, as the plant grows, it will be sunk up to 60cm/2ft below the surface. Do not use with waterlilies, as the *Aponogeton* will tend to take over.

APOROCACTUS

(ə-po-roh-**kak**-təs)

Rat's Tail Cactus

CACTACEAE

Once one of the most popular of Cacti for home use, the Rat's Tail, *Aporocactus flagelli-formis*, is now less widely seen, though it is very easy to grow from cuttings dried off a few days before planting. It is an epiphyte, native to Mexican jungles, so it needs a rich compost with plenty of leafmould, sharp sand and some charcoal. *Aporocactus* is best grown in small hanging pots because of its weeping habit, but is sometimes grafted onto a thicker tall cactus to make a weeping standard. The slim trailing stems are covered with brown spines and are not much more than 1 cm/½ in thick. They are frequently branched. The 4cm/1½ in cerise flowers appear in late spring. The Rat's Tail prefers only part sun, and makes an intriguing indoor plant.

Aporocactus flagelliformis. Rat's Tail Cactus

APTENIA

(ap-**teen**-ee-ə)

(SYN Mesembryanthemum)

Heartleaf

AIZOACEAE

You may still find *Aptenia cordifolia* listed under its old name, *Mesembryanthemum.* Whatever you call it, this prostrate South African is a delightful plant, its trailing stems adorned with succulent, heart-shaped leaves and tiny but brilliant daisy-like flowers in either magenta or crimson. The variegated form illustrated is perhaps the prettiest version, though it doesn't flower all that freely. The Heartleaf is an excellent fast-growing groundcover for a dry, sunny spot, but frost kills it instantly, and in cool to cold climates it is most often grown as a pot plant

Aptenia cordifolia 'Variegata'. Heartleaf

(it looks very pretty cascading from a window box) and taken indoors for the winter. It will happily live on a sunny window sill all year.

Seed can be sown direct in dryish soil in early spring and raked in. Thin out later to a spacing of 15cm/6in. Best in full sun.

AQUILEGIA

(ak-wil-**ee**-jee-ə)

Columbine, Granny's Bonnets

RANUNCULACEAE

Charming Columbines (*Aquilegia vulgaris*) seem to have dropped out of popularity and a revival is surely overdue. Modern types such as McKana Hybrids grow to 60cm/2ft in height, sending up tall stems of bright, long-spurred blooms from a loose rosette of

Aquilegia, McKana Hybrids. Granny's Bonnets

Aquilegia, Biedermeier Hybrids. Columbine

Aquilegia vulgaris cultivars. Columbine

Arachnis flos-aeris. Spider Orchid

ARACHNIS
(a-**rak**-nis)
(SYN Arachnanthe)
Spider Orchid
ORCHIDACEAE

In recent years, florists and fruitstands of the world have been dominated by a new type of cut flower imported largely from Singapore. These are long stems of rather wicked-looking orchids called *Arachnis* (from the Greek *arachne*, a spider), and they are often quite reasonably priced. Lasting for months, they can be an incredible bargain.

Growing these spider orchids has become quite a cottage industry in Singapore, where they grow like weeds in the equatorial climate. They are native to forests of Southeast Asia, where they sometimes produce hanging flower spikes up to 4m/13ft in length. Even in cultivation, they need a minimum temperature of 18°C/65°F.

The flowers appear in summer, and open one by one as the flower stem lengthens – but they are strictly a tropical subject.

Arabis caucasica 'Flore Pleno'. Double Rock Cress

delightful blue-green foliage resembling maidenhair fern. If seed is sown in earliest spring, germination may take up to 25 days. Plant out when 5cm/2in tall, at 30cm/12in spacings. Semi-shade is best, and an alkaline soil kept moist. Give plenty of liquid fertiliser during growth. In cold climates, *Aquilegias* are perennial and are cut to ground in late autumn. Elsewhere, fresh plants annually give best results.

ARABIS
(a-ra-bis)
Rock Cress
BRASSICACEAE

Charming but unspectacular plants for the rock or alpine garden, or for crevices in steps, walls and paving, the perennial Rock Cresses form dense mats of grey-green leaf rosettes and are often used to over-plant spring-flowering bulbs. They'll bloom from late winter through into summer, growing about 22cm/9in tall. Most commonly seen of about 120 species is the ubiquitous *Arabis caucasica* (also known as *A. albida* and *A. alpina*).

It is set out from divisions in autumn at a spacing of 40cm/16in but can also be grown from seed sown indoors at 21°C/70°F and left uncovered. *Arabis* likes sandy, well-drained soil and needs little water. It should be cut back hard when bloom is over. Like other members of the mustard family (Brassicaceae), it is prone to fungus diseases and should be watched in humid weather. There are both white and pink flowered forms.

ARAUJIA

(a-**rau**-jee-ə)

Cruel Plant, White Bladder Flower, Moth Vine

ASCLEPIADACEAE

There's something to be said for all of this plant's diverse popular names. Cruel Plant, because they have been observed to tear night-flying moths to shreds as they struggle to free themselves from the sticky pollen. Moth Vine because they are so attractive to these insects. White Bladder Flower because they develop great bladder-like seed pods which split to scatter silky-white seed for miles. *Araujia sericifera* is a twining vine from South America which grows altogether too well in warm temperate climates. The white, fragrant flowers are a little like related Stephanotis.

Propagate *Araujia* from seed, or from ripe-wood cuttings in autumn. Use care – it may become a pest.

ARBUTUS

(**ar**-byoo-təs)

Irish Strawberry Tree, Madrone

ERICACEAE

The name Irish Strawberry must be a hang-over from some earlier Irish joke. Birds, bugs and children playing games might appreciate the fruit, but hardly anyone else. But the tree itself is another matter! Seek out *Arbutus unedo* in autumn when the branches are almost weighed down with tiny, fragrant flowers, drooping just like Lily-of-the-Valley. The tree is evergreen, has beautifully gnarled, reddish branches and shiny, serrated, ellipti-cal leaves. The flowers are white or pink.

Arbutus unedo. Irish Strawberry Tree

Araujia sericifera. Cruel Plant

At the other end of Europe grows the simi-lar but taller *A. andrachne* of Greece and Asia Minor, with the flowers borne in erect spikes. Half a world away, in California, is *A. menziesii*, the Madrone or California Strawberry Tree. Tallest of all, reaching 30m/100ft, its decorative, terracotta bark peels away in large flaky patches, and the pink flowers appear in spring. Somewhere in between is *A. canariensis*, from the Canary Islands. Its leaves are softer and the flowers green and pink.

ARCTOSTAPHYLOS

(ark-toh-**staf**-il-os)

Manzanita, Bearberry

ERICACEAE

When the first European botanists in California enquired the uses of the plants they saw, local Indians told them that one particular genus of shrubs had a great attrac-tion for grizzly bears. So the botanists called the plants *Arctostaphylos*, from two Greek words meaning 'bear-grape'. Confined to western areas of North and Central America, they are mostly low, spreading bushes grow-ing to around 1m/3ft, with reddish stems and small, leathery leaves that are almost hidden in spring beneath a profusion of bloom. All 50-odd species are easy to grow from seed, autumn cuttings or by separation of self-layered branches which are easy to locate. Light watering and feeding are required, with regular pinching and pruning to control the sprawling habit.

ARCTOTHECA

(ark-**toth**-e-kə)

Cape Weed, Cape Dandelion

ASTERACEAE

I wonder if anyone weaves daisy chains any more? One of my earliest memories from a Tasmanian childhood was making them from the stringy stems and golden daisy flowers of the ubiquitous Cape Weed. This attractive and tough South African plant (*Arctotheca calendula*) has become natural-ised all over the temperate world and is even cultivated as a showy groundcover in California, particularly on hillsides. Not in the least fussy about soil, provided water is available in really dry spells, *Arctotheca* spreads rapidly by means of its runners, producing masses of deeply cut leaves that are greyish-green on their reverses. The 5cm/2in blooms appear on stems up to 15cm/6in high throughout the year, but most profusely in spring and summer. They have become common along roadsides in parts of Australia, and are obviously closely related to another African Daisy genus, Arctotis.

Arctotheca calendula. Cape Weed

Arctostaphylos densiflora. Bearberry, Manzanita

ARCTOTIS
(ark-**toh**-tis)
Aurora Daisy, African Daisy
ASTERACEAE

Bright, profusely blooming Aurora Daisies are unexcelled for groundcover or mass planting on sloping sites. They grow anywhere, prefer sandy soil with good drainage and a ration of fine, well-rotted compost. They grow to about 60cm/2ft and bloom continuously from spring to autumn. The 8cm/3in flowers of modern *Arctotis hybrida* include pinks, orange, red, white and yellow as well as some curious lilac and plum shades – all with contrasting black and gold centres.

Arctotis hybrids are really perennial, but are grown as annuals to preserve a bushy habit. Seed can be sown outdoors in earliest spring, or for quicker results, indoors, maintaining a temperature of 16°C/60°F. Germination should take 3 weeks. Allow 6 weeks till the long blooming season begins. Plant in full sun. *Arctotis* blooms close in the late afternoon or in dull weather and need continuous water.

Arctotis hybrida. Aurora Daisy

ARENARIA
(ar-en-**ar**-ee-ə)
Corsican Sandwort
CARYOPHYLLACEAE

One of the lowest-growing plants in the garden, the dainty *Arenaria balearica* rarely surpasses 5cm/2in in height, but may spread its mossy foliage for yards, showering itself with tiny white starry flowers throughout spring and summer. It will grow in sandy, well-drained soil in which it is planted from early spring divisions. Give it a modicum of shade and adequate water, and away she goes! Best confine it, though, to the spaces between paving stones or the shaded side of a rockery, for it can become very invasive and may smother other plants. Can be a useful lawn substitute.

Arenaria balearica. Corsican Sandwort

ARGEMONE
(ar-**gem**-o-nee)
Prickly Poppy, Mexican Poppy, Devil's Fig
PAPAVERACEAE

The *Argemones* (all 28 species of them) are a North American genus of the poppy family, named from the Greek *argema,* a cataract, because local Indians believed they could cure that affliction of the eye. All I can say is, don't go waving them at me! They have a *nasty* yellow sap, and quite uncomfortable prickles that make them impossible to pick without gloves. Sow seed in summer, transplant before winter to the mixed border, at least 45cm/18in apart. Blooming mostly in shades of yellow, white or purple, they'll grow in any soil in full sun. One species is naturalised in Australia.

ARGYRANTHEMUM
(ah-gai-**ran**-thə-mum)
Marguerite, Paris Daisy
ASTERACEAE

The Marguerites or Paris Daisies are old friends, and their transfer from *Chrysanthemum* to a genus of their own does not diminish their charm. Indeed it makes good sense, as these are 80cm/32in soft-wooded shrubs, while their former siblings are annuals or herbaceous perennials. The

Argemone mexicana. Prickly Poppy

Argyranthemum frutescens. Paris Daisy

Argyranthemum frutescens cultivar.
Marguerite

flowers can be either single, gold-centred
daisies, or double, like small chrysanthemums. Both types come in cheerful colours
from snow white through cream to yellow
and pink, the ferny leaves setting them off
very nicely. In frost-free climates they bloom
almost all year and put up with any soil so
long as drainage is perfect and the position
sunny. In frosty climates they are usually
struck from cuttings in autumn, over-
wintered in the greenhouse and planted
out for the summer when frost is no longer
a threat.

ARGYREIA
(ah-**gai**-ree-∂)
Elephant Vine, Silver Morning Glory
CONVOLVULACEAE

These rampant jungle vines from tropical
Asia are indeed related to the morning glory
(Ipomoea), and the flowers do resemble
them; but they are mainly some shade of
bright pink and you have to turn the leaves
over to see the silvery undersides to which
both common and scientific names refer.
They are handsome plants for a tropical
garden or a big greenhouse elsewhere, the big
bold leaves (those of the illustrated *Argyreia
nervosa* being about 20cm/8in wide, *A. splendens* even larger) and the year-round flowers
always attracting attention. Pruning in early
spring will keep the plants under control.

ARISAEMA
(ar-is-**ee**-m∂)
Jack-in-the-Pulpit
ARACEAE

Interesting as groundcover among shrubs
and trees, most species of *Arisaema* (about
150 of them) are native to Asia, with a few
found only in tropical Africa. They are
miniature relatives of the Arum Lily, to

Argyreia nervosa. Woolly Morning Glory

which they bear a strong resemblance,
though the tonings are often more like those
of an insect than a flower, stripes and spots
being the rule rather than the exception.
Illustrated species *A. sikokianum* is native to
the Japanese island of Shikoku, where it is
found among the leaf-litter of hillside forests.
In spring, dark compound leaves of up to
5 segments pop up from a deeply buried
tuber, followed by virtually stemless aroid
flowers of deep purple, striped with greenish
bands. The spathe's interior is greeny-white,
flecked purple; the spadix is snowy-white.
Keep moist and plant *deeply*.

Arisaema sikokianum. Jack-in-the-Pulpit

Aristea ecklonii. Blue Stars

ARISTEA
(a-ris-**tee**-∂)
Blue Stars
IRIDACEAE

Easy to grow from seed scattered in enriched,
well-drained soil, the showy *Aristeas* are Iris-
like rhizomatous perennials from South
Africa, and quickly naturalise to form a
striking show in the wild garden. The leaves
are evergreen, and appear in 2-ranked fans
from a creeping rootstock. During late spring
and early summer, 30cm/12in stems push
up to display their racemes of violet-blue
2cm flowers.

Clumps of *Aristea* look particularly decorative along woodland pathways or beside
pools and streams. They do best with shade
during the hottest part of the day, and need
plenty of moisture. In fact, lest you think they
are *too* easy to grow, it must be said that they
do not transplant well once established, and
must never be allowed to dry out. The 50 or
so *Aristea* species close their flowers at night,
so are of no use in arrangements. But let
them decorate the garden itself.

ARISTOLOCHIA
(ar-is-to-**loh**-kee-∂)
Dutchman's Pipe, Calico Plant
ARISTOLOCHIACEAE

Native to both the old and the new world,
the *Aristolochias* take their name from the
ancient Greek *aristos* and *locheia*, signifying
some long-forgotten medicinal use in child-
birth. Best known is the Dutchman's Pipe

Aristolochia littoralis. Dutchman's Pipe

(*Aristolochia macrophylla*), which needs training up a large trellis or over an archway, for it must make a considerable length of growth before flowers appear. It is a fast-growing twining plant, hiding its support beneath a mass of kidney-shaped crepe-textured leaves. The curious flowers often appear in pairs beneath the foliage in warm weather, pale yellowish-green outside, blotched deep purple inside. Native to North America, it seems hardy enough in English and coastal European climates. Prune back hard in winter.

Armeria maritima. Thrift, Sea Pink

Armeria maritima 'Vindictive'. Thrift

ARMERIA
(ar-**meer**-ee-ə)
Thrift, Sea Pink
PLUMBAGINACEAE

Evergreen perennials that look like grassy cushions all year, *Armerias* are mostly native to mountain meadows and rocky coasts of the Mediterranean and Asia Minor. They like gravelly, well-drained soil and need little water but appreciate an annual sprinkling of slow-release fertiliser. If spent flower stems are cut, they'll keep up a display of pink, white or deep rose bloom from spring through autumn. Propagate from winter division, summer cuttings, or in spring from well-soaked seed, which will germinate in less than 3 weeks at 18°C/65°F. Set plants out at 20–30cm/8–12in spacings. Watch 'rust' in spring, spray with fungicide.

ARPOPHYLLUM
(ar-poh-**fil**-lum)
Hyacinth Orchid
ORCHIDACEAE

This small genus of Central American orchids is less often seen than other members of the family, probably because the flowers are anything but spectacular, being so very small.

But they could certainly be called fascinating, because they are borne in incredibly large numbers all along the length of a crowded 60cm/2ft spike, which may last in good condition for a month or more. The popular name of Hyacinth Orchid would seem to be due to their appearance, for they are not fragrant. Treat as for Cattleyas. The name *Arpophyllum* means 'scimitar-leaf'.

Arpophyllum giganteum. Hyacinth Orchid

Arthropodium cirratum. Renga Renga

Arum italicum. Italian Arum

Aruncus dioicus. Goat's Beard

ARTHROPODIUM

(ah-throh-**poh**-dee-∂m)

Renga Renga

LILIACEAE

Not growing from bulbs in spite of their appearance, the graceful *Arthropodium* species (a dozen or so in the genus) are fibrous-rooted perennials, though included in the lily family. The best known are native to New Zealand, though some are found in Australia, one in New Caledonia. Purely for the temperate climate, they grow easily from seed or division and flourish in well-drained sandy soil with a little added peat or leaf-mould. The broadly lanceolate, arching leaves may be up to 60cm/2ft in length, and dainty many-branched panicles of white, starry flowers appear from leaf axils in spring. Light shade or filtered sun suits them best.

ARUM

(a-rum)

Italian Arum, Green Calla

ARACEAE

Though giving their name to a very large group of plants, the real members of the genus *Arum* are few. All of them enjoy rich soil, plenty of water and shade and are usually recognised by their arrow-shaped leaves and curious, hooded flowers.
A. italicum has a delicate, almost transparent green spathe and yellow spadix;
A. palaestinum (Black Calla) is green outside, purple-black inside, with a jet-black spadix; other species bear brown-violet and white flowers. The so-called Arum Lily is not an *Arum* – it is a Zantedeschia.

ARUNCUS

(a-**run**-kus)

Goat's Beard

ROSACEAE

A graceful woodland perennial that's at home in any shaded location, quaintly named Goat's Beard grows rather large (2m/6ft) and may best be set in a wild garden – though it looks sensational by a pool or creek. Wherever, it demands deep, rich soil to give of its best, and roots should be kept moist at all times. *Aruncus dioicus* (syn *A. sylvestris*) is a rose relative – there is a distinct resemblance in its handsome pale green leaves, each with many finely pleated, ovate leaflets. The flowers, however, are quite different: tiny, white and borne in plume-like panicles high above the dense foliage. Cut flowering stems back hard in autumn/fall, and plant out from divisions at the same time.

Asclepias incarnata. Swamp Milkweed

ASCLEPIAS

(as-**klee**-pee-∂s)

Milkweed, Butterfly Weed

ASCLEPIADACEAE

A large genus of plants from the Americas and Africa, *Asclepias* are represented in gardens by several perennial species. The Blood Flower, *A. curassavica*, is for warm-climate gardens only, a woody plant with bright, crown-shaped orange and red flowers in umbels at the upper leaf axils. It is grown from spring-sown seed, as is orange-flowered *A. tuberosa*, from cooler areas of eastern North America. Also from North America is *A. incarnata*, the Swamp Milkweed, which grows 60–120cm/2–4ft high, from cold-weather root divisions. All like a deep, rich soil with leafmould and peat. Regular water and an annual spring feeding help them remain fresh and green. The narrow leaves of all species are similar, but *A. incarnata's* tiny, flesh-pink flowers open from brick-coloured buds. The name Milkweed refers to the sticky sap, so attractive to butterflies. All species do best in full sun, and bloom for prolonged periods through summer. Several species bear attractive fruits during the autumn months.

Asclepias tuberosa. Butterfly Weed

Ascocentrum curvifolium. Ascocentrum

ASCOCENTRUM

(as-ko-**sen**-trəm)
(SYN Saccolabium)
Ascocentrum
ORCHIDACEAE

Until recently, this colourful group of tropical orchids was known as *Saccolabium,* which
was easy to translate – it means a flower with
a bag-like lip – and aptly described their
form, if not their beauty. But the taxonomists
decided that *Ascocentrum* would be a more
appropriate name, and if I only knew what it
meant, I might agree with them. Rarely seen

outside a glasshouse away from their exotic
homelands of New Guinea, the Philippines
and Java, they are all epiphytic and prefer a
winter temperature of not less than
15°C/59°F. Grow them in pierced pots filled
with chunks of treefern, fibre and bark chips,
anything in which their questing epiphyic
roots can get a grip. Low-growing
Ascocentrum curvifolium has fleshy, short,
curved leaves from which short spikes of
cinnabar red flowers appear in spring and
summer. Water sparingly in the cooler
months, shade from full sun in spring and
summer, removing the protection gradually
as the shorter days come.

ASPERULA

(as-**per**-oo-la)
Woodruff
RUBIACEAE

Classed in the same botanical family as more
tropical beauties like Bouvardia, Coffea,
Luculia, Pentas and Rondeletia – all popular
shrubs – the 90-odd species of *Asperula* are
mostly perennials, found naturally in Europe
and the Caucasus. They are hillside plants,
used to rough ground, and are most
commonly grown in pockets of the rock
garden, where they enjoy full shade and a
moist, compost-rich soil.

Grow them from seed or division of the
clumps in spring or early summer. Set out in
their final position in early autumn. *A. orientalis* produces terminal sprays of blue or
white 4-petalled flowers in summer. They
resemble Daphne. Most other species bloom
in shades of pink.

Asperula orientalis. Woodruff

Asphodeline lutea. Jacob's Rod

ASPHODELINE

(as-fod-el-**ee**-nee)
Jacob's Rod, King's Spear
LILIACEAE

Due to the tyranny of an imposed alphabetical order, I must describe this plant before
the following entry, which you are unlikely to
have absorbed at this time. Suffice it to say
that the two plants are almost identical, and
are constantly confused by horticulturists,
including myself. The main difference is that
the stems of *Asphodeline* are clothed with
grassy leaves for much of their length, while
those of Asphodelus are naked. *Asphodeline*
are also found over a more restricted area,
close to the Mediterranean. Plant them in
autumn or spring in any ordinary garden soil
and expect the 1m/3ft tall flower stems in
early summer.

ASPHODELUS

(as-**fod**-el-əs)
Asphodel
LILIACEAE

One of the soggier late-Victorian poets
managed to rhyme Asphodel with damosel
in a verse about knightly virtue – but he was
romanticising the daffodil anyway. The true
Asphodels (some 18 species of them) are
more connected with Greek myths; they are
said to grow plentifully in the afterworld.
Found wild in the crusader-haunted lands of
the Mediterranean, they grow to about
1m/3ft from a cluster of fleshy roots. These

Asphodelus albus. Asphodel

send up tufts of narrow, arching leaves, and in summer, tall stems bearing spikes of yellow or white 6-petalled flowers. Most effective planted in clumps in the woodland garden or mixed border, *Asphodelus* species are generally set out in early spring, and can be propagated by division. Half-shade suits them.

ASPIDISTRA

(as-pi-**dis**-tr∂)

Cast-iron Plant, Aspidistra

LILIACEAE

Aspidistra is famous as the house plant that will survive where almost anything else will die – hence the name Cast-iron Plant – but the dusty, starved specimens you so often see give little idea of the beauty the plant can achieve when it is happy. Then the shining

Aspidistra elatior. Cast-iron Plant, Aspidistra

leaves, rising from their rootstock like a greatly enlarged and polished version of those of their cousin, the lily-of-the-valley, create a picture of real elegance. In their native Japan one of the great tests of skill of a master of ikebana is to create an arrangement of aspidistra leaves only.

Treat your plant decently, giving it a reasonable amount of light, good potting mix, fertiliser in spring, and regular watering; and then it may even flower for you. The flowers are just 2.5cm/1in wide purplish affairs borne close to the soil in autumn, but they are a great conversation piece. As far as I know, they are the only flowers designed for pollination by snails!

ASTARTEA

(as-**tart**-ee-∂)

(SYN Baeckea)

Astartea

MYRTACEAE

Producing a never-ending display of bloom once established, the genus *Astartea* was named for a Phoenician goddess of fertility who was equally generous with her favours. Like many Australian plants, the *Astarteas* belong to the myrtle family and dislike extreme humidity. Otherwise they are highly adaptable, tolerating frost, salt air, drought and even waterlogged soil. They have minimal need for water or nutriment, and pruning is needed only to keep the 1m/3ft bushes compact. Illustrated *A. fascicularis* can be grown from tip-cuttings taken any time, or from ripe seed sown thinly on a sieved sand/peat mixture. The typical 5-petalled myrtle flowers are about 1cm/½in in diameter and may be white or rose pink. The needle-leaves are evergreen.

Astartea fascicularis. Astartea

Astelia banksii. Astelia

ASTELIA

(as-**teel**-ee-∂)

Astelia, Whara Whara, Kakaha

LILIACEAE

The *Astelias* are a genus of clumpy perennials related to the Cordylines, and if you imagine a dwarf Cordyline, with the same strap-shaped leaves and big, branching clusters of tiny, whitish flowers, you'll have the picture. They are equally fine house plants and can add a touch of tropical luxuriance to warm-temperate gardens. Most species, including the illustrated *Astelia banksii*, come from the southern hemisphere, with New Zealand having the largest number.

ASTER

(**ass**-t∂r)

Michaelmas or Easter Daisy

ASTERACEAE

Not the plant commonly called Aster or China Aster (*Callistephus chinensis*), the true

Aster novi-belgii 'Winston S. Churchill'. New York Aster

Aster ericoides. Heath Aster

Aster novi-belgii 'Patricia Ballard'. New York Aster

Asters are a vast genus of 500 and more perennial plants found on all continents except Australia. Though many have individual popular names, they are collectively known in the northern hemisphere as Michaelmas Daisies, because their peak flowering is around the end of September – conversely, south of the equator they are called Easter Daisies. Whichever name you use, they are, as a group, among the most rewarding of all herbaceous perennials, sending up tall panicles of showy daisy flowers year after year. Many species and colour varieties are grown. The Italian Aster, *A. amellus*, grows to 60cm/2ft, has rough-textured, greyish lanceolate leaves and blue-lilac flowers. North American *A. ericoides* or Heath Aster grows to 1m/3ft, bears many-branched stems of 1cm/½in white or pinkish bloom, and has very narrow leaves. *A. frikartii* is a Eurasian hybrid of 75cm/30in with dark, rough leaves and orange-centred violet-blue flowers,

5cm/2in across. *A. linosyris* (found around the Mediterranean) is known as Goldilocks; its bright yellow flowers appear in late summer right at stem tips. North American *A. novae-angliae* (the New England Aster) grows tallest, sometimes to 1.5m/5ft and is available in many colour varieties, with flowers from 2.5 to 5cm/1 to 2in across. *A. novi-belgii* (the New York Aster) is the parent of most commonly grown hybrids, in colour varieties of white, blue, mauve, pink, crimson and purple. All species are planted out from division of established clumps in late autumn. Grow in full sun except in very hot areas, where they will gratefully accept semi-shade. Soil must be well drained and preferably enriched with peat or leafmould. Plants should be kept moist at all times and benefit from a ration of complete plant food in spring and again in summer. After blooming, all flowering stems can be cut back to ground level. Replace plants every 3 years or so.

ASTERISCUS
(as-ter-**is**-kus)
(SYN Odontospermum)
Canary Island Daisy
ASTERACEAE

Now separated from its former genus of *Odontospermum*, the gaily coloured *Asteriscus maritimus* has been brought into cultivation in coastal areas of California, Hawaii and many other countries.

Propagated from seed, or more easily from cuttings, it should be set out in early autumn in a sunny position in well-drained soil that is rich in leafmould. With light watering and an occasional treat of dilute fertiliser it will grow to around 15cm/6in, spreading horizontally but keeping a compact shape. The silkily furred leaves are widest away from their stems. It is evergreen. The solitary daisy flowers, almost stalkless, appear at terminals.

Aster frikartii. Michaelmas Daisy

Asteriscus maritimus. Seaside Daisy

Astilbe 'Weisse Gloria'. White Astilbe

Astilbe, Mixed cultivars. False Spiraea

Astilbe 'Rotlicht'. Hybrid Astilbe

ASTILBE
(as-**til**-bee)
False Spiraea, Goat's Beard
SAXIFRAGACEAE

Spectacular when mass planted, *Astilbes* are easy to propagate and grow, require little attention, and really romp away in deep, rich soil with plenty of water. They can be naturalised under trees, used in the border or larger rock garden, and are specially effective set out in groups by a garden pool.

The foliage is magnificent – each shining leaf compounded of a number of finely pleated leaflets. A rich green at maturity, they are often distinctly pink or copper-toned when young. The flowers appear in 1m/3ft plume-like panicles, which may branch freely and consist of hundreds of tiny flowers. Colours range from white through every shade of pink to darkest red.

Most garden cultivars are grouped under the name *A. arendsii*, and are hybrids of various Asian species. They vary in height from 60 –100cm/2–3ft.

Astilbes are replanted from divisions set 60cm/2ft apart in early spring, and should be shaded in warm weather until their roots are well established. They can also be grown from seed, which is sown indoors in winter at a temperature range of 16–21ºC/60–70ºF. If this can be maintained, germination should take about 28 days. The only other species much grown are *A. chinensis* and its strain var. *pumila*, a dwarf rockery plant with erect panicles of rosy bloom, and the taller-growing *A. grandis* or Giant Spiraea, which may reach 2m/6ft in height, and should be planted at 60cm/2ft spacings. Its blooms are pure white but borne in spreading showy panicles.

Astilbes should be cut back to the ground in late autumn, and lifted and divided every 3 years. The flower stems of all varieties are good for cutting, and make as showy a display indoors as out.

Astragalus lusitanicus. Milk Vetch

ASTRAGALUS
(as-**trag**-a-lus)
Milk Vetch
FABACEAE

Remember an old song that runs 'The anklebone's connecka t'the shin bones'? Then you shouldn't have any trouble remembering the name of these small plants. *Astragalus* means 'ankle bone', and comes from the shape of the plant's seeds. Indeed, *Astragalus* are almost as common as ankle bones – there are around 2000 species of them scattered over the northern hemisphere, almost all perennials or annuals. Raise from seed – give them a sunny position in dry, well-drained soil, and do not over-water. Be warned – germination is slow. *Astragalus* rarely grow above 30cm/1ft.

ASTRANTIA
(as-**tran**-tee-ə)
Masterwort
APIACEAE

Several species of this small perennial genus (a division of the carrot family) have a great popularity with European gardeners. Native to Europe and the Near East, *Astrantias* grow well in any soil in part shade, but really sparkle in full sun so long as the soil is constantly moist. They grow 60–100cm/ 2–3ft tall. The attractive leaves are much divided and delicately pointed; the small starry flowers, borne all through summer in subdued combinations of pink, white and green, are arranged in many-branched umbels, each head surrounded by green-tipped white bracts.

Astrantias are propagated from divisions, between late autumn and early spring. They

Astrantia major. Masterwort

Asystasia gangetica. Ganges Bluebell

can also be raised from seed sown early autumn. The seedlings should be pricked out into boxes in spring, transferred to a nursery bed in summer and finally into the garden about 18 months after sowing. Flower stems are cut back in autumn.

ASTROPHYTUM
(as-troh-**fai**-təm)
Bishop's Hat, Star Cactus
CACTACEAE

Once included in the wickedly spined genus *Echinocactus*, the *Astrophytums* are now sensibly grouped on their own, for unlike most members of the cactus family, they are completely spineless and easy to handle. They are at least as easy to grow as other terrestrial cacti, being quite happy in a gritty, open compost with perfect drainage. This can be arranged in a raised rockery bed, or some sort of container. Indoors or out, water them regularly though infrequently, and leave them overall on the dryish side. They are ideal for a sunny window, terrace or open

Astrophytum myriostigma. Bishop's Hat

courtyard and make an effective contrast to other cactus types in a mixed planter. Viewed from above, the plants are shaped like a perfect star with 4–8 points. Each *Astrophytum* plant produces a single golden-yellow flower right on top. They grow up to 25cm/10in high.

ASYSTASIA
(a-sis-**tay**-shə)
Ganges Bluebell
ACANTHACEAE

A scrambling groundcover plant for the warmer climate (10°C/50°F is needed), *Asystasia gangetica* is from India, like others of the genus. It grows only 30cm/1ft in height, but can cover a considerable area in the tropical climates it loves. There it may bloom throughout the year, sending up erect spikes of Bignonia-like mauve flowers. It is used as an effective street planting in Hawaii. To propagate, take cuttings in early spring and strike in a sharp, sandy compost. When rooted, set out in a rich, well-drained soil and supply with ample water. Also effective in hanging baskets.

ATROPA
(a-**troh**-pə)
Deadly Nightshade, Belladonna
SOLANACEAE

Frankly, *Atropa belladonna*, a sprawling, 1m/3ft high perennial from central Europe, is no great beauty – its growth is weedy and its flowers are small, dull and scentless – but it has a remarkable history. I don't think any horror-movie sorcerer has failed to make use of deadly nightshade in one or other of his

potions, and 16th-century Italian belles used to squeeze a drop of its sap into their eyes to dilate their pupils and enhance their beauty – hence the name *belladonna*, beautiful woman. Don't try it: all parts of the plant are extremely poisonous, though modern medicine extracts drugs from its roots for the treatment of Parkinson's disease, among other things. If you fancy growing it, it likes a temperate climate, rich soil and a little shade.

AUBRIETA
(aw-**bree**-shə)
Rock Cress
BRASSICACEAE

Named for a prominent French botanical artist of the 18th century, *Aubrietas* are miniature trailing perennials used for paving chinks or border edges. They are easily grown from seed, or rooted cuttings. You can easily obtain the latter as follows: shear back the plant after spring bloom, work a quantity of leafmould and sand among the remaining stems and water lightly. Each stem will

Atropa belladonna 'Lutea'. Deadly Nightshade

Aubrieta cultorum. Rock Cress

sprout roots and can be separated for plant-ing in autumn. *Aubrietas* form dense mats of grey-green foliage which burst into flower for long periods in spring. Colours include pink, lilac and purple, both single and double in form. *Aubrietas* delight in sun, and prefer light, sandy soil in a sheltered posi-tion, where their roots can spread way down.

AURINIA

(aw-**rin**-ee-ə)
(SYN Alyssum saxatile)
Basket of Gold, Gold Dust, Madwort, Yellow Alyssum
BRASSICACEAE

So many of us have known and loved this plant as Yellow Alice or Alyssum, it may come as a shock to learn it is now *Aurinia saxatilis*! But no name change can detract from its incredible beauty in the spring and early summer garden. Then, its neat mound of greyish leaf-rosettes suddenly bursts into a blinding mass of tiny golden flowers, the display persisting for months. *Aurinia* is a woody-rooted, subshrubby perennial, grow-ing to 30cm/12in. It's evergreen and grown

Aurinia saxatilis. Basket of Gold

from seed or cuttings. The latter are taken after bloom ends, inserted in a mixture of sand and peat and potted up when rooted. Keep them under glass through winter. They should be ready to set out at spacings of 30–45cm/12–18in the following spring. Seed can be sown directly in the flowering position in spring, or indoors in winter, where it will germinate in about 2 weeks at a temperature of 13–24°C/55–75°F. The seed needs light to sprout and should merely be sprinkled on the surface. Shear the plant back hard when bloom is over. Seek out named colour varieties in every shade from cream to almost orange. The golden-yellow is the most eye-catching.

Azalea 'Alphonse Anderson'. Indica Azalea

AZALEA

(ə-**zae**-lee-ə)
(SYN Rhododendron)
Azalea
ERICACEAE

Though the world of botany now classes Azaleas as a section of the *Rhododendron* genus, we will stick to tradition and use the name every gardener knows – Azalea. There is more to this decision than taste. There are differences between them, and at one time these seemed to be sufficient to warrant separate classification. In addition to the actual structure of the flowers, the Azalea group thrive in a much wider climatic range than the other *Rhododendrons*, which are mostly mountain or cold climate plants. Azaleas, particularly the evergreen types, enjoy life anywhere the soil is light and acid.

The Azaleas we grow are nearly all hybrids, cross-bred from literally dozens of species, but even so, they fall into several main groups. By far the most common are the evergreen Indica Azaleas, mostly mauve, pink or white, which grow up to 3m/10ft in height and width. The Indicas also include a sub-category, the Belgian Indicas, mostly double, in a wider colour range and reaching only 1/m 3ft. The second most common group are the Kurume Azaleas – dainty mountain plants most often used in rock-eries. They often flower in both spring and autumn, some leaves colouring in winter.

Azalea 'Mme van Ackers'. Belgian Indica Azalea

Azalea 'Fairy Queen'. Kurume Azalea

Azalea 'Hotspur Yellow'. Mollis Azalea

Group three are the perfumed Mollis Azaleas, with blooms in yellow, orange and flame tones. These are deciduous, mostly grown in cool-climate gardens.

The Macrantha or Satsuki Azaleas are the popular types in Japan. They include many fancy flower shapes, some with multi-coloured blooms. This group encompasses the dwarf Gumpo types.

All Azaleas are shallow rooters and must be planted quite firmly to prevent wind damage. The Indica types are often disfigured by lacebug, which can be controlled by spraying *under* the leaves in warm weather with a suitable insecticide. The other principal problem is azalea petal blight, a fungus which causes the flowers to rot in humid weather. Spray regularly with a recommended fungicide, and burn all affected flowers.

Azalea 'Coronation Lady'. Knap Hill/Exbury Azalea

Azalea 'Seikai'. Satsuki Azalea

AZARA

(∂-**zar**-∂)

Oromo

FLACOURTIACEAE

Azaras are small trees or shrubs from Chile, bearing tiny golden flowers that have a rich, chocolaty perfume out of all proportion to their size. Local Chileans have always called them 'Oromo' in reference to their strong fragrance.

Several species are grown in sheltered areas of temperate gardens; all enjoy protection from strong sun and well-drained soil. Ample water and regular feeding are necessary to turn on a good blossom display. The ovate leaves of *A. dentata* are finely toothed and glossy above, slightly hairy on the reverse. The tree develops a rounded shape and branches densely; it can be pruned as a useful hedge. The small clusters of fluffy blossom are at their best in late spring. Related *A. lanceolata* blooms earlier, has larger, 6cm/2½ in leaves.

Azalea 'Coccineum Speciosum'. Ghent Azalea

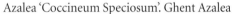

Azara dentata. Oromo

Babiana stricta. Baboon Flower

BABIANA
(bab-ee-**ah**-n∂)
Baboon Flower, Baboon Root
IRIDACEAE

Because the early Dutch settlers in South Africa observed baboons digging hungrily for the bulbs of these charming plants, they named them *babianer,* later adapted to the suitable botanical alternative *Babiana* by taxonomists. They are tender bulbs related to Freesia, Ixia, Sparaxis and many other flowers from the Cape. Unlike the others, however, their leaves are strongly pleated and very hairy. They add a useful range of blue and violet tones to the spring bulb spectrum, reproduce well from seed or from offsets formed around the old bulbs. Seed will bloom in 18 months, and bulbs should be planted out in autumn in sandy soil. With plenty of water, they'll bloom in spring. In cold areas, protect the planted bulbs with a thick winter mulch.

Baeckea ramosissima. Rosy Baeckea

Backhousia citriodora. Lemon-scented Myrtle

BACKHOUSIA
(bak-**hou**-zee-∂)
Lemon-scented Myrtle
MYRTACEAE

Backhousia citriodora is a tree with lemon fragrance in all its parts. It has attracted many common names, a proof of popularity not only in its native Australia, but worldwide: Sweet Verbena Tree, Sand Verbena Myrtle and Tree Verbena are among them.

Easily raised from half-ripe cuttings taken in spring, *Backhousia* grows fast in a good, rich, acid soil. It is deservedly popular not only for its shiny leaves with strong citrus fragrance, but also for the clouds of tiny 4-petalled white flowers produced in early summer. These fall in warm weather, but are outlived by tiny green calyces, the tree's principal display.

B. citriodora is raised commercially, the foliage being crushed to extract a volatile, citrus-scented oil. All six *Backhousia* species enjoy year-round moisture in climates no colder than 2ºC/36ºF in winter.

BAECKEA
(**bake**-ee-∂)
Baeckea
MYRTACEAE

Not very much grown, it seems, away from their native Australia (where they are found in all States) the dainty *Baeckeas* look rather like small Leptospermum (which see). They vary from 30cm–1m/1–3ft in height and bloom over a long period in spring and summer – something of a rarity among Australian flora. The small, heath-like leaves are very shiny, and may develop a coppery tone. The genus (which includes both upright and trailing plants) seems very adaptable to soil qualities provided drainage is good: they are susceptible to root-rot. Grow from ripe seed or cuttings of firm young growth, but keep a reserve of young plants, for they are generally short lived.

Banksia serrata. Saw Banksia

BANKSIA
(**bank**-see-∂)
Honeysuckle, Bottlebrush, Banksia
PROTEACEAE

There is no written proof that Sir Joseph Banks chose this genus to be his namesake. But he was known to be immensely proud of his discovery of these curious Australian plants, that first day ashore at Botany Bay, in April 1770.

At any rate, the first one he found was the tree species *Banksia serrata*, the Red

Banksia baueri. Possum Banksia

Banksia spinulosa. Hairpin Banksia

Banksia 'Giant Candles'. Banksia

Baptisia australia. False Indigo

Honeysuckle. About 70 more species were found in succeeding years in the southern continent.

The majority of *Banksia* species, however, are shrubs, the most spectacular of them from Western Australia. These include the Possum Banksia or Teddy Bear, *B. baueri*, a low-growing plant frequently less than 1m/3ft high. The very woolly flower spikes are brownish-grey in colour. *B. coccinea*, the Scarlet Banksia, produces short, bright red-stamened cylindrical spikes 8cm3in long and wide. *B. ericifolia*, the Heath-leaf Banksia,

Banksia coccinea. Scarlet Banksia

varies from shrub to almost tree size, some-times 4m/13ft wide and 5m/16ft tall. It is confined to the east coast, where it lights up the bushland with its orange flower spikes in the colder months.

Banksia flowerheads are the most inter-esting feature of the genus – stunning spikes of tubular flowers arranged in neat parallel rows. As these gradually open from the base upwards, the entire spike takes on a fuzzy appearance as wiry stamens emerge one by one. Banksia flowers are notably rich in nectar, hence the popular name of Honeysuckle.

All Banksias prefer sandy soil rich in leaf-mould, and can be propagated from seed or tip-cuttings. They are relatively slow-grow-ing, but turn on a long-lasting display. The spectacular inflorescences last for years in dried arrangements.

BAPTISIA
(bap-**tis**-ee-ə)
False Indigo, Wild Indigo
FABACEAE

A showy group of herbaceous perennials, all from North America, the *Baptisias* seem suited to any temperate climate, grow as well in Australia as they do in England or their native USA. They are lupin-like plants with trifoliate leaves similar to those of clover, and racemes of pea-flowers in various shades of blue, yellow and white. These are interesting

in arrangements, but even better left in the garden. *Baptisias* cope well in dry areas, though are seen at their best in a deep, well-drained soil rich in leafmould. Raise them from seed or winter division, and they'll grow fast to an average 1.2m/4ft high. Full sun suits them best. Blooms are produced in summer and all stems should be cut to the ground after flowers fade.

BARKLYA
(**bar**-klee-ə)
Gold Blossom Tree
FABACEAE

There is very little about *Barklya* to suggest at a distance that it is a member of the pea family, not even the tell-tale long pods. But that's what it is – a handsome but uncom-mon member of the rainforest flora in east coast Australia, named for a forgotten British colonial governor. It is a magnificent tree, the only one of its genus, and easily propagated from seed or cuttings.

B. syringifolia may reach 20m/65ft in a warm, sunny position. As its specific name suggests, its leaves are heart-shaped, exactly like those of lilacs (Syringa). The vivid orange-yellow flowers appear in long, stiff spikes in early summer, in superb contrast to the dark foliage and trunk. They are followed by small 5cm/2in pods with one or two seeds each.

Barklya seems able to withstand tempera-tures down to –2ºC/28ºF and has been

Barklya syringifolia. Gold Blossom Tree

Barringtonia asiatica. Hotu, Fish-poison Tree

Bauera rubioides. River Rose

raised successfully in France, South Africa and Hawaii, though not apparently on the mainland of the US. Not often stocked by nurseries but worth a hunt.

BARLERIA
(bar-**leer**-ee-ə)
Philippine Violet
ACANTHACEAE

Neither a violet nor from the Philippines, if the truth be known, this charming evergreen shrub is from tropical India and Burma. It may need winter protection under glass where the temperature drops below 7ºC/45ºF. *Barleria cristata* makes a spectacular tub plant for the sunny terrace, growing into a neat bush a metre or so tall. It is often seen trimmed into a hedge in the tropics and is ideal for hiding the bare lower branches of taller shrubs.

Propagate either by seed or from half-ripe cuttings struck in a sandy mix any time apart from winter. *Barlerias* grow fast and enjoy summer humidity, dry winters and an acid soil rich in leafmould and manure. Give them plenty of water all summer long and light shade protection if possible. Flowers appear for several weeks in summer; both white and mauve forms are available.

Barleria cristata. Philippine Violet

Barringtonia acutangula. Freshwater Mangrove

BARRINGTONIA
(ba-ring-**toh**-nee-ə)
Hotu, Fish-poison Tree, Indian Oak, Itchy Tree, Freshwater Mangrove
LECYTHIDACEAE

Scattered about seaside areas of the Indian and Pacific Oceans, there is a handsome tree resembling the American Magnolia (*M. grandiflora*). But the plump flower buds at branch's end open as brilliant pink and white puffballs of fragrant stamens up to 15cm/6in in diameter. I've often tried to photograph one on the tree itself, but alas, they never appear till late evening, and drop before dawn, littering the beach around with their fading beauty. The tree is *Barringtonia/asiatica*, and island fishermen sprinkle the grated seed into lagoons to stun the fish.

Closely related *B. acutangula* is the Freshwater Mangrove of creek banks in northern Australia and Southeast Asia. It bears elongated shiny leaves and hanging sprays of fluffy red blossom. A most spectacular tree in the dry season if you can keep up the water.

BAUERA
(bou-er-ə)
River Rose, Dog Rose
BAUERACEAE

Hating lime in any form, the delicate *Bauera rubioides*, in its native state, is usually found clinging to the sandy, peaty soil of mountain stream banks, in areas where the sun hardly ever reaches. In cultivation, it prefers much the same conditions, but will take more sun. *Baueras* propagate easily at any time from soft-tip cuttings, but may need bottom heat to strike in winter. They flower lightly all year round, but in spring are a mass of delicate 6-petalled pink flowers. Tidy up with a light pruning after bloom. Paler pink and white forms are sometimes seen.

BAUHINIA
(boh-**hin**-ee-ə)
Orchid Tree, St Thomas Tree, Butterfly Flower, Bauhinia
CAESALPINIACEAE

In the 18th century, when a new plant genus was discovered that bore uniquely twin-lobed leaves, a suitably paired name was lacking, until diligent search revealed the names of two 16th-century botanists – twins perhaps, brothers certainly! And so the obscure brothers Bauhin became immortalised in the curious foliage of these lovely trees and shrubs from tropical Africa, Asia, Australia and South America. Recent flora of Australia treatment puts the six native species back in *Bauhinia*, though not all botanists would agree. All *Bauhinias* have the characteristic twin-lobed leaves, but their biggest attraction is their floral display, which is both long and profuse. The flowers are simple, elegant and somewhat resemble an orchid or, as some would have it, a butterfly. In fact, both these resemblances are used as the basis for common names.

Bauhinia galpinii. Red Bauhinia, Pride of the Cape

Flowers can be any colour from white to yellow, through a range of pinks to a deep, rich purple. They can appear at any time of the year, depending on the species. Coming from subtropical regions, *Bauhinias* naturally do best in those parts of the world with similar climates. However, they are hardy enough to thrive in most temperate areas. Once established, they will not suffer from the occasional –3ºC/27ºF frost, but will succumb to frequent or severe freezing. Grow them in good, well-drained soil, enriched with organic matter, and prune lightly by shortening stems which have flowered. This prevents over-production of untidy seed pods. Grown from seed sown direct, *Bauhinias* push ahead fast. Illustrated *B. galpinii* is a sprawling shrub; the others are slight trees, to 6m/20ft or so.

Bauhinia monandra. St Thomas Tree

Bauhinia variegata 'Candida'. Orchid Tree

BEAUCARNEA
(boh-**kah**-nee-ə)
Ponytail Plant
AGAVACEAE

Beaucarnea recurvata, the Ponytail Plant, formerly *Nolina recurvata*, is most familiar as a striking house plant, its long narrow leaves

Beaucarnea recurvata. Ponytail Plant

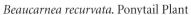

spraying out from the top of a curiously fattened stem like a giant bulb: but even indoors it sometimes produces its huge heads of little off-white flowers. Out of doors, in a frost-free but not tropical climate, flowering is a regular event, and there the plant slowly grows into a large, branching shrub. As a house plant it needs bright light and a wide, though not necessarily deep, pot to accommodate its girth, and should never be over-watered. Outdoors it likes fertile, well-drained soil and sunshine.

BEAUFORTIA
(boh-**fort**-ee-ə)
Swamp Bottlebrush, Gravel Bottlebrush
MYRTACEAE

Named for Mary, Duchess of Beaufort, an early patron of botany, *Beaufortia* is yet another spectacular Western Australian genus of the myrtle family, generally with tiny, stem-clasping leaves and bright scarlet flowers arranged in brush-like spikes.

B. sparsa will grow in a variety of climates from temperate to subtropical. Often found in swampy areas, it will also flourish in seaside gardens, even hot, dry areas. Prune lightly after bloom.

It is raised from cuttings of half-ripe shoots, or seeds from the previous year's capsules. These should be stored in a warm place until they open, and the seed scattered on a damp sand/peat mixture, barely covered.

Beaufortia sparsa. Swamp Bottlebrush

Begonia, Rex-cultorum Group, 'Fairy'. Rex Begonia

Begonia coccinea. Angelwing Begonia

Beaumontia grandiflora. Herald's Trumpet

Begonia, Tuberhybrida Group, 'Masquerade'. Tuberous Begonia

BEAUMONTIA
(boh-**mon**-tee-ə)
Herald's Trumpet, Easter Lily Vine
APOCYNACEAE

This evergreen, vining shrub climbs by twisting around its own growth to a height of 10m/33ft, and spreads just as wide. Well, that's what it does in a warm climate – elsewhere, in a sheltered, sunny position it can be pruned as a rather wonderful groundcover, or used as an espalier. The 22cm/9in leaves are heavily veined and semi-deciduous; the 12.5cm/5in white trumpet flowers are marked with green and very fragrant. *Beaumontia grandiflora* needs rich, deep soil, plenty of food and water. It does not bloom on new wood, so prune with care. It is neither frost hardy nor useful in containers.

BEGONIA
(be-**goh**-nee-ə)
Begonia
BEGONIACEAE

A large genus of perennial plants found in the subtropics of both hemispheres, most of the 1000-odd *Begonia* species can be grown in the open garden only in areas with temperate to subtropical climates. Their succulent stems and foliage are completely destroyed by frost; cooler-climate gardeners must be content to grow most of them in the greenhouse or as indoor plants with but a shadow of their tropical luxuriance. All *Begonias* are in fact perennial, though the ever-popular dwarf wax type (the Semperflorens group) is frequently used as an annual.

Wax Begonias prefer part sun, but do well in heavy shade. Soil needs to be rich and well drained but allowed to dry out between waterings. In cold areas, they can be dug up and potted for indoor use in winter. They will continue to flower as house plants.

Begonia, Semperflorens Group, 'White Comet'. Wax Begonia

Belamcanda chinensis. Leopard Lily

Gorgeous 'Masquerade' is a splendid example of the exotic tuberous-rooted or Tuberhybrida group. These are strictly summer-flowering types which produce large, rose-like blooms of every shade. Planted in spring, they reach a peak of perfection where summers are cool, moist.

Fibrous-rooted or cane-stemmed types such as *B. coccinea* prefer a light, sandy soil enriched with peat and leafmould. They are grown in full or semi-shade and need continual water. Propagate from divisions or cuttings which are taken just below a stem node; they can be rooted in water on a bright windowsill. These cane-stemmed *Begonias* flower mostly with small, satiny, 4-petalled blooms in brightly stemmed panicles. But their great joy is in their foliage, which is found in a wide range of shapes (mostly asymmetrical and ear-shaped) and many colours, often exotically marked with contrasting spots and streaks.

Rhizomatous *Begonias* include the richly toned Rex-cultorum group. These generally have wing-shaped leaves marked in pink, red, bronze, purple and silver. Some have an iridescent effect, others are quite translucent, and one or two have almost black leaves. All make striking summer bedding plants or spectacular potted specimens, but need the protection of a warm, bright room during winter months, anywhere out of the tropics.

BELAMCANDA
(bel-am-**kan**-də)
Blackberry Lily, Leopard Lily
IRIDACEAE

One of the less common members of the iris family, showy *Belamcandas* are tuberous-rooted herbaceous perennials, found in east Asia and Japan. In spring, they send up 1m/3ft fans of sword-shaped leaves which are joined, sometime in summer, by loose clusters of purple-spotted orange flowers,

each about 5cm/2in wide, borne on long stems. These are much valued for arrangements, as are the seed pods that follow. These burst open to reveal clusters of black seeds, which suggested the name Blackberry Lily. A rich, sandy loam and ample water in dry weather are advised. Shelter from wind and from winter cold are helpful. A brilliant gold cultivar of *Belamcanda chinensis* is called 'Hello Yellow'.

BELLIS
(bel-lis)
English Daisy, Bachelor's Button
ASTERACEAE

'Summer has come when you can set foot on seven daisies all at once' used to be an old English maxim, and it referred of course to the tiny white lawn daisy *Bellis perennis*. Nowadays, that English daisy has been improved out of sight, blooming more heavily and with larger flowers that may be fully double or even pompon-shaped. It comes in a wide range of pinks, reds and variegations as well as the original white, with a gold centre. It was this centre that gave the flower its name, 'Deus eye' or the eye of God – from a medieval belief that the Deity watched man's every move through the un-winking golden eyes of the omnipresent daisy.

Modern hybrids are used as bedding or rockery plants and may carry their blooms on stems up to 20cm/8in tall. Seed is sown outdoors in late spring in mild areas, otherwise indoors in very early spring. Sun or semi-shade suits them equally, but they need a rich, moist soil.

Belamcanda chinensis 'Hello Yellow'. Blackberry Lily

Bellis perennis cultivars. English Daisy

BERBERIDOPSIS

(bur-be-rid-**op**-sis)
Coral Vine
FLACOURTIACEAE

The name means barberry-like, though *Berberidopsis corallina* is not closely related to the barberries; unlike them, its chief attraction is not berries but showy coral-red flowers, borne in hanging bunches in summer. It is an evergreen, woody-stemmed twining vine, not overly rampant, and it can take a reasonable amount of frost. There aren't a great number of bright-flowered vines that won't take over the garden, and it is surprising this one isn't seen more often. In severe climates it makes a pretty pot plant for the greenhouse.

BERBERIS

(**bur**-bur-is)
Barberry
BERBERIDACEAE

About 450 species of these cool-climate shrubs are known. There are both deciduous and evergreen types, generally bearing sharp spines, gay yellow flowers in spring and attractive red fruit in autumn. Deciduous species are good in cooler districts where autumn tones develop. Illustrated *Berberis darwinii*, however, is an evergreen type with small, shining, holly-like leaves and racemes of golden flowers that bear an extraordinary resemblance to tiny daffodils. The succeeding blue berries last into autumn.

 Berberis like rich, well-drained soil, heavy watering only in a dry summer, and can reach 3m/10ft. They can be grown from autumn seed or late summer cuttings. A light pruning each year after flowering helps keep the bush attractively compact.

Berberidopsis corallina. Coral Vine

BERGENIA

(bur-**gen**-ee-ə)
Heartleaf Saxifraga, Megasea
SAXIFRAGACEAE

A useful winter cut flower in mild climates, *Bergenia* blooms a little later where winters are hard, as in its native Siberia. It grows easily in almost any soil, provided it is enriched with leafmould and receives plenty of water in hot weather. But you'll see these handsome plants at their best in damp, woodsy soil in semi-shade. There they make a splendid groundcover with great, leathery, toothed leaves up to 25cm/10in in diameter. The long, fleshy flower stems (usually drooping) bear massive panicles of 2.5cm/1in pink to lilac flowers with a charming perfume – that is, they do if you remember to protect

Bergenia schmidtii. Heartleaf Saxifraga, Megasea

them against marauding slugs and snails! *Bergenias* can be propagated from rooted divisions from autumn through to spring, or from seed, which can be sown outdoors in autumn for spring germination. They grow into dense clumps; these should be divided every few years. Spent flower heads should be removed to help prolong the flowering.

BESCHORNERIA

(be-shaw-**neer**-ee-ə)
Mexican Lily
AGAVACEAE

Though they are as Mexican as chili con carne or tequila, the showy *Beschornerias* have been grown successfully in the southwest of England, and are of course familiar in gardens of South Africa, California and

Berberis darwinii. Darwin Barberry

Beschorneria yuccoides. Mexican Lily

Australia. You'll find them growing anywhere you see Agaves doing well, for they like much the same conditions – first among which is a well-drained sandy loam and ample water when the flower spikes are developing in late spring or early summer. Full sun is advisable, to encourage blooming, which occurs on 1.4m/4ft unbranched red stems. They are a dull green in colour and subtended by rosy bracts. *Beschorneria yuccoides*, the most common of half a dozen species, develops about 20 leaves in a basal rosette.

BIFRENARIA
(bai-fre-**ne**-ree-∂)
Bifrenaria
ORCHIDACEAE

Here's a pleasant surprise – an orchid that's easy to grow without a glasshouse, can cope with temperatures down to 10°C/50°F and is over-poweringly perfumed as well!

Bifrenaria harrisoniae is its botanical name and it comes from Brazil. Plant in a small pot of fibrous, well-drained compost with plenty of sphagnum moss. Supply bright light (but not sun), water in the summer and keep up the humidity as best you can. The leaves are handsome, evergreen and rather like a pleated Aspidistra. The flowers (which may appear any time from late winter on) are rich buttery cream, with a handsome red-violet lip covered in silver hairs. Each one can be 7.5cm/3in wide.

BILLBERGIA
(bil-**bur**-j∂)
Flaming Torch, Queen's Tears
BROMELIACEAE

Among the easiest to grow of Bromeliads, *Billbergias* are striking plants indoors or out. Their humidity needs are not great, they're not fussy as to soil mix, and will actually grow sitting in a pot of stones or even a jar of

Billbergia nutans. Queen's Tears

Bifrenaria harrisoniae. Bifrenaria

water. In nature they anchor themselves to tree branches with small roots, collecting water and nutrients in the 'vase' formed by the rosette of leaves. In the garden or home these leaf-rosettes are always handsome, and striking flower displays appear at many times of the year. Just remember to keep the leaf vase filled with water, and grow in bright dappled shade or morning sun.

B. nutans, or Queen's Tears, produces slim, spidery grey-green leaves. In spring, tall, arching flower stems appear, decked with navy-blue and lime flowers in pink bracts. The Flaming Torch, *B. pyramidalis*, can grow to 1m/3ft, and features broad apple-green leaves and a tall stem of scarlet, gold and blue flowers with pink bracts. This may appear any time from midwinter on.

BIXA
(bik-s∂)
Lipstick Tree, Annatto
BIXACEAE

An ornamental in warm climates, the Lipstick Tree, *Bixa orellana*, is native to the Amazon region. Grown easily and quickly from seed or cuttings (cuttings flower sooner), it is inclined to be bushy in shape

Billbergia pyramidalis. Flaming Torch

Bixa orellana. Lipstick Plant, Annatto

and needs a certain amount of pruning and training to look like a tree.

Bixa may reach 10m/33ft in warm climates; through summer, charming pink and white flowers, like single wild roses, appear at the tips of branches. These are succeeded by clusters of almond-shaped red-brown fruit covered in soft spines.

An orange dye extracted from the seed coverings was used as body paint by South American Indians; now it's used industrially in products such as cheese, margarine, fabric and paint.

BLANDFORDIA
(bland-**for**-dee-ə)
Christmas Bells
LILIACEAE

Known as Christmas Bells in Australia, and widely sold during the festive season, this bright perennial is now popular in many other countries. At home, it often occurs on open heaths in soil that is well-drained but perpetually moist. Plant in autumn in acid, sandy soil enriched with leafmould. Full sun and consistent moisture are essential in either the open garden or large pots. *Blandfordias* colours include crimson, orange and yellow. Illustrated *B. grandiflora* is the most vivid of all. Propagate *Blandfordias* by seeds or offsets.

BLETILLA
(ble-**til**-lə)
Chinese Ground Orchid, Hyacinth Orchid
ORCHIDACEAE

The miniature Chinese Ground Orchid, *Bletilla striata*, is a charming terrestrial orchid for the open garden, easily grown in the shelter of large shrubs. Alternatively, raise in wide, shallow pots of peat and leafmould with rubble and coarse sand for drainage. Plant the snail-shaped corms in cool

Bletilla striata. Hyacinth Orchid

Blandfordia grandiflora. Christmas Bells

weather. The 30cm/1ft pleated leaves will appear in early spring, followed quickly by wiry stems, each with up to half a dozen miniature Cattleya-type blooms. These are a vivid cerise with a slight striped effect. Pots can be brought indoors as soon as the first shoots appear and should be watered regularly. *Bletillas* can cope with a winter temperature just above freezing, but they must be kept as dry as possible until the weather begins to warm up. They spread rapidly under ideal growing conditions.

BOEA
(bo-ee-a)
Rock Violet
GESNERIACEAE

Just think, if *Boeas* had been discovered before Saintpaulias, the entire garden world might have been growing *Australian* violets instead of their African cousins. The two plants are virtually indistinguishable, except that *Boea*'s mauve flowers appear on much longer, wiry stems. And it has developed a curious adaptation to the dry Australian climate. During the Queensland winter, it shrivels up to nothing – then sucks up water when the rains come, to resume its normal form. Otherwise, propagate and grow as with African Violets (see *Saintpaulia*).

Bolusanthus speciosus. African Tree Wisteria

BOLUSANTHUS
(bol-us-**an**-thəs)
Wisteria Tree, African Tree Wisteria
FABACEAE

There is only one species, *Bolusanthus speciosus*, a slow-growing deciduous tree or large shrub from South Africa. It grows about 5m/16 ft or so tall, and in autumn the crown of glossy leaves is lavishly adorned with pendent sprays of purple flowers which do bear a remarkable resemblance to wisteria blossoms – though without their glorious fragrance. It is resistant to heat and drought, though not to frost, and prefers fertile, well-drained soil and a place in the sun.

BOMAREA
(bom-**ah**-ree-ə)
Climbing Alstroemeria
ALSTROEMERIACEAE

Next time you see Alstroemeria flowers hanging on a vine, don't rush for the aspirin. Odds are, you just saw a *Bomarea*. There are

Boea hygroscopica. Rock Violet

Bomarea caldasii. Climbing Alstroemeria

Borago officinalis. Borage

Bomarea patacocensis. Climbing Alstroemeria

100-odd species, mostly from mountainous parts of tropical America where night temperatures drop below freezing. All species can be propagated by seed or division of the underground tuber, and thrive in well-drained sandy soil enriched with leafmould. During warm weather, *Bomareas* need copious water and regular feeding. Grow in a greenhouse or outdoors in bright, dappled shade. Where winters are frosty, cut down in autumn and protect roots with mulch.

BOMBAX
(**bom**-baks)
Red Cotton Tree, Silk Cotton Tree
BOMBACACEAE

From tropical forests of Asia, South America and Africa comes a genus of splendid trees called *Bombax* – an ancient Greek word for cotton. In truth, the filaments obtained from

their bulky seedpods are far too fine to spin, and are used instead as a substitute for kapok.

B. ceiba, the Red Cotton Tree from Southeast Asia, is commonly seen in gardens of northern Australia, Hong Kong, Hawaii, Africa and many other places. It is a tall tree, reaching 20m/65ft and more, with a widely buttressed trunk at maturity. Easily raised from seed, this *Bombax* needs deep soil and lots of moisture all year round to grow and produce its stunning crop of 12.5cm/5in flowers in early spring. These appear at the ends of branches shortly after the tree loses foliage for a brief period in winter. The Shaving Brush Tree, *B. ellipticum*, is smaller, rarely exceeding 15m/50ft. Its spring flowers resemble pink brushes, and the bark is grey-green, with a snake-skin pattern.

Bombax ceiba. Red Cotton Tree

BORAGO
(bor-**ah**-goh)
Borage
BORAGINACEAE

Grown for the cucumberish taste of its leaves in salads and summer drinks, Borage is also an attractive summer bedding plant, bearing star-shaped flowers resembling giant, furry forget-me-nots. Curiously, the odd pink flower may be produced on an otherwise all-blue cluster. There is a white strain, 'Alba', as well.

Borage grows fast and blooms for much of the year. It is a brittle plant, easily damaged by strong winds, so a sheltered spot is essential. It grows in sun or dappled shade, even in poor soil, and is sometimes used as a soil binder in sandy areas. Borage is best grown directly from seed – it doesn't transplant well, but it does re-seed itself reliably.

Bombax ellipticum. Shaving Brush Tree

Boronia heterophylla. Kalgan Boronia

Boronia megastigma. Brown Boronia

Boronia serrulata. Sydney Rock Rose

Bougainvillea 'Pink Champagne'. Bougainvillea

Bougainvillea glabra 'Variegata'. Variegated Bougainvillea

BORONIA
(bo-**roh**-nee-ə)
Boronia
RUTACEAE

There are almost 100 species of these dainty Australian shrubs, but they are not easy to grow away from their native bushland. They need sandy, acid soil that drains fast, yet is so rich in humus it never dries out. All have slender leaves with 3 leaflets and tiny flowers which vary from lantern shaped to fully open. They should be struck from firm tip-cuttings in coarse sand, as seed germination is highly erratic. They grow fast, varying at maturity from 30–150cm/1–5ft according to species.

Short-lived chartreuse and brown *Boronia megastigma* is the best-known species, exuding an enchanting perfume during its brief spring display; rosy-red *B. heterophylla* is popular in the cut flower trade; the delightful Native Rose, *B. serrulata*, a treasure of the NSW bushland in spring, is protected. Most *Boronias* can be grown as container plants; a light pruning of recently flowered shoots keeps them compact and has been shown to extend their life span.

BOUGAINVILLEA
(boo-gain-**vil**-le-ə)
Bougainvillea, Paper Flower
NYCTAGINACEAE

Growing *Bougainvilleas* is almost as easy as ABC. Plant them, water them and forget them. More of these gorgeous South American plants were killed by kindness than ever died of neglect. They enjoy well-drained soil, preferably of gravelly texture; sun, sun and more sun at all times; and hard pruning back when they get too leggy, to force the flower display. And if we didn't mention heavy watering, it's because they don't need it. Water forces leaf growth at the expense of bloom. I grow them myself in pots of crushed volcanic scoria with a little compost, and feed them with superphosphate. With the restricted root run they never stop flowering in hot weather.

Bougainvilleas are not true vines; they have no tendrils or suckers, but rather *lean* into taller plants and hang in there with sharp spines. To cover a wall, tie them to wire mesh or other support, or use heavy straps at intervals. Where the land is steep, plant at the top of retaining walls and let them hang down. This is *the* plant for the hot, dry garden, particularly near the sea. Plant in warm weather only in a position where the roots are always in full sun: do not use groundcovers or mulch. The greater the glare, the more flowering bracts will be produced. Grow as an espalier, to cover a pergola or train as a tree – provided you live in the right climate: a winter minimum of 2ºC/36ºF is needed.

Bougainvillea 'Scarlett O'Hara'. Red Bougainvillea

Bouvardia cultivars. Bouvardia

Brachychiton acerifolius. Illawarra Flame Tree

Bouvardia longiflora. Humboldt Bouvardia

BOUVARDIA

(boo-**vah**-dee-ə)
Bouvardia, Trompatella
RUBIACEAE

Often misunderstood, *Bouvardias* are really easy to grow in sheltered places with good soil. Just remember, they cannot stand frost and will always be untidy unless you cut them almost to the ground after flowering and then pinch back the growing tips regularly. Whatever you do, only the white species, *B. longiflora* (syn *B. humboldtii*), will ever develop that sweet perfume. A straggling evergreen shrub to about 1m/3ft, it enjoys a rich, well-drained loam, heavy watering in summer and dilute liquid fertiliser during flowering, which can go on from autumn to spring. Hardy down to 7°C/45°F, *Bouvardia* should be kept lightly shaded. The coloured species, hybrids of scentless *B. ternifolia*, may be single or double.

BRACHYCHITON

(brak-ee-**kai**-tən)
Kurrajong, Lacebark, Illawarra Flame Tree
STERCULIACEAE

Considered by many to be Australia's most spectacular genus of flowering trees, *Brachychitons* are maddeningly irregular in their flowering habits. But in a good early summer, a garden specimen of the Illawarra Flame (*B. acerifolius*) is a sight never to be forgotten – a vivid scarlet blur. The effect is heightened further if it is contrasted with the mauve flowers of a nearby Jacaranda, which blooms at the same time.

The *Brachychitons* are most variable trees – variable in size, shape of trunk and leaves, and size and colouring of flowers, which are generally bell-shaped. Those which are native to the semi-tropical forests of Australia's moist east coast tend to grow tall and flower profusely on the bare tree after leaf fall, in summer. Others, native to the dry Australian outback, are generally smaller in size and may have bloated, water-storing trunks. Their flowers are less showy and tend to appear under the new summer foliage.

All the Kurrajongs thrive in warm, dryish climates such as California, South Africa and the Mediterranean, but the desert species do not do well in the moister subtropics of Hawaii and Hong Kong. Evergreen *B. populneus* has small leaves which vary widely in shape, and becomes a mass of greenish-white, spotted bells. It is at home in quite desert conditions, even in alkaline soil. Deciduous *B. discolor* is a tropical giant of spreading proportions, its dull pink flowers covered with brownish fur on the outside. They grow well in the average garden, though only to a fraction of their forest height.

Brachychiton discolor. Queensland Lacebark

Brachycome multifida 'Break O'Day'. Cut-leaf Daisy

BRACHYCOME
(**brak**-ee-kohm, bra-kee-**koh**-mee)
Swan River Daisy, Cut-leaf Daisy
ASTERACEAE

Charming Australian annuals in the daisy family, *Brachycomes* make 10–30cm/4–12in mounds of finely cut foliage starred all over with hundreds of 2cm/1in daisy blooms in many shades of blue, mauve and white, centred in black and gold. The summer flowers are useless for picking, but make a delightful floral carpet, or are useful fillers for rock pockets and low containers. Plant seedlings in full sun in a light, warm soil, with a criss-crossing of fine-branched twigs for support. Pinch out early shoots to encourage branching and heavy flower yield; they are relatively short blooming, so sow extra batches of seed at monthly intervals to keep the show going. They revel in heat and stand dry conditions well – do not over-water.

BRACHYGLOTTIS
(brak-ee-**glot**-ǝs)
Shrub Groundsel, Dusty Miller, Shrub Daisy
ASTERACEAE

It remains to be seen whether the new, tongue-twisting name will harm the continued popularity of this versatile evergreen shrub, which gardeners in mild-wintered but drought-plagued climates have long admired under the name *Senecio greyii*. It is a bushy grower to a little more than 1m/3ft tall but spreading wider, and if its silvery, fuzzy foliage were not attraction enough, it covers itself for many weeks in late summer with golden-yellow daisyflowers. Clipped, it makes a very fine low hedge to set off bright flowers; it does well in pots; and I have seen it trained as a most elegant small standard. Give it sunshine and perfect drainage and don't starve it.

The cultivar *Brachyglottis* 'Sunshine' is most widely grown.

Brachycome iberidifolia. Swan River Daisy

BRACHYSEMA
(brak-ee-**see**-mǝ)
Swan River Pea, Scimitar Shrub
FABACEAE

An interesting member of the pea family from Western Australia, *Brachysema celsianum* (syn *B. lanceolatum*) can be preserved as a neat specimen by shaping regularly after each burst of bloom. Otherwise it flops, and will only look good sprawling on banks under light tree cover.

It can also be turned into a semi-climber by tucking the young shoots into a panel of wire netting. *Brachysema* prefers well-drained soil, but will withstand some waterlogging. Grow it from soft autumn tip-cuttings or seed scarified or soaked in hot water for 12 hours before sowing. The Swan River Pea grows well in California, and is hardy down to –5ºC/23ºF. Between blooming spurts, the foliage remains decorative, with lightly curled tips. A well-grown plant forms a rounded shrub about 1x3m/3x10ft.

Brachyglottis 'Sunshine'. New Zealand Shrub Daisy

Brachysema celsianum. Swan River Pea

BRACTEANTHA
(brak-tee-**an**-thə)
(SYN Helichrysum)
Everlasting Daisy, Straw Flower
ASTERACEAE

Everyone knows the Everlasting Daisy. There is no better flower for drying for decorating the house during flowerless seasons, the 'petals' (they are actually papery bracts that surround the cluster of tiny flowers) retaining their vivid tones of yellow, orange, hot pink or scarlet seemingly for ever. But beautiful as they are in death, they are even more splendid in life – few summer annuals can outshine the plant we all knew as *Helichrysum bracteatum* but must now learn to call *Bracteantha bracteata*. It is one of the few Australian plants that has been 'improved' by gardeners, but bigger flowers and more colours (in the wild the flowers are usually yellow) have been achieved at a price; most wild forms are perennial, at least in mild-wintered places, and much bushier in habit, with better foliage. Both they and the improved forms are sown in spring. Sunshine and perfect drainage are essential.

BRASSAVOLA
(bra-sa-**vole**-ə)
Ladies of the Night
ORCHIDACEAE

Poor Signor Brassavola! To be a botanist in 16th century Venice was only to dream about orchids like these. For all species of his namesake orchid *Brassavola* come from parts of South America that hadn't even been

Brassavola tuberculata. Ladies of the Night

discovered in his lifetime! They are real jungle beauties, allied to Cattleya and Laelia and capable of spontaneous hybridisation with them. Away from home, they need a winter minimum temperature of 13°C/55°F to survive and bloom. So a heated greenhouse is indicated. Grow them in baskets of firbark or osmunda fibre and tie the plant to the basket framework lest the weight of hanging growth up-end it. Species are variable, but mostly produce white or greenish summer flowers, strongly perfumed at night.

BRASSIA
(brass-ee-ə)
Spider Orchid
ORCHIDACEAE

A heated greenhouse will be needed to raise these slender, spidery beauties away from the real tropics. Like so many of the more exotic orchids, they grow naturally in the hottest parts of Central America, and cannot abide a winter temperature below 10°C/50°F. If you can arrange 15°C/59°F, they'll do even better, and bless you for it. The hotter it gets,

Brassia brachiata. Spider Orchid

the more moisture they need. Give them full sun except in summer, when a light shade is to be preferred, and grow them in the usual compost of firbark chips, renewed every 2 years.

Brassia brachiata is the sturdiest species, producing horizontal racemes of spidery greenish flowers spotted in black.

BRASSICA
(brass-ik-ə)
Rape
BRASSICACEAE

If you are asked the name of the showy biennial in our picture, please don't hesitate to cry Rape! The plant is quite uninteresting, and looks like a rather scraggy cabbage seedling until it bursts into glowing, golden blossom in early spring. To tell the truth, the whole plant smells no better than the edible cabbage, for they are closely related. The Rape plant is normally grown by Western farmers to harvest as the source of valuable canola or rapeseed oil. But the clever Japanese use it as a bedding plant to enjoy now, eat later.

Bracteantha bracteata cultivars. Everlasting Daisy

Brassica napus. Rape

X BRASSOCATTLEYA
(bras-soh-**kat**-lee-ə)
(No popular name)
ORCHIDACEAE

Brassocattleyas are possibly the most beautiful of all orchids – hybrids between the genera Brassavola and Cattleya – with great ruffled flowers up to 20cm/8in across. There are cultivars in delicious shades of mauve, lime, pink, crimson and white, usually with a fringed and contrasting lip. Some inherit the perfume of their Brassavola parentage.

They are grown under shelter except in the tropics, but can be raised successfully in a sunny room with mild winter heat (keep the temperature around 10°C/50°F). Epiphytic

X Brassocattleya. Unnamed hybrid

by nature, they are best grown in heavy pots or baskets filled with broken crocks, chunks of fern bark and other rough organic matter. *Brassocattleyas* need a lengthy rest in winter, so be sure to let them almost dry out during the cool weather. Give occasional deep soakings in dilute fertiliser as the weather warms up. Most species will produce flowers in late summer and autumn.

X BRASSOLAELIOCATTLEYA
(bras-soh-**lae**-lee-o-kat-lee-ə)
BLC Orchid
ORCHIDACEAE

Of all the plants in this book, this one is sure to win the prize for the longest botanical name – *Brassolaeliocattleya*. You'll probably come to refer to it as dedicated orchid fanciers do – BLC! It is the name of a group of orchids sharing a proven parentage of the three genera Brassavola, Laelia and Cattleya – though in varying degrees. Mostly, they are the work of man rather than nature, for the three parents of many hybrids often don't grow in the same part of the tropical Americas, or even bloom in the same season. Those species where the Cattleya parent predominates are easy to grow without special heat, provided you can give them the filtered light of a voile curtain and humidity of 50% or better in summer (a dish of moistened gravel will do it); in winter, proximity to a radiator on cold nights. Some others will need winter heat of 15°C/59°F.

Grow them in baskets of chunky compost including pats of old cow manure. They adore exploring with worm-like roots, bloom spring or autumn.

X Brassocattleya 'Madame Hye'. Brassocattleya Orchid

X Brassolaeliocattleya 'Crispum Royale'. BLC Orchid

X Brassolaeliocattleya 'Waikiki Gold'. BLC Orchid

BROWALLIA
(broh-**wol**-ee-ə)
Amethyst Flower, Bush Violet
SOLANACEAE

The true *Browallias* are a small genus of white or blue-flowered annuals related to Petunias. (The orange and yellow-flowered shrub of the same name is, in fact, a Streptosolen!) *Browallias* are mostly used as pot or basket plants, though they do grow well outdoors. Bushy, to about 30cm/12in, they bear clusters of white or white-centred blue flowers at branch tips. Outdoors, flowering occurs for many months in summer and early autumn; indoors it can occur at any time. For bedding, space the seedlings at 20cm/8in intervals in sun or semi-shade in late spring, preferably in rich soil with good drainage. Indoors, grow in diffused sunlight in a rich, moist compost. Night temperatures should not fall below 13°C/55°F.

B. speciosa will bloom about 12 weeks after sowing, and can be dug up and repotted in autumn for indoor use.

BROWNEA
(broun-ee-∂)
Rose of Venezuela, Panama Flame
CAESALPINIACEAE

The huge, cabbage-sized, orange-red flower clusters of the wonderful South American tree *Brownea ariza* (syn *B. grandiceps*) play hide-and-seek among its dense foliage. Look more closely and you will notice that each head is composed of dozens of tubular reddish blossoms with yellow stamens, fitted together very much like a hat-maker's tulle confection.

B. *ariza* is a tall tree, growing up to 20m/65ft in its jungle home, but not so high in cultivation. Even more spectacular in the warm-climate garden is the smaller Panama Flame, *B. macrophylla*. The flowers are inclined to open before the foliage and are a brilliant mass of gold, pink and scarlet long-stemmed blossoms that pop directly out of the slender trunk and branches.

BRUGMANSIA
(brug-**man**-zee-∂)
(SYN Datura)
Angels' Trumpets, Moon Flower
SOLANACEAE

A superb genus of evergreen flowering trees from cool areas of South America, the *Brugmansias* need wind protection for they are inclined to be top-heavy. They have 30cm/12in leaves and fragrant trumpet flowers to 25cm/10in in length, resembling giant Petunias. They grow very fast in almost any climate short of hard-frost areas. Mild frost will render them unsightly but, with a spring trim to remove damaged branches, they'll

Brownea ariza. Rose of Venezuela

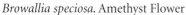
Browallia speciosa. Amethyst Flower

Brownea macrophylla. Panama Flame

Brugmansia candida. 'Knightii'

Brugmansia aurea. Golden Angel's Trumpet

Brugmansia insignis. Angel's Trumpet

Brunfelsia pauciflora. Yesterday, Today & Tomorrow

Brunfelsia americana. Dama de Noche

Brunsvigia josephinae. Candelabra Flower

soon recover as the warm weather returns. *B. suaveolens* bears enormous white flowers in summer and autumn – these are deliciously fragrant at night and are attractive to caterpillars and other chewing pests because of the plant's narcotic content. The tree develops many branches from a short trunk and grows 3–6m/10–20ft tall.

B. aurea has pale golden flowers; *B. sanguinea* has yellow to orange flowers with greenish veins; *B. insignis* has blooms of soft pink. *B. candida* includes handsome cultivars with double and hose-in-hose blooms.

BRUNFELSIA
(brun-**felz**-ee-ə)
Brazil Raintree, Yesterday Today & Tomorrow, Morning Noon & Night
SOLANACEAE

Handsome evergreen shrubs for the frost-free garden, most *Brunfelsias* take on a variegated appearance in spring and summer: the fragrant flowers open violet, fade to pale blue and finally white on successive days. There are some 30 species with this curious habit, all from South America and resembling one another except in the profusion of the flowers. From the nearby West Indies another group, including *B. americana*, noted for night fragrance, blooms in shades of white, green and pale butterscotch.

All *Brunfelsias* enjoy rich, well-drained soil and heavy water in summer. They make handsome patio or greenhouse plants, flowering better as their growing roots become more and more pot-bound. Strike cuttings of

new growth in a sandy mix at 21ºC/70ºF. Prune only after bloom, and then only to shape. *B. australis* and *B. pauciflora* (with larger flowers) will grow to about 2–3m/6–10ft in the garden, *B. americana* grows a little taller.

BRUNNERA
(brun-ner-ə)
Siberian Bugloss
BORAGINACEAE

Found all over the Russian steppes, hardy *Brunnera macrophylla* is a wonderful perennial for planting in large drifts or naturalising under trees. Its general appearance is that of a large Forget-me-not with heart-shaped leaves and arching sprays of pale-lilac flowers in spring and summer. Mature plants may be

Brunnera macrophylla. Siberian Bugloss

45cm/18in tall. *Brunneras* will thrive in ordinary garden soil and in almost any position, even full sun if you can keep up the water in summer. They are at their best, however, in leafy soil and semi-shade. Propagate from divisions of the root mass any time between late autumn and spring.

As with most herbaceous perennials, flowering stems should be cut as they fade, leaving just a few for seeding. *B. macrophylla* has an attractive variety with cream-variegated leaves which is most striking in a shaded position. The leaves are rough-textured, heart-shaped and prominently veined.

BRUNSVIGIA
(bruns-**vee**-jee-ə)
Candelabra Flower, Josephine's Lily
AMARYLLIDACEAE

Named for Napoleon's first Empress, Josephine, the stunning *Brunsvigia josephinae* sells for a truly regal price. I paid a tenth of an average week's salary for one bulb some years ago, and am still waiting for her to flower. They prefer a rich but sandy soil, with plenty of direct sun, and may condescend to

Bryophyllum delagoensis. Friendly
Neighbour

Buckinghamia celsissima. Ivory Curl Tree

bloom around 4 years after planting,
provided they are not disturbed. Plant with
half the bulb projecting above the soil; do
not over-water; *never* give them fresh
manure. In spite of all this studied neglect,
some autumn they will send up a 70cm/28in
stalk which will open into a veritable star-
burst of 60 or so Chinese-red lily blooms.

BRYOPHYLLUM
(**brai**-oh-fil-lɘm)
(SYN Kalanchoë)
Friendly Neighbour, Chandelier Plant
CRASSULACEAE

Botanically, these are now listed as
Kalanchoë, but gardeners and nurserymen
are hard to convince and most stubbornly
stick to the old name, *Bryophyllum.*
Whatever you call them, these 75cm/2½ ft
succulents are charming in any frost-free
garden. They're almost too easy to grow,
since dozens of tiny plantlets, complete with
roots, form all along the leaves. Where they
drop, a new plant springs up, and if a leaf
falls or a stem breaks, they too root readily.
Bryophyllums could almost be considered a
weed if it were not for the beautiful waxy red
flowers which shoot up on tall stems in
winter. Grow in sun or bright, dappled
shade, enriching sandy soil with compost.

BUCKINGHAMIA
(buck-ing-**ham**-ee-ɘ)
Ivory Curl Tree
PROTEACEAE

A slow-growing evergreen tree from the
rainforests of southern Queensland,
Buckinghamia is amenable to cultivation

Buddleja davidii. Summer Lilac

over a wide climatic range, though its size
is directly related to the annual amount of
heat it gets. It has flowered successfully
in areas where the temperature drops to
freezing point.

Like many of Australia's other flowering
trees, it is a member of the Protea family and
there is only one species. This may reach
20m/65ft in a suitably warm climate but
rarely passes 6m/20ft in cultivation.
The flowers, borne in late summer, consist
of long spikes of curled, creamy florets,
reminiscent of ostrich plumes. As the
florets open, the flower spikes weep under
their own weight until the entire tree is a
mass of fragrant blossom, which bees adore.
It grows successfully in Queensland and
New South Wales and should do equally well
in South Africa and the southern USA. It
grows best from seed.

BUDDLEJA
(bud-lee-yɘ)
(SYN Buddleia)
Butterfly Bush, Summer Lilac
LOGANIACEAE

Evergreen in warm climates, dropping leaves
in cold, the vigorous *Buddlejas* or Butterfly
Bushes need only water and good drainage
to grow like weeds. The fragrant spikes or
globes of tiny gold-throated flowers (white,
mauve, purple or orange according to variety) appear at various times from late winter.
Leaves are crepe-textured and quite large.

Chinese *B. davidii* should be pruned in
late spring to promote bloom. Other illustrated species are pruned right after flowering, in late summer or autumn. In all species,
flowering branches must be taken back to old
wood. Propagation by means of cuttings can

Buddleja globosa. Globe Buddleia

Buddleja 'Wattle Bird'. Butterfly Bush

Burchellia bubalina. Buffalo Horn, Wildegranaat

Bulbine frutescens. Stalked Bulbine

Bulbinella hookeri. Cat-tail Lily

be done in two ways. Use half-ripe cuttings in late summer, or try pieces of mature wood taken with a heel in autumn. Both are inserted in pots of a sand/peat mixture and struck under glass in a sheltered position. Species *B. globosa* and *B. tubiflora* need a warm temperate climate, *B. davidii* and *B. salviifolia* will survive winter frost as long as it's not too hard.

BULBINE
(bul-**bai**-nee)
Australian Leek

LILIACEAE

Despite its name, *Bulbine bulbosa* grows not from a bulb, but from a somewhat woody tuber. It is a modestly attractive plant, a native of Australia, admired in its native country for its 50cm/20in tall spikes of pale golden stars in spring, though gardeners elsewhere would prefer its showier relatives the Bulbinellas. Give it rather moist soil, and full sun or light shade. It can be grown from seed, and tolerates transplanting. Warm

climates are preferred. Most of the other species are South African natives, for example *B. frutescens* (syn *B. caulescens*), and some of these are grown by succulent collectors.

BULBINELLA
(bul-bi-**nell**-ə)
Cat-tail Lily, Maori Onion

LILIACEAE

Bulbinella is very closely related to the Australian genus Bulbine, so much so that some species have sometimes been included in it; but to a gardener's eye *Bulbinella* is quite distinct and superior. The flowers (almost always yellow) may be smaller, but they are clustered in dense spikes and make quite a show in their early spring season. The illustrated *B. hookeri*, a New Zealander, is typical and as fine a plant as any of them. Grow it in exactly the same way as outlined for Bulbine. In frosty climates it can be grown as a greenhouse plant, and if forced into winter dormancy by withholding water, it will flower in summer.

BURCHELLIA
(bur-**chel**-lee-ə)
Buffalo Horn, Wild Pomegranate, Wildegranaat

RUBIACEAE

Not very common away from South Africa, the showy Wild Pomegranate should be grown more widely. It is hardy down to −2ºC/28ºF, and likes soil that is well drained and enriched with compost. Raise from semi-hardwood cuttings taken in late summer or autumn and kept warm and humid until well rooted. *Burchellia* may also be raised from seed sown in late winter, but does not always flower true to colour. The glossy evergreen foliage is exactly like that of

Bursaria spinosa. Prickly Box, Blackthorn

TONY RODD

Butea monosperma. Dhak Tree, Flame of the Forest

the related Gardenia, and the bush develops into a broad, dense mound 3m/10ft tall and at least as wide. Showy orange-scarlet flowers are produced over a long period during spring and summer and appear only at the branch tips. They are quite fragrant. There is only one species, *B. bubalina*, formerly known as *B. capensis*.

BURSARIA
(ber-**sair**-ee-ə)
Prickly Box, Blackthorn
PITTOSPORACEAE

I had read so much in foreign horticultural publications about the beauty and value of Australia's lovely summer flowering *Bursaria spinosa* that I decided it just had to be included in this book. Only problem, I didn't have a picture of it and, even more remarkable, I wasn't aware of ever having seen it. It is supposed to grow in all our States, and is popular in California and in Mediterranean gardens. Even England's prestigious Royal Horticultural Society recommends planting it against a warm wall, and calls it 'charming' in both flower and fruit. Checking with country friends who lived in its native areas, I discovered this was the very same terror of the graziers, the dreaded Blackthorn that bloodies cattle with its spines, and snags the wool of passing sheep. More surprisingly, to Tasmanians it is their beloved Christmas Bush. If you really want to grow it, try seed or summer cuttings. Seriously, *Bursaria* blooms best in areas where shale is found, and the clouds of minute blossom are very fragrant indeed.

BUTEA
(byoot-ee-ə)
Dhak Tree, Flame of the Forest
FABACEAE

A brilliantly flowering specimen tree for the warm-climate garden, the *Butea* or Dhak Tree will tolerate a wide range of soil conditions. It is a slow-growing, 15m/50ft, rather gnarled tree of stark appearance until the flowers burst open in spring. These are arranged in 15cm/6in racemes of curved, orange-red pea-flowers with a marvellous silvery sheen to their exteriors. They are followed by typical long pea pods which are grey and furry. The blueish-green foliage has a rather silky texture.

In its native Bangladesh and Burma, *Butea* is also known as the Palas tree and Flame of the Forest.

A splendid choice for warm coastal gardens, *B. monosperma* will resist a degree of salt. It is also suited to saline desert soils and will even put up with an occasional light frost.

BUTOMUS
(**byoo**-tə-məs)
Flowering Rush, Water Gladiolus
BUTOMACEAE

An elegant aquatic perennial, *Butomus umbellatus* is the only member of its genus and found in many parts of temperate Europe and Asia. It is hardy almost anywhere provided the water doesn't actually freeze. Revelling in a warm, sunny position, it may be planted in a shallow pool pocket or close by in a boggy, marginal position. This is best

done in early spring before renewed growth begins, and propagation is generally by division of the parent plant at that time.

Tall stalks of rose-pink flowers arise to 90cm/3ft in summer, and should be cut carefully, for the plants' leaves are razor sharp. The botanical name refers to this – 'a plant that cuts the mouth of oxen when grazing' is what it means.

Butomus umbellatus. Water Gladiolus

CAESALPINIA
(seez-al-**pin**-ee-ə)
Dwarf Poinciana, Bird of Paradise
CAESALPINIACEAE

The genus *Caesalpinia* includes several handsome shrubs for warmer climates. The most
often seen of these is *C. gilliesii*, a rather
sparsely branched, semi-deciduous plant that
grows to about 3m/10ft and is sometimes
used for bedding in the tropics. It also makes
a handsome wall-shrub, with 20cm/8in
bipinnate leaves and terminal racemes of
yellow-petalled blooms, each centred with
arching scarlet stamens. In well-drained,
leaf-rich soil with light but regular water, the
shrub grows fast and produces flowers over a
long period in summer. It is easily grown
from seed, which should be soaked in warm
water before sowing. Semi-hardwood tip-
cuttings can also be struck in a very sandy
mixture with high humidity and heat. Native
to Uruguay and Argentina.

   Taller-growing *C. pulcherrima*, Barbados
Pride, is small-tree sized, blooms in several
colours, of which the scarlet variety is the
most common.

CALANTHE
(kal-**an**-thee)
Christmas Orchid
ORCHIDACEAE

Though Christmas Orchid is the recognised
popular name (in the southern hemisphere
at least), I wouldn't count on these charming
terrestrials coming in on time. I have grown
them and learned that the big display seems
to be just when it suits the individual plant –
anywhere from mid-spring to early autumn.
Calanthe species are widely distributed in
Asia, Africa and Australasia, and are very
popular hobby plants in Japan. The
Australian *C. triplicata* is evergreen, prefers
to grow in a well-drained soil rich in leafmould. Outdoor culture is possible only in a
frost-free climate, as the plant is native to
subtropical rainforests. Try it in a sheltered
position protected from wind. Leaves are
pleated, up to 60cm/2ft long, and either two
or four to a pseudobulb. The snow-white
flowers are very sweet.

CALATHEA
(ka-lə-**thee**-ə)
Peacock Plant
MARANTACEAE

Native to South America and nearby
Caribbean islands, *Calatheas* have always

Caesalpinia gilliesii. Bird of Paradise

Caesalpinia pulcherrima. Barbados Pride,
Peacock Flower

Calanthe triplicata. Christmas Orchid

Calathea louisae. Slender Calathea

been popular with indoor plant growers
because they romp ahead in the generally
low light levels of the home. They come by
this habit naturally: in the wild they grow in
dense jungles where the sun is never seen
and light of any sort is hard to come by. In
areas where even winter nights are never
colder than 5°C/41°F, *Calatheas* can be safely
grown in a shady part of the garden; but the
rest of us will have to remove them to the
safety of a heated greenhouse or indoors if
we are to enjoy their fancy leaves and curiously attractive flowers. Of the illustrated
species, *C. louisae* is grown more for its
handsome foliage than its small but pretty
flowers. But *C. burle-marxii* 'Ice Blue' is a
different story. Its 10cm/4in spire of pale
turquoise bracts is its most striking feature.

Calceolaria, Herbeohybrida Group. Ladies' Purses

Calendula officinalis 'Sunset'. Calendula

Calliandra haematocephala. Red Powder Puff

Calceolaria integrifolia. Slipper Flower

Calendula officinalis. Pot Marigold

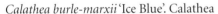
Calathea burle-marxii 'Ice Blue'. Calathea

CALCEOLARIA

(kal-see-o-le∂r-e-∂)
**Ladies' Purses, Slipper Flower,
Pocketbook Plant**

SCROPHULARIACEAE

Calceolaria is familiar to most as the curiously shaped, gaily coloured Ladies' Purses (Herbeohybrida group). These charming spring annuals are sold by the millions, potted up in bloom for indoor use. They're difficult to germinate, grow slowly to 15–35cm/6–14in and seem far too fragile for outdoor planting except in sheltered parts of mild-climate gardens.

Another 300 or so species exist, including *C. integrifolia*, an evergreen, subshrubby perennial which is a more attractive and versatile subject in almost every way, though

without the colour range. It grows outdoors in most climates and while not completely frost hardy, it will generally survive with a minimum of damage. *C. integrifolia* and the Fruticohybrida group (of which it is a parent) prefer crowded conditions, an acid, moderately rich soil, and only occasional water.

CALENDULA

(ka-**len**-dyoo-l∂)
Pot Marigold, Gold Daisy, Calendula

ASTERACEAE

Pot Marigolds (*Calendula officinalis*) are surely the easiest of annuals to propagate and bloom, and though their scent is not to everyone's taste, they are almost unexcelled for bedding at many times of the year. As well as the familiar orange, there are now shades of gold, yellow, apricot, cream and even a white, many of the strains fully double. You can sow or plant them outdoors in spring for summer display or again in summer for autumn and winter bloom. Leave a few flower heads to ripen and they'll resow without any help from you at all. Flowers can be expected in 10 weeks from seed provided they're planted in full sun in a soil that's rich, fertile and well watered.

CALLIANDRA

(kal-lee-**an**-dr∂)
**Powder Puff, Tassel Flower, Lehua Haole,
Fairy Duster**

MIMOSACEAE

There are some 200 species of *Calliandra*, mostly with pink or white powderpuff flowers. Bolivia's *C. haematocephala* grows into an open, spreading 3m/10ft shrub dotted with big pinkish-red flowers throughout summer and early autumn. *C. tweedii* is a smaller bush with finer, fern-like foliage and

Calliandra tweedii. Red Tassel Flower

Callistemon 'Little John'. Bottlebrush

Callistemon viridiflorus. Green Bottlebrush

Callicoma serratifolia. Blackwattle

Callistemon viminalis. Weeping Bottlebrush

Callistemon 'Reeves Pink'. Pink Bottlebrush

flowers like crimson pompons all through spring and summer. *Calliandras* enjoy light soil with heavy summer water and should be pruned in late winter for more compact growth. Propagate from ripe seed in spring, kept warm and moist.

CALLICOMA
(kal-lə-**koh**-mə)
Blackwattle
CUNONIACEAE

From the appearance of its fluffy cream flower clusters, it is easy to see why this tree was also given the name 'wattle' in Australia's early colonial times. They certainly do resemble the flowers of Acacia but in fact belong to quite a different family, the Cunoniaceae.

At one time, *Callicomas* grew densely around Sydney Harbour, but they virtually disappeared with the spread of suburbia, because they enjoy shady places and the shelter of other trees.

The 15cm/6in serrated leaves, long oval in shape, are a pleasant, light green when young. The Blackwattle ranges from shrub size to 10m/33ft in height. It is shallow-rooted, enjoys the same acid soils and humid conditions as Azaleas, Rhododendrons and Camellias, but grows over a much wider climatic range and is now a popular garden specimen in many countries away from its native land. *C. serratifolia* is the only species; its name means it has serrated leaves.

CALLISTEMON
(kal-**lis**-tem-ən)
Bottlebrush
MYRTACEAE

Evergreen shrubs and small trees from Australia which have become popular in frost-free areas throughout the world, *Callistemons* are often somewhat weeping in habit, their branches tipped in season with exciting brush-like flowers of red, pink, green, white or mauve-purple. From the ends of these, new leaves grow, bypassing a patch of woody seed capsules which persist for years. Leaves vary from needle-like to spear-shaped with a silken hairy texture – young foliage is often tinted red or pink. All prefer a light, deep soil that is well-drained

but damp, and are found naturally on banks of streams. They may be propagated from spring seed or from short, leafy tips taken in autumn and struck in a humid atmosphere. Most tolerate wind, some frost and occasional waterlogging.

The species *C. montanus* is one of the hardiest, able to tolerate several degrees of frost and strong wind. The main flush of flowers occurs in spring, with a secondary blooming in autumn. Flowers may also appear at other times, especially after periods of heavy rain.

CV 'Captain Cook' forms a dense, pendulous bush about 2m/6ft tall. It flowers profusely in spring, with a second flush in autumn, and makes a good specimen for a large tub or an attractive and unusual informal hedge.

CV 'Harkness' (also known as 'Gawler Hybrid') is altogether larger, growing to at least 3m/10ft and up to 6m/20ft in ideal conditions. The flowers are bigger, too – often 20cm/8in long and generously produced. CV 'Harkness' thrives in acid or alkaline soils and under a wide range of climatic conditions.

Green-flowered *C. viridiflorus* will tolerate light frosts, and enjoys moist soils that are occasionally flooded and the shelter of other shrubs.

Callistephus chinensis 'Southcote Single'. China Aster

Calochortus venustus. Mariposa Lily

Callistephus chinensis 'Totem Pole'. China Aster

CALLISTEPHUS
(kal-lis-**tef**-ᵊs)
Aster, China Aster
ASTERACEAE

China Asters (*Callistephus chinensis*) are more often bought as cut flowers than grown in the garden, as they have a reputation for being 'difficult'. But modern improvements have worked wonders. The secret is in the soil, which should be light and sandy, with added lime where there is natural acidity, and heavy manure. On no account should they be planted where Asters have been grown the previous year. As they have a short flowering season, stagger sowing times at 2-week intervals. Keep well watered and mulch around the plants in hot weather to keep the root system cool. Asters can be 15–100cm tall (6in–3ft) and bloom in early autumn. Modern strains have a wide colour range and are wilt resistant; they can be double or single, pompon forms or loose shapes with long curled petals; there are dwarf growers that flower profusely.

Callistephus chinensis hybrid. Dwarf Aster

CALLUNA
(kal-**loo**-nᵊ)
Heather, Ling
ERICACEAE

Most familiar to inhabitants of the northern hemisphere, the genus *Calluna* is the famous Scottish Heather of many a grouse moor and romantic legend. There is only one species, a densely spreading bush with innumerable varieties blooming in shades from white to crimson and with foliage of silver, gold or green. Mature plants are 50–100cm/20–36in tall and prefer a gritty, well-drained, acid soil with regular water. A cool root run is an asset and the plants do well in rockeries or when mulched with pebbles. Flowers appear in spring and a second flush usually follows in autumn. Shear after bloom to keep compact.

CALOCHORTUS
(kal-oh-**kor**-tᵊs)
Mariposa Lily, Globe Tulip
LILIACEAE

Charming and rather uncommon away from their native American Southwest, the Mariposa Lilies are rewarding if you can afford the endless vigilance they demand. Found mostly in mountainous areas of California, they prefer a cool climate, tolerate frost, and require particular attention to drainage. Soil should be light and sandy, and a winter mulch will help protect the bulbous roots, which can be divided in autumn. Spring moisture is essential, but let them dry out after blooming. They can be yellow, white, pink, lilac, maroon and bicolors, and are often fragrant. You'll probably have to grow them from seed: plants are scarce. *Calochortus* means 'beauty grass'.

Calluna vulgaris 'Elegantissima'. Scottish Heather

Calodendrum capense. Cape Chestnut

Calostemma purpureum. Garland Lily

CALODENDRUM
(ka-loh-**den**-drum)
Cape Chestnut
RUTACEAE

One of Africa's most delightful trees, *Calodendrum capense*, the Cape Chestnut, is now seen in gardens all over the world where winter temperatures fall no lower than –5ºC/23ºF.

Best propagated from cuttings, it will grow rapidly to 7m/23ft and more slowly thereafter, particularly in cooler areas, reaching a maximum height of about 15m/50ft. The handsomely spotted leaves are evergreen in warm climates, but may be deciduous elsewhere. It will usually flower in either late summer or early spring and possibly at other times, too.

The 10cm/4in flowers, which appear in open spikes at branch ends, each have 5 curling pink petals, 5 crimson spotted petaloids and 5 rigid pink stamens. They are highly perfumed, pick well and are reminiscent of Rhododendron blooms.

Calodendrums like water at all times and are not for dry areas. They prefer the company and shelter of other trees, where they will grow to taller and more striking specimens. When exposed they tend to grow too horizontally and may fall over in strong wind.

CALOMERIA
(kal-oh-**meer**-ee-∂)
(SYN Humea)
Incense Plant
ASTERACEAE

The interesting Incense Plant, *Calomeria amaranthoides* (syn *Humea elegans*) is, surprisingly, another Australian member of the daisy family, though certainly untypical.

Calomeria amaranthoides. Incense Plant
TONY RODD

It is native to damp forest areas of southeast Australia, and grows best in cool conditions.

Calomeria is slow growing and rises to a height of 2m/6ft. At the back of a mixed border or behind lower plants would be an ideal position from which the plume-like, dull red flowers might be exhibited.

Truly biennial in habit, it is necessary to sow the seed in early summer for flowers 15 months later. Sow direct in lightly raked soil and water regularly. Spicily perfumed foliage and flowers will be your reward.

CALOSTEMMA
(kal-oh-**stem**-m∂)
Garland Lily
AMARYLLIDACEAE

Calostemma is Greek for 'beautiful crown', although the Greeks themselves never knew these lovely Amaryllids from warmer parts of Australia. The name refers to the curious way the gold stamens are united at the base, giving the appearance of a tiny, gold coronet placed in the heart of every flower.

Garland Lilies, as they are known in Australia, thrive in rich, well-drained soil kept moist until the leaves begin to yellow. They should then be allowed to dry out until new flowers appear the following summer. Plant in full sun and increase by seed or division. Feed once per year when new leaves appear. *C. purpureum* is purple-red; there are white and yellow species as well.

CALOTHAMNUS
(kal-oh-**tham**-n∂s)
Netbush, One-sided Bottlebrush
MYRTACEAE

Untidy in growth, never truly spectacular, *Calothamnus* are useful wherever climatic conditions approximate those of their native Western Australian desert. Highly drought resistant, they can be relied on in poor or sandy soil, or wherever wind and salt are a problem. Even light frosts do not faze them, for while the growing tips may be destroyed, flowers are invariably produced on older wood. A light pruning any time will help

Calothamnus quadrifidus. Netbush

Calotropis gigantea. Giant Milkweed, Crown Plant

keep the bush compact; it is inclined to grow leggy, though not much taller than 2m/6ft.

Leaves of most species are needle-like and 3–8cm/1–3in long. The flowers are produced for months in spring and summer in one-sided clusters, each flower consisting of several bundles of gold-tipped stamens united at the base.

CALOTROPIS
(kal-o-**troh**-pəs)
**Giant Milkweed, Crown Plant,
Bowstring Hemp, Kapal, Pua Kalaunu**
ASCLEPIADACEAE

Native to Africa and southern Asia, the Giant Milkweed, *Calotropis gigantea*, has become naturalised in warmer climates worldwide and is a declared noxious weed in parts of Australia. It is a fast-growing, rather leggy shrub, 1.5–4.5m tall (5–15ft). Branches are few and clothed with wedge-shaped, mealy leaves. The unremarkable flowers have a charming fragrance and greatly resemble those of the related Stephanotis. They may be easily grown from seed or cuttings, which should be struck under glass and kept dryish. Good drainage is a necessity and regular heavy pruning after bloom will help promote bushiness and reduce height. *Calotropis* flowers throughout the warm weather. Its bark yields a strong fibre and the sap makes a type of gutta-percha.

Calpurnia aurea. East African Laburnum

CALPURNIA
(kal-**pur**-nee-ə)
East African Laburnum, Gold Tassels
FABACEAE

No, this is not named after Caesar's wife, she who had to be above suspicion, but after a minor Roman poet called Calpurnius, an imitator of Virgil – the significance being that *Calpurnia aurea* is very closely related to

Caltha palustris. Kingcup

South Africa's Virgilia and was indeed at one time included in that genus. It is a tall shrub, to about 3m/10ft, very fast growing but short lived, and makes a fine display in late summer, when it covers itself in small golden flowers. Occurring wild from Ethiopia to South Africa, it must have a frost-free climate, though it is not at all fussy about soil or position.

CALTHA
(kal-tha)
Kingcup, Marsh Marigold
RANUNCULACEAE

What a collection of popular names this showy perennial has totted up! Kingcup, May-blob, Meadow-bright, Marsh Marigold – but the first describes *Caltha palustris* best, for what is it but a king-sized buttercup? This hardy herbaceous perennial grows wonderfully by the margins of a pool, in boggy soil – even in water, if it's no deeper than 15cm/6in. It sends up masses of hollow-stemmed, handsome, rounded leaves, each up to 18cm/7in wide and lightly toothed. These are joined in late spring by a profusion of generally golden-yellow cup-shaped flowers (though there are paler varieties). *Caltha* produces plenty of seeds and seedlings, but may also be propagated by division of the roots soon after flowers fade.

The fully double strain 'Flore Pleno' is sometimes available. It is usually smaller, but what it lacks in size it makes up for in bloom – it is one of the loveliest of the hardy waterside plants.

Rust, if it is a problem, will occur in spring and should be treated with a fungicide.

Calycanthus occidentalis. California Allspice

CALYCANTHUS
(ka-li-**kan**-thus)
California Allspice, Sweet Shrub

The two or three species of *Calycanthus*, all from North America, are deciduous, frost-hardy bushes to about 3.5m/12ft, bearing long glossy leaves that are ovate, pointed and downy on the reverse. The fragrant flowers are borne singly on terminal twigs. For much of the summer they look like many-petalled Magnolias (though they are not related), and in the illustrated *C. occidentalis* flowers are 7.5cm/3in in diameter. Like related species, they have purplish-red petals, tinged brown. They may be raised from seed, divisions or, most readily, by layering. Best in full sun.

CALYTRIX
(**kal**-i-triks)
Fringe Myrtle
MYRTACEAE

Though the Fringe Myrtles hail mainly from Western Australia, the illustrated *Calytrix tetragona* (syn *C. sullivanii*), one of the best-known and most cold resistant of them, occurs in most Australian States. It is typical in being an open-growing shrub, to about 1.2m/4ft tall, with small, heather-like leaves and clusters of pale, starry flowers that cover the bush in late spring. After the petals fall, the bronzy pink calyces remain to give further colour for some weeks. These are not difficult plants to grow in a mild climate, sandy soil and light shade; but they do look best when several plants are grown together in a clump. Most species are easily propagated from cuttings.

Calytrix tetragona. Fringe Myrtle

CAMASSIA
(ka-**mas**-see-ə)
(SYN Quamassia)
Quamash, Camass
LILIACEAE

A genus of striking bulbous plants from North America, *Camassias* have become popular in many other cool-climate areas for their tall stems of late spring flowers. These bring a welcome touch of blue to the mixed border. They can be propagated from seed,

Camassia leichtlinii 'Electra'. Quamash

but as it can take up to 4 years before the plants reach blooming size, bulbs are to be preferred. A heavy, even damp soil is desirable, and they look most attractive reflected in the water of garden pools. Like Miss Greta Garbo, however, they like to be alone, and resent disturbance. Give them full sun, and a climate verging from cool temperate to cold, and *please*, after all that trouble, do not follow the example of the Native Americans who found them very tasty and nutritious.

Camellia reticulata 'Curtain Call'. Reticulata Camellia

CAMELLIA
(ka-**meel**-ee-∂)
Chinese Rose, Japonica, Sasanqua
THEACEAE

Though *Camellias* will always be associated with Japanese culture, most of the 250-odd species have been found in China, nearby islands and Indochina. They are woody plants – trees in every sense of the word – generally with glossy leaves. Their usual habitat is mountainous and subtropical, where they grow in partial shade.

The flowers of the vast majority of the genus *Camellia* are neither large nor spectacular, but less than 4cm/1½in in diameter and plain white. Even smaller are the blooms of the most widely cultivated *Camellia* species, *C. sinensis*. This is the plant we know as tea, found naturally over a wide range centring on Assam, where it has been known to reach 16m/50ft.

When tea reached Europe in the mid-17th century, it was immediately adopted by fashionable society. The British East India Company, sensing a commercial bonanza, tried to export some of the tea plants by bribing Chinese officials. But it seems the Chinese outsmarted the company and substituted plants of the more decorative *C. japonica*, the leaves of which were useless for tea making. Those first plants of *C. japonica* arrived in England early in the 18th century, and their blooms immediately caught the fancy of nurserymen. Their rapid growth in popularity may be judged by the fact that the number of *Camellia* hybrids bred since, from these few early plants, is estimated to be as high as 20,000.

Camellia japonica 'Margaret Davis'. Japonica Camellia

Far and away the majority of ornamental *Camellias* are descended from the wild *C. japonica*, a rather scraggy-looking tree of 9m/30ft found naturally in Japan, Korea and eastern China. Today, its descendants look better, flower better, and are pruned to a more compact height and width. All Japonicas prefer protection from full sun and a deep, neutral to slightly acid soil. Reproduce their natural forest surrounds of shade, good drainage and humidity and you can't go wrong!

The third most widely cultivated species of *Camellia* is *C. sasanqua*, a slender, densely foliaged tree (to 6m/20ft) from southern Japan and nearby islands. Originally white flowered, there is now a wide range of colours; the blooms are smaller and often lightly fragrant but they do not last well. It extends the *Camellia* season by several months. The Sasanquas can take more sun than Japonicas.

The fourth widely grown *Camellia* species is a relative newcomer, *C. reticulata*,

Camellia lutchuensis. Fragrant Camellia

Camellia nitidissima. Yellow Camellia

Camellia sasanqua 'Paradise Sayaka'. Sasanqua Camellia

found naturally in the forests of southern China at altitudes of 2000–3000m/6500–9800ft. It is an open-growing tree up to 15m/50ft, with large, heavily veined leaves and pink blooms up to 9cm/3½in across in the wild.

It was introduced to Western gardens only in the 1930s and used largely to increase the size of Japonica blooms – until the discovery in 1948 that gigantic Reticulata cultivars had been grown in southern China for centuries. Some of these plants were imported into the USA and elsewhere in 1948–49, and when they bloomed with flowers up to 15cm/6in across, the rest was botanical history. Now it is these enormous *C. reticulata* cultivars and their Western-bred hybrids that catch the eye at all *Camellia* shows.

One of maybe 25 yellow-flowered species of *Camellias*, *C. nitidissima* (syn *C. chrysantha*) is the only one in widespread cultivation. Alas, yellow has not yet found its way into the colour range of available *Camellia* cultivars. *C. lutchuensis*, however, has been generous in donating its delicious fragrance to many of today's hybrid *Camellias*.

Camellia japonica 'Bob Hope'. Japonica Camellia

Camellia 'Shiranui'. Higo Camellia

CAMPANULA
(kam-**pan**-yoo-lə)
Bellflower, Bluebell, Canterbury Bell
CAMPANULACEAE

A popular genus of about 300 species, the *Campanulas* or Bellflowers mostly originate from Europe and have been hybridised to produce an enormous range of useful garden plants for the rockery, border, wild garden or even hanging baskets. All of the popular species except one are perennial, and though their blooms vary greatly in size, shape and height of inflorescence, all provide a welcome range of blue tones for every garden use. They can be propagated from seed sown outdoors in late spring or summer; the perennial types may also be increased by division of the clumps or by striking stem cuttings of firmer wood under glass in a mixture of sand and peat.

All enjoy a rich, well-drained soil that is kept constantly moist, and most perform best in full sun. But *C. rotundifolia* and *C. persicifolia* are also useful in part-shade, where colours remain brighter. *C. latifolia* is tall growing, sending up stems of open, bell-shaped flowers in dense, terminal panicles to a height of 2m/6ft. *C. latiloba* is satisfied to reach 1m/3ft in height and is decorative toward the front of the border. *C. carpatica* and *C. rotundifolia* are popular for rock gardens, where they rarely pass a height of 30cm/1ft but form dense clumps. The only annual species, *C. medium*, towers 1m/3ft over a neat rosette of leaves and produces a spire of lovely bell-shaped, blue, pink or white blooms.

Taller-growing perennial species should be divided every 3–4 years or whenever they show signs of crowding.

Campanula lactiflora. Bellflower

Campanula medium. Canterbury Bell

Campanula carpatica 'Chewton Joy'. Carpathian Bellflower

Campanula latifolia 'Alba'. Giant Bellflower

Campsis tagliabuana. Chinese Trumpet Creeper

Cananga odorata. Ylang Ylang

CAMPSIS

(**kamp**-sis)

(SYN Tecoma, Bignonia)

Chinese Trumpet Creeper

BIGNONIACEAE

This handsome creeper will cling to almost any surface by means of aerial rootlets and is a useful, fast cover. Brick, wood and other plants all give generous support. It can also be trained as a shrub or hedge with regular pruning. The dark, shining leaves are attractive in themselves and the flowers appear in summer clusters at the ends of new shoots. Sometimes these persist to winter in warmer areas. Deciduous where winters are cold, it will endure several degrees of frost and once established easily withstands dry summers. It is inclined to be rampant.

CANANGA

(ka-**nan**-jə)

Perfume Tree, Ylang Ylang

ANNONACEAE

Even the poor sighted could hardly overlook *Cananga odorata* planted nearby, or even in a garden several houses away, for its appeal is as much to the nose as to the eye.

Unfortunately, it is purely for the warmer climate – it is found naturally over a wide area, from Burma through Malaysia and Indonesia to the north of Australia.

A tall, rather narrow tree with weeping, brittle branches, it bears the long, drooping rippled leaves of the custard apple, to which it is related. But in the leaf axils, in autumn, appear clusters of the most striking, long-lasting flowers. They are up to 7.5cm/3in across, with 5 thin, curiously drooping petals. These are lime-green at first, ripening to a warm orange after a few days, and are overpoweringly fragrant, particularly in the early morning.

In parts of its native range, *Cananga* is also known as the Perfume Tree or Ylang Ylang (which means the same thing), and individual blossoms are worn about the person or placed in cupboards to perfume linen. Earlier this century they were used to scent coconut oil for a men's hairdressing known as macassar oil. Elsewhere, the tree's trunk was used to carve drums and canoes, the bark was used for rope and the flowers to make medicine palatable. *Cananga* is now widely grown in Hawaii, but it is rare in Australia south of Rockhampton.

CANNA

(**kan**-na)

Indian Shot

CANNACEAE

Popularly named for its hard, round seeds which resemble gun shot, only a few of the 60 or so species of *Canna* are commonly grown. Most garden cannas are hybrids, derived long ago from several of the wild species, notably *C. indica*, *C. glauca*, and *C. flaccida*. Most are lumped under the botanical name of *C. × generalis*. They bring a tropical touch to any garden with their big green, bronze or reddish leaves and flowers in a dazzling range of either plain shades or with mottled and spotted variations. *C. iridiflora* is a taller species, reaching 3m/10ft, and its large flowers are carried on drooping, arching stems.

In temperate climates *Cannas* can be planted out at any time, but wait until all danger of frost has passed in colder areas. Increase *Cannas* by division of the rhizome and cut flowered stems to ground level in late autumn. In cold areas, protect roots with mulch.

CANTUA
(kan-too-∂)
Sacred Flower of the Incas, Magic Flower
POLEMONIACEAE

Whether this gorgeously blooming shrub really was sacred to the Incas I do not know, but it may well have been since it comes from the Andes, is scarce in cultivation and very, very beautiful indeed. It enjoys a light, leaf-rich, well-drained soil and a sunny, sheltered position; it is remarkably drought resistant. *C. buxifolia* is said to be reasonably hardy and is grown with wall shelter in many parts of England. In Australia, I have seen it only in mountain gardens where the drainage is above suspicion. It develops a rather leggy habit, with slender branches bowed down by the weight of long, tubular flowers that appear continuously for many weeks in spring. These are purplish-red at their flared tips, with the tubes striped yellow and borne in dense terminal corymbs. The shrub can grow to 2m/6ft, needs staked support for best display, and should be lightly tip-pruned after bloom. *Cantua* makes a dazzling basket plant when young, but must eventually go into the garden.

Cantua buxifolia. Sacred Flower of the Incas

Canna × *generalis* 'Pandora'. Indian Shot

Canna iridiflora. Iris-flowered Canna

Canna × *generalis* 'Lucifer'. Indian Shot

CAPPARIS
(kap-pər-əs)
Caper Tree, Cat's Whisker

CAPPARACEAE

A most variable genus, 300-odd species of *Capparis* are found in subtropical or tropical areas of both the old and new worlds. All are evergreen and include herbs, shrubs, trees and climbers, often with exquisite flowers. Shrubby Mediterranean species *C. spinosa* is raised commercially and its pickled flower buds are the tangy capers with many culinary uses.

The Jamaica Caper Tree, *C. cynophallophora*, is popularly grown in the Caribbean and southern USA. It bears leathery, elliptical 10cm/4in bronze leaves, single fragrant flowers and bean-like fleshy fruits.

The Cat's Whisker, *C. micrantha*, is widely distributed from India through Malaysia to the Philippines. It is an erect, thorny, small tree to 5m/16ft in height with drooping branches. The delightfully fragrant flowers appear in summer, right along the branches. The small petals are only 1cm/½in long and generally white, though one may be marked in red or yellow. From the centre of the flower emerges a group of fine white stamens in a spectacular display.

CARAGANA
(ka-ra-**gah**-nə)
Pea Tree

FABACEAE

Admirers of these deciduous shrubs or small trees, mainly from central Asia, say that their remarkable thorns are among their chief attractions. Maybe so: but I find them most uncomfortable plants to deal with. So, it seems, do most people, for despite their often lavish spring or summer displays of pea flowers in shades from white to yellow, and their pretty foliage, they are rarely seen. There are quite a few to choose from, the illustrated *Caragana arborescens* 'Lorbergii', which grows about 4.5m/15ft, being usually thought among the best of them. All are frost hardy and require sun and sharp drainage.

CARDIOCRINUM
(kar-dee-oh-krai-nəm)
Giant Lily

LILIACEAE

A giant among lilies – but perhaps not *quite* a lily! Taxonomists are still arguing whether this wonderful flower is a real Lilium or a *Cardiocrinum*, which merely means a lily with heart-shaped leaves! So far as you and I

Caragana arborescens 'Lorbergii'. Pea Tree

are concerned, the important differences are that it grows to 3.5m/11ft, and the football-size main bulb dies after flowering, leaving offsets to bloom another year. Obviously, because of its size, *Cardiocrinum giganteum* is suited only to large, woodland gardens with the rich acid soil and deep root run it needs. You, on the other hand, will need lots

Capparis micrantha. Cat's Whisker

Cardiocrinum giganteum. Giant Lily

Carissa macrocarpa cultivar. Natal Plum

Carpenteria californica. Tree Anemone

of patience, for it takes 7 years to bloom from seed, or 4 years from offsets. Seed is best! Choose an area with dappled shade, fertilise heavily and regularly as the plant develops a leaf-rosette several feet in diameter. From this, one summer when it's good and ready, a tall stem of fragrant white trumpet flowers will shoot up – way up!

CARISSA

(ka-**riss**-ə)
Natal Plum, Christ's Thorn
APOCYNACEAE

I'd answer queries on how to handle a *Carissa* with the words 'very carefully'. All 20-odd species have wickedly forked spines which can inflict a painful injury. They are very useful plants for a people-proof hedge in warm climates. Warmth is a key to their culture, though the smaller-flowered species *C. bispinosa* can be grown elsewhere in an unheated greenhouse. The 5-petalled flowers are as fragrant as related Frangipani, and in illustrated *C. macrocarpa* are 7.5cm/3in in diameter. The main flush is in late spring but flowering continues through most of summer. They are fairly drought resistant, good seaside plants and need heavy pruning. Propagate from autumn seed (set in the pulpy, scarlet, edible fruit) or from semi-hardwood cuttings struck with heat. In time, they may reach 4.5m/15ft.

CARPENTERIA

(kar-pen-**te**ər-ee-ə)
Tree Anemone
SAXIFRAGACEAE

Often hard to find because it's difficult to strike from cuttings, slow-growing *Carpenteria californica* is best propagated from suckers or layered in a damp mixture of sand and peat. It will thrive only in full sun (though a semi-shaded position may bring success in hot climates). *Carpenteria* is ever-green, quite drought resistant and can be killed by over-watering in cold weather. You'll grow it to its full height of 2.5m/8ft

Carpobrotus edulis. Hottentot Fig

only in a rich, well-drained soil, but prune regularly after bloom to counteract its rather untidy habit. The dark leaves are spear-shaped and rather downy. The white, poppy-like, fragrant flowers are borne for a short time in summer.

CARPOBROTUS

(kar-poh-**broh**-tus)
Hottentot Fig, Sour Fig, Gouna
AIZOACEAE

Native to coasts of Australia, South Africa, North and South America, some 30 *Carpobrotus* species are large, succulent

plants much used for sandbinding of coastal dunes, in both private residences and public projects. Spreading rapidly from runners, they can be propagated from seed or cuttings, which should be pinned down until they get a grip on soft, sandy soil. So succulent and water retentive they rarely need sprinkling, *Carpobrotus* species, particularly *C. edulis*, have become naturalised on the famous white cliffs of Dover, and around the entrance to Sydney Harbour. Leaves are three-angled and fleshy: the scantily borne yellow flowers fade to pink.

Carruanthus ringens. Karroo Star

Caryopteris incana. Bluebeard

Cassia javanica. Apple Blossom Tree

CARRUANTHUS
(ka-roo-**an**-thəs)
Karroo Star
AIZOACEAE

Similar in appearance to many of the other South African succulent genera, the 2 *Carruanthus* species vary considerably where it doesn't show – they grow from a rhizome!

Propagated from seed or sections of the running root, *C. ringens* spreads rapidly, forming a thick mat of foliage, covering its long stems with 4 rows of 6cm/2½ in succulent leaves. These are slightly triangular in sections, resemble those of Carpobrotus (which see). They make splendid groundcovers in hot, dry areas (where summer moisture is a must) or in exposed seaside positions. The 5cm/2in golden flowers are petal-tipped in bright red, and appear singly during summer weather. They don't open on dull days.

CARYOPTERIS
(kar-ee-**op**-ter-is)
Blue Spiraea, Bluebeard
VERBENACEAE

A popular group of deciduous shrubs from Japan and China, the *Caryopteris* genus bloom in very late summer or autumn, when flowers are often scarce. Suited to the cool temperate garden, they are *not* frost hardy and are useless in the northern and midwest United States. In marginal areas, they can be treated as perennials and cut back hard in very early spring. Grow them in ordinary soil, and keep them moist in the warmer months, cosily mulched in the cold. Propagate from seed or semi-hardwood cuttings struck under glass. The simple grey-greenish foliage is aromatic, the small long-stemmed flowers fragrant and borne in cymes at the leaf axils. Grow them in full sun, prune in early spring.

CASSIA
(kas-see-ə)
Shower Tree, Indian Laburnum
CAESALPINIACEAE

The pan-tropical genus *Cassia* used to include both shrubs and trees, but most of the shrubs and some of the trees have been decanted into their own genus, *Senna*. Just which depends on which authority you consult: but there seems to be agreement that *Cassia* still holds two of the most desirable of all tropical trees, *C. javanica,* the Shower Tree, and *C. fistula,* the Indian Laburnum.

C. javanica is an airy tree that covers itself in late summer with soft pink flowers, the tropics' nearest equivalent to apple blossom, while the Indian Laburnum turns 'rich in streaming gold' when in spring the long hanging chains of flowers appear, to be followed by the heavy, glossy leaves and the long seed pods that give it the unromantic name Pudding-pipe Tree. Neither is at all difficult to grow, and there are few tropical gardens without one or the other – or both!

CASTANOSPERMUM
(kas-tan-oh-**spur**-m∂m)
Moreton Bay Chestnut, Black Bean
FABACEAE

Named Moreton Bay Chestnut by early British settlers, these handsome Australian trees have only one resemblance to the European Chestnuts – the size and shape of their seeds, which are mildly poisonous.

Botanists followed the settlers' lead and christened the tree *Castanospermum*, meaning chestnut-seeded. Beyond that there is no relationship at all. *C. australe* is a handsome tree with dense, dark foliage becoming partly deciduous as the flowers appear in summer. It is slow growing, propagated from seeds or ripe cuttings, and is now raised in many warm temperate parts of the world.

Strictly a tree for frost-free areas, *Castanospermum* makes a striking specimen or street tree where there is room. It is variable in habit, but generally wide and spreading, and up to 12m/38ft tall.

CATALPA
(ka-**tal**-p∂)
Indian Bean, Cigar Tree, Southern Catalpa
BIGNONIACEAE

Showy *Catalpa bignonioides* is a lush tree of a most tropical appearance and it comes as something of a surprise to learn that, in fact, it hails from the southeastern part of the USA. *Catalpas* are deciduous and quite

Castanospermum australe. Moreton Bay Chestnut

Cassia fistula. Golden Shower Tree

Catalpa bignonioides. Indian Bean, Southern Catalpa

Catananche caerulea. Cupid's Dart

Catharanthus roseus 'Bright Eyes'. Madagascar Periwinkle

resistant to moderate frosts – the ideal tree for a sunny lawn. The huge heart-shaped leaves can be 30cm/12in across, purplish when young and fresh in spring, maturing to either green or gold depending on variety. They have a slightly furry texture and a rather unpleasant smell when crushed. The foxglove-like summer flowers appear in large fragrant clusters or spikes – white, pink or lemon according to species, and generally marked in purple or yellow. These are followed by long, dangling pods which give *Catalpas* their popular names.

CATANANCHE
(kat-an-**an**-chee)
Cupid's Dart
ASTERACEAE

From southern Europe comes this lovely 'everlasting' type of daisy, useful for drying and somewhat resembling the cornflower. *Catananche caerulea* (or Cupid's Dart, as it is commonly known) is a fast-growing perennial that usually blooms in the first year from spring-sown seed. It grows about 60cm/2ft tall and produces masses of deep purple-blue flowers in late summer. These are long lasting when cut for indoor use.

    Catananches are easy to grow in all climatic and soil conditions provided they are raised in full sun. They are particularly successful in dry areas. Faded blooms should be removed promptly to prolong flowering. Propagation is by division or from seed. A yellow-flowered species, *C. caespitosa*, is sometimes available.

CATHARANTHUS
(kath-ar-**an**-thəs)
Madagascar Periwinkle
APOCYNACEAE

A small African relative of Plumeria, *Catharanthus roseus* is often sold incorrectly as *Vinca rosea*. Originally a shrubby perennial, it has been refined to a more dwarf type of plant which is widely used for annual display. As *Catharanthus* is frost-tender, seed should be sown indoors in mid-winter, keeping up a temperature of 24°C/75°F during germination. After all danger of frost is passed, set the young seedlings out in a well-drained, compost-enriched garden soil. Sun or semi-shade are equally suitable, and the little plants will tolerate considerable heat. Different strains have white, pink or red blooms, each with a darker red eye. Replace plants annually, as they become untidy over winter.

Cattleya Bob Betts. Hybrid Cattleya

Cattleya Irene Holgium 'Brown Eyes'. Hybrid Cattleya

CATTLEYA

(kat-**lae**-ə)
Cattleya
ORCHIDACEAE

Gorgeous orchids from tropical South and Central America, *Cattleyas* are really not difficult to grow if you can meet their three main requirements: softly filtered light, heat of around 15ºC/59ºF in winter and humidity of 50% or better in summer. *Cattleyas* are usually grown in hanging baskets filled with a compost of bark chunks, broken terracotta, treefern and other fibrous material.

There are two principal types. The first are related to the giant-flowered *C. labiata* and have swollen pseudobulbs with a single leaf. The second type have tall, cane-like bulbs with a pair of leaves and generally bear smaller flowers in clusters. They both grow from a creeping rhizome which roots at intervals. All *Cattleyas* are tree dwellers, like free circulation of air and occasional top-dressing with old manure.

CAVENDISHIA

(kav-en-**dish**-ee-ə)
Colombian Heath
ERICACEAE

One of the most magnificent gardens in Britain is that at Chatsworth, the seat of the dukes of Devonshire, whose family name is Cavendish. They are honoured by this genus of some 40 evergreen shrubs from the mountains of South America. *Cavendishias* enjoy the same conditions as the vireya rhododendrons – that is, leafy lime-free soil and a cool spot outdoors in frost-free climates, or a gently warmed greenhouse in cold ones. Their beauty resides as much in the bright colour of their young leaves as in their small flowers, pretty as these can be. Most are a bit straggly in habit and benefit from pruning after the late-spring flowering is over.

Cattleya aurantiaca (yellow form). Golden Cattleya

Cavendishia pubescens. Colombian Heath

CEANOTHUS

(see-an-**oh**-thәs)

California Lilac, Red Root, Wild Lilac

RHAMNACEAE

Though originating in the western United
States and Mexico, lovely California Lilacs
(*Ceanothus* species) seem to do best in
slightly cooler areas. In particular, they enjoy
a chilly winter, and do very well in many
parts of England. In Australia, they do best in
Victoria, Tasmania and mountain districts.
They are of course, not lilacs at all. Certainly
they do not share the lovely fragrance, so
their popular epithet is due to a similarity in
flower colour. In fact, the 50-odd species of
Ceanothus bloom in every imaginable shade
of blue, violet, mauve, pink and purple, and
there are whites and greyish tones as well.
Some species are deciduous, some evergreen,
but the latter are most popular. The tiny
flowers develop in showy terminal umbels
or panicles.

Grow *Ceanothus* in light, gravelly, fast-
draining soil in full sun. Tip-prune regularly
in early years to force a denser habit, then
prune away dead flower masses annually.
Named hybrids are propagated from semi-
hardwood cuttings in spring or autumn.

CELMISIA

(sel-**mee**-see-ә)

Mountain Daisy

ASTERACEAE

A genus of 60-odd daisy species from alpine
areas of New Zealand with a few representatives in similar regions of Australia. *Celmisias*
are delightful plants for colder areas,
flourishing in the scree garden or on sunny
banks. They do not like wet winters, preferring the dry cold of frozen soil. All *Celmisias*

Ceanothus papillosus. California Lilac

are covered with a thick, silvery fur, making
them attractive plants at any time and
providing a suitable background for their
profuse summer display of yellow-centred
white flowers.

They grow easily from seed sown in
autumn or from cuttings taken at the same
time. Grow in full sun in a well-drained,
compost enriched alkaline soil.

Celosia argentea, Plumosa Group,
'Pyramidalis'. Prince of Wales Feathers

CELOSIA

(sel-**oh**-see-ә)

**Cockscomb, Prince of Wales Feathers,
Chinese Wool Flower**

AMARANTHACEAE

Showy, fast-growing annuals from tropical
Asia, *Celosias* do well where summers are
hot. They need a well-drained, sandy soil,
rich in humus and manure, and kept
constantly moist. Two main strains are
grown. The Plumosa group (often known as
Prince of Wales Feathers) bear tall, feathery
inflorescences like sprays of plumes; these are
generally blood-red or bright yellow but
many intermediate shades are now available.
The Cristata group (also called Cockscomb)
have fan-shaped, rippled flower heads reminiscent of some corals, generally in vivid
cerise, but also found in other shades.
Flowers of both types are extremely long
lasting and may remain in good condition
for up to 2 months. They cut splendidly for
indoor decoration.

Celmisia spectabilis. Mountain Daisy

Celosia argentea, Cristata Group. Cockscomb

CENIA
(see-nee-ə)
Bachelor's Buttons, Brass Buttons
ASTERACEAE

The genera *Cenia* and *Cotula* are closely related and alike to the gardener's eye: both specialise in creeping or tufted rock-garden perennials with small button flowers, and both come from the temperate southern hemisphere. Botanists tend to transfer the species from one to the other, and they may be sold under either name. The illustrated *Cenia turbinata*, a South African native, will serve to give you an idea what they are like. They make useful carpeting plants to cover for small spring bulbs, providing flowers and pleasant foliage after the latter have gone.

Cenia turbinata. Bachelor's Buttons

TONY RODD

CENTAUREA
(sen-**tor**-ee-ə, ken-**tor**-ee-ə)
Knapweed, Centaury, Cornflower, Bachelor's Button, Sweet Sultan, Blue-bottle
ASTERACEAE

Native to Europe and the Middle East, the *Centaureas* have been grown since ancient times and may have been used in medicine, since one of them, the illustrated *C. macrocephala*, or Globe Centaury, is said to have healed a wound in the foot of Chiron, the wisest of all centaurs and mentor of Hercules. It is a perennial and bears its big yellow summer flowers on stems up to 1.5m/5ft in height.

But the annual varieties are more widely grown. For years known only in a particularly vivid ultramarine blue, the Cornflower

(*C. cyanus*) now comes in a vibrant mixture of shades including pale and deep pink, cerise, crimson, white and powder blue. They are easy to grow from seed or seedlings and turn on a splendid though rather short display. In mild climates, like those of Australia, South Africa or southern California, they bloom in late winter and earliest spring, but where winters are hard, summer sees their peak display. Flowering takes 14 weeks from seed sown in full sun or light shade. Choose a light but rich soil and keep up the water while buds are forming.

Related *C. moschata* or Sweet Sultan (sometimes listed as *Amberboa moschata*) may bloom in purple, white, pink or yellow, and has sweet perfume. It is not very common nowadays.

Centaurea moschata. Sweet Sultan

Centaurea cyanus. Cornflower, Bachelor's Button

Centaurea macrocephala. Globe Centaury

Centranthus ruber. Jupiter's Beard, Red Valerian

Cephalophyllum species. Red Spike

Cephalaria gigantea. Tartar Pincushion

CENTRANTHUS

(ken-**tran**-thəs)
(SYN Kentranthus)
Red Valerian, Jupiter's Beard, Fox's Brush
VALERIANACEAE

Native to Europe, North Africa and Asia Minor, old-fashioned Jupiter's Beard or *Centranthus* has been in cultivation for centuries and makes one of the showiest displays in adverse conditions. It will thrive in walls, on steep banks or in unwatered seaside areas, for it is quite drought resistant. Keep an eye peeled, though, for it has a reputation for seeding far and wide and has become naturalised in several countries.

Sow seed direct in the garden, or, in frosty areas, indoors in flats in early spring. Plant out or thin to a spacing of 30cm/12in. *C. ruber* is bushy and fast growing with 10cm/4in grey-green leaves topped with 60cm/2ft stems of densely clustered pink or ruby-red flowers in warm weather. These should be dead-headed to prolong the display. A useful cut flower, *Centranthus* grows anywhere except in a damp position, and likes dryish soil on the alkaline side.

CEPHALARIA

(kef-a-**le**ər-ee-ə)
Tartar Pincushion
DIPSACACEAE

Looking at the many beautiful plants that come from Siberia, we may spare a thought for the many Russian scientists who spent long, involuntary vacations there. The Giant or Tartar Pincushion (*Cephalaria gigantea*) is one of these plants, a beautiful 2m/6ft herbaceous perennial for the larger border or as a naturalised subject. It will grow in any soil, is naturally frost hardy, and resembles a large, yellow Scabious, to which it is related. Grow from autumn divisions or seed. Plants are set out at 45cm/18in spacings and will certainly need light staking as they grow beyond the 1m/3ft mark. Dead-head regularly to prolong the already generous summer display and cut back to ground after the first frost, or in late autumn.

CEPHALOPHYLLUM

(kef-a-loh-fil-əm)
Red Spike
AIZOACEAE

Like many of South Africa's succulent genera, the attractive *Cephalophyllums* are lazy risers, not opening their flowers for business before noon. Colours are dazzling – rich reds, oranges, salmons and warm creams – and blooming is best in well-drained soils of poor quality where the plants will not bolt to leaf. Strike them from cuttings, use in rockeries or as groundcover, in seaside positions of warm temperate climates. They'll grow with great speed into a prostrate mass with leaves crowded in tufts at branch ends and rooting joints.

CEPHALOTUS

(kef-ə-**loh**-təs)
Australian Pitcher Plant
CEPHALOTACEAE

Apart from television's once-popular ghoul-friends, the Addams family, these showy Western Australian carnivorous novelties are grown only by hobbyists, for they require very special treatment. Native to damp, peaty areas, they are raised in shallow pans of a saturated sphagnum-peat mixture, out of direct sun and usually covered by a glass jar. A minimum winter temperature of

Cephalotus follicularis. Albany Pitcher Plant

7°C/45°F is required, and the water supply is tapered off during winter. The plant's *real* flowers are tiny clusters of petal-less white stamens. But their *display* is a series of specialized leaves which develop into colourful pitchers into which insects are lured by nectar-secreting glands.

CERASTIUM
(sur-**ass**-tee-ə m)
Snow-in-summer
CARYOPHYLLACEAE

A fast-growing blanket of silver for ground-cover or rockery, *Cerastium* is planted from divisions in autumn, and may spread to 1m/3ft across in a single year. Cold climate or hot, it enjoys them both. Any soil will do so long as the position is sunny and well drained. Water regularly, but allow to dry out between soakings, and scatter packaged fertiliser twice a year. The snowy-white flowers appear in spring and summer, so densely that they sometimes hide the plant itself and give it the common name of Snow-in-summer. After bloom, shear lightly to remove spent flowers. Propagate by striking leafy tip-cuttings in a sand/peat mix any time, or separate rooted sections in autumn.

CERATOPETALUM
(ke-ra-toh-**pet**-ə-lə m)
Christmas Bush
CUNONIACEAE

In the coastal bushlands of New South Wales, the summer Christmas season is announced by a small, slender tree, *Ceratopetalum gummiferum* or Christmas Bush. As the longest day approaches, the tree becomes powdered with tiny white flowers that soon drop, leaving their calyces behind to enlarge until they are almost 1cm/½in in diameter. These then begin to change colour, darkening in some local varieties to a brilliant cherry red, sometimes suffused with royal purple.

So eyecatching is the display, few people ever notice that behind it is a slender tree with distinctive, 3-lobed leaves of softest green. In positions with deep, rich, sandy soil it may reach 12m/40ft in height.

C. gummiferum is hardy down to –2°C/28°F and is now grown in the southern USA, usually from ripened cuttings.

Cerastium tomentosum. Snow-in-summer

Ceratopetalum gummiferum. Christmas Bush

CERATOSTIGMA
(ker-at-oh-**stig**-m∂)
Chinese Plumbago
PLUMBAGINACEAE

Commonly pruned back to half its normal height of 120cm/4ft, the dense-growing Chinese shrub *Ceratostigma willmottianum* makes an interesting groundcover or low hedge; it is starred from late spring to autumn with striking, plumbago-like single flowers coloured pale to mid-blue. Soft-tip cuttings taken throughout the warm weather will strike easily; *Ceratostigma* should be set out in a friable, fertile soil and kept perpetually moist. It is hardy down to −5°C/23°F; colours beautifully in a cool climate and tolerates considerable drought. Shear heavily after bloom to prevent a plague of seedlings in all directions.

CERBERA
(**sur**-bur-∂)
Sea Mango, Tanghin
APOCYNACEAE

Closely related to the Frangipanis and resembling them in many particulars, the gawky Sea Mangoes or *Cerberas* are often used in tropical seaside gardens where the red-marked white flowers make a pleasant summer display. These appear in clusters at the ends of the branches and are followed by tennis-ball-sized fruits.

It would be an unfortunate person who *did* mistake these for mangoes, for all parts of the plants are poisonous. *C. odollam* may reach 15m/50ft, *C. manghas* grows to about 12m/40ft, while *C. venenifera* rarely tops 7m/23ft. All have red to blue or purple fruits. They are propagated from seed or cuttings. *Cerberas* are salt resistant.

Cerbera venenifera. Tanghin

Ceratostigma willmottianum. Chinese Plumbago

Cerbera manghas. Sea Mango

Cercis canadensis. Redbud

CERCIS
(**kur**-kis)
Judas Tree, Redbud
CAESALPINIACEAE

There are 6 *Cercis* species from Europe, Asia and North America, all with a strong family resemblance. They are deciduous trees or shrubs, growing 5–15m/16–50ft tall in the wild. The leaves are kidney-shaped, and small pea-flowers, generally pink but sometimes white or purple, appear on bare wood (often from the trunks or older branches) in stalkless clusters. They are followed by absolute masses of 10cm/4in flat pods which persist well into winter.

The botanical name is from the Greek *kerkis*; the original name of the European species, *C. siliquastrum*. In contrast to its cousins, it is fast growing and may develop a columnar or round-headed shape. The North American Redbud, *C. canadensis*, is a many-branched tree, often spindly, and covered in every part with brilliant rose-pink blossom.

CEREUS
(**se**-ree-∂s)
Torch Thistle
CACTACEAE

Once one of the larger genera in the cactus family, *Cereus* is now reduced to some 25 species, mostly night-flowering species with a strong architectural effect. Larger plants of *Cereus uruguayanus* are often seen in gardens of 19th-century villas or country houses,

Cercis siliquastrum. Judas Tree

Cereus uruguayanus. Torch Thistle

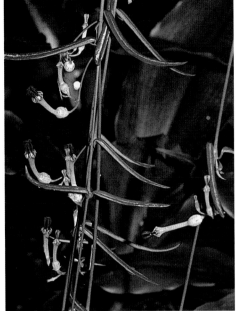

Ceropegia linearis subsp. *debilis.* String of Hearts

Cestrum endlicheri. Scarlet Jessamine

Cestrum nocturnum. Night Jessamine

where they certainly make a stunning feature with their clumps of 3m/10ft spiny-ribbed grey-green trunks. These are sometimes branched, but more often simply columnar. There is some controversy about the plant's name, *Cereus*: Latin in origin, it may refer to the waxen texture of the dazzling white nocturnal flowers. Grow from large cuttings in deep, well-drained soil, and do not water except in severe drought. Originally from the banks of the River Plate in northern Argentina and Uruguay, it makes a large clump in just a few years. You'll never see blooms without a flashlight – they're dead by dawn.

Ceropegia linearis subsp. *woodii.* Rosary Vine

CEROPEGIA

(ser-oh-**pee**-jee-ə)

Rosary Vine, String of Hearts

ASCLEPIADACEAE

Not so much vines as small, succulent trailing plants, *Ceropegias* grow from tubers which form at intervals along the wiry stems, much in the fashion of beads on a rosary. They are very popular novelty plants for the conservatory or humid plant house, where they are normally planted many to a hanging basket. They grow at a great rate in warm weather, blooming singly or in clusters from stem nodes. The blooms are small, tubular and purplish – bent upwards like a Dutchman's pipe. The name *Ceropegia* means 'fountain of wax' – an apt description. *C. linearis* subsp. *woodii* has heart-shaped leaves, subsp. *debilis* small cylindrical foliage.

CESTRUM

(**ses**-trəm)

Night Jessamine, Purple Cestrum

SOLANACEAE

Easy to strike from slips, *Cestrums* grow fast in any well-enriched, fast-draining soil and can be 2–4m/6–13ft tall, depending on species. They all need lashings of water and regular doses of fertiliser during the warm weather. Removing a few of the oldest canes each winter will force plenty of new growth. Evergreen, *Cestrums* are hardy to 1ºC/34ºF and need wall protection in cold areas. *C. nocturnum* is noted for its rich night fragrance, which can fill the air on summer evenings. *C. parqui* is another strongly perfumed type, but is best hidden among

Cestrum cultum. Purple Cestrum

other shrubs as it is not particularly attractive and is easily damaged by frost. If you don't like the perfume (and it can be cloying at times), you can still enjoy the flowers. Unscented species such as scarlet *C. endlicheri* and dark *C. elegans* (syn *C. purpureum*) both bear masses of flowers in late spring and summer and the latter lends itself to espaliering. Where winters are frosty, cut to the ground after early frosts and mulch roots heavily.

Chaenomeles × superba. Japonica

Chaenomeles speciosa 'Nivalis'. White-flowering Quince

CHAENOMELES

(kae-**nom**-ə-leez)

Flowering Quince, Japonica, Japanese Quince

ROSACEAE

Dense, spiny shrubs often 2m/6ft tall and as wide, the Japonicas commence blooming in winter and continue for months. Four species only are known, but many cultivars have been raised, blooming in shades and combinations of white, pink, red and orange. *Chaenomeles* are raised easily from leaf semi-hardwood cuttings taken in summer or autumn, or by division of the suckering stems. They romp ahead in any well-drained soil, provided the position is in full sun and the plants are kept moist during summer. They are hardy down to at least –10ºC/14ºF

Chamaecereus silvestrii. Peanut Cactus

but in such climates flowering is delayed until spring. Complete removal of at least a third of the oldest stems each year after bloom will ensure profuse flowering the following spring. Flowers appear on bare branches and are usually single, though semi-doubles are also available. The hard autumn fruit which follows makes a delicious, tangy jelly.

CHAMAECEREUS

(ka-mae-**seer**-ee-əs)

Peanut Cactus

CACTACEAE

Argentina's gay little Peanut Cactus is seen all over the world, growing in small pots at sunny windows. The prostrate tubular stems are covered in silvery spines and grow in every direction. They should be handled carefully for they break easily, although severed pieces will root again in a few weeks. The stems of *Chamaecereus* take on a reddish tone in cold weather and if allowed to dry out (even to the point of shrivelling) in winter, they will tolerate several degrees of frost and the late spring flowers will be even more profuse. Grow them in shallow pots in a standard, gritty cactus mix. Keep moist in spring and summer.

CHAMAEMELUM

(ka-mee-**meel**-əm)

(SYN Anthemis)

Chamomile, Roman Chamomile

ASTERACEAE

It seems odd in a book like this to have to note that the most highly recommended cultivars of *Chamaemelum nobile* are those that don't flower. That is because its chief use these days is the making of chamomile lawns in imitation of the famous one at Buckingham Palace – a use for which this tough, almost prostrate perennial is well suited, at least in cooler climates. Alternatively, it is grown to make chamomile tea, for which purpose the flowers are picked and dried as soon as they are fully open. Either way, you miss out on the pleasure of seeing its carpets of greyish, aromatic foliage studded with little white and gold daisies for much of the summer. A pity!

Chamaemelum likes sunshine and rich soil, and should be divided every few years to keep it vigorous.

Chamelaucium megalopetalum. White Waxflower

Chamelaucium uncinatum. 'Purple Splendour'. Purple Wax Plant

CHAMELAUCIUM

(kam-e-**lor**-kee-∂m)

Waxflower, Wax Plant, Geraldton Wax

MYRTACEAE

Western Australia's *Chamelauciums* are widely grown down under, but deserve worldwide popularity since their 'hard-to-grow' reputation is really quite undeserved. They simply prefer a gravelly soil of a rather alkaline balance – given that, they will grow fast into open, twiggy shrubs, anything up to 3m/10ft tall. Acid soil and too much water are sure to cause premature death and they do have very brittle roots, so must be planted with extreme care. *Chamelauciums* are members of the myrtle family, have tiny, aromatic leaves and bear their honey-rich, 5-petalled flowers for weeks in early spring. Prune lightly after bloom. *C. uncinatum*, the Geraldton Wax Plant, is the most commonly grown.

Chamaemelum nobile. Chamomile, Roman Chamomile

CHASMANTHE

(kas-**man**-thee)

(SYN Antholyza)

Pennants, African Cornflag

IRIDACEAE

Waving gaily from branched stems up to 1.5m/5ft tall, *Chasmanthe*'s one-sided flower spikes may well remind some people of pennants fluttering on board ship. The blooms (pretty rather than spectacular) are tubular, but open their gaping throats for a short period only. Related to Gladiolus, they are propagated from small offsets of the rather larger corms. Give them full sun in the well-watered soil of a frost-free area, and set out in early spring for midsummer bloom. They are from South Africa and can be allowed to dry out during late summer dormancy. All species bloom in shades of red, yellow and orange.

Chasmanthe aethiopica. Pennants

CHIMONANTHUS

(kim-on-**an**-th∂s)

(SYN Meratia)

Winter Sweet

CALYCANTHACEAE

Not exciting in appearance, the dainty brown and yellow flowers of *Chimonanthus praecox* are grown and treasured for the rich, rare scent they bring to the winter garden, when blooms are scarce.

These appear on leafless stems which may be cut to open indoors in water. One or two will perfume a whole room.

Strictly a subject for the cold to cool temperate climate, *Chimonanthus* is a clump-forming native of China and Japan, and does best in a fairly rich, well-drained soil. Seed takes so long to bloom that the plant is almost invariably propagated from layers, which will still take up to 2 years before severance is wise.

Set the plant out in full sun in colder areas, and with afternoon shade where the climate is warmer. Prune lightly to thin in

Chimonanthus praecox. Winter Sweet
TONY RODD

winter – the plant looks better kept at two-thirds of its natural 4.5m/15ft height. *Chimonanthus* foliage turns a light yellow before it falls in autumn.

CHIONANTHUS
(kai-on-**an**-thᴐs)
Fringe Tree
OLEACEAE

An ideal choice for the cool to temperate garden, the slim and delicate Fringe Trees will never grow too large and outwear their welcome. Only 2 of the 100-odd species are seen in cultivation, neither likely to top 4.5m/15ft. Both are deciduous, one from China, the other from North America. The Chinese species, *Chionanthus retusus*, is the more dainty, with slim, pointed 10cm/4in leaves, dense panicles of pure white flowers in summer, and later, dark blue fruits about the size of a grape. It is frost hardy, loves a good, woodsy soil in full sun and is usually propagated from seed. The American species, *C. virginicus*, is sometimes known as Old Man's Beard, for its flower panicles may droop in a pointed fashion to 20cm/8in. Its leaves are larger and so are the fruit. *Chionanthus* is from old Greek and means 'snow flower'.

CHIONODOXA
(kai-on-oh-**dok**-sᴐ)
Glory of the Snow
LILIACEAE

Popping out of the winter snowdrifts in Asia Minor in earliest spring, the delightful *Chionodoxas* are dainty members of the lily family whose appearance is cause for celebration throughout their natural area.

In cultivation (cool to cold temperate climates only), they are set out in well-drained, loamy soil in autumn. Left to them-

Chionanthus retusus. Fringe Tree
TONY RODD

Chionodoxa forbesii. Glory of the Snow

selves, they spread rapidly from seed and offsets, soon forming most attractive clumps which are especially useful in the rock garden or beneath the outermost branches of deciduous trees. Sparse foliage appears with the flowers.

Illustrated *C. forbesii* (syn *C. luciliae*) is the preferred variety.

CHIRANTHODENDRON
(kai-**ran**-thoh-den-drᴐn)
(SYN Cheirostemon)
Monkey Hand Tree, Hand-flower Tree
BOMBACACEAE

Cultivated in southern California and other subtropical regions is the curious Monkey Hand Tree, *Chiranthodendron pentadactylon*, long attributed magical qualities by Mexican Indians. Fast growing, with gnarled, woody

Chiranthodendron pentadactylon. Monkey Hand Tree

branches and furry leaves, it bears some of the most remarkable flowers in the world. Borne in clusters at the leaf axils, often well hidden by the foliage, a series of bronze, furry buds appear. One by one, these develop into cup-sized dull red flowers from the centre of which emerges a blood-red appendage, complete with sharp, curved claws which really do look like a monkey's hand. *Chiranthodendron* needs rich soil and plenty of water. It is a variable tree, usually spreading in habit and anything from 8–25m/26–80ft tall; while it is evergreen in frost-free areas, it may be partly deciduous where winters are harder. Flowers are borne year-round in the tropics but only in spring and summer at the cooler end of its range. It is hardy down to –5ºC/23ºF.

Choisya ternata. Mexican Orange Blossom

CHIRITA
(chi-ri-tə)
Malay Gentian, Cheryta
GESNERIACEAE

Perhaps least common of the Gesneriads in cultivation, the *Chiritas* are certainly among the most beautiful of that family. All native to the Indo-Malaysian area, including jungles of Sri Lanka, their temperature needs are so high they are unlikely to be found outside expensively heated greenhouses. A minimum 15ºC/59ºF at night keeps them happy, and up to 6ºC/10ºF higher during the day helps them bloom well. Porous soil rich in leaf-mould is best for their cultivation, with high air-moisture in summer. Propagate from leaf cuttings set in damp sand. Bright shade produces showy clusters of mostly mauvish bell-flowers in winter.

Chirita sp. Cheryta

Chlidanthus fragrans. Sea Daffodil, Fairy Lily

CHLIDANTHUS
(klid-an-thus)
Fairy Lily, Sea Daffodil
AMARYLLIDACEAE

There are only two species of these dainty early summer flowering bulbs: *Chlidanthus ehrenbergii* from Mexico and the much better known *C. fragrans* from Chile. Both grow about 25cm/10in tall, both have yellow flowers, and both are sweetly fragrant. They dislike frost, and in cool climates are best grown as pot plants, treated in exactly the same way as their distant cousin the hippeastrum. In the garden they like a sunny spot and can be left undisturbed to build up into clumps. Plant in early spring.

CHOISYA
(choi-see-ə)
Mexican Orange Blossom
RUTACEAE

There are about 8 species of these elegant, evergreen shrubs, and yes, they are closely

Chonemorpha penangensis. Malay Jasmine

related to the Citrus, whose perfume they share. A great favourite in temperate climate gardens, *Choisya ternata* needs a certain amount of attention to bloom satisfactorily. Acid soil, rich in humus, is a good starting point, and the shrub's root junction should be set above the surrounding soil level. It is propagated from cuttings of firm tips taken in autumn. Regular pruning produces more bloom and keeps the bush to a dense, rounded, 2m/6ft 'bun'. The thin, leathery leaves are aromatic, each consisting of 3 rounded, glossy leaflets. The sweetly fragrant flowers appear in spring and draw bees. Hardy down to –9ºC/15ºF.

CHONEMORPHA
(kon-e-mor-fə)
Malay Jasmine
APOCYNACEAE

Not true Jasmines, the 13 species of *Chonemorpha* are gigantic tropical vines from Indo-Malaysian forests. Several do quite well in warm temperate areas of Australia and California, where their size is, fortunately, much reduced. They have been proven hardy down to –3ºC/27ºF. Try one in full sun with leaf-rich, well-drained soil and plenty of warm-weather water. It may need some support, for in the absence of a truly tropical climate it is more likely to run along the ground than up a tree. *C. penangensis* bears very large glossy leaves up to 37.5cm/15in long and almost as wide, while the creamy blossoms, borne in cymes, are highly fragrant. *Chonemorpha* is closely related to the popular Star Jasmine, *Trachelospermum jasminoides.*

Choricarpia leptopetala. Brush Turpentine

CHORICARPIA

(ko-ri-**kah**-pee-∂)
Brush Turpentine
MYRTACEAE

A fine ornamental for warm coastal areas, *Choricarpia leptopetala* has been little known outside Australia, though it would suit many climates.

The leaves are smooth, leathery and wavy-edged, rust coloured when young but ripening to a soft green with rusty reverses. The spring blossoms appear in large arching clusters – great puffballs of creamy stamens similar to Acacia but much larger.

Choricarpia (the name means separate fruits) flowers when quite young, at which stage it could be mistaken for Callicoma (which see). However, the leaves are totally different.

The beautiful Brush Turpentine has proven itself an ideal street tree in warm temperate parts of Australia, where it grows to 16m/53ft.

Chorisia speciosa. Floss Silk Tree

Chorisia insignis. Spiny Chorisia

CHORISIA

(ko-**ris**-ee-∂)
Floss Silk Tree, Chorisia
BOMBACACEAE

Successful anywhere winter temperatures stay above –7ºC/19ºF, *Chorisia* remain inexplicably rare in gardens everywhere. Yet the sight of one in full bloom is food for the soul – no two of them have flowers exactly the same. That is their peculiarity. The 15cm/6in flowers on one giant tree will always differ

Chorizema cordatum. Heart-leaf Flame Pea

from those on another, both in colour and in structure. In the case of the best-known species, the Brazilian *C. speciosa*, the flowers will be 5-petalled and basically pink, but beyond that they may vary from reddish to salmon, their centres white or yellow, marked in deep red or brown, the petals plain or with rippled edges. The related *C. insignis* from Peru has basically white flowers, marked with gold, but they may also be all yellow or marked in various other colours.

Both species grow tall, 15m/50ft and more, and have tapering trunks up to 2m/6ft in diameter at ground level, liberally studded with thorns and spines. Both are deciduous in late summer, the flowers appearing in early autumn.

CHORIZEMA

(ko-ri-**zee**-m∂)
Flame Pea, Flowering Oak
FABACEAE

The gaudiest pea-flowers imaginable have brought wide popularity to this small genus of evergreen Australian shrubs. They enjoy a sandy loam, regular water and annual pruning to keep them from becoming untidy. Unpruned, they grow into an open, semi-climbing shrub 1m/3ft or so tall. Well-grown specimens can be attractive as sprawling groundcovers, rockery subjects or among other lightly foliaged shrubs. *Chorizemas* are hardy down to –4ºC/24ºF and grow well in full sun, though it must be said that the colours of the flowers, which appear over a long period in spring, are brighter in semi-shade. Firm tip-cuttings strike easily any time from summer to midwinter if kept warm and humid. Alternatively, raise from seed, which must first be scarified or soaked for a day in warm water.

CHRYSANTHEMOIDES
(kris-an-them-**oi**-dees)
Bitou Bush, Bone Seed, Bush-tick Berry
ASTERACEAE

'Who would imagine that such a pretty plant could become such a *pest!*' Famous last words, presumably from some early Australian settler who brought in the seed from South Africa. Now, as it is well on its way to taking over the entire east coast of Australia, decimating the native vegetation as it grows, we have learned to be more careful. Named as a noxious weed in Victoria and New South Wales, it can still be grown elsewhere and is a wonderful cover for dry banks or poor sandy soil. Plant it (in Australia at least) only if you have the time to dead-head regularly before the seeds form, and pull out any seedlings that pop up. *Chrysanthemoides monilifera* is recognised from its irregularly toothed waxy leaves and somewhat untidy yellow daisy flowers.

CHRYSANTHEMUM
(kriz-**anth**-ə-məm)
(SYN Dendranthema)
Chrysanthemum
ASTERACEAE

In recent times botanists have divided up *Chrysanthemum* in the old sense into more easily recognised groups. In this book you will find some former Chrysanthemums under *Ajania, Argyranthemum, Leucanthemum* and *Tanacetum*. But there is still one important group of plants that remain as the true Chrysanthemums, and happily this coincides with the popular use of the name, that is, for the 'Florists' Chrysanthemums' sold worldwide as potted and cut flowers. The breeding of the innumerable cultivars began centuries ago in China, the chief parent species believed to be *Chrysanthemum morifolium*, but they are now grouped under the hybrid name *C. grandiflorum*. News of these gorgeous plants reached the West in the 18th century and soon strenuous efforts were being made to introduce as many as possible of the Chinese cultivars. Breeding continued apace in both East and West, so that today there are many thousands of recorded cultivars, and numerous societies devoted to growing and exhibiting them.

The Florists' Chrysanthemum ranks with the rose and the carnation as the world's biggest-selling flower, thanks to its rich variety of sizes, shapes and colours (everything but blue, though the genetic engineers

Chrysanthemoides monilifera. Bitou Bush

Chrysanthemum 'Bendigo'. Quill-shaped Chrysanthemum

Chrysanthemum 'Morning Star'

Chrysanthemum 'Apricot Cream'. Single Chrysanthemum

Chrysanthemum 'Cheddar'. Incurved-form Chrysanthemum

Chrysanthemum 'Pink Poolys'. Intermediate Chrysanthemum

Chrysanthemum 'Bridesmaid'. Spoon-shaped Chrysanthemum

brought into flower at any time of year. That is not a trick we can do at home. It calls for special greenhouses equipped with blackout curtains, drawn to a precise schedule to fool the plants into thinking that autumn, their natural flowering season, is on the way.

Nor is it easy to emulate the florists in the way they get their potted versions to flower when only a handspan high. In the garden, the plants can grow much taller, and according to the variety and whether you thin out the flower buds, they can bear either sprays of many little flowers or solitary ones almost the size of saucers; and they can be single daisies, great mop-headed affairs, or spidery in their long, quilled 'petals'. The flowers last in beauty for weeks, either on or off the plant – and they have a delicate, spicy fragrance.

The plant is a herbaceous perennial; plant in spring, either from divisions or cuttings of young shoots, giving the plants rich soil and sunshine and a stake or two lest they flop. Where winter arrives early, the big exhibition types are best grown under glass.

But there is also a small group of annual species that, for the meantime at least, are kept in *Chrysanthemum* though not closely related to the Florists' Chrysanthemums. They include the Crown Daisy, *C. coronarium*, whose leaves and flower buds are used in Chinese cooking, and the Painted Daisy or Tricolor Chrysanthemum, *C. carinatum*, from Morocco – this makes a sensational bedding plant in cooler climates, and cuts superbly.

Chrysanthemum carinatum 'Court Jesters'. Tricolor Chrysanthemum

Chrysanthemum 'White Spider'. Spider Chrysanthemum

Chrysanthemum 'Xenia Noelle'. Reflexed-form Chrysanthemum

Chrysocephalum apiculatum. Yellow Buttons

Chrysogonum virginianum. Golden Star

CHRYSOCEPHALUM
(kris-oh-**sef**-∂-l∂m)
Yellow Buttons
ASTERACEAE

First it was *Gnaphalium apiculatum*, then for a long time *Helichrysum apiculatum* – and now it is *Chrysocephalum apiculatum*! A lot of longwinded names, and I wonder if they have not blinded gardeners to the very real merits of this shrubby perennial – you don't see it very often even in its native Australia. It is a charmer, especially in summer, when the silvery leaves almost vanish under clusters of little brilliantly golden buttons which can, if you wish, be dried as everlastings. The species includes a range of growth forms, some almost prostrate but none more than 60cm/2ft high and wide. It will endure quite a lot of frost as well as the hardest drought. Just give it full sunshine and perfect drainage.

CHRYSOCOMA
(kris-oh-**koh**-m∂)
Goldilocks
ASTERACEAE

Closely related to Michaelmas and Easter daisies, this dainty South African evergreen can put on an almost blinding display in the rock or paved garden. It enjoys a gritty, well-drained soil and light but regular water, more generously applied in the warmer months. A little fertiliser at monthly intervals in spring will bring on the maximum display of golden pompon flowers and prolong the already long show. Shear the dwarf bush all over after bloom to keep it a compact 60cm/2ft mound. Cuttings of half-ripened shoots are easy to strike under glass in late summer. *Chrysocoma coma-aurea* is the preferred species.

CHRYSOGONUM
(kris-**og**-on-∂m)
Golden Star
ASTERACEAE

A charming little perennial plant from the eastern United States, *Chrysogonum virginianum* is not widely grown elsewhere, merely because it has such competition from other, more spectacular members of the daisy family. But if you have a position in dappled shade that needs extra summer colour – then the Golden Star will turn on a great show in ordinary well-drained soil, and can be propagated from seed or spring divisions. Rarely reaching 30cm/1ft high, it grows fast in the warm weather of cool temperate climates, blooming over a long period. The foliage is slightly hairy, with bluntly toothed leaves up to 7.5cm/3in long. The plant is completely deciduous – the daisy flowers are 5-petalled and a soft gold in colour.

Chrysocoma coma-aurea. Goldilocks

CHYSIS
(kai-sis)
Chysis
ORCHIDACEAE

Not grown as widely as the more spectacular Cattleyas and their many crosses, the several *Chysis* species have an important plus – a rich, memorable perfume that can scent an entire orchid-house. You'll need a minimum glasshouse temperature of 15°C/59°F, but give them just enough water to prevent shrivelling. In warmer weather, keep them humid and partly shaded and look out for thrips and red spider-mites, either of which can do a lot of damage. The 7–9 waxen flowers open on a short spike around spring. Grow in a fibre-rich compost. The name *Chysis* is Greek for melting, referring to the fused appearance of the pollen-masses.

Chysis bractescens. Chysis

Cirsium rivulare 'Atropurpureum'. Plumed Thistle

CIRSIUM

(**kur**-see-∂m)

Plumed Thistle

ASTERACEAE

Native to many cooler parts of the northern hemisphere, there are literally thousands of *Cirsium* species. And their name may well be appropriate, for they are cursed by farmers who find them among the most intractable of weeds. But city gardeners value them for their beauty and rich colours in the mixed border. Both annual and perennial types grow in ordinary well-drained garden soil with average moisture. *C. rivulare* may reach 120cm/4ft in height and produce its typically thistle-type flowers throughout the summer. They are a rich crimson, borne on long stems and splendid for cutting. The name is from the ancient Greek *kirsos*, a swollen vein, for which they were once used medicinally.

CISTUS

(**sis**-t∂s)

Rock Rose

CISTACEAE

Wonderful evergreen shrubs from the sun-baked shores of the Mediterranean, the 20-odd species of *Cistus* are a perfect choice for poor or sandy soil, for exposed banks or seaside cliffs. Most of them remain compact,

Cistus populifolius. Poplar-leaf Rock Rose

particularly when pinched back regularly. They are remarkably drought resistant, and need little water once established – but as a corollary, they do not like humidity. They are hardy down to –9º/15ºF.

C. 'Silver Pink' develops into a 1x1m/3x3ft compact shrub bearing thick, textured leaves and lovely, clear pink single flowers at the end of spring. *C. populifolius* is twice the size, and more open and erect.

CITRUS

(**sit**-r∂s)

Orange, Lemon, Grapefruit, Lime etc

RUTACEAE

In a world of orange juice, eau de Cologne and lemon-scented detergents, it's hard to imagine life without *Citrus* trees. All 15-odd

Citrus blossom

Cistus 'Silver Pink'. Sage-leaf Rock Rose

species are native to tropical Southeast Asia, but most are happy with an outdoor winter temperature as low as 7ºC/45ºF. They have even been known to resist short frosty spells – especially oranges and lemons.

Citrus grow best in a moist, humid atmosphere and appreciate a daily spray of the foliage in dry weather, which also keeps at bay the innumerable pests attracted by their volatile leaf-oils. They like a deep, rich soil that's very well drained, and use plenty of manure and other fertiliser during the growing season.

All *Citrus* species have similar dark, glossy leaves, often with curiously bladed or winged leaf-stalks. The white or sometimes mauve-tinted flowers may appear at any time but are most heavy in spring, filling the air with their fragrance.

Clarkia amoena. Farewell-to-spring, Godetia

Cleistocactus straussii. Silver Torch

Clarkia unguiculata 'Flore Pleno'. Garland Flower, Clarkia

CLARKIA

(klah-kee-ə)
(SYN Godetia)
Rocky Mountain Garland, Godetia, Satinflower, Farewell-to-spring
ONAGRACEAE

I am really quite confused about Clarkias and Godetias – English and Australian nurseries seem to sell them as different plants, but Americans class them both as *Clarkia* and I expect they should have the last word, as these are among the most colourful of their native plants.

C. *amoena*, commonly called Farewell-to-spring because of its late-blooming habit, bears open, cup-like flowers, 7–12cm/3–5in across, in combinations of red, white, pink and lilac. These are sometimes double or ruffled, and open in bunches at the top of stems. C. *pulchella*, the Rocky Mountain Garland, is a taller-growing annual with generally double, ruffled flowers of about 2.5cm/1in diameter, borne in the leaf axils.

C. *unguiculata*, the Garland Flower, is similar, but with flowers usually in shades of pink or mauve. There are also many hybrids between the three species, which further adds to the confusion. All of them are among the most charming of annual blooms, and need the same treatment in both propagation and cultivation. They make splendid cut flowers, and do best in a light, sandy soil that has perfect drainage and low fertility. Sow the seed only outdoors where they are to grow. In frost-free areas, sowing can take place in autumn for early spring bloom. Dry out between waterings – they are originally desert flowers.

CLEISTOCACTUS

(klai-stoh-kak-təs)
Silver Torch, Pizzle Plant
CACTACEAE

A small genus from South America, *Cleistocactus* grow tall and straight, though rather slowly. This is something of an advantage for pot culture as they do quite well in a container of standard, gritty cactus mix. Ample water is welcome during the warm months, with little moisture during the winter resting period.

The commonly grown species C. *straussii*, the Silver Torch, grows into a simple, lightly ribbed column, its areoles producing compact groups of spines and fine woolly hairs. The flowers (which appear only on mature plants) are tapered, phallic cylinders, covered with silvery hair. The vivid cerise petals open only far enough to reveal the stamens and make fertilisation possible. Taller potted specimens will need the

support of a light stake, for they quickly become top-heavy. Alternatively, grow in very heavy pots. *Cleistocactus* is propagated by severing and replanting the offset branches which form at soil level.

CLEMATIS

(klem-ə-tis)
Virgin's Bower, Travellers' Joy
RANUNCULACEAE

Widely known in cool-winter climates as beautiful, deciduous climbers, the genus *Clematis* is available in a staggering variety of forms and colours. With over 200 species, there are many worthwhile subjects for the garden, including at least a dozen types which do not climb and can be truly classified as herbaceous perennials for the bed or border.

These other *Clematis*, often with smaller, more subtle blooms and interesting foliage, rarely grow taller than 120cm/4ft. They flourish in neutral to alkaline soil that is well drained and thoroughly enriched with leaf-mould before planting takes place in the colder months. Herbaceous *Clematis* also

Clematis 'Vyvyan Pennell'. Double Clematis

Clematis montana. Anemone Clematis

Clematis 'Twilight'. Hybrid Clematis

Clematis aristata. Traveller's Joy

Clematis integrifolia. Leather Flower

need their roots in a cool, moist position, say on the shaded side of a small shrub or evergreen perennial. There, with minimum support, they will rapidly rise to their full height over the spring months. They are grown from divisions or 8cm/3in basal cuttings taken in spring and rooted under glass in a mixture of peat and sand. Herbaceous *Clematis* do not appreciate cultivation around the root area but do benefit from a deep summer mulch. They are cut back to ground level in winter. Illustrated *C. integrifolia* is inclined to be weak-stemmed and so requires more support than some others.

Of the climbing types, large-flowered cultivars such as illustrated 'Vyvyan Pennell' and 'Twilight' are the most popular, but they are really only suited to cool, moist areas, for they cannot cope with hot summers and drying wind. The twining stems should be directed onto their support and lightly pruned only after th e plant has reached the desired size. Thereafter, a proportion of the oldest wood should be removed each year.

Himalayan *C. montana* is a light, deciduous creeper producing perfumed pink flowers in spring. In cool climates it can reach 12m/38ft and spread 6m/20ft.

Australia boasts about 8 species; all are suitable for the hotter climate provided they can be grown in dappled shade. The small but profuse flowers are followed by decorative fruits. *C. aristata*, the best known, is a vigorous evergreen best displayed on a fence.

CLEOME
(klee-**oh**-mee)
(SYN Gynandropsis)
Spider Flower
CAPPARACEAE

Spectacular though rather large plants (1.5m/5ft), *Cleome hassleriana* (syn *C. spinosa*) can be used for bedding or background display, or singly as an occasional feature in the smaller garden. They quickly produce great mounds of 7-lobed leaves that look for all the world like marijuana! These are topped in summer with heads of airy pink, white and lavender blooms like long-whiskered orchids. They are strongly scented and will last to autumn if you let them. It is

Cleome hassleriana 'Rose Queen'. Spider Flower

Clerodendrum paniculatum. Pagoda Flower

Clerodendrum speciosissimum. Glory Bower

Clerodendrum thomsoniae. Bleeding Heart Vine

Cleome isomeris. Bladder Bush

best to sow them well after the last frost, or earlier if you can maintain a temperature of 24ºC/75ºF, for they are tropical plants. Thin seedlings to 60cm/2ft spacings in a warm, dry position that receives full sun. With regular water, they'll revel in the hottest weather. Different strains bloom in white and many shades of pink. Shrubby *C. isomeris*, the Bladder Bush, is a colourful native of California and Mexico.

CLERODENDRUM
(kler-oh-**den**-drəm)
Glory Bower, Butterfly Bush, Pagoda Flower
Verbenaceae

Hailing from parts of Africa and Southeast Asia where around 400 species grow, the *Clerodendrums* are variable in habit and appearance. Often shrubby, there are also climbing and tree-like species among them. Most can be grown from ripe seed, but are usually propagated from semi-hardwood cuttings in autumn. They do well in a rich, leafy soil, need year-round water, more

generous in summer. Out of the tropics, grow against a sunny wall, but where summers are hot, light dappled shade will prevent the flowers from fading.

Shrubby *C. paniculatum* grows just over 1m/3ft and bears pagoda-like terminal spikes of scarlet blooms which account for the epithet Pagoda Flower. *C. splendens*, a dwarf climber, can reach 3.5m/11ft in equatorial regions, but less in cooler climates; a gorgeously flowering plant, it well deserves its popular name Glory Bower. *C. thomsoniae*, the Bleeding Heart Vine, has long clusters of white calyces that seem to exude drops of blood. *C. ugandense*, the Blue Butterfly Bush, is a wonderful example of vegetable mimicry.

Clerodendrum ugandense. Blue Butterfly Bush

Clerodendrum splendens. Glory Bower

Clethra arborea. Lily-of-the-valley Tree

CLETHRA
(kleth-rə)
Sweet Pepper Bush, Lily-of-the-valley Tree
CLETHRACEAE

Clethra is the ancient Greek name for the alder, and though this is no relative, the leaves *do* look similar, and both like rather damp soil. The best-known species is the Sweet Pepper Bush, *Clethra alnifolia*, a deciduous shrub about 2m/6ft tall, with spikes of little white bells in late summer; these are not really showy, perhaps, but very sweetly fragrant. It is quite hardy to frost, but the larger-growing, and in most people's eyes more beautiful *C. arborea*, the Lily-of-the-valley Tree, is doubtful in cool temperate climates. It is happiest in the kind of warm temperate ones, and in the sort of acid soils where such plants as sasanqua camellias flourish.

Clianthus puniceus 'Albus'. Kaka Beak

Clianthus puniceus. Kaka Beak

CLIANTHUS
(klee-**an**-thəs)
Kaka Beak, Parrot's Bill
FABACEAE

Among the showiest members of the pea family is New Zealand's *Clianthus puniceus*, the Parrot's Bill or Kaka Beak, a shrubby vine which may reach 4m/13ft with good support. The leaves are compound with 12–24 leaflets. The showy racemes of 6–15 pendant red pea-flowers appear from the leaf axils in spring. It has several colour varieties, including pure white. Inclined to be short-lived, the Kaka Beak benefits from an all-over pruning after flowering.

C. puniceus is now the sole member of its genus, since its former companion, the Sturt Desert Pea from the dry outback of Australia, has been reclassified as *Swainsona*.

CLITORIA
(kli-tor-**ree**-ə)
Butterfly Pea, Pigeon-wings
FABACEAE

An interesting member of the legume family, the Butterfly Pea, *Clitoria ternatea*, is grown for its singly borne, open pea-flowers of vivid cobalt blue, quite a rare colour in the botanical world. Tropical in origin, it should be grown in a humid glasshouse except in frost-free areas, where it can be used outdoors. If it does not survive the winter,

this fast-growing plant can be raised as an annual from seed sown indoors in late winter in a heated propagating box.

The flowers appear throughout the warm weather, their magnificent blue contrasting with white and gold throats. Double and white-flowered forms are known but are rarely seen.

CLIVIA
(klai-vee-ə)
Kaffir Lily, Fire Lily, Clivia
AMARYLLIDACEAE

Spectacular bulbous plants with yellow-throated orange flowers, *Clivias* grow well outdoors in any place where the ground does not freeze. Even the lightest frost will damage leaves, but this usually only sets the flowering back from spring to summer. Where winters are severe, or for indoor use, the rather massive roots can be forced into a relatively small pot (say 20cm/8in). This is done in summer to get them established in time for early spring flowers.

Clivias like a shady position in well-drained soil containing plenty of humus. During winter they rest, and want very little water. After the coldest weather has passed, gradually increase water and keep them moist all summer.

Clivia nobilis. Natal Clivia

Clitoria ternatea. Butterfly Pea

Clivia miniata. Fire Lily

Cobaea scandens. Cathedral Bells   *TONY RODD*

Two species are grown: *C. miniata* with open, orange and yellow (sometimes cream) trumpet flowers, and *C. nobilis*, the Cape Clivia, with more tubular flowers, orange tipped with green.

CLYTOSTOMA
(**klai**-toh-stoh-mə)
Violet Trumpet Vine
BIGNONIACEAE

Clytostoma callistegioides is a fast-growing evergreen vine that climbs up any support by means of coiling tendrils. Once established, it will resist quite severe frosts and prolonged drought, though it is undoubtedly seen at its best in more congenial climates. It grows strongly to at least 3m/10ft and produces a profusion of purple-streaked mauve flowers in late spring and summer. Grow in full sun

(or dappled shade in very hot areas) in humus-enriched, acid, well-drained soil and be prepared to prune out some of the oldest stems each year after flowering to keep the vine within bounds.

COBAEA
(**koh**-bee-ə)
Cathedral Bells, Cup and Saucer Vine
POLEMONIACEAE

The drooping bell-shaped flowers in a large green calyx give this rampant vine one of its common names, Cathedral Bells, but turn the flowers upside down and you'll see why it's also called Cup and Saucer Vine. It grows fast from seed sown indoors in late winter, so you'll have plenty of flowers by summer. In fact, raising it as an annual is the best way, for it never flowers as well again after the first

season or two. Grow on a trellis against a sunny wall, sheltered from cold winds, and treat to a rich well-drained soil, kept moist. The big blooms open green and change through mauve to violet-purple as they age.

COCHLIOSTEMA
(kok-lee-oh-**ste**-mə)
Blue Jenny
COMMELINACEAE

Perhaps the most spectacular of the Wandering Jew family, the 2 species of *Cochliostema* are also among the least typical. They do not run, hang or climb, merely develop into a rosette of large leaves, much in the manner of a Bilbergia. In the species *C. jacobianum*, these have a narrow purple margin. From Ecuador, they need at least subtropical temperatures, and grow well in dappled shade with a well-drained, leaf-rich soil. Propagate from seed or spring divisions, keep moist all year round, though less so in winter. The flowers, appearing in a crowded terminal cyme, remind one of grape hyacinths, in both colour and perfume. They would probably pick well, if you were lucky enough to have a tropical garden.

Cochliostema jacobianum. Blue Jenny

Clytostoma callistegioides. Violet Trumpet Vine

Cochlospermum vitifolium. Maximiliana, Wild Cotton

Codonanthe carnosa. Brazilian Bellflower

COCHLOSPERMUM

(**kok**-loh-spur-m∂m)
Buttercup Tree, Maximiliana, Wild Cotton
COCHLOSPERMACEAE

At home wherever the climate is really hot, *Cochlospermum* grows easily from cuttings or seed in warm weather.

A slender and deciduous tree, it will begin flowering when a mere 1m/3ft high and may ultimately reach 9m/30ft. Rather sparse and stiff-looking, its leaves are larger than a dinner plate. They are 5-lobed (rather like those of a grape vine or Liquidambar), and appear in spring after the tree's 3-month blooming period.

It is in late winter that the *Cochlospermum* achieves its finest moment, as golden-yellow, cup-sized blossoms open a few at a time, rapidly carpeting the ground as they fall. *Cochlospermum* are 5-petalled, with a mass of golden stamens.

C. vitifolium, the best-known species, is seen in hot climate gardens of India, the Philippines, Africa, California and Florida. Its cousin *C. religiosum,* from India, is virtually identical. Australian *C. gillivraei* has bright red stamens.

CODONANTHE

(koh-don-**an**-thee)
Brazilian Bellflower
GESNERIACEAE

Trailing members of the Gesneriad family, the charming *Codonanthes* are native to fully

tropical latitudes of South America, mostly Brazil. Yet because they normally grow at high altitudes, we are able to raise them outdoors in temperate climates. As they like to trail and hang, they are often seen in baskets, where they can spill over the edge and produce their blooms at eye level. They enjoy an organically rich but fast-draining compost, and can be raised from leaf-cuttings struck in sharp sand. The trailing stems branch and root readily, producing single white tubular flowers at leaf axils. These bear orange markings in the throat, and flare into 5 lobes. Leaves are waxy and pointed.

CODONOPSIS

(koh-don-**op**-sis)
Chinese Bellflower
CAMPANULACEAE

It's blue, it twines, it has bell-like flowers. Really, it's hard to decide whether the showy *Codonopsis convolvulacea* looks more like a Campanula, a Clematis or (as the specific name suggests) a Convolvulus! Certainly a treasure for the cooler garden, it comes from western China, and likes a well-drained acid soil that stays fairly moist.

Sow seed in early spring, and plant out in autumn to bloom the following summer. It's best if you can arrange shrubby support for its twining activities or plant it in a high position where the flowers can hang down to be viewed close up. On second thoughts, not *too* close up, for they smell distinctly 'off'.

COELOGYNE

(k∂-**loj**-∂-nee)
Angel Orchid
ORCHIDACEAE

Beautiful Angel Orchids are certainly among the easiest to grow. My prized specimen of *Coelogyne cristata* is thoroughly crowded into a 40cm/16in pot, and spills its long strings of bright green pseudobulbs over the rim. It lives out of doors in a breezeway sheltered from the hottest sun, and is watered only occasionally with the garden hose. I bring it indoors in winter as the

Codonopsis convolvulacea. Chinese Bellflower

Coelogyne cristata. Angel Orchid

Coelogyne flaccida. Angel Orchid

flower spikes develop from last season's pseudobulbs. These open into perfect hanging sprays of icy-white flowers, 8cm/3in across, with 3 to 7 per spray. The display lasts for up to 6 weeks. *C. cristata* grows in a well-drained mix of old coke, leafmould and treefern bits, and likes an occasional dose of diluted fish emulsion. Related *C. flaccida*, with sprays of beige and yellow flowers, grows under similar conditions with perhaps a fraction more winter protection. It also flowers in winter and spring.

Coelogynes survive winter temperatures down to 1ºC/34ºF, for they are native to the high mountain valleys of northern India.

COFFEA
(kof-fee-ə)
Coffee
RUBIACEAE

Everyone who enjoys a morning cup of coffee has seen the brown coffee beans from which it is prepared: but few people know that if you plant an unroasted bean it will grow quite fast into a small evergreen tree with attractively glossy leaves. In a frosty climate it will need to spend its life indoors – and it makes a fine house plant – but in not-too-hot yet frost-free climates it can be planted in the garden, where after a couple of years it will adorn itself in early autumn with little scented white stars that are followed up by the red to black berries that contain, yes, coffee beans! The ardent coffee lover will want several trees, however – 1kg/2lb of ground coffee per tree is regarded as a bumper harvest.

Coffea arabica. Arabian Coffee

(kol-chik-ə m)
Autumn Crocus
LILIACEAE

Often called Autumn Crocus, *Colchicums* in fact belong to quite a different botanical family and are incredibly easy to grow. Newly bought bulbs will bloom as readily sitting on a saucer of pebbles as they do planted in the most exotic bulb fibre or soil mixture. Set them out in summer (with the neck of the bulb at soil level if planted) and the flowers will often appear with the first cold snap – usually more than one to a bulb. Plant them properly after flowering is over, so that the leaves can grow and help ripen the bulb; otherwise they won't put on a repeat performance the following year.

The species *C. autumnale*, *C. byzantinum* and *C. speciosum* are similar, with white to mauve flowers. The more exotic *C. agrippinum* has a distinct chequered appearance on its wide pink and mauve flowers. *Colchicums* are not affected by cold so long as they are covered against frost.

Colchicum autumnale. Autumn Crocus

Coleonema pulchellum. Breath of Heaven

Coleonema album. White Diosma

COLEONEMA
(koh-lee-o-**nee**-mə)
Diosma, Breath of Heaven, Confetti Bush
RUTACEAE

Neat evergreen shrubs from South Africa, *Coleonemas* have aromatic heath-like foliage, though they belong to the Citrus family. They grow best in a rich but well-drained soil, and are popular for planting on banks or in groups as lawn specimens. With continuous light pruning, they can be trained as low, informal hedges, though flower loss will result. Winter moisture stimulates bloom, but mature plants will endure drought along the coast. *Coleonemas* are easily propagated from soft-tip cuttings taken in late summer. These should be struck in a sharp sand/peat mixture with bottom heat and misting. The tiny flowers appear in many shades of pink in spring. There is a white-flowered species and one with golden foliage. Non-dwarfed forms can reach 1.5m/5ft.

COLLETIA
(kol-**let**-ee-ə)
Anchor Plant
RHAMNACEAE

Colletia is a group of spiny shrubs from South America, rarely met with in gardens but quietly charming when their clusters of small flowers appear, and useful for making hedges and barriers in a large garden. They are all white, the illustrated *C. paradoxa* being typical. It usually doesn't flower until late in the summer, when most other shrubs have finished. The cruelly shaped flattened segments are actually adapted spines, and the name *paradoxa* refers to the way the stems zig-zag. Mild, not too frosty climates, sunshine and good drainage are required.

COLLINSIA
(kol-**lin**-zee-ə)
Innocence, Chinese Houses
SCROPHULARIACEAE

Collinsia bicolor (syn *C. heterophylla*) is a California wildflower more commonly seen in the gardens of other countries. A dainty plant found wild in shaded places, it will grow fast and bloom profusely in a semi-shaded position in almost any type of soil. Temperatures, however, are important. They do not tolerate heat and like night temperatures that drop below 18°C/65°F. Sow outdoors anytime in autumn, or as early in spring as frost will allow. *Collinsia* sends up spikes on which the flowers open in whorls or layers, like the roofs of a Chinese Pagoda. There is a white cultivar as well.

COLUMNEA
(kol-**um**-nee-ə)
Column Flower
GESNERIACEAE

Columneas or Column Flowers belong to the same family as African Violets, but bear little resemblance to them. They are mostly raised in hanging baskets where the beauty of their

Colletia paradoxa. Anchor Plant

Collinsia bicolor. Chinese Houses

Columnea banksii 'Variegata'. Column Flower

Colvillea racemosa. Colville's Glory

Combretum coccineum. Red Combretum

trailing stems of red, orange or yellow flowers can be seen. Grow in a porous, leafy compost containing sphagnum moss or similar material. Regular moisture and feeding with soluble fertiliser is necessary in the growing season, and they should be repotted every other year. *Columneas* like winter sun, and semi-shade in really hot weather. Flowers appear in spring or autumn depending on type. Illustrated *C. banksii* 'Variegata' has leaves variegated in grey-green and white. Its flowers are a duller orange than most and it is less trailing in habit.

Colutea media. Bladder Senna

COLUTEA
(kol-**yoo**-tee-ə)
Bladder Senna
FABACEAE

Senna is the old name for the cassias (and the new botanical name for some of them), and the bladder part of the name comes from the inflated seed pods, which are modestly decorative in autumn – but the chief beauty of these fast-growing, drought-hardy shrubs is their lavish summer-to-

autumn display of pea-flowers, which are usually cassia-yellow, as in the best-known species, the southern European *Colutea arborescens*, but orange in its hybrid with *C. orientalis*, *C. media*. Flourishing in any temperate climate and sunny position, this is to my mind by far the most attractive member of the genus.

COLVILLEA
(kol-**vil**-ee-ə)
Colville's Glory
CAESALPINIACEAE

Colvillea racemosa is one of the most spectacular of all flowering trees, though its gorgeousness is reserved for the tropics – it won't take the slightest frost and you'd need a very big greenhouse to accommodate its height of 12–15 m/38–50ft and its wide, spreading branches. But where it flourishes it is a magnificent sight in early summer, the fresh green of its ferny leaves making a perfect backdrop for the long hanging sprays of brilliant orange flowers, as many as 200 in each spray. It comes from Madagascar, and its name honours Sir Charles Colville, governor of Mauritius from 1828 to 1834.

COMBRETUM
(kom-**bree**-təm)
Paintbrush Plant, Combretum
COMBRETACEAE

Extremely variable tropical climbing shrubs, many *Combretum* species are suited to frost-

Combretum fruticosum. Paintbrush Plant

free gardens of temperate areas. In nature, they are confined to the southern hemisphere – South Africa, South America and Southeast Asia. They may be propagated from stiff side shoots taken with a heel and struck in sand, preferably under glass. Rooted plants should be set out in a well-drained position in leaf-rich soil and kept moist during warm weather. They are most effective scrambling up a wall (with support) or hanging over banks. *Combretum fruticosum* blooms orange yellow. *C. decandrum* is greenish-white; most other species show paintbrush-type flowers in shades of red. Average height is 2m/6ft, but *Combretums* may spread several times as wide.

Congea tomentosa. Pink Sandpaper Vine

CONGEA

(**kon**-jee-ə)
Pink Sandpaper Vine
VERBENACEAE

This very rampant vine from Southeast Asia is rarely seen outside conservatories except in fully tropical parts of the world, though it can in fact be grown in a sunny, sheltered position elsewhere. Soft tip-cuttings strike well, and should be grown in a compost-rich, fast-draining soil. Both water and fertiliser should be applied lavishly during its warm-weather growing season. The leaves are velvety, 12.5cm/5in long; the insignificant flowers make way for a showy display of bracts which change from grey to a rich pink as they age.

CONOSPERMUM

(**koh**-no-spur-məm)
Smokebush, Smoke Grass
PROTEACEAE

Common xerophytic plants in the Australian outback, the 50-odd species of *Conospermum* belong to the Protea family. Not often grown in the home garden, even in their native land, they are sold widely as cut flowers, and last for months. They are, however, useful in drought-stricken areas with dry, gravelly soil, where they may be raised from summer cuttings and need little water except in the hottest weather. Shrubby plants, the *Conospermums* mostly grow to 2m/6ft in height – though *C. stoechadis* is barely half that size. The curious woolly flower heads are mostly grey, and look like a puff of smoke when seen from afar.

Conostylis aculeata. Woolly Grass

CONOSTYLIS

(**koh**-no-stai-ləs)
Woolly Grass
HAEMODORACEAE

Popular among rocks of Australian native gardens, several of the 40-odd *Conostylis* species make a pleasing if unspectacular display. They are virtually foolproof, surviving both frost and drought, provided the soil is well drained. Grow them from divisions taken in winter, but kept under glass till spring comes – or from seed sown on sandy soil with the minimum suggestion of cover. Planted out, they make rapid growth into a clump of grassy leaves, producing a long-lasting show of small woolly flower heads in spring and summer. These may be pink, grey or, as in *C. aculeata*, a dull yellow-green.

CONSOLIDA

(kon-**sol**-i-də)
Larkspur, Sweet Rocket
RANUNCULACEAE

For a long time classed as Delphiniums (which they do resemble), the charming Larkspurs now have a genus of their own as *Consolida*. Of the 40-odd species, *C. ajacis* (syn *C. ambigua*) is the most commonly

Conospermum stoechadis. Smokebush

grown. Native to southern Europe, they have bright green, fern-like foliage, and bear spikes of many-petalled open flowers in a wide range of white, pinks, blues, mauves and purples, all excellent for cutting. Several styles have been bred: branching strains, which produce a number of stalks per plant and may grow 30–45cm/12–18in tall, and the taller column strains, with one large flower stem to a plant (these make excellent cut flowers).

Plant out in clumps, in well-fertilised, loose and slightly alkaline soil. Add lime or dolomite if the soil is inclined to acidity. The plants like full sun, but in exposed positions will need light bamboo stakes or twigs for support. Pull weeds and feed often, especially when buds appear. Dead-head to stop self-seeding.

CONVALLARIA

(kon-və-**le**ər-ee-ə)
Lily of the Valley
LILIACEAE

Native to all continents of the northern hemisphere, Lily of the Valley is the very symbol of spring in many lands. For the French, May Day would never be the same without its fragrance. Try it as a short-term house plant yourself. Nurseries sell plump 'pips' (budding roots) in late autumn or early winter. These can be forced into early bloom by being planted in bowls of damp sphagnum moss or a light, peaty mix. Keep

Consolida ajacis 'Imperial Mix'. Larkspur

Convallaria majalis. Lily of the Valley

them moist in a dim, warm spot (about 15°C/59°F) until the flower spikes appear, then move to a brighter place. After flowering, the pips will be exhausted. Set out in a shady spot, they'll ultimately bloom again, though not for about 3 years – and only if you have cold winters.

CONVOLVULUS
(kon-**vol**-vyoo-ləs)
Bush Morning Glory, Silver Bush
CONVOLVULACEAE

Think of *Convolvulus* and you normally visualise the pink or blue flowered Morning Glory vines twining around cottage doors. But in fact they are Ipomoeas, while in this genus belong better-behaved annuals, creepers and neat shrubs, many of which make marvellous garden plants. *C. tricolor* is a neat, bushy annual with open, 4cm/2in trumpet flowers banded in yellow, white and shades of pink, blue and mauve. It grows to 30cm/12in, spreads a little wider and is excellent for sunny beds as well as rockeries, hanging baskets and window boxes. It grows in most soils and blooms continuously through the warm weather.

Southern European *C. cneorum* is a compact, bushy shrub 60–120cm/2–4ft tall and about as wide. It can be propagated from seed but is easier to grow from heeled cuttings of basal shoots taken in summer for striking in a damp mixture of peat and sand. The Silver Bush likes to sunbake in a light, sandy soil where it will grow into a compact, densely foliaged plant in no time at all. The pointed lance-shaped leaves have a satiny texture and are covered with silver-silky hairs on both sides. The white 2.5cm/1in trumpet flowers are flushed with pale pink and appear in dense terminal clusters in spring and summer.

CORDIA
(kor-dee-ə)
Bird Lime Tree, Kou, Geiger Tree
BORAGINACEAE

Cordia are showy tropical relatives of the temperate gardener's forget-me-nots and Heliotrope and as easy to grow. All 250 species are found between the tropics in Africa, Asia, Australia and particularly in the Americas.

The commonly seen species is *C. sebestena*, the Geiger Tree from the Caribbean. This is notable for rough, oval leaves, whose dark colouring makes a perfect foil for vivid orange-scarlet flowers, borne in terminal clusters throughout the year. The Geiger Tree grows easily from seed or cuttings in a subtropical climate, reaching 10m/33ft in a few years.

Its paler-flowered cousin *C. subcordata* is the sacred Kou tree of Polynesia, found by the seashores throughout the Indian and

Convolvulus cneorum. Silver Bush

Convolvulus tricolor. Bush Morning Glory

Pacific Oceans. There is a legend that when a downpour threatened to extinguish fire, the god Maui told the flames to take refuge in the Kou tree, hence the colour of its blossom! *C. subcordata* has smooth, paler, wavy-edged leaves and slightly less gaudy flowers than *C. sebestena*. The flowers are followed by green and yellow grape-sized fruits.

Cordia sebestena. Geiger Tree

Cordia subcordata. Kou

Cordyline fruticosa. Ti

CORDYLINE

(kor-də-lain, kor-də-**lai**-nee)

Ti, Cabbage Tree

AGAVACEAE

In the Pacific Islands, Polynesian firewalkers attach the flame red leaves of the Ti plant to their ankles to ensure a painless passage across the glowing embers. Western gardeners are also drawn to the plant, *Cordyline fruticosa* (syn *C. terminalis*), because of its leaves, which can be strikingly coloured in bright green, dark red and mixtures of pink, scarlet, white, yellow, purple and bronze. It *does* have flowers, but as you can see, the sprays of small mauve or greenish-white summer flowers would hardly turn heads. Outdoors, the Ti plant is only for frost-free gardens, but it makes a colourful indoor specimen where winters are cold. Propagate by laying stems in a sand/peat mix kept warm, moist and humid.

Coreopsis tinctoria. Tickseed

Coreopsis lanceolata. Calliopsis

COREOPSIS

(ko-ree-**op**-sis)

Tickseed, Calliopsis, Sea Dahlia

ASTERACEAE

Coreopsis are so easy to grow, details of any sort should be unnecessary. Perennial, golden-flowered *C. lanceolata* has become naturalised all over the world and might be considered a pest if it were not so beautiful. It grows from a rosette of simple, slender, dark green leaves and self-sows freely.

Annual *C. tinctoria* grows just as easily in lightly cultivated, well-drained soil, but for best display it should be supported either by branched twigs or fine bamboo stakes. Dead-head regularly, and right through summer and autumn great clusters of dazzling daisy flowers in shades of bright red, mahogany, yellow, pink and purple will appear. A dwarf variety with spectacular banded blooms grows only to a height of 15cm/6in and is brilliant in rockeries.

Cornus florida. Dogwood

Coreopsis maritima. Sea Dahlia, Winter Marguerite

California's native Sea Dahlia, *C. maritima* (syn *Leptosyne maritima*), thrives in dry, well-drained soil and is usually grown as an annual. The clear yellow flowers, 10cm/4in in diameter, open on 30–40cm/12–16in stems, and are great for cutting. They appear over a long period in spring. Sow seed direct in early spring.

CORNUS

(kor-nəs)

Dogwood, Cornel, Crackerberry

CORNACEAE

I shall never forget my first train ride to Virginia, speeding through the Allegheny Mountains in the clear light of an April morning. All along the track, the landscape was touched with spring – a riot of lime-green foliage and here and there the brilliance of flowering dogwoods, white, pink and almost-red.

Cornus canadensis. Dwarf Cornel, Crackerberry

It was only later in a friend's garden that I discovered that the inflorescence of the common Dogwood (*Cornus florida*) is not a flower at all, but a whole composite head of tiny greenish flowers with 4 spectacularly marked bracts enclosing the group. When the bracts fall, the flowers develop into a cluster of bright red fruits which persist into autumn, joining the foliage in a fiery farewell to summer.

C. florida is a slim, dark-trunked tree growing 5–12m/16–40ft in height, its crepy, pointed leaves marked with conspicuous parallel veins. There are around a hundred species of Dogwood found in cool-winter parts of America and Asia, many of them shrubs with brilliantly coloured winter bark, and a few perennial herbs. One such is *C. canadensis*, the Bunchberry, Dwarf Cornel or Crackerberry. It grows only 20cm/8in tall, a whorl of leaves sprouting a cluster of typical, bracted flowers in latest spring. It makes an interesting groundcover for moist, dappled shade.

COROKIA
(kə-**roh**-kee-ə)
Wire-netting Bush
CORNACEAE

Hardy down to –5°C/23°F, New Zealand's dainty Wire-netting Bush makes an interesting informal groundcover, but is probably more effective when pruned regularly to force denser growth. In this guise it can make an effective hedge, or a useful addition to the sheltered seaside garden. Flowering best in full sun, it likes a moderately rich soil and light water year-round. *Corokia cotoneaster* grows every which way, zigging and zagging in all directions, producing tiny, roundish leaves and, in spring, a veritable cloud of bright yellow, star-shaped, lightly fragrant blooms. Unpruned it will reach 3m/10ft.

Coronilla valentina subsp. *glauca.* Crown Vetch

CORONILLA
(ko-ro-**nil**-lə)
Crown Vetch
FABACEAE

Among the most brilliantly flowering of the pea family are the *Coronillas*. The Crown Vetch, *C. valentina* subsp. *glauca*, is mostly seen as a dense, 1m/3ft evergreen bush, always with an odd number of leaflets on either side of each leaf. The yellow pea blossoms literally cover the plant for a brief period in late spring, and are quite fragrant in daylight hours. Grow *Coronillas* from seed, cuttings, layers or divisions – they are remarkably easy to propagate. All species are native to the Mediterranean region and prefer open, well-drained soil.

Corokia cotoneaster. Wire-netting Bush

Correa reflexa 'Salmon'. Australian Fuchsia

CORREA
(**kor**-ree-ə)
Australian Fuchsia, Native Fuchsia
RUTACEAE

Related to citrus and many other popular genera, the handful of *Correa* species are mostly native to southeastern Australia and Tasmania.

Not difficult to grow (except from seed), they are usually raised from firm young cuttings struck in an alkaline sandy mixture. Before planting out, the chosen position should also be sprinkled with powdered limestone. They prefer soil that is light, well drained and moist at first, though dryer conditions are acceptable to mature plants.

Grow all species in part shade, except in cooler climates, where more sun is welcome. *Correas* grow fairly fast, producing their dainty bell-shaped blooms most heavily in winter and early spring, but sporadically at other times. They can be pruned lightly to keep them reasonably compact. Flower colours are mostly red, green or white.

Correas are now grown in many countries outside Australia.

Cortaderia selloana. Pampas Grass

Corydalis lutea. Fumitory

Cosmos bipinnatus. Mexican Aster

CORTADERIA
(kor-ta-**deer**-ee-ə)
Pampas Grass
POACEAE

The tall, silvery plumes of giant Pampas Grass gathered dust in many a Victorian parlour and a few years back they were again all the rage as accent plants. Thankfully, fewer are seen these days, for these are vigorous plants that form huge clumps. Their long, narrow leaves have razor-sharp edges which effectively deter any attempt to prune them. The only way to control the plant's size is to burn to the ground periodically, but this can only be done if it is planted well away from other shrubs, buildings and fences. The striking flower plumes appear in autumn and persist into winter, releasing countless seeds which establish the plant in neighbouring gardens and bushland areas.

Cosmos bipinnatus Sensation Series
CV Cosmos

CORYDALIS
(ko-**rid**-a-lis)
Fumitory
FUMARIACEAE

How strange that these delicate-looking relatives of the poppies have never acquired an attractive common name! They are certainly one of the most widespread of perennial genera, with some 300 species found in the northern hemisphere and South Africa. They can be planted almost anywhere in a rich, damp soil that is also well drained. Growing them in wall crevices is one popular technique – getting them to stop is rather more of a problem, for they self-seed with abandon. Be sure to root out excess plants to keep them within bounds. If you don't have them already, sow seeds (where you want them) in late winter.

Charming *Corydalis lutea* has grey-green foliage, rather like that of a maidenhair fern, and tubular yellow flowers that appear in profusion from spring to autumn. It can reach a height of 40cm/16in.

The botanical name seems to be Greek in origin, from *korydalos*, a lark. But why?

COSMOS
(**kos**-mos)
Mexican Aster, Cosmos, Bidens
ASTERACEAE

Splendid annuals for late summer and autumn cutting, *Cosmos* are from Mexico. *C. bipinnatus* used to be very tall, often seen peeping over suburban fences in hot weather, its great 10cm/4in daisy flowers waving in

the breeze. But modern hybrids with larger blooms are now available. These rarely exceed 60cm/2ft in height, are most successful for bedding, and come in a range of warm colours in single shades or striped. Sow where they are to grow in spring, cover lightly and expect seedlings in 5–10 days, flowers in around 12 weeks. They'll grow fast in any soil and flower more happily if it's on the dry side. Taller strains need shelter from wind, or staking. Later-blooming *C. sulphureus* has coarser foliage, and blooms in many shades of yellow and orange.

COSTUS
(**kos**-təs)
Crepe Ginger
ZINGIBERACEAE

Costus are a genus of rhizomatous perennials within the ginger family. The majority are South American, but the more commonly seen Crepe Ginger (*C. speciosus*) is found

Costus speciosus. Crepe Ginger

Cosmos sulphureus cultivar. Golden Cosmos

Cotyledon orbiculata. Pigs' Ears   TONY RODD

over the entire Indo-Malaysian area as far north as the Philippines. *Costus* grows in frost-free temperate areas but really thrives only in the subtropics or tropics or in a warm, humid greenhouse or conservatory. Potted specimens can be brought into the house or a sheltered patio at flowering time in the warm months. Crepe Ginger grows best in a moist, peaty compost and needs shade from direct sun. The tissue-thin white blossoms have the finely pleated effect of crepe fabric and are marked in orange.

COTONEASTER
(ko-toh-nee-**as**-tə)
Rockspray, Cotoneaster
ROSACEAE

Evergreen and deciduous shrubs with many garden uses, the *Cotoneasters* are extremely hardy. In spring they are dusted with a covering of tiny white flowers. Individually these are quite unremarkable, though necessary for the production of the autumn berries which are the plants' chief appeal. The blooms are attractive in a mass, however, especially when they begin to fall, carpeting the ground like snow.

All *Cotoneasters* grow fast and are not particularly fussy about soil so long as it is well drained. Too much water encourages excessive new growth, which hides the berries. *C. salicifolius* grows to 5m/16ft, bears masses of summer flowers; prostrate *C. cashmiriensis* (syn *C. microphyllus*) is ideally suited to positions where it can spill over banks or walls.

COTYLEDON
(koh-til-**ee**-don)
Pigs' Ears
CRASSULACEAE

Mostly South African, the succulent, fleshy-leaved *Cotyledons* are great for open terraces, patios, rockeries, or the succulent garden – anywhere you can give them full sun and fresh air. They grow in a sandy, well-drained compost and need regular water in the warmer months – never apply water from above, for it will spot the leaves. In winter, water only to prevent the leaves from shrivelling and bring indoors if the temperature drops below 10°C/50°F. *Cotyledons* produce

Cotoneaster salicifolius. Cotoneaster

drooping stems of red, yellow and orange flowers in spring but are usually grown more for the sculptural quality of the rounded leaves, which are interesting and attractive year-round. They can be raised easily from seed or increased by tip-cuttings taken in late spring and summer and struck in a 50/50 mix of sand and peat moss.

Couroupita guianensis. Cannonball Tree

Crambe cordifolia. Colewort

COUROUPITA
(koo-**roop**-i-tə)
Cannonball Tree
LECYTHIDACEAE

Thank goodness Cannonball Trees are not to be found in every garden! Dodging the head-size fruit as they came cannonading down the trunk in every rainstorm could be a real hazard, and the less said about the smell of its decaying droppings the better! They are a sight, though, that every tree-lover wants to see at least once in a lifetime, and all the great warm climate arboreta make sure that we have the chance.

What a stunning botanical conversation piece! A 17m/55ft column decked with slender flower stems all twisted and tangled like Medusa's snake-hair. In season, these bear hibiscus-sized flowers of rich apricot-pink and gold. These have a curious lopsided mass of stamens and exude a strong fruity fragrance that can be smelt from afar. Brown, velvety fruits appear in winter, clustered from top to bottom of the tree. They consist of a mass of seeds embedded in sickly pulp, which to Westerners smells distinctly

'off'. South American Indians, however, find it delicious and squeeze a popular brew from it.

The Cannonball Tree is known botanically as *Couroupita guianensis* after its native land. It has foliage, of course, but this is hard to see. The leaves are great blunt-ended oblongs up to 30cm/12in long and are borne on separate branches right at the very top of the tree.

Craspedia uniflora. Billy Buttons

CRAMBE
(**kram**-bee)
Colewort
BRASSICACEAE

Only a cabbage in fancy dress really, *Crambe cordifolia* is stunning at the back of the border, or naturalised in the wild garden. Everything about it is enormous except the flowers. In rich, well-drained, neutral to alkaline soil, it will shoot up fast to more than 2m/6ft, with deeply lobed heart-shaped basal leaves of 60cm/2ft in diameter. Come early summer, the stout flower stems begin to rise, branching and rebranching until they reach their maximum height, when they burst into a cloud of tiny, fragrant, white, 4-petalled flowers, rather like Virginia Stock. *Crambe* is propagated by root division in earliest spring, or can be grown from spring-sown seed, which will take about 3 years to reach flowering size. Grow it in full sun in cool climates, semi-shade where summers are hot. Like other cabbages, *Crambe* is attractive to slugs, snails and grubs.

CRASPEDIA
(kras-**pee**-dee-ə)
Billy Buttons
ASTERACEAE

Craspedia is a genus of half a dozen or so low, tufted perennials from southern Australia and New Zealand, occasionally seen in alpine gardens in Europe (they don't seem to have won favour in America) and in rockeries in their native lands. They flower in spring or early summer, and the flowers are daisies without the ray florets – just round, fuzzy buttons. The best known at home is probably the yellow-flowered *C. glauca*; in other places you more often see the illustrated *C. uniflora*, which grows fast enough to be treated as a half-hardy annual. Its flowers can be white, yellow or orange. All the species like rich, leafy soil and just a little shade.

CRASSULA

(kras-yoo-lə)

Jade Plant, Sickle Plant, Crassula

CRASSULACEAE

Native to South Africa, *Crassulas* make splendid rockery subjects where only the lightest frost may be expected, if any at all. They can cope with dry conditions and careless owners but remember, too much water makes the leaves bloat, then they shrivel and become unsightly when moisture is withheld. Grow in a sandy, well-drained compost with some leafmould added, preferably in full sun. Propagate from stem cuttings or seed.

The Sickle Plant, *C. perfoliata* var. *minor*, is the showiest of all, being spectacular in bloom and sculpturally decorative at other times. It needs plenty of water in winter and just enough to prevent shrivelling in summer.

The Fairy Crassula, *C. multicava*, must be one of the easiest of all to grow. Just give it a well-drained but shady spot and it will largely look after itself. It blooms in winter.

French Crassula, *C. coccinea* (syn *Rochea coccinea*) grows well in pots of gritty cactus mix, or in the open in frost-free gardens. It rarely exceeds 30cm/12in in height and develops many branching stems massed with 4 rows of thick, fleshy, triangular leaves. These stems are topped in late spring with clusters of 4-petalled scarlet flowers, which last for a month or more.

CRATAEGUS

(kra-**tae**-gəs)

Hawthorn

ROSACEAE

Gives not the hawthorn bush
a sweeter shade than doth
a rich embroidered canopy?

Good old Shakespeare! As usual, he said it all in signalling his approval of the ubiquitous hedgerow tree of English fields, the common Hawthorn or May, *Crataegus monogyna*.

Yet the common Hawthorn is but one of more than 200 species of these deciduous members of the rose family, found principally in North America, but with flourishing groups native to Europe, Asia Minor and north Africa. They all prefer a cool climate and are frost hardy. The variations between them are principally in height of growth, from 5–15m/16–50ft, and in size and colour of fruit, varying from currant to small apple size, in every shade of red, white and pink, plus a few in orange and yellow.

Crassula coccinea. French Crassula

Crassula multicava. Fairy Crassula

Crataegus monogyna. Hawthorn

Crataegus laevigata 'Paul's Scarlet'. English Hawthorn

The English Hawthorn *C. laevigata* (formerly known as *C. oxyacantha*) is a tree-like shrub that can reach 6x5m/20x16ft. It has many varieties, both single and double, red, pink and variegated, all of which make handsome lawn trees, especially in areas with frosty autumns. Illustrated cultivar 'Paul's Scarlet' is just one example. Others include: 'Plena' with double white flowers; 'Coccinea' with single bright red flowers; 'Rosea', a single pink variety; and 'Rosea Flore Pleno' with magnificent double pink flowers. All species grow easily from seed, which takes 2 years to ripen. Grafting is used for cultivars.

Crinodendron hookerianum. Lantern Tree

Crocosmia crocosmiiflora. Falling Stars

CRINODENDRON

(krai-noh-**den**-drən)

Lantern Tree

ELAEOCARPACEAE

Related to several Australian genera, both species of *Crinodendron* are found exclusively in Chile, where they grow to 7.5m/25ft in height. Elsewhere they tend to be much smaller.

Crinodendrons are certainly not frost hardy, but have been raised in the British Isles against the shelter of a sunward-facing wall. Grow them from semi-hardwood cuttings taken with a heel in midsummer. Strike in a sandy mix, then keep in a pot till large enough for transplanting. They like a moist, rich, acid soil, and a semi-shaded position in warm temperate climates. The evergreen foliage is leathery and coarsely toothed. Scarlet lantern-shaped blooms grow on arching stems from the leaf axils.

Crinum moorei. Veld Lily

CRINUM

(krai-nəm)

Veld Lily, Poison Lily

AMARYLLIDACEAE

Semi-tropical members of the Amaryllis family, *Crinums* grow easily from their gigantic bulbs, planted with at least the neck above soil level. They can and should be left undisturbed for years, as lifting them is hard work and they often respond by refusing to flower for a couple of years afterwards. *Crinums* are fairly hardy plants, resisting several degrees of frost but not frigid conditions for weeks on end. In milder climates they can be grown outdoors in deep, rich soil. Full sun suits them where summers are not extreme, though they always seem to do well in dappled shade. *C. moorei* looks a lot like the Belladonna Lily, but it blooms in late summer to early autumn. *C. asiaticum*, the Poison Lily, forms a huge clump, from which shoots a tall stem of fragrant white flowers in summer; its bulbs, once used as an emetic, are somewhat poisonous.

Crinum asiaticum. Poison Lily

CROCOSMIA
(krok-**oz**-mee-ə)
Falling Stars, Montbretia
IRIDACEAE

Whenever I think of *Crocosmias* I think of neglected country gardens, with which they seem to be synonymous.

Perhaps they were more popular in bygone days, but they have always been fussy plants to get established. From South Africa originally, they are now seen in all climates from cool temperate to subtropical. Set the corms out in winter in well-drained soil rich in leafmould, and in a position open to morning sun. Water heavily in summer for best results, but they will survive drought to bloom another year. Multiplying through runners and offsets, they spread rapidly to form large clumps, from which 1m/3ft stems of curved, tubular flowers can be cut in summer. Flowers fall rapidly indoors.

CROCUS
(kroh-kəs)
Meadow Saffron, Crocus
IRIDACEAE

Delightful little flowers that pop straight out of the ground in earliest spring, *Crocus* appear through melting snow in northern lands with a cold winter. Silver-striped leaves follow the cup-shaped blooms. They are not widely grown in countries where spring can be warm to hot, as such conditions prevent the corm from forming the following season's flowers.

All species thrive in sun or light shade in leaf-rich, well-drained soil. They need plenty of water from the time flowers appear until

Crocus sibieri 'Violet Queen'. Crocus

Crocus tommasinianus 'Ruby Giant'. Crocus

the leaves begin to yellow, when drier conditions must prevail. Increase by lifting overcrowded clumps in summer and separating the offsets. These can be replanted in autumn. Autumn-sown seed takes 3 years to bloom.

Colours include mauve, blue, white, cream, yellow and beige – also striped bicolours.

Crocus olivieri subsp. *balansae* 'Zwanenburg'. Crocus

CROSSANDRA
(kros-**san**-drə)
Firecracker Flower
ACANTHACEAE

Useful shrubs for the tropical garden where they may grow to 1m/3ft tall, *Crossandras* will even do well enough in frost-free warm temperate areas, but will not come close to that size. They can be used as house or conservatory plants anywhere. Grown in acid, sandy soil, rich in decayed compost, *C. infundibuliformis* will develop into a neat bush of glossy, dark green leaves, topped at intervals during summer with clusters of pleasant, salmon-pink to orange-red flowers. Keep uniformly moist while temperatures remain above 15ºC/59ºF, but taper off water as winter approaches.

Crossandra infundibuliformis. Firecracker Flower

Crocus vernus 'Queen of the Blues'. Dutch Crocus

Crotalaria agatiflora. Canary Bird Bush

Crowea exalata. Crowea

CROTALARIA
(kroh-tə-leər-ee-ə)
Canary-bird Bush, Rattlebox
FABACEAE

Tender shrubs for warm climates, *Crotalarias* do well in moderately rich, well-drained soil. They should be pruned after bloom to keep them compact and induce a second flush. They can be grown either from seed, which should first be soaked in warm water for at least 12 hours, or from soft-tip cuttings taken in spring.

The Canary Bird Bush, *C. agatiflora* (syn *C. laburnifolia*) has soft green leaves, just like the European Laburnum. Before opening, its yellow-green flowers look exactly like birds suspended by their beaks.

The Indian Rattlebox, *C. semperflorens*, has simple, heavily ribbed leaves with golden pea-flowers in a terminal spike. The ripe, puffy seed pods have given rise to the name Rattlebox.

CROWEA
(kroh-wee-ə)
Crowea
RUTACEAE

Showy relatives of Boronia and Citrus, *Croweas* flower sporadically throughout the year, but most heavily when the lookalike Boronias are not in bloom, as though out of deference. They are as showy as the latter, but can't compete in the matter of fragrance. There are only 3 species, all of which can be

grown from semi-hardwood cuttings struck in a sand/peat mixture from late summer to the end of autumn. They'll root faster with high humidity. In their native Australia, they are considered frost hardy, but they are unlikely to stand up to more severe winters. Grow them in semi-shaded places in sandy, leaf-rich bush soil. Keep slightly damp and prune lightly in winter to keep compact. The more sun, the more water is needed.

CRYPTANTHUS
(krip-**tan**-thəs)
Earth Stars
BROMELIACEAE

Cryptanthus are small members of the Bromeliad family, low-growing and earth-hugging for the most part. They are incredibly easy to grow and are usually raised in pots for the year-round decorative value of

Cryptanthus sp.

their leaves – the greenish-white, long-stamened flowers being a pretty enough bonus. They can be grown in any standard potting soil, pebbles mixed with moistened peat or even straight sphagnum moss. So long as regular moisture and humidity are there, the leaves stay fresh. *C. bivittatus*, the Green Star, is much admired for its olive green leaves flushed pink and its simple but appealing flowers.

CUPHEA
(koof-ee-ə)
Firecracker Plant, Cigar Flower
LYTHRACEAE

The dainty Cigar Flower, *Cuphea ignea*, is really an evergreen sub-shrub, but becomes so untidy in later life that it is often used as an annual bedding plant. For best results, sow seed in flats 6–8 weeks before outdoor planting in early spring. Seeds need light to germinate, so leave them uncovered. Plant them out at 20–30cm8–12 in intervals for a dense display, choosing a light, well-drained soil in sun or part shade – but don't expect flowers in much under 4 months from sowing. Then, the 30cm/12in bushes will be literally covered with black-and-white-tipped, scarlet tubular flowers, which will continue to appear until cold weather puts an end to their usefulness. In frost-free areas they can flower year-round.

Cuphea ignea. Cigar Flower

CURCUMA
(kur-**koo**-mə)
Zedoary, Turmeric
ZINGIBERACEAE

Cultivated in the Far East, the 40-odd species of *Curcuma* are valued for their rhizomes, the source of turmeric, dyes, East-India arrowroot and cheaper grades of ginger. Grow them in a warm temperate to tropical

Curcuma zedoaria. Zedoary

Cyclamen persicum cultivar. Florist's Cyclamen

climate, setting out sections of rhizome in a warm place and watering lightly until growth starts. The 75cm/30in flower spikes of *C. zedoaria* appear most heavily in summer, highlighting the golden blooms with a display of flashy pink bracts. Each spike will last an entire season. Away from the tropics, they make good glasshouse plants.

CYBISTAX

(**sib**-is-tax)
(SYN Tabebuia)
Primavera
BIGNONIACEAE

From its popular name, you would expect this magnificent tropical tree to bloom in spring. So it does in some places – but in summer or even winter elsewhere. Nobody has yet worked out its system. Where it *does* flourish (and that may even be in a warm temperate climate) the gorgeous golden flowers appear after the leaves have fallen, littering the ground for weeks. In Central America, *Cybistax* may reach 23m/75ft in height, but only a third of that in less tropical areas. The tree likes summer moisture, but is also good in a hot, dry climate. Grow from seed.

The deciduous foliage is compound, with 5 leaflets to a leaf.

CYCLAMEN

(**sai**-klǝ-men, but correctly **kik**-lǝ-men)
Cyclamen, Sowbread, Alpine Violet
PRIMULACEAE

Cyclamens are ideal winter-flowering plants, mostly sold for indoor use. However, in areas where winter temperatures remain above freezing, they may be used as bedding plants. The many hybrids of the principal species, *C. persicum*, grow from fleshy, circular tubers pressed into a compost rich in leafmould,

charcoal and sand, for they are woodland plants and need perfect drainage. Water regularly until leaves appear and then give diluted liquid fertiliser at fortnightly intervals until the flower buds develop during the colder months. Mist the plants regularly in dry indoor conditions, but do not over-water. An occasional deep soaking in the sink is of far more value. Indoors they dislike central heating, so put them into an unheated room at night or outdoors in mild areas.

Cybistax donnell-smithii. Primavera

Cyclamen persicum cultivar. Florist's Cyclamen

Cyclamen hederifolium. Alpine Violet, Sowbread

Most plants are discarded after a single season, but they can be used again if you leave the pots on their sides in a dry, cool place for the summer. When leaves begin to reappear, repot and start the cycle over again. *C. persicum*, the Shooting Star or Florist's Cyclamen, makes a 30cm/12in plant with leaves often marbled in white and silver. *C. hederifolium*, the Alpine Violet, is much smaller, with pink or white violet-sized autumn flowers.

CYDONIA

(sai-**doh**-nee-ə)

Quince

ROSACEAE

Called *Cydonia* after the old Cretan city where it grew, the Quince is native to eastern Europe and western Asiatic countries and has been cultivated since time immemorial.

The tree is deciduous, with woolly young shoots and leaves rather like those of an apple. It may reach 7m/23ft and is usually of a rather shrubby appearance unless pruned. The flowers are perfumed and charming, single and rose-like, a delicate blush-pink. The great, irregularly shaped fruits ripen in autumn, often persisting on the tree after leaves have yellowed and fallen.

CYMBALARIA

(sim-ba-le**ə**r-ee-ə)

(SYN Linaria)

Ruin of Rome, Kenilworth Ivy, Pennywort, Wall Toadflax

SCROPHULARIACEAE

It's hard to imagine this dainty, creeping perennial bringing the Roman forum crashing into ruin … but some writers insist that it did. Certainly it should be introduced with care unless you're prepared to set aside part of your life for a perpetual clean-up. It has an incredible capacity for seeding in the tiniest crevices, will even root right into old mortar. For all that, it's pretty harmless, needing both shade and moisture to trail far; and it just can't survive in perpetually hot, dry places. Leaves are kidney-shaped, amd the blue flowers resemble tiny snapdragons, to which they are related.

Cymbalaria muralis. Ruin of Rome, Pennywort

Cydonia oblonga. Quince

CYMBIDIUM
(sim-**bid**-ee-əm)
Cymbidium
Orchidaceae

Most improved of all the orchid genera, modern *Cymbidiums* are the result of extensive hybridisation over the last 80 years. They do not thrive in a tropical climate, preferring temperate areas where the winter temperature does not fall below 2ºC/36ºF. There they can be grown in the garden, preferably in large pots which can be moved to a favourable position, even indoors, at flowering time.

Cymbidium hybrids like full sun in the cooler months, light shade in summer. They are grown in a special compost available at any nursery. It is moisture retentive yet free draining and should be kept moist during spring and summer when new growth develops. Flower spikes up to 1.5m/5ft long appear at varying times from midwinter to summer, according to type.

Cymbidium 'Miretta'. Cymbidium

Cymbidium 'Nonina'. Miniature Cymbidium

Cymbidium 'Buxom Irene'. Cymbidium

Cymbidium 'Lustrous Betty'. Cymbidium

Cymbidium floribundum. Miniature Cymbidium

Cynara cardunculus. Cardoon

CYNARA
(sai-**nah**-rə)
Cardoon
ASTERACEAE

Tall, spectacular Cardoons are great value in the larger perennial border or as feature plants almost anywhere. Grown mostly from spring-planted suckers, they soon sprout metre-long silvery leaves, looking much like silver treefern fronds and developing into an enormous rosette over 2m/6ft in diameter. Finally, after regular water and feeding, the heavy flower stalks begin to rise and keep growing until they're taller than any gardener. At full summer height, the mauve blooms, like giant Scotch thistles, appear. These consist of multiple rows of spiny over-lapping bracts topped with a pompon of long-stamened tubular flowers. Botanically, the Cardoon is known as *Cynara cardunculus*, and it's no accident that the blooms resemble that great delicacy, the Globe Artichoke, for those are the buds of related *C. scolymus*. Grow the Cardoon in deep, heavily enriched soil with free drainage – and as a bonus you can cook and eat the root and leaf stalks. Grow them from spring-sown seed, too, but they won't reach flower-ing size the first year. Cardoons die back and look very sad in winter but can be easily tidied up in spring.

CYNOGLOSSUM
(sai-noh-glos-səm)
Hound's Tongue, Chinese Forget-me-not, Beggar's Lice
BORAGINACEAE

Cynoglossum amabile is a rather weedy annual that blooms briefly but is popular because of the valuable splash of blue it brings to the mixed border. Often called Chinese Forget-me-not because it's from China and resembles a large Forget-me-not with 1cm/½in flowers. Of its other names, 'Hound's Tongue' is a reference to the long, floppy leaves and 'Beggar's Lice' to the burr-like seeds which stick to anyone brushing past the plant. Seed can be scattered outdoors in raked soil in early spring and thinly covered to protect it from light. With warm sun and moisture, young seedlings can appear in 5–10 days. Thin to 22cm/9in inter-vals and water regularly. *Cynoglossum* will grow anywhere: in wet or dry soils, cold or warm climates.

Cynoglossum amabile 'Blue Beard'. Chinese Forget-me-not

CYPRIPEDIUM
(sip-rə-**pee**-dee-əm)
Lady's Slipper Orchid, Moccasin Flower
ORCHIDACEAE

Once used as a general name for all the popular Slipper Orchids now called Paphiopedilum (which see), *Cypripedium* has been retained as the scientific epithet for the frost-hardy deciduous species found mostly in North America and Europe. These are grown in a lightly shaded position in a neutral but leaf-rich and well-drained soil. Moisture is essential for continued growth, and a cold winter ensures maturity of the embryo flowers. *C. calceolus*, the Yellow

Cyrilla racemiflora. Leatherwood

Lady's Slipper, is one of the more popular types in cool-climate gardens, blooming from late spring into summer on stems up to 60cm/2ft tall. The plant's name has been adapted from the Cypriot name for Venus, the Mediterranean love goddess.

CYRILLA
(si-**rill**-ə)
Leatherwood, Titi, Myrtle, He-huckleberry
CYRILLACEAE

A most decorative shrub, the single species of *Cyrilla racemiflora* grows naturally from southern parts of the United States right across the Caribbean to northern Brazil. But that one species has many decorative forms, all easily raised from cuttings struck under glass in a mildly heated sandy compost. In the northern parts of its range the *Cyrilla* tends to be deciduous, and presents a creditable display of autumn colour. But further into the tropics it turns evergreen, grows almost to treesize. In all varieties, there is a summer flower display as long, drooping tassels of tiny white blossom appear from leaf axils.

Cypripedium calceolus. Lady's Slipper Orchid

CYRTANTHUS

(sur-**tan**-thəs)

Fire Lily, Ifafa Lily, Scarborough Lily, George Lily, Knysna Lily

AMARYLLIDACEAE

Originating in southern Africa, Fire Lilies are an interesting group of bulbs. The Ifafa Lily, *Cyrtanthus mackenii,* is the best known and produces a clump of grassy leaves which may disappear over a short period of winter dormancy. Through spring and summer, flower stalks arise topped with tubular, curving, sometimes fragrant flowers that can be cream, pink, red or salmon-toned depending on the variety.

Cyrtanthus mackenii. Ifafa Lily

Long grown around Scarborough in northern England, the Scarborough Lily, *Cyrtanthus elatus* (formerly *Vallota speciosa)* was once thought to be native to the district. Now we believe they were washed ashore from an early Dutch shipwreck, for they certainly grow wild at the Cape of Good Hope. These are truly spectacular flowers – open funnels of glowing orange-scarlet, 8cm/3in across and clustered together atop a thick 30cm/12in stem. They flower in late summer and do well in pots.

Plant bulbs with their necks at ground level in a well-drained, compost-enriched, sunny spot. Alternatively, crowd them into low, wide pots. Feed often and water freely except during winter, when they like to be dryish. Increase by seed or offsets separated from infrequently divided clumps.

Cytisus battandieri. Atlas Broom

Cytisus multiflorus 'White Gem'. White Spanish Broom

Cyrtanthus elatus. Scarborough Lily

CYTISUS

(**sit**-iss-əs)

Broom

FABACEAE

What Crotalarias are to the warm climate, so *Cytisus* is to cool temperate areas. A smaller genus, with all 50 species native to the Mediterranean and Atlantic islands, *Cytisus* has similar showy pea-flowers, though borne in greater profusion over a longer period. The colour range is also wider, including shades of pink, white, cream, tan and mahogany red as well as basic yellow. The Warminster Broom, *C. praecox*, is propagated from ripe shoots taken in autumn; Atlas Broom, *C. battandieri* (a much larger plant, up to 5x4m/16x13ft), grows better from seed. Both are deciduous, with a generally weeping habit. The Scotch Broom, *C. scoparius*, is evergreen. All have silky leaves of 3 leaflets and a strong smell that's not necessarily pleasant. Flowering occurs in spring. *Cytisus* enjoy poor-quality, slightly acid soil and need regular water throughout spring and summer.

Daboecia cantabrica. St Dabeoc's Heath

Dahlia 'Don Jose'. Formal Decorative Dahlia

DABOECIA
(dab-oh-**ee**-sh∂)
Irish Heath, St Dabeoc's Heath

ERICACEAE

Two species of low, evergreen shrubs in the heath family, native to Ireland, France, Spain and the Azores. Like all heaths, *Daboecia* needs a lime-free soil, preferably including sand and peat. The flowers, much larger than on other heaths, appear in spring and early summer towards the end of slender twigs. There are several hybrids in shades of white or rosy-purple. Dwarf-growing and wide-spreading, *Daboecias* are suited to the semi-shaded rock pocket or in the foreground of larger shrubs. Illustrated *D. cantabrica* is hardy in the UK but needs protection in colder parts of North America. It grows to only 40cm/16in.

Dactylorhiza elata. Hyacinth Orchid

Dahlia 'Alwyn Trimmer'. Semi-cactus Dahlia

DACTYLORHIZA
(dat-til-oh-**rai**-z∂)
(SYN Orchis)
Marsh Orchid, Spotted Orchid

ORCHIDACEAE

Named for its finger-shaped tubers, *Dactylorhiza* is a group of deciduous terrestrial orchids from Europe, North Africa, western Asia and North America. The Hyacinth Orchid, *D. elata* (syn *Orchis elata*), from southwestern Europe and the Algerian hills, grows widely in moist, shaded gardens of Europe and similar cool temperate areas.

If you find a source, plant them in drifts where you can't fail to notice the dazzling spikes of red-violet blooms that appear on leafy stems in late spring. They resemble giant Grape Hyacinths, and may reach 60cm/2ft in height in a suitable position. A deep, rich, slightly limey soil suits them best, and they resent disturbance. If you must transplant, do it in autumn, when tubers are fully grown.

DAHLIA
(**dah**-lee-∂)
Dahlia

ASTERACEAE

With *Dahlias*, there is no half measure – you either love them or loathe them. I make no secret of my own feelings, but in all fairness, the bulk of the gardening public seems to like them a great deal. I will concede one point. The small annual varieties grown from seed make splendid bedding plants, and my taste for these is increasingly well catered for.

They are normally sown in flats in spring or earliest summer. Those from later sowings will peak in autumn and probably give you a more brilliant display. Seeds, covered by moistened vermiculite, should germinate in 5–10 days. Plant the young seedlings out 4–6 weeks later at 30cm/12in spacings. Feed and water well.

The more spectacular, taller-growing *Dahlia* hybrids are usually grown from

Dahlia 'Bertie Bromley'. Cactus Dahlia

Dahlia 'Wootton Cupid'. Pompon Dahlia

potato-like tubers planted around the middle of spring or when all danger of frost has passed. Do *not* separate tubers from the stem of an old clump, but split vertically through the stem, of which each tuber needs a portion to develop new growth. *Dahlias* are gross feeders and need full sun to thrive. The planting site should be well prepared: this is mostly a matter of digging in a generous amount of rotted manure, compost and other old organic matter plus a ration of complete plant food. Drive stout 2m/6ft stakes firmly into the worked soil then plant three tubers of the taller-growing types around each. New shoots will appear within a few weeks and should be tied loosely to the stake as soon as they've reached about 45cm/18in. In really hot weather, they will benefit from a mulch of straw around the stems of each plant to keep the roots cool and the ground moist and free of weeds.

Dahlia Unwins Dwarf Group. Bedding Dahlia

If quantity of blooms is your wish for cutting or garden display, pinch out the growing centre of each plant when it has passed 40cm/16in in height and the laterals have appeared. Pinching produces a lower, shrubbier bush with plenty of bloom.

If you prefer quality blooms, you will need to disbud. This means snipping away all but the largest bud on each stem, so that this bud receives all the plant's growth energy.

Dahlia blooms come in many sizes and arrangements of petals, as our photographs demonstrate.

Dais cotinifolia. South African Daphne

Dahlia 'Meira'. Small Decorative Dahlia

DAIS
(dae-əs)
South African Daphne
<small>THYMELAEACEAE</small>

Though definitely a tree in the hot, dry areas of South Africa to which it is native, lovely *Dais cotinifolia* often tends to adopt a shrubby, multiple-trunked habit in the home garden – probably due to the absence of leaf-eating animals that prey on its young foliage in the wild. Best follow nature's example and force it into a single trunk when young – though it still may not grow above 4m/13ft in height. It is a handsome, slender treelet with reddish bark and blue-green leaves to 8cm/3in in length and broadest towards the tip. Though South Africans insist it is ever-green, I find it loses its foliage briefly in both Australia and the United States. Apart from some commercial use of the tough bark fibres, *Dais* is grown most for its fragrant, unusual blossom. Tubular pink flowers appear in a dense pompon-shaped cluster in late spring, and tend to hang on the tree long after they've faded. A charmer for the small temperate garden.

Dampiera trigona. Blue Boys

Daphne cneorum. Garland Flower

DAMPIERA
(**dam**-pee-er-∂)
Blue Boys
GOODENIACEAE

True blue, as befits a plant named for a British naval officer (Captain William Dampier RN), the showy *Dampiera trigona* is only one of 60-odd species known to science. *All* of them are likely to have open-faced blue flowers. *Most* of them are native to Western Australia. They are a subshrubby lot, enjoying a fairly well-drained site where they grow easily from stem cuttings or divisions of the root system. There are varieties for climates from cool to subtropical, mostly 30–60cm/1–2ft in height. Sun to light shade, please!

DAPHNE
(**daf**-nee)
Daphne, Garland Flower
THYMELAEACEAE

A long time ago, in far-off Arcadia, there lived a nymph named Daphne. One day, while working on her all-over tan, she caught the eye of Apollo, the sun god. He was beside her in a flash, and Daphne, fearing the worst, began praying to her favourite goddesses for help. Her prayers were answered as her arms turned to sleek branches with shining leaves, her feet took root and she became one of the prettiest flowering shrubs you ever saw! That, according to Greek legend, was the origin of the charming European *Daphne laureola*, a species not much grown since the discovery of its more beautiful Asian cousins, such as *D. odora*. We now know there are some 50 species of these fragrant winter and spring flowering shrubs, popular everywhere short of the subtropics. Most are of hillside, woodland origin and hardy down to –8°C/17°F. They like dappled shade and well-drained, slightly acid soil, though *D. cneorum* will tolerate limey soil provided

Daphne oleoides. Olive-leaf Daphne

there's plenty of leafmould mixed in. Only light watering is needed, with a meagre ration of complete fertiliser immediately after bloom. Over-watering in summer will lead to collar rot, which will put paid to an apparently healthy plant in no time. Best grow *Daphnes* in a raised position, with the root junction above soil level and let the surface dry out between summer waterings. *Daphnes* are evergreen and propagated from tip-cuttings struck in summer. *D. cneorum* will grow from seed.

Daphne odora. Sweet Daphne

Daphne laureola. Spurge Laurel

DARLINGTONIA
(dar-ling-**toh**-nee-∂)
Cobra Lily, California Pitcher Plant
SARRACENIACEAE

Back arched, head forward, forked tongue out – one toot from a snake-charmer's flute and you'd expect this remarkable plant to rise and bite. It is even marked exactly like the cobra with which it shares a popular name – the flowers, in contrast, are a plain yellow-green. *Darlingtonia californica* is

Darlingtonia californica. Cobra Lily

Darwinia taxifolia. Scent Myrtle

found only in the wet sphagnum bogs of North America's western mountains, and is commonly cultivated only by carnivorous plant fans who raise them in containers of damp moss set in a tray of water. They are normally propagated from seed and repotted in summer every second year. Constant moisture is essential, and only liquid manure can be used. Insects are attracted by nectar glands inside the hood, then slide down the smooth interior to be drowned and digested by the stickiness within. Ugh!

DARWINIA
(dah-**win**-ee-ə)
Scent Myrtle
MYRTACEAE

Compact, heath-like plants of the myrtle family, Australia's 40-odd species of *Darwinia* are useful 1m/3ft shrubs for sandy, acid soil. Easily propagated from lateral cuttings taken in spring or autumn and struck in sharp sand, they like a well-drained position and thrive with minimum water and an occasional light dressing of organic fertiliser. The evergreen leaves are small and aromatic, generally sharply pointed and linear. Flowers appear in terminal and axillary clusters and their petals are so inconspicuous they are often mistaken for leaves. The showy part is a cluster of 10 red and white stamens which protrude in a pincushion effect. All species feature this same colour scheme.

Davidia involucrata. Handkerchief Tree

DAVIDIA
(dae-**vid**-ee-ə)
Handkerchief Tree, Dove Tree
NYSSACEAE

Almost a century ago, the beautiful *Davidia involucrata* caused a botanical sensation when it flowered for the first time in the West in the garden of a French collector named de Vilmorin. This came as the climax of a race between French and English botanists to find and flower a tree reported from western China by a French missionary, Father David. It had ghostly white flowers fluttering among the foliage like handkerchiefs, or so he reported.

The race and its result are botanical history, but even before the trees were located and taken back to Europe, the botanical name was never in doubt – *Davidia*.

Davidia, though deciduous, will grow in any frost-free area short of the subtropics,

preferring a deep, rich, acid soil. It may reach 13m/40ft but is usually only half that in the average garden. The flower heads are less than 2cm/1in wide and consist of a number of greenish filaments topped with red or dark brown stamens. These heads are each surrounded by 2 unequal bracts, the larger as big as a human hand.

The floral display starts just as the tree opens its spring foliage and lasts for several weeks, after which inedible purplish fruits appear on long stems.

DELONIX
(**del**-on-iks)
Poinciana, Flamboyant
CAESALPINIACEAE

Believed to have originated on the island of Madagascar, home of so many wonderful plants, *Delonix regia*, the Poinciana or Flamboyant, has been hailed as the showiest

Delonix regia. Poinciana, Flamboyant

flowering tree in the world. But gardeners living further than 30° from the equator will have to be content to dream about it, for it won't flower anywhere else.

When it does condescend to bloom, the whole tree drops its foliage and lights up literally overnight into a canopy of bright scarlet flowers, each about the size of a rose. These are quite variable in colour, shading from almost crimson to almost orange, in each case with one petal heavily spotted in either white or yellow. There is even a much rarer form, which I photographed in Tahiti, where the entire flower is yellow, one petal marked in cream.

The Poinciana (its botanical name *Delonix* is from the Greek *delos*, meaning 'obvious' and it certainly is hard to miss!) is not tall, as trees go – its limit is about 10m/33ft – but it may ultimately reach three times that in width, a great, spreading umbrella that makes wonderful shade in tropical gardens.The smooth, grey trunk often develops large supporting buttresses; the pinnate leaves are feathery and delicate, rather like those of a Jacaranda.

The flowers are followed by a mass of long, bean-like pods that may persist for months.

DELOSPERMA
(de-loh-**spur**-mə)
(SYN Mesembryanthemum)
Delosperma, Vygie
AIZOACEAE

Yet another of the seemingly innumerable African Ice Plant genera, the 150-odd species of *Delosperma* tend to have a woodier growth than many of their succulent relatives, and bloom on and off throughout the year, but most heavily in summer. The Pink Vygie, *D. cooperi,* is found naturally in the Orange Free State. It likes a warm temperate climate, rich though dryish soil and winter moisture. Seaside positions suit it well, as do sunny, dry banks. Grow from seed or cuttings and allow it room to sprawl. Other Ice Plants may offer better value.

DELPHINIUM
(del-**fin**-ee-əm)
Candle Larkspur
RANUNCULACEAE

Think blue – think *Delphiniums*! These tall and stately perennials of cooler-climate gardens are one of the glories of the summer border, producing great clumps of hand-shaped leaves, ingeniously divided and mostly of an elegant, pale green. From

Delosperma cooperi. Pink Vygie

among them appear 2m/6ft spire-like stems completely covered with 3cm/1in cup-shaped blooms in every imaginable shade of blue and mauve, from palest baby-blue to darkest indigo. Earlier hybrids were single but now, with hybridists busy year after year, we have semi-double and ruffled varieties – some even fully double – while the range of colours has been widened to include white, pink and (even more recently) a few in lemon and cream shades.

Hybrids of Eurasian *D. elatum* with several other species, these are known as the

Elatum Group. Although they can be grown as annuals from seed, the really spectacular cultivars come true only from vegetative propagation. Crowns or clumps consisting of a mass of fleshy roots can be purchased in autumn or early spring from specialist nurseries. Plant them in deep, lightly alkaline soil in full sun, but preferably sheltered by taller plants or hedges, for they are very prone to wind damage without strong staking. They can also be propagated, from cuttings taken close to the rootstock when growth has begun in spring. These are struck in a

Delphinium nudicaule. Scarlet Larkspur

Delphinium 'Magic Moment'. Delphinium

Delphinium, Elatum Group. Candle Larkspur

Dendrobium bigibbum. Cooktown Orchid

sand/peat mixture under glass, set out in a nursery area when rooted and transplanted to final position in late summer for bloom the following year.

To grow from seed, sow under glass in winter at a temperature of 18–24ºC/65–75ºF: germination takes about 2 weeks. Prick the seedlings into boxes and plant out in spring or autumn. Cut the main flower spike for indoor use or when faded; smaller spikes will often appear towards autumn. Many other perennial *Delphinium* species are also grown, including the dwarf Californian *D. nudicaule* with scarlet flowers. This has a long blooming season during spring and summer, and is grown from fresh summer seed and planted out in autumn for bloom the following year. This species can cope with semi-shade and looks great in a naturalised woodland setting.

DENDROBIUM
(den-**droh**-bee-əm)
Dendrobium

ORCHIDACEAE

Undoubtedly the most diversified of orchid genera, *Dendrobiums* are native to the Pacific and Asia, where more than 1400 species have been catalogued. Many of them are tree-dwellers, and can be potted for indoor bloom. There are two principal divisions – the evergreens (including most of the Australian natives), which should never be allowed to dry out completely, and the deciduous, tropical group, which need a definite rest from water corresponding to the dry tropical winter. The cane-stemmed types are usually grown in heavy pots of porous, well-drained compost. Hanging types such as *D. aphyllum* and *D. bigibbum* need glass protection, for they flower around winter. The small Australian epiphytic types such as *D. kingianum* do well in a shallow pan of packaged orchid compost and small firbark pieces, or can be wired onto pieces of paper-bark trunk.

D. bigibbum (Cooktown Orchid) produces showy, arching flower stems lined with deepest cerise butterfly flowers that have marvellous, crepe-like texture.

D. nobile, from north India, a 45cm/18in cane-stemmed type, flowers candelabra-style in early spring. There are many hybrids in

Dendrobium nobile hybrid. India Dendrobium

Dendrobium speciosum. Rock Lily

Dendromecon rigida subsp. *harfordii.* Tree Poppy

shades of pink, white and mauve with dark, velvety lip markings.

D. *speciosum* (Rock Lily) is found from the tropics to the temperate zone in mountainous and lowland areas of Australia, and thus is extremely variable. It grows on rocks or in trees in shade or sun and blooms late winter or early spring.

D. *thyrsiflorum* (Golden Dendrobium) is another cane-stemmed species, from Burma, with hanging clusters of cream and egg-yellow flowers in late spring.

Dendrobium thyrsiflorum. Golden Dendrobium

DENDROMECON
(den-**drom**-ee-kən)
Tree Poppy
PAPAVERACEAE

One of California's most beautiful native shrubs, *Dendromecon rigida* is sometimes known as the California Tree Poppy. And that's exactly what it is – a member of the poppy family that has adapted into a 3m/10ft hard-wooded perennial form. There is only one species, though with many local varieties, including subsp. *harfordii*, which grows to a height of 6m/20ft. *Dendromecon* likes dry, gravelly soil and a sheltered, well-drained position. It can be propagated from seed (very slow to germinate) or cuttings of well-ripened summer shoots struck in sharp sand with some heat. The evergreen leaves are simple, leathery, generally pointed and a curious shade of grey-green. The masses of pleasantly fragrant 8cm/3in poppy flowers appear in warm weather.

DESFONTAINEA
(des-fon-**tae**-nee-ə)
Peruvian Holly
LOGANIACEAE

This decorative shrub from the South American Andes is the only one of its genus, presenting every appearance of being a fruitless holly bush for much of the year. But come midsummer, it surprisingly produces

masses of vivid 4cm/1½in tubular flowers from the leaf axils, revealing its true identity. These blooms are scarlet lined with yellow, and make a grand display in the mild, moist climates which *Desfontainea* prefers. It is best raised from semi-hardwood cuttings of 10cm/4in lateral shoots, taken with a heel in summer. Plant it in a cool, acid soil and keep slightly moist at all times. It may grow slowly to 3m/10ft, but usually reaches only half that. It is not truly frost hardy.

Desfontainea spinosa. Peruvian Holly

DEUTZIA
(doit-zee-ə)
Wedding Bells, Bridal Wreath
SAXIFRAGACEAE

Splendid oriental shrubs that bloom with the late spring bulbs and continue to early summer, *Deutzias* are closely related to Philadelphus, but are without their rich perfume. As compensation, their long, arching canes literally bend under the weight of hanging flower clusters.

Most of the 60-odd species need rich, fast-draining soil and grow readily from semi-hardwood cuttings taken in summer. Deciduous and frost hardy, *Deutzias* produce pointed leaves about 10cm/4in long, with terminal panicles of single starry blooms in white, pink or mauve. After bloom, prune away a third of the older canes. Allow plenty of room: *Deutzias* are normally far wider than they are high.

DIANELLA
(dai-an-**el**-lə)
Flax Lily
LILIACEAE

Dianella species of one sort or another are found right up the east coast of Australia; also in Tasmania, Polynesia and, more rarely, Southeast Asia. They are fibrous-rooted perennial plants, spreading from underground rhizomes and sending up fans of tough, flax-like foliage at regular intervals. These may reach 1.2m/4ft in height. *Dianella* grows readily from fresh seed or divisions and is very adaptable in terms of soil type, provided moisture is available. In early spring, colonies of these decorative plants commence a prolonged display of bloom. This consists of blue or purple small starry flowers borne in sparse panicles. Shining dark blue berries follow. The ancient woodland goddess Diana is commemorated in the name of these forest plants.

DIANTHUS
(dai-an-thəs)
Carnation, Pinks, Gillyflower
CARYOPHYLLACEAE

The name *Dianthus* means heavenly flower and was used in Ancient Greece to describe the annual and perennial Carnations and Pinks.

The perpetual flowering Carnations (*D. caryophyllus* hybrids) can be grown under glass to produce cutting blooms the entire year. Most named hybrids are grown from winter cuttings of healthy sideshoots.

*Deutzia scabra.*Wedding Bells

Deutzia longifolia. Longleaf Deutzia

Deutzia gracilis. Slender Deutzia

Dianella revoluta. Flax Lily

Dianthus 'Doris'. Modern Pink

Dianthus deltoides. Maiden Pink

Dianthus arenarius. Prussian Pink

These are potted up when rooted, then set out in late spring. Pinching will produce bushier growth. They love full sun, perfect drainage and grow best in neutral, sandy soil. Regular water and twice-monthly feeding produce fine blooms, but watch for aphids, thrips and caterpillars.

Smaller *D. plumarius* includes all the old-fashioned clove-scented pinks. They are lower, untidier plants, but propagated in the same way and used at the front of the border or in rockeries.

D. arenarius and *D. deltoides* are dwarf, mat-forming plants, easily grown from seed or cuttings. They do well in gritty soil, and bloom best when you use a high potassium fertiliser and give regular water. *D. arenarius* is happiest in semi-shade.

Most popular of the annuals is the Indian Pink, *D. chinensis*. This is a colourful, dwarf, bushy plant growing about 22cm/9in tall with masses of sweetly scented, flat, open flowers, either single or double. There are many hybrids.

Next in popularity are the biennial Sweet Williams (*D. barbatus*). These have dark green foliage with flat clusters of 2cm/1in flowers. The dwarf types rarely grow over 15cm/6in.

Dianthus 'Lemon Sim'. Carnation

Dianthus barbatus. Sweet William

Diascia rigescens. Twin Flower

Dicentra spectabilis. Bleeding Heart

DIASCIA

(dai-**ass**-kee-∂)
Twin Flower, Twinspur
SCROPHULARIACEAE

Not very common anywhere except in their native South Africa, the 50-odd species of *Diascia* (both annual and perennial) are useful additions to the temperate garden. Related to Linaria, Nemesia and Torenia, all of which they resemble to some degree, they do best in a sunny position in almost any soil and have no special requirements beyond a light ration of fertiliser when flowers are forming, and regular water. Sow seed in trays in earliest spring and plant out when frost has passed. The short flowering period occurs in summer. Pinching out the growing tips will make the 20–45cm/8–18in plants bushier, and a second flush can be promoted if the stems of the twin-spurred flowers are cut back after they fade.

DICENTRA

(dai-**sen**-tr∂)
Bleeding Heart, Locket Flower
FUMARIACEAE

Graceful, old-time perennials, the handful of *Dicentra* species can only be grown with success in cool or cold winter areas. They are delicate herbaceous plants for the semi-shaded shrubbery with deep, woodsy soil, where they grow up to 75cm/30in tall. They shrivel up in full sun or dry conditions. *D. spectabilis* is the preferred species, native

to Japan – but south of the equator you will only find it doing well in gardens of elevated districts. A tangle of fleshy roots when planted in autumn, *Dicentra* sends up ferny, green foliage in spring and then arching stems hung with heart or locket-shaped blossoms. On these, the outer petals are red or pink, the inner white. *Dicentra* can be propagated from winter divisions replanted immediately, or by seed sown in moist peat and sand then refrigerated for 6 weeks. The plants die back completely in late summer.

Dichelostemma ida-maia. Firecracker Flower

DICHELOSTEMMA

(dai-**kel**-oh-stem-m∂)
(SYN Brevoortia, Brodiaea)
Firecracker Flower, Floral Firecracker
AMARYLLIDACEAE

Showiest of a small genus of bulbous species found only through North America's western states, *Dichelostemma ida-maia* has been in and out of fashion over the years, though mostly sold under the name of Brodiaea. It will grow in climates from warm temperate to cold, though in the latter a winter mulch is recommended. Well-drained soil and lots of water in winter and spring give best results. Let the bulbs dry out completely after summer bloom. Bright, dappled shade is ideal. Expect results only from large bulbs; offsets take years to bloom.

DICHORISANDRA

(dai-kor-i-**san**-dr∂)
Purple Ginger
COMMELINACEAE

A striking tropical perennial from Brazil, *Dichorisandra thyrsiflora* can be grown in far more temperate climates with winter protection for the succulent stems. It is definitely not frost hardy. A tall growing plant (to 1.5m/5ft), it is related to the common Wandering Jews. Grow under trees, in shade houses or containerised on a sheltered patio; you may need to stake the tall stems. Well-drained soil with plenty of leafmould is ideal. Regular water and high humidity are

Dichorisandra thyrsiflora. Purple Ginger

Dicliptera suberecta. Orange Justicia

Dictamnus albus. Burning Bush, Dittany

expected in summer, tapering right off in winter. It can be grown from seed, cuttings, root divisions or by detaching the small, rooted plantlets that form on main stems.

The glossy green leaves are spirally arranged, with vivid violet-blue blooms borne profusely on tall spikes to give a long display through summer and early autumn.

DICLIPTERA

(dai-**klip**-ter-∂)

Orange Justicia

ACANTHACEAE

A charming but little-known dwarf shrubby perennial for the warm-climate rock garden or bank, Uruguayan *Dicliptera suberecta* retains a reminder of earlier nomenclature and relationships in the popular name Orange Justicia. Grow it in well-drained, sandy soil in full sun and propagate from cuttings struck in sharp sand.

When not in bloom, the plant forms a neat mound of velvety-grey foliage – but then 25cm/10in arching flower stems develop and suddenly the whole plant is covered in a mass of firecracker-orange blossom. The display may last from spring to autumn. *Dicliptera* can also be grown in pots or baskets for terrace display and needs plenty of water as the flowers develop.

DICTAMNUS

(dik-**tam**-n∂s)

Gas Plant, Burning Bush, Dittany, Fraxinella

RUTACEAE

This may not be the burning bush that Moses ran across, but it will certainly do until the real thing comes along! A strongly aromatic herbaceous perennial of the citrus family, with shining, dark green compound leaves, it is an ornament to any border and has a peculiarity that will fascinate your friends and charm the children to distraction. In hot, still weather, the entire plant

Dietes grandiflora. Wild Iris

exudes a volatile oil in the form of an invisible vapour. One touch of a match near the base of a flower spike and pff! – a sudden burst of flame may startle you, but won't damage the flowers at all.

A native of southern Europe and Asia, *Dictamnus albus* bears attractive long-stemmed white blooms in terminal summer racemes. It likes a rich, well-drained soil with regular water. Propagate from root-cuttings taken in early spring or from seed sown outdoors in late autumn for spring germination. Plant at 1m/3ft spacings in full sun or part shade.

Dierama pulcherrimum. Fairy Fishing Rod

Digitalis purpurea. Foxglove

DIERAMA

(dai-er-**ah**-m∂)

Wand Flower, Fairy Fishing Rod, Fairy Bells

IRIDACEAE

Dieramas are South African members of the Iris family, thriving only in rich, moist, well-drained soils. In nature they usually grow in the dappled shade of open forests.

Once established, *Dieramas* quickly form clumps of narrow grassy leaves from which appear delicate, arching flower stems in late spring or early summer. These are hung with pendant pink blooms, seen to best advantage against a background of dark shrubbery. They make delightful poolside or rockery plants. Propagate from seed or by offsets separated from the mother bulb. Disturbance is resented, so leave clumps alone for years.

DIETES

(dai-**et**-eez)

(SYN Moraea)

Fortnight Lily, Wild Iris

IRIDACEAE

The evergreen, sword-like foliage of South Africa's *Dietes* makes an attractive garden feature at any time of the year – but warm weather is when they come into their own, sending up many long flower stems to produce blooms for several weeks at a time. All *Dietes* are extraordinarily drought resistant and so tough they can be used as low hedges. Once established, they self-seed into dense clumps.

The species *D. bicolor* has 5cm/2in yellow and brown flowers. *D. grandiflora* blooms are larger, white marked with mauve and orange-yellow. *D. iridoides* is a smaller version of *D. grandiflora*, growing only to about 60cm/2ft tall. It forms dense clumps under tall, open trees.

DIGITALIS

(di-ji-**tah**-lis)

Foxglove, Thimble Flower

SCROPHULARIACEAE

Marvellous plants for generations of gardeners, Foxgloves (*Digitalis purpurea*) have been revolutionised by the development of new strains which are grown as annuals. These do not grow as tall as older biennial types but the 70cm/28in flower spikes are adequate for

Dietes bicolor. Fortnight Lily

modern gardens, and less prone to wind damage. The colour range is wide, including magenta, purple, white, cream, yellow, pink and lavender, all with beautifully spotted yellow or white throats.

Seeds should be sown in late summer or autumn for bloom the following spring and summer. Germination will take 15–20 days at a maintained temperature of 21°C/70°F, provided seed is lightly covered and kept moist. Prick seedlings out to a wider spacing during winter; when danger of frost is past, set plants out in well-fertilised soil, in part shade, 30–45cm/12–18in apart. Blooming begins about 5 months from sowing, so plan accordingly. Foxgloves will self-seed regularly in a moist, sheltered position. If the main flower stem is cut, a number of secondary spikes will develop.

DILLENIA

(dil-**len**-nee-∂)

Dillenia

DILLENIACEAE

Linnaeus named the genus after his friend Johann Dillenius, professor of botany at Oxford University, comparing the enormous flowers of *Dillenia indica*, the Elephant Apple, to Dillenius's spectacular contributions to botany. The flowers are indeed magnificent: nearly as big as dinner plates, shining white, sweetly fragrant and borne among equally

Dillenia alata. Red Beech   TONY RODD

spectacular glossy deeply corrugated leaves. But gardeners in temperate regions must be content to drool over pictures: the 10m/33ft tree on which they grow is strictly tropical in its preferences. It is a native of India, where its juicy, vaguely lemon-flavoured fruit is eaten either fresh or in curries.

The yellow-flowered *D. alata* is a common beachfront tree in northern Australia.

DIMORPHOTHECA

(dai-mor-**foth**-ee-kə)
Star of the Veldt, Namaqualand Daisy, African Daisy
ASTERACEAE

Bright, free-flowering daisy plants from South Africa, now naturalised in many temperate lands; *Dimorphotheca sinuata* (often listed as *D. aurantiaca*) was originally perennial but has been hybridised with many close relatives to develop a truly annual habit and colours in the cream-yellow-apricot-orange range, often with petals reversed in pink or mauve. They are a wonderful bedding choice for hot, dry areas, and drifts of them make an unforgettable sight along the California coastal highways. They adore full sun and a dryish, well-drained soil. Unfortunately they are useless for cutting, as they close on cloudy days and remain closed indoors.

Scatter seed (ideally where the plants are to grow) after the last cold snap of early spring, or start indoors a month earlier. Germination should take 10–15 days at a temperature of 16°C/60°F. Plant out as soon as possible: flowering begins as soon as 9 weeks from sowing, and in a dry year will continue until the plants are destroyed by frost. In frost-free areas, they may even revert to their original perennial habit.

DIONAEA

(dee-o-**nee**-ə)
Venus Fly-trap
DROSERACEAE

Here I am breaking the rules again. The curious Venus Fly-trap is not grown for its flowers – nor does my picture show them. They are very small, white and are removed in cultivation to stimulate growth of the decorative leaves. *Dionaea* was the first plant recognised as carnivorous, and watching the speed with which its leaves snap shut on some helpless insect gives one food for thought … can any living thing set and spring such an elaborate trap without a brain? *Dionaea* is found only in a small area of America's Carolinas, and can be grown in shallow containers of a compost of sand and mostly peat. Stand this in a dish of water for constant saturation. Buy from specialists.

Dionaea muscipula. Venus Fly-trap

Dimorphotheca sinuata. African Daisy

Dipelta ventricosa. Shield Flower

DIPELTA

(dai-**pel**-tə)
Shield Flower
CAPRIFOLIACEAE

This genus of deciduous shrubs from China contains several species, but the one usually seen in gardens is *Dipelta floribunda*. It is a most attractive shrub, almost smothering itself in early summer with clusters of palest pink, bell-shaped flowers with a delicate touch of gold in their throats. If it reminds you a bit of a coarse-leafed Weigela, you are spot on – it is a close relative, and you can grow it in precisely the same way (see Weigela). It can grow some 3m/10ft tall, though in my opinion it looks its best when kept at half that size by annual pruning immediately the flowers are over. Grow from summer cuttings.

Dipogon lignosus. Hyacinth Bean

Dipsacus fullonum. Teasel

Distictis buccinatoria. Mexican Blood Trumpet

DIPOGON

(dai-**poh**-gon)

(SYN Dolichos)

Australian Pea, Hyacinth Bean

FABACEAE

Easiest to grow of all vines, requiring only a scattering of seed in winter, *Dipogon* will rapidly climb any support or hide unsightly fences, tanks etc. It is evergreen in mild climates where its rampant growth and self-seeding habit can make it something of a pest. It should be cut back hard immediately after bloom to prevent seed formation or, better still, pulled out completely. In cold-winter areas it is less of a problem as the frosts quickly dispose of it. Despite its common name it is not an Australian native, hailing instead from southern Africa.

DIPSACUS

(**dip**-sə-kəs)

Teasel

DIPSACACEAE

Really, *Dipsacus* is not very exciting to grow, the tiny white or pink flowers hardly adding much colour to the garden, though when they have faded the 8cm/3in flower heads can be dried for use in flower arrangements. They turn a very pleasant beige and there is no need to dye them garish colours as is sometimes done. But it is a plant of great interest as one of the few old industrial plants that has not been replaced by machinery. The fullers who finished woollen cloth used to stroke it with dried teasel heads to tease and raise the nap – hence the specific name *D. fullonum* – and they are still used in the manufacture of the very best fabrics.

The plant grows to about 2m/6ft. A biennial, raised from seed, it is easily cultivated in temperate climates in fairly moist soil.

DISA

(**dee**-sə)

Pride of Table Mountain

ORCHIDACEAE

Found in many parts of Africa and its offshore islands, there are 120-odd species of

Disa hybrid. Pride of Table Mountain

these showy little terrestrial orchids, and many more hybrid varieties have been developed. They do not enjoy life in a glasshouse, and can be grown well only in a cool, airy, moist atmosphere out of doors, in a temperate climate. A lath house should be ideal. Tuberous-rooted, they are propagated from offsets in well-drained, leaf-rich soil. Keep them moist, except for a short 6 weeks after bloom. Even then, do not let them dry out completely. Morning sun is to be preferred, but whatever the aspect, *Disa* species will never produce a big display, for only one flower at a time opens on each stem. Leaves appear in a low rosette from which the flower stem may rise 60cm/2ft.

DISTICTIS

(di-**stik**-tis)

(SYN Phaedranthus)

Mexican Blood Trumpet

BIGNONIACEAE

Away from Mexico, the marvellous *Distictis* grows best in full sun, and is a sight never to be forgotten with its blood-coloured trumpet flowers opening generously from spring through summer. Propagate from semi-hardwood cuttings in warm weather, and plant in leaf-rich soil. When established, it will climb very fast, clinging with wiry tendrils. Cut it back hard after bloom to force new growth. Try it over a pergola, as it grows top-heavy clinging to a vertical surface.

Dodecatheon meadia. Shooting Stars

DODECATHEON

(doh-dee-**kath**-ee-∂n)

Shooting Stars

PRIMULACEAE

Beautiful, woodsy Primula relatives from North America, *Dodecatheons* are not often seen in the southern hemisphere, but would be quite at home in hillside or mountain gardens – for they really need cold weather. To raise from seed, sprinkle on a moist soil mix and keep in the freezer for 3 weeks. Then place the tray in a propagator at 21°C/70°F for up to a month. Prick seedlings out and grow them on under glass for 2 years before planting out. Established plants can be divided in autumn.

D. *meadia* is most commonly seen in leafy, well-drained soil, where it produces handsome rosettes of light green, toothed, primula-type leaves. The 45cm/18in flower stalks pop up in late spring, each topped with an umbel of cyclamen-pink 2.5cm/1in blooms whose petals are strongly reflexed from a yellow centre. They look like tiny Cyclamen blooms. All 14 species of *Dodecatheon* are difficult to transplant as disturbance is resented.

DODONAEA

(doh-d∂-**nee**-∂)

Hopbush, Ake Ake

SAPINDACEAE

Dodonaea is a genus of some 60 species of evergreen shrubs, all but a few confined to Australia, very easily grown from cuttings in warm temperate climates. They do best

Dodonaea viscosa 'Purpurea'. Hopbush

in well-drained soil, in full sun to part shade. Be sure to pinch back in early spring to keep the plant bushy.

Australian Aborigines and Maoris used the leaves and fruits of several species medicinally, and early European settlers found the resinous fruits useful for flavouring beer, hence the name Hopbush. Nowadays, Hopbushes are valued for their fast growth even in dry, poor soils, their pretty foliage, which is often tinted with russet, purple or bronze, and the clusters of little flat fruits which can be as decorative as flowers in late summer. The flowers themselves (male and female on different plants) are usually greenish and insignificant.

DOMBEYA

(dom-**bae**-∂)

Natal Cherry, Wild Pear, Cape Wedding Flower

STERCULIACEAE

Native exclusively to eastern Africa and the islands of the Indian Ocean, the *Dombeyas* are handsome but very variable trees and shrubs, now grown in many lands and climates.

Dombeya cayeuxii. Cape Wedding Flower

Dombeya rotundifolia. Wild Pear

Striking D. *tiliacea*, the Natal Cherry, is a slim, many-branched tree which may reach 8m/26ft. It grows easily from seed or cuttings and produces a magnificent display of bloom in autumn when the entire tree becomes weighed down with clusters of white, long-stemmed, fragrant flowers. This species is sometimes listed as D. *natalensis* after its native South African province.

D. *rotundifolia*, the Wild Pear, is a deciduous tree with glossy, pear-like foliage, rusty on the underside. The white or pale pink blossoms form dense panicles in spring, often before the leaves arrive.

D. *cayeuxii* is a shrubby small tree with enormous heart-shaped leaves. Its pretty pink flowers in drooping clusters appear throughout the warm weather.

Dombeya tiliacea. Natal Cherry

Doritis pulcherrima. Esmeralda

DORITIS

(dor-**ai**-təs)
Esmeralda
ORCHIDACEAE

In Southeast Asian gardens you'll find a small, clump-forming terrestrial orchid that develops like Jack's beanstalk: growing and blooming, growing and blooming, up and up so that it produces delightful hyacinth-pink blooms throughout the year. It is called *Doritis* (though many still know it as Esmeralda from an earlier name). It is planted out from offsets in leaf-rich compost. There are 3 species, but many varieties localised variously in Burma, Indochina and Malaysia. If you can keep up a winter temperature of 16°C/60°F, you can raise them in a heated greenhouse, using small pots of a compost that is largely osmunda fibre. In summer, the sky's the limit, in both temperature and humidity.

DORONICUM

(dor-**on**-ik-um)
Leopard's Bane
ASTERACEAE

Some 35 species of Leopard's Bane or *Doronicum* grow wild from England to Iran. They like deep, damp soil, and should be planted 30–45cm/12–18in apart in dappled shade. They are most variable, some growing from fibrous roots, others from runners.

Doronicum excelsum 'Harpur Crewe'.
Leopard's Bane

Heights range from 30–100cm/1–3ft. All species have glorious golden-yellow daisy flowers with brilliantly shining petals, suitable for cutting. To propagate, lift, divide and replant the root masses between autumn and spring every 2–3 years. They can also be raised from seed sown on the surface and left uncovered. Plants should be dead-headed regularly for a second blooming in autumn. Cut back hard in late winter.

DOROTHEANTHUS

(dor-oh-thee-**an**-thəs)
Livingstone Daisy, Mesembryanthemum
AIZOACEAE

Rare among succulents, Livingstone Daisies (*Dorotheanthus bellidiformis*) are genuinely annual and produce a magnificent display

Dorotheanthus bellidiformis. Livingstone Daisy

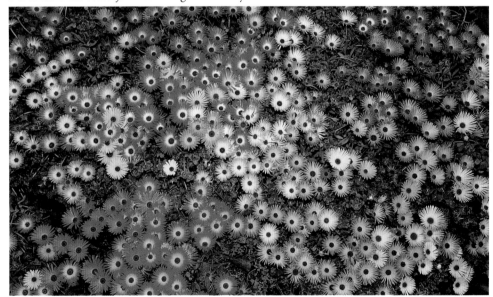

from seed. Their dazzling 3cm/1in flowers range through crimson, purple, pink, apricot, lemon, white, buff and red, centred in a paler tone and with a red eye.

Sow seed in early winter, maintaining a temperature of 18°C/65°F. Do not cover the seed but let it germinate in a dark place – it will take about 15–20 days. After cold snaps are over, plant out at 20cm/8in spacings in poorer than average, well-drained soil. Ideal for seaside gardens because of their salt resistance. Do not over-water.

DORSTENIA

(dor-**steen**-ee-ə)
Counter-herb
MORACEAE

Dorstenia is a genus of evergreen perennials mainly from tropical America, more often grown (and that not very often) for their handsome foliage than for their flowers, strange and interesting though these are. The individual flowers are very tiny and borne on flattened disks, looking just like

Dorstenia turnerifolia. Counter-herb

Doryanthes excelsa. Gymea Lily

what they are – figs opened out flat. But they are definitely not edible! The whole genus (including the species pictured) is poisonous, which will probably cut short their promising career as house plants. Native Americans used the poison of *D. contrajerva* to counteract that of venomous snakes, hence the strange name Counter-herb.

DORYANTHES
(dor-ree-**an**-thƏs)
Gymea Lily, Giant Lily, Spear Lily
AGAVACEAE

Out of bloom, Australia's Gymea Lily (*Doryanthes excelsa*) is a huge clump of up to 100 sword-shaped leaves, 2.5m/8ft long. But in early spring a dramatic change begins to take place. Spear-like spikes shoot up as high as 7m/23ft before bursting into an enormous head of long-lasting red flowers.

Doryanthes prefers semi-shade and a moist, woodsy soil. It makes a striking feature plant. The flowers drip with honey, attracting insects and both insect- and honey-eating birds from far and wide. Fairly slow-growing, Gymea Lilies won't begin to flower until they are well established, which may take up to 10 years. Propagate by seed, division or separation of the suckers which form occasionally.

DRABA
(**drah**-bƏ)
Whitlow Grass
BRASSICACEAE

Such a big genus of such little plants! There are over 300 species of these delightful mat-forming alpine plants, found in cold regions of the northern hemisphere. They love full sun, a soil that's light, sandy (even gravelly)

Dracocephalum nutans. Dragon-head

and moist all year. *Drabas* are happy in the moraine garden, which mimics their natural home. Mostly perennial, they bloom profusely in all hues, often hiding the foliage.

DRACOCEPHALUM
(drak-oh-**kef**-Ə-lƏm)
Dragon-head
LAMIACEAE

Like the previous subject, the many species of *Dracocephalum* are found all around the upper northern hemisphere. There are around 50 species, all members of the great mint family and bearing that family's typical inflorescence, with the flowers arranged in whorls around a stem that produces leaves in opposite pairs.

Draba myrtinensii. Whitlow Grass

Dracunculus vulgaris. Dragon Arum

Grow them from root divisions set out in spring or autumn in a well-drained sandy loam that is both damp and rich. They like a little shade at midday. They'll spread and shoot up as high as 60cm/2ft, doing best in a cool temperate to cold climate. They are ideal for mountain gardens.

DRACUNCULUS
(drak-**unk**-yoo-lƏs)
Dragon Arum, Snake Plant
ARACEAE

The name *Dracunculus* – a little dragon – comes to us from the ancient Romans, and there is something of the surreal about this plant, a common wildflower in Greece and Italy. There is the lizard-skin pattern on the stalks of both leaves and flowers, the intricate design of the many-lobed leaves, and the extraordinary shape and colour of the flower of *D. vulgaris*. There is a rare white version, and *D. canariensis* from the Canary Islands is pale green.

Fascinating plants indeed, provided you hold your nose – the flowers stink! The bright berries that follow in autumn before the plant dies down for the winter are most attractive but dangerously poisonous. Grow them from offsets or seed.

DREGEA
(**drae**-gee-Ə)
(SYN Wattakaka)
Dregea
ASCLEPIADACEAE

Dregea sinensis is a climbing plant from southern China, related to the Hoyas. I photographed it at the Royal Horticultural

Dregea sinensis. Dregea

Society's garden at Wisley, where I was much taken by its lavish display of small star-shaped flowers, hanging in large clusters and looking at a little distance as though they were pale pink. Close inspection revealed that they are white, delicately spotted in red – and pleasantly fragrant. The people at Wisley tell me that given a warm spot it endures the British winter and needs no special care apart from a tidy-up after its summer season is over. In mild-winter climates it is quite vigorous, and I think it deserves more attention there.

DRIMYS
(**drim**-is)
Winter's Bark
WINTERACEAE

Members of this handsome, variable genus of some 30 species are found in Central and South America, in Australasia and Indonesia – but only one tree species, the delightful *Drimys winteri,* from Chile and Argentina, is

Drimys winteri. Winter's Bark

much cultivated. Mildly frost tender, it prefers a moist, coastal climate, but will grow well in a sheltered position in warmer areas given plenty of water. Growing to 15m/50ft in the wild, it will rarely pass half that in cultivation. It is a slender, red-trunked tree that is fragrant in all its parts. It often tends to a multi-trunked habit, but can easily be pruned and trained to a single trunk with gracefully drooping branches.

Both shining, leathery leaves and young, red bark are pleasantly aromatic, while the creamy-white 3cm/1in blossoms are considered to share the fragrance of Jasmine. Each flower has between 6 and 12 petals, and they are borne in long-stalked clusters of 7 or 8 blooms.

DROSANTHEMUM
(droh-**san**-th∂-mum)
Redondo Creeper
AIZOACEAE

Smallest-flowered of the succulent group known as Ice Plants, the dainty Redondo Creeper is also the loveliest, and a very useful groundcover for hot, open places and steep banks. Plant *Drosanthemum candens* 45cm/18in apart and they'll quickly form dense carpets of sparkling grey-green leaves. In late spring or early summer these leaves almost disappear under an icing of delicate pink daisy flowers which bring the bees from near and far. *Drosanthemum* is easily propagated from cuttings struck in pots of sandy soil and the fully grown plants require little or no maintenance. They cannot, however, be walked on, for the juicy leaves just crush into a green pulp.

Drosanthemum candens. Redondo Creeper

DRYANDRA
(drai-**an**-dr∂)
Bush Rose
PROTEACEAE

The Western Australian *Dryandras* include some of the most spectacular blooms in the Protea family. Unfortunately, few of the 60 species can be grown away from their natural conditions of dry heat and sandy soil, but the smaller flowered *D. polycephala* has been grown on Australia's east coast and elsewhere. It must be propagated from seed and should be planted in a sheltered spot and left to its own devices. It cannot abide lime, and does not like cultivation nearby. The 10cm/4in leaves are thin and saw-toothed, the golden flower heads borne both terminally and on laterals. When picked, *Dryandras* last for years, only the foliage fading.

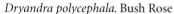

Dryandra polycephala. Bush Rose

Dryandra nobilis. Great Dryandra

Dudleya caespitosa. Chalk Lettuce

Dyckia altissima. Dyckia

Duranta erecta 'Alba'. Pigeon Berry

DUDLEYA

(**dud**-lee-ə)

(SYN Echeveria, Stylophyllum)

Chalk Lettuce, Live Forever

CRASSULACEAE

Native exclusively to the western part of North America and much used in desert gardens there, the genus *Dudleya* includes about 40 species that are highly resistant to both drought and salt spray. They are suitable only for mild to warm temperate climates, and can be rendered quite unsightly by frost, or even a prolonged rainy spell. The oblong leaves (up to 20cm/8in long and a third as wide) are arranged in a rosette and covered with a chalky substance that is easily marked. The multi-branched flower stem (up to 60cm/2ft long) develops in late spring, bearing many scarlet to yellow 5-petalled blooms that never open fully.

DURANTA

(dyoo-**ran**-tə)

Pigeon Berry, Golden Dewdrop, Golden Tears, Sky Flower

VERBENACEAE

A useful, fast-growing shrub, often used as a hedge or windbreak, *Duranta* is attractive at any time of the year. In summer *D. erecta* is speckled all over with thousands of tiny blue-violet flowers. These are soon followed by a spectacular crop of orange berries which persist for months. Unfortunately, the berries are poisonous, the branches spiny. *Durantas* demand only good drainage and prefer a mild climate where temperatures never drop below –2°C/28°F. They are easily propagated from cuttings, either soft-tips taken in spring

Duranta erecta 'Variegata'. Golden Dewdrop

or harder autumn or winter wood. Foliage is plain, dark green but a variegated cultivar makes an attractive change.

DYCKIA

(**dai**-kee-ə)

Dyckia

BROMELIACEAE

A spectacular group of Bromeliads that grow well in the same open, sunny aspect that suits Agaves and Yuccas, the *Dyckias* range from low, creeping groundcovers to 3m/10ft giants. They spread from rhizomes as do Flag Iris and produce dense rosettes of stiff, spiny, succulent leaves. The flower stalks can be single stems or many-branched, in the form of a candelabra. The flowers themselves are orange or yellow and appear in spring. Perfect drainage is vital for success, and regular water is required only in summer. *D. altissima* grows to around 1–1.2m/3–4ft and comes from the drier, elevated parts of Brazil.

Dymondia margaretae. Dymondia

Eccromocarpus scaber. Chilean Glory Flower

Echeveria species. Hen and Chickens

DYMONDIA

(dim-**mon**-dee-∂)

Miniature Gazania

ASTERACEAE

This genus of a single species, *Dymondia margaretae*, was discovered in the mountains of South Africa and named in 1953, but has only become well known in gardens in more recent years. A delightful ground-hugging plant, it has foliage like a Gazania in miniature but the yellow daisy flowers are much smaller and remain half-hidden among the leaves. In open, well-drained soil and with plenty of sun it spreads fairly quickly to make a dense mat up to 60cm/2ft across but only about 2.5cm/1in high, sparsely dotted with flowers in spring – like those of Gazania, they open fully only in sunny weather. *Dymondia* will survive a few degrees of frost, or in cold climates can make an interesting conservatory subject, shown to best advantage in a hanging basket.

ECCREMOCARPUS

(ek-krem-oh-**kah**-p∂s)

(SYN Calampelis)

Chilean Glory Flower

BIGNONIACEAE

A small genus of lightweight climbers from Chile and Peru. Only a couple of species of *Eccremocarpus* are occasionally seen in gardens – *E. scaber,* with red flowers, and *E. longiflorus,* with yellow. They grow fast in any temperate climate, but can be raised as annuals where frost would kill them off. Try in full sun in a well-drained soil that's light but rich, and keep moist during the growing season. They'll need the support of light sticks to twine their way to the main trellis, and bloom through late summer into autumn. Foliage is evergreen, with dainty leaflets; flowers are tubular. They grow sparsely to 3m/10ft.

ECHEVERIA

(ech-e-**ver**-ree-∂)

Echeveria, Mexican Snowball, Hen and Chickens

CRASSULACEAE

Popular rockery plants, for both their spreading rosettes and useful red and yellow winter flowers. The 150 species of *Echeveria* are hard to identify as they hybridise quite indiscriminately, both with each other and with other succulent species. However, they are all among the easiest of succulents to grow, needing only a gritty soil with some rotted organic matter added and a fully sunny position. Drainage must be perfect and the plants should be kept moist during spring to early autumn and fed occasionally with low nitrogen fertiliser. All are native to southwest USA and Mexico, and hardy to just above freezing point.

ECHINACEA

(ek-in-**ae**-see-∂, ek-in-**ae**-sh∂)

Purple Coneflower

ASTERACEAE

Native to the great prairies of North America, the showy Purple Coneflower prefers plenty of sun and thrives in average garden soil with good drainage. It will even tolerate dry conditions and exposure to wind, and should do well both inland and in coastal gardens. Most commonly grown of only three species, *Echinacea purpurea* can be multiplied from autumn divisions, or from winter root-cuttings grown under glass for planting when the weather is warm. Seed is sown indoors in winter, and the 1–1.2m/3–4ft plants will flower late the following season.

Echinacea purpurea. Purple Coneflower

Flowers are produced during summer and regular dead-heading will prolong the display even further. In colder climates the entire plant can be cut back in autumn. Its roots are hardy even to severe frosts.

The dried and powdered rhizome of *E. purpurea* is used in herbal medicine.

ECHINOCACTUS
(ek-**ain**-o-kak-tƏs)
Ball Cactus
CACTACEAE

Echinocactus was once used in a broad sense to include most of the larger ball and barrel cacti of North America, but most of the species have been split off into other genera, such as *Ferocactus*, leaving only six species from southwestern USA and northern Mexico still in *Echinocactus*. Some are small and clustering, others can grow into massive barrel-like plants. A favourite species is the Golden Ball Cactus, *E. grusonii*. Botanical gardens often have it on display as groups of mature plants up to 80cm/32in high and almost as much in diameter, of striking appearance with their regular rows of fierce yellow spines along many vertical ribs. This size takes decades to achieve, but tennis ball-sized plants are readily obtainable and will make steady growth in a hot, sunny position. As long as soil is very open and free-draining, plants will respond to watering and fertilising through summer, and may eventually produce a central cluster of bright yellow flowers.

Echinocactus grusonii. Golden Ball Cactus

ECHINOCEREUS
(ek-in-oh-**see**-ree- Əs)
Hedgehog Cactus, Rainbow Cactus
CACTACEAE

Echinocereus are also known as Hedgehog Cactus or occasionally as Rainbow Cactus because of the brilliance of the flowers in many species. They are ribbed, cylindrical growers, sometimes up to knee-high, and easily grown in standard, well-drained cactus mix. Give them full sun and feed twice monthly with low-nitrogen fertiliser during the growing season. The summer flowers may be white through pink to red-violet and even purple, with several in shades of yellow-green. Hardy down to 10°C/50°F, all species are native to Mexico and southwestern United States.

Echinocereus subinermis. Yellow Hedgehog Cactus

Echinocereus scheeri (red flowers), *E. salmdyckianus* (orange). Rainbow Cactus

Echinops ritro. Globe Thistle

ECHINOPS
(e-**kin**-ops, **ek**-in-ops)
Globe Thistle
ASTERACEAE

Found naturally from the Mediterranean eastwards as far as India, many of the 120-odd species of *Echinops* or Globe Thistles have been tamed to become favourite plants worldwide. Most popular species are the 120cm/4ft *E. bannaticus* from Hungary, and the smaller 60cm/2ft *E. ritro*, which is found in southern Europe and in Asia. Both can be grown from root divisions taken in colder weather, or from seed. *Echinops* like plenty of water over the long summer blooming period, which will be extended if flowers are cut regularly. Those of *E. ritro* have a steely lustre and can be cut and dried for winter decoration. Leaves are thistle-like and downy beneath, and the plants are very drought resistant.

Echinopsis oxygona. Easter-lily Cactus

Echinopsis 'Green Gold'. Sea-urchin Cactus

Echium candicans. Pride of Madeira

Echium wildpretii. Tower of Jewels

ECHINOPSIS

(e-kin-**op**-sis)
Easter-lily Cactus, Sea-urchin Cactus
CACTACEAE

Of all the cactus family, the genus *Echinopsis* must be the richest in delightful garden plants, especially now that the old genera *Lobivia* and *Trichocereus* have been brought under its wing. South American in origin, the species have been much hybridised, and you are as likely to find plants bearing names like 'Princess Diana' as ones in Latin. The hybrids are mainly small plants, quite comfortably accommodated on a windowsill, and range from spherical to shortly columnar in shape. The Greek *echinos* from which the name derives meant either sea-urchin or hedgehog – take your pick!

Boring? Not when they flower – the flowers can be as big as the plant itself, and they come in the most gorgeous colours imaginable. Like all cacti they like rich, perfectly drained soil and sunshine. Water them freely in spring but not at all in winter. If grown in the open rockery, a pebble mulch will prove both beneficial and attractive.

ECHIUM

(ek-ee-ə̀m)
Pride of Madeira, Viper's Bugloss, Paterson's Curse, Blue Devil
BORAGINACEAE

A varied genus including annuals, perennials and shrubs, *Echiums* are native to the Mediterranean, west Asia and some islands of the eastern Atlantic. All are easy to grow, flowering best in poor-quality soil, kept dryish. When the going is rich or damp they bolt to foliage and grow unwieldy. Pride of Madeira, *E. candicans,* is a splendid feature plant in seaside gardens, for its long-pointed, parallel-veined leaves are covered with salt-resistant, silver-silky hairs. Leaves are borne in great profusion all up the rather woody branches, each of which is tipped in late spring and summer with a long panicle of purple-blue bell-shaped flowers, honey-rich and attractive to bees.

Both annual and perennial species are propagated rather too easily from seed sown directly in place – faded flower heads should be pruned before they have a chance to self-seed in every direction.

Australian country gardeners would probably be aghast at the idea of cultivating the lovely annual *E. vulgare,* for its close relative, Paterson's Curse (*E. plantagineum*) is a Mediterranean weed which has taken over huge areas of pasture in its rampantly growing blue-violet form. But *E. vulgare* is a lovely garden plant, particularly in its dwarf, multi-coloured modern forms. Grow in a well-drained, dry area of the garden in full sun. Shrubby *E. wildpretii,* from the Canary Islands, branches freely to form a 3m/10ft softly hairy bush with thick clusters of pale-red flowers appearing over a long period in summer. Propagate by layers or cuttings of firm tips struck in sandy soil. All *Echiums* are frost tender.

EDGEWORTHIA

(edj-**wur**-thee-ə̀)
Paper Bush, Yellow Daphne, Mitsumata
THYMELAEACEAE

Closely related to Daphnes, the Paper Bush, *Edgeworthia,* strongly resembles them except in colour, for the silky grey-green buds open in late winter to reveal snowy 4-petalled blooms lined with rich egg-yolk yellow. Their perfume, too, is equally rich, but the show is brief.

Edgeworthia is deciduous, bursting into leaf as the flowers fade. The foliage is crowded mostly towards the ends of branches, which are so flexible they can be knotted without

Edgeworthia gardneri. Paper Bush

breaking. *Edgeworthia* is frost hardy only in sheltered positions and must be grown in well-drained, acid soil, where it can reach a height and spread of 2m/6ft. Plenty of summer water is needed and propagation is from cuttings struck in sand under glass, or by layering. The tough and fibrous plant was once used for papermaking in Japan.

EDRAIANTHUS
(ed-rae-**an**-thəs)
(SYN Wahlenbergia)
Rock Bluebell, Grassy Bells
CAMPANULACEAE

These tiny relatives of the stately Campanulas are sometimes listed as Wahlenbergia – though in Australia that name is reserved for the wiry-stemmed Austral Bluebells (see Wahlenbergia). All species of *Edraianthus* are perennial, though

Edraianthus dinaricus. Rock Bluebell

short lived. They grow only inches high, and are found naturally in Europe's mountainous Balkan peninsula, where they send their stout roots down into the rich soil of rock crevices. Preferring a cool climate, they need full sun to produce an absolute profusion of bell-shaped blue flowers during spring and summer. Their foliage is greyish and grass-like, and more profuse where limestone chips are present.

EICHHORNIA
(aikh-**hor**-nee-ə)
Water Hyacinth
PONTEDERIACEAE

This unusual floating aquatic plant is native to tropical America but has become natu-ralised in many warm countries, with disas-trous results for lakes and streams. Grow only where it can be controlled and *never* in open watercourses, for the plants, kept afloat by bladder-like stems, multiply at an aston-ishing rate, quickly choking large areas. It is a declared pest in many parts of Australia and cannot even be grown in home ponds. Where it is legal, it makes a charming pool plant bearing spikes of gold-spotted mauve flowers all summer. Cold nights quickly kill it, but a couple overwintered indoors will soon multiply in spring.

Eichhornia crassipes. Water Hyacinth

ELAEAGNUS
(el-ee-**ag**-nəs)
Wild Olive, Silverberry
ELAEAGNACEAE

Known commonly for its many shrubby species, the genus *Elaeagnus* also includes several flowering trees, notably *E. angustifolia*, the Oleaster, and *E. umbellata*, the Chinese Silverberry or Wild Olive. This is a hand-some, spreading tree with a silver-scaled effect on both young wood and leaf reverses. In spring, clusters of creamy, tubular flowers

Elaeagnus umbellata. Chinese Silverberry

spread fragrance all around. These are followed by tiny fruits, which also have a silver-scaly appearance until they ripen to pink. It is found naturally from the Himalayas to Japan.

Of the shrubby species, *E. pungens* is one of the most popular. Evergreen, it forms a dense, horizontally inclined bush 4x6m/13x20ft at most. The wavy-edged leaves are shiny, dark green above and silvery-white beneath, though there are cultivars with variegated foliage. Cream flowers appear from late summer and are pleasantly perfumed.

Elaeocarpus reticulatus. Blueberry Ash

ELAEOCARPUS
(el-ae-oh-**kar**-pəs)
Blueberry Ash, Hinau, Silver Quandong
ELAEOCARPACEAE

Elaeocarpus is a genus of 200-odd evergreen warm-climate and tropical flowering trees of Asia and Australasia. Mostly slender, graceful and rather slow-growing at the outset, they bear laurel-like leaves, sometimes toothed. The fragrant flowers are borne in small sprays like lily-of-the-valley. They are usually white or pink and most delicately fringed.

Embothrium coccineum. Chilean Firebush

This spring display is followed by a heavy crop of brilliant blue fruits which persist into winter.

Species in cultivation include: *E. dentatus*, New Zealand's Hinau, with pale yellow flowers; *E. grandis*, the Silver Quandong from eastern Australia, with creamy flowers; and the Blueberry Ash, *E. reticulatus*, with pink or white blossom.

EMBOTHRIUM
(em-**both**-ree-əm)
Chilean Firebush
PROTEACEAE

This rather large evergreen shrub from Chile suckers heavily, and will in time develop into a dense planting up to 5m/16ft tall. It demands a loose, peaty soil that is either neutral or acid, and will not tolerate lime or animal manures. Its propagation is not easy as cuttings do not seem to strike; so the slower alternative of seed should be sown early spring in a standard seed-raising mix. Prick out into individual pots when large enough, and grow on for 2 years before finally setting out in spring. Suckers from a large plant can also be severed and grown on. A member of the Protea family, *Embothrium* bears leathery, spear-shaped leaves and produces startling racemes of tubular orange-scarlet flowers over a few weeks in late spring and early summer. Strictly for the cooler climate, *Embothrium* is fairly hardy but appreciates shelter from strong winds.

Emilia coccinea. Flora's Paintbrush

EMILIA
(em-il-ee-ə)
Tassel Flower, Flora's Paintbrush, Cacalia
ASTERACEAE

Found naturally right round the tropics of both hemispheres, the showy Tassel Flower, *Emilia coccinea*, takes to culture in almost any climate and adds a dazzling splash of colour to annual displays. It is a member of the daisy family that went slightly wrong, as the gaudy orange-scarlet flowers never open fully, remaining like clusters of blazing tassels atop wiry 45cm/18in stems.

The plants from which these spring are simple rosettes of arrow-shaped leaves that enjoy crowding in sandy soil in sun. Well fed and watered, *Emilias* will keep blooming away just as long as you dead-head spent flower stems. They make useful cut flowers and may be dried for more permanent arrangements.

Emilia is widely naturalised in warm climates and there is a hybrid, 'Lutea', which has yellow flowers, as well as many variations between.

ENKIANTHUS
(en-kee-**an**-thəs)
(SYN Melidora)
Chinese Bellflower
ERICACEAE

Grow Azaleas and Ericas and you can grow the dainty bellflower *Enkianthus*, a slow-moving lover of semi-shaded places where acid to neutral soil is rich in leafmould and always well drained. A background of evergreen shrubbery helps disguise the rather spidery habit and accent the pale flowers

Enkianthus quinqueflorus. Chinese Bellflower

which appear in spring and again in autumn. *Enkianthus* species are hardy down to –8ºC/17ºF, and do best in country gardens, for they resent air pollution. Most species are deciduous; they grow 1–2m/3–6ft tall and in cooler areas the sharply pointed leaves colour brilliantly in autumn. The lightly fragrant bell-flowers, like lilies-of-the-valley, hang from a slender stem.

Propagate *Enkianthus* from seed, or from autumn cuttings of lateral shoots taken with a heel. Dip in hormone powder and strike in a standard sand/peat mix under glass. Flowers may be white, pink, red or green.

EPACRIS
(e-**pak**-ris)
Australian Heath, Native Fuchsia
EPACRIDACEAE

Ideal plants for a sunny or lightly shaded rockery, this Australian genus of 40-odd species includes some extremely showy shrubs. All *Epacris* need perfectly drained, acid, sandy soil, kept consistently moist. This

Epacris impressa. Australian Heath

can be achieved by laying flat stones around the plant, providing a cool, moist root-run. Cutting flower stems encourages dense, bushy growth and many more blooms the following year.

Seed is hard to germinate; semi-hardwood cuttings taken in summer to strike in moist, sandy soil are the best method of increase.

E. impressa is a straggly shrub to 1m/3ft, greatly improved by pruning. Flowering occurs throughout the year but mostly in spring. *E. microphylla* is smaller and more open, with pretty white starry flowers most of the year.

EPIDENDRUM
(ep-i-**den**-drəm)
Crucifix Orchid, Baby Orchid
ORCHIDACEAE

Epidendrums form a large and widely variable genus of the orchid family, and their name means simply 'upon a tree'. Beyond the fact that they all originate in the tropical Americas, they differ more widely among themselves than any other orchid group. The vast majority are specialist plants. The minority group with which we are concerned are the Crucifix Orchids, *E. radicans*. These send up tall, leafy cane-like stems, supported by worm-shaped aerial roots. The stems may ultimately reach 2.5m/8ft in frost-free gardens. Where winters are cold the plants are grown in large containers with the support of a wire frame. The small flowers are produced in a cluster at the end of each stem and open progressively for many months in warm weather. Thanks to the work of hybridists, they are available in many shades of red, pink, orange, yellow, white and mauve.

Epidendrum radicans. Crucifix Orchid

Epilobium angustifolium. Fireweed, Willow Herb

EPILOBIUM
(ep-ə-**loh**-bee-əm)
Fireweed, French Willow, Willow Herb
ONAGRACEAE

Rather invasive, *Epilobiums* are native to the northern hemisphere, with a few outliers in New Zealand and Australia. Most widely seen is lovely *E. angustifolium* whose popularity can best be judged by its wide range of popular names, those above being just a few.

Plant from divisions, from grown-on cuttings of spring basal shoots, or from spring-sown seed which should be pricked out after germination and set in final position in autumn. Any light, well-drained soil suits, and regular water is a necessity. The 1–2m/3–6ft stems, clothed in willowy foliage, are topped in summer with terminal racemes of open, rose-pink flowers like Evening Primroses, to which they are related.

Epimedium youngianum. Bishops' Hats

EPIMEDIUM
(ep-i-**mee**-dee-əm)
Bishops' Hats, Barrenwort
BERBERIDACEAE

Hardy dwarf perennials, the 30-odd species of *Epimedium* are evergreen, make a charming display most of the year, differing in every season. They grow from spreading underground roots which send up the foliage on wiry stems in early spring. Leaves of the hybrid *E. youngianum* are prickly edged and brightly marked with red. In late spring, when bright green, they are joined by wiry, compact stems of tiny white or pink flowers – something like miniature daffodils. In autumn, the leaves turn orange and red. Plant from spring or autumn divisions, or sow seed in summer soon after ripening. Old or damaged leaves should be removed in spring to accent the flower display. Mature plants are 20cm/8in tall and at least as wide.

EPIPHYLLUM
(e-pi-**fil**-ləm)
Orchid Cactus
CACTACEAE

No plant collection should be without the gorgeous Orchid Cacti, which are incredibly easy to grow in a rich, fast-draining compost. They strike easily from severed branchlets of the flattened stems and should be grown in heavy pots or hanging baskets. Given semi-shade and plenty of water and humidity in summer, they'll survive temperatures of 2ºC/36ºF.

In nature, *Epiphyllums* are usually night flowering, but they have been crossed with other genera to produce daytime flowers as

Epiphyllum oxypetalum. Belle de Nuit

Eranthemum pulchellum. Blue Sage

Epiphyllum 'Pink Nymph'. Orchid Cactus

Episcia dianthiflora. Lace Flower Vine

ERANTHEMUM
(e-**ran**-thәm-әm)
Blue Sage, Limeng-sugat, Guerit Petit
ACANTHACEAE

This charming evergreen shrub from Southeast Asia is easy to grow anywhere the minimum day temperature stays above 10ºC/50ºF. It has handsome, heavily veined leaves and pushes ahead from spring cuttings rooted in a glass of water. For maximum display, plant several cuttings as a clump in a leaf-rich well-drained soil with a dressing of manure. Fertilise every 3 months; keep up the water in warm weather, tapering off until flowering is over, after which you can prune heavily, resting them until late spring. The purple-eyed blue flowers appear in long terminal spikes from among pale green bracts. *E. pulchellum* grows 60–100cm/2–3ft and prefers dappled shade. It makes a good container plant.

well. These are unbelievably beautiful – up to 23cm/9in across with iridescent petals in a wide spectrum of colours. Some are entrancingly perfumed. The night-flowering species *E. oxypetalum* is one of the easiest to grow; its giant flowers unfurl on summer nights, spreading their fragrance all around.

EPISCIA
(e-**pis**-kee-ә)
Flame Violet, Carpet Plant
GESNERIACEAE

Another dazzling group of Gesneriads, the *Episcias* are jungle dwellers that revel in humidity. Grow them outdoors in humid, frost-free or tropical gardens or in warm, bright rooms elsewhere. They'll do best in pots of peaty, porous soil where they can trail about and hang over the edge. If you can keep up the warmth (15ºC/59ºF minimum) they'll keep going throughout winter, otherwise get new plants for old from cuttings or divisions in spring.

E. cupreata 'Acajou' is a 40cm/16in mound of big, dark green leaves, handsomely marked in silver, topped in summer with bright red flowers. *E. dianthiflora* produces long, trailing stems of velvety leaves, interspersed in summer with charming fragrant white flowers.

Episcia cupreata 'Acajou'. Flame Violet

Eranthis hyemalis. Winter Aconite

ERANTHIS
(e-**ran**-this)
Winter Aconite
RANUNCULACEAE

Dwarf relatives of Ranunculus from the fast-disappearing wilds of southern Europe and Asia, the pretty little Winter Aconites are rarely seen away from cold-winter areas, where they burst into glowing, golden bloom at the first sign of spring – sometimes even in the middle of a mild winter. Plant from divisions of the tubers, which can be lifted during summer dormancy, setting the segments 2cm/1in deep beneath deciduous trees or in shallow rockery pockets where they'll get full winter sun. The light green leaves are much-divided, and surround the open blooms like an Elizabethan ruff. They're frost hardy, and like damp, fast-draining soil.

Eremophila maculata. Emu Bush

Eremophila sturtii. Poverty Bush

EREMOPHILA
(e-re-**mof**-fil-ə)
Emu Bush, Poverty Bush
MYOPORACEAE

Found exclusively in Australia, many of the 180-odd species of *Eremophila* have been exported to other drought-prone areas, producing an invaluable display where almost nothing else will grow. They are quite drought resistant, adore hot dry climates and reward a minimum of care with a welcome sprinkling of flowers at any time of the year. Drainage must be perfect (especially in well-watered gardens), and best growth will occur in very sandy, just-alkaline soil.

Eremophilas come in all sizes, with flowers in many different colours, but the most attractive and typical species are spreading bushes with grey-green, lightly haired foliage and tubular heath-type flowers of vivid scarlet. *Eremophilas* grow easily from cuttings taken with a heel in autumn and struck in a sharp sandy mix. Grow on for a year or two before planting out. Water sparingly if at all.

EREMURUS
(er-em-**yoo**-rəs)
Foxtail Lily, Giant Asphodel
LILIACEAE

The 50-odd species of *Eremurus* are not seen as often as they deserve, for the 2m/6ft spikes of flowers make a fine display in any garden. They like full sun, well-drained soil and must not be disturbed by deep digging or unnecessary lifting, as the fleshy roots break easily. Flower colours are yellow, pink and white; the illustrated species *E. robustus* may bear 100 or more peach-tinted blossoms on a single stem. They look best against a background of dark foliage; flower stems need staking. *Eremurus* are generally hardy in cold winters of the northern USA provided the roots are protected by a layer of mulch.

Eremurus robustus. Foxtail Lily

ERICA
(**er**-ik-ə, e-**rik**-ə)
Heath, Heather
ERICACEAE

A most variable shrub genus, the *Ericas* include 700-odd species, all but 30 of them from South Africa. They are beautiful, extraordinarily floriferous evergreen plants with some species in bloom at any time of the year.

Erica arborea var. *alpina.* Alpine Tree Heath

Erica cerinthoides. Fire Heath

Erica vagans 'Lyonesse'. Cornish Heath

They are also, with rare exceptions, extraordinarily fussy plants, with a very pronounced group of likes and dislikes. For this reason, in European gardens, they are usually grown on their own in raised beds sited in full sun. The beds are raised because *Ericas* must have the perfect drainage of their native mountainsides. The ideal growing medium will be slightly acid, porous yet water-retentive. A good mix consists of two parts fibrous peat and one part silver sand. They cannot abide lime or any type of animal manure and are best kept moist with pure, unpolluted water. They need constant moisture and a year-round mulch of pebbles or other lime-free material. Most species can be raised easily (if slowly) from seed – though plants are unlikely to come true if you grow more than one species. The practical gardener will propagate them from 2cm/ 1in tip-cuttings taken in autumn or early winter and struck in a constantly moist sand/peat mix.

Species vary widely in both habit and height, from *E. vagans* 'Lyonesse' (a 50cm/20in spreading mound) to *E. arborea* (a 4.5m/14ft tree-like plant) and *E. regia*, a 2m/6ft bushy shrub. All have small linear or needle-leaves and flowers that are either tubular or bell-shaped. These are slightly fragrant en masse and much liked by bees.

Erica hybrida. Hybrid Cape Heath

Erica regia. Elim Heath

Erigeron pulchellus. Midsummer Aster

Eriocephalus africanus. Wild Rosemary

ERIGERON

(e-**rij**-er-ən)

Fleabane, Midsummer Aster, Vittadenia

ASTERACEAE

Showy *Erigerons* differ from other daisy genera in surrounding their compound flower heads with two or more rows of fine, thread-like petals. The most popular species for perennial border work are all North American, relatively low-growing plants that quickly form large clumps from division in autumn or early spring. Prairie plants, they prefer a sandy, light-textured soil of average to poor quality. They also need regular water and good drainage.

The most popular bedding species is *E. speciosus,* from the western United States,

where it is often called the Midsummer Aster. It has many colour varieties including pale and deep pink, pale blue, mauve and purple. *Erigerons* make good cut flowers and bloom prolifically when regularly dead-headed. In cold areas they should be cut back to ground level in late autumn; where the climate is more temperate they will remain evergreen.

Mexican *E. karvinskianus* is different altogether, blooming year-round in warmer climates. It is a wiry, subshrubby sort of plant, spreading widely. The 2cm/1in flowers open white then change first to pink and finally to wine red. Useful for groundcover or rockery work, it should be cut back hard from time to time.

ERIOCEPHALUS

(e-ree-oh-**kef**-a-ləs)

Wild Rosemary, Kapok Bush

ASTERACEAE

South Africa's *Eriocephalus* species are members of the daisy family, though they don't much look like it. The commonly seen species, *E. africanus,* is a dwarf shrub 50–100cm/20–40in tall but usually spreading much wider. It likes sandy acid soil, full sun and will even stand a certain amount of frost in a sheltered position. Useful at the seaside, it is also drought tolerant.

Grow it from cuttings of young shoots and give room to spread. Its needle-like leaves are silky, the late winter flowers white with gold or purple centres, and borne for quite a few weeks in dense terminal umbels. They are quite fragrant, and after bloom the seed heads expand into woolly balls that are sometimes dried for decoration. Prune occasionally to restore a neat shape.

ERIOGONUM

(e-ree-oh-**goh**-nəm)

St Catherine's Lace, Umbrella Plant

POLYGONACEAE

Useful little plants for arid places in cool temperate climates, the many species of *Eriogonum* flower naturally in mountainous regions of western America, principally California. They abhor humidity and wet winters, but protect themselves against dry cold with a dense, woolly covering. Grow from seed in dry, gravelly soil of a rockery

Erigeron speciosus. Quaker Daisy

Erigeron karvinskianus. Vittadenia, Santa Barbara Daisy

Eriogonum umbellatum var. *torreyanum.* Woolflower

Erodium reichardii. Stork's Bill

Eryngium bourgatii. Sea Holly

pocket – water very lightly until established. Alternatively, try divisions taken in autumn. The plants grow 30–100cm/1–3ft in height according to variety, and bear attractive grey-green foliage in whorls. Tiny flowers appear in dense clusters – yellow in almost every species.

ERIOSTEMON
(er-ee-**oss**-tem-∂n, er-ee-oh-**stem**-∂n)
Waxflower, Native Daphne
RUTACEAE

There are 30-odd species of the delightful Waxflowers in Australia, but the favourite by far is *Eriostemon myoporoides*. At a distance, it resembles the Asiatic Daphnes, but the leaves are narrower and the flowers not as fragrant, though they do have a sharp, citrus perfume.

E. *australasius*, the Pink Waxflower, is a taller, more open shrub, to 2m/6ft. Its pink flowers are larger, too, and abundantly produced from late winter into spring. *Eriostemons* can be grown from seed soaked for 24 hours before sowing, or from semi-hardwood cuttings taken in autumn. They are all susceptible to root rot and need perfect drainage.

Eriostemon australasius. Pink Waxflower

ERODIUM
(e-**roh**-dee-∂m)
Stork's Bill, Alpine Geranium
GERANIACEAE

Less commonly grown than their close relatives the Geraniums and Pelargoniums, 60-odd species of *Erodium* are for the most part dwarf rockery plants from alpine areas of all continents except the Americas. They grow best in slightly alkaline, well-drained soil, and you can raise them from seed or 5cm/2in root-cuttings taken in spring. These should be grown in a tray of damp soil until 3 or 4 leaves have formed, after which they can be set out in a sun-drenched rock pocket. Slow-growing, they'll ultimately produce dainty 5-petalled flowers from spring to autumn. The long, pointed seed heads do resemble a stork's head and bill.

Eriostemon myoporoides. Native Daphne

ERYNGIUM
(e-**rin**-gee-∂m)
Eryngo, Sea Holly
APIACEAE

Spiky, formidable-looking members of the carrot family, the *Eryngiums* or Sea Hollies are found on every continent, but most cultivated species come from Europe or North America. Valued for their interesting foliage and their spiny-collared blooms, which have a bluish metallic sheen, all can be grown from winter root-cuttings planted under glass until they produce foliage. These are planted out the following autumn. Seed sprouts in 5–10 days when sown at a temperature of 24ºC/75ºF. *Eryngiums* prefer sandy, well-drained soil, and with light but regular water may reach 60cm/2ft.

The long flowering period begins in summer and stems may be cut and dried for winter decoration indoors. Handle cautiously! The spines are very sharp.

ERYSIMUM
(e-**riss**-i-m∂m)
(SYN Cheiranthus)
Blister Cress, Treacle Mustard, Wallflower
BRASSICACEAE

The popular names of these interesting perennials and annuals remind us that they once had medicinal uses as counter-irritants. There are about 80 species found in all parts of the northern hemisphere, where they thrive in areas with poor soil. In the garden, given a well-drained, average, even slightly alkaline loam with regular water, they'll turn on a dazzling display for months on end, starting in spring.

Erysimum cheiri. Annual Wallflower

Erysimum perofskianum. Treacle Mustard

Erythrina crista-galli. Cockscomb Coral Tree

Perennial and shrubby species can be anything from 15–60cm/6–24in tall and are propagated from heeled cuttings taken in summer. They can also be raised from seed; the seedlings are planted out in autumn in milder areas or early spring where the winters are cold. Once established, they self-seed freely, returning reliably year after year.

Annual wallflowers (formerly Cheiranthus, now *Erysimum cheiri*) are available in many rich new shades of gold and red as well as older colours of yellow, orange and brown. They are as fragrant as ever, but now blooms are larger and more profuse. Their peak display is still late winter and spring, but the blooming range can be extended to include summer and autumn in milder climates. Good drainage, rich soil and full sun are needed in winter; semi-shade in summer.

Erysimum 'Bowles' Mauve'. Blister Cress

Erysimum mutabilis. Madeira Wallflower

ERYTHRINA

(e-rith-**rai**-n∂)
Coral Tree, Tiger Claw, Kaffirboom
FABACEAE

There are some who say the gaudy *Erythrinas* make an appropriate floral symbol for Los Angeles – all show and magnificence on top, they stand on a rather shaky foundation. For *Erythrinas* really are pretty vulnerable. Their wood is poor, weak stuff. The trees are likely to drop a branch without notice, or fall over

Erythrina speciosa. Coral Tree

Erythrina vespertilio. Batswing Coral Tree

in a high wind. At any rate, Los Angeles has adopted them, though none is native, and they are planted widely there.

Coming from many warm temperate and tropical areas of the world, they are mostly gnarled and rugged-looking trees with vicious thorns. They enjoy a climate on the warm, dry side, but seem indifferent to winter cold short of frost. The flowers are mostly brilliant scarlet, in some species shading to crimson or orange; many flower in midwinter when the trees are bare of foliage.

The ubiquitous Indian Coral Bean, *E. sykesii* (syn *E. indica*), can be struck from large branches as an 'instant tree', but is just as likely to fall over without protection from windy weather. Its large, heart-shaped leaves give wonderful summer shade.

Leaves of the Variegated Tiger Claw, *E. variegata* 'Parcellii', are strongly marked in yellow.

Erythrina variegata 'Parcellii'. Variegated Tiger Claw

Erythrorchis cassythoides. Climbing Orchid

Escallonia exoniensis. Pink Escallonia

The picturesque *E. crista-galli*, or Cockscomb Coral Tree, will in time develop a wonderfully gnarled trunk, but needs annual pruning back to the main branches. It bears spring spikes of scarlet-to-crimson pea-blossoms at branch ends, and self-seeds rather too freely.

E. caffra, the Kaffirboom from South Africa, makes a tall, handsome foliage tree and is deservedly popular. Its flowers are vermilion, borne in rounded clusters.

The Batswing Coral Tree, *E. vespertilio*, bears trifoliate leaves (that do resemble a bat's wing when seen at an angle) and salmon-pink flowers.

ERYTHRONIUM
(e-rith-**roh**-nee-əm)
Dog-tooth Violet
LILIACEAE

The dog's tooth of the popular name refers to the shape of the bulb rather than the flower. *Erythronium dens-canis* is the only

Erythronium dens-canis. Dog-tooth Violet

widely cultivated species of many from all over the northern hemisphere. The bulbs are planted 8–13cm/3–5in deep in autumn in part or full shade in well-drained soil, rich in rotted organic matter. The 5cm/2in mauve and white flowers appear in early spring, and the entire plant dies down to rest in summer. *Erythroniums* can be increased by seed or offsets from the mother bulb. Clumps can be left undisturbed for years.

ERYTHRORCHIS
(e-rith-**ror**-kis)
(SYN Galeola, Ledgeria)
Climbing Orchid
ORCHIDACEAE

I should warn those of you who may take a fancy to this strange plant – nobody has yet figured out how to grow or bloom an *Erythrorchis* in cultivation. Occasionally found anywhere on the east coast of New South Wales and southern Queensland, it is a

saprophyte, depending for its very life on a symbiotic root fungus found only in rotting vegetation. A kind friend led me to a headland of Sydney Harbour some years ago, where it had appeared almost overnight. I was amazed to see a tangle of reddish-brown leafless stems twisting every which way on a pile of rotting teatree brush, to which it was attached by adventitious roots. Generally, *Erythrorchis* grows in semi-shade, and produces hundreds of dainty, soft golden orchid flowers in spring. These are faintly fragrant, resembling upside-down Cattleyas.

ESCALLONIA
(es-kal-**loh**-nee-ə)
Escallonia
SAXIFRAGACEAE

All but one of 60 *Escallonia* species are evergreen and come from Chile or Brazil.

Sturdy, glossy-leaved shrubs, hardy to –9°C/15°F, they enjoy a well-drained but compost-rich soil and plenty of moisture in summer. They are best propagated from 10cm/4in cuttings of half-ripe, non-flowered shoots taken with a heel in late summer.

A light pruning to remove spent flowerheads is advisable, though they can be pruned more heavily if you are prepared to sacrifice many flowers. These vary from white to red, are lightly fragrant and borne in terminal, hanging clusters.

Eschscholzia californica. California Poppy

Eschscholzia cultivar. California Poppy

ESCHSCHOLZIA
(esh-**sholt**-zee-ə)
California Poppy, Calce de Oro
PAPAVERACEAE

Brilliant California Poppies are hard to transplant, so should be sown directly where they are to grow. But they readily make up for this early inconvenience by germinating in about 10 days, provided the temperature remains a regular 13°C/55°F. So broadcast the seed in bed, rockery or container in earliest spring (even autumn in frost-free areas). No fancy soil preparation is needed; just loosen up the surface of any well-drained, dryish spot and scatter seed mixed with a little sand to help it spread. Follow up with a light watering and then sit back and wait for results. Thin out the seedlings when they appear, maintaining a spacing of about 20cm/8in, and scatter a little snail bait – the finely cut, fern-like foliage attracts them.

Eschscholzia caespitosa. Amapola del Campo

The 30cm/12in mature plants are very decorative mounds of grey-green leaves even before they commence sending up flower stems as high again. Bloom starts in about 8 weeks from plant emergence and, once sown, they are inclined to naturalise from seed in the most unlikely places; patches of them can often be found blazing away along country roadsides. Although *Eschscholzias* will survive without distress in semi-shaded places, they prefer full sun, being native to the dry and sunny coastal hills of California.

The natural colour of the species *E. californica* is a satiny orange, but many colour varieties and forms have been discovered and hybridised for today's garden beauties. California's state flower now comes in shades of gold, bronze, yellow, cream, deep red, rose-pink and scarlet as well, with some cultivars edged or splashed with contrasting tones.

A dwarf species, *E. caespitosa*, is also available for rockery and alpine garden work. Its popular name is Amapola del Campo (Field Poppy) and it rarely passes 12cm/5in in height. The 4-petalled flowers are pale, clear yellow.

ETLINGERA
(et-lin-ger-ə)
Torch Ginger, Rose de Porcelaine, Philippine Waxflower
ZINGIBERACEAE

One of the most splendid flowers in the world, Indonesia's Torch Ginger has become an outstanding feature in tropical gardens everywhere.

Walking among a well-grown clump is like a trip through an exotic jungle, for here and there you will find tall, cane-like stems bearing fantastic 25cm/10in flowers that bear an extraordinary likeness to Australia's Waratah (see Telopea). Like that totally unrelated plant, they are a cone-shaped mass of bracts (in the case of *Etlingera elatior*, formerly *Nicolaia elatior*, red, with white margins). The real flowers appear from among these and several of them, scarlet with a gold edge, can be seen in our picture. The inflorescences of the Torch Ginger are approximately the size of a pineapple, which their fruit cluster does indeed resemble. They are borne on 1.5m/5ft stalks, the leaf stems developing separately to a height of 6m/20ft.

Far from the tropics, *Etlingera* grows only in the largest heated greenhouses.

Etlingera elatior. Torch Ginger

(yoo-**an**-thee)
Euanthe
ORCHIDACEAE

There is only one species, *Euanthe sanderiana* from the Philippines, but that is one of the most glorious and important of all orchids. A magnificent flower in its own right, it is even more important as the parent of innumerable beautiful hybrids with various species of *Vanda*, from which genus it is separated only by very minor differences in the structure of the labellum (lip). Its hybrids (classed as Vandas) inherit its beautiful shape and rich colouring. It is grown in exactly the same way as Vandas are.

Euanthe 'Nellie Morley' is derived mainly from *E. sanderiana*.

EUCALYPTUS
(yoo-ka-**lip**-təs)
Eucalypt, Gum Tree
MYRTACEAE

In Australia, the ubiquitous Gum Tree is king. The great bulk of the continent's natural tree life consists of one or another of the 700 and more recorded species of *Eucalyptus*. Often localised by species, the Gums as a group are highly adaptable and now dominate every type of environment except rainforests and true deserts.

Eucalypts were one of Australia's earliest exports, and these days you'll find them all over California, in Israel, in north, east and southern Africa, all about the Mediterranean and on islands as far apart as Hong Kong and Hawaii.

Their flower display is often quite stunning, though somewhat irregular, and the range of colour goes all the way from crimson

Euanthe 'Nellie Morley'. Hybrid Euanthe

through scarlet to palest pink, from white through yellow to orange, though cream is the most common by far. Species from the drier central and western regions generally produce the most vividly coloured flowers but the plants themselves are often low, straggly shrubs or small, crooked trees. There are exceptions, of course, such as *E. ficifolia*, which can grow into a handsome broad-crowned tree, 10m/35ft tall, producing one of the most spectacular displays of the whole genus; it thrives in California's dry heat but doesn't take to the moist, acid soils of the east coast of its homeland.

E. caesia is a slim, pendulous, small tree to around 5m/16ft; it looks best if forced to form several trunks from an early age and prefers acid soil and light to moderate rainfall. The cool-season flowers can be pink or red, and are pretty rather than spectacular.

E. rhodantha, the Rose Mallee, is an open, rather straggly shrub with blue-grey, roundish leaves, but its flowers are among the largest in the genus. They can be 8cm/3in across and are usually bright red and gold, appearing in flushes throughout the year. *E. macrocarpa*, the Rose of the West, has the largest and most spectacular flowers of all. They are brilliant red, tipped gold, can be 10cm/4in across and are set off beautifully against the silvery leaves.

Eucalyptus caesia. Gungunnu

Eucalyptus microcorys. Tallow-wood

Eucalyptus erythrocorys. Illyarie

Eucalyptus calophylla × *ficifolia*. Pink Flowering Gum

Eucalyptus ficifolia. Red Flowering Gum

Eucalyptus macrocarpa. Rose of the West

Eucharis amazonica. Amazon Lily

E. erythrocorys can be a handsome, small tree on dryish, alkaline soils. Its autumn display is dramatic, the distinctive red buds contrasting with brilliant yellow open flowers. *E. microcorys* hails from the wet, eastern forests and grows into a tall, straight feature tree. Its flowers are typically cream and make a pretty display from late winter into spring. Other good species include *E. calophylla*, a 20m/65ft tree with pink or white flowers in late summer; *E. camaldulensis*, a grand, imposing tree periodically dusted with cream flowers; *E. eximia*, with striking clusters of cream flowers against dense, rich green foliage; *E. pauciflora*, from the alpine areas, is one of the few gums that can withstand ice and snow. Picturesquely crooked, it flowers profusely in summer.

Eucomis comosa. Pineapple Lily

EUCHARIS

(**yoo**-kə-ris)
Amazon Lily

Amaryllidaceae

The magnificent Amazon Lily can be flowered up to 4 times per year if you ensure summer humidity, a minimum temperature of 10ºC/50ºF and dryish rest periods between bursts of bloom. If that is beyond you, keep it dryish and above freezing point in winter; increase water and fertiliser as the weather warms and you should get a fine crop of summer flowers. Grow in well-drained peaty compost, with extra quantities of sand, leafmould and manure, or in large pots if winter temperatures ever fall below freezing. Flowers of *Eucharis amazonica* are sweet-smelling, and resemble snow-white daffodils with lime green markings.

EUCOMIS

(**yoo**-kə-mis)
Pineapple Lily

Liliaceae

The Pineapple Lily, *Eucomis comosa*, is an unusual plant in or out of bloom. In autumn it sends up 60cm/2ft cylindrical purple-spotted stems bearing hundreds of greenish flowers, sometimes tinged with mauve. And to top them all off is a tuft of leaves just like a

Eupatorium megalophyllum. Mist Flower

Eucryphia lucida. Tasmanian Leatherwood

pineapple top. The flowers last for weeks, even when cut for indoor use. Set out bulbs in early spring for autumn flowers, and be sure to plant them in a group for striking effect most of the year.

They prefer full sun and should be left alone for years. Being South African natives, they are not hardy where the ground freezes but can be grown in pots.

EUCRYPHIA
(yoo-**krif**-ee-ə)
Leatherwood
EUCRYPHIACEAE

Separated by the vastness of the Pacific Ocean, there are about four natural species of the elegant *Eucryphia* – two in Chile, one each in Tasmania and mainland Australia. These are the only plants in their family. You may know the Tasmanian species as the source of delicious Leatherwood honey, but in a cool temperate climate they are worth growing for the beauty of their flowers alone. Hardy down to at least –5°C/23°F, they enjoy a sun-dappled sheltered spot in leaf-rich soil. They can be grown from ripe seed or from summer cuttings taken with a heel and struck in sandy compost. In suitably cool, moist places, or in mountain gardens, they may grow to 7m/23ft, spreading about one-third as wide. Flowers are 6cm/2½in across.

Euonymus japonicus 'Aureopictus'. Japanese Spindle Bush

EUONYMUS
(yoo-**on**-e-məs)
Spindle Bush
CELASTRACEAE

Quite a large genus, *Euonymus* includes some 170-odd species from almost all continents, mostly shrubs, but a few lightweight trees and climbers are included – both deciduous and evergreen. They are grown only in cool temperate climates, where they produce a vivid display of autumn colour, both from their foliage and from long-stemmed, spindle-shaped fruits which last through winter. Often used as decorative background 'greenery', they are rarely planted for their flower

display – yet evergreen *E. japonicus* 'Aureopictus' produces quite a respectable show of tiny white blooms, rather like privet.

Propagate them from ripe seed, or semi-hardwood cuttings struck in early summer. Keep moist, and prune lightly to keep compact. *Euonymus* make splendid hedges, especially in windy areas. Plant in deep, well-drained soil.

EUPATORIUM
(yoo-pa-**tor**-ee-əm)
(SYN Hebeclinium)
Mist Flower, Thoroughwort, Boneset
ASTERACEAE

A genus of about 40 shrubs and herbs, mostly from the Americas, *Eupatoriums* are frequently mistaken for overgrown Ageratums, which they strongly resemble. Mauve-flowered *E. megalophyllum* from Mexico offers a splendid contrast to pink spring blossom. Making a dense mound 2m/6ft tall but much wider, it is often planted in a mixed border. It needs a winter temperature above freezing to look at all happy, so is probably not familiar to many northern hemisphere gardeners.

For cooler climates, *E. purpureum*, from eastern USA, provides a handsome alternative, bearing its deeper violet-purple blooms from late summer into autumn.

Well-drained soil and plenty of water are needed to develop the large (up to 20cm/8in) furry leaves and massive panicles of mauve or violet puffball flowers. After blooming, prune flowered stems lightly. Propagate from semi-hardwood cuttings with short internodes struck under glass in summer.

Euphorbia leucocephala. White Poinsettia

Euphorbia pulcherrima 'Henrietta Ecke'.
Double Poinsettia

Euphorbia polychroma. Cushion Euphorbia

EUPHORBIA

(yoo-**for**-bee-ə)
**Poinsettia, Crown of Thorns, Snow on the
Mountain, Fire on the Mountain**
EUPHORBIACEAE

Familiar enough to house plant fans everywhere, the shrubby species of *Euphorbia* are
probably the best-known members of the
genus, which also includes more than 2000
annuals, perennials and succulents – many
with little resemblance to the illustrated
species. What do they have in common?
First, an unpleasant milky sap, usually poisonous. Second, spectacular flower-like
arrangements which are not flowers at all,
but a series of highly coloured bracts or
modified leaves.

Of the shrub species, the hollow-stemmed
Poinsettia, *E. pulcherrima*, is the showiest, its
dazzling display stimulated by the shortening
days of winter. Widely sold as 'potted colour'
by florists, in the garden it likes well-drained
soil and plenty of water. It is normally grown
from soft-tip cuttings taken in summer and
autumn. Prune heavily after bloom, shortening flowered stems by at least half.

The Crown of Thorns, *E. milii*, is a spiny,
succulent plant, deciduous in cooler areas.
Propagate from spring cuttings, dried off
before striking in sharp sand. Drought resistant and hardy down to 1°C/34°F, it likes
regular water in summer, tapering off in its
winter resting period. The scarlet bracts
appear in spring with the foliage, and inter-
mittent blooms are borne throughout the
warm months.

Euphorbia milii. Crown of Thorns

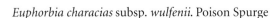

Euphorbia characias subsp. *wulfenii.* Poison Spurge

Euphorbia marginata. Snow on the Mountain, Ghostweed

E. leucocephala, the Flor de Niño (Flower of the Christ-child), is from Central America, and propagated in the same way as the Poinsettia. It can also be grown from seed. Its bracts are always white.

The annual species turn on a grand show in most temperate parts of the world. Two are commonly grown – *E. cyathophora* (syn *E. heterophylla*), known as Fire on the Mountain, and *E. marginata*, known as Snow on the Mountain or Ghostweed. Both are native to central areas of North America ranging from Minnesota to Mexico, with *E. cyathophora* being the more tropical of the two. Both grow to 60cm/2ft in the poorest of soils and thrive equally well in sun or part shade. Seed should be sown outdoors where the plants are to bloom, after all danger of frost has passed, or, for an earlier display, indoors some 2 months earlier. Both make a spectacular garden display, with Fire on the Mountain looking better in partial shade.

Of the perennials, European *E. characias* subsp. *wulfenii* is a shrubbier plant, growing to 130cm/4ft, each stem clothed with linear, blue-green foliage topped with flowers surrounded by yellow and green bracts.

The Cushion Euphorbia, *E. polychroma*, is a bushy evergreen subshrub that makes neat mounds of bright green foliage. It is decked with small multiple heads of bright yellow bracts in late spring.

All perennial *Euphorbias* can be propagated from division between autumn and spring, or from seed or cuttings as detailed above.

EURYOPS
(**yoo**-ree-ops)
Yellow Marguerite, Brighteyes
ASTERACEAE

Shrubby evergreens from South Africa, almost 100 *Euryops* species are grown in temperate climates and are hardy down to –2ºC/28ºF. All are quite similar except in minor botanical details. Their habit of growth is rather spreading, with stems reaching about 1m/3ft before sprawling onto the ground. Pruning after bloom helps keep them in some semblance of shape.

The alternately-borne leaves are 6–9cm/ 2½–3½ in long and deeply lobed; in some species they're a dark grey-green; in others they're covered with fine silver hair. The golden daisy flowers appear singly on long stems for many weeks during late winter and spring and cut well for small bouquets. A gravelly, well-drained soil suits best, with ample water in dry weather. Propagate from short, semi-hardwood cuttings taken in late autumn and struck in sandy soil over bottom heat.

Euryops pectinatus. Bright Eyes

EUSTOMA
(yoo-**stoh**-mə)
(SYN Lisianthus)
Prairie Gentian, Tulip Gentian, Lissie
GENTIANACEAE

Very popular in the world's cut-flower trade, gorgeous Prairie Gentians (*Eustoma grandiflorum*) are native from America's midwest right on down to Texas and New Mexico.

Eustoma grandiflorum. Lisianthus, Prairie Gentian

Eutaxia obovata. Sunshine

There they bloomed quietly away until discovery by the Japanese seed merchants. I first saw them (expensively priced) in a Tokyo florist's window in 1976, and could not believe the rich purple of their tulip-like blooms. Some years later they turned up in Australia as cut flowers and container plants, and now double and bicolor forms abound in shades of pink, mauve and purple with white. Best raised as annuals from spring seed or summer cuttings, they prefer full sun and good drainage, growing to 90cm/3ft in a warm temperate climate and blooming in summer. Cut flowers last up to 3 weeks.

EUTAXIA

(yoo-**tak**-see-ə)
Sunshine
FABACEAE

Endemic to Australia, several species of *Eutaxia* have been transported in reverse, and now adorn gardens in England and California. They are but one genus of Australia's seemingly endless range of pea-flowers – but notable for the sheer abundance of golden bloom which has led to their popular name. *E. obovata* is easy to grow in a well-drained, sandy soil – from either cuttings or scarified seed. It does not much like humidity, is frost hardy down to –6°C/20°F, and is not particularly long-lived. The dazzling display commences in spring, and persists for months in a position with midday shade. Feed once a year with slow-release granules only.

Exacum affine. Persian Violet

EXACUM

(eks-ə-kəm)
Persian Violet, German Violet
GENTIANACEAE

A showy and uncommon miniature annual from the island of Socotra, *Exacum affine*, the Persian Violet, has been known to indoor plant specialists for many years, but is now achieving popularity as an annual for outdoor, semi-shaded positions. It is

Exochorda racemosa. Pearl Bush

compact and bushy, 30cm/12in high at most, with shining, oval, dark leaves. Masses of small, fragrant, 5-petalled blue-violet flowers develop throughout summer.

Sow the dust-like seed indoors in early spring and do not cover; they need light to germinate. *Exacums* enjoy rich, moist soil, and can be planted out in a warm, shaded garden spot when the seedlings are 6cm/2½in across. Space at 20cm/8in intervals and keep moist. Indoors, they like diffused sun and a night temperature not below 15°C/59°F.

EXOCHORDA

(eks-oh-**kor**-də)
Pearl Bush
ROSACEAE

This very small genus of the rose family includes only 4 species, all surpassingly lovely. Considering their ease of propagation, it is surprising they are not seen more often – but then they dislike humid summers. Raise them from spring-sown seed, kept warm and moist, or from semi-hardwood cuttings taken in autumn and misted regularly; even by separating and potting up suckers.

Exochordas are 3–6m/10–20ft, sparse, open shrubs preferring a rich, well-drained soil, and should be kept constantly moist except in cold weather. They are deciduous, and the lightly toothed ovate leaves produce a delicate display in autumn. *Exochorda racemosa* bears terminal racemes of snowy-white 4cm/1½in flowers for a brief period in spring.

FAGRAEA

(fag-**rae**-ə)
Pua Keni-keni, Ten-cent Flower
LOGANIACEAE

Found naturally right across the Pacific from Queensland to Hawaii, *Fagraea berteroana* is relatively uncommon in cultivation, though universally admired for its fragrant flowers. The tree itself is most variable, ranging from a single-trunked, 12m/40ft giant down to a shrubby, many-trunked bush where the soil is not so rich.

Short-stemmed leaves are widest at the outer end and up to 15cm/6in long; the fragrant, long-tubed blossoms (cream changing to orange) resemble those of Australia's Hymenosporum, and appear at any time during warm weather. They are followed by smooth, oval 2.5cm/1in fruit, each containing many seeds. The fruit ripens from green to red if the birds leave it alone.

Fagraea berteroana. Ten-cent Flower

FARADAYA
(fa-ra-**dae**-ə)
Buku, Pitutu
VERBENACEAE

One of the glories of Queensland's fast-vanishing rainforests, where it may climb up into the highest trees, the splendid *Faradaya splendida* is most aptly named. Tropical in nature, it reduces in size the further from the equator it grows. I have seen it in subtropical Brisbane as a spectacular lawn shrub, perhaps 2m/6ft high and twice that across. Planted out in a hot climate in rich soil with plenty of summer moisture, it will positively bolt into growth. You can grow it from cuttings and enjoy dense panicles of showy and very fragrant white blossom in spring. Roots should be shaded; *Faradaya* will reach up to the sun.

FATSIA
(**fat**-see-ə)
Aralia
ARALIACEAE

More commonly known as Aralia in many countries, *Fatsia* is a shrubby plant that produces magnificent leaves in almost any conditions. It is ideal for shaded gardens or indoors and grows well in fast-draining soil. Raised from suckers, seed or cuttings, it can be cut back hard if it becomes too leggy. Give *Fatsia* regular water and liquid fertiliser, but never let it remain sodden. It produces terminal clusters of greenish-white flowers in autumn. There are several varieties in leaf-shape, including a variegated type which is particularly effective in shaded places.

Faradaya splendida. Buku, Pitutu

FAUCARIA
(fou-ke ə r-ee-ə)
Tiger Jaws
AIZOACEAE

Savage-looking succulents from South Africa, *Faucarias* are best planted at eye level, where they can be clearly observed. On top of a dwarf wall would work well – so long as they are in full sun. Plant out in a well-drained, gritty compost. Water lightly, except in summer, when you can be generous. As the plants grow, plump green leaves will appear in pairs, their spiny, jagged edges interlocked like clenched jaws. As they grow, each leaf-pair opens wide. There are 5cm/2in golden daisy flowers in autumn, and the plants are hardy down to 5ºC/41ºF in winter. *F. tigrina* has about 10 hooked teeth to each leaf; related *F. tuberculosa* rarely has more than 5.

Fatsia japonica. Aralia

Faucaria tigrina. Tiger Jaws

Feijoa sellowiana. Pineapple Guava

FEIJOA
(fae-**joh**-ə)
Pineapple Guava, Fruit-salad Plant
MYRTACEAE

Not a true Guava, *Feijoa sellowiana* is never-theless related, and produces a popular autumn fruit in cooler climates. It can reach small tree size in southern England, but in Australia seems content to remain a rounded shrub. Wherever grown, 4m/13ft seems to be about its maximum height, with a slightly smaller spread. It needs rich, well-drained soil and ample water in dry summers to develop its ovoid, 5cm/2in green fruit, which have a tangy, guava-like taste when ripe. The 7cm/3in shiny oval leaves have woolly reverses. The decorative 4cm/1½in flowers are borne over a long period in spring. They appear in twos at the base of new season's growth and have white, reflexed petals and deep-red stamens. Propagate from seed or semi-hardwood cuttings in autumn, struck with heat and humidity.

FELICIA
(fə-**lee**-see-ə)
(SYN Agathaea)
Kingfisher Daisy, Blue Marguerite
ASTERACEAE

Felicias add much sought-after blue and mauve to the spectrum of daisy flowers. The Kingfisher Daisy, *F. bergeriana*, is a charming annual. It rarely grows above 15cm/6in and is almost obscured by a mass of bright blue daisy flowers for months. It can be used for bedding or edging, and because of its wind resistance is useful in window boxes or balcony planters. The blooms, however, close in cloudy weather.

The Blue Marguerite, *F. amelloides*, is a sturdy little plant that grows so fast in temperate climates it is often treated as a bedding plant and struck afresh from soft-tip cuttings at any time. It can also be raised from seed. A low, generally tidy shrublet, it makes a brilliant warm-weather display in rock gardens, as a path edging, or by the seaside. It is also useful in hillside gardens, and is hardy down to –3ºC/27ºF. The showy, bright blue flowers are borne at tip ends and cut well for posies.

Both species need full sun and prefer dryish, very well-drained gravelly soil, enriched with organic matter. They bloom spring and summer, and the already long season can be further prolonged by regular dead-heading of spent blooms.

FEROCACTUS
(fer-oh-**kak**-təs)
Hedgehog Cactus
CACTACEAE

At one time most of the shorter and fatter ribbed cacti of Mexico and southern USA were placed in the genus *Echinocactus*, but many have now been removed to *Ferocactus*. Common features of the latter are the very strong spines that are frequently hooked or at least strongly curved, and day-blooming summer flowers in reds, pinks or yellows clustered around the central growing point. They have mostly solitary stems that can reach up to 60cm/2ft in diameter with age, the height seldom more than twice the width. Some of the smaller species can be flowered in pots, but the big ones do best in a sunny rockery in open, gritty soil, and take decades to reach their mature size. Unless you live in a hot, dry climate, withhold water gradually as winter approaches, stopping it entirely over the coldest months. Most will tolerate very light frosts if kept dry.

Felicia amelloides. Blue Marguerite

Ferocactus viridescens. Hedghog Cactus

Forsythia intermedia. Golden Bells

FILIPENDULA

(fil-i-**pen**-dyoo-lə)

Meadowsweet

ROSACEAE

Related to both Aruncus and the shrubby Spiraeas, *Filipendulas* have very large and striking leaves, 3–5 lobed, doubly serrated and diagonally pleated. They thrive at the back of the larger perennial border provided the soil does not dry out, but look and grow even better in waterside positions where the soil is both damp and well drained.

Propagate by dividing the crowns around winter. *Filipendulas* can be raised from seed sown in early spring, but may take 3 years to reach flowering size. Then they produce plumes of tiny, fragrant flowers each year in early summer. Watch for powdery mildew among the dense foliage, and cut back to the ground in winter in colder areas.

FORSYTHIA

(for-**sai**-thee-ə)

Golden Bells

OLEACEAE

Hardy down to $-15^{O}C/5^{O}F$, the beautiful golden-flowered *Forsythia* lights up cold-climate gardens at the first breath of spring, its slender branches arched with the sheer weight of blossom. Bare stems cut in bud will even open indoors in plain water. Easy to grow in rich, well-drained soil, *Forsythias* are also easy to propagate, either from divisions or from semi-hardwood tip-cuttings taken in summer and struck in a cool, humid place. *F. suspensa* is conveniently self-layering, and well-rooted layers may be severed and lifted in late winter.

Forsythia species don't like subtropical conditions, and should be tried only where the winters are cold. In such places, they

form dense, many-stemmed bushes up to 4m/13ft tall. The bell-shaped flowers appear in small clusters from lateral buds of the previous year's wood, so annual pruning should only be undertaken immediately after flowering – or by judicious cutting of blooms, which last well indoors.

FOTHERGILLA

(fo-thər-**gil**-lə)

Mountain Snow

HAMAMELIDACEAE

Only two species of *Fothergilla* have been discovered, in secret mountain places of the eastern United States, southward from the Alleghenies. *F. major* is typical of these

Filipendula purpurea. Meadowsweet

Fothergilla major. Mountain Snow

exquisite shrubs, which are treasures for the cool climate or mountain garden. It grows about 1m/3ft in height, spreading a web of tangled branches close to the ground. From mid-spring, puffballs of white stamens open from bare wood, followed by slightly downy, pleated leaves, 8cm/3in in length. These are an attractive light green but blaze into orange and crimson in autumn. Plant from layers or semi-hardwood cuttings taken with a heel in midsummer. All *Fothergillas* prefer a lime-free soil and constant moisture.

Fouquieria splendens. Ocotillo

FOUQUIERIA

(foo-kwee-**eer**-ee-ə)
Ocotillo, Coachwhip
FOUQUIERIACEAE

The Ocotillo, *Fouquieria splendens,* is a remarkable shrub from the deserts and semi-deserts of the south western USA and adjacent parts of Mexico. When not in bloom it can resemble a cactus, but closer inspection reveals that among the ferocious thorns which stud its fleshy branches are small leaves, at least during the rainy season; and the flowers are quite different in structure and borne in small clusters. They are scarlet, and in their early summer season the bush blazes with them. Ocotillo hedges are very popular in the plant's native region – all you have to do is stick branches in the ground in spring and they take root almost at once, rapidly becoming impenetrable to man or beast. No other attention is required.

Fragaria chiloensis. Wild Strawberry

FRAGARIA

(frə-**ge**ə**r**-ee-ə)
Wild Strawberry
ROSACEAE

Wild Strawberries are used for groundcover, bed edging and pot culture. They are actually perennial but grow so quickly from seed they make a useful annual display. For the biggest plants, sow seed in a warm room in mid-winter, then set the young plants out in earliest spring in soil that is well drained, rich and cultivated. Where there is no danger of frost, seed may be sown direct. *Fragaria chiloensis* is one parent of the commercial, fruiting type, and native to the whole west coast of the Americas. It has decorative leaflets in groups of three, white flowers, red fruit and a respectable autumn colouring. *F. vesca* is the European Alpine Strawberry, with smaller fruits. Wild Strawberries flower in flushes throughout summer.

FRANCOA

(fran-**koh**-ə)
Bridal Wreath, Maiden Wreath
SAXIFRAGACEAE

In reality a perennial, the charming Bridal Wreath, *Francoa ramosa,* is a native of Chile, but grows so easily from seed it is used for annual display among Azaleas and Camellias. It enjoys the same rich, acid soil and woodsy conditions as Foxgloves and Primulas. Sow direct in late autumn or early spring, in a

position with broken sunlight for summer display. Young plants should be thinned out to at least 30cm/12in spacings, for they make a considerable growth of wavy-edged leaves resembling those of Gerberas. Flower spikes vary from about 30–100cm/1–3ft in height, and consist of tall stems topped with polyanthus-like clusters of 5-petalled pink and white blooms, quite useful for cutting. These appear over a long period in summer.

Francoa ramosa. Bridal Wreath

Freesia hybrids. Freesia

FREESIA
(**free**-zhə)
Freesia
IRIDACEAE

These dainty members of the iris family would be worth growing even if their charming spring flowers weren't so deliciously perfumed. Where frosts are light, they can be grown in almost any soil, provided it is well-drained and sunny. In cold climates they can only be grown in pots, sheltered against the worst excesses of winter.

Freesia lactea. Sweet Freesia

Freesias grow easily and quickly from seed, flowering in only 8 months – or half that if raised from autumn-planted corms. They look best when grown in clumps and, once established, can and should be left undisturbed for at least 3 years. Keep moist from the time growth begins in autumn until the leaves turn yellow in late spring, then let go dry. Creamy-white *F. lactea* (once known as *F. refracta)* is still the most common *Freesia* grown, but many hybrids in brilliant colours are available, some of them semi-double.

Fremontodendron californicum. Tree Poppy

FREMONTODENDRON
(free-**mon**-tə-den-drən)
Tree Poppy, Fremontia, Flannel Bush
BOMBACACEAE

Fremontodendrons make ideal specimens for dryish, sheltered gardens with well-drained, sandy soil, where they may reach 7m/23ft. Usually evergreen, they produce woolly, grey-ish leaves and hibiscus-like flowers on short spurs along the branches. *Fremontodendrons* cannot abide a humid climate, but in the right position can be expected to bloom several times a year. Even in England, they will produce quite a spectacular summer show on a south-facing garden wall. They are propagated from seed or softwood cuttings and need regular pruning to shape.

FRITHIA
(**fri**-thee-ə)
Babies' Toes, Fairy Elephant's Feet
AIZOACEAE

I can imagine playing 'This little piggy …' with these cute succulents – but the mere thought of a Fairy Elephant is too much for a grown man. *Frithias* are very low-growing, clump-forming plants with stubby, cylindrical leaves of varying lengths arranged in a

Frithia pulchra. Babies' Toes

Fritillaria meleagris and *F. meleagris* 'Alba'. Snake's Head

Fritillaria imperialis 'Lutea'. Crown Imperial

rosette. Each of these leaves ends in a translucent window-like organ that reveals the plant's interior. The entire plant is stemless and slow-growing, and prefers sandy, well-drained soil. Seed is the only way to grow them, in a sun-drenched position. They can take a light frost, and produce bright purple daisy flowers in winter. These open properly only on the brightest days.

FRITILLARIA
(fri-til-**lar**-ee-∂)
Snake's Head, Fritillary, Crown Imperial
LILIACEAE

Not common at the best of times, the curious *Fritillarias* are true collector's plants, related both to the Lily and the Tulip. In nature, they are found from Syria through Asia Minor to the foothills of the Himalayas. Most spectacular is *F. imperialis*, the Crown

Fritillaria imperialis. Crown Imperial

Imperial, a tall-growing bulb with yellow or orange bells arranged in a whorl atop a 1m/3ft stem crowned with a rosette of shiny leaves. Plant it in heavy soil in a cool temperate climate.

The daintier Snake's Head, (*F. meleagris*) is found wild all over Europe, including Great Britain. It rarely exceeds 35cm/14in tall, bears usually a single bell-flower, checkered in mauve or green and white. It resents disturbance, and may take 7 years to bloom from seed.

Fuchsia 'Jean'. Hybrid Fuchsia

FUCHSIA
(**fyoo**-sh∂)
Ladies' Eardrops
ONAGRACEAE

Driving in western County Cork on a recent visit to Ireland, I couldn't believe my eyes – those scarlet-blooming hedges were really thickets of *Fuchsia* arching over the roads! The climate of southern Ireland is their ideal. Warmed by the Gulf Stream, it has humid summers and frost-free winters. Frequent mists and cloudy skies raise the humidity, and soft rains drench the plants at any time of the year.

Fuchsia 'Beacon'. Hybrid Fuchsia

Fuchsia triphylla 'Gartenmeister Bonstedt'. Honeysuckle Fuchsia

Fuchsia arborescens. Tree Fuchsia

Fuchsia 'Flash'. Hybrid Fuchsia

Fuchsias will grow in almost any soil, as long as it contains plenty of organic matter and is not too acid. If your Azaleas bloom beautifully, add half a cup of dolomite to the square metre/yard for Fuchsias and feed them regularly with bone-meal. They have a terrible thirst, too. Water deeply and often, but never while the sun is directly on them. They will grow best among other shade-loving shrubs in the shelter of deciduous trees. In hot, dry areas, raise in containers in a lath or shade house and keep the humidity high.

Varieties with a weeping habit make elegant basket plants in a sheltered position; those with stronger, upright growth can be trained as standards or espaliered. They even make showy (if temporary) indoor plants, but suffer from the dry indoor atmosphere. Raise them outside, in the shade, and bring inside for a few days only when they are in full bloom – and they mostly are from midsummer to autumn. Prune while dormant in late winter, and begin pinching back new shoots in spring for a compact, bushy habit and more flowers. New plants are easily raised from tip-cuttings of 2 to 4 nodes, taken from spring to autumn.

Hybrids of *F. triphylla* take more sun than most and bloom well in the semi-tropics. The Tree Fuchsia, *F. arborescens*, is a handsome, wide tree reaching 8m/26ft in a suitable spot. Grow sheltered from frost in the dappled shade of taller, open trees for winter and spring bloom.

Fuchsia 'Dollar Princess'. Hybrid Fuchsia

Fuchsia 'Heidi Weiss'. Hybrid Fuchsia

Gaillardia aristata. Blanket Flower

GAILLARDIA

(gal-**lar**-dee-ə)
Blanket Flower, Indian Blanket
ASTERACEAE

A genus of vividly coloured daisies originally
from central and western United States,
Gaillardias come in both annual and perennial species. Both are more commonly
raised as annuals in cooler climates. They are
easy to grow, proving useful in areas where
the soil is poor and dry. Taller strains may
need staking.

    The annual *Gaillardia pulchella* should be
sown in autumn or early spring at a temperature of 21ºC/70ºF. Germination takes
15–20 days and flowering time is summer.
Space plants 20cm/8in apart, and do not be
too disappointed when you discover the
main petals or rays are lacking: in
G. pulchella the composite centre develops
into a mass of tubular flowers, giving a
pompon effect. Other *Gaillardias* grow to a
height of 30–75cm/12–30in; the *G.* × *grandiflora* hybrids reach an even greater height.
Perennial *G. aristata* grows to 60cm/24in.

    G. × *grandiflora* is grown from spring
divisions or cuttings, and will bloom from
spring right through to winter, with regular
dead-heading. Different strains widen the
colour range from burgundy to rich reds and
golds, and produce more compact growers to
25cm/10in. Like all *Gaillardias,* they romp
through heat, producing flowers in the gay
and gaudy colours of an Indian Blanket.

Galanthus nivalis. Snowdrop

GALANTHUS

(gal-**an**-thəs)
Fair Maid of February, Snowdrop
AMARYLLIDACEAE

One of the earliest bulbs to bloom, as its
charming popular name suggests, *Galanthus*
is rarely seen away from its native Europe,
which is just as well. Below the equator it
would bloom in August, and the name
Snowdrop is reserved there for the related
but larger Leucojum, which flowers somewhat later. The 19 *Galanthus* species grow
7.5–20cm/3–8in high, damp, rich soil
producing the taller stems. They prefer
dappled shade except in the coldest districts,
and take quite a few years to establish.
Propagate from seed or offsets, but don't
keep the latter out of the ground for long.
They're quite frost hardy.

Galega officinalis. Goat's Rue

GALEGA

(ga-**leeg**-ə)
Goat's Rue
FABACEAE

These easy-to-grow perennials resemble the
farmer's lucerne, and from their quaint,
oldtime popular name, one must wonder
if they have the same bloating effect on
ruminant beasts!

    Galega officinalis grows wild right across
the goat country of southern Europe and
Asia Minor, and is at home in any deep soil,
where it thrives for years without division. It

Galphimia glauca. Rain of Gold

does even better, of course, with special feeding and plenty of water, growing into great mounds of handsome pinnate foliage; each leaf has up to 17 leaflets.

The flowers appear in summer, pea-shaped in mauve, pink or white according to variety, providing a long display.

Galegas grow to a height of 1–1.5m/3–5ft. Propagate them by division of roots from autumn to spring and cut faded flower stems to the ground.

GALPHIMIA
(gal-**fim**-ee-ə)
(SYN Thryallis)
**Rain of Gold, Rama de Oro,
Mexican Gold Bush**
MALPIGHIACEAE

The first popular name of this showy Mexican shrub is an understatement. On a mature specimen in full flower, the red stems are literally weighed down by terminal spikes of tiny golden star-flowers for weeks at a time.

Galphimia grows fast to 2m/6ft and is strictly a subject for the warm temperate to tropical climate, needing a rich, well-drained soil and regular water to keep the roots damp.

The shrub's very long display is enhanced by the rapid fall of individual blossoms, which turns the surrounding garden a vivid yellow. Opposite leaves are ovate, shiny, about 5cm/2in long and evergreen. Propagate from seed or cuttings of ripe wood, which should be struck in a sharp, sandy mix with warmth and humidity.

Galphimia can be clipped into a hedge.

Galtonia candicans. Summer Hyacinth

GALTONIA
(gorl-**toh**-nee-ə)
Summer Hyacinth, Berg Lily
LILIACEAE

South Africa is home to this tall summer beauty. Closely related to that perfumed favourite, *Galtonia candicans* is, nonetheless, not a true Hyacinth at all, and differs in both size and scent.

Galtonias make a splendid feature behind lower plants. Their large bulbs need to be planted 15cm/6in deep in autumn. They

resent disturbance and in cooler districts need a deep winter mulch, as they are sensitive to frost.

They bloom for about 6 weeks in midsummer and are most attractive if planted in clumps of about 6 or 8, about 25cm/10in apart.

Needing a compost-rich soil that drains freely, *Galtonias* should be watered and fed during the spring and summer but allowed to dry out in winter. Divide every 3 years; and protect from eager slugs and snails.

GARDENIA
(gah-**deen**-yə)
Gardenia, Cape Jasmine, Tiare
RUBIACEAE

Gardenias are cherished in every temperate part of the world for their perfume, their snowy-white perfection! Though native to hot climates, they bloom elsewhere in a sheltered position. Temperatures down to 5–9ºC/41–48ºF are not uncommon where I live, for instance, and I enjoy *Gardenias* for most of the year.

They love humidity, it is true, so I spray the foliage regularly and have planted them near a garden pool. A rich, well-drained soil is best, and they are easily raised from 5–8cm/2–3in semi-hardwood cuttings, taken with a heel in the cooler months. At this stage they strike better with warmth and humidity, but while a hot summer is their

Gardenia augusta 'Florida'. Florist's Gardenia

Gardenia augusta 'Professor Pucci'. Giant Gardenia

Gardenia thunbergia. Star Gardenia

prime requirement, they also need plenty of water and feeding with complete plant food at least once a month.

The most commonly seen varieties are cultivars of *G. augusta*: 'Radicans' is a dwarf with 2.5cm/1in flowers; 'Florida' has 7.5cm/3in flowers; and 'Magnifica' features asymmetrical flowers to 12.5cm/5in. Picking the blooms serves as sufficient pruning for all types.

The height of *Gardenias* also varies, from the 25cm/10in dwarf *G. augusta* 'Radicans' to the 3.5m/11ft *G. thunbergia*, and all of them may bloom sporadically the whole year.

'The flower of sweetest smell is shy and lowly,' observed the poet, and the legendary Tiare Tahiti makes truth of his observation. A wide-spreading, low-growing shrub, its flowers open late in the day, their perfume magnificent, for this joy of the dark-eyed Vahines is also a true *Gardenia*, *G. taitensis*.

GARRYA
(**gar-ree-y**ə)
Silk Tassel, Curtain Bush
GARRYACEAE

Like gardeners, California's *Garrya* comes in two sexes and like many other plants and animals, the male of the species is the showier. During winter it produces spectacular curtains of greenish-yellow catkins that can each be 20cm/8in long. Female flowers are barely noticeable, but their grape-like

clusters of purplish-black berries are pleasant enough and provide a summer-long feast for the birds – that is, if a male and female are planted together.

G. elliptica varies in habit according to its position. In good, deep, moist soils it may reach 6–9m/20–30ft and take on the appearance of a tree, while in poor soil or exposed sites it is more usually seen as a 2m/6ft shrub. Either way it's a fine foliage plant that thrives in sun or part shade, on the coast or inland.

Garrya elliptica. Curtain Bush

Gardenia taitensis. Tiare

Gaultheria wisleyensis. Wintergreen

GAULTHERIA
(gorl-**theer**-ee-∂)
(SYN Pernettya, Gaulnettya)
Salal, Wintergreen
ERICACEAE

Strictly speaking, the Native American name Salal belongs to *Gaultheria shallon*, a prickly, thicketing shrub from the Pacific coast of the USA and much grown there as a dense groundcover, but I sometimes hear it applied to the other species also, whose homelands range from North and South America to the Himalayas and even to Australia and New Zealand. Some grow into small trees, some are tiny enough for the rock garden, but all display leathery evergreen leaves, little white bell-flowers, and edible pea-sized berries, which range in colour from white through pink to purple or even blue, and are another good reason for growing the plants. They all like a temperate climate, moist lime-free soil and just a little shade – too much makes them leggy.

Gazania Sunshine Giant Hybrids. Treasure Flower

GAZANIA
(g∂-**zae**-nee-∂)
Treasure Flower, Black-eyed Susan
ASTERACEAE

Modern *Gazanias* or Treasure Flowers have been hybridised from a number of South African species, some perennial, some annual. Favouring full sun, in warm climates they can be grown either way, but in districts where frost can destroy, it is preferable to sow annually, or regrow them from cuttings kept in a warm position indoors over winter. Originally orange with a black-bordered centre (today's *Gazania rigens*), they now come in mixtures that contain every conceivable colour short of a true blue (though there are lavenders, greens and pinks, as well as the common autumn shades).

Of the two main types, trailing and clump-forming, the apricot-bronze *G. uniflora* is the most notable trailer. *G. rigens* is the only original clumping species seen these days; there are many mat-forming hybrid perennials. With shining dark green leaves that are often lobed and invariably silver-grey and woolly beneath, their flowers can be banded, rayed or bordered with contrasting colour.

Gazanias grow to about 30cm/12in and favour a temperate climate. Either sow seeds indoors in midwinter, at 20–30ºC/68–86ºF, or outdoors, later, when cold snaps have passed. With either method, thin plants out, and set 20–30cm/8–12in apart in a sun-drenched position. Light, sandy soil with some blood and bone is suitable; coastal gardeners will find them quite resistant to salt.

Gazania rigens. Black-eyed Susan

Gazania Sunshine Giant Hybrids

Geleznowia verrucosa. Geleznowia

Genista tinctoria. Dyer's Greenweed

GELEZNOWIA
(gel-ez-**noh**-ee-ə)
Geleznowia
RUTACEAE

Australian native shrubs, striking in a hot, sandy position, *Geleznowias* are closely related to both Boronia and Citrus. When drainage is perfect and soil to the plant's liking, they branch heavily, each woody stem becoming crowded with round, grey-green leaves and the whole developing into a 60x60cm/2x2ft rounded shrub.

Small, yellowish flowers cluster in dense masses at stem tops from early to mid-spring, each bloom about 2.5cm/1in across. Grow from seed sown in spring or autumn, with smoke treatment.

Gelsemium sempervirens. Carolina Jasmine

GELSEMIUM
(gel-**see**-mee-əm)
Carolina Jasmine
LOGANIACEAE

Suitable for smaller gardens and cooler, even frosty climates, the Carolina Jasmine, *Gelsemium sempervirens,* has much to recommend it. First and foremost, shiny yellow trumpet flowers, pleasantly scented, appear over a long period from late winter (or as early as autumn in especially mild areas). Secondly, although a climber, it is not particularly rampant, and will provide a rewarding show on the smallest trellis or support. It's also useful as groundcover, spilling down banks and walls. *Gelsemium* grows quite well with minimum care and water, and can be easily controlled by pinching away the soft new shoots it produces in spring. Semi-deciduous and virtually pest-free, it is also entirely toxic.

Genista sagittalis. Winged Broom

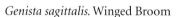

GENISTA
(jen-**is**-tə)
(SYN Spartium)
Genet, Broom, Dyer's Greenweed
FABACEAE

Valued worldwide for the brilliance of their golden pea-flowers, most *Genistas* are native to the Mediterranean area. They revel in hot weather but are surprisingly hardy in the cold, suffering damage only in lengthy freezes. They thrive by the sea and bloom in drought-stricken areas too.

Grow them from seed sown in spring after a 24-hour soak in water, or propagate from 10cm/4in cuttings of semi-hardened wood taken with a heel in late summer.

All 90-odd species should be tip-pruned to encourage bushiness. They mostly grow to about 30–100cm/1–3ft, have a perfume, are many-branched, and are sparsely foliaged even in the growing season. *G. canariensis,* the Canary Island Broom, seeds continuously once given space.

Gentiana acaulis. Trumpet Gentian

Gentiana septemfida. Fringed Gentian

Geranium renardii. Cranesbill

GENTIANA
(jen-tee-**ah**-n∂)
Gentian
GENTIANACEAE

Gentians are natives of alpine meadows throughout the world, including Australia and New Zealand. And though they have given their name to a particular shade of deep blue, many of the over 400 *Gentiana* species bloom in red, white and yellow. They all enjoy a damp, gravelly soil which drains well, and suit pockets of sloping hillside gardens. Nearly all species are propagated by division in early spring; but autumn-sown seed, frozen for 3 weeks, can also be germinated at a constant 24°C/75°F. This may take a month; then prick out seedlings and pot them up singly for planting out the next autumn.

Their name derives from Gentius, a king of Illyria who discovered the value of their bitter roots which are still used medicinally.

GERANIUM
(jer-**ae**-nee-∂m)
Cranesbill
GERANIACEAE

It is entirely possible that the majority of the world's Geranium hobbyists have never seen one in their lives! For the whole range of plants popularly known as Scented, Zonal, Fancy Leaf, Ivy and Martha Washington Geraniums do not belong to the genus at all, and you will find them listed correctly, later in this book, as Pelargoniums.

But yes, there are real *Geraniums*, botanically so named, and popularly called Cranesbills on account of the long beak-like projection on their seeds.

Geranium cinereum 'Ballerina'. Cranesbill

True *Geraniums* include some 300 species of perennial plants found all over the world in cool temperate and alpine regions. Used mostly in the rock garden, they are also good informal groundcovers or loose mounding plants for the front of the border.

All species enjoy a damp, well-drained soil, and should be lifted for division in winter before being immediately replanted. Seed should be sown fresh at 21°C/70°F and will take up to 40 days to germinate. The young plants are potted up and ultimately planted out in autumn at 25cm/ 10in intervals.

There is some variation in height, and their general practice is to spread fast and provide a long display in summer.

Geraniums bloom in both temperate and colder areas. Their colour range is limited to mostly mauve, pink or blue. They produce open 5-petalled flowers, and require little attention, but a regular snipping will encourage growth and a bushy habit.

Geranium ibericum. Caucasus Geranium

Geranium psilostemon. Armenian Cranesbill

Gerbera jamesonii cultivars. Barberton Daisy

Geum chiloense 'Mrs J. Bradshaw'. Scarlet Avens

Gilia capitata. Blue Thimble Flower

GERBERA

(jer-ber-ə)

African Daisy, Barberton Daisy, Transvaal Daisy

ASTERACEAE

Surely the most decorative of all daisies, *Gerberas* come in a wide colour range from crimson to pink, yellow and many other tones. Both single and double hybrids have derived from the original Barberton Daisy, a small orange species from the Transvaal. Other species are also found here and there around the Indian Ocean.

Gerberas are not frost hardy, demand full sun and need perfect drainage. Plant from autumn divisions, or grow from seed germinated in early spring without soil covering.

Their height is only 45–50cm/18–20in. They bloom for a long time, but plant them 60cm/2ft apart, as they grow into large clumps.

GESNERIA

(gez-**neer**-ee-ə)

Firecracker

GESNERIACEAE

Though these delightful plants give their name to the entire Gesneriad family, they are among the least common of its members. Native to the islands of the Caribbean, they need a temperature range of 18–27°C/ 65–80°F to turn on much of a show. Propagate from seed, stem cuttings or divisions set in a sandy peat mixture with warmth and humidity – plant out later into pots of well-drained, leaf-rich compost, and feed regularly with a high phosphorus fertiliser. They'll bloom around midsummer. The scarlet tubular flowers, the size of a small firecracker, appear from leaf axils. *Gesnerias* rarely grow more than 15cm/6in high.

GEUM

(jee-əm)

Avens, Indian Chocolate

ROSACEAE

Less often seen in these days of mini-gardens, old-fashioned *Geums* produce masses of red, orange and yellow flowers but do require sprawling room to produce a good display. Their foliage is rather like a strawberry's – the flower not unlike a small, single Ranunculus.

The once-popular bedding species in mixed colours is *G. chiloense* (formerly *G. quellyon*) from South America. *G. coccineum*, from Asia Minor, however, is a better gamble for the small garden.

All *Geums* can be propagated from division in early spring, or from seed sown in winter, germinating at 28–30°C/68–86°F. They prefer full sun and good drainage.

Gesneria cuneifolia. Firecracker

GILIA

(gil-ee-ə)

Blue Thimble Flower

POLEMONIACEAE

Endemic to the western mountains of North and South America, there are some 30 species of *Gilia*, few of them yet introduced to the world's gardens. Annuals, biennials and perennials, they prefer a cool climate and will romp along without fuss in a well-drained soil . To propagate, they must be sown from seed in the position you wish them to grow. Early autumn is best, while the seed is fresh. Seedlings can be thinned out in early spring.

Gilia capitata grows 45cm/18in tall, likes full sun and light but regular water. Its leaves have a fern-like appearance, and are tripinnately dissected. The tiny blue flowers appear in a pincushion-like mass in summer; they are good cut flowers. Other species bloom in red, white, lilac and yellow.

GILLENIA

(gil-**len**-nee-ə)

Indian Physic, Bowman's Knot

ROSACEAE

There are two species of *Gillenia*, both from North America, the one usually seen in gardens being *G. trifoliata* or Indian Physic. It is a herbaceous perennial, very elegant indeed in early summer, when it becomes an airy froth of white starry flowers with red calyces which remain decorative for some time after the petals have fallen. Growing to about 1m/3ft, it is easy to grow (from seed or root division in spring) in any temperate to cool climate; it needs sun or light shade and moist but well-drained soil. The common name comes from its having been used in medicine by Native Americans.

Gladiolus communis subsp. *byzantinus.*
Eastern Corn Flag

Gladiolus carneus. Sword Lily

Gladiolus 'Elvira'. Miniature Gladiolus

GLADIOLUS

(glad-ee-**oh**-ləs)
Gladiolus

Florists' favourites for presentation sheafs,
the tall, multi-coloured spikes of *Gladiolus*
are hybrids of many species, mostly from
Africa. Many of these older species, though
small in size, are still grown for their charming flowers, and they too have been
hybridised and improved. *G. communis*
subsp. *byzantinus* is hardy and should be left
undisturbed for years; it grows to 60cm/2ft,
and blooms in summer. *G.* 'Cherbourg' is a
large-flowered hybrid that can reach 1.2m/4ft
or so and usually blooms in the latter half of
summer. Hybrids of *G. natalensis* have a
more tropical origin, and produce hooded,
primrose-yellow flowers that last well when
cut. They are widely used in hybridisation.

All *Gladiolus* are easy to grow from flat
corms, which can be planted most of the
year, ensuring a regular succession of bloom.

Gillenia trifoliata. Indian Physic, Bowman's
Knot

Gladiolus 'Charm'. Miniature Gladiolus

Gladiolus 'Summer Gold' and 'Summer
Sunshine'. Hybrid Gladiolus

GLAUCIUM

(**glou**-kee-əm)
Horned Poppy, Sea Poppy

Glauciums or Horned Poppies are an interesting genus within the poppy family,
Papaveraceae, several of which make particularly decorative summer annuals.

They are native from the Mediterranean
area to Central Asia, and have become naturalised in many other regions including the
Canary Islands and the United States. They
are remarkably drought-resistant, and grow
with a will in dry areas or in sandy soil close
to the coast.

All *Glauciums* are straggly plants, making
low rosettes of grey, fern-like leaves from
which appear the gorgeous 7.5cm/3in
blooms, like a cross between a poppy and a
tulip. The flowers are followed by bean-
shaped pods, up to 30cm/12in long.

Sow seed in early spring, in dryish, well-
cultivated soil, later spacing the young plants
to 30cm/12in. Alternatively, sow indoors
somewhat earlier, in standard flats, keeping
up a temperature of 21°C/70°F.

Gladiolus 'The Bride'. Hybrid Gladiolus

Glaucium flavum. Horned Poppy

Glechoma hederacea. Runaway Robin

GLECHOMA

(gle-**koh**-m∂)

(SYN Nepeta)

**Ground Ivy, Gill-over-the-Ground, Runaway
Robin, Ale-hoof**

LAMIACEAE

Delightful in its native Europe as a woodland
groundcover, this charming old plant's
popular names suggest how easily it can take
off to become a pest, as it has in parts of
North America. Still, so long as we are
warned, we can make our own choices,
preferring to keep it away from heavily
planted beds, but letting it run elsewhere.

Propagate from divisions set out in damp
soil in a lightly shaded place. Keep moist and
stand back. Runaway Robin will spread fast,
rooting as it does from stem-joints and
producing small clusters of aromatic mauve-
blue trumpet flowers throughout the warm
months. Evergreen where winter temperatures remain above −7ºC/19ºF, it makes a
good basket plant.

Gliricidia sepium. Madre de Cacao

GLIRICIDIA

(gli-ri-**sid**-ee-∂)

Madre de Cacao

FABACEAE

Though not the source of cocoa itself, the
picturesque Madre de Cacao (Mother of
Cocoa) is regarded in Central America as
indispensable for the cultivation of the
Cocoa plant. Sometimes thought a fiction,
this natural 'companioning' or symbiosis is a
fact. The *Gliricidia*, like many of the legume
family, is especially rich in nitrogen, both in
its root nodules and in the fallen leaves
which are turned in as green manure for the
Cocoa plants.

Madre de Cacao grows to 8m/26ft and
has a short, gnarled trunk. Its leaves are
compact and fern-like, with 13 to 15 pairs of
leaflets, and an odd one on the end.

The tree is very sensitive and will drop all
its leaves overnight in dry or cold weather;
but in the early spring it bursts into perfect
pea-flowers, mauve-pink with a yellow eye,
from the trunk and branches. Its botanical
name, *G. sepium*, indicates the use of its
seeds as rat poison.

GLOBBA

(**glob**-b∂)

Fishhook Ginger

ZINGIBERACEAE

There are 30-odd species of these delicate
gingers from Southeast Asia, but only one,
Globba winitii, is found in cultivation. It is
worth growing for the colourful but somewhat bizarre flower spikes it puts up through
summer and autumn. Each spike curves over
at the tip and bears slender flowering

Globba winitii. Globba

branches, each with a pretty pale pink to
purple bract at the base. At the tip of each
branch a succession of small tubular yellow
flowers of intricate structure appears, each
fine tube uncoiling to a fishhook shape
before the flower falls. The soft, heart-shaped
leaves taper to fine points; in humid weather
drops of clear water are exuded from the
leaf tips, a phenomenon termed *guttation*
by botanists.

Frost tender, *Globba* is easily grown
indoors. Water freely as new shoots emerge
in early summer, feed with soluble fertiliser
during the growing period, and withhold
water as foliage yellows in winter. The plant
dies back to a mass of fleshy roots, which can
be divided when dormant.

GLOBULARIA

(glob-yoo-**lah**-ree-∂)

Globe Daisy, Blue Daisy

GLOBULARIACEAE

Not really daisies of any sort, *Globularias* are
dainty, rather dwarf plants found in many
parts of central Europe and down to the
Mediterranean. They include perennials,
shrubs and subshrubs, such as illustrated
G. cordifolia, which is the perfect plant for
sunny rockeries in cool temperate climates.

Propagate them from cuttings, then set
out rooted plants in dryish, neutral to alkaline
soil and water infrequently. Plants will spread
gradually, scarcely topping 15cm/6in high and
producing solitary heads of fluffy mauve
stamens from late spring to early summer.
The unusual leaves are rather spoon-shaped.

Globularia cordifolia. Globe Daisy

GLORIOSA
(glor-ee-**oh**-z∂)
Gloriosa Lily, Glory Lily
LILIACEAE

Exotic climbing members of the lily family, *Gloriosas* grow from tuberous roots and cling to the nearby support of dense shrubs or trees with the wiry tendrils that tip their leaves.

They need little attention once planted in a deep, rich soil in early spring. Give them bright light and regular water, and the first leaves should appear within 2 weeks. If possible, keep up the humidity at all times, and watch out for slugs and snails as the first flower buds appear in the summer. Blooms have reflexed petals, and are rather like an attenuated Tiger Lily.

Gloriosas are native to Uganda, so it is not surprising that they are frost tender, and need a minimum winter temperature of 10ºC/50ºF.

Gloriosa superba 'Rothschildiana'. Gloriosa Lily

GLOTTIPHYLLUM
(glot-ti-**fil**-l∂m)
Tongue-leaf
AIZOACEAE

Regarded for many years as just another Mesembryanthemum species, this small group of plants now rejoices in a botanical name of its very own – *Glottiphyllum*, which means exactly the same as its older popular name of Tongue-leaf. Tongues are certainly what they look like – the leaves flat, wide and succulent, with turned-up tips. They come in pairs and loll on the ground, resembling a butcher's display of calves' tongues in all but colour. The short-stalked flowers open in midsummer, bright yellow in all species and up to 10cm/4in wide. Grow them in sandy, well-drained soil in a sun-drenched rock pocket. Water infrequently.

Glottiphyllum uncatum. Tongue-leaf

GMELINA
(mel-**ai**-n∂)
Spiny Gmelina
VERBENACEAE

My reference books tell me that there are *Gmelinas* with lilac flowers, but the only one I have encountered on my travels is the yellow *Gmelina asiatica*. This 3.5m/11ft shrub is for subtropical and warmer climates only, but there it is a striking sight with its many hanging clusters of flowers, the sulphur-yellow bells emerging from among contrasting mahogany-coloured bracts. I am told it is easily grown in sunshine and rich soil, and can be pruned in early spring. In colder climates it would be a handsome pot plant for a well-heated greenhouse.

Gmelina asiatica. Spiny Gmelina

GOMPHOLOBIUM
(gom-foh-**loh**-bee-∂m)
Glory Pea, Wedge Pea
FABACEAE

Gompholobium is a small Australian genus of about 25 species. Nearly all are low shrubs, their narrow, linear leaves signalling their origins in the sandy, coastal heaths. Some, such as *G. grandiflorum*, are extremely showy in spring when fully decked with 3cm/1in bright yellow pea-flowers. Oddly, they seem to have a greater following in countries other than their own, for they are widely grown in mild-climate gardens elsewhere. They are fussy, though, and demand humus-rich, sandy soil, always just moist yet well drained. Dappled shade during the hottest part of the day seems to suit them best. Grow from scarified seed.

Gompholobium grandiflorum. Golden Glory Pea

Gomphrena globosa. Globe Amaranth

Gordonia axillaris. Gordonia

GOMPHRENA

(gom-**free**-n∂)
Globe Amaranth
AMARANTHACEAE

Purple clover might be your first impression of the dainty Globe Amaranths, but the plants are actually stiffer and more branching, and 7–30cm/3–12in high, according to variety.

Rather leggy plants, these members of the amaranth family provide flowers which are useful for bedding, and for drying as 'everlastings' for indoor arrangements.

Gomphrena globosa is available these days with a dwarf habit and in many mixed shades, from pink to lavender, white, putty, orange and yellow. Seed should be sown some 2 months before planting out time. It will germinate in 15–20 days at a constant temperature of 21ºC/70ºF. The plants take 3 months to reach flowering size; they should be spaced 25cm/10in apart in light, well-drained soil. Mulch in hot weather.

GONGORA

(gon-**gor**-∂)
Punch and Judy Orchid, Helmet Orchid
ORCHIDACEAE

For years I have grown *Gongora galeata* in my little greenhouse, and it attracts comment every summer when I bring it indoors so as to enjoy the scented cinnamon-and-beige flowers, which are among the most remarkably formed of all orchids. Its pot has to be stood on a tall pedestal so the long chains of flowers can dangle freely on their string-like stems; but that is the only special attention it ever gets. A little fertiliser in spring, regular

Gongora galeata. Helmet Orchid

watering in summer but almost none in winter – that's all. Like all South American orchids, it will not stand the slightest frost. A winter temperature of at least 12ºC/50ºF is ideal.

GORDONIA

(gor-**doh**-nee-∂)
Gordonia
THEACEAE

Showy *Gordonias* are found in both Asia and North America and can easily be mistaken for their close relatives, Camellias. *G. axillaris*

is the most common species and spends years as a shrub before finally developing into a handsome, rounded tree 10m/33ft tall. Its leaves are glossy dark green, and although evergreen, it produces a sort of autumn and winter colour as isolated leaves turn rich scarlet and gold.

But it is the flowers that are the *Gordonia*'s claim to fame. Each 7–10cm/3–4in across, they are simple blooms made up of creamy-white crepe-textured petals surrounding a golden-yellow boss of stamens that is faintly fragrant and draws bees from all directions. The flowers are borne profusely from late summer or early autumn and continue for 2 or 3 months, carpeting the ground beneath the plant with fallen but still perfect blooms. It is this feature that makes them particularly appealing lawn specimens.

Gordonias are hardy to light, infrequent frosts only, and prefer a deep, rich, acid soil kept consistently moist. They are grown from seed, cuttings or layers.

GOSSYPIUM

(gos-**sip**-ee-∂m)
Cotton Plant
MALVACEAE

The most important members of this genus are the two or three species that provide cotton: florists sometimes display branches adorned with the fluffy white puffs of fibre in which the seeds are embedded. But the most beautiful flowers that the genus offers are undoubtedly those of the Sturt's Desert Rose, *Gossypium sturtianum*, a shoulder-high shrub from central Australia and the floral emblem of the Northern Territory. They appear in late winter and spring and are normally a lovely shade of mallow-pink, with maroon blotches in the centre. Frost-free semi-desert (or at least dry-summer) climates suit it best.

Gossypium sturtianum. Sturt's Desert Rose

GRAPTOPETALUM
(grap-toh-**pet**-ə-ləm)
(SYN Tacitus)
Graptopetalum
CRASSULACEAE

This dainty succulent plant was discovered in the Mexican desert only in 1972. Just a few inches high at maturity, *Graptopetalum bellum* (syn *Tacitus bellus*) doesn't take long to sprout from seed (or from one of the offset leaf-rosettes that appear behind the main plant). Sandy soil is the rule, plus absolutely arid conditions: you must grow it under glass in an area with regular rain. Warm temperate climates are best: scant water only during extreme drought. You'll love the stems of 5-petalled pink flowers that appear from the blue-green leaf-rosettes in late spring.

Graptopetalum bellum. Graptopetalum

Graptophyllum excelsum. Scarlet Fuchsia

GRAPTOPHYLLUM
(grap-toh-**fil**-ə m)
Scarlet Fuchsia, Caricature Plant
ACANTHACEAE

The most commonly seen species of *Graptophyllum* (from Indonesia and New Guinea) are grown mainly for the beauty of their curious foliage. The leaves are marked with irregular scrawls that resemble rough drawings or ink-blot tests. They may be green and yellow or pink and red, according to variety, and have given rise to the popular names Caricature Plant and Letter Leaf. Small heads of purple-crimson flowers form in warm weather, but they are not sufficiently showy to be considered a feature.

Graptophyllums strike easily from cuttings, and should be renewed regularly, as they tend to become too straggly.

In Australia there is a colourful species grown just for the spectacle of its scarlet blossoms, which are far larger than the small glossy leaves. This is *G. excelsum*, the Scarlet Fuchsia, which may reach 3m/10ft in a rich, well-drained soil. It needs a warm temperate climate, regular water, and is improved by a light pruning after its summer bloom.

Grevillea 'Robyn Gordon'. Spider Flower

Grevillea 'Sandra Gordon'

GREVILLEA
(grə-**vil**-lee-ə)
Spider Flowers
PROTEACEAE

Most attractive and floriferous of the antipodean shrub genera, *Grevilleas* are also the most improved, having long attracted the attention of hybridists. Now they bloom in a rainbow of colours, often for much of the year. California gardeners have discovered them in a big way; they are grown in Africa, New Zealand, and all around the Mediterranean. In a word, they have caught the imagination of modern gardeners just as they once did the early plant hunters of the southern continent.

This almost exclusively Australian genus is so variable in flower, foliage and habit, it is hardly surprising to learn that it belongs to the family Proteaceae, named for the demi-god Proteus, who could change his shape at will. Thus they are included with many other plants of bizarre appearance found in Australia, South Africa and South America, offering some proof of a prehistoric continental connection.

Grevillea 'Pink Surprise'

Grevillea pteridifolia. Toothbrush Grevillea

Grevillea curviloba. Woolly Grevillea

Grevillea robusta. Silky Oak

Grevillea lavandulacea. Lavender-leaf
Grevillea

Grevillea triloba. Three-lobed Grevillea

Grevillea 'Poorinda Queen'

Grevilleas seem to prefer full sun, and grow best in a well-drained soil that is rich in leafmould and somewhat gravelly. It must also be slightly acid and on the dryish side – species from inland Australia in particular abhor humidity. Grevilleas appreciate a light ration of balanced fertiliser from time to time. An excess of phosphorus can cause very unhappy plants.

While it is possible to grow them from absolutely fresh seed, the preferred method of propagation is from firm tip-cuttings, taken in late summer. These should be treated with a rooting hormone and set in a fast-draining sand/peat mixture. Warmth and humidity at this stage will promote rooting in no time. They can also be grafted.

G. 'Robyn Gordon' is a popular cultivar, and moderately frost hardy. It is a low, spreading plant with deeply divided leaves and arching sprays of scarlet bloom all year. These resemble those of one parent, the tree species G. banksii. Its stablemate G. 'Sandra Gordon', of tall, open habit, has similar foliage and golden-yellow flower spikes.

Among the lower-growing species is the splendid 'Poorinda Royal Mantle', which makes a very showy weeping feature with its eucalyptus-style foliage and single-sided toothbrush-type flower sprays. It is sometimes grafted onto a tall stock of the tree species G. robusta and makes a spectacular weeping standard. West Australian G. curviloba is also used for groundcover, growing to about 50cm/20in high, and bearing clouds of white perfumed flowers in spring. Random upright branches should be pruned away.

All Grevilleas are attractive to birds, particularly honeyeaters, which find rich sustenance among their flower-laden branches. There are over 250 species of these lovely shrubs, and innumerable hybrids, all of them lovely.

Grewia occidentalis. Lavender Star

GREWIA
(**groo**-ee-ə)
India Star
TILIACEAE

I first encountered *Grewia occidentalis*, the Lavender Star, at Disneyland many years ago, and wondered why such a delightful shrub was not grown in Australia, as it was obviously suited to our warm climate. Well, it duly arrived and is now very popular for its ease of culture, pleasant evergreen leaves and summer-long display of starry flowers, each about the size of a watch-face and either lilac or pink. It can grow into a small tree, but pruning in late winter easily keeps it shoulder-high and bushy. No fads about soil and position, but it dislikes frost. There are about 150 species in various parts of the Old World; this one, by far the most attractive, is from southern Africa.

GREYIA
(**grae**-ee-ə)
Mountain Bottlebrush, Baakhout
MELIANTHACEAE

A small South African genus, *Greyia* was named after a one-time governor of the Cape Colony. All three species are hardy to occa-

Greyia radlkoferi. Mountain Bottlebrush

sional frost, but need protection where the winters are really cold. They prefer fast-draining soil and should be watered sparingly except in summer, their main growth season.

Grow from seed if you can get it or from cuttings of half-ripe wood struck under glass. They do best in hot, exposed positions, and often develop a sprawling habit. The semi-deciduous leaves resemble those of the edible fig, and cluster at branch tips, where the spectacular orange-red inflorescences appear any time in winter or spring. In autumn, some leaves may colour before falling.

G. sutherlandii is the most widely grown species, though *G. radlkoferi* is also attractive and worthwhile. Both grow well in containers, flowering at an early age in large pots.

GUZMANIA
(gooz-**man**-ee-ə)
Guzmania, Red Cockade
BROMELIACEAE

Guzmanias are grown for their long-lasting cockades of red, green or yellow bracts that surround a shorter-lived spike of whitish flowers. They are raised in pots of open, rubble-filled compost and make agreeable house plants, though somewhat more demanding than other Bromeliads.

They begin to deteriorate during long spells of temperature below 10°C/50°F and need to be misted daily to maintain high humidity. The leaf vases should be kept filled with water all through the summer months, until the flowers and bracts appear. Each stem flowers only once and should be replaced after bloom with one or more of the suckers, freely produced. The illustrated species has leaves marked thinly in red.

Guzmania lingulata var. *minor*. Golden Cockade

Gymnocalycium saglionis. Chin Cactus

GYMNOCALYCIUM
(gim-noh-ka-**lik**-ee-əm)
Chin Cactus
CACTACEAE

Chin Cactuses are easy to identify by their pronounced bump or 'chin' underneath each group of spines. Dwarf plants, cylindrical, and with well-defined ribs, they are easily grown in small, shallow dishes.

They also produce flowers of pale green through to white and pink. The plants should be grown in a standard gritty cactus mix, watered regularly through the winter months.

G. mihanovichii 'Redhead' (formerly 'Hibotan') is the weirdest of the *Gymnocalyciums*, as it has no chlorophyll, and can only survive by being grafted onto another cactus. There it looks like a spiny orange-red fruit.

These strange plants are not frost hardy, and need dry winter conditions.

GYPSOPHILA
(jip-**sof**-il-ə)
Baby's Breath, Chalk Plant
CARYOPHYLLACEAE

A short life but a delightful one is the story of *Gypsophila paniculata*! It grows from seed, reaches flowering size, and dies, all within 10 weeks. For this reason it is resown every 3 weeks for continuous warm-weather bloom. Curiously (for such an airy-fairy plant), it is related to the sturdy Carnation, with which it is often sold in mixed bunches.

G. repens, by contrast, is a small, shrubby perennial that forms large mats of many-branched wiry stems. It produces tiny 6mm/2½ in flowers in loose bunches all over the plant in summer. Propagate from 5cm/2in spring cuttings of small lateral shoots; it is best to root these in a sand/peat mixture before planting out in early autumn.

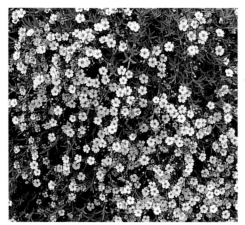

Gypsophila repens. Baby's Breath

Gypsophila paniculata 'Bristol Fairy'. Baby's Breath

Gypsophila tenuifolia. Baby's Breath

Haberlea rhodopensis. Bulgarian Primrose

Habranthus robustus. Pampas Lily

Haemanthus albiflos. Paintbrush

Haemanthus coccineus. Blood Lily

All *Gypsophilas* prefer well-drained alkaline soil and need little water. They are popular plants in rockeries, and will bloom repeatedly if sheared back when the flowers fade.

HABERLEA
(ha-**bur**-lee-ə)
Bulgarian Primrose
GESNERIACEAE

This dainty perennial comes from Bulgaria's mountains – and you'll need to reproduce its native terrain for successful growth. Seek out the shaded side of your rock garden, and plant in a leaf-rich crevice so water will drain away fast. Or grow them in pots in a gravelly mix.

Propagate from autumn leaf-cuttings, just like related African Violets, keep them moist all the time, and look forward to stems of mauve spring flowers.

HABRANTHUS
(hab-**ran**-thəs)
Pampas Lily
AMARYLLIDACEAE

Found naturally from Texas down to Argentina, some 10 species of *Habranthus* pop gaily out of the bare earth in summer to present mildly fragrant trumpet flowers in a variety of colours. They are sometimes listed as Hippeastrum or Zephyranthes, but vary from both genera through a difference in the spathe or budsheath.

Best-known *H. robustus*, native to the Argentine pampas, needs a warm temperate climate. It is grown from seed or bulb offsets, preferably in a leaf-rich, well-drained soil. Regular moisture produces the best flowers, which are tinted a rosy mauve, but fade to white on their 25cm/10in stems. Very showy!

HAEMANTHUS
(hee-**man**-thəs)
Blood Lily, April Fool, Scadoxus
AMARYLLIDACEAE

Over 20 species of vividly coloured bulbous flowers from southern Africa, *Haemanthus* are easy to grow and perfectly amenable to pot culture. The group was bigger, but tropical members have been moved to Scadoxus (which see).

The large bulbs should be planted out in a light, sandy compost with a little animal manure, the neck of the bulb at soil level. Set out or pot up in earliest spring in semi-shade and water regularly till roots have developed, allowing them to dry out between soakings.

Hakea laurina. Pincushion Tree

Hakea sericea. Needle Hakea

The plump flower stems will appear while the plant is bare of leaves. In *Haemanthus coccineus*, the stem bursts into a mass of red florets enclosed by showy scarlet bracts; *H. albiflos* has delicate greenish-white florets and green bracts.

Leaves appear later, but will die back in the plant's winter dormancy, when water should taper off completely. Keep at 10°C/50°F in winter. *Haemanthus* should be top-dressed and manured annually.

HAKEA
(**hae**-kee-ə)
Pincushion Tree, Sea Urchin Flower
PROTEACEAE

'Spectacular' is a good word to describe *Hakea laurina*, most interesting of yet another Protead genus!

It is happy down to –7°C/19°F and even produces its flower display in cold weather. Not a large tree, you can expect a maximum height of 7m/23ft, and then only in dry, gravelly soils, the conditions it enjoys in its original West Australian setting. This *Hakea* is widely grown as a decorative shrub in the Mediterranean area, southern California and New Zealand, and is prized for its perfume. Occasionally seen pruned to shrubby size as a street tree in Melbourne, in nature it is a loose, gangling sort of plant, with branches often weeping and densely covered with 10cm/4in leathery leaves of an interesting blue-green. The eye-catching flower clusters appear in early winter to spring. *H. sericea* has stiff needle leaves and silky white or pink flowers.

Hakeas can be grown from either seed or ripened cuttings. Acid soil, plenty of sun and sharp drainage are ideal, and they really take off close to the coast.

The entire group was named for Baron von Hake, an 18th-century professor of botany, and there are 130 or so species in the genus.

HALESIA
(hae-**lee**-see-ə)
Silver Bell, Snowdrop Tree
STYRACACEAE

In cold climates, the five species of *Halesia* just have to be among the most beautiful of flowering trees. One is from China, the others grow naturally in eastern USA. *H. monticola* has been measured to 30m/100ft in the wild, but is only a fraction of that in the home garden. It enjoys a deep, damp root-run in rich, acid soil. *Halesias* are often pruned to compact size after bloom to protect next season's delicate bell-flowers. Propagate from seed or cuttings, and bless with full sun.

Halesias are deciduous, and have no great display of autumn colour.

Halesia monticola. Silver Bell

HALIMIUM
(ha-**lim**-ee-um)
Great Sunrose
CISTACEAE

Rarely acclaimed for a wide variety of native plants, the Iberian peninsula does produce a few of great decorative value, among them the illustrated *Halimium lasianthum* or Great Sunrose. It is closely related to the subshrubby Helianthemums, but grows in a warm climate to 120cm/4ft or more – a dazzling sight in spring or summer, when it is decked with 5cm/2in red-marked golden flowers.

Grow *Halimium* from seed or soft-tip cuttings, and plant in well-drained alkaline soil. It is evergreen, upright in habit, and needs little water except in drought. Not truly frost hardy.

Halimium lasianthum. Great Sunrose

HAMAMELIS
(ham-a-**mel**-əs)
Witch Hazel, Chinese Witch Hazel
HAMAMELIDACEAE

Stunning in winter flower arrangements, the strap-like golden petals of Chinese Witch Hazel resist frost and icy winds to drape the bare zig-zag branches all through the cold months.

Hamamelis mollis. Chinese Witch Hazel

The shrub grows happily enough among deciduous trees where winter sunlight can reach, preferring sun for only part of the day. Choose a well-drained acid soil, enriched with plenty of leafmould and ground bark. Its growth is as slow as its blooming is brief, but it offers a charming fragrance when used indoors.

Hamamelis mollis is from China, and spreads gradually into a sparsely furnished bush clothed with 13cm/5in leaves that are widest near the tips. They are coarsely toothed and deciduous; blossom can be cut in bud.

Seed germination is very slow; heeled cuttings 10cm/4in long, taken in autumn, prove more successful.

Hamelia patens. Firebush

HAMELIA

(ha-**mel**-lee-ə)
(SYN Duhamelia)
Firebush, Scarlet Bush
RUBIACEAE

Not truly spectacular, the 40 or so *Hamelia* species are native to the Caribbean area and Bolivia – and grow tall enough (to 7.5m/25ft) to make a useful background in subtropical gardens. Elsewhere they'll reach only half that size.

Growing fast (in warm climates), they may be propagated from seed or semi-hardened cuttings struck over heat. Water regularly, feed occasionally to replace nutrient leached out by tropical rains, and give plenty of sun. Flowers are sparse, tubular, and come in various shades of orange and scarlet, at branch tips.

HARDENBERGIA

(hah-den-**bur**-gee-ə)
False Sarsaparilla, Australian Lilac
FABACEAE

A dainty groundcover for dappled shade or full sun, the False Sarsaparilla (*Hardenbergia*

Hardenbergia comptoniana. False Sarsaparilla, Native Wisteria

violacea) will also climb if given support. Only lightly foliaged and not at all rampant, it will wander harmlessly through and over shrubs or up and around verandah posts, wire fences or trellises. Native to eastern Australia, it is more frost hardy than its cousin from southwestern Australia, the illustrated *H. comptoniana*.

The small, pea-type flowers occur during the warmer months and are almost always purple, though pink or white forms are sometimes seen. *Hardenbergia* is not a demanding plant and requires only well-drained soil to thrive. Water only if rainfall is inadequate and go easy on the fertiliser. The seed coat is hard and must be filed or softened in warm water for 24 hours before sowing.

Hatiora salicornioides. Bottle Plant

HATIORA

(hat-ee-**or**-ə)
Drunkard's Dream, Bottle Plant
CACTACEAE

I suppose it *is* the drunkard's dream – a plant made up of green wine bottles! But *Hatiora salicornioides* wouldn't offer him much to drink when he woke up – each bottle-shaped segment of the stems of this bushy epiphytic cactus from Brazil is only about 2cm/1in long. It grows very slowly, eventually cascading gracefully from its pot, and looks delightful in spring when each stem is tipped with a tiny golden flower. The flowers last for weeks and are succeeded by little yellow berries. There are no thorns. Give the plant rich but perfectly drained soil and a spot in light shade, water it freely in summer (but not in winter), and protect it from frost.

HEBE

(**hee**-bee)
Veronica, Shrub Speedwell, Koromiko, New Zealand Lilac
SCROPHULARIACEAE

A diverse shrub genus for the cool temperate garden, *Hebe* includes some 100 species, mostly native to New Zealand. Evergreen, bearing dense spikes of tiny 4-petalled flowers, mostly in shades of purple, white and cerise, they thrive in the frost-free coastal garden. There they are used as thick groundcovers, in massed shrubberies or trimmed as dense hedges. They are completely resistant to salt and sea winds and favour a semi-

Hebe diosmifolia. Shrub Speedwell

Hebe 'Amy'. Veronica

Hedychium coccineum. Red Ginger Lily

Hebe salicifolia. Koromiko

Hebe hulkeana. New Zealand Lilac

HEDYCHIUM
(he-**dik**-ee-ə m)
Kahili Ginger, Ginger Lily, Garland Flower, Butterfly Flower, White Ginger Blossom
ZINGIBERACEAE

Luxuriant tropical plants for semi-shaded corners, the Ginger Lilies are deliciously perfumed and can be grown in rich, peaty compost, with a little sand for drainage. They must be kept constantly moist after early spring planting until the flowers appear in summer.

Hedychiums grow from shooting sections of rhizome, as do Flag Iris, and will reach 1.5–2m/5–6ft. Cut right back to the ground after blooming, and keep barely moist over the winter months, preferably at around 13°C/55°F. All *Hedychiums* are native to India, and really do best with high humidity.

shaded spot. *Hebes* are fast-growing and will bloom both winter and summer.

Commonly planted garden types are mostly cultivars which can only be propagated by means of cuttings taken in midsummer. Trim these to 10cm/4in and insert in a mixture of peat and sand, keeping in a cool place. Generally rooted by the following spring, they should be potted up individually, hardened up outdoors and finally planted in a permanent position in early autumn.

Hebe subalpina. Veronica

Hebes are not at all fussy as to soil, accepting even a little lime, and are remarkably maintenance-free. Few require regular pruning, though an occasional shearing in earliest spring will improve their vigour. Take branches back to half their former length, feed over the root area and new growth will break from the cut twigs within a few days. Even pests are inclined to leave *Hebes* alone, only downy mildew causing much of a problem.

All *Hebe* species and cultivars prefer a well-drained soil. There is marked variation in height. The low-growing types such as *H. pinguifolia* and *H. subalpina* make decorative groundcovers, for they normally grow less than 30cm/1ft in height and spread widely.

Variably taller *H. elliptica*, *H. diosmifolia*, *H. hulkeana* and *H. salicifolia* can be allowed to have their heads, be clipped as dense hedges or bun-shaped specimens. Most *Hebes* have decorative foliage, each alternate pair of glossy leaves being borne at right angles to its neighbour.

Hebe, these lovely plants' namesake, was the Greek goddess of youth.

Hedychium gardnerianum. Kahili Ginger

Hedychium coronarium. Garland Flower

H. gardnerianum, the Kahili Ginger, is the most commonly grown, producing 45cm/18in spikes of scarlet and yellow blossom all summer. *Hedychium* means 'Sweet Snow', aptly describing the Garland Flower, *H. coronarium,* fragrant and satiny-white with a touch of pastel yellow.

HELENIUM
(hel-**ee**-nee-∂m)
Sneezeweed
ASTERACEAE

Sneezeweeds – *Helenium autumnale* and its cultivars – are daisy-bearing plants from North America, with brownish pompon centres that set them apart from other daisy flowers. They revel in hot summers, and though perennial in nature, are raised as annuals in temperate climates.

Seed should be sown outdoors the year before blooming, any time up to 2 months before frost. Indoor sowing is also possible in cooler climates, if a temperature of 21°C/70°F can be maintained during germination, which takes only 7–10 days.

Helenium 'Moerheim Beauty'. Sneezeweed

Helianthemum 'Fire King'. Scarlet Sunrose

The plants are slow-growing and must have rich, moist soil in a warm, sunny position, as their natural preference is for swampy places. Space them 30–45cm/ 12–18in apart and at flowering time, deadhead regularly to force extended bloom and avoid unwanted seedlings.

Growing to 1m/3ft in height, they require little attention. They come in shades of yellow, beige, tan and red.

HELIANTHEMUM
(hel-ee-**an**-th∂-mum)
Sunrose
CISTACEAE

Small relatives of the handsome and shrubby Cistus or Rock Roses, *Helianthemums* are classed as subshrubby perennials. Low, mound-forming evergreen plants with attractive foliage that varies from deep to greyish green, they enjoy a dryish well-drained sunny spot with slightly alkaline soil. In spring they become a carpet of dazzling bloom in warm reds, pinks, oranges or yellows. When flowers fade, shear the plants all over to promote a second flush.

Helianthemum 'Golden Queen'. Yellow Sunrose

Helianthemums survive well in cold winter areas and temperate climates. Heeled 7.5cm/3in cuttings of lateral shoots taken in summer root rapidly in a sandy mix. Pinch out to develop a bushy habit and plant out the following spring.

Watch for powdery mildew in hot weather. They grow 10–45cm/4–18in high, and can spread to 1m/3ft wide.

HELIANTHUS
(hel-ee-**an**-th∂s)
Sunflower
ASTERACEAE

Giants among the annuals, Sunflowers are possibly the easiest of all to grow. Just take some large black seeds, scatter in weed-free, cultivated soil, rake in, water regularly and await results! Because they grow so fast, children love them, and are reminded of Jack and the Beanstalk.

Helianthus annuus varies greatly in height, and can reach 4m/13ft in some cultivars. They are all coarse, leggy plants with heavily veined leaves that have a sticky feel to them. For success, they need full sun and a protected position, as wind can play havoc with them.

H. multiflorus has spectacular cultivars featuring huge flowers, double blooms or

Helianthus multiflorus. Double Sunflower

Helichrysum orientale. Golden Buttons

compact plants, as well as colours ranging from palest creamy yellow to bronze and brownish tones.

Sunflowers will grow in any soil, but prosper in heavily composted ground enriched with manure and packaged fertiliser. Snails are the principal menace.

Giving a long display from summer to autumn, in both cold-winter and temperate climates, these glorious golden flowers were once worshipped by the Incas of Peru as living images of their Sun God.

Helianthus annuus. Sunflower

HELICHRYSUM
(hel-i-**krai**-sǝm)
Paper Daisy, Curry Plant
ASTERACEAE

Most of the Australian plants once included in this genus have been transferred to *Bracteantha*, *Chrysocephalum* or *Ozothamnus*, leaving Africa and the Mediterranean as the main home of true *Helichrysum*.

The plants are mostly perennials, prostrate or spreading, with small woolly or silver-haired leaves. The elaborate daisy-like blooms are borne in clusters, and have a

crackly finish. What appear to be petals are actually papery bracts, while the true flowers make up the centre.

Offering a stunning outdoor display in most garden soils, the flower yield is enhanced by the application of packaged fertiliser. *Helichrysums* prefer warm, sunny, sheltered sites; they can survive hot summers better than most plants, but regular watering is vital.

Seed can be sown direct in early spring but quicker results can be gained by sowing indoors in flats in late winter, at a steady temperature of 21°C/70°F. Germination should only take 7–10 days if the seeds remain uncovered and moist. Plant out seedlings at 25–35cm/10–12in spacings, in well-drained soil, and blooming should start in about 16 weeks.

There are also perennial types, mostly native to southernmost Africa. Dwarf *Helichrysum milfordiae,* with yellow-centred white blooms, is sometimes known as the Silver Straw Flower. *H. orientale,* from the eastern Mediterranean and Greece, bears shiny yellow flower heads in summer.

Helichrysum milfordiae. Silver Straw Flower

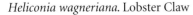

Heliconia rostrata. Fishpole Heliconia

HELICONIA
(hel-i-**koh**-nee-ə)
Lobster Claw, Parrot Flower
MUSACEAE

This remarkably beautiful group of plants from the tropical banana family is difficult to bring to flower any distance from the humid tropics. To do them justice in temperate areas you really need a warm greenhouse or conservatory, although the

Heliconia wagneriana. Lobster Claw

Heliconia caribaea 'Gold'. Golden Heliconia

smaller species *Heliconia psittacorum*, or Parrot Flower, can be managed as a window plant where constant warmth and humidity can be provided.

Heliconias are best planted in earliest spring in a rich, peaty compost and watered generously throughout the warmer months, with the accompaniment of an occasional ration of decayed manure; they prefer filtered sun. While the flowers are generally insignificant, they are hidden inside dazzlingly coloured bracts.

Originally hailing from South America, *Heliconias* need a 13°C/55°F winter minimum to produce their splendid show. Needless to say, if you live in such a climate, you should seek them out without delay. *H. bicolor* has orange-scarlet bracts and grows to 90cm/3ft; *H. rostrata* (called the Fishpole Heliconia) reaches 2.5m/8ft, with bracts of scarlet, green and yellow; *H. bihai*, at 2m/6ft, glows red and dark green; *H. caribaea* has red and yellow bracts; *H. wagneriana* has pinkish-red, cream and green bracts. What splendid decorations they make, arranged indoors!

HELIOCEREUS
(hel-ee-oh-**see**-ree-əs)
Sun Cactus
CACTACEAE

Heliocereus, the Sun Cactus, is an epiphyte from Central America which has been much hybridised with Epiphyllums and others to produce red colour breaks.

Because of their sturdy nature, they are also used as stocks for the weeping standards of Aporocactus, Rhipsalidopsis and Schlumbergera. But *Heliocereus mallisonii* is well worth growing for itself. Planted in wide containers of gritty but moist compost, the stems of the Sun Cactus will spill over the edge and bloom generously in early summer. The flowers, mostly in tones of orange-pink, vermilion and scarlet, remain open for several days. They require full sun and regular water, and a minimum winter temperature of 4°C/40°F.

Heliopsis helianthoides subsp. *scabra* 'Incomparabilis'. Ox-eye Daisy

HELIOPSIS
(hel-ee-**op**-sis)
Ox-eye
ASTERACEAE

Another fine North American daisy genus that puts on a dazzling display in the summer border, or naturalised in wild parts of the garden. *Heliopsis* grow in any soil and are particularly useful in dry areas where their blooming will continue for months, with a minimum of water.

They are commonly planted from root divisions taken in cold weather, but can also be grown from seed, germinated under glass at a temperature of 21°C/70°F. If started early enough, the *Heliopsis* plants may even bloom the first year. Set them out 60cm/2ft apart, preferably in a moist but well-drained

Heliocereus mallisonii. Sun Cactus

Helleborus argutifolius. Corsican Hellebore

position. They'll reach a height of 1–2m/ 3–6ft and spread far and wide.

Regular dead-heading will prolong the display well into autumn, when they should be cut back to ground level.

HELIOTROPIUM
(hel-ee-oh-**troh**-pee-ǝm)
Heliotrope, Cherry Pie
BORAGINACEAE

Sweetly fragrant, the old-time Heliotrope or Cherry Pie of cottage gardens is actually an exotic South American import – tender to frost and fast-growing in mild climates. So fast, many people set out cuttings in early spring and treat them as annuals. In fact, Heliotrope is one of those borderline plants some authorities list as a subshrub, others as a shrubby perennial.

Growing in any enriched, well-drained garden soil, in full sun, *Heliotropium arborescens* enjoys humidity. In very hot, dry areas, it is best raised in semi-shade, with the foliage sprinkled regularly. Reaching a height of up to 120cm/4ft, it requires regular weak liquid fertiliser while growing, and should be cut back by half in very early spring to promote bushiness.

HELLEBORUS
(hel-lǝ-**bor**-ǝs)
Winter Rose, Lenten Rose, Hellebore, Christmas Rose
RANUNCULACEAE

Useful winter and spring flowering perennials for the cooler climate, Hellebores provide unusual and exciting colorations for the flower arranger. Apple green, greenish-white and many shades of purple are the principal tones.

Heliotropium arborescens 'Marine'. Cherry Pie

Plant them in drifts or massed in the shade of deciduous trees during autumn, making sure the soil is heavily enriched with organic matter. Then give them several years to establish, and they'll reward you year after year with masses of fascinating flowers when blooms are hard to come by.

All species of *Helleborus* are native to southern Europe and western Asia. If their names are seasonally illogical south of the equator, they are popular everywhere. They are closely related to the Ranunculus. Like Miss Greta Garbo, they want to be left alone, although a top-dressing of well-rotted compost or manure after flowering seems to have an improving effect.

To propagate, lift and divide the roots immediately after flowering, but risk a year's loss of bloom. Ripened seed can be sown in

Helleborus orientalis. Lenten Rose

Hemerocallis fulva 'Flore Pleno'. Double Daylily

early summer, under glass. Prick out when large enough, and grow on; the seedlings will be unlikely to flower before the third year.

Growing to a height of 25–60cm/ 10–24in, Hellebores are evergreen and hold their handsome, deeply-lobed and divided leaves all year, those of *Helleborus argutifolius* being rather spiny. There's one cardinal rule: never let the plants dry out over the summer months: always keep them moist.

HEMEROCALLIS
(hem-ər-oh-**kal**-ləs)
Daylily, Spider Lily
LILIACEAE

A useful genus of perennial bulbs for any climate or type of soil, old-fashioned Daylilies need little care but should be positioned carefully when planting, as the blooms will always turn towards the equator and the sun. Individual blooms last only one day, but as they come in clusters, a single flower head may be in bloom for weeks.

Daylilies are much hybridised, but they're of two principal types: evergreen and deciduous. The evergreen *Hemerocallis aurantiaca*, for example, produces lush clumps of pale-green leaves and has been hybridised to include lemon, pink and purple blooms with the original orange. The deciduous *H. fulva* is usually seen in double form: orange flowers marked with mahogany.

Hemerocallis. Hybrid Daylily

Hemerocallis minor. Dwarf Daylily

Hermodactylus tuberosus. Snake's Head Iris
TONY RODD

Plant from divisions in winter. Part-shade gives brighter colours: blooms are inclined to fade in full sun. *Hemerocallis* will do well even in rather poor, exhausted soil and will grow in any temperate climate.

HEPATICA
(hep-**at**-ik-ə)
Liverleaf
RANUNCULACEAE

Hepatica comes from the Latin word for the liver, and might suggest a flower in some horrid brownish colour – but in fact these diminutive spring-flowering perennials are admired for the clarity and delicacy of their tints, and the name refers to their supposed usefulness in treating liver problems. They resemble miniature anemones, and indeed many botanists prefer to include them in that genus.

The best-known species is *H. nobilis* (syn *H. triloba*), in cultivation for so long that it can now be bought in a number of varieties, with single or double flowers in shades from white to blue and deep pink. They like a semi-shaded place in humus-rich soil in temperate to cool climates.

HERMODACTYLUS
(her-moh-**dak**-til-əs)
Snake's Head Iris
IRIDACEAE

Rather sinister both in name and in colouring, the Snake's Head Iris is not a real iris at all, for reasons that interest only serious botanists. Rather, it is a tuberous-rooted perennial with striking iris-like flowers in a strange combination of green and near-black. These are much valued for flower arrangements.

Native to well-drained, rocky but fertile soil in central and eastern Europe, it can withstand cold but not cold and wet winters; it is not suitable for tropical gardens.

Grow *Hermodactylus tuberosus* in sun or dappled shade. In cold climates, flowering occurs in earliest spring. Elsewhere, expect bloom in late winter.

HESPERIS
(**hess**-per-is)
Dame's Rocket, Damask Violet,
Sweet Rocket, Night-scented Stock
BRASSICACEAE

Favourite flowers in northern hemisphere gardens, the 30-odd species of *Hesperis* are almost unknown in the south. Just why is a mystery: they are invaluable for their fragrance on long summer evenings.

All cultivated species are biennial or perennial, and are normally raised from seed. (When established they'll self-sow with abandon.)

Hepatica species. Liverleaf

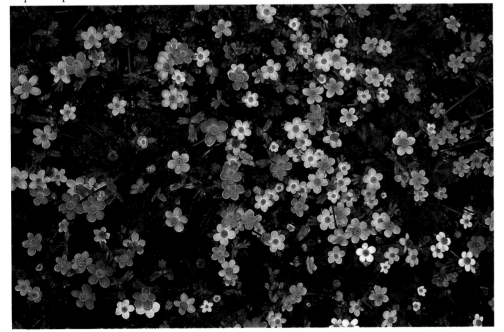

Hesperis matronalis. Dame's Rocket

Heterospermum xanti. Desert Stars

They are not fussy about soil (so long as it drains well), and need little water, but must never be allowed to dry out. Favourite *H. matronalis* comes in single and double varieties, in shades from white to purple. The Sweet Rocket grows 60–120cm/2–4ft, likes full sun and a coolish climate.

Heterocentron elegans. Spanish Shawl

HETEROCENTRON
(het-ur-oh-**sen**-trən)
(SYN Heeria)
Spanish Shawl, Trailing Lasiandra, Creeping Fuchsia
MELASTOMATACEAE

Best known in warm climate gardens for the brilliantly flowered groundcover known as Spanish Shawl (*Heterocentron elegans*), the genus includes several shrubby perennial species of great value in both warm and temperate gardens.

Heterocentron macrostachyum. Heeria Rosea

Heterocentron macrostachyum (known for many years as Heeria or *H. roseum*) is a handsome plant which may reach 1m/3ft in favourable conditions. Native to Mexico and Guatemala, this plant does best in a sandy soil enriched with peat, and demands regular water.

It is best propagated from root divisions or cuttings in early spring, and spreads by means of suckers. In autumn, the stems of red-edged elliptical leaves are topped with panicles of bright cerise 2.5cm/1in flowers, rather similar to those of the creeping species. Cut back old flower stems in early spring.

HETEROSPERMUM
(het-ur-oh-**spur**-m∂m)
Desert Stars
ASTERACEAE

Related to the more commonly grown
Coreopsis, a handful of *Heterospermum*
species are found principally in the southwestern desert areas of the United States, and
in nearby Mexico, where they'll turn on a
dazzling display a few weeks after spring
rains. *H. xanti* from Baja California is occasionally found in cultivation, being easy to
grow from seed and useful in cool-climate
gardens with perfectly drained soil. Its leaves
are finely divided, fern-like and borne in
opposite pairs; the 5-petalled golden daisy
flowers are borne on long, wiry stems.

HEUCHERA
(**yoo**-kur-∂)
Coral Bells, Alum Root
SAXIFRAGACEAE

Heuchera species seem somewhat out of
fashion today and are often hard to find,
though they make splendid edgings for
perennial borders or a charming massed
planting. They form neat clumps of scalloped leaves, a little like Geraniums, but in
spring and early summer the tall, wiry stems
appear, laden with nodding bell-flowers.
These may be white or crimson, but are
commonly coral pink.

Delicately rising to about 45cm/18in,
they should be planted out in autumn in
light, neutral to alkaline soil. Full sun is best,
except in dry climates, where light tree shade
is preferred.

Hibbertia procumbens. Guinea Flower

Hibbertia scandens. Guinea Gold Vine

HIBBERTIA
(hib-**bur**-tee-∂)
Golden Guinea Flower
DILLENIACEAE

Hibbertia is one of the showiest genera of
Australian native plants, with 120 or more
species found on the continent. They include
both shrubs and climbers, and *Hibbertia
scandens* in particular has become popular
all over the world. A shrubby vine with evergreen leaves, it likes sandy, well-drained soil.
It thrives on sand dunes, covers rocks and
will climb a sturdy wall or fence.

H. procumbens, on the other hand, prefers
to stay close to the ground and makes an
excellent rockery subject in well-watered, cool
temperate gardens. The spring and summer
flowers are large and freely produced.

HIBISCUS
(hib-**is**-k∂s, hai-**bis**-k∂s)
**Rose of China, Rose Mallow, Rosella,
Rose of Sharon, Shrub Althaea**
MALVACEAE

Pioneer botanist Linnaeus first used the
name Rose of China in the 18th century,
when he christened these fantastic tropical
flowers *Hibiscus rosa-sinensis.* He believed
they came from China itself (they were
certainly grown there at the time of the earliest European contacts), but modern research
suggests the Indian Ocean area as the most
likely original home. Species sufficiently
compatible to cross are found in East Africa,
Malagasy and Malaysia, and also throughout
the Pacific islands. Other species, native to
the Middle East and China itself, do not

Heuchera sanguinea. Coral Bells

Hibiscus 'Canary Girl'

Hibiscus 'The Path'

Hibiscus 'Ben Lexcen'

cross with *H. rosa-sinensis*. At any rate, hybrid *Hibiscus* reach their full glory only in warm to tropical gardens, the flowers peaking in size at about 25cm/10in diameter with the advent of autumn rains.

The spiritual if not the actual home of the ornamental *Hibiscus* is Hawaii, whose floral emblem it has become. The Hawaiian Islands have several native species and these have been crossed with at least 33 other species from different tropical areas to produce the stunning hybrids we know today. At one time there were over 5000 named cultivars grown there, but island gardeners became bored with them and reserved their enthusiasm for other flowers. There has been, however, a revival of interest in them.

Hibiscus species range all the way from small annuals to trees, but the popular types illustrated on these pages are mostly shrubs. *H. syriacus* (which really does come from Syria) is a favourite in European and North American gardens. It has single and double

Hibiscus 'Red Robin'

Hibiscus 'White Picardy'

Hibiscus schizopetalus. Skeleton Hibiscus

Hibiscus moscheutos 'Southern Belle'

Hibiscus tiliaceus. Sea Hibiscus

varieties in shades of pink, white and mauve, often with a deep red blotch. It is not compatible with any of the others illustrated, but they will rarely be found in gardens with the same climate anyway. *H. calyphyllus* and *H. schizopetalus* are native to East Africa.

Uncommon *H. insularis* has been found only on Norfolk and Phillip Islands in the South Pacific, but grows particularly well in coastal areas elsewhere. All are best propagated from 10cm/4in cuttings taken in spring or summer and struck in a peat/sand mixture at a temperature of around 18°C/65°F. If living in a borderline climate, don't hesitate to grow *Hibiscus* as a compact pot shrub that you can bring indoors in the cooler months, and pot up from time to time.

Where climates are not warm enough for the splendid Hawaiian hybrid *Hibiscus* to do their thing, gardeners must be content with *H. moscheutos*, a herbaceous perennial species from the eastern United States. These flower in a respectable colour range of red, pink and white, usually with contrasting centres, and are planted from division in autumn or spring. Deep, damp soil is best, enriched with compost and leafmould, and they should be fed complete fertiliser every 6 weeks during the growing season. Staking will probably be required unless the clumps are dense. Never allow them to dry out, and cut back hard in winter.

The tree species, *H. tiliaceus,* is found in coastal areas all about the Pacific Ocean.

Hibiscus syriacus 'Ardens'. Blue Hibiscus

Hieracium murorum. Hawkweed

HIERACIUM

(hai-er-**ak**-ee-ɘm)
Hawkweed, Golden Lungwort
ASTERACEAE

With very rare exceptions, the many Hawkweeds (*Hieracium* spp.) are native to Europe and North Africa, where over 250 species have been catalogued. They are a puzzling example of the artificial dichotomy between flowers and weeds. Easy to propagate and grow, frost hardy, rarely fussy about soil and water, Hawkweeds turn on a stunning display of rectangular-petalled daisy blooms in shades from lemon to red. Often in the wild they light up an entire field or hillside, but how often are they allowed to blaze away in the garden? Try some in a mixed border and you may well change your ideas about weeds! Raise them from summer seed or division of clumps in autumn; water and feed well and you'll have a show to remember. Dead-head regularly.

HIPPEASTRUM

(hip-pee-**ass**-trɘm)
Barbados Lilies
AMARYLLIDACEAE

The striking Barbados Lilies or *Hippeastrums* (once classified as *Amaryllis*), native to tropical America, make gorgeous house plants, and are usually raised that way.

Buy the fist-sized bulbs in early spring, and plant them up in individual 15cm/6in pots, always ensuring that there is at least 2.5cm/1in of space for compost all around. This should be a rich, loamy mixture with slight additions of sand and charcoal, and a layer of crocks below for drainage. Leave a third of the bulb showing above the surface.

Soak the pots deeply and put them away in a dim, cool place, not watering again until the flower spike is 5–8cm/2–3in high. Then acclimatise gradually to bright light.

When blooming is over, store bulbs dry until the first signs of next year's growth, when you must repot with fresh soil.

Indoors at any time, or out in the open garden, there are few bulbs which give a more spectacular display, and come in such a wide range of shades as the modern *Hippeastrum* hybrids. These are the result of crossing many of the 80 different species.

Snails, unfortunately, find the buds and leaves irresistible – so keep watch!

Hippeastrum 'Cocktail'. Hybrid Amaryllis

HOHENBERGIA

(hoh-en-**berg**-ee-ɘ)
Red Stars
BROMELIACEAE

One of the less common Bromeliads, *Hohenbergia* is more likely to be seen in tropical gardens than in glasshouse collections. Its spiny leaf-rosettes are up to 2.5m/8ft in diameter, making it too hard to handle in a pot. Showy *H. stellata* is from Brazil and Trinidad, needs a minimum temperature of 16–30°C/60–86°F to survive, and high humidity to flourish. Mist it often, and keep the leaf-vase full at all times. *Hohenbergias* look best in shade, where the vivid red bracts last for months. Actual flowers are violet, and appear sporadically in summer.

HOHERIA

(hoh-**heer**-ee-ɘ)
Lacebark, Houhere
MALVACEAE

The name is a Latin version of the Maori name, *hoihere*, and indeed these elegant shrubs or small trees come from New Zealand. The best known are *Hoheria lyallii* from the South Island and *H. populnea* from the North Island, the first deciduous, the second evergreen (and available in a most attractive version with variegated leaves), but otherwise alike in their slender, upright habit and their lavish displays of white flowers which bring a touch of springtime to the very end of summer. *H. lyallii* is the hardiest of the five species, though even it will not take severe cold and is happiest in a warm temperate climate. Good soil and shelter from the strongest winds and hottest sun are desirable, and no pruning is required.

Hohenbergia stellata. Red Stars

Hoheria lyallii. Lacebark

Holmskioldia sanguinea. Chinese Hat Plant

HOLMSKIOLDIA
(hohm-**shohl**-dee-ə)
**Chinese Hat Plant, Parasol Flower,
Mandarin's Hat, Cup-and-saucer Plant**
VERBENACEAE

Delightful little shrubs for warm coastal climates, or sunny, sheltered positions, *Holmskioldias* are fast-growing and bloom right through the warm weather

H. sanguinea is rather untidy and makes a considerable growth of slender weeping branches, even in poor soil. A single plant may spread wider than its 3.5m/11ft height, and the curious orange-scarlet flowers appear in autumn, clustered in dense terminal and axillary racemes. Each is small and tubular, backed with a thin, disc-like bract. A mature *Holmskioldia* can be kept vigorous

Hoheria populnea. Houhere

with a light annual pruning. Eliminate several of the oldest canes entirely. Propagate new plants from semi-hardened tip-cuttings struck over heat in spring or summer.

Pink and lime-yellow forms are also in cultivation.

HOMERIA
(hoh-**meer**-ee-ə)
Rooitulp, Salmon Homeria
IRIDACEAE

In many parts of Australia, the eye-catching *Homeria* is declared a noxious pest due to the stomach upsets it is claimed to cause in cattle. This quaint example of pressure from the rural lobby is hard for a gardener to understand. I'd protest that any cow that eats

Homeria collina. Rooitulp, Homeria

Hosta plantaginea. Plantain Lily

them deserves to throw up, and should stay out of my garden anyway. *Homerias* are tall, cormous perennials blooming in shades of apricot, salmon and yellow, and very spectacular in the mixed border.

Plant them from offsets, set out in early autumn. They need well-drained soil, plenty of winter water, none in summer, and are only marginally hardy. Their heir fragrant spring flowers close at night and in cloudy weather, and so are useless for picking.

Homoranthus flavescens. Homoranthus

HOMORANTHUS
(hom-∂-**ranth**-∂s)
Homoranthus
MYRTACEAE

Homoranthus flavescens is not widely grown even in its native Australia, and it is true that the lemon-yellow flowers are rather tiny. But they make up for that by coming in great abundance in spring and summer, by harmonising very nicely with the greyish leaves, and by wafting a very strong and pleasant scent of honey. Naturally, this attracts honey-eating birds, and the horizontal branches seem designed to display them to perfection. The shrub grows about 50cm/20in tall but spreads to twice that width and isn't fussy about soil or position, though it must have a frost-free climate. It grows well in tubs. Grow from cuttings.

HOSTA
(**hos**-t∂)
(SYN Funkia, Niobe)
Plantain Lily
LILIACEAE

Elegant Plantain Lilies produce luxuriant foliage effects in cool, shaded positions. They're equally effective in a courtyard or garden room. They are herbaceous perennials from Japan and China and are propagated by division of the root mass in autumn. Set *Hostas* out in a rich, peaty compost, with good drainage, and just hope you'll survive the suspense of waiting for the new leaves to appear in spring.

These develop in many shapes and sizes – up to 50cm/20in long according to variety – and in combinations of white and gold as well as many shades of green. *H. plantaginea* has large oval leaves of blue-green, distinctively pleated, and *H. fortunei* has longer pointed leaves in many colour variations.

Tall stems of nodding bell-flowers appear in warm weather, in shades of white, pink or mauve, but eternal vigilance against snails and slugs is necessary.

Feed *Hostas* regularly while in growth, but don't be startled when the entire plant dies back to the roots in autumn.

HOVEA
(**hoh**-vee-∂)
Hovea
FABACEAE

Lovely, lightly branched and foliaged shrubs that thrive in the dappled shade cast by open trees or in the shelter of other, taller shrubs, *Hoveas* deck themselves in early spring with masses of blue-purple pea-flowers. These appear along the entire length of every stem but, sadly, are not particularly long lived. The whole show comes and goes inside a month.

Hovea lanceolata. Shrub Hovea

Hoya lanceolata subsp. *bella*. Beautiful Honey Plant

Hoya carnosa. Wax Flower

HUNNEMANIA

(hun-nə-**mae**-nee-ə)

Mexican Tulip Poppy, Golden Cup

PAPAVERACEAE

A close relative of the California Poppy, the lovely Mexican Tulip Poppy, *Hunnemania fumariifolia*, is just as easy to raise, but often taller-growing.

Hunnemanias naturalise easily, but transplanting is difficult. Seed should be sown direct into lightly raked soil that has a slight alkaline balance. Do this in early spring, or after frost in cooler areas. Germination takes 15–20 days and young plants need thinning out to 25–30cm/10–12in intervals.

Hunnemania is drought resistant, and enjoys full sun in a warm location. The decorative foliage is blue-green, with flowers a glorious satiny yellow. Dip stems of unopened buds in boiling water. They will last a week.

Hoveas demand well-drained soil and prefer it on the sandy side as well. And if their roots can be kept cool by a large, flat stone nearby, so much the better! *H. lanceolata* is an understorey shrub of the moist forests of eastern Australia. It cannot stand dryness at any time, is hardy down to at least −5ºC/23ºF and is grown from pre-soaked seed.

HOYA

(hoi-ə)

Wax Plant, Honey Flower

ASCLEPIADACEAE

The Wax Plants or *Hoyas* are incredibly beautiful plants from Australia and neighbouring areas. Hardy outdoors only to 10ºC/50ºF, they grow easily inside, preferably on a glassed-in balcony, as they make an incredible mess of furniture with the sticky honeydew that drips from every flower. Most are summer-blooming trailers, with superbly scented blossoms that look like wax dipped in powdered sugar.

Plant *Hoyas* in small containers of standard compost and repot only when you must, for they resent disturbance. They should never be pruned, as new flowers always appear from the remains of the old, and next year's blossoms will flourish in exactly the same place as previously. This is

always so with the most popular of the *Hoyas*, *H. carnosa*. Pink-flowered, it has two variegated leaf forms, one with pink edges fading to cream, and the other gold-centred foliage edged with dark green.

Hoya lanceolata subsp. *bella*, the Beautiful Honey Plant, is very suitable for growing in a hanging planter. It is a lightweight plant with trailing branches and bears umbels of starry, snowy-white flowers with an alluring perfume.

Hunnemania fumariifolia. Mexican Tulip Poppy

Hyacinthoides hispanica. Spanish Bluebell

Hyacinthoides non-scripta. English Bluebell

HYACINTHOIDES

(hai-ə-sin-**thoi**-deez)

(SYN Endymion, Scilla)

Bluebell

LILIACEAE

The English Bluebell is one of the best-loved of all spring flowers, and it is a pity that the rules of botanical nomenclature oblige us to call it by the cumbersome name *Hyacinthoides non-scripta*, which suggests that it closely resembles a hyacinth. Perhaps it does, to a botanist's eye; but to mine the slim stems hung with softly scented bells are very different. It needs a frosty winter to flower well.

In mild-winter climates the Spanish bluebell, *H. hispanica*, is a better choice. A larger and showier plant, it unfortunately lacks scent. Both species can be bought in white and soft pink as well as blue. They are happiest in woodland, or at least in shade and leafy soil; and the pretty old name *Endymion*, alas now obsolete, was appropriate. Endymion was, you recall, the young man loved by the forest goddess Diana.

Showy Spanish Bluebells, *Hyacinthoides hispanica*, grow easily in moist, woodsy soil and are ideal for planting under deciduous or open evergreen trees. They grow equally well in shallow pots of rich, acid compost – but be sure there's a good layer of broken crocks and charcoal for drainage.

Plant the succulent white bulbs 5cm/2in deep in late autumn. Water deeply once and not again until the leaf shoots appear. Thereafter, keep just moist until the spring flowers fade. The leaves will then begin to yellow and drier conditions will stop the

Hyacinthus orientalis 'Hollyhock'. Hyacinth

bulb rotting. English Bluebells (*H. non-scripta*) are similar but smaller all round. Both are hardy enough to withstand European winters but also grow well in frost-free areas.

HYACINTHUS

(hai-ə-**sin**-thəs)

Hyacinth

LILIACEAE

Favourite spring bulbs for indoors or out, Hyacinths are sold all over the world, often already potted up and in bud.

For bowl culture, buy the largest bulbs you can find in autumn and plant 5 or 6 to a wide container. Fill with standard indoor compost and a little granulated charcoal. Put the bulbs with their tops right at soil level,

Hyacinthus orientalis 'Grand Maître'. Hyacinth

Hydrangea paniculata 'Grandiflora'. Pee Gee Hydrangea

soak, then hide the container away in a dark, airy place. Check from time to time and when the shoots appear, bring gradually into stronger light and re-water. The flowers will open in early spring.

Hyacinths can also be grown in plain water. They are the most deliciously fragrant of the spring-flowering bulbs and Dutch Hyacinths are the result of hybridising the old-fashioned Roman Hyacinth, *H. orientalis* var. *albulus*. The original single whites and blues have been improved to include pinks, purples, creams and reds, many of them double-flowered.

Outdoors, they are best planted in clumps in an open, sunny position.

Hyacinthus orientalis 'Ostara'. Hyacinth

Hyacinthus orientalis 'City of Haarlem'. Hyacinth

Hydrangea macrophylla. Massed Hydrangeas

HYDRANGEA

(hai-**draen**-jə)

(SYN Hortensia)

Hydrangea, Hills of Snow, Lacecap, Pee Gee, Hortensia, Christmas Rose

SAXIFRAGACEAE

Favourite shrubs for the large, shaded border or sunless aspect, *Hydrangeas* produce big, showy flower heads in midsummer, and are often used for Christmas decoration in the southern hemisphere. There are over 30 deciduous species from China, Japan and North America; and one evergreen species, *H. integerrima*, which hails from Chile and generally develops a climbing habit. All enjoy deep, porous soil and ample water, making massive growth in the warmer months. Their terrible thirst is clearly indicated by their botanical name, which is adapted from the Greek *hydor aggeion* or 'water vessel'.

Hydrangeas of all types can be planted in autumn or early spring. They need overhead shelter from frost in colder areas, and look better in a position where morning sun cannot damage damp foliage. All species do best in semi-shade, except in generally cloudy areas, where full sun is readily accepted.

The most commonly grown species is *H. macrophylla*, from China and Japan. It has many flower forms, which must be propagated from cuttings to come true, and have one very striking peculiarity. While they do equally well in acid or alkaline soil, their colour is quite changeable. Generally mauve or blue in acid soils, in alkaline they become pink or red. And it is possible to switch from one colour range to the other by repeated chemical additions to the soil. Aluminium

Hydrangea aspera. Lacecap Hydrangea

Hydrangea macrophylla 'Parsifal'. Hybrid Hydrangea

Hydrangea quercifolia. Oak-leaf Hydrangea

Hydrangea macrophylla. Hortensia Hydrangea

sulphate turns them blue; lime turns them pink; it is as simple as that. But there are also white and greenish varieties which rarely tone at all.

All *macrophylla* Hydrangeas have two sorts of flower: one tiny and fertile with minute petals surrounding a cluster of stamens; the other sterile, with large, showy sepals and no stamens at all. Varieties consisting almost entirely of the sterile florets are known as 'Hortensias', and are most commonly sought after. Heads with a large proportion of fertile florets are known as 'Lacecaps'. Both types are pruned heavily during late winter: cut each cane back to a pair of plump growth buds. The ultimate size of each bush can be controlled in this way.

The second most popular *Hydrangea* species are the 'Pee Gee' types, such as *H. paniculata* 'Grandiflora', which grow taller than the *macrophyllas* (to 5m/16ft) and bear terminal panicles of white bloom up to 45cm/18in in length. These are greenish at first, gradually fading to pink. Rarely seen in the southern hemisphere is climbing *H. petiolaris*, which can scale a rough-barked tree or textured wall, and which produces flat heads of creamy-white blossom in summer.

All *Hydrangeas* can be propagated from 15cm/6in cuttings of unflowered shoots taken in early autumn. These should be struck in a peat/sand mixture, preferably over heat, and planted out the following autumn. Keep watch for aphids and red spider-mites, which can defoliate entire plants where the air is dry.

In cold, winter areas, both flowers and foliage of some *Hydrangea* varieties may turn gorgeous shades of red, green or rust, and make wonderful indoor displays.

Less commonly, there are fancy-leaf species such as *H. quercifolia*, or Oak-leaf Hydrangea, and variegated-leaf varieties of several other species. These are striking, but rarely bloom well.

HYDROCLEYS
(**hai**-droh-klaes)
(SYN Limnocharis)
Water Poppy
LIMNOCHARITACEAE

The South American Water Poppy, *Hydrocleys nymphoides*, is not really a poppy in spite of its name. Useful for flooded areas or water gardens in warm climates, it produces masses of floating heart-shaped leaves, and in warm weather long-stemmed, golden flowers. Provided you can guarantee a position in full sunlight, it is not at all difficult to grow.

Propagate from divisions of the tuberous root system, set in containers half-full of rich compost. Sink the pots carefully in a sunny pond, only a few inches below the water surface.

Hydrocleys is from Brazil. There are several other species, which are rarely grown.

Hydrocleys nymphoides. Water Poppy

Hylocereus undatus. Princess of the Night

HYLOCEREUS
(**hai**-loh-see-ree-əs)
Princess of the Night, Honolulu Queen, Night-blooming Cereus
CACTACEAE

The royal title 'Princess of the Night' is perfectly appropriate for the gorgeous blooms of this untidy, sprawling plant.

In warmer climates, *Hylocereus undatus* grows easily from stem pieces thoroughly dried off before they are dipped in rooting hormone and set in a sharp, sandy mixture. Later, after roots have developed, they need an acid compost, rich in leafmould, and will soon go climbing up the wall of a terrace, patio, or even sunny living room, sending out clinging roots that support them for years. The main triangular stem will branch and the creamy 23cm/9in flowers form on these branches, opening all on the one summer night after dark, filling the air with magnificent perfume.

HYLOMECON
(hai-**lom**-ee-kon)
Wood Poppy
PAPAVERACEAE

A delightful dwarf perennial from woodland areas of Japan and Southeast Asia, *Hylomecon japonica* is a monotypic species which only reaches a height of 30cm/12in but romps away in deep, acid, woodsy soil with plenty of peat and leafmould.

Though classed as a member of the poppy family, you would be hard put to place the relationship until the 5cm/2in 4-petalled golden flowers opened in late spring. Its leaves are compound, with 2 or 3 pairs of toothed leaflets, and quite hairy when young. To propagate, sow seed outdoors in spring in a sheltered position, or use autumn divisions. Keep moist in the growing season and cut back in autumn.

Hymenocallis littoralis. Filmy Lily

HYMENOCALLIS

(**hai**-men-oh-kal-lǝs)
Filmy Lily, Spider Flower
AMARYLLIDACEAE

A valuable bulbous plant from South America, fragrant *Hymenocallis* thrives in almost all conditions, wet or dry, from warm to hot.

Bulbs are planted out in early spring; choose a sunny position in cooler areas of its range, light shade in the tropics. Given good drainage and summer water, it rapidly forms a large clump of rich green, strap-like leaves. The spidery white flowers, 10cm/4in across, appear on 75cm/30in stems in summer.

They take their name from Hymen, the Greek god of marriage and son to Apollo by one of the Muses, described in legend as a youth of such delicate beauty that he might be taken for a girl. The pure white, fragrant *Hymenocallis* seems appropriately named – a botanical perfection.

Hylomecon japonica. Wood Poppy

Hymenosporum flavum. Australian Frangipani

HYMENOSPORUM

(hai-men-oh-**spor**-ǝm)
Sweet Shade, Native Frangipani
PITTOSPORACEAE

Sweet shade indeed! If fragrance is your fancy and you live in a climate as warm as coastal Australia, plant a graceful *Hymenosporum flavum*, and watch it grow to a height of perhaps 5m/15ft, though it can reach 27m/90ft in the wild.

The foliage is glossy and evergreen, massed alternately to one side or the other of the tree, and at various heights, giving it a marvellous asymmetrical appearance. And in the spring, masses of creamy frangipani-type flowers tumble out on long stems, in a profusion that almost hides the foliage. Delicately marbled with red and green, these blooms ripen to a rich butterscotch shade and spill delicious perfume everywhere.

When mature, *Hymenosporum* is reasonably frost resistant and is found even in mountainous districts up to 1000m/3300ft and more.

Hypericum cerastioides. St John's Wort

Hypericum 'Rowallane'. Rose of Sharon

The Sweet Shade apparently tastes as good as it smells, for I once made the mistake of planting one too close to a garden wall, where hungry possums regularly made short work of every flower and leaf.

A very fast grower, with a tall, sparse habit, it bears its flowers high above the ground in both cool and coastal districts. It is easily propagated from either seed or suckers. The botanical name combines two Greek words: *hymen*, a membrane, and *sporum*, a seed. The seeds have a winged membrane.

HYPERICUM

(hai-**pe**-rik-ǝm)
St John's Wort, Aaron's Beard, Goldflower, Rose of Sharon
HYPERICACEAE

This wonderfully showy genus is represented on every continent, mostly in the form of shrubs. Sometimes evergreen, sometimes deciduous, they provide year-round colour in a mild temperate climate and are easy to grow. Full sun is a must for at least part of each day, and a fast-draining soil will give good results.

Hypericum inodorum. Goldflower

Hypoëstes aristata. Velvet Plant

Small species should be propagated from 5cm/2in cuttings taken in late spring. Taller varieties grow best from 12.5cm/5in summer cuttings of non-flowered shoots. Both types are set in a final position when well rooted, about 10 months later. All species need annual winter pruning to maintain shape.

Pests do not seem to be a bother, but leaves are occasionally attacked by rust – spray with a fungicide when this occurs.

More than 400 *Hypericum* species are recognised, with the most spectacular blooms being found among the cultivars. Those of 'Rowallane' may be 7.5cm3in in diameter. Smaller-flowered *H. inodorum* makes the best mass display, while dwarf-growing *H. cerastioides* (syn *H. rhodoppeum*) is a showy plant in rock gardens or at the front of the mixed border. Seed pods should be removed to maintain the plant's vigour, and most species benefit from a deep winter mulch over the root area.

HYPOCALYMMA
(hai-poh-ka-**lim**-mə)
White Myrtle
MYRTACEAE

This is a genus of a dozen or so species of small evergreen shrubs from Western Australia, related to the Geraldton Wax (*Chamelaucium*) and rather resembling it, though a couple add yellow to the palette of white and pink. I must say I don't find them all that exciting out of flower – in most there isn't enough foliage to stop the plants looking like heaps of brushwood – but in their winter/spring flowering season they are transformed into sheets of soft colour, so abundant are the little flowers. They're useful for cutting, which also helps keep the plant tidy. Mediterranean climates with warm, dry summers and cool, wet winters suit them best, and they enjoy dappled shade.

HYPOËSTES
(hai-poh-**ess**-tees)
Polka-dot Plant, Freckleface, Velvet Plant, Ribbon Bush
ACANTHACEAE

If you live in the right climate, you pays your money and you takes your choice! *Hypoëstes aristata* gives plenty of bloom and uninteresting foliage; *Hypoëstes phyllostachya* is very much the opposite.

The first named comes from southern Africa, the second from Malagasy, and both of them need a minimum winter temperature of 10°C/50°F to survive. They are not frost hardy but in the right climate seem to grow happily in any soil, developing dense, deep-rooted clumps and self-seeding regularly. Both species reach a height of 30–100cm/1–3ft and give a long display. Cuttings are struck easily when you cut back the faded flower stems in autumn.

Hypocalymma angustifolium. Peach Myrtle, White Myrtle

Hypocalymma robustum. Swan River Myrtle

Hypoxis villosa. Star Grass

Iberis amara 'White Spire'. Hyacinth-flowered Candytuft

HYPOXIS

(hai-**pok**-sis)

Star Grass

AMARYLLIDACEAE

Too seldom seen in the average garden, the many species of *Hypoxis* are well worth searching out. All have star-shaped flowers, mostly in a brilliant, glossy yellow tending to green on the undersides, but there are also species with lilac or white flowers.

Hypoxis needs a humus-rich but well-drained soil, slightly acid in reaction, and once established is fairly drought resistant. Flowers appear in autumn but open only in bright sunlight, so the corms should always be planted in a fully sunny spot. *H. villosa* has distinctly hairy, greyish-green leaves and yellow flowers. It can be increased from seed or by separation of offsets from clumps lifted and divided in winter. This, however, should be done only once in every 3 or 4 years.

IBERIS

(**ai**-bur-is)

Candytuft, Wryflower

BRASSICACEAE

Two types of Candytuft are commonly grown as annual bedding plants. *Iberis amara*, the Rocket or Hyacinth-flowered Candytuft, has tall heads of fragrant white bloom. *I. umbellata*, the Globe Candytuft, has flat umbel-shaped heads of bloom; these are unperfumed, but compensate with a rainbow of colours.

Both are used for edging, rock gardens or bedding displays. Each may be sown direct as spring warms up, or 2 months earlier indoors, with a temperature of 20°–30°C/ 68°–86°F in the seed-raising compost. Germination takes 10–15 days, and young plants should be spaced 15–30cm/6–12in apart in well-drained garden soil, preferably in full sun.

Less spectacular, but similar to the annual Candytufts, is perennial *I. sempervirens*. A dwarf, mat-forming plant much favoured in rock gardens, it will grow in full sun in any ordinary garden soil if the drainage is good. This *Iberis* has trailing stems tipped with rosettes of dark, oblong leaves from which issue flat heads of white bloom in late spring.

ILEX

(**ai**-leks)

Holly

AQUIFOLIACEAE

If this were a book about berries, the picture below would be full of them, and instantly recognisable as the glossy fruit of English Holly, or *Ilex aquifolium*, a magnificent pyra-midal tree that will grow to 25m/80ft in height, though not in an average lifetime.

But many gardeners can't get their Hollies to fruit at all, and wonder why. It is because

Iberis umbellata. Globe Candytuft

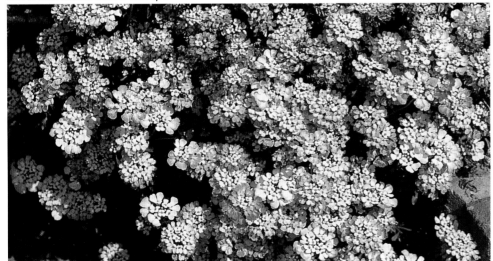

Ilex aquifolium. Common Holly

Hollies are dioecious by nature. That is to say, while all Holly trees produce small clusters of rather charming white or greenish blossom with 4–6 petals and a faint fragrance, there are two sexes, just like us. The boy flowers are on one tree, the girls on another, and unless you have both – no berries! Plant Hollies in autumn, in a sunny spot.

Impatiens balsamina. Balsam

IMPATIENS
(im-**pae**-shəns)
Busy Lizzie, Patient Plant, Snapweed, Balsam, Touch-me-not, Patient Lucy
BALSAMINACEAE

The many varieties of Busy Lizzie are virtually indestructible, their botanic name being an allusion to the impatience with which they grow and multiply. Pot-planted groups in mixed colours can be pinched back continuously to keep them within bounds, and they will flower all winter long inside a sunny window. Hanging baskets, too, can be grown in a glassed-in room all year.

A wide spectrum of colours may be found among the hybrids between several varieties of *Impatiens walleriana*. Even yellow and orange have now joined the range of reds, whites, pinks, mauves and cerises – while the leaves may be striped or variegated with pink, white, cream and gold. Double-flowered cultivars are available and some with variegated and picoteed blooms.

Grow them in a well-drained peaty mix with sand, and water well through the warm weather. Strike cuttings in damp sand or a glass of water at any time.

Impatiens walleriana. Busy Lizzie

The flowers of *I. walleriana* hybrids are followed by elastic pods which scatter seed. They are the shade gardener's best friend, giving an endless display from spring to late autumn. Sow direct at any time in warmer weather, thinning out later.

An entirely different species is the Camellia-flowered *I. balsamina*, an erect-growing 30cm/12in annual much used for bedding in full sun. Especially for baskets, there is the trailing species, *I. repens.* This is known as Golden Dragon.

Impatiens repens. Golden Dragon

Impatiens New Guinea Hybrid. Butterfly Impatiens

Incarvillea delavayi. Pride of China

INCARVILLEA
(in-kah-**vil**-lee-ə)
Pride of China, Hardy Gloxinia
BIGNONIACEAE

Beautifully marked trumpet blooms in bright cerise, scarlet and yellow are the main attraction of this perennial genus from high places in several areas of Tibet and China. Growing from a mass of fleshy roots, in cool temperate climates, they send up exquisitely formed foliage and elegant flower stems in the spring. Some species have fern-like leaves, though in *Incarvillea delavayi* they are merely compound, with up to 4 pairs of leaflets.

Grow them in the sun, in rich well-drained soil. Seeds germinate in a month at a temperature of 13º–18ºC/55º–65ºF, but they will take 3 years to bloom. Better and faster to plant out from autumn divisions. Mulch the root areas in winter or, in really cold places, lift and store roots in a dry place.

Inocarpus fagifer. Mapé, Tahiti Chestnut

Indigofera australis. False Indigo

INDIGOFERA
(in-dig-**off**-er-ə)
Summer Wisteria, False Indigo
FABACEAE

Found in many warmer areas of Asia, Australia and Africa, *Indigoferas* are a genus of dainty weeping shrubs bearing long sprays of wisteria-type blossom in the warmer months. They are drought resistant, and very useful in drier gardens where the soil is poor.

Grow them in full sun, in sheltered pockets of large rockeries, or where they can be attached to stone walls. The flower display is improved by a heavy pruning each winter. There are over 700 species altogether, of which *I. australis* is an Australian representative, growing to 1.2m/4ft. Himalayan *I. heterantha* (syn *I. gerardiana*) is more commonly grown in the northern hemisphere; it is frost hardy and grows to about 3m/10ft.

INOCARPUS
(in-oh-kah-pəs)
Mapé, Polynesian Chestnut
FABACEAE

The Mapé or Polynesian Chestnut, *Inocarpus fagifer* (syn *I. edulis*) is a tall, handsome evergreen tree from humid valleys of Tahiti and nearby islands.

Its leathery leaves are dark, the winter flowers small, white and fragrant, appearing in spikes from the leaf axils. They strongly resemble those of the Macadamia (which see), though they're unrelated. In spring, there are fibrous 5cm/2in pale orange pods. These each contain one large seed or nut which, when cooked, has all the flavour of the European Chestnut. The Mapé is propagated from half-ripened cuttings.

INULA
(in-yoo-lə)
Eye of Christ
ASTERACEAE

Known and grown since the most ancient of days (their name *Inula* was bestowed by old Roman botanists), this showy genus of daisy flowers includes some 100 perennial species from Asia, Africa and Europe, ranging in height from 5cm/2in rock plants to an impressive 2m/6ft. You can grow them in any part of the garden so long as you like yellow flowers, for they don't come in any other hue! Most will romp in any soil so long as it is fertile and moisture-retaining, but they must have full sun. They generally develop into dense clumps of unbranched stems with broad basal foliage and spear-shaped stem-leaves gradually reducing in size as the stems gain height.

Inula oculus-christi. Eye of Christ

The style of inflorescence varies from type to type, the daisy blooms being borne singly or in corymbs, racemes or panicles. *Inulas* are propagated by division in spring and autumn, and can also be raised from seed sown as soon as possible after ripening. Illustrated *I. oculus-christi* is relatively small, rarely passing 60cm/2ft, with flowers 8.5cm/ 3½ in wide; *I. magnifica*, an Asian species, is altogether larger, reaching 2m/6ft in height, with 30cm/12in leaves and multiple heads of orange-centred cup-shaped flowers borne in corymbs. A peculiarity of all *Inula* species is the multiple row or involucre of heavy bracts at the back of each flower. These are particularly noticeable in unopened buds.

Iochroma grandiflorum. Violet Tubeflower

IOCHROMA
(ai-oh-**kroh**-m∂)
Tubeflower
SOLANACEAE

Long tubular flowers, in shades of purple, blue, red, yellow and white, hang all summer and autumn on these fast-growing shrubs, of which about 20 species are grown in temperate and tropical climates.

Iochromas are easily raised from cuttings and grow best in a warm, sheltered spot with plenty of water. As summer hots up, they will send out succulent stems and felty 20cm/8in leaves, quickly becoming untidy and straggly unless kept in shape with a regular trim. *Iochromas* grow to 3m/10ft in height and

should be used as wall shrubs or espaliers for maximum display value. Plant in a sheltered spot for protection against winds, and cut back hard in winter.

I. grandiflorum and *I. cyaneum* bloom in varying shades of purple. *I. coccineum* is scarlet, while *I. flavum* is a pale yellow. *I. fuchsioides* has a broader flower, tinted a rich orange-scarlet.

IONOPSIDIUM
(ai-on-op-**sid**-ee-∂m)
Violet Cress, Diamond Flower
BRASSICACEAE

Delightful dwarf annuals from Portugal, *Ionopsidium* or Violet Cress make a charming display in moist, shaded rockeries, in paving, or as indoor or conservatory plants. They form small mounds of watercress-like foliage, just 7.5cm/3in high, from which single 4-petalled flowers pop up continually throughout late spring and summer. These are white, tinged with pale mauve, and are scarcely 5mm/¼in across. Sow the seed direct in early spring, barely covering it, or sow indoors in early autumn for greenhouse use. Young plants of *I. acaule* are spaced at 5cm/2in intervals, and can be kept through winter if the temperature does not drop below 7°C/45°F. This dainty charmer deserves greater popularity in gardens of cool and temperate climates.

Ionopsidium acaule. Violet Cress

Ipheion uniflorum. Glory of the Sun

Ipomoea indica. Blue Dawn Flower

Ipomoea alba. Moon Flower, Belle de Nuit

Ipomoea coccinea. Red Morning Glory

Ipomoea horsfalliae. Cardinal Creeper

IPHEION
(if-ee-∂n)
(SYN Triteleia)
Glory of the Sun, Spring Star Flower
LILIACEAE

Useful and charming small bulbs for groundcover in neglected areas, *Ipheions* multiply and spread with astounding speed, from both bulb and seed. Native to the Argentine pampas, they like hot, dry summers and wet, frost-free winters, but will grow in literally any soil, sunny or shaded, provided the drainage is good.

Plant the thumbnail-size bulbs out in autumn, burying them little more than their own depth in light soil to which a ration of bonedust has been added. In late winter they will send up flat, blueish-green leaves with a distinct onion smell, and later, in spring, starry pale blue blooms in profusion. These are borne singly on 15cm/6in wiry stems.

IPOMOEA
(ip-oh-**mee**-∂)
(SYN Calonyction, Mina, Pharbitis, Quamoclit)
Morning Glory, Moonflower, Dawn Flower
CONVOLVULACEAE

Several groups of species split off 100 or more years ago have recently been returned, so this tropical and subtropical genus of climbing plants is now bigger than ever.

The most important member is still *Ipomoea batatas*, the sweet potato, but many species are delightful in flower, even those such as the perennial *I. indica* (syn *I. learii*), the Morning Glory, that make horrible pests of themselves in warm climates. Like most of them, this one opens its pure blue flowers in the early morning; by midday they have faded to purple and are beginning to crumple away. Alternatively, *I. tricolor* 'Heavenly Blue', a much more restrained plant and a still purer colour, can be grown as an annual.

Ipomoea nil 'Scarlett O'Hara'. Crimson Morning Glory

Ipomoea tricolor 'Heavenly Blue'. Morning Glory

Iris sibirica 'Orville Fay'. Siberian Iris

Iris 'Professor Blaauw'. Dutch Hybrid Iris

Rather in the same manner are the Japanese hybrids which usually go under the name *I. imperialis,* and whose cultivation was very fashionable among the samurai of old, who vied with one another in producing the largest flowers and most *recherché* colours – mauve, lilac, pink, even *café-au-lait* , often edged or marbled with white. All will grow in almost any climate, flowering right through summer from spring-sown seed.

Then there is a series of red-flowered perennial vines for hot climates, such as the glossy-leaved, carmine-flowered cardinal vine, *I. horsfalliae,* and the cypress vine, *I. quamoclit,* with scarlet flowers and leaves like lace.

The Moonflower, formerly known as *Calonyction aculeatum* but now called simply *I. alba,* the white ipomoea. This is a rampant perennial in frost-free climates, an annual elsewhere, and opens its flowers not at sunrise but at sunset, to glow in the moonlight and breathe a fragrance that is the very essence of a tropical evening.

IRIS
(ai-ris)
Iris, Orris, Fleur de Luce, Flag
IRIDACEAE

A vast group of bulbous plants with stiff, sword-like leaves, the *Irises* include both desert and water plants and grow from

Iris crocea. Golden Iris

true bulbs or tuberous rhizomes. They may also be evergreen or die down completely each winter.

The flowers, while differing widely in shape and colour, do have a family similarity: 3 vertical petals, called 'standards', alternating with 3 drooping ones, called 'falls'. The flowers may appear singly or in groups, and many are highly perfumed. For convenience they are often grouped into 3 classes: Bulbous, Bearded, and Beardless.

Bulbous Irises, planted in autumn, are represented in most gardens by the English, Dutch and Spanish types, all hybrids of species *I. reticulata, I. xiphium* and *I. xiphioides.* They bloom in early spring in tones of white, blue, yellow and bronze.

Iris 'Nashborough'. Tall Bearded Iris

Iris japonica. Crested Iris

Iris ensata 'Yuki-Asobi'. Japanese Iris

Iris Louisiana Hybrid

Iris unguicularis. Algerian Iris

The Bearded Irises, popularly known as Flags, are further divided into dwarf, intermediate and tall types. Modern varieties are very much ruffled, with broad falls. Colours now include pink, red, yellow, bronze, purple and tan, in addition to the original mauves and whites. They grow from rhizomes, flower in early summer, and like a touch of lime.

Beardless Irises include most other species and vary too widely for general description. Notable are the gorgeous *I. ensata* (syn *I. kaempferi*); the dwarf winter-flowering *I. stylosa* and the quickly spreading *I. sibirica* and *I. laevigata,* which love water.

I. ensata – the Japanese or Higo Iris – has been in cultivation for several thousand years, and prefers to grow with its roots actually below water. Gardeners in Japan choose a position which can be flooded in the summer blooming season to produce the finest flowers. These are flat and triangular and there are varieties in every imaginable combination of white, blue, purple, pink and crimson.

Appropriately enough, *Irises* were named for the Greek goddess of the rainbow; and they have left their mark in European heraldry – one local variety probably inspired the French royal emblem, the *fleur de lys.*

Isatis tinctoria. Woad

Isopogon anethifolius. Drumsticks

ISATIS
(ai-**sat**-is)
Woad, Asp of Jerusalem, Common Dyer's Weed
BRASSICACEAE

When the Romans first landed in Britain they were met by a horde of barbaric warriors, dyed bright blue with a herb called woad. Not that this ceremonial camouflage did them much good. The more heavily armed invaders gave them a good scrubbing and sent them in chains to Rome for the Victory triumph. Woad, then, has some interesting historical associations, but is rarely grown except by dyers of trendy homespun wool. Botanically *Isatis tinctoria*, it grows from seed in average soil, likes moisture, and may reach 120cm/4ft in height. Related to Cabbage and Rape (see Brassica), it is a mass of golden flowers in summer.

ISOPLEXIS
(ai-soh-**plek**-sis)
Bush Foxglove
SCROPHULARIACEAE

Though *Isoplexis canariensis* is related to the foxgloves (*Digitalis*), so closely indeed that botanists once included it in that genus, it isn't really a shrubby version of the familiar purple foxglove. The flowers, borne in early summer, are two-lipped rather than bell-shaped, and they are a most unusual terra-cotta shade. The greyish-green leaves set

Isoplexis canariensis. Canary Islands Foxglove

them off very nicely, and the whole thing grows to about chest-high. It does come from the Canary Islands (as the specific name suggests), which indicates a preference for warm temperate climates. Give it well-drained, fertile soil and a place in the sun, dead-head to prolong blooming and trim gently after the flowers fade.

ISOPOGON
(ai-**sop**-ə-gon)
Coneflower, Drumsticks, Conebush
PROTEACEAE

A small group of evergreen Australian shrubs, this genus of the extraordinary Protea family is less well known than others outside their native Australia. The 30-odd species of *Isopogon* are found mostly on the west coast of the continent, but with several useful representatives in the east.

They like an acid, sandy soil, with regular water in the growing season. Cultivated successfully in California, the Mediterranean area and England's Scilly Isles, they all produce cone-shaped flower heads from winter on, and have stiff, needle-like foliage. The blooms vary in colour from yellow to pink, purple and white. They cut well and are useful for adding bulk to large arrangements. Propagate from well-ripened seed sown in winter, or from cuttings struck in sharp sand and peat.

ITEA
(**ai**-tee-ə)
Sweetspire
SAXIFRAGACEAE

A small genus of slim, decorative trees found in moist, temperate climates, the *Iteas* include evergreen species from Asia, and one deciduous member from North America. The species commonly cultivated is the

Isopogon dubius. Rosy Coneflower

Hollyleaf Sweetspire, *I. ilicifolia*, from western China, which is most at home in the deep rich soil of humid coastal gardens, or in a sheltered position in the hills, well protected from frost. As both its popular and botanical names suggest, the foliage resembles that of the European Holly (Ilex), although individual leaves are both longer and narrower than those of most holly varieties.

The delicate greenish-white summer flowers are lightly fragrant, and crowded in hanging racemes up to 40cm/16in long. These racemes appear both from the leaf axils and as terminal clusters.

I. ilicifolia rarely passes 5m/16ft in height, and can be struck from cuttings of ripe wood taken in summer. The botanical name, *Itea*, is the classical Greek name for the willow, with which it shares a certain grace.

Itea ilicifolia. Sweetspire

IXIA
(ik-see-ə)
African Corn Lily, Corn Lily
IRIDACEAE

Graceful spring-flowering bulbs for the temperate climate, *Ixias* are found naturally in various parts of southern Africa and are most effective naturalized in lawns, where they can be left in the ground season after season. Just be sure to plant them in clumps so they can be allowed to ripen seed naturally without upsetting the mowing.

The small bulbs are set in position in late summer, after the soil has been enriched with a liberal dressing of blood and bone. *I. maculata* bloom in early spring on tall wire-like stems up to 60cm/2ft in height. The heavily clustered flowers are generally in shades of cerise, pink, orange and yellow, often with darker centres. The less common turquoise-flowered species *I. viridiflora* reaches almost 1m/3ft in height.

Ixia 'Yellow Prince'. Corn Lily

Ixia viridiflora. Green Ixia, Blue Ixia

Ixia maculata 'Vulcan'. African Corn Lily

IXIOLIRION
(iks-ee-oh-**lir**-ee-ən)
Tartar Lily, Siberian Lily, Lily of the Altai
AMARYLLIDACEAE

I don't see any resemblance to Ixias myself, but some earlier botanist did, and he got in first with the naming privileges. *Ixiolirion* is Greek for 'ixia-lily' though they're not even in the same botanical family.

Raise them from seed or offsets in well-drained quality soil. Set mature bulbs out in

Ixiolirion tataricum. Tartar Lily

Ixora chinensis. Jungle Flame

Ixora coccinea. Jungle Geranium

autumn 7cm/2½in deep. Though from Siberia, Tartar Lilies need the protection of a winter mulch, and in very cold areas should be raised in containers and set under shelter. In full sun, stems of brilliantly blue flowers shoot up in spring to 40cm/16in, then die back with the grass-like leaves as the bulbs go dormant.

IXORA
(ik-sor-ə)
Jungle Flame, Jungle Geranium, Flame of the Woods
RUBIACEAE

Colourful shrubs from all over Southeast Asia and many Pacific islands, *Ixoras* are related to the Gardenia and to many other tropical favourites. Admirably suited to their popular name of Jungle Flame, they are striking plants for gardens where the humidity is high.

Grow them in a sandy soil rich with leaf-mould, and give them plenty of moisture throughout the summer. Cut back to shape in winter, when they can be allowed to dry out a little. Standing 1–2m/3–6ft high, *Ixoras* bloom over a long period, though as equatorial natives they need warmth and protection in less-than-tropical winters. Even indoors *Ixora* may grow to 1m/3ft, and can be propagated from summer cuttings struck in sharp sand. *I. chinensis* 'Prince of Orange' is often used as a bedding plant in the tropics, but its flowers fade badly. *I. coccinea* (Jungle Geranium) has deep scarlet blooms, with golden-green foliage – a splendid sight. New cultivars bloom in diverse shades of pink, orange, red, yellow and white.

JACARANDA
(jak-ər-an-də)
Blue Haze Tree, Fern Tree
BIGNONIACEAE

The *Jacaranda* is found naturally in the high and dry deserts of Brazil, and many temperate gardeners have noticed that its late spring display is measurably better in a dry year, or in a neglected part of the garden. Give it too much water and the lacy leaves (like pale-green ostrich plumes) appear first, somewhat spoiling the startling effect of mauve trumpet flowers on bare grey branches.

Jacarandas seed readily, grow fast and transplant easily. One in my own garden, 13 years from seed, is 10m/33ft high and nearly as wide. Another, in an old garden opposite, has developed a strange horizontal shape as it grows away from the cold southerly winds. *Jacarandas* will always do this and need protection from whichever direction your coolest wind blows from if they are to grow straight and strong.

The trees are deciduous, though they do not drop their leaves until late winter, often turning a rich yellow first in cooler areas. There are white, pink and red flowered species, but these are not half so lovely as the beautiful mauve-blue *J. mimosifolia*.

Jacaranda mimosifolia. Blue Haze Tree

Jasione laevis. Shepherd's Scabious

JASIONE
(jae-see-**oh**-nee)
Sheep's Bit, Shepherd's Scabious
CAMPANULACEAE

Dainty little meadow plants from the Mediterranean area, several species of *Jasione* are grown in rock gardens for their charming clover-like heads in a particularly attractive shade of Jacaranda blue. These appear in summer and, though generously produced, their massed display quickly peters out. Perennial *J. laevis* (syn *J. perennis*) is the most popular, growing to 30cm/12in from a small rosette of hairy leaves that are widest at their outer ends.

A sandy, even gravelly soil suits all types best, for perfect drainage is essential. Perennial species are planted out at 30cm/12in intervals and can be divided in autumn. They also grow well from autumn-sown seed. Don't overfeed – the plants tend to flop in rich soil.

JASMINUM
(**jas**-min-ǝm)
Jasmine, Jessamine, Pikake, Pitate
OLEACEAE

Think of fragrance, think of Jasmine! Delicate starry flowers in yellow, white or pink according to species, and native to all the fabled lands of the East. You can have Jasmine scenting your house and garden the whole year round if you pick the right species from among the 200-odd listed by taxonomists. Just give them a partially shaded or sunny position, reasonable soil, a regular ration of water and watch them take off. They'll need occasional going over with the secateurs to keep them in bounds, though, for almost all Jasmines love to turn climber if you let them have their heads.

Jasminum nudiflorum is the first to bloom, opening single 1cm/½in flowers from

Jasminum polyanthum. Pink Jasmine

Jasminum mesnyi. Primrose Jasmine

its bare twigs in the winter sunlight. In its native Japan they call it 'the flower that welcomes spring'. *J. mesnyi* (with much larger semi-double golden blooms on arching canes) follows at the first sign of warm weather; and you'll know spring has truly arrived when pink-budded *J. polyanthum* bursts into bloom. It is strictly a climbing shrub, and will cover a wall in no time with light support. *J. azoricum* and *J. officinale* keep up the fragrance throughout summer and will bloom continuously till the following winter. In warmer climates, *J. sambac* and *J. multiflorum* (often misidentified as *J. sambac*, Arabian Jasmine) will bloom intermittently through the warm weather. Almost all Jasmines are easy to propagate: from 8cm/3in cuttings of nearly ripe wood in summer; by layers; even from seed when it is produced.

Jasminum nudiflorum. Winter Jasmine

Jasminum multiflorum. Pikake

Jasminum humile 'Revolutum'. Yellow Jasmine

Jatropha integerrima. Peregrina, Spicy Jatropha

Jovellana violacea. Chilean Figweed

Justicia carnea. Brazilian Plume Flower

JATROPHA

(ja-**tro**-fə)
Coral Plant, Jatropha
EUPHORBIACEAE

Several of the 170-odd *Jatropha* species were credited by the herbalists of tropical America with remarkable medical powers – the purple-flowered *J. gossypifolia* was even reputed to cure leprosy. It is a spreading soft-wooded shrub from the Caribbean. Spicy Jatropha, *J. integerrima*, is a taller shrub, to about 3m/10ft tall, bearing its coral-red flowers almost year-round in the tropics, in summer in greenhouses elsewhere.
J. podagrica is the Guatemalan Rhubarb or Gout Plant, chiefly admired in greenhouses for its curiously swollen stem, which makes the 1m/3ft tall bush look like a miniature baobab tree; but it is quite decorative in summer when it bears its scarlet flowers. You can't eat it like ordinary rhubarb; like most of the genus, it is violently purgative.

JOVELLANA

(joh-vel-**lah**-nə)
Chilean Figweed
SCROPHULARIACEAE

The species you are most likely to encounter in gardens is *Jovellana violacea* (syn *Calceolaria violacea*) from Chile, a pleasing shrubby perennial with summer clusters of small mauve flowers with darker spots. Though it rather resembles one of the shrubby Calceolarias, it is less hardy than they, preferring a warm temperate climate and rich, leafy soil, which should not be allowed to dry out in summer. Should the plant get straggly, it can be pruned quite severely in early spring. The name has nothing to do with Jupiter (Jove) but honours Don Caspari Melchiori de Jovellanos, a Peruvian botanist. The genus occurs in New Zealand as well as in Chile.

JUSTICIA

(jus-**tis**-ee-ə)
(SYN Beloperone, Cyrtanthera, Drejerella, Jacobinia, Libonia)
Plume Flower, Paradise Plant, Prawn Plant, Shrimp Plant
ACANTHACEAE

As you'll see from the list of synonyms, this genus has expanded in recent years. It now includes about 420 species of subtropical and tropical shrubs and perennials, mainly from the Americas, many of them popular subjects in the frost-free garden and cool-climate greenhouse.

The showy Brazilian Plume Flower, *Justicia carnea*, produces tall spikes of bloom in flushes, starting in late spring and continuing all through summer and into autumn. Each flush is short, but prompt removal of faded flower heads, coupled with well-

Justicia rizzinii. Libonia, Paradise Plant

Justicia brandegeana. Shrimp Plant

drained, acid soil and regular fertiliser will quickly initiate the formation of new buds. The colour range is wide – pink, red, orange, yellow and white.

In tropical or subtropical climates the Shrimp Plant, *J. brandegeana*, is almost continuously in bloom, but it also flowers well in coastal areas where temperatures don't drop below 7ºC/45ºF. In cooler climates it can be raised as a container plant and taken under glass during winter. Another good conservatory subject is Libonia, *J. rizzinii*, which grows neatly to about 60cm/2ft tall and wide; all through winter and spring it bears tubular red flowers, each with a golden tip.

Prune *Justicias* back hard in earliest spring to encourage branching or they will grow tall and scruffy. Even well-grown specimens can reach 3m/10ft, though 1.5m/5ft is far more usual. They prefer dappled shade and can be increased from 10cm/4in cuttings of young growth taken in spring and potted up under heat. Spray with a suitable insecticide to prevent caterpillars making a meal of both flowers and foliage, and lay snail-bait regularly or the dark green leaves will soon be ruined. In areas with cold winters, grow in wide pots, brought indoors in winter.

Justicia aurea. King's Crown

KAEMPFERIA
(kamp-**fur**-ee-ə)
Oriental Crocus, Resurrection Lily
ZINGIBERACEAE

One of the most surprising of the ginger family, the lovely Oriental Crocus belongs in a genus of some 50 species scattered from Africa to the Philippines. Many of them are cultivated for the spice content of their

Kaempferia pulchra. Dwarf Ginger Lily

aromatic roots, but *Kaempferia rotunda* generally escapes this fate due to the serendipitous display of its flowers and foliage. The stemless, fragrant blossoms appear in clusters of 4–10, beautifully patterned in white and violet. The leaves which follow are patterned like a peacock's tail. Deep, rich soil, constant moisture and filtered light are best.

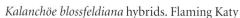

Kalanchöe blossfeldiana hybrids. Flaming Katy

Kaempferia rotunda. Oriental Crocus, Resurrection Lily

KALANCHÖE
(ka-lan-**koh**-ee)
Friendly Neighbour, Flaming Katy
CRASSULACEAE

Popular flowering succulents for winter and early spring, *Kalanchöes* require frost-free conditions for permanent planting outdoors. However, they take to life in pots of gritty,

Kalanchöe manginii. Basket Kalanchöe

Kalanchöe 'Wendy'. Hybrid Kalanchöe

Kennedia coccinea. Coral Vine

well-drained soil enriched with organic matter, and can thus be grown in the coldest climates if given winter protection and heat.

Kalanchöes need full sun year-round and can be grown from seed or cuttings of leaves or stems. In fact, they root so readily that in warm, sheltered positions they may even become something of a problem, for every leaf that drops will form a new plant within weeks. Cuttings can be taken in spring and dried out before planting in damp sand. When rooted, they can be potted up in containers of perfectly drained compost including 50 per cent sand and brick rubble. Water freely in summer, but hold off in winter until the leaves show signs of distress.

K. blossfeldiana is one of the best winter house plants, with many cultivars in white and shades of red, pink and yellow. *K. manginii* forms a neat mound of spreading and trailing stems decked with pinkish-red tubular flowers.

KALMIA

(**kal**-mee-ə)
Mountain Laurel, Calico Bush
ERICACEAE

Garden treasures away from their native American mountains, the slow-growing *Kalmias* are a small genus of evergreen shrubs that enjoy exactly the same conditions as their Rhododendron relatives: part shade, humidity, an acid soil rich in leaf-mould and an assured supply of water. The laurel-like leaves are dark and glossy, the flowers (white, red or apple-blossom pink

according to variety) have a curious sticky feel and are borne profusely at the ends of last season's growth, during spring.

Kalmias are completely hardy and will survive temperatures well below −18ºC/0ºF. In fact, they seem to need frosty winters to do well and are not recommended for mild areas. They develop into a broad, densely foliaged shrub, 2–3m/6–10ft tall and about as wide. Plant out in late spring or early autumn and don't prune except to remove faded flower heads. They are best propagated by layering new wood in late summer, but may also be struck from cuttings, though this is far less reliable.

Kalmia latifolia. Mountain Laurel

KENNEDIA

(ken-**ned**-ee-ə)
Coral Vine
FABACEAE

Kennedia is an Australian genus of fairly rampant vines in the pea family, mostly from the forests and sandy heaths of the south-west corner of Western Australia. *K. coccinea*, the Coral Vine, is one of the showiest species, producing an abundance of yellow-centred orange-red flowers over quite a few weeks in spring. It's a vigorous climber but seems best suited to large-scale groundcover in full sun or light, dappled shade. It propagates easily from scarified seed and grows fast in any well-drained, preferably (though not essentially) alkaline soil. It is not hardy but can be used as an annual.

KERRIA
(ke-ree-ə)
Japanese Rose, Jew's Mallow, Globe Flower, Bachelor's Button
ROSACEAE

A decorative, deciduous member of the rose family, *Kerria japonica* is the only species of its genus, and a great favourite in cooler-climate gardens for its profusion of golden spring blooms. Easily grown from cuttings, layers or divisions, it spreads rapidly, needing at least a 2m/6ft diameter space to display its graceful arching branches. These are festooned with doubly toothed leaves from early spring, and glow with autumn colour, seen at their best in suitably chilly areas. The single flowers (double in CV 'Pleniflora') cut well for indoor display.

Kerria needs a rich, fast-draining soil and occasional heavy watering. It is hardy to –6°C/20°F and needs a heavy pruning after flower fall. In cold-climate gardens it can be grown in light shade or full sun and thrives with wall shelter. Where winters are mild, grow in part or full shade.

Kerria japonica 'Pleniflora'. Japanese Rose

KIGELIA
(kai-jeel-yə)
Sausage Tree
BIGNONIACEAE

Grown more as a novelty than anything else, and then only in gardens with at least a subtropical climate, the bizarre *Kigelia pinnata* has no practical use in commerce. It is a heavy-trunked tree to about 16m/52ft, bearing compound leaves consisting of 7–11 hand-sized leaflets. From the uppermost branches, long, hanging stems descend many

Kigelia pinnata. Sausage Tree

metres, punctuated by large, velvety, red-brown flowers, more curious than showy. The result is a long chain of flowers, but as they open only at night you may never see them unless you're an early-bird. And since they also exude a distinctly unpleasant smell, you probably wouldn't want to! The smell attracts night-flying insects which perform pollination.

What follows is a botanical wonder! Long, hard, inedible, gourd-like fruits up to 1m/3ft in length are produced to dangle and sway on cord-like stems. Grow *Kigelias* from the encased seeds or from cuttings of half-ripened wood struck under glass.

KNAUTIA
(nou-tee-ə)
Gypsy Rose, Field Scabious
DIPSACACEAE

A popular wildflower all around the Mediterranean area and as far east as the Caucasus, *Knautia arvensis* is often known as Blue Buttons because of its pale blue, Scabious-lookalike flowers which appear in summer. It was in fact once included in the genus Scabious until botanists found some significant differences. *K. macedonica* has dark red or purple-red flowers.

Plant *Knautias* 25–35cm/10–14in apart in rich, sunny, well-drained soil, preferably slightly alkaline in makeup. They can be propagated from autumn divisions or from seed sown in spring – this will germinate in about 2 weeks. Regular summer water improves flower yield and the plants (1.2m/4ft tall for *K. arvensis*, half that for *K. macedonica*) can be kept tidy and compact by staking.

Knautia macedonica. Field Scabious

KNIPHOFIA
(nip-hoh-fee-ə)
Red-hot Poker, Torch Lily
LILIACEAE

Southern Africa's striking *Kniphofias* are hardy enough to be grown in the milder parts of the UK. They are stately plants, producing long-stemmed torches of bloom from clumps of stiff, grassy leaves. In mild climates like that of their homeland, flowering usually begins in spring, but where winters are severe, summer is more usual. *K. uvaria*, with its spikes of vivid red and yellow flowers, is one of the best species, but hybrids such as 'Bees Lemon' are today far more commonly grown.

Propagate by seed or division of the roots after flowering. Grow in light soil with plenty of water in the months before bloom.

Kniphofia uvaria. Red-hot Poker

Kniphofia 'Bees Lemon'. Torch Lily

Kohleria amabilis. Fiesta Bells

Kolkwitzia amabilis. Beauty Bush

Kniphofia 'Atlanta'. Red-hot Poker

KOHLERIA

(koh-**lee**-ree-ə)

(SYN Isoloma)

Fiesta Bells, Tree Gloxinia

GESNERIACEAE

Spectacular South American perennials, *Kohlerias* have somewhat the appearance of European Foxgloves. They like warmth and humidity, and are best grown in glasshouses in cold climates, or in shaded, moist positions or pots in warm temperate zones. Raise them either from summer stem cuttings struck in sand or from divisions of the rhizome potted up in early spring. Use a moist, loamy compost with sand to improve drainage. They scorch in full sun and the soft, velvety leaves can spot badly from spraying or from overhead watering.

Kohleria eriantha. Tree Gloxinia

KOLKWITZIA

(kolk-**wit**-zee-ə)

Beauty Bush

CAPRIFOLIACEAE

The graceful Chinese Beauty Bush, *Kolkwitzia amabilis*, is surely one of the loveliest of deciduous garden plants. Grow it in a well-watered, sunny position with roots partially shaded – but allow plenty of room, for the tall, arching stems will soon form a 2–3m/ 6–10ft fountain, covered in spring with spicily fragrant masses of palest pink trumpet flowers, their throats spotted orange-yellow. *Kolkwitzia* is in every sense a year-round plant. When not in bloom it displays attractive winter bark, soft autumn leaf colour and foliage that remains decorative throughout the summer. Prune out a third of the oldest stems annually to keep mature plants vigorous. Hardy down to −10ºC/14ºF.

KOPSIA

(kop-see-ə)

Kopsia

APOCYNACEAE

Beautiful 7.5cm/3in periwinkle-type flowers coloured like strawberry ice-cream assure *Kopsia fruticosa* a favoured place in warm, humid gardens. An erect shrub, fast-growing to around 6m/20ft tall, it needs a sunny position sheltered from strong winds. Leaves are an attractively glossy dark green and the flowers have a fragrance reminiscent of related Frangipani. *Kopsia* generally does not need pruning, though cutting flowering branches for indoor use helps to control its size. Firm young shoots can be struck fairly easily under glass and plants should be grown in an acid, sandy soil, rich in humus. Needs a warm winter.

Kopsia fruticosa. Kopsia

Kunzea capitata. Tick Bush

Kunzea parvifolia. Violet Kunzea

Lachenalia bulbifera. Soldier Boys

KUNZEA

(**kun**-zee-ə)
Kunzea
MYRTACEAE

Closely related to Callistemon and
Leptospermum, the *Kunzeas* are a small
Australian genus of evergreen shrubs. All
species are clothed with tiny, heath-like
leaves and produce showy masses of fluffy,
long-stamened flowers that can be red, pink,
cream, mauve or white. *Kunzeas* are usually
increased by firm tip-cuttings, which strike
easily in moist, sandy soil during the
warmer months.

K. *capitata* is a small, rounded shrub
1m/3ft high and as wide, occasionally larger,
generously decked with clusters of pinkish
flowers for most of the spring and summer.
Odd flushes may also occur at other times of
the year. K. *baxteri*, from Western Australia,
grows a little taller, produces dark red flower
spikes from late summer to early spring and
does best in very well-drained, sandy soil.

Kunzea baxteri. Scarlet Kunzea

LABURNUM

(lə-**bur**-nəm)
Golden Chain Tree, Golden Rain
FABACEAE

The spring glory of cool-climate gardens,
where it contrasts to perfection with the pink
and white blossom of peach and apple, the
graceful *Laburnum* or Golden Chain Tree
is a native of central Europe and parts of
Asia Minor.

Laburnums are small deciduous trees of
slim, graceful habit and compound leaves.
The chains of golden pea-flowers (very variable in their brightness) are followed by
simple brown pea-type pods.

All species and varieties grow well in
almost any position and in any type of soil,
provided the winters are cold and the atmosphere moist. They self-sow from seed, but
named varieties are normally budded. All
parts of the tree are poisonous; in country
gardens they should be placed out of the
reach of stock.

Laburnum anagyroides. Golden Chain Tree

Lachenalia aloides var. *quadricolor.* Cape
Cowslip

LACHENALIA

(lak-ə-**nael**-ee-ə)
Soldier Boys, Cape Cowslip, Soldier Lily
LILIACEAE

Easily grown bulbs that can remain in the
ground for years, *Lachenalias* are just as
happy potted up and brought indoors in
bloom. Planted in autumn, they quickly
sprout a couple of strap-like leaves, from the
centre of which develop the spikes of pendulous, tubular flowers. These can be pinkish-
red, orange-yellow or combinations, tipped
green. They are striking in clumps but if
planted in neat rows you'll soon see why
they're called Soldier Boys! Flowering usually
begins in winter and may continue until
earliest spring.

Being from southern Africa, *Lachenalias*
cannot survive outside where the ground
freezes solid, but they enjoy being crowded
into pots of loamy compost and can be
grown in a sunny window in cold climates.
Keep moist from the time foliage appears
until after flowering, when the leaves will
begin to wither. At this point, gradually
reduce watering and keep dry over summer.
They should be lifted where summer rainfall
is high, unless drainage is perfect.

Laelia purpurata. Laelia

Laeliocattleya. Chit Chat

Laeliocattleya. Florence Patterson

LAELIA
(lae-lee-ə)
Laelia
Orchidaceae

Tropical American orchids closely related to Cattleyas, *Laelias* share the same cultural requirements. Species of Mexican origin safely survive a winter temperature of 10°C/50°F. Brazilian and Central American types need slightly higher temperatures all round; *L. purpurata*, for example, deteriorates fast in temperatures below 13°C/55°F.

All *Laelias* prefer moderately bright light but must have a well-drained compost, such as bark chips, orchid fibre and charcoal. Flowers usually appear in late winter.

LAELIOCATTLEYA
(lae-lee-oh-**kat**-lae-ə)
(**No popular name**)
Orchidaceae

The *Laeliocattleya* group are bigeneric hybrids between the two orchid generas Laelia and Cattleya; there are well over 2000 named cultivars. High humidity is needed for successful flowering and they demand the same chunky, well-drained compost and temperatures as do Cattleyas. They do not like a close atmosphere, so grow them in an airy but not draughty spot.

LAGERSTROEMIA
(lah-gur-**stroh**-mee-ə)
Crepe Myrtle, Pride of India
Lythraceae

Native to Southeast Asia and some islands of the western Pacific, the showy Crepe Myrtles, *Lagerstroemia*, include some 50 species of the most ornamental flowering trees in the world. Illustrated *L. indica*, the Chinese Crepe Myrtle, is a deciduous, slim tree to 7m/23ft, with 4-sided, small branches and smooth oval leaves not more than 5cm/2in long. These may put up a good autumn colour display in cool districts. The large flower panicles develop at branch tips only, with each flower about the size of a peach blossom. On every flower there are six round, wrinkled petals on narrow bases, a mass of gold stamens and a glossy green calyx. There are named flower varieties in red, purple, pink, mauve and white.

The key to Crepe Myrtle culture is that they flower only on new season's wood, so it's in your hands whether you lop them back hard and get a compact flower display or let them have their heads and end up with a gracefully branched tree with sumptuously mottled bark and a floral canopy out of reach of flower arrangers. I prefer the latter. All species can be grown easily from seed, but only cuttings will assure the colour you want.

LAGUNARIA
(lah-gyoo-**ne**ər-ee-ə)
Norfolk Island Hibiscus, Cow-itch Tree, Primrose Tree, Pyramid Tree
Malvaceae

First discovered on the lonely Pacific penal colony of Norfolk Island in 1792, *Lagunaria patersonia* has a seaside ancestry stretching back thousands of years, and has proven to be one of the few trees that can really cope with the salt-laden air of coastal gardens.

Propagated easily from seed, it grows quickly in a warm climate into a handsome pyramidal shape, with a maximum height of 16m/52ft on old trees. Throughout the warm weather, the trees are decked with pretty flowers exactly like small Hibiscuses, to which they are closely related.

Flower colour varies from deep rose, through soft-pink to almost white, sometimes with a tendency to mauve. These are followed by a rough, inedible fruit about the size of a ping-pong ball and lined with barbed hairs which can be irritating to both man and beast.

Lagerstroemia indica. Crepe Myrtle

Lamium galeobdolon. Yellow Archangel

LAMBERTIA
(lam-**bur**-tee-ǝ)
Mountain Devil, Honey Flower, Honeysuckle
PROTEACEAE

An Australian shrub in the Protea family, all but one *Lambertia* species are found in Western Australia. The odd one out, illustrated *L. formosa*, occurs a continent away on the east coast. Its clusters of red flowers top every stem during spring and summer and are very attractive to honey-eating birds and butterflies. The strange, woody fruits that follow, like horned animal heads, are very attractive to tourists when made into bizarre dolls. Grows from seed; needs full sun, well-drained soil.

Lagunaria patersonia. Norfolk Island Hibiscus

Lambertia formosa. Mountain Devil

LAMIUM
(lae-mee-ǝm)
(SYN Galeobdolon, Lamiastrum)
Deadnettle, Archangel, Snowflake
LAMIACEAE

Common hedgerow plants and weeds in many parts of Europe and the Middle East, few of the 50-odd species of *Lamium* have found their way into cultivation, but these few have become worldwide favourites for flowering groundcover in spite of their invasive habits.

The cultivated species are: *L. album*, the Archangel or Snowflake, which is a densely foliaged, 60cm/2ft perennial with coarsely-

Lamium maculatum 'Beacon Silver'. Silver Deadnettle

toothed leaves and spikes of white flowers arranged in whorls; and *L. maculatum*, the Spotted Deadnettle, which grows only to 45cm/18in, has deeply toothed leaves often spotted white along the midrib, and sports spikes of pink or purple flowers. It has gold and white variegated garden cultivars. *L. orvala*, the Giant Deadnettle, is less invasive, and has purple blooms. *L. galeobdolon*, the Yellow Archangel, produces 60cm/2ft spikes of golden-yellow flowers in early summer on long trailing stems of silver-marked and coarsely-toothed leaves.

All do well in any soil with regular water, and are propagated from winter divisions of the root mass. Remember, though, to give them plenty of room.

Lampranthus aurantiacus. Orange Iceplant

Lantana montevidensis. Polecat Geranium

Lampranthus productus. Pigface

Lantana camara 'Chelsea Gem'. Shrub
Verbena

LAMPRANTHUS

(lamp-**ran**-thəs)
Iceplant, Pigface, Mesembryanthemum
AIZOACEAE

Winter and spring flowering succulents that
literally disappear under a dazzling blanket
of flowers, *Lampranthus* are the most brilliant of all the iceplants usually tossed
together under the catch-all name of
Mesembryanthemum. (You will find others
listed under Carpobrotus, Dorotheanthus
and Drosanthemum).

Mostly low, creeping groundcovers, the
genus also includes rounded, densely
foliaged subshrubs up to 45cm/18in tall. All
species are very drought resistant and usually
thrive on rainfall alone, however scant it may
be. During extended hot, dry spells, the
leaves may begin to droop, but a single deep
soaking will revive them for weeks.

Iceplants grow easily from cuttings and
should be planted at 45cm/18in intervals for
groundcover work – but not where they will
be trodden on. Most species have cylindrical

or triangular leaves and 5cm/2in flowers that
can be purple, orange, pink, red, yellow or
virtually any shade in between. There are
many recorded species, the shown *L. aurantiacus* and *L. productus* being fairly typical. So
similar are these plants, even botanists have
difficulty distinguishing between the species.
They also hybridise freely.

LANTANA

(lan-**tah**-nə)
Shrub Verbena, Lantana
VERBENACEAE

These splashy flowered shrubs really do
appear to be sprinkled with posies of tiny
verbena flowers in mixed or separate colours.
Native mostly to the Americas, they have
become a great favourite in mild winter
areas, but many species can quickly become
unwelcome guests. Mauve-flowered *Lantana
montevidensis* is the exception – its dainty
arched stems make a wonderful groundcover
or small hedge and never become trouble-
some; there is also a white cultivar.

The more robust *L. camara* is a different
story. It has been proclaimed a noxious weed
in many countries where it has been spread
by birds, which excrete seeds from the juicy
black fruit. But while the species is a hated
weed, there are many sterile hybrids of
L. camara – in marvellous colours, including
cream, white, pink, yellow, orange, red and
bicolours which are useful hedging shrubs in
the warm climate garden. They also make
handsome standards.

These cultivars must be propagated from
8cm/3in cuttings, taken in summer and
struck in sharp sand and peat. They should
be pinched back several times as they grow,
to encourage bushiness, and set out early the
following spring in their final positions.
They need to remain above freezing to
survive winter happily and should be
allowed almost to dry out during that
season. Plenty of summer water is needed,
but too rich a soil makes the plants bolt
to leaf rather than bloom. Tip-prune to
keep compact.

Lapageria rosea. Chilean Bellflower

Lathyrus latifolius. Perennial Pea

Lathyrus grandiflorus. Two-flowered Pea

LAPAGERIA
(lar-pa-**jeer**-ee-∂)
Chilean Bellflower
LILIACEAE

Introduced from Chile in 1847, the gorgeous climbing *Lapageria* was named for Napoleon's beloved Joséphine. She had been born Marie Josèphe Rose Tascher de la Pagerie on the island of Martinique, and is still remembered as Europe's arbiter of floral excellence.

Rare and unusual plants in cultivation, *Lapagerias* enjoy high humidity and well-drained leafy soil in the acid to neutral range.

Lasthenia coronaria. Goldfields

For this reason, they are often raised in a glasshouse, but in fact do well outdoors provided temperature does not fall below –5ºC/23ºF.

Propagate them from ripe seed sown in sand, or layer strong, firm shoots which will root readily. Growing plants need the support of wire mesh or trellis, and are particularly effective trained over arches, where the great bell-flowers droop through in summer and autumn. Stems may grow to 4m/13ft long, but won't even get off the ground unless you swear eternal vigilance against slugs and snails!

LASTHENIA
(las-**thee**-nee-∂)
(SYN Baeria, Actinolepis)
Goldfields
ASTERACEAE

Goldfields is an apt popular name for these small Californian plants, for fields of gold they certainly make. They are so widely seen in the golden state in early summer that nobody even bothers to grow them there. Fewer than 20 species have been classified – all from the Pacific coast of the USA or Chile, all of them annual and growing less than 30cm/12in high.

They should be raised from seed sown in spring, directly where the display is planned, the soil being well cultivated first. Mist regularly until the first leaves appear, and thin out later to a 10cm/4in spacing. They love full sun, but don't take to humidity.

LATHYRUS
(la-**thai**-r∂s)
Perennial Pea, Sweet Pea
FABACEAE

What gardener does not know and love the fragrant Sweet Pea (*Lathyrus odoratus*) and take pride in the ability to grow it well? Germination and growth are easy, but guaranteeing quality and quantity of bloom is another thing. Fortunately, hybridists have made it all easier, and modern Sweet Peas would be almost unrecognisable to the

Lathyrus odoratus. Sweet Pea

Lavandula angustifolia. English Lavender

Victorian railway gardeners who first brought them into popularity. There are more flowers to a stem, a wider range of colours, *and* they can be raised almost the entire year from midsummer – even in winter in mild areas.

Sweet Peas demand a loose, well-drained soil, prepared in advance with plenty of lime and a fertiliser rich in phosphorus and potash. They should be sown in rows running north/south so sun can reach all parts of the plant. If this is not possible, well-staked wire cylinders will give adequate support.

Of course Sweet Peas are only one of some 150 species in the genus, most of the others being perennial, such as the semi-climbing *L. grandiflorus*, with dense heads of magnificent rosy-red, cerise or white unscented blooms. Grow it from seed sown in spring and planted out the following autumn by an old stump or evergreen bush, or propagate from divisions of the rootstock. It will lean or scramble over the host plant or stump and bloom endlessly through the warm weather in fertile, well-drained soil. Shear to ground in autumn.

LAVANDULA
(la-**van**-dyoo-l∂)
Lavender
LAMIACEAE

French Lavender, English Lavender, Italian Lavender, Dutch Lavender, Spanish Lavender – take your pick! But let it not be on nationalistic grounds, for all of the 25-odd species are native to areas from the western Mediterranean across to India, and there are many cultivars.

Lavandula angustifolia (syn *L. spica*) is the mounded, silvery-leafed type with long-stemmed heads of bloom that are so easy to strip for sachets. *L. stoechas* is a dense shrub to 1m/3ft with many branches from the base, thickly clothed with aromatic grey-green leaves. The others tend to be leggier, with shorter flower spikes. All are hardy down to –5°C/23°F, and none of them appreciates humidity.

Propagate from autumn cuttings of ripened shoots with a heel and set out the following spring. Grow in light, gravelly soil on the dryish side. Dead-head regularly and shear new growth frequently to keep compact, but don't cut into old, woody stems.

LAVATERA
(la-**vat**-er-∂)
Rose Mallow, Tree Mallow
MALVACEAE

Native to the Mediterranean, Tree Mallows strongly resemble the related Hibiscus, grown south of the equator. They are

Lavandula stoechas. Spanish Lavender, French Lavender

Lavatera trimestris. Tree Mallow

Layia platyglossa. Tidy Tips

shrubby annuals with maple-shaped leaves. Modern hybrids are well worth growing for summer display now that seed is more readily available.

Lavatera trimestris grows in any well-drained soil in a sun-drenched position. The silken pink, mauve or white cup flowers are 8cm/3in across, and though short-lived, are borne in profusion for much of the summer – longer still if you remove flowers as they fade.

Sow seed (where they are to bloom) in early spring. Thin seedlings to 60cm/2ft spacings and feed monthly with balanced fertiliser. Stake for support, for they easily reach 1.3m/4ft in no time – though there are dwarf hybrids. Grow them only in a temperate climate that's not too cold, not too hot.

Lechenaultia formosa 'Sunrise'. Red Lechenaultia

LAYIA
(**lae**-ee-∂)
Tidy Tips
ASTERACEAE

A popular wildflower in much of the western USA, the lovely *Layia platyglossa* is more widely cultivated in Europe than in its native land. (A classic case of familiarity breeding contempt, perhaps, though how anyone could be contemptuous of this dazzling annual plant it is hard to imagine.)

Given full sun and a rich, well-drained soil with plenty of moisture, it quickly develops a broad, many-branched mound of fine grass-like foliage that becomes hidden by a galaxy of starry 5cm/2in golden daisy flowers with white-tipped petals.

Lechenaultia biloba. Blue Lechenaultia

Seed is best sown direct in early spring. Thin seedlings to 60cm/2ft spacings. Feed monthly, keep roots consistently moist and cut the flowers regularly for indoor use. *Layia* makes a brilliant garden display and can also be stunning in large window boxes or terrace planters.

LECHENAULTIA
(lesh-en-**orl**-tee-∂)
Lechenaultia
GOODENIACEAE

Generally so low-growing they can most accurately be described as subshrubby, Western Australia's gorgeous *Lechenaultias* turn on a dazzling spring display wherever conditions suit them. They'll accept most

Ledebouria cooperi. Striped Squill

X Ledodendron 'Arctic Tern'. Ledodendron

climatic variations from cool to warm temperate, and demand drainage that's top quality. This is best done by planting them in a raised rockery bed (or even a container) of soil with sand or gravel and a degree of acidity. They may be propagated from firm tip-cuttings or divisions at any time in mild-winter areas – English enthusiasts confine their propagation to the warmer months, using a sand/peat mixture.

Though American garden books make no mention of them, *Lechenaultias* would seem to be ideal subjects in California, where the climate brings out the best in so many West Australian natives.

Of around a dozen species, the most popular is *L. formosa*, ranging from 5–30cm/2–12in in height, generally with open scarlet blooms, though there are cultivars in orange, yellow and rose-pink as well. *L. biloba* may grow 15–50cm/6–20in tall, often with a straggling habit, and has open flowers in many shades of blue, including some of the most intense colours known.

In cultivation, *Lechenaultias* are not long-lived, and regular replacement from cuttings is advised. They will cope with a little light shade.

LEDEBOURIA
(led-ə-**boo**-ree-ə)
Striped Squill
LILIACEAE

This is one of those charming plants that suffers from too many names. *Ledebouria cooperi* (syn *L. adlamii, Scilla cooperi*) is, however, a very distinctive small spring bulb, with its grey-green leaves boldly striped in purple and its clusters of starry flowers in some shade of purple or violet. One plant doesn't look much – you need a good-sized clump. Plant the bulbs in autumn, in sun or

light shade, and ensure that the drainage is excellent. Warm temperate climates are preferred. The Striped Squill makes a very pretty pot plant to be brought indoors in flower so you can admire its intricate detail in close-up.

Ledebouria socialis (syn *L. violacea, Scilla violacea*) has grey-green leaves spotted with dark purplish green, and green or purple-green flowers.

X LEDODENDRON
(lee-doh-**den**-drən)
(**No popular name**)
ERICACEAE

The genus *Ledum* (see next entry) is sufficiently closely related to the Rhododendrons to have allowed hybridists the possibility of creating a bigeneric cross of great beauty – and one that can be grown through a much wider climatic range than either of its parents. Using cold-loving *Ledum glandulosum* as the pollen parent, and *Rhododendron trichotomum* from Yunnan as the female parent, we now have a charming shrub that nature never intended. It is formally called *X Ledodendron* 'Arctic Tern'. It grows a little taller than the male parent, and has tiny, narrow leaves, and small rose to white spring flowers.

Acid soil is necessary, preferably a mixture of peat and sand, but with good drainage. Propagation must be from cuttings or layers, since the plant is sterile. It has not been around long enough to acquire a popular name.

LEDUM
(lee-dəm)
Labrador Tea, Hudson's Bay Tea
ERICACEAE

Not widely seen in nature or cultivation, the *Ledums* are a small genus of evergreen shrubs native to Arctic areas of Eurasia and North America. The illustrated *L. groenlandicum* may even be the only plant from Greenland that is grown elsewhere in the world. Rarely reaching 1m/3ft in height, and commonly half that, it is a small-leafed ever-

Ledum groenlandicum. Labrador Tea

Leonotis leonurus. Lion's Ear

green shrub that thrives in moist, peaty soil of cold climates, and is propagated from seed, layers or division.

The dainty late-spring flowers are snowy-white, appear in terminal clusters on rusty stems. Though the plant prefers an open site, shade from morning sun will prevent discoloration of the blooms. The leaves were brewed into a mild-tasting tea during America's revolutionary days.

LEONOTIS
(lee-on-**oh**-tis)
Lion's Ear, Lion's Tail, Dagga
LAMIACEAE

Leonotis, a small genus from Africa, consists mainly of annuals and perennials, but one shrub species, *L. leonurus*, is popular throughout the temperate world. Tall and striking (if kept well groomed), it sends up 2m/6ft flowering stems decked with regularly spaced whorls (or layers) of velvety orange or white flowers. This process will continue throughout the warm months.

Plant *Leonotis* in a warm, sunny, well-drained position with good-quality soil, and do not over water. It is fairly drought resistant except in very hot weather. Growing tips may be damaged by prolonged frost, but the plant will generally recover quickly, for it is quite hardy down to –2ºC/29ºF. You can grow it from seed, divisions, or semi-hardwood tip-cuttings struck under glass in winter.

Leontopodium alpinum. Edelweiss, Lion's Paw

LEONTOPODIUM
(lee-on-toh-**poh**-dee-∂m)
Edelweiss, Lion's Paw, Flannel Flower
ASTERACEAE

After all those years of listening to 'The Sound of Music', one's first sight of the over-romanticised Edelweiss comes as something of a disappointment. I dare say it has some significance to young lovers scrambling about the mountains of central Europe, but that is surely where it should remain.

It is not hard to grow in well-drained, gravelly soil in a cool climate, but what have you got? A 15cm/6in mound of small, narrow, green leaves and, in late spring or early summer, a short display of small, greyish daisy flowers. These are pleasant enough but much inferior to the Australian Flannel Flower (see *Actinotus*). The name is Greek, meaning lion's foot, from some fancied similarity of the flowers. They tend to be short-lived but propagate readily from seed.

Leptinella sp. Water Buttons

LEPTINELLA
(lep-tin-**el**-l∂)
(SYN Cotula)
Water Buttons
ASTERACEAE

I am not sure what the distinction between the genera *Cotula* and *Leptinella* is, or why botanists should transfer the species back and forth between them but under whichever name, they are pretty carpeting plants to grow between paving stones or to fill gaps in the rockery with their deeply slashed but diminutive leaves. The little button flowers, rayless daisies, are of less account, but charming enough in late spring when they appear in large numbers. In the best-known species, the sometimes-invasive *L. squalida*, they are white, but some of the others offer pink to red shades.

Almost all *Leptinellas* come from New Zealand and like a temperate climate and rather moist soil.

Leptosiphon hybrida. Stardust

Leptospermum polygalifolium 'Pacific Beauty'. Tantoon

LEPTOSIPHON

(lep-toh-**sai**-fǝn)

(SYN Gilia)

Stardust

POLEMONIACEAE

A dainty dwarf annual from California, *Leptosiphon hybrida* or Stardust is sometimes listed as *Gilia lutea*, and outside the United States it seems available only in the English Thompson and Morgan range; their 'French Hybrids' mixture includes a variety of colours: creams, yellow, orange, rose and cyclamen.

Leptosiphon is a tiny plant just 20cm/8in tall, with much the habit of Malcolmia (which see). It is a charming miniature for edging beds, growing in paving cracks or for groundcover where traffic is not heavy. It is wind resistant and useful in window boxes and planters of all sorts. It has fine, deeply divided foliage and vividly coloured 1cm/½in star-shaped blooms that appear right through summer. Its only requirements are a dryish soil and plenty of sun. Sow directly outdoors after cold snaps have passed. Thin to a 10cm/4in spacing

LEPTOSPERMUM

(lep-toh-**spur**-mǝm)

Tea Tree, Manuka

MYRTACEAE

Ever since Captain Cook brewed a beverage from the tiny leaves of a *Leptospermum*, the whole genus has been blessed with the name of Tea Tree. More than 80 species are recognised, all of them native to Australia and New Zealand. *Leptospermums* are now deservedly popular shrubs all over the temperate world – not, I hasten to add, for

Leptospermum scoparium cultivar. Pink Tea Tree

Leptospermum scoparium 'Red Damask'. Manuka

Leptospermum 'Lambethii'. Hybrid Tea Tree

Leucadendron discolor. Gold Tips

their value as a tea substitute, but for the graceful habit and soft, casual appearance that makes them ideal subjects for the informal landscape garden.

Grown in full sun, they resist drought, wind and even salt spray. In fact the larger forms thrive on coastal cliffs or in sand dunes, where they assume a horizontal, contorted shape. In spring, all make a profuse display of small white, pink or red flowers, quite like peach blossom. Propagate from half-ripe cuttings struck in summer in a sandy mix.

The species always produce single flowers, but hybridists have produced a range of spectacular double cultivars.

LEUCADENDRON
(loo-kə-**den**-drən)
Gold Tips, Geelbos
PROTEACEAE

Increasingly popular in the cut flower trade, southern Africa's 70-odd species of Leucadendron are remarkably decorative shrubs, along with their more spectacularly floriferous cousins, the Proteas. In Protea, the flower is all-important: in the case of Leucadendron the foliage is decorative as well – stiff, upward-pointing leaves that may be smooth or silky and are sometimes tinted silver, gold or pink as well as green.

They demand acid, well-drained soil and a sunny hillside position with plenty of leaf-mould or peat but not animal manure. Humidity keeps the plants thriving – even ocean breezes. The actual flowers are not

Leucadendron salignum. Geelbos

spectacular, but most are surrounded by modified leaves (called bracts) which persist for many months and can be attractively coloured, especially in winter and spring.

LEUCANTHEMUM
(loo-kan-thə-mum)
Ox-eye Daisy, Shasta Daisy
ASTERACEAE

It used to be a bit confusing to learn that the Shasta Daisy, the big white one with the yellow centre that you see on every flower

Leucanthemum superbum. Shasta Daisy

Leucanthemum vulgare. Ox-eye Daisy

Leucanthemum superbum 'Chiffon'. Hybrid Shasta

Leucanthemum superbum 'Esther Read'. Hybrid Shasta

Leucochrysum albicans subsp. *alpinum.* Alpine Daisy

TONY RODD

seller's stand in summer, was in fact a type of chrysanthemum, so the recognition of a distinct genus for it is rather welcome (French and Italian botanists have always recognised it!). The double forms do look a bit like white Florists' Chrysanthemums but the plant is quite different, being a regular herbaceous perennial which makes tufts of radical leaves from among which the flower stems rise to a height of 60cm/2ft or so. If you cut stems immediately after the flowers fade, plants will flower repeatedly through summer and autumn. They are easily grown in any temperate climate in rich soil and sun.

The Shasta Daisy is the masterpiece of the great American plant breeder Luther Burbank, who bred it from crosses including, it is believed, the Ox-eye or Moon Daisy, *Leucanthemum vulgare.* This woody-stemmed perennial, a common wildflower in Europe, is a charmer in its own right. The name *Leucanthemum* means 'white flower' – the pale pink, blue or even green Shastas you sometimes see in the flower shops are dyed after cutting.

LEUCOCHRYSUM
(loo-koh-**krai**-s∂m)
(SYN Helipterum)
Alpine Everlasting, Alpine Daisy
ASTERACEAE

Leucochrysum albicans, formerly known as *Helipterum albicans,* is one of Australia's most charming alpine plants. It grows almost on the summit of the continent's highest mountain, Mount Kosciuszko, carpeting the ground in small fuzzy silver-grey leaves and studding itself with little everlasting flowers

Leucocoryne ixioides. Glory of the Sun

Leucospermum cordifolium. Nodding Pincushion

Leucojum aestivum. Summer Snowflake

Leucospermum tottum. Firewheel Pincushion

in summer. At high altitudes they are white, at lower ones yellow. You need to be sure which form you are getting, as the lowland versions are short-lived and best grown as annuals, while the high-alpine ones are perennial. Lovers of sunshine and good drainage, they are beautiful plants for the rockery in mild climates, for the alpine house in cold, wet ones.

LEUCOCORYNE
(**loo**-koh-**cor**-**ai**-nee)
Glory of the Sun
LILIACEAE

Though the first *Leucocorynes* were brought from Chile in 1826, it was a full century before bulbs were available in quantity, and even now they are not common anywhere, due to the difficulty of propagation. Magnificent flowers, mostly pale blue, purple or white and 5cm/2in across, are borne in umbels at the top of 45cm/18in stems. They like a light, sandy, acid soil, humidity and constant moisture until the flowers fade. Seed will take years to bloom; bulb offsets are better, but increase is slow. Some years, the plants remain dormant altogether. Plant in full sun for early spring bloom in a cool climate.

LEUCOJUM
(**loo**-koh-j∂m)
(SYN *Acis*)
Snowflake, Snowdrop
AMARYLLIDACEAE

Delicate, green-tipped snowy bells, sharply fragrant, appear by the hundred in earliest spring when you plant the Snowflake, *Leucojum vernum.* The more you crowd them, the better they seem to bloom, sending up hollow stems of nodding flowers among masses of stiff leaves. Set the Snowflake bulbs at twice their own depth in the shelter of

deciduous trees, where winter sun can reach them and stimulate growth. They'll multiply at a great rate, provided the soil is rich, deep and welldrained. Propagation is simply a matter of detaching bulb offsets and replanting in the dormant summer season, but this should not be done too often, as these dainty plants do best when undisturbed.

The Summer Snowflake, *L. aestivum,* is similar, but with longer leaves; the Autumn Snowflake, *L. autumnale,* is smaller, with reddish-tinged flowers.

LEUCOSPERMUM
(loo-koh-**spur**-m∂m)
Pincushion
PROTEACEAE

Many of southern Africa's about 50 species of *Leucospermum* have been raised successfully in the western United States, Australia and other warm temperate parts of the world. They are striking and handsome in both flower and foliage, and enjoy a soil that is light and fast-draining, enriched with leafmould but not animal manure.

Leucospermum reflexum. Rocket Pincushion

L. *reflexum*, the Rocket Pincushion, has unusual soft-grey leaves which make a stunning contrast to the dazzling red flowers. In mature plants, these can appear continuously from midwinter to early summer. A spreading bush, L. *reflexum* needs an area of at least 3x3m/10x10ft. The Nodding Pincushion, L. *cordifolia*, reaches about 2m/6ft tall and wide. The Firewheel Pincushion, L. *tottum*, flowers from mid-spring till the latter half of summer. It is much more compact, being just 1m/3ft tall and about the same across.

LEUCOTHÖE
(lew-kə-**thoh**-ee)
(SYN Andromeda)
Dog Hobble, Fetter Bush, Switch Ivy
ERICACEAE

Named for one of the God Apollo's many lady friends, the decorative genus *Leucothöe* includes some 45 woodland plants, mostly

Leucothöe fontanesiana 'Rainbow'. Dog Hobble

Lewisia rediviva. Bitter Root

from North America, but with others native to Asia, Malagasy and South America as well. Most are evergreen, with strongly reflexed leaves and showy racemes and lily-of-the-valley type flowers suspended from arching stems. These look sensational in large arrangements.

Grow them from semi-hardwood tip-cuttings taken in late spring and struck over heat, or from spring-sown seeds germinated in a warm, humid place.

They like a moist, humus-rich, acid soil, regular summer water and part shade; even the evergreen types colour well in autumn. Hardy down to –8°C/18°F, L. *fontanesiana* grows into a rounded shrub about 2m/6ft tall and slightly wider. Its waxy flowers appear during the latter half of spring.

Lewisia cotyledon 'White Form'. Bitter Root

LEWISIA
(loo-**wis**-ee-ə)
Bitter Root
PORTULACACEAE

Charming perennials from the northwest United States, *Lewisias* are sometimes raised in stone sinks or other wide containers where light, loamy soil can be brought to perfect drainage with sand and grit. They are lime haters, so make sure the soil is acid.

Lewisia species vary greatly, and there are many hybrids both in nature and in cultivation. They form dense rosettes of strap-like leaves, sometimes toothed, usually dark green. The clusters of starry flowers appear on stems 12–30cm/5–12in in length; each plant produces many stems simultaneously. The flowers may be white, cream, pink, apricot or mauve and have a delightful waxy sheen similar to Portulacas, to which they are related. *Lewisias* are completely hardy, so are suitable for even the coldest areas.

LEYCESTERIA
(less-ess-**te**ər-ee-ə)
Himalaya Honeysuckle
CAPRIFOLIACEAE

A small genus of Himalayan shrubs, the *Leycesterias* are closely related to the Honeysuckles (Lonicera) and, like them, are mostly deciduous.

They enjoy a moderately rich, well-drained soil with high humidity and are hardy down to –5°C/23°F in a sheltered position. In appropriately woodsy locations,

Leycesteria formosa. Himalayan Honeysuckle

Libertia umbellata.

Libertia grandiflora. New Zealand Iris

they send up closely packed, arching stems, rather like bamboo, but decked with hanging spikes of claret-bracted white flowers. These are lightly fragrant and followed by purplish, many-seeded fruits that are attractive to birds. The lightly toothed leaves, covered with fine hair when young, colour well in autumn. They should be propagated from 20cm/8in hardwood cuttings which are grown on for 12 months before autumn planting. Cut back flowered canes in early spring.

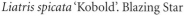

Liatris spicata 'Kobold'. Blazing Star

LIATRIS
(lee-**at**-ris)
Blazing Star, Button Snakeroot, Gayfeather
ASTERACEAE

Hailing from the middle and eastern parts of the United States, *Liatris* is really only a daisy in disguise. For most of the year the woody rootstock shows just a tuft of grassy foliage, but in summer tall, fine-leafed spikes of fluffy rose-purple (or, more rarely, white) flowers shoot up to 75cm/30 in.

Liatris are indifferent to heat and cold, but do best away from high-humidity areas. They are wonderfully hardy perennials for the mixed border, thriving with minimal care and attention, even in poor soil. Propagate by seed or division of old clumps in winter.

LIBERTIA
(li-**bur**-tee-ə)
New Zealand Iris
IRIDACEAE

About 20 species of these easy-to-grow rhizomatous perennials are scattered on both sides of the Pacific Ocean – Chile, Australia and New Zealand. They spread from a creep-ing rootstock, average around 45cm/18in

high and produce tall, wiry stems of minia-ture white iris-like flowers in spring and summer. All species are so much alike it takes a specialist to identify them for sure.

Libertias are easy to grow in a temperate climate, provided you can give them well-drained peaty soil and constant moisture over the spring and summer months. They enjoy full sun and naturalise freely once they find a spot to suit them. A great feature in many English gardens.

LIGULARIA
(lig-yoo-le ə r-ee-ə)
(SYN Senecio)
Chinese Rocket, Leopard Plant
ASTERACEAE

A marvellous daisy genus that is often the highlight of any perennial display – particu-larly in damp or shaded positions. The *Ligularias* are closely related to the genus Senecio and have been included in it by some taxonomists; the general opinion, however, is that they are quite distinct. But these are matters that concern only botanists, and to the rest of us their appeal is in their beautiful foliage and showy heads of golden daisy flowers.

Ligularia przewalskii. Chinese Rocket

Lilium 'Enchantment'. Asiatic Hybrid Lily

Ligularia dentata 'Golden Queen'. Ligularia

LIGUSTRUM
(li-**gus**-trəm)
Privet

OLEACEAE

I do not greatly care for Privets myself, having once spent a year or so hauling them out of a neglected garden to which I had moved. The trunks were like cast iron, the roots like a strangling boa constrictor with a grip on everything in sight. And for years afterward my every gardening effort was thwarted by a crop of tiny new trees from long-discarded berries.

There are small and large leafed Privets but their flowers are much the same whatever the species – dense clusters of small creamy-white flowers with a rather sickly honey smell, which appear for about a month in summer. Pictured *L. sinense* makes a fast-growing hedge plant, reaching 4m/13ft in a few years, but it and other species can become weeds in warm climates.

Ligustrum sinense. Privet

Lilium speciosum. Pink Tiger Lily

LILIUM
(**lil**-ee-əm)
Lily

LILIACEAE

Longer in cultivation than any other plant, the tall and stately Lily was known in gardens 3000 years ago. This was the still-popular *Lilium candidum*. But most of today's popular *Liliums* were developed in the last 60 years. Many are hybrids of the two Japanese species, *L. auratum* and *L. speciosum*; others cross a number of North American natives. Our photographs show the fantastic range of colours and styles available today.

Liliums grow from scaly bulbs and are planted deep in rich, well-drained soil, preferably on the acid side. They like shade around the roots and filtered sun at flowering height. Most do extremely well in large containers which can be moved about when the flowers come into bloom – any time from spring to autumn depending on type.

L. speciosum, the Japanese or Pink Tiger Lily, grows up to 1.5m/5ft tall and produces waxen pink or white fragrant flowers, the petals of which are strongly recurved. Blooming is towards the end of summer.

Mostly, they are quite tall plants, such as *L. dentata* which generally grows to around 120cm/4ft and needs 1m/3ft of lateral growing space. It forms dense clumps of 30cm/12in leaves like those of a giant violet; these are slightly cupped and heavily veined with red or purple. In summer, branched, dark red flower stems shoot up higher than the leaves and produce large heads of drooping daisy flowers, generally orange in colour.

Most striking of all is *L. przewalskii*, a stunning waterside perennial from north China, sometimes called the Chinese Rocket. Its long-stemmed 60cm/2ft leaves are basically triangular, but deeply and irregularly divided and lobed. Hairy, purple-brown flower stems tower up to 2m/6ft, each covered with a dazzling display of sparsely-petalled daisy flowers. The effect is that of a display of blazing rockets shooting skyward from the foliage.

All *Ligularias* can be lifted and replanted from divisions in late spring. They should be cut back to ground in early winter.

Lilium regale. Regal Lily

Lilium longiflorum. Trumpet Lily, November Lily

L. *regale,* the Regal Lily, seems to have been made somewhat obsolete by big, modern, more colourful hybrids. But its yellow-throated pure white summer flowers are still as striking and fragrant as ever atop their 2m/6ft stems.

L. *longiflorum,* the November or Christmas Lily of the southern hemisphere, turns out to be the Easter Lily in the north. A wonderful cut-flower, the pure white blooms filling the house with fragrance, this lily is worth a place in any garden.

L. *auratum,* the Golden Rayed Lily, is one of the most spectacular of all. It can grow well over 2m/6ft tall and yield an incredible crop of sweetly fragrant flowers, each up to 25cm/10in across. Blooming usually occurs in the latter half of summer.

Modern *Liliums* are fairly expensive, so take the trouble to supply their specialised needs. Be sure the bulbs you buy are fresh, plump and the largest available. Set them at the depth specified and insert a thin bamboo supporting stake before covering with soil.

Lilium 'America'. Asiatic Hybrid Lily

Lilium cultivar. Asiatic Hybrid Lily

Lilium 'Casablanca'. Oriental Hybrid

Lilium 'Imperial Crimson'. Oriental Hybrid Lily

Limnanthes douglasii. Poached-egg Flower

LIMNANTHES

(lim-**nan**-theez)
**Meadow Foam, Poached-egg Flower,
Fried Eggs**
LIMNANTHACEAE

How strange that so many annuals are
ignored for cultivation in their native land! It
is so with most Australian annuals and again
with the delightful North American Meadow
Foam, *Limnanthes douglasii.* Delicate plants
just 15cm/6in high, with pale-green fern-like
foliage, they are decked for most of spring
and summer with lightly perfumed 2.5cm/
1in white flowers, golden-centred. There is a
pure golden yellow form as well.

While open sun suits them best, they also
like a cool root-run and can be used along
path edgings, in rockeries, and among paving
stones. Seed is sown direct in autumn or
early spring and should only be lightly
covered. Staggered sowing will give a continued display. Damp soil suits them.

Limonium sinuatum. Statice

Limonium latifolium. Sea Lavender

LIMONIUM

(lim-**ohn**-ee-∂m)
(SYN Statice)
Statice, Sea Lavender, Marsh Rosemary
PLUMBAGINACEAE

Once a popular dried subject for winter
arrangements, Statice is easily grown in the
mixed border from seeds or seedlings, both
planted out in autumn. Full sun and well-
drained soil suit it best; no special cultivation
is needed beyond a sprinkling of packaged
fertiliser in the spring while flower heads
are developing.

Sea Lavender (*Limonium latifolium*)
bears 45cm/18in spikes of tiny pink-mauve
flowers that are often corkscrew-shaped and
make brilliant indoor decorations. Blooming
is 20 weeks from seed, and as the plants are
resistant to drought and salt spray they are a
blessing for country and seaside gardens.

Statice, *L. sinuatum*, is a frost-hardy,
woody perennial, its tough rootstock
producing dense rosettes of oblong, deeply

waved leaves up to 30cm/12in and more in
length. From among them, in warm weather,
emerge the many-branched stems of papery
flowers in blue-violet, white, yellow and
pink. When fully open, these are so densely
covered in bloom they almost hide the plant.
This species is also resistant to drought and
salt spray.

All *Limoniums* can be grown from seed
sown in autumn and just covered with soil.
They will germinate in about 3 weeks but the
seedlings must be sheltered from frost in that
first winter. Plant out in permanent positions
the following spring.

LINARIA

(lin-e∂r-ee-∂)
**Eggs and Bacon, Toadflax, Spurred
Snapdragon**
SCROPHULARIACEAE

A gay and adaptable little annual with flowers like miniature Snapdragons (to which
they are related), the humble Toadflax,
Linaria maroccana, is a native of Morocco but
has become naturalised in many places.

Used for bedding and edging, in rock
pockets (or, at its most charming, in the wild
garden), it needs good drainage, rich, porous
soil and only moderate water. Sow seed direct
in the chosen position in autumn or earliest
spring and expect germination in under
15 days. Thin seedlings to 15cm/6in spacings
and remove weeds, as *Linaria* plants are very
fine and easily overshadowed. They grow to
around 45cm/18in tall, producing their tiny
blooms in masses over many weeks. Shearing
plants back after the first flush often produces
more flowers. 'Fairy Bouquet' is the best
strain, blooming in gold, pink, mauve,
apricot, cream, purple and yellow.

Linaria maroccana. Eggs and Bacon

Lindelofia longiflora. Chinese Borage

Liriodendron tulipifera 'Aureomarginatum'. Tulip Tree

Lithodora diffusa 'Heavenly Blue'

LINDELOFIA

(lin-də-**lof**-ee-ə)
Chinese Borage
BORAGINACEAE

There are around a dozen species of *Lindelofia*, widely separated between two homelands in Africa and the Himalayas. They are related to the Hound's Tongue (Cynoglossum) and (less obviously) to the herb Borage. Not universally cultivated, they are popular in England's perennial borders. Raise them from seed or root divisions, plant in any soil and keep moist. Leaves are up to 2.5cm/1in long and furry; the plants may grow 60cm/2ft high. Small flowers are a vivid purple-blue.

LINUM

(**lai**-nəm)
Scarlet Flax, Flowering Flax, Flax
LINACEAE

Another lightweight annual from North Africa, the Scarlet Flax, *Linum grandiflorum*, is from Algeria, once of a large family of related plants found all round the Mediterranean basin. (The taller *L. usitatissimum* or Common Flax is useful in commerce as the origin of linseed oil and linen thread.) *L. grandiflorum* demands a light, well-drained soil and plenty of sun, and puts on its best display in a cool summer. The flowering period is rather short, but a continuous display can be had by sowing additional seed at monthly intervals.

Sow seed direct in autumn or early spring in chosen places. Germination is fast and seedlings should be thinned to 20cm/8in spacings. Water moderately. The 60cm/2ft plants branch freely and will need no support apart from each other. 'Grand Rubrum' is an improved strain.

LIRIODENDRON

(li-ree-oh-**den**-drən)
Tulip Tree, Tulip Poplar
MAGNOLIACEAE

Closely related to Magnolias, the Tulip Tree, *Liriodendron*, is native to the mid-eastern seaboard of the United States. A fast grower, slow to flower, it may reach 7m/23ft in as many years and ultimately the straight trunk may top 25m/80ft.

The deciduous leaves, long-stemmed and 4-lobed, unfurl quite late in spring, well after the maples, and turn to a blaze of molten gold in autumn. The name Tulip Tree is a reference to the handsome flowers, which are indeed like tulips. They are coloured a rich lime-green with orange centres and appear well after the foliage, often at too great a height to pick.

Linum grandiflorum. Scarlet Flax

There are exquisite varieties with the leaves beautifully margined, though lighter areas tend to darken in late summer. Its botanical name is *L. tulipifera*, meaning the tulip-bearing lily tree.

LITHODORA

(lith-oh-**dor**-ə)
(SYN Lithospermum)
Puccoon, Gromwell
BORAGINACEAE

There's no richer blue in nature than that found in the flowers of many *Lithodora* species, though there are white and yellow varieties of these attractive rockery plants as well. Some are perennials, some subshrubs, some true shrubs. Most prefer alkaline soils, but *L. diffusa* 'Heavenly Blue' can't abide lime in any form.

It's a 10–30cm/4–12in tall, spindly sort of plant, and in cool temperate mountain gardens it makes a stunning ground or rock cover in contrast with white Arabis and golden Aurinia, seeming to reflect the intense blue of mountain skies for months. It prefers full sun except in hot areas, and demands a well-drained soil and only light watering, even in summer. Grow from cuttings of last year's growth struck in a shaded mix of peat and sand. Shear after blooming to keep compact and to promote a dense display the following year.

Lithops karasmontana. Living Stones

LITHOPS
(lith-ops)
Living Stones
AIZOACEAE

Lithops, the curious little plants known as Living Stones, are often hard to distinguish from the pebbles scattered about them in nature. You can reproduce their environment in shallow containers of sandy potting soil with extra gravel for super drainage. Top with a layer of river pebbles and place a few larger, polished stones here and there.

Lithops will never grow much above 2.5cm/1in or so, but will slowly spread from the roots to form clumps in colour combinations of green, grey and brown. The single, daisy-like flowers, which may be twice as big as the plant, appear in autumn. From southern Africa, they are not hardy and like a warm, dry position in winter and regular moisture in summer.

LITTONIA
(lit-toh-nee-ə)
Climbing Lily, Climbing Bell
LILIACEAE

Most intriguing for pot or terrace culture, the Climbing Lily, *Littonia modesta*, can also be grown in the open where winters are mild. It climbs like the related Gloriosa (which see) by means of leaf tendrils. Thus it will need the support of either a small, inconspicuous trellis or a larger plant around which it can twine.

Littonias enjoy moist, peaty composts with plenty of leafmould, loam and a little sand. Plant out their tubers in early spring and the first shoots should appear a month or so later. Regular water is appreciated and, later in growth, spraying, to increase the humidity. Flowers appear in early summer when stems have climbed to about 1m/3ft. They are bright, orange-yellow bells.

Lobelia erinus. Edging Lobelia

LOBELIA
(loh-beel-yə)
Lobelia, Heavenly Blue, Cardinal Flower, Indian Pink
LOBELIACEAE

A large and variable genus of about 370 species, both annual and perennial, *Lobelia* is represented in the annual catalogues only by dainty *L. erinus*, the Edging Lobelia.

A dwarf, spring-blooming plant, it introduces to the gardener's palette some of the most intense blues of any known flower. A stunning edging to beds of taller plants, it is used too in rockeries, hanging baskets and window boxes, where one sees it all over Europe with Geraniums, Pinks and Petunias. The tiny plants grow in full sun or part shade, in moist or dryish soil, so long as it is rich and porous. Blooming improves when the soil is enriched with a complete fertiliser and cow manure. Water sparingly but regularly and feed with soluble fertiliser as buds begin to appear. Flowering normally begins 14 weeks from seed.

The taller perennial species hold their colour best in a position that is shaded for part of the day. They are not hardy, and in

Littonia modesta. Climbing Lily

Lobelia cardinalis. Cardinal Flower

Lobularia maritima. Sweet Alice, Alyssum

cold areas must be cut back in autumn, dug up and stored under cover until spring, when signs of new growth appear. Then divide, pot up and water well to stimulate feeding roots before planting out. New plants can be started from seed in early spring, taking about 3 weeks to germinate at a constant temperature of 21°C/70°F.

L. cardinalis likes damp soil and plenty of water. It has open flowers of brilliant scarlet. L. laxiflora is a woody plant with masses of tubular red and yellow flowers on arching canes. It can be grown in warm temperate and tropical climates, where it will form dense clumps up to 120cm/4ft in height.

Lobelia laxiflora. Torch Lobelia

LOBULARIA
(lob-yoo-le∂r-ee-∂)
Sweet Alice, Alyssum, Madwort
BRASSICACEAE

One of the most widely grown of annuals, Sweet Alice is also one of the most widely misnamed. An Alyssum it is not, but correctly *Lobularia maritima*. The specific epithet betrays its origins as a seaside plant, a native of southern Europe where it is often seen clinging to coastal cliffs, blooming happily despite the battering of salt-laden winds.

Correctly classed as a perennial, Sweet Alice becomes so tatty late in the season that it is preferred everywhere for annual display, being used for edging, basket work, rock gardening or just plain bedding, particularly in its more dwarf varieties, which rarely exceed 8cm/3in.

Seed can be sown direct outdoors in early spring or indoors in late winter. Germination will take around 10 days at a constant temperature of 21°C/70°F. The first blooms can be expected 8 weeks from seed and will continue right through till late autumn, especially if you shear them back occasionally. Seedlings should be thinned to 15cm/6in intervals; they do best in full sun and well-drained soil. *Lobularia* prefers moisture but will tolerate both drought and heat. Different strains offer blossoms in a choice of deep purple, white, rosy-red or mixed colours. All types self-sow freely but may not come true.

LOMATIA
(lo-**mae**-sh∂)
Rust-bush, Crinkle-bush
PROTEACEAE

Lomatia is a genus of evergreen shrubs and small trees, with a few members in South America and a few more in eastern Australia. Related to the Grevilleas, they have rather less colourful flowers, but their slightly greater hardiness and often attractive foliage win them admirers in cooler countries. Best known

Lonas annua. Golden Ageratum

Lonicera hildebrandiana. Giant Burmese Honeysuckle

Lomatia ferruginea. Rust-bush

Lonicera japonica var. *repens.* Japanese Honeysuckle

is the rust bush, *L. ferruginea*, a small tree from Chile, rather resembling the Australian Silky Oak (*Grevillea robusta*) but with bunches of red and greenish-yellow flowers set close along its branches in summer. The Australian species are almost all shrubs with white flowers.

LONAS
(**loh**-nəs)
Golden Ageratum, African Daisy
ASTERACEAE

Not the most exciting of annuals, *Lonas annua* (syn *L. inodora*) has no perfume and generally displays more foliage than flowers. So why bother? Because it brings a nice touch of bright yellow to bedding displays, is completely tolerant of salty winds in coastal gardens and not fazed by dryness either. (It is native to Sicily and North Africa, not the lushest regions on Earth.)

Lonas resembles in every way the related Ageratum except that the fluffy 5cm/2in flower heads are golden. It will bloom almost anywhere from late spring to late autumn. Sow the seed indoors in midwinter and cover well – they need darkness to germinate, which will take 5–7 days at a temperature of 21ºC/70ºF. Plant out in early spring at a spacing of 15cm/6in in a sun-drenched position. Any well-drained soil will do. *Lonas* is most effective sown in drifts.

LONICERA
(lon-**iss**-ur-ə)
Honeysuckle, Woodbine
CAPRIFOLIACEAE

The scented, nectar-rich flowers of the Honeysuckles bring birds and bees and small children, all eager for a taste. And the twining, evergreen stems and leaves of most types make useful cover for sheds and fences. Grow them from cuttings or layers taken in late summer, but remember, these are rampant plants, ideal where there's plenty of room or where they can be cut back easily.

Lonicera japonica is a vigorous climber, and makes a splendid groundcover, while *L. japonica* var. *repens* or Hall's Honeysuckle is an attractive and vigorous form, its red buds opening white then slowly becoming yellow. *L. hildebrandiana* is a giant, and for frost-free gardens only. It has stems as thick as your arm and 15cm/6in tubular flowers of rich cream changing to orange. *L. fragrantissima* is a different type of plant. Completely deciduous, it flowers in midwinter on long, arching canes of the previous year's wood.

LOPHOSTEMON
(lof-**ohs**-tem-ən)
(SYN Tristania)
Brush Box, Brisbane Box
MYRTACEAE

The handsome *Lophostemons* were known until quite recently as Tristania. They are a small genus of about 5 species, of which by far the most important is *L. confertus*, the Australian Brush Box. A good-natured giant with lofty, reddish trunk and branches, it can reach 40m/130ft in the temperate rainforests that are its natural home. In the garden, though, it rarely passes 15m/50ft, preferring to spread into a short-trunked, broadly crowned tree, wonderfully shady in summer. The flowers, borne profusely among new foliage at the branch tips in late spring, are creamy-white, 5-petalled and honey-scented, with masses of feathery stamens. They are small and not particularly showy.

Although native to rainforests, *Lophostemon* is surprisingly resistant to dry conditions and is a very popular street tree in Australian cities. As well as the type, there is a beautifully marked variegated form, most eye-catching against a dark background.

Loropetalum chinense. Fringe Flower

Lotus maculatus. Parrot's Beak

LOROPETALUM

(lor-oh-**pet**-ǝ-lum)
Fringe Flower, Strap Flower
HAMAMELIDACEAE

Don't believe all the things you read about *Loropetalum*! I was so used to hearing it described as a 'dwarf shrub for rockeries' that I was almost shocked to see it growing to 7m/23ft in Japan. Now we understand each other and it looks most elegant in my garden

Lophostemon confertus. Brush Box

as a series of dark, woody trunks, layered with horizontal branches, topped with clouds of dainty foliage. The plant has downy twigs and leaves and in spring produces masses of fragrant, cream blooms with strap-like petals. These resemble the flowers of Hamamelis, to which it is related, and with which it is often confused.

Grow from semi-hardwood cuttings taken in winter or summer and struck with bottom heat. Plant in a moderately rich soil and keep the roots moist. Hardy down to at least –3ºC/27ºF, it needs little pruning except to remove twiggy growth. Keep its shape in mind when pruning.

LOTUS

(**loh**-tǝs)
Parrot's Beak, Pelican's Beak, Coral Gem
FABACEAE

Not the dramatic water plant commonly known as Lotus, but a group of useful perennials or subshrubs, usually with prostrate stems. The most frequently grown are *Lotus berthelotii*, with scarlet or orange flowers, and *L. maculatus*, with rich golden flowers. Both have a silver-grey waterfall of fine needle-leaves, perfect for hanging baskets, rockeries, banks or the tops of walls.

Grow them in full sun or light dappled shade in well-drained soil. Evergreen where winters are mild, they die back during frosty weather, usually reviving in spring; where winters are very severe, they are best grown in pots brought under cover for the coldest months. The vivid pea-flowers appear all over trailing stems in spring and summer.

LUCULIA

(loo-**kool**-ee-ǝ)
Luculia
RUBIACEAE

Most desirable and infuriating of autumn-flowering shrubs, the Himalayan beauty we call *Luculia* has broken many gardeners' hearts. Just why does it die out so suddenly? Every expert has his own opinion! It adores warmth and humidity but likes its roots to be cool at all times and left undisturbed. The colder the winter, the drier it should stay. It may be hardy down to –3ºC/27ºF, but should be protected from frost with a root cover of deep, organic mulch.

L. gratissima (one of 5 species) can be grown from seed or tip-cuttings struck in spring or summer in individual pots. Cut it back heavily after bloom and tip-prune to shape except when flower buds are forming. One of the most fragrant of flowers.

Luculia gratissima. Luculia

Lunaria annua. Honesty

LUDISIA

(loo-**dis**-see-ə)

(SYN Haemaria)

Jewel Orchid

ORCHIDACEAE

This plant has a most unusual distinction among the vast orchid family, as it is grown almost exclusively for the beauty of its foliage. *Ludisia discolor* produces leaves which are a rich, velvety green with fine red parallel lines and red reverses.

The tuberous roots are planted in early spring in a rich compost, with sand and charcoal for good drainage. They need constant warmth, a minimum winter temperature of 10ºC/50ºF, bright light – but not sun – and high humidity.

Often mixed with other plants in minia-ture gardens, regular feeding will keep the leaves healthy and produce the 30cm/12in spikes of tiny white flowers.

LUNARIA

(loo-**ne**ə**r**-ee-ə)

Honesty, Money Plant, Moonwort

BRASSICACEAE

Every gardener knows the old-fashioned Honesty, *Lunaria annua*, (syn *L. biennis*), but hardly anyone seems to sell the seeds or plants! Its sin is probably that it is too easy to grow, for once you have it, you have it for ever! It is valued for its handsome, toothed

Ludisia discolor. Jewel Orchid

foliage, its colourful pink, white or purple flowers and most of all for the stems of silvery, circular seed pods which are so popu-lar in dried arrangements.

But if you *do* get some seed, sow direct in very early spring (indoors in frosty areas). Plant out or thin to 30–40cm/12–16in spacings in any soil with good drainage. Flowering is in spring; the seed pods appear in late autumn, and next year you'll have it again, and again … The cultivar 'Alba Variegata', with white-marked leaves, is less invasive.

LUPINUS

(loo-**pee**-nəs, loo-**pai**-nəs)

Lupin, Texas Bluebonnet, Russell Lupin, Lupine

FABACEAE

Dense spikes of pea-flowers in showy colours identify the tricky-to-grow Lupin genus, which includes several hundred annual, perennial and even shrubby plants.

The ancient Romans named them after *lupus*, the wolf, because they were believed to ravage garden soil. Now we know the oppo-site is true – crops of annual Lupins are often grown to be dug in so they can enrich the soil with precious nitrogen. But today's popular perennial Russell Lupin hybrids are not for digging in. They are much used for bedding display, though they take from 16 to 30 weeks to bloom from seed and must be picked in bud to last for any length of time.

If Lupins are to be sown direct (which must be done in autumn), the soil should be prepared well ahead of time. Lime will be needed at a rate of 1 cup to the square metre/yard in average garden soil. Also, turn in plenty of compost and a packaged fertil-izer high in phosphorus. The position should be well-drained and in full sun. Nick or file

Lupinus Russell Hybrids. Hybrid Lupin

the hard seed coatings before sowing and drench with fungicide. Broadcast the seed and rake in lightly. If the soil is reasonably moist there is no need for further water until the young plants appear. Best sow more than you need so you can thin out later to a spacing of 45cm/18in: they have deep taproots and don't move well.

Named strains will not come true to colour from seed, so must be propagated from cuttings taken with a piece of rootstock in early spring. These are rooted in sandy soil, potted up and finally planted out in late autumn for bloom the following spring.

Lupins enjoy high humidity and in drier areas a mulch should be laid to keep the roots cool and moist. Tall (1.5m/5ft), thirsty plants, they are strictly for the cooler climate and are not worth considering in frost-free gardens.

Russell Hybrid Lupins produce a magnificent clump of handsome grey-green compound leaves, the perfect foil for spires of bloom that can be had in a rainbow of colours. They are the most popular strain by far, but some annual species, such as *L. hartwegii* and *L. nanus,* are worth trying.

LYCASTE
(lai-**kas**-tee)
Lycaste
ORCHIDACEAE

Unusual orchids from Central and South America, *Lycastes* appear to have 3 petals, arranged in the form of a triangle, point up. In fact these are sepals, and closer observation will reveal 3 undeveloped petals between them.

Lycastes include both epiphytic and terrestrial species, but both can be grown in baskets or pots of fir chips or chunky mixtures of treefern, orchid fibre, leafmould and rubble.

They rest during winter and are not greatly worried by cool temperatures provided they are sheltered from frost and kept dryish. Flowering begins in late winter or early spring, and additional water should not be given until this is completed and the days begin to warm up. During summer, water lavishly and place in bright light, but not direct sun. Good ventilation is essential at all times.

Lycaste deppei. Lycaste

Lychnis coronaria. Rose Campion

Lycoris aurea. Golden Spider Lily

Lychnis chalcedonica. Maltese Cross

Lychnis viscaria. German Catchfly

LYCHNIS
(**lik**-nis)
(SYN Viscaria)
Campion, Catchfly
CARYOPHYLLACEAE

Known and cultivated throughout Europe and Asia since ancient times, the colourful summer-blooming *Lychnis* has been through endless reclassification and sorting out, and many plants once included in it are now listed as Agrostemma, Silene, Coronaria, and Viscaria. But the most worthwhile plants of the genus seem still to be included.

They grow in any well-drained garden soil (in sun or part shade), but the species *L. chalcedonica,* or Maltese Cross, will often grow taller, and put on a better display where the soil is really moist in summer. Conversely, they can't bear to be water logged in winter, so that poses a bit of a problem. A tall-growing plant (often 1m/3ft) with mid-green lanceolate foliage, it bears tall, hairy

flower stems topped with flattened heads of orange-scarlet bloom, each with notched petal tips like a Maltese Cross.

The much lower-growing *L. flos-jovis*, Flower of Jove, is from the European Alps; the entire plant is a wonderful shade of silver-grey until the brilliant pink or purple flowers appear all over it in loose clusters during the summer months.

Very similar is the Rose Campion, *L. coronaria*, which makes denser rosettes of an even lighter grey, and somewhat larger single blooms on branched stems held high above the foliage. These are either a vivid magenta shade or white.

The German Catchfly, *L. viscaria*, is a useful bedding plant found all the way from Europe to Japan. It bears narrow green leaves on hairy stems that may reach 50cm/20in in height, and spikes of carmine-pink flowers that are good for cutting. The double 'Splendens Plena' is most often grown.

All perennial *Lychnis* species self-seed readily and should be dead-headed if this is undesirable. A spring mulch and regular water in the flowering season will keep them growing well. Seed of most species sown in winter at 21°C/70°F will germinate in less than a month and plants will flower the first season.

LYCORIS
(lai-**kor**-iss)
**Spider Lily, Resurrection Lily,
Golden Hurricane Lily**
AMARYLLIDACEAE

Lycoris are a beautiful genus of bulbs from China and Japan which strongly resemble and are often confused with Nerines. However, *Lycoris* flowers first, usually in late summer or earliest autumn, and its blooms have much longer stamens projecting from the backward-curling petals.

The bulbs can be planted any time between midsummer and early autumn when they are dormant, but may not flower that first season. Soil must be well drained and fairly rich in rotted organic matter. *Lycoris* need full sun and regular moisture while in active growth, but when dormant in summer they should be kept as dry as possible to ripen the bulbs and produce a good crop of flowers. Where summers are wet, grow them in pots that can be sheltered from rain; but still remember to expose the dormant bulbs to full sun.

Lysichiton americanus. Skunk Cabbage

Lysimachia ephemerum. Moneywort

Lysiphyllum hookeri. Pegunny

LYSICHITON
(lai-si-**kai**-tən)
Skunk Cabbage
ARACEAE

Spectacular plants for boggy waterside positions, *Lysichitons* come in two lookalike species: *L. americanus* from the western United States and Alaska, and the smaller *L. camtschatcensis* from Siberia and northern Japan. They belong to the family Araceae, and produce typical aroid flowers, bright yellow in the first, whiter and smaller in the second. Both are propagated from sections of the thick rhizome, set out in autumn. Flowers appear first in spring, followed quickly by the enormous, elliptical leaves.

Why Skunk Cabbage? Well, bruise the leaves and you'll soon find out.

LYSIMACHIA
(lai-si-**mak**-ee-ə)
Loosestrife, Moneywort, Creeping Jenny
PRIMULACEAE

In the Middle Ages, when personal hygiene was somewhat lacking and insecticides unknown, *Lysimachias* were called Louse-strife, and grown primarily to repel those vile pests. In these squeaky clean days, we call them Loosestrife and value them as useful and decorative perennials for constantly damp soil. Most species are propagated from autumn or winter divisions and can become quite invasive unless volunteer plants are regularly pulled out.

L. ephemerum can easily reach 1m/3ft, producing tall spikes of star-shaped, pink-centred white blooms in summer. *L. punctata* bears cup-shaped golden flowers arranged in whorls. In rich soil, both species may need twiggy support, which will soon be hidden by the flower stems. Space plants 45cm/18in apart. *L. nummularia* or Creeping Jenny is a miniature creeping perennial with open golden flowers.

LYSIPHYLLUM
(**lai**-si-fil-ləm)
(SYN Bauhinia)
Pegunny, Mountain Ebony
CAESALPINIACEAE

Formerly classified as a species of Bauhinia (*B. hookeri*) this showy small tree is a gem for the subtropical garden, where it blooms most heavily in spring. Growing to 10m/33ft in the wild, it is smaller and blooms later in cooler climates. Deciduous in the tropics, it is only partly so elsewhere.

Lysimachia punctata. Loosestrife

Lysiphyllum hookeri enjoys full sun and heavy, moist soil. Very frost tender, it must be grown from scarified seed. New foliage is copper-coloured – the white flowers have showy scarlet stamens.

LYTHRUM
(lith-rəm)
Purple Loosestrife, Spiked Loosestrife
LYTHRACEAE

Lythrum salicaria is the perfect plant for that damp, hard-to-drain area, where it will soak up all the water and convert it into tall spikes of mauve, pink, crimson and red-violet flowers that are grand for picking. It is native to temperate areas all over the world, including Australia.

Lythrum salicaria 'Firecandle'. Purple Loosestrife

Lythrum salicaria. Purple Loosestrife

In nature perennial, it is often grown as an annual in warmer areas and will flower in a single season if sown early enough. Sow direct in autumn – or early spring in warm temperate climates. Choose a heavy, rich, constantly moist soil in sun or light shade. Though colours vary widely, most seed sold seems to be of the rose-pink variety, which is quite attractive. *Lythrum* can be grown by pools or ponds, even in large pots *in* a pool with the soil surface above water.

MACADAMIA

(mak-∂-**dae**-mee-∂)
Queensland Nut, Australian Nut
PROTEACEAE

Native to the north-eastern coast of Australia, the *Macadamia* is now grown in many tropical and warm temperate parts of the world, not for its insignificant flowers, but for the mouth-watering nuts that follow.

Three species are grown, all handsome, evergreen trees. *M. integrifolia* grows to 20m/65ft tall but not as wide and has relatively smooth-edged adult leaves; *M. tetraphylla* is not so tall, but is wider in the spread of its branches; *M. ternifolia* is the runt of the genus, a mere 5m/16ft, with pink new growth. Its nuts are smaller than the others, somewhat bitter and inedible. All three bear long, hanging racemes of tiny flowers; *M. integrifolia's* are white, the others a soft pink.

Macadamias are propagated from grafted cuttings and grow fast. I have one that

Macfadyena unguis-cati. Cat's Claw

fruited in its fifth year, and now, at 14 years is about 8m/26ft tall. The nuts ripen in late summer in a temperate climate, but the trees flower and fruit continually in the tropics. When in bloom, it is essential that the roots be kept moist or the clusters of dark brown, hard-shelled nuts will simply not appear.

MACFADYENA

(mak-**fad**-y∂n-∂)
(SYN Bignonia, Doxantha)
Cat's Claw, Hug-me-tight
BIGNONIACEAE

At one time, this beautiful climber was known as *Bignonia tweediana*, then for a time it became *Doxantha unguis-cati*. These days you should find it listed as *Macfadyena*, but the old names occasionally pop up. Whatever you call it, it's a vigorous climber that can be extremely invasive in tropical and

Macadamia integrifolia. Queensland Nut

subtropical climates. In cooler districts, though, it is far better behaved and a really worthwhile subject for covering walls and fences.

It flowers briefly but brilliantly, usually towards the end of spring, producing golden sheets of clear yellow flowers. *M. unguis-cati* clings by means of clawed tendrils and finds its own support. Grow it in full sun in soil that is well drained. Prune hard after bloom.

MACKAYA

(ma-**kai**-∂)
(SYN Asystasia)
Mackaya
ACANTHACEAE

Growing best in the warm temperate to tropical garden, *Mackaya bella* makes a delightful feature where climatic conditions are to its liking. It enjoys light though leaf-rich soil, and while it will take full sun, the hotter the climate the more shade it needs to maintain a rich blue-mauve colour in its flowers, which are borne all through the warm months. Where frost might be expected, tree shelter is essential.

Propagate from semi-hardwood cuttings taken in summer, and keep moist after the rooted plants are set out. Its growth is not fast, but ultimately *Mackaya* may reach 1.5m/5ft – its display of open bell-flowers will then be quite spectacular. The shining leaves have distinctly sinuate edges.

Mackaya bella. Mackaya

Macleaya microcarpa 'Coral Plume'. Plume Poppy

MACLEAYA

(mak-**lae**-ə)

(SYN Bocconia)

Plume Poppy, Tree Celandine

PAPAVERACEAE

Tallest member of the poppy family by far, the Plume Poppy, as *Macleaya* is popularly known, can reach 2.8m/9ft, and should be grown only at the back of a very large border, or on its own among shrubs and trees – anywhere there is shelter from strong wind. Fortunately, its stems are so thick and tough that staking is seldom needed.

Deep, rich soil is a necessity, plus lashings of water in the growing season – but be warned, *Macleaya* spreads from underground stems and can become quite invasive! Set individual plants out over winter at a

Macropidia fuliginosa. Black Kangaroo Paw

Magnolia grandiflora. Bull Bay

spacing of 1m/3ft at least. The leaves are splendid, 20cm/8in in diameter, deeply lobed and sometimes with a bronze toning. The pinkish-buff flowers are very small but appear in profuse panicles at the top of 2.8m/9ft stems over much of the summer.

The entire plant exudes a uniquely yellow sap when cut. It should be taken right back to ground level in late autumn. A thick mulch, scraped away in spring, protects the roots from winter frost.

MACROPIDIA

(mak-roh-**pid**-ee-ə)

Black Kangaroo Paw

HAEMODORACEAE

Nobody has ever explained to me why *Macropidia fuliginosa* is not just another variety of Anigozanthos (which see). Except in colour, it appears identical. The same clump of flax-like leaves, the same tall (1.3m/4ft) flowering stems, the same likes and dislikes. It even comes from the same part of Western Australia. But ah, those flowers! Black as darkest velvet, their petals are slashed to reveal an interior coloration of brilliant lime-green.

Away from Australia you'll rarely find them, for seed is quite unreliable. They prefer a dry, gravelly position, need water only in drought and bring honey-eating birds from far and wide.

Magnolia denudata. Yulan

MAGNOLIA

(mag-**nohl**-ee-ə)

Bull Bay, Yulan, Cucumber Tree, Chinese Tulip Tree, Saucer Magnolia

MAGNOLIACEAE

Through a tremendous range of climates from cold temperate to subtropical, the ultimate flowering tree is a *Magnolia* of one sort or another. This is thanks to the fact that the genus has two homelands – the cold far west of China in the vicinity of the Himalayas, and the southern USA and Central America surrounding the warm Gulf of Mexico. Generally speaking, the Chinese species are deciduous and spring flowering; those from America are evergreen and bloom in summer.

Magnolia stellata. Star Magnolia

The most commonly seen species in temperate climates is undoubtedly the giant American Bull Bay or southern Magnolia, *M. grandiflora*, which may reach 25m/80ft where the winters are warm enough. It is evergreen, with very large simple leaves that look as if they have been lacquered on top and sprayed with brown flock beneath. The dinner plate-sized flowers, with 6–12 petals, open continually in the warm weather, spreading a rich, citrusy perfume all around. It is especially effective planted away from the house on a downward slope, so that the enormous flowers can be seen from above.

The deciduous Chinese species grow particularly well in acid, woodsy soil of hill areas, where one of the most commonly seen is *M. denudata* (syn *M. heptapeta*) the Yulan, a gorgeous, rounded tree that grows to 13m/40ft and produces white goblet-shaped flowers on its bare branches almost at the end of winter.

Where you see the Yulan, you're also likely to find its hybrid, *M.* × *soulangeana*, the result of a cross with *M. liliiflora*, a dark purple-pink flowering species that blooms later, well after its foliage has developed. *M.* × *soulangeana* is available in a wide range of shades, from almost white to almost purple. CV 'Rustica Rubra' is particularly vivid, especially seen against a clear blue sky.

The giant of the family is the Chinese Tulip Tree, *M. campbellii*, reaching an unbelievable 50m/160ft in its home mountains, but so slow-growing that we still have no idea of its ultimate size in cultivation. It is not likely to flower in much less than 20 years, so it's a real heirloom plant – but what an heirloom! For the impatient, a hybrid has been produced, *M.* × *veitchii*. Its flowers aren't as gorgeous, but they appear much sooner on a faster, growing, hardier plant.

At the other end of the scale is *M. stellata*, a slim, twiggy shrub to around 2.5m/8ft with starry, open flowers 8cm/3in across – a much more practical suggestion for the small garden.

Magnolias are named for Pierre Magnol, a director of the French Botanic Gardens in the 18th century.

Magnolia liliiflora 'Nigra'. Lily Magnolia

Magnolia × *soulangeana.* Saucer Magnolia

Mahonia aquifolium. Oregon Grape

Mahonia lomariifolia. Fern-leaf Mahonia

MAHONIA
(mah-**hoh**-nee-ə)
(SYN Berberis)
Oregon Grape, Holly Grape, Holly Barberry
BERBERIDACEAE

Shiny-clean evergreen shrubs with spiky, holly-like leaves and plumes of golden blossom in spring or even earlier, the *Mahonias* are useful plants for hard conditions. Frosty or hot, shaded or sunny, moist or dry, any position seems to suit them; and the flowers are usually followed by blue-black berries that look like grapes and often make a good jelly.

Grow them in full sun in cool, mountain places, and in semi-shade where the temperatures are higher. They enjoy a rich, well-drained soil where they can sucker to their heart's content, producing a dense thicket of bamboo-like stems. Most are easily propagated from rooted divisions, but they can

Mahonia nevinii. Nevin Mahonia

also be increased from firm winter or autumn cuttings struck in a cool, moist place. Hardy down to at least –10°C/14°F, *Mahonias* can be rejuvenated by cutting spindly shoots right back. All species are from China or North America.

M. lomariifolia grows 3–4m/10–13ft. Smaller *M. aquifolium* may reach 1.5m/5ft. Its flowers are lightly fragrant.

MALCOLMIA
(mal-**koh**-mee-ə)
Virginia Stock, Malcolm Stock
BRASSICACEAE

For fast, fast, fast colour, rely on Virginia Stock (*Malcolmia maritima*). With only 4 weeks from seed to full bloom in a warm,

Malcolmia maritima. Virginia Stock

sunny position, it's the perfect spring-blooming annual for gardeners with purple thumbs. Grow them around larger tubbed plants, in window boxes, in rockeries, as edgings, in paving, in odd corners anywhere – even over spring-flowering bulbs. The tiny root systems are so shallow they'll never upset other plants. They prefer sun but grow well in shade.

Just prepare the soil with fertiliser, scatter seed lightly and water with care. They'll germinate in a matter of days any time except midsummer. Plants are so fine that thinning is hardly necessary, but liquid fertiliser will help the 2cm/³/₄in flowers open in shades of mauve, pink, white and primrose. Wonderful for emergency colour-up any time.

Malope trifida. Annual Mallow

Malus floribunda. Japanese Crab

MALOPE
(mal-**oh**-pee)
Mallow Wort
MALVACEAE

Not common annual plants away from their
native Europe (*Malope trifida* grows wild in
Spain), the Mallow Worts are closely related to
both Malva and Hibiscus, as you can see when
you look at the illustrations for those entries.

Malpighia coccigera. Singapore Holly

M. trifida is a bushy plant growing to
1m/3ft in height, with many-branched stems
and lobed, pale green foliage. The clustered
blooms – 8cm/3in in diameter – are, in the
wild species, rosy-mauve with deeper red
veining. Cultivated varieties can be white or
pink and bear more profusely.

Sow seed where the plants are to grow in
early spring, covering them sparingly. Thin
seedlings out later to 30cm/12in spacings;
with regular water, they'll grow very fast.
M. trifida prefers full sun and light, and
sandy soil, but will grow almost anywhere
and bloom for up to 4 months.

MALPIGHIA
(mal-**pig**-ee-ə)
Singapore Holly, Miniature Holly
MALPIGHIACEAE

Not a holly, nor from Singapore either, this
fine example of botanical misnaming is a
very worthwhile plant for the warm-climate
garden, where it can be clipped into shape
as a neat hedge or low mound. The leaves
are small, sharp and spiny, the feathery
flowers (which appear for most of the
summer) are white to pink with a blur of
golden stamens – and sometimes there are
tiny red fruits to follow.

Malpighia coccigera (one of about
45 species) prefers well-drained, moderately
rich soil that is kept continuously moist. It is
a slow-growing plant, but regular feeding will
speed it along into a dense mass of cane-like
trunklets, 2m/6ft tall at most. These should be
pruned to different heights if a good foliage
cover is desired. Propagate from cuttings of
almost-ripe shoots struck over heat.

MALUS
(mal-əs)
Apple, Crabapple, Purple Chokeberry, Crab
ROSACEAE

If the cost of medical insurance continues to
rise it may pay us to remember the old saying
'an apple a day keeps the doctor away', and
plant an apple tree in our own gardens. That
is, if we are prepared to take the trouble to
combat such hazards as fruit fly, the codling
moth and many other pests!

Alternatively, we could plant one of the
many lovely varieties of flowering Crabapples
or Crabs, feed our souls on the beautiful
spring blossom and enjoy the tangy fruit later.

From the vast number of Apples and
Crabapples listed, it is hard to believe that
they are all varieties of just 35 species. The
rest are cultivars, including over 1000 named
strains of the eating apple, *Malus domestica*,
alone. Apples are all native to the temperate
zone of the northern hemisphere, though
they are now grown in cooler climates everywhere. They are deciduous members of the
rose family, a fact which isn't surprising if you

Malus ioensis 'Plena'. Prairie Crab

the European species' popularity. The Japanese Crab is a graceful, heavily flowering tree that scarcely reaches 8m/26ft, an ideal size for the average garden. Depending on local climate, flowering begins any time from early to mid-spring, with deep carmine buds opening to rosy flowers which finally turn almost pure white. Usually all three colours are displayed at once.

The Prairie Crab, *M. ioensis*, is an American species, 10m/33ft in the wild, but often quite dwarfed in cultivation. It has hairy, often lobed leaves and sweetly fragrant, semi-double pink and white flowers like Cherry blossom. Flowering occurs from mid to late spring.

M. purpurea 'Eleyi' is the Purple Crab, a decorative, small tree that may reach 8x6m/26x20ft. It has a short single trunk and pendulous branches, resulting in a fountain effect. Leaves are a bronzy colour and flowers of deep purple-pink appear early in spring. The dark-red fruits ripen in summer but hang on the tree well into autumn.

Other species and cultivars are grown more for the decorative effect of the fruits than for their floral display. The fruits are too tart to eat but most can be made into tasty jams and jellies.

Malus, the botanical name of both Apples and Crabapples, is the original Roman name of the wild European species.

look closely at their flowers and leaves. Apples are only a larger, juicier version of rose hips. The original European Crab, *M. sylvestris*, has white flowers and is rather thorny. But the introduction of the Japanese Crab, *M. floribunda*, in 1862 quickly put an end to

Malus purpurea 'Eleyi'. Purple Crab

Malva sylvestris 'Brave Heart'. Musk Mallow

MALVA
(**mal**-v∂)
Musk Mallow, Cheeses, Mallow
MALVACEAE

A group of rather coarse plants, several of which are grown as annuals. Their generally pink or white blooms show affinity to the Hibiscus, but they have elegantly lobed foliage with a sticky, hairy texture. When crushed, both flowers and foliage have a musky, cheesy odour.

Sow seed in spring, and germinate it at a temperature of 16°C/60°F. Raise the young plants in flats or nursery beds and plant out in autumn. Except in the coldest climates, they'll survive winter and have a head start to bloom the following spring. *Malva sylvestris* is a common species, also *M. moschata*, which has a white variety. All are prone to rust disease, which can be treated by spraying with a fungicide.

MALVAVISCUS
(mal-v∂-**viss**-k∂s)
(SYN Achania)
Turk's Cap, Cardinal's Hat, Sleepy Mallow, Fire-dart Bush
MALVACEAE

If your scarlet-flowered Hibiscus fails to open, but produces many vivid, hanging buds, it is probably not a Hibiscus at all, but the related *Malvaviscus* or Turk's Cap. This showy South American plant blooms from early summer right through till winter in frost-free or subtropical climates. It is

Mammillaria rhodantha. Nipple Cactus

Mandevilla laxa. Chilean Jasmine

Malvaviscus penduliflorus. Turk's Cap

particularly stunning where the humidity stays high and the sun is slightly filtered.

Fairly fast-growing, it can reach its maximum size of 3x3m/10x10ft in just a few years. Propagate from semi-hardwood cuttings struck in winter or early spring in a warm, moist place, or layer from naturally low-growing branches tied down in winter and severed from the main plant when roots have formed, usually just over a year later.

Enriched, sandy soil is best if it can be kept well drained, but *Malvaviscus* can also be raised in large containers. Flowers are generally scarlet but there is a pink type.

MAMMILLARIA
(mam-il-e∂r-ee-∂)
Nipple Cactus
CACTACEAE

Mammillarias are bought by the million because they are almost completely foolproof and flower reliably year after year. All species are native to Mexico and the American southwest, and the great majority of them remain small enough all their lives to be grown on a sunny windowsill. They can be readily identified because exaggerated tubercles (or bumps from which the spines grow) are arranged in spiral rows rather than vertical ribs – this gives them the popular name of Nipple Cactus – and many species are densely downy or hairy. The flowers appear in a ring or crown around the top of the plant in early spring and can be any colour from white through yellow to pink, orange or red. They may be small and dainty or large and showy.

Mandevilla sanderi 'Red Riding Hood'. Brazilian Jasmine

Mammillarias start into growth as soon as the weather warms up in spring. From then on, they should be given consistent moisture and regular doses of soluble fertiliser. With the arrival of cooler autumn weather, watering should be gradually reduced, and withheld entirely during winter unless plants begin to shrivel. All species need full sun and temperatures above freezing. They can be propagated by separating the offsets which form around their bases.

M. rhodantha grows into a cylinder 30cm/12in high and 10cm/4in thick. It produces both coloured spines and whitish wool, which contrasts well with the purplish-pink flowers.

MANDEVILLA
(man-d∂-vil-∂)
(SYN Dipladenia)
Chilean Jasmine, Mexican Love Vine
APOCYNACEAE

Charming if somewhat rampant vines for frost-free gardens, *Mandevillas* can also be grown in pots in greenhouses, conservatories or sunrooms where winters are cold – just be sure to plant them in a big container, for they have large root systems.

Mandevillas demand good drainage, but apart from that they're not overly fussy plants, thriving in average garden soil. With regular water and occasional liquid fertiliser they really take off, and twine closely around everything in sight. A small trellis attached to a wall will suit ideally, or grow them over a pergola or fence. The scented white flowers of *M. laxa* appear in profusion all through the summer months, followed by bean-like seed pods. The soft-pink Mexican Love Vine, *M. splendens*, will flower almost continuously in a warm climate, except perhaps in the coldest months. *M. amoena* 'Alice du Pont' is similar but has a richer flower colour. *M. sanderi*, the Brazilian Jasmine, has shiny leaves and mauve-pink flowers; its CV 'Red Riding Hood' has rich red flowers, while CV 'My Fair Lady' has pink buds, opening white to pale pink.

Keep *Mandevillas* moist all through the growing season; in winter they can be allowed almost to dry out. Prune hard in winter to control size.

Manettia luteorubra. Firecracker Flower

MANETTIA
(man-**ett**-ee-ə)
Firecracker Flower, Brazilian Firecracker
RUBIACEAE

Gay little tubular flowers, seemingly made from scarlet and gold velvet, shine like Christmas baubles among the felty leaves of this attractive small twiner. Evergreen and tropical in origin, *Manettias* flourish in any warm to temperate climate provided you give them sun for at least part of the day. Sandy, acid soil enriched with organic matter and kept moist will produce the best and fastest growth and keep the plant in bloom all year round. Not at all rampant, *Manettia luteorubra* (syn *M. bicolor*) is a good choice when a light cover only is required.

Masdevallia coccinea. Crimson Masdevallia

MASDEVALLIA
(mas-də-**val**-lee-ə)
Masdevallia
ORCHIDACEAE

Not among the best known of orchid genera, the *Masdevallias* would undoubtedly be more frequently grown if collectors realised that they are quite happy with a minimum winter temperature of 10ºC/50ºF. They will in fact tolerate lower temperatures than that if you water cautiously.

Start them from divisions set in the smallest available pots of leaf-rich compost, and pinch out any flower buds forming in the first year. They'll do well in an unheated glasshouse in most areas, and they enjoy bright shade in summer, with a touch of sun

Matthiola incana, Cinderella series. Stock

Matthiola incana, Column series. Stock

in the cold months. The sparse leaves are leathery and up to 30cm/12in long. The showy flowers appear singly on long stems, and have a most curious (apparently one-petalled) shape. There are 340-odd species.

MATTHIOLA
(mat-ee-**ohl**-ə)
Stock, Gillyflower
BRASSICACEAE

Deliciously scented Stock are rarely grown to good quality in the home garden, because their needs are difficult to meet. First, they should never be grown where Stock have flowered before. Plant in new soil, deeply dug and enriched with lime, fertiliser and all the old manure you can lay claim to. They need good drainage, regular water and feeding to produce picking-size flower spikes.

Set seedlings 30–40cm/12–16in apart and feed monthly with balanced fertiliser, except for column-flowering types, which may branch if overfed. Cultivate lightly between the plants as they grow and do not overdo the watering.

The most popular strain for bedding is Ten Week Mixed, but there are other good strains, both dwarf (30cm/12in) and mammoth (75cm/30in) heights, with mostly double blooms in a wide range of colours, including buff, lilac and brilliant red. Column styles produce a single flower spike and can be spaced more closely.

Maurandya barclayana. Climbing Snapdragon

MAURANDYA
(mor-**and**-y)
Climbing Snapdragon
SCROPHULARIACEAE

Here's a lightweight climber you can grow from seed in a single season! Once classed as an Antirrhinum (whose popular name it still shares) and then as Asarina, *Maurandya barclayana* was separated from the original genus because of the climbing habit, which it has in common with several other species. Sow seed in well-drained pots of damp, sandy soil in earliest spring – just cover the seed scantily with sand, sprinkle with water and cover the pot with clear plastic, keeping it at 7ºC/45ºF until sprouting is observed. Then remove the plastic and introduce to stronger light. Pot up several times until you set them out or plant them in hanging baskets. Handsome leaves and mauve trumpet flowers appear in profusion as the young plants twine rapidly around supports all through the warm weather. Cut them back in autumn, where climate is warm enough, or grow fresh plants from seed the following spring.

Maxillaria picta. Painted Maxillaria

MAXILLARIA
(maks-∂-**le**∂r-ee-∂)
Maxillaria
ORCHIDACEAE

This is not one of the famous genera of tropical American orchids, but if you come across any of the 250-odd species (there are surprisingly few hybrids) it will be well worth growing. The plants are usually neat in habit, with their flowers borne singly or in clusters on short stems among the long leaves. They go in for quiet colours – pale yellow, lime green, dark red or purple, many showing attractive blotches and marblings of a contrasting tone. They flower in spring (from growths they made the previous summer) and they like generous watering in hot weather. Keep them moist all year, don't over-pot, and fertilise about once a month.

MAZUS
(mae-z∂s)
Teat Flower
SCROPHULARIACEAE

Dainty creeping relatives of the Mimulus, *Mazus* are charming plants for the rock garden from cool, mountain areas of Australia, New Zealand and India. Like Mimulus, they prefer a soil that is constantly moist but not boggy, and can be propagated easily from seed or divisions of the creeping rootstock. *M. pumilio* is the most readily available species, preferring dappled shade where summers are hot, but full sun in cool temperate climates. The spatula-shaped leaves are slightly hairy and up to 7.5cm/3in long. The mauvish flowers are only 1cm/½in or so in diameter. Himalayan *M. reptans* is more reliably frost hardy.

Mazus pumilio. Teat Flower

TONY RODD

MECONOPSIS

(mek-on-**op**-sis)

Himalayan Poppy, Bastard Poppy,
Welsh Poppy, Satin Poppy

PAPAVERACEAE

Many gardeners' hearts have been broken in an attempt to flower these superb hardy perennials. The problem is that, with the exception of the Welsh Poppy (*Meconopsis cambrica*), which will grow anywhere, they must not be allowed to bloom the first time they produce buds, for they will then promptly die. But some clever person discovered that if you block the flowering the first year, they'll turn perennial and bloom for a few years in succession.

For best results, grow in a lightly shaded, wind-sheltered spot in soil that is open but rich and well drained. Native to high mountain climes, *Meconopsis* need plenty of summer water, but almost none in winter. The plants may take several years to grow to blooming size, so to avoid disappointment, it is recommended that you sow seed several years in succession. This can be done outdoors in autumn for spring germination,

Meconopsis cambrica. Welsh Poppy

or indoors in a seed-raising mix. Set the seedlings out in spring at 30cm/12in spacings and you'll gradually build up a patch of varying-sized plants which should guarantee bloom for some years. But still the plants are short-lived and will not last overlong.

M. grandis produces silky, sky-blue blooms of large size and is one of the most sought-after types. It is virtually impossible to grow where winters are mild. *M. napaulensis* is variably pink, purple or white, while *M. cambrica* is yellow or orange.

Meconopsis grandis. Blue Tibetan Poppy

Meconopsis napaulensis. Satin Poppy

Medicago arborea. Moon Trefoil

Medinilla magnifica. Medinilla

Megaskepasma erythrochlamys. Brazilian Red-cloak

MEDICAGO
(med-ik-**ah**-goh)
Alfalfa, Lucerne, Medick

FABACEAE

Not common in horticultural display, Alfalfa (*Medicago sativa*), with its small clusters of mauve flowers, is in fact a useful garden plant. It is grown from seed, and turned in as green manure to enrich poor soil with nitrogen. On its own behalf, it will grow anywhere the soil is neutral to alkaline and well drained. In almost any climate it will rapidly reach 1.5m/60in high.

Shrubby *M. arborea*, the Moon Trefoil, grows to about 2m/6ft. Its greyish-green leaves are tripinnate (with 3 leaflets), and the tiny summer pea-flowers are a brilliant golden yellow. It needs full sun.

MEDINILLA
(med-in-**il**-l∂)
Medinilla
MELASTOMATACEAE

Unless you live in the tropics or can afford to run a heated conservatory, you're not likely to enjoy the showy blooms of this most gorgeous of tropical plants. For *Medinillas* are fussy growers, and even in winter demand a night temperature of at least 21°C/70°F if they're to do at all well. And as anyone with a recent central heating bill can testify, winter temperatures like that don't come cheap.

There are some 100 species of these remarkable shrubs, mostly native to Southeast Asia and certain of the Pacific islands, but the only one much seen away from its native lands is the slow-growing *M. magnifica*, sometimes called the Javanese Rhododendron, though in fact it comes from the Philippines.

It is propagated from cuttings of half-ripened wood in spring. These are potted up in a mixture of sifted peat, sand and fine charcoal, and kept in a humid glasshouse until they strike. *Medinillas* can be kept permanently in containers of moderate size, but must be repotted regularly to freshen up the soil. Fertilise from time to time, prune to shape after bloom and syringe with miticide to discourage red spider-mite. The fantastic pendent flower clusters appear in late spring and continue throughout summer. They combine strawberry-pink flowers and mauve-pink bracts with purple and yellow stamens.

MEGASKEPASMA
(meg-∂-skee-**paz**-m∂)
Brazilian Red-cloak, Megas
ACANTHACEAE

A spectacular shrub for mass display in the *very* warm-climate garden, tongue-twisting *Megaskepasma erythrochlamys* (gasp!) is sometimes known as Brazilian Red-cloak, though in fact it comes from Venezuela. It is a member of the Acanthus family and bears

more than a passing resemblance to Aphelandra, Justicia, Pachystachys and Sanchezia, all popular house plants in recent years.

They enjoy a light, leaf-rich soil with regular water and fertiliser and look best in semi-shade, which reduces transpiration from their large leaf areas. The showy panicles of crimson bloom appear in autumn in warm temperate gardens, but much earlier in the tropics. Plants form spreading clumps of erect stems, each topped with flowers. Snails seem particularly attracted to the leaves and quickly render them unsightly. *Megaskepasmas* are easily increased from cuttings rooted in a warm, humid spot.

Melaleuca lateritia. Robin Redbreast

Melaleuca fulgens. Scarlet Honeymyrtle

Melaleuca linariifolia. Snow-in-summer

MELALEUCA
(mel-∂-**loo**-k∂)

**Honeymyrtle, Bottlebrush, Cajeput,
Paperbark, Robin Redbreast**

MYRTACEAE

To all intents and purposes exclusively
Australian, *Melaleucas* are particularly noted
for their showy blossoms and decorative,
peeling bark. Most species are evergreen and
provide a dense foliage cover or windbreak.
They make do with only occasional watering
in dry times, need little or no fertiliser and
are not at all particular about soil provided
the drainage is reasonable – and even that
isn't always essential.

Melaleucas can be grown from seed sown
in spring in a light, peaty mix with scant
cover, or from 5cm/2in semi-hardwood

Melaleuca armillaris. Bracelet Honeymyrtle

cuttings struck over heat from summer to
midwinter. The shown species have a sweet,
honey scent and attract birds from afar. They
grow well by the coast, where they often
adopt picturesque shapes. But probably their
most popular use is sheared to a compact
shape for a windbreak. In this form their
profusion of bloom is greatly stimulated.
M. linariifolia can reach 10m/33ft on a short,
twisted trunk. It is a handsome tree, its fine,
light-green leaves disappearing in summer
beneath a mass of creamy-white flowers.
M. violacea, a small shrub, has a curious flat-
topped form – just 50cm/20in tall but
spreading as much as 1.5m/5ft across. Its
small mauve flowers appear in spring.
M. lateritia, Robin Redbreast, usually grows
into an open bush less than 3m/10ft tall. Its
flowers are a vivid orange-scarlet.

Melaleuca violacea. Dwarf Honeymyrtle

MELASTOMA
(mel-∂-**stoh**-m∂)

**Pink Lasiandra, Blue Tongue, Indian
Rhododendron**

MELASTOMATACEAE

Found in most tropical areas except the
Americas, the 40-odd species of *Melastoma*
greatly resemble related Tibouchina (which
see) and have a flowering season centring
on summer in temperate climates. So, the
hotter it gets, the longer they bloom –
tropical gardeners can expect flowers most
of the year.

The leaves are typically spear-shaped and
leathery, with strongly delineated parallel
veins. Open 5-petalled flowers cluster at the
ends of branches and may be pink, purple or
(rarely) white. They are followed by edible
blue-black berries that stain the mouth and
tongue and have led to one of the plant's
popular names.

Melia azedarach. Persian Lilac

Melastoma affine. Blue Tongue

Propagate all species from semi-hardwood cuttings struck in late winter under warm, humid conditions. They grow quickly and should be pruned lightly to shape. Mature plants will reach 2m/6ft in height with a slightly smaller spread. Not hardy at all.

MELIA
(**mee**-lee-ə)
White Cedar, Persian Lilac, Pride of India
MELIACEAE

Pride of India, Persian Lilac, Texas Umbrella Tree, Australian White Cedar – a partial list of names collected by the decorative *Melia azedarach* serves to underline the confusion as to its original home. Today, there is hardly a country on Earth where it is not known and grown.

In tropical climates it shoots up to 20m/65ft and more, with a spreading crown. In Texas, Australia and Persia it grows usually wider than its height. In all areas it bears handsome leaves that resemble those of the European Ash.

In spring, with the new foliage, *Melia* produces sprays of small lilac and purple flowers, 5 or 6-petalled and fragrant. *Melia* is of particular use in dry, semi-arid areas,

Mentzelia lindleyi. Bartonia

though it is happiest in deep, rich, well-watered soils. Deciduous, it easily copes with frosts down to −5°C/23°F – and can stand lower temperatures still, but not months of ice and snow.

MENTZELIA
(ment-**zeel**-ee-ə)
Blazing Star, Bartonia
LOASACEAE

A desert plant from southern California, the Blazing Star (*Mentzelia lindleyi*, syn *Bartonia aurea*) may be hard to locate, but is worth ordering from the United States if necessary. I have seen it growing to perfection in Europe but never in the southern hemisphere, where it should do well. The golden, shining 5-petalled flowers have an orange eye and long stamens and are sweetly scented, especially at night. They appear for months in summer on 60cm/2ft plants with deeply divided, decorative foliage. Full sun and good drainage are musts, but any type of soil seems to suit. Sow direct in early spring. Thin later to 25cm/10in spacings. Flowers open late afternoon, last till next noon.

MENZIESIA
(men-**zees**-ee-ə)
Mock Azalea, Minniebush
ERICACEAE

Found naturally in both Japan and North America, *Menziesia* are delightful small shrubs for the shaded, woodsy, lime-free

Menziesia ciliicalyx. Mock Azalea

garden. They are deciduous, grow to around 70cm/27 in and perhaps, when not in bloom, could be mistaken for small Azaleas. But when the terminal flower clusters open in spring, the likeness disappears immediately, for the blooms are distinctly urn or bell-shaped.

Easily propagated from winter-sown seed, layer or 8cm/3in cuttings taken with a heel in summer, they have only two needs: humidity and perfect drainage. They are almost completely hardy, at least when planted under trees. Keep their roots continuously moist in warm weather and shop around for flower colours: these include red, pink, cream and greenish-white, according to species.

Merremia tuberosa. Hawaiian Wood Rose

MERREMIA

(me-r∂-**mee**-∂)
(SYN Ipomoea, Operculina)
Hawaiian Wood Rose, Spanish Woodbine, Yellow Morning Glory
CONVOLVULACEAE

There is evidence of taxonomic confusion in the many names of this decorative Morning Glory. *Merremia tuberosa* is seen all around the tropics, but has left a special mark in Hawaii, where it twines into the highest trees, almost hiding them beneath curtains of handsome 7-lobed leaves and golden-yellow spring and summer blooms. The fertilised

flowers are followed by globular seed pods which split as the seed ripens. Together with the persistent sepals, these split pods form the novel 'wood-rose' used in many dried flower arrangements. Planted in semi-shade, *Merremia* doesn't seem anxious to flower away from the tropics.

METROSIDEROS

(met-roh-**sid**-∂r-os)
Ironwood, Pohutukawa, Rata, Ohi'a Lehua
MYRTACEAE

Scattered about the islands of the Pacific is a splendid group of flowering trees and shrubs related to the Eucalypts; their generic name is *Metrosideros*, meaning heart of iron, a tribute to the glorious red heart-wood, which was used for intricate carving in earlier days.

Most splendid of all is *M. excelsus* (syn. *M. tomentosus*), aptly called Pohutukawa, or 'sprinkled with spray', by the Maoris, for its habit of clinging to sea-washed cliffs or growing with roots actually in salt water. It is both salt and sand resistant, and in exposed positions will become gnarled and picturesque, trailing a tangle of aerial roots from every branch. Its dark, leathery 10cm/ 4in leaves have silver reverses and in midsummer (Christmastime in the southern hemisphere) it bursts into dazzling bloom as masses of scarlet-stamened, pincushion flowers open on woolly white stalks.

Metrosideros excelsus. Pohutukawa

Metrosideros kermadecensis. Variegated Rata

Michelia doltsopa. Wong-lan

Taller, with flowers of duller red, is the Northern Rata, *M. robustus*, from forests of New Zealand's North Island, while *M. carmineus* is an infrequently seen climber despite its clusters of striking, carmine-red flowers. It makes a splendid groundcover.

A fourth New Zealand species is *M. kermadecensis*, sold in a number of varie-gated leaf forms. Less useful in coastal areas but at home in humid mountain districts is *M. collinus*, the Ohi'a Lehua, found high on the slopes of Tahiti and the Hawaiian Islands, where it has been recorded at 35m/115ft in height. It is crowned with a blanket of vivid orange bloom.

Michelia alba. Pak-lan

MICHELIA
(mi-**kei**-lee-ə)
Port Wine Magnolia, Banana Shrub, Pak-lan, Wong-lan, Cham-pak

MAGNOLIACEAE

Evergreen and closely related to the Magnolias (which see), the 50-odd Asiatic species of *Michelia* are commonly repre-sented in Western gardens only by shrubby *M. figo*, the Port Wine Magnolia or Banana Shrub; its small, buff and crimson spring flowers smell strongly of ripe bananas to some and rich, fruity port wine to others. But in gardens of Asia, Hawaii, South America and Africa, several of the tree species are among the most beloved of garden ornamentals. The following three of these trees are generally available and worth seeking out.

M. alba, the Pak-lan, is a handsome pale-trunked tree of 10m/31ft with slender, pointed, apple-green leaves to 25cm/10in long. The snowy-white flowers are about the size of a Gardenia, though with narrow petals of an irregular length. They are very fragrant and popular among Chinese communities everywhere. Alas, they are hard to pick, as the tree tends to be rather high-branching.

M. doltsopa, the Wong-lan, is a fast-grow-ing pyramidal tree to 13m/40ft. Its pointed leaves are a darker green and the branches often develop a convenient weeping habit. The flowers are very large, up to 15cm/6in across, with long, floppy petals of white, changing to a butterscotch colour. They are fragrant at first but develop an unpleasantly heavy perfume after a day.

M. champaca, the Cham-pak, is a larger-growing tree from Tibet and Yunnan. It may reach 30m/100ft in nature, but much less in the garden. The fragrant, often 12-petalled flowers are 8cm/3in wide and a creamy-buff shade, or sometimes yellow.

Michelia figo. Port Wine Magnolia

Micromyrtus ciliata. Fringed Heath Myrtle

All *Michelias* bear their flowers in the leaf axils (unlike Magnolias). They can be grown from semi-hardwood cuttings taken in summer and autumn, and all species enjoy fairly rich, well-drained soil with plenty of summer water. Prune *M. figo* lightly all over after bloom to keep the plant smaller than normal. All *Michelias* tolerate light frosts but are not recommended where winters are severe. The name commemorates a 17th-century Italian botanist, Pietro Micheli.

MICROMYRTUS
(mai-kro-**mur**-t∂s)
Heath Myrtle
MYRTACEAE

I suppose you could call *Micromyrtus ciliata* Australia's version of heather. It isn't even closely related, but in its small leaves and little flowers which cover the plant for many weeks in late spring it does present much the same picture – except that the leaves are pleasantly aromatic and the flowers white, turning pink as they age. There are two versions in cultivation, one completely prostrate and making an excellent groundcover for a sunny bank, the other more upright and up to about 1m/3ft tall. Both like a warm temperate climate (though they will stand mild frosts), perfect drainage and a sunny position, and both are usually propagated from cuttings.

MILLETTIA
(mil-**let**-ee-∂)
Umzimbiti, Tree Wisteria
FABACEAE

A spectacular flowering tree from southern Africa, the Umzimbiti (*Millettia grandis*) can be grown in any warm temperate to tropical climate. Like others in the pea family, it is raised from seed, which should first be soaked 24 hours in warm water.

Millettia may ultimately reach 7m/23ft in a leaf-rich sandy loam, and develops a broad crown of pinnate leaves. Young foliage is a soft grey, ripening to the rich, dark green which highlights the upright racemes of violet-blue flowers. These appear in midsummer, but the display fades fast. *Millettia* likes regular moisture, and high humidity. It is not frost hardy.

Michelia champaca. Cham-pak

Millettia grandis. Tree Wisteria

Miltoniopsis hybrid. Pansy Orchid

Mimulus 'Whitecroft Scarlet'. Red Monkeyflower

MILTONIOPSIS
(mil-**toh**-nee-op-səs)
Pansy Orchid
ORCHIDACEAE

Vibrantly coloured South American orchids that can be flowered with little or no heat, *Miltoniopsis* bloom in unusual shades of crimson, purple, pink and brown, but so variously are they patterned that the range seems almost endless. The large, single, pansy-like flowers last well (often appearing twice a year) and in most species they are sweetly fragrant.

Miltoniopsis (there are many hybrids) can be grown in a compost of fine firbark and charcoal, or orchid fibre and sphagnum moss. They need shade from bright sun, moist conditions all year except winter, and very high humidity in summer. Good ventilation is also important, but draughts must be avoided. Keep above freezing for the most and the best flowers.

Miltoniopsis 'Mrs J.B. Crow'. Pansy Orchid

MIMOSA
(mim-**oh**-sə)
Sensitive Plant, Touch-me-not, Action Plant, Humble Plant
MIMOSACEAE

Does it have feelings? Only a novelty away from the tropics, the famous Sensitive Plant, *Mimosa pudica*, has been the subject of more scientific research than any other plant, and has left as many botanists goggle-eyed as it has children! A short-lived subshrub, it is usually grown as an annual away from the tropics. Decorative, sprawling, with leaves like Jacaranda and clusters of dainty but short-lived pink puffball flowers in summer, it has the remarkable habit, when touched, of snapping leaves shut like a fan and drooping its stalks. Then, when your back is turned, it becomes normal again!

Mimosa pudica. Sensitive Plant

Keep the plants well ventilated and moist, feed with liquid fertiliser but don't expect them to grow much above 8cm/3in. They enjoy strong light but rarely survive even temperate winters without becoming unsightly.

MIMULUS
(**mim**-yoo-ləs)
Monkeyflower, Monkey Musk
SCROPHULARIACEAE

Far and away the majority of *Mimulus* species seen in the gardens of the world are perennial or annual. But North America, particularly the western part, is home to a number of shrubby species, formerly classified as Diplacus. These include *M. aridus*, *M. aurantiacus*, *M. longiflorus* and illustrated *M. puniceus* – a many-branched shrub growing to 1.5m/5ft and with a clammy, even sticky feel to all its parts. Fast-growing, it produces its single, coppery-red flowers for much of spring and summer. In frosty areas, cut it right back to the ground in late autumn and protect the roots with a thick layer of mulch.

More commonly seen are the species grown as annuals, most of them hybrids between *M. luteus*, *M. cupreus* and *M. moschatus*, all from cool Pacific coastal areas of Chile and the United States. They are really frost-tender perennials, but because they rarely survive winter, they are grown as annuals. Particularly suited to damp, boggy places in semi-shade, they do well around pool margins. Many of them spread from running stems.

Mimulus moschatus. Monkey Musk

Mimulus puniceus. Bush Monkeyflower

Plants should be set out after frosts are gone in a moist, well-drained soil, thoroughly enriched with compost and old manure; space them at 15cm/6in intervals. They can also be used indoors, where they enjoy bright, diffused light, a constantly moist, well-drained compost and night temperatures not below 10ºC/50ºF. Popular strains include 'Whitecroft Scarlet', 'Red Emperor' and 'Queen's Prize'. *M. luteus* grows to 30cm/12in and more, and spreads from runners as well as seed. Its yellow flowers on long stems are good for picking.

MIRABILIS

(mi-**rab**-il-is)
Marvel of Peru, Four O'clock Flower, Umbrella Wort, Beauty of the Night
NYCTAGINACEAE

These curious plants from tropical America are known as Four O'clocks because their flowers open at that gentlemanly time – give

Mirabilis jalapa. Four O'clock Flower

or take an hour for daylight saving! Their jazzy cerise or yellow blooms (sometimes both on the one plant) remain open for business all night and collapse in a heap at dawn (except on cloudy days). In their native tropics, they are tuberous, rooted perennials, but in cool temperate climates they are grown from seed annually.

They can be raised as pot specimens, bedding plants or as a dwarf hedge, where they make a stunning display. Give them full sun, a light, well-drained soil and they'll grow to around 1m/3ft tall. Water regularly (they are inclined to flop) and feed monthly. In very cold areas the tuberous roots of *Mirabilis jalapa* can be dug and stored like Dahlias, but as a rule, the plant self-sows generously. Flowering occurs throughout summer and into autumn.

Mitraria coccinea. Creeping Mitraria

MITRARIA

(mit-re∂r-ee-∂)
Creeping Mitraria
GESNERIACEAE

There is only one species, *Mitraria coccinea*, a rather soft-wooded evergreen shrub from Chile. It is happiest in warm temperate climates, where it flourishes best in well-drained soil and a lightly shaded position. It is apt to be rather straggly and is seen best espaliered against a wall, which it will adorn from spring to autumn with hanging bells, not unlike miniature foxgloves but in a dazzling shade of scarlet. The glossy leaves provide a nice contrast. In colder climates it is best grown as a greenhouse plant or even as a house plant if you can keep the humidity up – if the air dries out it will protest by dropping its flowers and then its leaves.

MOLUCCELLA

(mol-uk-**kel**-l∂)
Bells of Ireland, Molucca Balm, Irish Bell Flower, Shell Flower
LAMIACEAE

How this curious plant acquired its popular names is something of a mystery – it is neither Irish nor from the Moluccas, but from Syria! At any rate, it is a great favourite with flower arrangers, who use full stems of the shell-like green calyxes (the actual flowers are insignificant) after snipping away their nettle-like leaves.

Moluccella laevis. Bells of Ireland

Moluccella laevis is best sown direct into its flowering position in early spring, though since it takes 12 weeks and more to reach flowering size, many gardeners jump the gun and sow indoors in winter. Set seedlings 30cm/12in apart in average garden soil. Water moderately, feed monthly with a balanced fertiliser and expect plants 60cm/2ft tall.

MONARDA
(mon-**ah**-d∂)
Bergamot, Bee Balm, Oswego Tea, Horsemint
LAMIACEAE

In his 1571 book *Joyful Newes out of the New Found World*, botanist Nicolas Monardes introduced a genus of aromatic perennials that was later given his name – *Monarda*. We should gratefully remember him every time we see it grown and smell its fascinating fragrance!

Monardas thrive in full sun in damp, well-drained soil and send up 1m/3ft high stems of mint-like foliage, topped in summer with dense heads of tubular flowers surrounded by colourful bracts. These do not come true from seed, so *Monardas* are commonly planted from outer divisions of the root mass in early spring. Cut back hard in late autumn and replant every three years. Principal colours are pink, crimson, white and mauve.

Monarda didyma. Bergamot, Bee Balm

Monardella odoratissima. Pennyroyal

Monarda citriodora. Lemon Mint

MONARDELLA
(mon-ah-**del**-l∂)
Pennyroyal, Coyote Mint, Lemon Mint
LAMIACEAE

A small genus of North American perennials, *Monardellas* are most commonly used in the rock garden or border with light, damp, sandy soil. They can be grown from seed sown *in situ* in autumn, or from spring divisions of the spreading rootstock.

The 40cm/16in stems are noticeably square in cross-section, the leaves narrow, dark and sometimes serrated. The flowers of most species are mauve, pink or white and borne in spring and summer in dense globular masses, both terminally and at various positions on the stems. *Monardellas* are hardy but grown mostly in temperate climates. They demand ample water from spring to autumn.

Monopsis lutea. Yellow Lobelia

Moraea neopavonia. Peacock Iris

MONOPSIS
(mon-**op**-sis)
Yellow Lobelia
LOBELIACEAE

These small herbaceous plants from Africa are close allies of *Lobelia*, as the common name indicates, and their small flowers betray this relationship. They come mostly in shades of yellow, mauve or purple and are borne singly on weak, scrambling stems along with small, narrow leaves. Only the South African *Monopsis lutea* is ever grown: in mild climates it will spread freely in a rockery, spilling over boulders or retaining walls and decked throughout summer with a profusion of golden-yellow flowers. A hanging basket displays it equally well, but it must have a position in bright light.

Montanoa bipinnatifida. Tree Daisy

MONTANOA
(mon-tan-**oh**-ə)
Tree Daisy, Daisy Tree
ASTERACEAE

Growing right through Central America is a large and spectacular genus of daisies, some of which must reach 6m/20ft in height. They make truly sensational background plants in the subtropical garden, with their winter-long display of gold-centred, snowy daisy flowers on long, branching stems. Don't even attempt them in cold winter areas though, for the brittle, pithy stems collapse at the first touch of frost.

Montanoa species can be grown from seed and from stem or root cuttings struck with heat. Being such large plants, they need a heavy, well-enriched soil and plenty of water. Dead-head regularly to maintain appearance.

MONTEZUMA
(mon-te-**zoo**-mə)
(SYN Thespesia)
Aztec Tree
BOMBACACEAE

One of the most spectacular trees from a land of spectacles, *Montezuma* was of course named for Mexico's Emperor at the time of Spain's bloody invasion. You'll only find it in warm to tropical gardens, an evergreen tree that needs plenty of water and will flourish in a well-drained, leaf-rich soil.

Propagate it (if you have a chance) by striking semi-hardwood cuttings in sharp sand over bottom heat. The drooping leaves are almost round and up to 20cm/8in in diameter. The scarlet hibiscus-like flowers are shaded to rich purple, and droop beneath the foliage.

MORAEA
(mor-**ae**-ə)
Peacock Iris, Natal Lily, Butterfly Iris
IRIDACEAE

Beautiful bulbous flowers from southern Africa, *Moraeas* are members of the iris family and need similar conditions to do well. There are around 120 species known, but only a few are commonly grown, including *M. spathulata* and *M. neopavonia.*

M. spathulata produces a single sword-shaped leaf up to 60cm/2ft long and clusters of rich, butter-yellow flowers on stems that can be 120cm/4ft tall. The individual flowers are nearly 8cm/3in across and pleasantly

Montezuma speciosissima. Aztec Tree

Moraea spathulata. Yellow Moraea

Murraya paniculata. Mock Orange

Musa coccinea. Red Banana

fragrant. A tough and fairly hardy plant, *M. spathulata* tolerates wet or dry soil and several degrees of frost.

M. neopavonia, the Peacock Iris, is a daintier plant with a single, narrow, grass-life leaf and flowers of white or orange-red, the petals each stamped with a dramatic glossy black and blue 'peacock eye'. *Moraeas* are planted in autumn and need plenty of water during the spring growing season but dryness during summer.

MUCUNA
(moo-**koo**-nə)
**Scarlet Jade Vine, Garland of Garnets,
New Guinea Creeper**
FABACEAE

Possibly the most gloriously flowering vine in the world, *Mucuna* is also useless away from a tropical climate. I have seen it rampantly climbing the tallest trees in Tahiti and Hawaii, and covering a large shade-house in Singapore. Shade indeed seems to be the key to its culture; it does not like any sun at all in the root area. The spectacular flower clusters seem at their best in the shade of the handsome foliage, which resembles that of a gigantic bean plant – not surprising really, when you consider that that is exactly what *Mucuna* is. If you live in the right climate, grow it from seed or air layers and keep it moist always.

MURRAYA
(**mur**-rae-yə)
**Mock Orange, Cosmetic Bark, Satinwood,
Orange Jessamine, Chinese Box**
RUTACEAE

Jasmine fragrance and clustered flowers like orange blossom earn *Murraya* a place in any frost-free garden. And as if all that were not enough, in any one year *Murraya* will repeat the display several times during the warmer months, following each blooming with a sprinkling of orange-scarlet fruits like tiny citrus. Full sun brings on the best flowering, except in really hot areas, where semi-shade is best.

M. paniculata likes well-drained soil rich in leafmould, and constant summer water. It should be sheared after the last autumn blooming to encourage heavy flowering the following season. *Murraya* is easily struck over heat from heeled cuttings taken in winter, and grows into a densely foliaged bush 3m/10ft tall. Fruit may not set out of the subtropics.

Mucuna bennettii. Scarlet Jade Vine

MUSA
(**myoo**-sə)
Banana, Plantain, Fe'i, Manila Hemp
MUSACEAE

The Bananas (*Musa* spp.) are not trees but giant tropical perennials that send up fruit-bearing stems from suckers. In the garden, their spectacular leaves are the chief attraction, but they must be grown only where they are protected from wind or the splendid 1.5m/5ft foliage is soon reduced to tatters. Dwarf varieties are often planted in sheltered courtyards, and in cold areas can even be potted up to brighten sunny rooms or heated greenhouses.

Banana plants *do* flower, but their large inflorescences are more curious than showy. They are produced at the ends of stems, pendulous in some types, erect in others, the bracts slowly opening to reveal the rows of insignificant flowers which attract hordes of insects, notably flies. Grow in sun or shade in rich soil kept moist. Invasive in warm gardens.

MUSCARI
(**mus**-kə-ree)
Grape Hyacinth
LILIACEAE

Charming early spring bulbs for cold-climate gardens, the dainty blue flowers of Grape Hyacinths (*Muscari armeniacum*) make a wonderful contrast to Daffodils, which appear at the same time. Planted in clumps in early autumn, Grape Hyacinths produce their long,

Musa ornata. Flowering Banana

Mussaenda erythrophylla. Ashanti Blood, Red Flag Bush

narrow, dark green leaves right away and are only without them for a short period during summer, when they are dormant. Flowers appear on low, leafless stems and the plants are ideal for edgings, rockeries, pots or for natural-ising in meadow gardens or in the dappled shade cast by lightly foliaged deciduous trees.

Plant *Muscari* in rich, open, well-drained soil and leave undisturbed until natural increase congests the clump. Lift and divide in summer.

MUSSAENDA
(mus-sae-**en**-də)
Buddha's Lamp, Flag Bush, Ashanti Blood
RUBIACEAE

These curious shrubs put on a brilliant display year round in the tropics, reducing to summer only with increasing distance from the equator. On close inspection, though, the colour is supplied largely by occasional over-sized sepals, the flowers being quite insignifi-cant. Spectacular cultivars include several

named for the wives of regional rulers, e.g. 'Queen Sirikit', 'Dona Imelda'.

In the right climate, all species can be propagated from thin hardwood cuttings taken in midwinter and kept both warm and humid. A light, fibrous soil with ample summer water produces a spreading shrub, to 3m/10ft in tropical gardens but less else-where. Prune heavily after bloom to force further flowers. African *M. erythrophylla* is quite drought resistant.

Muscari armeniacum. Grape Hyacinth

Mussaenda 'Dona Leonila'. Buddha's Lamp

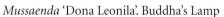

Myoporum floribundum. Boobialla

Myosotis alpestris. Forget-me-not

MYOPORUM

(mai-oh-**por**-ðm)

Ngaio, Boobialla, Manatoka

MYOPORACEAE

Asia, Australia, New Zealand and islands of
the Pacific are home to more than
120 species of *Myoporum*, but few compare
with Australia's slender 4m/13ft Boobialla,
M. floribundum. A small, spreading tree, its
branches are draped with fringes of dark,
hanging leaves, and in spring, a frosting of
white flowers that make the tree look as if it
has been caught in an unlikely blizzard. It
enjoys light, acid soil and grows well in sun
or dappled shade.

New Zealand's Ngaio, *M. laetum*, is a
5m/16ft tree with 10cm/4in lanceolate leaves
and masses of purple-spotted, white 2cm/³/₄ in
flowers, followed by red-violet fruit. Hawaii's
M. sandwicense or Bastard Sandalwood

Myoporum laetum. Ngaio

reaches 20m/65ft in the wild. It bears white
or pink flowers, and its hard, yellow-green
timber is used as a sandalwood substitute. All
species are evergreen and inclined to be
slow-growing.

MYOSOTIDIUM

(**mai**-oh-soh-**tid**-ee-ðm)

Chatham Island Forget-me-not

BORAGINACEAE

There is only one species, *Myosotidium hortensia*, a remarkable perennial from the
Chatham Islands in the Pacific, a long way
east of New Zealand's South Island and one

Myosotidium hortensia. Chatham Island
Forget-me-not

of the world's more remote places. It has
bold leaves, not unlike those of a hosta but
glossy, and in late spring bears giant forget-
me-not flowers in clusters like those of a
small hydrangea on 40cm/15in stems. They
are pure, vivid blue, sometimes white. It has
a reputation for being difficult to grow, liking
cool but not cold climates with plenty of
moisture – and, so its original introducers
claimed, a twice-yearly mulch of dead fish!
Squeamish gardeners can try fish emulsion
fertiliser instead.

MYOSOTIS

(mai-oh-**soh**-tðs)

Forget-me-not, Scorpion Grass

BORAGINACEAE

It would be very difficult to forget Forget-
me-nots, if only because they keep popping
up every year with their charming baby-blue
flowers to remind us that it is spring again.
Very easy to establish from seed in a damp,
semi-shaded spot with morning sun, they
will reappear for years to come, where the
soil is open and rich in compost. They are
sweet in rockeries, as bed edgings or just
allowed to naturalise among shrubs in a
shaded spot.

Myosotis sylvatica is the popular species –
it has many strains, some pink or mauve.
Shown *M. alpestris* differs in that it is altogether smaller than the typical Forget-me-
not. Scatter seed outdoors in late summer
and cover lightly to bloom the following
year. Germination is slow.

Myrtus communis. Greek Myrtle

MYRTUS

(mer-t∂s)

Myrtle, Greek Myrtle

Myrtaceae

The sweetly fragrant, fuzzy white flowers that appear from summer to winter are merely an extra added attraction, for the Myrtle's aromatic bright-green leaves are its chief charm. The shrub will grow in any soil provided drainage is good, and takes either full sun or partial shade without complaint. Hardy down to –8°C/17°F, it can be clipped into a formal hedge, or allowed to develop itself into an irregularly shaped but attractive bush up to 4m/13ft tall – but not quite as wide.

Myrtus communis is easily propagated from hardened tip-cuttings taken in the warm weather and struck in moist sandy soil. The cultivar 'Variegata' produces a mass of foliage with contrasting creamy-white edges.

NANDINA

(nan-**dee**-n∂)

Sacred Bamboo, Heavenly Bamboo

Berberidaceae

The many erect, cane-like stems of clump-forming *Nandina domestica* have earned it the common names of Sacred or Heavenly Bamboo, though it is not even distantly related to those giant grasses. In rich, well-watered soil, the evergreen stems can grow to nearly 3m/10ft, and *Nandina* is very popular in modern landscape gardening for the vertical effect of its growth.

Narcissus bulbocodium. Hoop-petticoat Daffodil

It thrives equally well in sun or shade, although the handsome, reddish foliage which is a feature of the plant in autumn and winter does not develop without full sunlight. Naturally, the colder the climate, the more pronounced this colouring will be, and *Nandinas* are hardy down to about –10°C/14°F. Sprays of small and unremarkable yellow-centred white flowers are produced in summer and autumn, followed by shiny, persistent, bright red berries.

Nandina domestica. Sacred Bamboo

NARCISSUS

(nah-sis-∂s)

Daffodil, Jonquil, Campernelle, Hoop Petticoat, Pheasant's Eye

Amaryllidaceae

Daffodils, Jonquils, Narcissus and Campernelles are all part of the genus *Narcissus* so far as botanists are concerned. All grow from autumn-planted bulbs; all produce long, flat or hollow leaves and a single stem of flowers. Blooms of all species

Narcissus 'Harbour Lights'. Small-cupped Daffodil

Narcissus 'Soleil d'Or'. Tazetta Hybrid Daffodil

Narcissus 'Grand Monarque'. Tazetta Hybrid Daffodil

Narcissus 'Tête à Tête'. Hybrid Daffodil

have 6 petals and a central trumpet protecting the stamens. Beyond that, they vary widely in colour, perfume and numbers of flowers per stem.

Native to the northern hemisphere, these popular bulbs have evolved to cope with very cold winters and are often short-lived where winters are mild. Many gardeners in warm climates accept this and crowd their Daffodils and Jonquils into pots for a single, spectacular display that can be brought indoors in bloom. The bulbs are then discarded and new ones bought the following autumn.

But where winters are at least frosty, the plants can be grown permanently in the garden. A sunny position is best, but where summers are hot, the shade of deciduous trees is an advantage. Plant the bulbs in autumn 15cm/6in apart, in drifts, in any average soil so long as it is well-drained. Water deeply once and not again until shoots have appeared. From then on, keep the soil moist but not wet. After bloom, continue to water and feed the plants, which will be forming next year's flower buds within the bulb. Never cut green leaves from the plant and don't tie them into 'neat' knots! As the leaves begin to yellow, gradually reduce watering to nothing. After a few years, the drift will become congested and will need to

Narcissus 'Russ Holland'. Trumpet Daffodil

Nasturtium officinale. Watercress

be lifted, and the bulbs separated and replanted. Do this in early summer and store the biggest bulbs in a cool, dark, airy place for replanting in autumn. You will have many small bulbs to give away or to increase the size of your planting.

These days, the range of Daffodils, Jonquils and other members of the *Narcissus* genus is almost endless, with those illustrated being just a few. Colours vary from the traditional yellow to white, pink and apricot shades, with many bicoloured blooms. Flowers can be small or large, single or double, solitary or clustered together on a stem; the more unusual species such as *N. cyclamineus* and *N. bulbocodium* (shown) are worth having for their novelty value alone.

The strains sometimes known as Jonquils are varieties of *N. papyraceus,* and differ from Daffodils in that they produce clusters of small, richly fragrant flowers on each stem. They flower earlier than Daffodils, sometimes as early as autumn. They are the best choice for frost-free gardens, returning reliably year after year, especially if planted where they will be shaded from the hottest summer sun.

All *Narcissus* species are dormant during summer and liable to rot where rainfall is heavy unless the soil is extra well-drained.

NASTURTIUM
(nas-**tur**-shəm)
(SYN Rorippa)
Watercress
BRASSICACEAE

Not the popular orange-flowered climbing plant – not even a member of the same botanical family – the true *Nasturtium* belongs with cabbages and cauliflowers in the family Brassicaceae. It is, in a word, the sharply flavoured, delicious Watercress – perfect accompaniment to a fine steak! Found all over the northern hemisphere in

Neillia thibetica. Neillia

streams and rivers of limestone areas, it is not truly a garden plant, though you can propagate it by rooting cut stems in fresh water. These will grow for a time in the fishpond or boggy garden area. *Nasturtium* needs bright, dappled shade, blooms in summer, and is edible all year round.

NEILLIA
(**nee**-lee-ə)
Neillia
ROSACEAE

I must confess that of this small genus of deciduous shrubs from the Himalayas, the only one I have ever seen is the one illustrated – *Neillia thibetica,* which sat for my camera in London's Chelsea Physic Garden. It looked most attractive there with its long sprays of little pink flowers and beautifully cut foliage waving in the spring breeze on their slender, arching stems, the whole thing just under 2m/6ft tall and wide. I am told it is of easy culture in a cool temperate climate, in sun or part shade; prune after flowering. The other species resemble it except that their flowers are white or different shades of pink. The name honours a Scottish horticulturist, Patrick Neill (1776–1851).

Nelumbo nucifera. Sacred Lotus

NELUMBO
(ne-**lum**-boh)
Lotus, Sacred Lotus
NYMPHAEACEAE

Great blue-green umbrella leaves held high above the still water provide a perfect back-drop to pale rose-tipped flowers held higher still. This is *Nelumbo nucifera*, the Sacred Lotus of Buddhism, a flower of unparalleled delicacy and all of 25cm/10in across.
It is the giant of the water lily family. If you've a big, deep pond, plant them in extra-rich soil in at least 30cm/12in of water that's exposed to full sun.

To Buddhists, this glorious blossom proves that virtue and purity can triumph in spite of the world's wickedness. This, because the Lotus rises from foul mud through polluted waters and yet produces a miracle of perfection in its flower. The Buddha himself is often depicted in religious artworks seated in the centre of a golden Lotus.

NEMATANTHUS
(nem-ə-**tan**-thəs)
(SYN Hypocyrta)
Clog Plant
GESNERIACEAE

Less colourful than other popular Gesneriads, the Clog Plant or *Nematanthus* makes a stunning basket specimen when it can be treated to dappled shade within a temperature range of 18–27ºC/65–80ºF. Any colder and it will collapse – much higher and it can develop a stem rot.

Grow these Brazilian exotics from firm cuttings or divisions struck in dryish sand. Plant out later in mildly acid sandy soil with some leafmould. Keep up the humidity but do not over water. Treat to a monthly ration of high-phosphate fertiliser.

NEMESIA
(ne-**mee**-shə)
Cape Jewels, Cherub's Lips, Nemesia
SCROPHULARIACEAE

Showy winter–spring blooming annuals (early summer in cooler climates), *Nemesia* are shallow-rooted and particularly valuable for planting between and over summer-flowering bulbs. They are unsurpassed for spring bedding because of their compact, many-branched habit and incredible range of jewel-like colours – yellow, orange, scarlet, crimson, cream, white, pink, lavender and several shades of blue. Their flowering is profuse, to say the least, if somewhat short-lived, and individual blooms may be flecked, spotted or edged with contrasting tones.

While they adapt to almost any soil, they do best with a really fertile loam enriched with every sort of organic matter and complete fertiliser. Good drainage is impera-tive, plus a sunny position with shelter from prevailing winds, as plants are inclined to flop.

With all this going on. why are they not seen more? Because they can't tolerate heat and do really well only in areas where the night temperature drops below 18ºC/65ºF. Sowing seed direct gives best results in frost-free climates. This should be done in early

Nematanthus gregarius. Clog Plant

Nemesia stremusa 'Blue Gem'. Blue Nemesia

Nemesia strumosa. Cape Jewels

Neomarica caerulea. False Flag

winter or autumn, several weeks after the bed has been prepared. In cold climates, seed can be sown indoors in both autumn and spring, and set out at 15cm/6in spacings when chills have passed. Pinch back to encourage bushiness, water regularly and feed at fortnightly intervals as flowers develop. This will be about 14 weeks from seed.

Many hybrids are available, ranging from colourful mixtures to bicolours. 'Blue Gem' is a 20cm strain, with flowers in many shades of blue; others are taller-growing.

NEMOPHILA
(nem-**off**-il-∂)
Baby Blue-eyes, Five Spot
HYDROPHYLLACEAE

California native *Nemophilas* are a relatively uncommon annual genus for winter–spring bedding, and particularly effective over-planted in a bed with spring bulbs. They dislike heat and transplanting, and should be sown where they are to grow. A well-drained, sandy soil suits them and while they'll survive sun, they look better, and grow better in light, broken shade.

Two species are seen: *N. maculata* or Five Spot has white, open blooms with a purple spot on each petal; *N. menziesii* or Baby Blue-eyes has a brilliant sapphire-blue flower with a white eye. Both have fern-like foliage. Sow *Nemophila* in a lightly raked soil in early spring. Germination takes 7–12 days; the plants should then be thinned to 15cm/6in spacings.

NEOMARICA
(nee-oh-**ma**-rik-∂)
(SYN Marica)
Walking Iris, Apostle Plant, Fan Iris, Twelve Apostles, False Flag
IRIDACEAE

The short flowering span of these tropical iris-relatives relegates them to curiosity status only. The fragrant summer flowers (blue, yellow or white according to species) seem to open before dawn and close as the sun hits them. They are pleasant enough, but useless for cutting. Plants are propagated from divisions set out in spring, and grow well in rich soil of any warm to tropical area.

Nemophila menziesii. Baby Blue-eyes

Where does the curiosity status come in? Well, *Neomaricas* travel, would you believe! The weight of the blooms bends flowering stems down so they take root. A new plant grows in that position – the old one dies. In a year or two, they may travel a metre this way. Hence, 'Walking Iris'.

NEOREGELIA
(nee-oh-r∂-**jee**-lee-∂)
Heart of Flame, Blushing Bromeliad, Painted Fingernail
BROMELIACEAE

In this spectacular genus of Bromeliads, the leaf-vase itself bursts into glowing summer

Neoregelia carolinae. Heart of Flame

Nepeta faassenii. Catmint

Nepenthes maxima. Pitcher Plant

colour! This effect is obviously designed to attract fertilising insects to the tiny flowers, which are almost invisible, barely showing above the water collected and stored in the well of the leaves.

Neoregelias are usually grown in pots of leaf-rich compost for indoor decoration, and where winter temperatures drop below freezing this is the only way to raise them, for they are not at all hardy. In milder climates they can be grown outdoors, but wherever, they should be displayed low down, where the eye can see into the vivid centre of the plant.

Water regularly, keeping the central leaf-hollow full at all times, and grow in full sun in winter and where summers are mild. In hot areas, dappled shade from midday on is appreciated in summer.

Illustrated *N. carolinae* or Heart of Flame is one of the loveliest. It features light olive-green leaves and small blue flowers highlighted by a splash of rich copper-red.

NEPENTHES
(ne-**pen**-theez)
Pitcher Plant
NEPENTHACEAE

In the subtropical or warmer garden, carnivorous Pitcher Plants thrive in the open, for they are found naturally from Southeast Asia down to north Queensland. Elsewhere, most *Nepenthes* species are strictly for the heated glasshouse, where they enjoy filtered sun, high humidity and a minimum 16°C/60°F.

They are usually grown in hanging baskets filled with spaghnum and orchid bark, from which they trail up to 15m/50ft,

hanging on via tendrils which develop at leaf ends. Some of these develop into brightly lidded pitcher-shaped traps, lined with nectar glands. Curious insects are lured into the trap and drown in the sticky liquid within. Hours later they have been digested and absorbed by the plant as food.

NEPETA
(**nep**-e-tə)
Catmint, Catnip
LAMIACEAE

Aromatic perennials of the mint family, *Nepetas* are low-growing plants that form spreading mats of greyish leaves. They are useful in the rockery or as a groundcover.

Flowers are small and blue, mauve or white, produced freely whenever the weather is mild. Planted out in light, well-drained soil, they spread rapidly and are said to be irresistible to cats, though no one seems to have told mine that. Growth is vigorous and compact in full sun but the plant still performs satisfactorily in part shade. Catmints largely look after themselves if given water in dry times. Cut back to tidy up in winter.

NERINE
(nə-**reen**, nə-**rai**-nee)
Guernsey Lily, Nerine, Spider Lily
AMARYLLIDACEAE

Charming and easily grown bulbs, *Nerines* have been known as Guernsey Lilies since European botanists first found them on that island in the 17th century. Years later, when they were found to be widespread in southern Africa, it was realised the bulb must have established itself on the Channel Island following the wreck of a Dutch ship bound for Holland from the new Cape Colony.

Nerine bowdenii. Pink Spider Lily

Nerium oleander 'Algiers'. Red Oleander

Nerium oleander 'Petite Salmon'. Dwarf Oleander

Nerines enjoy a light, sandy soil of average fertility and flower best in full sun. Naked flower spikes shoot up from the bare soil any time from summer on, depending on species. From then on, the plant should be kept moist and fed with soluble fertiliser. In spring, the leaves begin to die off; as they do, water should be reduced, and withheld entirely over summer. Summer rain will not rot the dormant bulbs unless it is excessive. Where summers are very wet or winters frigid, *Nerines* should be grown in pots sheltered from the worst extremes of the weather. They must be grown in sun but can come indoors in bloom.

Offsets are freely produced and this is the best method of increase, though plants resent disturbance. Replanted bulbs may not flower in the first year after lifting.

Spangled *N. sarniensis* and *N. bowdenii* are the two most common species.

NERIUM

(**neer**-ee-ə m)
Oleander, Rose Bay, Pink Laurel
APOCYNACAE

Most useful of shrubs wherever the climate is warm enough (above -5°C/23°F), the Mediterranean's sturdy Oleanders (*Nerium oleander*) are astonishingly resistant to neglect and thrive in the toughest of conditions, blooming away for months even in the most polluted of industrial areas, where they are often used for street plantings.

They are the perfect choice in seaside gardens, where they seem unworried by salt air, and equally spectacular in dry, semi-desert places or in soils with poor drainage and heavy salinity. Where the going is good they are unmatched in the profusion of their bloom. Oleanders are somewhat bulky plants, sending up many erect suckers. But

Nerium oleander 'Soeur Agnès'. White Oleander

Nerium oleander 'Punctatum' (pink) and 'Delphine' (red). Oleander

Nerium oleander 'Yellow'. Yellow Oleander

Neviusia alabamensis. Snow Wreath

Nicotiana sanderae 'Salmon Pink'. Flowering Tobacco

Nicotiana alata. Flowering Tobacco

with regular pruning they can be trained to single-trunked shape or forced into an almost two-dimensional hedge. If space is short, dwarf cultivars such as 'Petite Salmon' are now available. These rarely grow more than 1m/3ft tall, and are perfect miniatures of their full-sized brothers.

All parts of Oleander are poisonous, however, and they are best not planted where stock might be tempted to feed on them. The dark, glossy, evergreen leaves are spear-shaped and 10–15cm/4–6in long; the flowers, 5–7.5cm/2–3in in diameter, are clustered densely at branch ends and come in a variety of colours – white, pink, apricot, red and pale yellow. They may be single or double, and improve in both size and colour as the weather warms up. All colour varieties are easily propagated from 8–10cm/3–4in semi-hardwood cuttings taken in autumn and set in containers of standard sand/peat mixture with warmth and humidity. Heavy pruning of old flowered wood is done in early spring. Watch and spray for aphids.

NEVIUSIA

(nev-ee-y**oo**-see-∂)
Snow Wreath
ROSACEAE

There is only one species, *Neviusia alabamensis.* It comes, as its name suggests, from Alabama, where it was discovered in 1858 by the Reverend R.D. Nevius. Even in its home country it is not often seen in gardens, but it is a very pretty deciduous shrub, growing to about 1.5m/5ft tall and inclined to spread. It bears sprays of crystal-white flowers in spring. They have no petals, their beauty coming from the long stamens which give each flower the appearance of a 2.5cm/1in-wide powder puff. I'm told that in Britain the flowers are cream rather than white, though that is due to the climate, not to British gardeners having a different variety. The plant itself is happy in a sheltered spot in any temperate climate and soil. Prune after flowering.

NICOTIANA

(nik-oh-tee-**ah**-n∂)
Flowering Tobacco, Tobacco Plant
SOLANACEAE

Several ornamental species of tobacco are grown for the delicious evening fragrance of their warm-weather flowers. Seed, however, is sometimes hard to find, as many authorities in tobacco-growing countries discourage them for fear of cross-pollination with commercial tobacco crops.

Nicotianas are really short-lived perennials, but rarely survive winter. *N. alata* and *N. sanderae* are most popular. Sow outdoors when frost has gone or indoors in late winter at a temperature of 20–30°C/68–86°F. Germination should take about 15 days if the fine seed is left uncovered. Plant out in light shade, in moist but well-drained soil, 30cm/12in apart. *N. sanderae* 'Salmon Pink' is popular, while varieties of *N. alata* are 'Lime Green' and colourful 'Sensation Mixed'. Plants grow 30–100cm/1–3ft tall, depending on type.

NIEREMBERGIA

(nee-ur-em-**bur**-jee-∂)
Cup Flower, White Cup
SOLANACEAE

A small, mound-forming perennial that is commonly grown as an annual bedding plant, Argentina's charming *Nierembergia caerulea* (syn *N. hippomanica*) is a great favourite for window boxes, rock gardens, and bed edging. Seed should be sown in spring or summer, when average daytime temperatures of 21°C/70°F can be maintained. Seedlings will appear within 20 days and should be set out at 15cm/6in spacings. They will grow fast to 30cm/12in. *Nierembergias* prefer an enriched, light,

Nierembergia caerulea 'Mont Blanc'. White Cup

Nolana paradoxa. Chilean Bellflower

Nierembergia caerulea. Blue Cup Flower

well-drained soil that is kept continually moist, and do best in sun except where summers are hot and hard. There, afternoon shade is better. Among the easiest of all bedding plants to grow, they produce masses of violet-blue, 2.5cm/1in flowers on wiry stems all through the warm weather. They can also be multiplied from summer cuttings, which strike readily in sandy soil. There is also a white hybrid, 'Mont Blanc'.

A small creeping, white-flowered species (N. repens) is less often seen.

NIGELLA
(nai-jel-lə)
Love-in-a-Mist, Devil-in-a-Bush, Wild Fennel
RANUNCULACEAE

Most often seen in its baby-blue form, Love-in-a-Mist is also available in white, purple, rose and deep pink forms, the latter more appropriately known as Devil-in-a-Bush. It is a lightweight, airy annual, never more than 45cm/18in in height, that does well in average soil in a sunny position.

As the plant has a short blooming season, make successive sowings outdoors from early spring to summer for months of warm-weather flowers. Germination takes 10–15 days at a temperature of 18ºC/65ºF. Growth is fast and the first flowers will appear in weeks, almost hidden in a mist of fine foliage. Thin to 20cm/8in apart, water regularly and fertilise monthly. Once established, Nigella damascena self-seeds regularly.

NOLANA
(noh-lah-nə)
Chilean Bellflower
NOLANACEAE

Of the 18 species, the one usually seen in gardens, and that not nearly as often as it deserves to be, is Nolana paradoxa, a summer-flowering annual from Chile. It trails along the ground, covering it with

Nigella damascena, Persian Jewels series. Love-in-a-Mist

soft green, slightly fleshy leaves, and at the height of its season smothers itself in 5cm/2in flowers. Resembling small petunias, they are a very pleasing shade of lavender, with a neat circular zone of white surrounding an old-gold centre. A seaside plant in nature, it revels in sunshine and doesn't mind how poor the soil is, so long as it is perfectly drained. Sow in spring, preferably where the plants are to grow.

NOPALXOCHIA
(noh-pəl-soh-shə)
(SYN Epiphyllum, Lobeira)
Empress Cactus, Orchid Cactus
CACTACEAE

A truly magnificent plant for a hanging basket or pot, the tongue-twisting Nopalxochia phyllanthoides is an epiphytic cactus from high Mexican mountains.

Nopalxochia phyllanthoides. Empress Cactus

Grown in a rich, well-drained compost of peat, loam and sand and fed regularly, it will produce masses of 8cm/3in spring blossoms right along the spineless, flattened stems. These flowers shade from rich carmine to delicate rose.

Nopalxochia (Empress Cactus for short) strikes easily from large leaf cuttings severed with a very sharp knife, the cut end being allowed to callus over before replanting. Tolerant only of temperatures above freezing, it likes warm, humid conditions in summer. It grows best in part shade.

NOTHOLIRION
(noh-thoh-**lir**-ee-∂n)
(SYN Fritillaria)
Afghan Lily, False Lily
LILIACEAE

Once included with the true Liliums, the *Notholirion* were placed in a genus of their own some years back, because of several distinct differences in growth habit. First, the fleshy bulb is enclosed in a dry, brown sheath; second, the main bulb dies after blooming in early spring – though not before producing a mass of bulbils from which new plants may be grown.

Strictly for a cool to cold climate, *Notholirions* do well in a leaf-rich, cool and moist soil. They need year-round water, except in the months after flowering.

N. thomsonianum blooms are mauvish-pink and very fragrant.

Notospartium carmichaeliae. Pink Broom
GEOFF BRYANT

NOTOSPARTIUM
(noh-toh-**spar**-tee-∂m)
New Zealand Broom, Pink Broom
FABACEAE

Every bit as graceful as its northern hemisphere counterparts, the New Zealand Broom differs in the colour of its flowers – a beautiful cool pink. There are 3 species, the most admired being *Notospartium carmichaeliae.* This grows into a small tree with almost weeping green branches and twigs, leafless like all brooms and adorned their full length with flowers in mid-spring. Like all Brooms, it is fast-growing but inclined to be short-lived and prefers warm temperate climates; prolonged, severe frost will kill it. The name means 'southern broom'.

Notholirion thomsonianum. Afghan Lily

Nuytsia floribunda. Golden Bough, Fire Tree

NUYTSIA
(noit-see-∂)
**Fire Tree, Golden Bough,
Western Australian Christmas Tree**
LORANTHACEAE

Although none of us will ever see a Fire Tree in flower unless we happen to be in Western Australia around Christmas, it could not be omitted from this book.

In bloom, *Nuytsia floribunda* is one of the most beautiful trees in the world, a splash of brilliant gold that blazes away in the drab olive-green of the Australian bush. But it is a root parasite, a tree-sized relative of the humble mistletoe, with no means of feeding except through the roots of established nearby host plants with which it has grown to maturity.

You can sow the seed and it will sprout, but stay at seedling size for years. In nature it will send feeding stems for literally hundreds of metres in every direction, battening onto every plant in sight – and partaking delicately from each of their life support systems: a true vegetable Dracula!

NYMPHAEA
(nim-fee-∂)
Water Lily, Egyptian Lotus, Blue Lotus
NYMPHAEACEAE

A splendid genus of aquatic plants requiring a considerable depth and area of water to do well, most Water Lilies are a little beyond the range of the average garden. Nevertheless, they are so attractive that flower lovers go to extraordinary lengths to grow them in all manner of containers and small pools.

There are two main types, hardy and tropical. Both require a fairly large, stillwater pool and need to be planted at least 30cm/12in apart and preferably 45cm/18in beneath the surface. All species are gross feeders and have extensive roots, so large

Nymphaea capensis. Blue Lotus

Nymphaea gigantea. Australian Water Lily

Nymphaea 'Escarboucle'. Water Lily

Ochagavia carnea. Ochagavia

OCHAGAVIA

(ok-ə-**gah**-vee-ə)
(SYN Rhodostachys)
Ochagavia
BROMELIACEAE

Unlike most Bromeliads, the Chilean *Ochagavia* is firmly terrestrial in its habits. It shares a strong resemblance to the Pineapple plant (see Ananas), if only in the recurved, spiky leaves and dense head of flowers. But Pineapple blooms are purple, while those of *Ochagavia carnea* (syn *O. lindleyana*) are pink or gold, and they do not develop into the juicy syncarp (or multiple fruit) when fertilised.

Ochagavia enjoys a temperate climate, in a compost of acid, leafy loam with sand for good drainage. Propagate by division of suckers, and keep moist except when in bloom.

Nymphoides geminata. Star Fringe

containers or bags of good soil enriched with generous quantities of well-rotted manure are essential.

Hardy Water Lilies come in shades of white, gold, pink and red, and are planted in early spring. They bloom throughout the warm weather, both flowers and foliage floating on the surface.

The tropical types add blue and violet to the colour range – these can only be successfully flowered in relatively warm water. Their tubers must be lifted and stored over winter, out of the subtropics. Tropical Water Lilies bloom later in the season than their temperate cousins and hold their flowers high above the water on long stems.

Most Water Lilies, be they temperate or tropical natives, are delightfully fragrant, but none are suitable for pools with fountains or cascades, for the splashing water quickly spots and ruins the delicate flowers.

NYMPHOIDES

(nim-**foi**-deez)
(SYN Limnanthemum)
Floating Heart, Star Fringe
MENYANTHACEAE

Found in warmer areas of most continents, the dainty *Nymphoides* species are particularly useful in the cooler climate watergarden, for they are relatively frost resistant.

For once, their popular names are quite apt and descriptive. The leaves are heart-shaped and they do float; and the dazzling golden flowers are star-shaped, finely fringed and about 2.5cm/1in across.

N. geminata, a native of watercourses right down Australia's east coast, can be grown in pots of muddy compost sunk up to 50cm/20in below the water surface. It needs sun at least part of each day and flowers right through summer to early autumn.

Ochna serrulata. Carnival Bush

OCHNA

(ok-n∂)

Carnival Bush, Mickey Mouse Plant, Bird's Eye Plant

OCHNACEAE

No worries about propagating this one – any friend who has an *Ochna* bush will soon find seedlings everywhere, though that is only likely to happen in a warm climate. The common species is *O. serrulata*, an evergreen bush from southern Africa, but other species are quite similar. All can be grown from fresh seed or from cuttings of half-ripened wood taken in summer or autumn.

Ochnas will grow fast in full sun in almost any soil so long as it is well drained, but a slightly acid pH is preferred. It positively thrives in seaside salt air with regular water and will tolerate one or two degrees of frost. Bronzy new spring foliage is followed by yellow buttercup flowers which soon fall, leaving the persistent sepals to turn a bright scarlet. Within these appear shining black berries. Prune just before fruit fall to induce more compact growth and to prevent a carpet of unwanted seedlings which become deep-rooted and hard to pull out.

ODONTOGLOSSUM

(oh-**don**-t∂-**glos**-∂m)

Tiger Orchid, Lace Orchid

ORCHIDACEAE

In Europe, *Odontoglossums* are popular orchids for indoor culture. They flourish in low temperatures, short of actual freezing, because they are native to mountainous parts

Odontoglossum crispum hybrid. Lace Orchid

of the Andes. Romping along in pots of firbark, fibre or charcoal, they need year-round water except for a few weeks either side of flowering time, which varies according to species.

O. crispum usually flowers in spring or autumn but sprays can appear suddenly at any time. Flowers are large and waxy and each can be 10cm/4in across. They open one by one and blooming may extend over several weeks.

Odontoglossums need cool, moist, fairly shaded conditions.

ODONTONEMA

(oh-don-toh-**nee**-m∂)

(SYN Thyrsacanthus, Justicia)

Red Justicia

ACANTHACEAE

Although tropical in origin, *Odontonemas* will adapt to life in frost-free, temperate gardens, forming spreading masses in either sun or shade. True, where winter temperatures drop to near freezing, they tend to look somewhat tatty by winter's end, but hard pruning at the first hint of spring quickly encourages fresh new growth, revitalising the plant for its role in the summer garden.

O. strictum is the only one of 30 species you are likely to see. Its shiny, elliptical leaves are borne in opposite pairs all the way up tall, dark stems. The warm-weather flower display is spectacular, but useless for cutting, as the narrow tubular flowers open irregularly and drop all over the place.

Oenothera laciniata. Evening Primrose

Odontonemas enjoy moderately rich soil with good drainage, and can be grown from soft tip-cuttings struck at any time through the warmer months. A sheltered spot is essential as the brittle stems are easily damaged by winds.

OENOTHERA

(ee-**noth**-ur-∂)

Evening Primrose, Rose of Mexico, Rose of Heaven, Sundrop

ONAGRACEAE

This widely varied genus of about 120 species includes both annuals and perennials. Native to North America (but widely naturalised elsewhere), the genus includes the Mexican Evening Primrose (*O. laciniata*),

Odontonema strictum. Red Justicia

Oenothera speciosa 'Rosea'. Rose of Mexico

a 60cm/2ft annual with toothed green foliage and 5cm/2in faintly fragrant golden flowers borne in the upper leaf axils. These open in the evenings and turn reddish as they age. More commonly seen are varieties of day-blooming *O. speciosa* or Rose of Mexico, spectacular dwarf plants that pop up from running rhizomes with 8cm/3in pink flowers. Many of the loveliest species remain open during the day. These are sometimes referred to as Sundrops, and the showiest of them is 1m/3ft tall *O. fruticosa* subsp. *glauca*. It should be massed in open, well-drained soil and given plenty of water in the warmer months. Leaves of the basal rosettes are dull green, generally oval in shape and 20cm/8in long. As the red stems grow upward, the leaves become smaller and narrower. Golden, cup-shaped flowers 3cm/1in across open from scarlet buds.

All *Oenotheras* can be raised from seed sown direct during the warm weather.

OLEARIA
(ohl-ee-e∂r-ee-∂)
(SYN Eurybia)
Daisybush, Tree Aster, Mountain Holly
ASTERACEAE

Scarcely to be numbered among the more spectacular plants of the Australasian flora, *Olearias* or Daisybushes have won a northern hemisphere following out of all proportion to their beauty. True, they mostly hail from cooler parts of Australia and New Zealand and might be expected to be climatically

Olearia ilicifolia. Hakeke, Mountain Holly

Omphalodes cappadocica. Navelwort

suited to the UK and parts of the US, but even cold parts of those southern lands are positively mild by northern standards.

Olearias are evergreen and bloom profusely from spring till late in the season. They enjoy well-drained loam in full sun and are quite useful in seaside gardens. Of over 130 species, the majority have white daisy flowers, with a few in washed-out mauve. Some have no petals around the central disc at all. *Olearias* do better without cultivation around the roots but need annual pruning and regular dead-heading to prevent them from becoming woody and straggly.

OMPHALODES
(om-fa-**loh**-deez)
Navelwort, Blue-eyed Mary
BORAGINACEAE

The navel business (both in English and in botanists' Greek) comes from the shape of the seeds, which are of interest to gardeners only as a means of propagation. What we admire is the intense, pure blue of the flowers, like large Forget-me-nots, that precede them in spring.

There are about 30 species, whose homes range from the Mediterranean region to western China and Mexico. Most significant are Blue-eyed Mary, *Omphalodes verna*, a low-growing but creeping perennial from southern Europe with vivid blue flowers; *O. cappadocica*, rather like it but a shade taller and with slightly greyish leaves, from Turkey; and *O. luciliae*, a neat tufted perennial from Greece (for the rock garden) with paler blue flowers. It likes sun, the other two prefer light shade and a soil that doesn't dry out too much in summer. Cool temperate climates are preferred.

Oncidium Sultamyre. Dancing Dolls

ONCIDIUM

(on-**sid**-ee-ǝm)
Dancing Ladies, Dancing Dolls
ORCHIDACEAE

In subtropical areas, *Oncidiums* are quite often grown outdoors in hanging containers for their arching flower sprays (as long as 120cm/4ft). On a breezy day, the moving flowers explain the popular names Dancing Ladies and Dancing Dolls.

Away from the subtropics, they thrive on a glassed-in balcony or in a sunny room; some tolerate low but not freezing temperatures, while others need more heat. All need constant humidity.

Onixotis triquetra. Dipidax   TONY RODD

Plant in shallow baskets or pots placed high up where the flowers can spill forward. Grow them in any porous, perfectly drained combination of treefern fibre, osmunda, charcoal and sand. Water only occasionally, for the pseudobulbs store water and the roots rot easily. Most of the many species of *Oncidium* are similarly marked in brown or yellow (though there are a few pink and white types). They vary principally in the size and number of the flowers.

ONIXOTIS

(on-ik-**soh**-tǝs)
Dipidax, Water-flower
LILIACEAE

Onixotis triquetra may be better known to gardeners under its old name *Dipidax triquetrum* – not that it can really be said to be very well known to gardeners outside its native South Africa. Its tenderness has cost it popularity: in cool temperate climates it is strictly a greenhouse plant, and even in warm temperate ones it needs a sunny spot, lots of water in the winter growing season but much less in summer, and after the bulbs are planted it takes a while to settle down before producing its flowers. When they do appear, from early spring, they are very pretty in their combination of white with dark red centres, and the rush-like leaves are modestly decorative.

Ononis aragonensis. Restharrow

ONONIS

(on-**oh**-nis)
Restharrow
FABACEAE

A tough, untidy member of the pea family, Fabaceae, *Onois aragonensis* is found sporadically in poor soil from the Pyrenees through Spain to Algeria. It is a pretty enough shrub, with 3-lobed leaves and stems of typical yellow pea-flowers, faintly fragrant. Its main attraction is the fact that it is tough, survives in poor soil where not much else will grow, and needs water only in drought.

Grow from semi-hardwood cuttings struck in midsummer, or from spring-sown seed, which sprouts easily enough but is hard to transplant thanks to a long, brittle taproot. *Ononis* suits sunny banks or rock gardens of cool to cold climates. It grows to 60cm/2ft, and blooms in midsummer.

ONOPORDUM

(on-oh-**por**-dǝm)
Scotch Thistle, Cotton Thistle
ASTERACEAE

A scourge in many farmers' fields, *Onopordum acanthium* (Cotton Thistle) is raised in many perennial gardens as a cut flower. The leaves are viciously lobed and spined and are best kept well away from paths. But the spring and summer flower heads are another story: reminiscent of the larger Cynara (which see), they are typical thistle blooms – 5cm/2in across and tinted a charming mauve.

Onopordon branches heavily to a height of 2m/6ft and regular dead-heading will keep

Onopordum acanthium. Cotton Thistle

it blooming for months as well as reducing indiscriminate self-seeding. Deep, rich soil produces the largest plants, which are easily grown from seed sown directly in the flowering position.

ONOSMA

(on-**oz**-mə)
Onosma, Golden Drop
BORAGINACEAE

Said to be most attractive to donkeys, the genus *Onosma* is scattered about Europe and Asia Minor. They are stiffly hairy plants with bell-shaped flowers borne in the leaf axils. They enjoy rich, well-drained, sandy soil and make splendid plants for the rock garden, since few of them exceed 20cm/8in in height. Nearly all bloom in shades of yellow, though a few are white, pink and mauve.

Onosma echioides. Golden Drop

Ophiopogon jaburan 'Vittatus'. Snakebeard

European *O. echioides* is best propagated from softwood cuttings taken after flowers fade. Root them in sand and peat, then pot up until winter's passed. Plant out in spring for summer flowers but be patient, for seed is slow to germinate.

OPHIOPOGON

(off-ee-o-**poh**-gən)
Mondo Grass, Snakebeard
LILIACEAE

Popular with landscape gardeners, the tough *Ophiopogon* has great value as groundcover in hard or heavily shaded areas, although it does tend to become a harbour for snails and other pests.

Opuntia vulgaris. Smooth Prickly Pear

Two species are commonly grown, the illustrated *O. jaburan* and *O. japonicus*, Mondo Grass. Both form neat tufts of grass-like leaves that can be plain dark green or variegated but are always less than 30cm/12in tall. Both bloom in summer, *O. jaburan* producing loose, drooping sprays of snow-white flowers while *O. japonicus* has lilac blooms. Neither is particularly showy but both add colour to shaded areas.

OPUNTIA

(oh-**punt**-ee-ə)
Indian Fig, Prickly Pear
CACTACEAE

Said to have been introduced by an enthusiastic gardener charmed by their gorgeous flowers, several species of *Opuntia* once devastated vast tracts of Australian pastoral land. The scourge was finally controlled, but *O. stricta* (syn *O. inermis*) is still a declared noxious weed down-under.

There are about 300 other species, though, and most are brilliantly flowered plants of dramatic appearance. Their flattened stems or pads spring one from another, branching readily. The flowers (typically yellow but also pink or red) appear in spring, and are followed, on many species, by edible fruits. Best in pots against a sunny terrace wall, *Opuntias* survive near freezing temperatures.

Orbea variegata. Starfish Flower, Toad Cactus   *TONY RODD*

Ornithogalum thyrsoides. Chincherinchee

ORBEA
(**or**-bee-ə)
Carrion Flower, Starfish Flower, Toad Cactus
ASCLEPIADEACEAE

The name is a new one, for a genus formed by splitting off several species from the South African genus *Stapelia*. They include the best known, *S. variegata*, now to be known as *Orbea variegata*. This is a remarkable flower, a flat star up to about 7.5cm/3in across, in an extraordinary colour scheme of pale yellow all mottled and streaked with brown and purple. Unfortunately for the grower, it smells of rotting meat, the better to attract the flies that pollinate it, though, to be fair, the smell does not carry any distance. The plant itself looks a bit like a small, soft-bodied cactus, flowers in early summer, and is grown in exactly the same way as cacti are. The other species resemble it, the differences to the gardener being the size of the flowers and the precise shade of their beef steak-coloured flowers.

ORIGANUM
(or-**rig**-ə-nəm)
Oregano, Marjoram
LAMIACEAE

The various species of *Origanum*, small perennials, sometimes bushy, sometimes creeping, come from southern Europe. Their late spring flowers are modestly pretty, but they are best known for their use as culinary herbs.

Origanum 'Kent Beauty'. Ornamental
Oregano   *TONY RODD*

There are, however, several varieties whose foliage or flowers are more colourful than the norm, such as the golden-leafed form of the creeping *O. vulgare*, and the illustrated hybrid, *O.* 'Kent Beauty', a bushy plant about 20cm/8in tall, whose small pink flowers are accompanied by decorative pink and creamy-green bracts. Like all the genus, it likes a temperate climate, full sun, and sharp drainage.

ORNITHOGALUM
(or-nith-**og**-ə-ləm)
Chincherinchee, Star of Bethlehem, Nap-at-Noon, Summer Snowflake, Star of Africa, Chinks, Ink Flower
LILIACEAE

Not the most spectacular of spring flowering bulbs, *Ornithogalums* are popular in warm climates because of their extreme reliability. Plant them in autumn in a light, well-drained soil in full sun. They should be kept moist from the time growth begins until the leaves wither at the end of spring, but must be kept as dry as possible during summer dormancy, or they may rot.

The species *O. arabicum* or Star of Bethlehem is most often sold as a cut flower, the tall stems being capped by lightly fragrant white and gold flowers with centres like polished jade.

The quaint *O. thyrsoides* or Chincherinchee, has several useful peculiarities – the flowers last for many weeks, even out of water, and also absorb colour when the stems are rested in a pot of dye or ink. They are often sold in bunches dyed in an assortment of colours such as pink, blue and green.

O. umbellatum, called Nap-at-Noon or Summer Snowflake, is shorter-growing, and has become naturalised in the USA.

Golden-flowered *O. dubium* is known as Star of Africa.

Ornithogalum arabicum. Star of Bethlehem

Orthosiphon stamineus. Cat's Whisker

ORONTIUM

(o-**ron**-te-ǝm)
Golden Club
ARACEAE

Called after the fabled Syrian river Orontes, which pre-World War II travellers will remember also gave its name to a famous ocean liner, *Orontium* is a remarkable aquatic plant in the arum family. It grows underwater and rhizomes must be set at least 30cm/1ft below the surface in heavy pots of deep loam.

At its best in cold to cool-temperate climates, *Orontium aquaticum* revels in full sun. Come spring, 30cm floating blue-green leaves appear from the root mass, later joined by curious flower stems that look more than anything else like gold-tipped earthworms. These are actually elongated versions of the Arum Lily's spadix.

Orontium aquaticum. Golden Club

OROTHAMNUS

(or-roh-**tham**-nǝs
(SYN Mimetes)
Marsh Rose, Soldaat
PROTEACEAE

One of the rarest of the Proteaceae in cultivation, *Orothamnus* are seldom seen outside southern Africa. The 16 species have stem-clasping, leathery leaves, overlapping like fish scales. Those towards branch tips colour a rosy-pink in winter and early spring and part slightly to reveal a mass of red or pink-tipped stamens largely protected by a colourful bract.

Orothamnus zeyheri. Marsh Rose

O. zeyheri, the Marsh Rose, is covered with silvery hairs on all its parts.

Like other *Orothamnus*, it needs an acid soil, enriched with vegetable compost but not animal manure. Drainage should be fast but the soil must never dry out. Given these conditions the plant will grow into a rounded bush 1.2m/4ft tall. Hardy to –8ºC/17ºF.

ORTHOSIPHON

(or-thoh-**sai**-fǝn)
Cat's Whisker, Whisker Plant
LAMIACEAE

Unusual shrubs and perennials from Africa, Asia and Australia, the Cat's Whiskers are attenuated members of the mint family, growing to more than 1m/4ft and bearing spidery, whorled racemes of pale lilac-blue flowers.

These appear in summer, and are noted for their extremely long stamens. *Orthosiphon stamineus* is named in recognition of them. In nature it often occurs on alluvial soils prone to flooding. In cultivation it enjoys sandy, well-drained soil, and is easily grown from seed or cuttings – provided, of course, the climate's at least warm temperate.

OSBECKIA

(oz-**bek**-ee-ǝ)
(SYN Lasiandra, Melastoma)
Rough-leaf Osbeckia
MELASTOMATACEAE

These brilliantly coloured 1.5m/5ft shrubs look so much like Tibouchinas (which see), one wonders why they have been given

Osbeckia kewensis. Rough-leaf Osbeckia

Osmanthus delavayi. Devilweed

Osmanthus fragrans. Kwai-fa, Fragrant Olive

Osteospermum 'Whirlygig'. Whirlygig Daisy

another name. And then, checking in my library, I see *Osbeckias* come from Asia and Africa, whereas the lookalike Tibouchinas are from tropical America. Still, a difference in origin is not usually sufficient reason to give a plant a different name, so there has to be more than meets the eye to these eye-catching flowers.

They're easy to grow from soft-tip cuttings taken in spring and prefer a light soil that's friable, moist and enriched with organic matter. They're inclined to grow naturally sparse if you don't give them an all-over trim in late winter. Flowers are pink, purple or red and borne for months between spring and autumn.

OSMANTHUS
(oz-**man**-th∂s)
Fragrant Olive, Kwai-fa, Chinese Holly, Devilweed
OLEACEAE

To many people, the most delicious fragrance of all is the unforgettable perfume of *Osmanthus fragrans* – a blend of Jasmine, Gardenia and ripe apricots. A rather sparse shrub with glossy, toothed leaves that almost hide the minute flowers (which are used in China to make jasmine tea), it can be trained as a small tree, an espalier, even as a rough sort of hedge. I keep mine in a large pot in a sunny, sheltered spot outside the kitchen door, where its fragrance is a joy from autumn right through to spring.

O. delavayi is altogether smaller, usually under 2m/6ft. Its leaves are dark green, and while the small white flowers are fragrant, they're not in the same league as *O. fragrans.*

Propagate both from leafy tip-cuttings set over heat during autumn and winter. The growing plants will enjoy a moderately rich, well-drained soil with plenty of water in dry weather.

OSTEOMELES
(os-tee-oh-**meel**-eez)
Osteomeles
ROSACEAE

The three species of *Osteomeles* are found variously in east Asia, Hawaii and New Zealand. Best known is *Osteomeles schweriniae,* an elegant evergreen shrub from China. It grows about 2–3m/6–10ft tall and wide, with ferny leaves and sprays of 12mm/ ½in starry white flowers in summer. These are often set off by scarlet tints among the older leaves, and are followed by quite attractive small fruits, vaguely like those of their cousins the Cotoneasters, which start out green, turn red, and finally ripen blue-black. Warm-temperate climates and rich soil are preferred, and the shrub can be given a trim in winter to keep it bushy.

OSTEOSPERMUM
(oss-tee-oh-**spur**-m∂m)
(SYN Dimorphotheca)
Sailor-boy Daisy, Trailing Daisy, African Daisy, Freeway Daisy
ASTERACEAE

Shrubby evergreen perennials related to the annual Dimorphotheca (and often sold under that name), *Osteospermums* make a wonderful display in almost any position. They prefer a warm temperate climate like that of their native southern Africa, and will produce a carpet of colour for many weeks in winter and spring. However, most species can tolerate some frost and in colder climates they can be grown as summer and autumn blooming annuals.

Osteospermums are easy to grow from seed (sown *in situ* early spring, or indoors during winter if you can maintain a temperature of 16–21°C/60–70°F).

Osteomeles schweriniae. Bone Fruit

Osteospermum fruticosum. Trailing Daisy

Otacanthus caeruleus 'Amazon Blue'. Blue Ear-flower

Leaves should appear in less than 2 weeks. Named colour varieties should be propagated from cuttings or, in the case of *O. fruticosum*, from rooted sections of trailing stem. Plant out in a well-drained position in full sun. While all species are seen at their best in good, rich soil with regular water, they are really drought resistant and will continue to reward with a dazzling display of blue-centred daisy flowers through the driest season. Dead-heading will ensure repeat bloom, as will cutting back old,

spindly branches to thicker wood. Try them spilling over banks or walls, as a low ground-cover along driveways or by the pool.

O. fruticosum spreads at a great rate by trailing stems that root as they go, and will cover a square metre of space in a single year. The original species is white; colour varieties include mauve 'Nairobi Purple' and cerise 'Burgundy Mound'. It is a particularly valuable plant in coastal gardens, and looks sensational along southern California freeways.

Osteospermum 'Nairobi Purple'. African Daisy

O. barberae and *O. ecklonis* are more shrubby, mounded plants. The former has lilac-pink flowers with deeper-toned reverses, but they close on cloudy days. The latter's blooms are pure white, tinged blue on the reverse. All species can be pinched back to become bushy, and a sunny position gives the longest display.

OTACANTHUS
(oh-ta-**kan**-th∂s)
Ear-flower

SCROPHULARIACEAE

There are four species of these evergreen shrubs, all from Brazil, and one is now quite widely grown in tropical gardens. The attraction of *Otacanthus caeruleus* is the colour of the flowers – there aren't many blue flowers in the tropics, and few as rich and attractive as this one. The plant is a subshrub with weak, erect branches, rather like one of the New Guinea hybrid impatiens in style, though the leaves are plain green and bear small prickles on their edges. It is easily grown in a frost-free climate, liking fertile soil and shelter from the hottest sun and flowers for a very long period through summer and autumn. In frosty climates it makes an attractive conservatory plant.

OTHONNA
(oh-**thon**-n∂)
Little Pickles

ASTERACEAE

A gaily coloured southern African perennial for the warm-climate rockery, pots or hanging baskets, succulent *Othonna* grows well from cuttings in sand and needs perfect drainage at all times. *Othonna* trails rapidly, making it a good choice for growing along the tops of walls or in raised beds and, more than anything else, resembles clusters of juicy green jelly beans. The bright yellow

Othonna capensis. Little Pickles

Oxalis pes-caprae. Bermuda Buttercup

Oxyspora paniculata. Oxyspora

daisy flowers appear any time, but most heavily in winter. On wiry stems, they can be picked for posies, as they do not close up at night.

OXALIS

(oks-ə-lis)
Soursob, Bermuda Buttercup, Wood Sorrel, Mountain Soursob, Lucky Clover
OXALIDACEAE

Oxalis has something of an image problem to overcome, at least in the warmer parts of the garden world. There, the mere mention of its name seems to strike a raw nerve; while it is true some species are invasive, hated weeds, the genus is not all bad. Those pictured, for example, are among the most charming of perennials. And for 'once bitten' gardeners, these species are happy to prove

Oxalis adenophylla. Mountain Soursob

their worth in pots and make delightful flowering house plants for sunny windowsills.

O. adenophylla or Mountain Soursob forms neat little mounds of grey-green leaves just 10cm/4in high. Flowers appear over a long period and are each nearly 2.5cm/1in across. From the mountains of Chile, it prefers a cooler climate, needs extra well-drained, gravelly soil and full sun. It is an ideal rockery plant. *O. pes-caprae*, the Bermuda Buttercup, should definitely be kept in pots, where its brilliant, golden-yellow flowers can be enjoyed but its expansionist nature can be controlled. The flowers appear in winter and spring, and in California it is used as a sensational groundcover.

O. crassipes flowers sporadically throughout the year, making it an ideal house plant. Flowers are deep pink in the type, but white and pale-pink cultivars are sometimes available.

Ozothamnus obcordatus. Yellow Rice Flower
TONY RODD

OXYSPORA

(oks-ee-**spor**-ə)
Oxyspora
MELASTOMATACEAE

Most members of the Melastomataceae family are strongly marked with the family likeness – one expects to see quilted leaves and silky-petalled flowers with long, curving stamens, in some shade of pink or purple, and to learn that the plants are best grown in frost-free climates. *Oxyspora paniculata* is no exception, and it remains only to say that it comes from Bangladesh; that it is a shrub growing to about 1.5m/5ft tall; and that the flowers are shocking pink. They appear in autumn, in long, slightly drooping clusters. It makes a handsome pot plant, one for the well-warmed greenhouse in cold climates.

OZOTHAMNUS

(oh-zoh-**tham**-nəs)
Rice Flower, Wild Rice
ASTERACEAE

These bushy but soft-wooded shrubs from southeastern Australia, Tasmania and New Zealand have sometimes been included in *Helichrysum*, but botanists have now given them back their own genus. There are several species, all rather alike – they grow about waist-high and are densely bushy, with small leaves and clusters of tiny everlasting-daisy flowers, so abundant that they can almost obscure the foliage. Most, such as *O. ledifolius* and *O. diosmifolius*, have white flowers opening from red or pink buds, but *O. obcordatus* is golden yellow in both bud and flower.

They prefer mild-winter temperate climates; the hardiest is *O. ledifolius*, which succeeds in a sheltered spot in Britain. All love sharp drainage and sunshine.

Ozothamnus diosmifolius. Rice Flower
TONY RODD

PACHIRA
(pə-**kai**-rə)
**Guiana Chestnut, Shaving-brush Tree,
Dragon's-tooth Tree**
BOMBACACEAE

A genus of about 20 species of trees from tropical America, with handsome palmate leaves and large flowers whose chief attraction is their many long stamens. They are not commonly seen outside the tropics, being very sensitive to cold and generally too big for most greenhouses, but where they can be grown they are a magnificent ornament to the garden. Individual flowers open at sunset and are fading by dawn. They are extremely rich in nectar, and a tree in full bloom in early summer attracts honey-eating birds from far and wide. The trees range in size from large-shrub size to 20m/65ft, and in flower colour from white through yellow and pink to brilliant red.

Pachira aquatica. Shaving-brush Tree

Pachystachys lutea. Golden Candles

PACHYPODIUM
(pak-ee-**poh**-dee-əm)
Halfmens
APOCYNACEAE

'Like a cross between a cactus, a palm tree and a frangipani' would describe the *Pachypodium*. Most remarkable shrubs from the deserts and dry hillsides of southern Africa and Madagascar, for much of the year they are leafless, their swollen, bolt-upright branches adorned only with formidable spikes. But when the rains come, each branch crowns itself with a spray of bright green leaves and beautifully shapely flowers in pale pink, white or yellow. They dislike extreme cold, but in my mild climate I have grown *Pachypodium geayi* as a pot plant on my balcony for years, treating it as I would a cactus. I may wait for years more to see the flowers, however – on some plants they do not appear until it is at least 30 years old!

PACHYSTACHYS
(pak-ee-**stak**-əs)
(SYN Justicia)
Golden Candles
ACANTHACEAE

Peruvian *Pachystachys lutea* is obviously a close relative of the Prawn Plant (Justicia, which see). Striking in photographs, I have found it disappointing in performance, even though I give it the warm shade and humidity

it requires. However, I must admit that my garden, though rarely colder than 5ºC/41ºF, is a far cry from the plant's tropical homeland. My main objection is that the admittedly handsome golden bracts and white flowers last such a short time, after which the entire spike drops off completely. But in the right climate (or in heated greenhouses), *Pachystachys* produces many stems up to 1m/3ft tall, each topped with a spike of golden bracts.

Pachypodium geayi. Halfmens

Paeonia lactiflora 'Magic Orb'. Peony Rose

Paeonia lactiflora 'Bower of Roses'. Peony Rose

PAEONIA

(pee-**oh**-nee-ə)

Peony, Tree Peony, Moutan

PAEONIACEAE

Two thousand years ago the Chinese called these silken-flowered, perfumed beauties 'the king of flowers'. They are not hard to grow, given the deep, rich soil they need, but a cold winter is the real key to success, for they originate in hard-winter areas of Tibet, western China, Siberia and Mongolia. They grow to perfection in Britain, Canada and colder parts of the USA, and in mountainous areas of other countries. Peonies can be divided into two main classes: the shrubby or tree species and the herbaceous perennials.

The majority of plants in cultivation are cultivars of the Chinese perennial *Paeonia lactiflora*. They like well-drained soil, deeply dug and heavily enriched with well-rotted compost and manure, and resent disturbance

Paeonia lactiflora 'Postillion'. Peony Rose

once established. Planting takes place in the colder months (except where the soil is frozen), and the crown of the tuberous root mass must be set no more than 2.5cm/1in below the surface. Dress the area liberally with bonemeal, water well and mulch to protect the young shoots as they come through.

Peonies are most effective in mass plantings at 1m/3ft intervals and can be propagated from division of the root mass in autumn. You'll need a really sharp knife for this operation and must exercise great care if the brittle roots are to escape damage. Make sure each split section includes both roots

Paeonia humilis. European Peony

and dormant growth buds. Peonies can also be grown from seed, though named varieties will not come true, and it will be years before the first flowers are seen.

Many *P. lactiflora* cultivars have red stems and dark red or purplish foliage. All have beautifully divided compound leaves, sometimes with lobed leaflets. They must be watered deeply and often throughout the summer. Flowers should be dead-headed as they fade to prolong bloom and to conserve growing energy which would otherwise be channelled into seed production. Stems are cut back to the ground in autumn. All Peony cultivars are deliciously fragrant. Stems should be cut just as the blooms begin to

Paeonia lemoinei 'L'Espérance'. Golden Tree Peony

Paeonia tenuifolia. Lace-leaf Peony

Paeonia suffruticosa 'Chromatella'. Yellow Tree Peony

open and laid in a cool place for 24 hours. Then the stems should be lightly trimmed before being immersed up to their heads in water. Leave overnight before arranging.

Other herbaceous Peonies such as P. humilis and P. tenuifolia should be grown and treated in much the same way. They vary mostly in height and in the complexity of their foliage which, is often fine and fern-like or may have long, attenuated leaf divisions. Unlike the hybrids, they invariably have single blooms. Some taller species may need staking.

The so-called Tree Peonies are a handful of species of sparse, woody, deciduous shrubs that grow 2m/6ft tall. They are best planted among other shrubs, with protection from morning sun, which damages the dew-wet blossoms. Tree Peonies of most species bear the larger flowers (up to 22cm/9in across) but have fewer petals than the perennial types. They also have a wider range of colours – every shade from darkest red to white, with some in tones of purple, orange and yellow. The shown cultivars of P. suffruticosa and P. lemoinei are just a few examples. Tree Peonies are usually bought as grafted plants, but can be grown from 20cm/8in hardwood cuttings taken in autumn. They are slow-growing plants but long-lived. Little care is needed except to prune out any dead wood in spring.

Paeonia suffruticosa 'Suzakuman'. Moutan, Tree Peony

Paeonia suffruticosa subsp. rockii. Moutan, Tree Peony

Paeonia suffruticosa 'Jim Prentice'. Tree Peony

Pandorea jasminoides. Bower Vine

Pandorea pandorana 'Snow Bells'. Wonga-Wonga Vine

PANDOREA

(pan-**dor**-ee-ə)

(SYN Bignonia, Tecoma)

Bower Vine, Wonga-Wonga Vine

BIGNONIACEAE

Showy-flowered twining plants from the Malay Archipelago down into Australia, species of *Pandorea* are now popular in temperate areas of Africa and the United States.

The beautiful Bower Vine, *P. jasminoides*, is especially valued by gardeners; it is still often sold as *Bignonia jasminoides*, a name that is no longer valid. Preferring a deep, rich soil that is also well drained, it can be raised from cuttings or seed sown in spring. The shining leaves are compound, with 5–9 oval leaflets, and the 5cm/2in trumpet flowers are blush pink with a deeper throat and appear right through the warm weather.

The Wonga-Wonga Vine, *P. pandorana*, is less showy but far more vigorous, twining high into tall trees. The dark, glossy leaves are also compound, and may be reddish when young. The tubular flowers borne in dense panicles are creamish, streaked with purple. Recent cultivars are yellow 'Golden Showers', and pure white 'Snow Bells'. Neither species has any noticeable fragrance.

Papaver croceum. Iceland Poppy

Papaver orientale 'Picotee'. Oriental Poppy

PAPAVER

(**pap**-av–ə)

Iceland Poppy, Arctic Poppy, Oriental Poppy

PAPAVERACEAE

There can be few gardeners unfamiliar with the big, open, crepe-textured blooms of the Iceland Poppy, *Papaver croceum* (syn *P. nudicaule* of gardens) but there are another 50 species, many extremely showy.

Although well known in cooler, north-ern hemisphere gardens, these are rare and exotic in warmer climes.

The showiest of all must be *P. orientale*, the gigantic Oriental Poppy from Armenia, and its many hybrids. Those unfamiliar with them can only gaze in wonder at the sight of these enormous blooms shrugging away their hairy sepals and unfolding wrinkled, crepe-like petals, in the manner of a butterfly emerging from its chrysalis. The petals may take days to reach their full diameter of up to 30cm/12in, a silken cup brimming with the purple-black stamens that protect a many-sided seed capsule. The fragrance is acrid and somewhat disturbing, as well it may be, for these and other larger poppies (such as *P. somniferum*) are the source of opium and its derivatives.

Where winters are suitably cold, these magnificent blooms grow from a mass of fleshy roots planted out in autumn at 45cm/18in intervals. They spread thickly and should not be disturbed for several years. Coarse, hairy foliage will appear in late autumn but will not really push ahead until early spring, when it rises 60–120cm/2–4ft, depending on variety. In late spring the plump, furry flower buds appear singly at the ends of stems, opening to full display in early summer. If spent flowers are removed quickly, plants may produce a second, smaller flush of bloom in autumn. Otherwise, the foliage will yellow and die down almost immediately, not resuming growth until the following autumn.

Oriental Poppies are short-lived in warmer climates, but elsewhere may be propagated by division of the root mass in early spring. Named varieties will not come true from seed, but if you wish to experi-ment, sow in spring, right on the surface. Given plenty of light, germination should take about 2 weeks.

Papaver somniferum. Opium Poppy

In many parts of the world Iceland Poppies are the most popular bedding flowers for late winter and spring. Their long-stemmed blooms are produced in great profusion and make splendid arrangements. Some recent strains include bicoloured and picoteed flowers.

Another species worth growing as an annual was made famous by World War I. A symbol of remembrance ever since, the Corn Poppy, *P. rhoeas*, is the original poppy that 'blew in Flanders fields' – and for that matter, in fields all over Europe and much of the East. Its petals could be made of scarlet satin – with or without the brilliant black markings that reflect the blue of the sky. Its cultivars include the Shirley series.

All poppies like full sun, a rich soil and perfect drainage.

Papaver rhoeas. Field Poppy, Corn Poppy

Papaver somniferum 'Paeony Flowered'. Opium Poppy

PAPHIOPEDILUM
(paf-ee-oh-**pee**-də-ləm)
Slipper Orchid, Paph
ORCHIDACEAE

Popularly known as Slipper Orchid because of the curious pouch that is a feature of the flowers, *Paphiopedilums* are one of the easiest of Orchid genera to raise. In frost-free gardens many species can be grown outdoors in any bright spot sheltered from wind and strong sun. They seem unconcerned by temperatures as low as 3ºC/37ºF, despite the fact that most books refer to their need for temperatures above 10ºC/50ºC. However, there are some truly tropical types and these definitely would suffer if regularly exposed to low night temperatures.

Fairly small plants, *Paphiopedilums* enjoy being crowded in small pots in a moisture-retaining mix of sandy soil, ground bark and charcoal. They bloom mostly in winter or early spring but have no real resting period. Paphs (as they are often called) rarely need repotting, but should be kept in a humid, shady place in the summer months, and watered often. Strip off any old yellowed leaves periodically and check the plants for snails.

Paphiopedilum insigne. Slipper Orchid

Paphiopedilum sukhakulii. Slipper Orchid

Paphiopedilum hybrid. Slipper Orchid, Paph

P. insigne is the most common type. Its blooms are light green blotched with brown, or white and yellow in some varieties. *P. venustum* is a small tropical species with variegated blue-green leaves and maroon-tipped white flowers, striped green.

PARAHEBE
(par-ə-**hee**-bee)
Parahebe, Veronica
SCROPHULARIACEAE

When the botanists decided many years ago to divide the old genus *Veronica*, leaving the herbaceous perennials (mostly from the northern hemisphere) as Veronicas and giving the shrubby species, all from New Zealand the new genus *Hebe*, they included with the hebes a number of species that are really best described as bushy perennials. These have now been given their own genus, *Parahebe* – 'almost a *Hebe*' – whose 30 or so species are mostly from New Zealand and New Guinea (one in southeastern Australia). They are charming plants, mostly rather

Parahebe lyallii. Veronica

sprawling in habit, with blue, white or pink flowers in sprays rather than the compact spikes of their relations. *P. catarractae* is perhaps best known; but for display my pick of the genus is the illustrated *P. lyallii* from New Zealand, which spreads to form a dense groundcover, covered in early summer with small pink flowers. Moderately frost hardy, they grow best in a moist, sheltered spot in the rock garden and do not like too much soil disturbance.

PARKINSONIA
(pah-kin-**soh**-nee-ə)
Jerusalem Thorn, Mexican Palo Verde
CAESALPINIACEAE

This versatile shrub (or small tree) from tropical America has nothing whatsoever to do with the oft-quoted Parkinson's Law! In fact it is absolutely *against* the law to grow it in some subtropical areas, for it spreads like mad along watercourses, where its spiny stems become a nuisance to thirsty cattle. Plant it in a dry or desert garden, though, and you have a slender, well-mannered, lightweight tree that is almost impossible to dislike.

Parkinsonia aculeata. Jerusalem Thorn

Parkinsonia aculeata is deciduous, quickly dropping its minute leaves in dry spells, and in midwinter. But they soon appear again with rain, followed in spring (or at other times) by racemes of showy yellow blossom. You couldn't really call it a shade tree, for its foliage is so fine it barely casts a shadow. *Parkinsonia* tolerates alkaline soil.

PAROCHETUS
(pa-roh-**kee**-təs)
Blue Oxalis, Shamrock Pea, Blue Pea
FABACEAE

Here's a true botanist's fantasy – obviously one of the pea family when in bloom (though flowering in a most unlikely colour), you'd swear it was a clover or Oxalis at other times. *Parochetus* is from the Himalayas (home of so many unlikely plants) but is also found in Mozambique.

Use it in damp, leaf-rich soil of shaded rockeries, or as a groundcover between pink-flowering shrubs. *P. communis* is easy to raise from spring divisions, blooms most of the year in a cool temperate climate, and rarely passes 8cm/3in tall; but a single plant can easily cover a 60cm/2ft circle.

Parochetus communis. Blue Oxalis

Parodia formosa. Ball Cactus

PARODIA
(par-**roh**-dee-ə)
Parodia, Ball Cactus
CACTACEAE

Small and slow-growing, *Parodias* take up little space in the cactus collection and reward the grower with clusters of fairly long-lasting spring flowers in a range of warm colours. The spines of some species are decorative as well, and this adds to their value, year-round.

Grow *Parodias* in standard, gritty cactus mix, kept just moist in spring and summer but allowed to dry out for long periods between waterings in winter. Light shade is an advantage where summers are hot, with increasing sun as the weather becomes cooler. *Parodias* tolerate cold but not freezing conditions.

PASSIFLORA
(pas-i-**flor**-ə)
Passionflower, Granadilla, Lilikoi, Apricot Vine, Banana Passionfruit
PASSIFLORACEAE

Despite their torrid appearance, there is nothing salacious about the passion which named these tropic beauties! They were so named by Spanish Jesuit missionaries who discovered them in the jungles of South America and were amazed to observe in one blossom so many reminders of the Passion or suffering of Christ.

The 5 petals and 5 sepals were said to symbolise the 10 apostles who remained faithful to the end. The showy corona was said to represent either the crown of thorns or the halo, depending on the situation, and the 5 stamens represented the 5 wounds. The plants' climbing tendrils were said to represent the cords or scourges, and the handsome palmate leaves to remind us of the hands of Christ's tormentors. It was a foregone conclusion the plants would later be named *Passiflora*.

All Passionflowers are at least *sub*tropical in origin, and most bear their tart–sweet fruit only in favourably warm locations. In marginal climates they should be grown against a sheltered sunny wall in extra-rich but well-drained soil kept moist throughout the warm weather. Where central heating is a way of life, many species of Passionflower make spectacular indoor plants. They can be raised in a sunny, glassed-in sunroom, or in the background of a massed indoor planting. They'll grow in 25cm/10in pots of rich, loamy compost, and need light support to which their climbing tendrils can become attached. Water well in the warm weather, and fertilise when they really start to climb. The popular edible species *P. edulis* has weak roots and is commonly grafted onto stock of *P. edulis* f. *flavicarpa* or *P. caerulea*.

Most species grow rampantly in warm climates unless pruned back annually during the warmer months. Summer is the peak flowering period.

Patersonia glabrata. Leafy Purpleflag

Passiflora caerulea. Blue Passionflower

Passiflora mollissima. Banana Passionfruit

PATERSONIA
(pat-ur-**soh**-nee-ə)
Wild Iris, Native Iris
IRIDACEAE

The delicate mauve flowers of this Australian Iris last just a few hours, but *Patersonias* produce several 40cm/16in stems, each containing a number of blooms that open in succession. Flowering usually begins in late spring and continues into summer and, in the bush, all the plants in any one area have a curious ability to bloom simultaneously.

Patersonias spread from creeping rhizomes, sending up clumps of grassy leaves at intervals. They prefer an acid, sandy soil, well drained but moist, and need full sun to look their best. *P. glabrata* has purple flowers, *P. fragilis* very pale blue, while *P. sericea* has deep blue-violet blooms with woolly bracts.

Passiflora × *exoniensis.* Hybrid Passionflower

PAULOWNIA
(por-**loff**-nee-ə)
Princess Tree, Mountain Jacaranda
BIGNONIACEAE

Named for a princess, and a true princess among trees, China's noble *Paulownias* are sometimes mistaken for the American Catalpa – and not surprisingly, for they are closely related. The principal similarity is in the green, heart-shaped, fuzzy leaves, which may reach 30cm/12in in length and almost as much across. Both tree genera bear large trumpet-shaped flowers, but those of the *Paulownia* are carried in vertical spikes.

Paulownia tomentosa. Mountain Jacaranda

Pedilanthus tithymaloides. Red Bird

Another difference is in the seeds. Catalpa carries them in hanging pea-type pods; in *Paulownia* they are in pointed, oval capsules about 3cm/1in across.

Paulownias flower best in a cool climate and will happily survive a winter minimum of −12°C/10°F. In mild countries such as Australia, New Zealand and South Africa, they are most often seen in high country gardens, where they are sometimes known as Mountain Jacaranda because of the appearance of the flowers. Even in cold climates they do best where summers are also cool and moist.

P. tomentosa is the commonly seen species, reaching 13m/40ft in a good position and bearing 5cm/2in mauve flowers, spotted violet and very fragrant. The buds appear in late summer but don't open until the following spring.

Smaller *P. fortunei* blooms earlier, and rarely passes 7m/23ft. Its flowers are oyster-white marked with purple and yellow. Both species are usually propagated from seed.

Pelargonium hortorum 'Schöne Helena'. Zonal Geranium

PEDILANTHUS

(ped-ə-**lan**-thəs)
Ribbon Cactus, Zig-zag Plant, Red Bird, Jewbush, Slipper Flower
EUPHORBIACEAE

Ribbon Cactus, Devil's Backbone, Zig-zag Plant, Red Bird, Jewbush and Slipper Flower. Just look at the range of names collected by this very popular West Indian plant! *Pedilanthus tithymaloides* should be seen in any warm climate garden or collection of indoor or terrace plants. The waxen leaves are variegated and tinted pink; the stems (often striped) are formed in a perfect zig-zag; and the flowers consist of vivid scarlet bracts like tiny red slippers.

Grow it from summer cuttings, hardened thoroughly. Plant in a compost of normal loam and gritty sand over some good drainage material. Keep the temperature above 10°C/50°F – this is not a difficult task, for it likes the dry air of heated rooms.

PELARGONIUM

(pel-ah-**goh**-nee-əm)
Geranium, Pelargonium
GERANIACEAE

Is there a garden anywhere without at least one of these free-flowering perennials? Blazing away in pots, trailing from baskets, spilling over the ground, even climbing up panels of wire mesh – their garden uses are without number.

Pelargoniums (or Geraniums, as we call them, quite incorrectly) are so easy to grow that even the most purple-thumbed of gardeners is usually rewarded with success.

Pelargonium hortorum 'Minipel Orange'. Zonal Geranium

Water regularly in summer and treat them to a weak dose of liquid fertiliser in the growing season – that's all there is to it! And they're so easy to propagate! Just tidy up older plants in early spring and insert the cuttings firmly in pots of sand. Pinch out growing tips as the plants begin to move, allow a few weeks, then plant them out or pot them up.

Pelargoniums fall basically into two types: those grown for fancy, scented foliage and those grown for their flowers. The former are mostly original species, the latter all hybrids. Of these, the following three types are especially popular.

The bushy Zonal Geraniums (*P. hortorum* hybrids) have velvety round or kidney-shaped leaves, usually marked with a band or zone of contrasting colour.

The Ivy-leaf Geraniums (*P. peltatum* hybrids) have glossy, fragrant, waxy leaves of ivy shape and a distinct climbing or trailing habit.

Pelargonium peltatum 'L'Elégante'. Ivy-leaf Geranium

Pelargonium domesticum hybrid. Martha Washington Geranium

The Regal Pelargoniums (*P. domesticum* hybrids), sometimes called Martha Washington Geraniums, have a spreading, bushy habit, and sharply toothed hand-shaped leaves that are very fragrant when crushed. The flat heads of larger blooms are often beautifully marked in contrasting colours. These spectacular plants have a shorter flowering season – spring and summer only.

None of the *Pelargoniums* is frost hardy. In cold-winter climates they are usually kept under glass, or cuttings are taken and struck indoors where they remain until spring. Dead-head all types to prolong bloom.

Their principal pest is budworm, small caterpillars that drill holes in unopened flower buds. Spray with your nurseryman's recommended chemical. Rust is a common fungus disease of leaves. Pull away rust-marked foliage, and spray with a fungicide.

Pelargonium peltatum hybrid. Ivy-leaf Geranium

Peltophorum pterocarpum. Yellow Flamboyant, Flame Tree

PELTOPHORUM
(pel-**tof**-or-ǝm)
Yellow Flamboyant, Golden Flame Tree, Copperpod
CAESALPINIACEAE

The Yellow Flamboyant, *Peltophorum ptero-carpum*, is the best-known member of this small genus of tropical trees. Native to a large area of Southeast Asia, from Sri Lanka and the Philippines through Indonesia and into northern Australia, it is now cultivated all over the tropics. It is a stately tree, growing fairly rapidly to 12m/40ft or more in cultivation, with most attractive ferny leaves which sometimes fall during a severe dry season. In late spring or early summer it is a sight to behold as the great sprays of rust-coloured buds open to innumerable golden flowers and waft heady fragrance upon the air. The

Pennisetum 'Burgundy Giant'. Fountain Grass

season lasts for a good month, after which conspicuous dark brown seed pods develop. Alas, it is very sensitive to cold and thrives only in the tropics and subtropics.

PENNISETUM
(pen-ni-**see**-tǝm)
Fountain Grass
POACEAE

With the fashion for growing ornamental grass among the flowers, the Fountain Grasses have become very popular indeed. They are graceful plants, with long, feathery flower spikes and pleasing foliage.

The best known is *Pennisetum alopecuroides,* with its white or purplish flowers in early summer. It comes from parts of Asia and Australia and grows about 1m/3ft tall given the rich soil and regular summer watering it likes. And unlike many grasses, it stays put, neither creeping all over the place nor coming up everywhere from self-sown seed.

The African Fountain Grass, *P. setaceum* (syn *P. ruppellii*), has given rise to several varieties which feature red or bronze foliage, but it tends to self-seed in warm climates. Both will grow happily in any climate from the subtropical to the cool temperate.

Penstemon gloxinioides. Beard Tongue

Penstemon 'Alice Hindley'. Penstemon

PENSTEMON

(**pen**-stem-ǝn)

Beard Tongue, Mountain Pride, Penstemon

SCROPHULARIACEAE

The Border Penstemons, *Penstemon gloxin-ioides*, are hybrids of several perennial species from Texas and Mexico, but are often grown as annuals, especially where winters are cold. They are rather bushy plants, resembling related Antirrhinum. The flowers are open and bell-like and appear on tall spikes throughout summer and autumn, but they seem somewhat out of fashion these days. Even so, they still come in many shades of scarlet, dark red and pink with beautifully marked white throats, and make excellent cut flowers.

Other worthwhile species include *P. davidsonii* and *P. barbatus*, the Beard-lip Penstemon; both are frost hardy and look splendid in large rock gardens or hillside areas. They can be propagated from 8cm/3in cuttings of lateral shoots in late summer. Strike these in peat and sand mix, and plant out the following spring. Seed can be sown in winter at a temperature of 13°C/55°F.

Recent years have seen a glorious range of new cultivars, both tall (to 1.2m/4ft) and dwarf or mat-forming in habit.

Most *Penstemons* prefer a loose, gravelly soil with fast drainage and a position in full sun but sheltered from wind.

PENTAS

(**pen**-tǝs)

Egyptian Star Cluster

RUBIACEAE

A colourful genus of compact shrubs from tropical Africa, *Pentas* somewhat resemble Bouvardia and are easily grown from soft-tip cuttings. These may be taken any time from spring to early autumn and must be struck with heat and humidity. In spite of its tropical origin, *Pentas* will grow in any frost-free climate, but prefers a wet summer and a warm winter. Well-drained, sandy soil is best (ideally rich with leafmould), and regular pinching back will encourage a neat, bushy habit and many more clusters of flowers.

Pentas lanceolata. Egyptian Star Cluster

Be sure to dead-head regularly and shorten flowered stems slightly in early spring.

Pentas species are very much at home by the sea, in rock gardens or as a massed bedding plant. Well-grown specimens can be expected to bloom from spring to autumn. *P. lanceolata* blooms in rosy-mauve, pink, white or scarlet, and there are some interesting two-tone cultivars. All grow fast, reaching 60–100cm/2–3ft in a couple of seasons at most, and grow well in pots.

PEPEROMIA

(pep-ǝ-**roh**-mee-ǝ)

Peperomia, Radiator Plant, Yerba Linda

PIPERACEAE

In frost-free gardens, *Peperomias* can be used as a groundcover, but most of us know them as indoor plants used in terrariums, mixed planters or on warm, sunny windowsills. They are waxy plants with beautifully shaped and marked leaves, and this is a big attraction for year-round display, since the long-stemmed flower spikes are produced only in warm weather. These, although not particularly colourful, are, in their own way, quite charming, reminding one of attenuated Anthuriums or Arum Lilies. They do, in fact, consist of a myriad small flowers arranged along arching stems that are sometimes tinted red or brown.

Indoors, in cooler climates, grow *Peperomias* in a standard house plant mix, moist yet porous. Keep continually damp in the warm weather, and dry off in winter. Always water from below.

Peperomia caperata. Peperomia

They grow easily from stem cuttings and should be repotted annually. Many dozens of species are sold but you are most likely to see the following: *P. caperata* 'Emerald Ripples' with pinkish stems, rippled heart-shaped leaves and twisted stems of greenish flowers; *P. maculosa* (Radiator Plant) with long, oval leaves and 30cm/12in maroon flower spikes; *P. marmorata*, with silvery blue-green leaves and 10cm/4in green flower spikes.

Pereskia aculeata. Barbados Gooseberry

PERESKIA

(pə-**res**-kee-ə)
**Lemon Vine, Barbados Gooseberry,
Leaf Cactus**
CACTACEAE

Unusual for cactuses, *Pereskias* produce leaves, though these are deciduous should the winter temperature drop much below 7ºC/44ºF. They are grown in well-drained soil enriched with rotted organic matter. In pots, charcoal chips help sweeten the soil – and improve drainage, too. *Pereskias* have woody, spiny stems, are easily grown from cuttings, and on fences they are excellent plants for discouraging intruders.

Give them plenty of water in summer, sufficient in winter only to stop the leaves from wilting and, of course, full sun. *P. aculeata*, the Lemon Vine or Barbados Gooseberry, is most commonly seen. Its leaves are a rich golden yellow with cerise reverses, and the open cactus flowers in pink, pale green or yellow appear during summer.

PERICALLIS

(pe-ri-**kal**-ləs)
Florist's Cineraria
ASTERACEAE

Under this unfamiliar name we must now seek the familiar Florists' Cineraria, until recently known to science as *Senecio*

cruentus, but now as *Pericallis hybrida*. A short-lived perennial (always grown as an annual), it originates from the Canary Islands, and was originally magenta-red but has been developed by hybridists into wonderful colours from white through pink to crimson and the richest shades of blue, as well as spectacular bicolours.

The modern hybrids grow about 30cm/12in tall and at least as wide, with the daisy-flowers ranging in size from about 3–5cm/1–2in wide. They crown the plant in great branching heads in spring, completely obscuring the foliage, and whether they are grown as pot plants in the greenhouse in cold climates, displayed on the coffee table or massed out of doors in frost-free temperate areas, they present a most magnificent sight. Either way, they love the richest soil and dappled shade.

PERISTROPHE

(pe-**ris**-troh-fee, per-is-**troh**-fee)
Violet Mint
ACANTHACEAE

Vividly flowered perennials that brighten frost-free gardens or heated greenhouses in colder climates, *Peristrophes* enjoy similar conditions to related *Justicia* – that is, rich, moist, loamy soil and a position sheltered from wind and at least partly shaded. The plants have fairly weak stems and assume a floppy habit unless staked or supported with a criss-crossing of twigs (these are hidden as the plants grow). Flowers appear in winter in clusters of 2 or 3 and quite resemble Honeysuckle, but in shades of pink to purple.

Pericallis hybrida. Florist's Cineraria

PERSICARIA

(pur-si-**ke**ər-ee-ə)
(SYN Polygonum)
Snakeweed, Prince's Feather, Knotweed
POLYGONACEAE

The Snakeweeds are a group of spreading perennials, formerly included in the large, diverse genus Polygonum, the Knotweeds, and are still often found in nurseries under that name. The best known is *Persicaria bistorta*, a splendid not-too-rampant groundcover for a sunny spot in temperate climates. (It is native to Europe and western Asia.) It hugs the ground with pleasant oval leaves and raises short spikes of white or pink flowers all summer. The rose-pink cultivar 'Superba' is taller-growing.

P. capitata is a sprawling, creeping perennial from northern India, a great standby in milder climates – it seems to grow anywhere, in the poorest soil, so long as its spot isn't too shady, though it is too invasive for a choice flower bed. The leaves are marked with purple, the little globes of flowers mauve-pink.

Peristrophe speciosa. Violet Mint

Persicaria orientalis. Prince's Feather

Petrophile linearis. Conesticks   *TONY RODD*

PETROPHILE

(pet-**roff**-il-ee)

(SYN Petrophila)

Drumsticks, Conesticks

PROTEACEAE

Yet another interesting genus of the Protea family, this time almost exclusively from Western Australia, the *Petrophiles* huddle in dry, perfectly drained, rocky places and make up in texture what they lack in colour. Illustrated *P. linearis* both looks and feels like a mass of pink pipe cleaners. The leaves are thick, sickle-shaped and about 5cm/2in long. The stems are woody, and the spring flower clusters are followed by interesting fruits that have the texture of pine cones.

Petrophiles are mostly grown from seed, which germinates in about 2 months. They grow best in continually warm, sandy soil and do not care for humidity. Prune by picking flowers.

Persicaria capitata. Knotweed

Petrorhagia velutina. Tunic Flower

PETRORHAGIA

(pet-roh-**rah**-gee-ə)

Coat Flower, Tunic Flower

CARYOPHYLLACEAE

A small genus within the Carnation family, the 20 species of *Petrorhagia* are found naturally from the Canary Islands through the Mediterranean and eastward to Kashmir. They are all annual or perennial plants, thriving in alkaline soil on the dry or sandy side.

Annual species are propagated from seed, sown direct; the perennials by autumn division. Illustrated *P. velutina* is annual, rarely passing 30cm/12in in height, and occasionally grown as a posy flower. The fine-petalled pink blooms are less than 1cm/¼in wide, almost hidden in large bracts. It is grown in South Africa, parts of America and Australia. *P. illyrica* is a little taller, and blooms in yellow; *P. saxifraga* (syn *Tunica saxifraga*) blooms in pink. Plant in full sun.

PERSOONIA

(per-**soon**-ee-ə)

Geebung

PROTEACEAE

Even in their native Australia, the Geebungs are not commonly seen in gardens, though they are graceful shrubs with pleasant leaves and clusters of small yellow flowers followed by small yellowish or greenish berries, which are edible (if sharp-tasting). To my mind the most attractive is *Persoonia pinifolia*, with soft pine-like leaves – a pleasant change from the prickly leaves of

Persoonia pinifolia. Pine-leaf Geebung

so many Australian plants – and abundant flowers in summer and autumn. It comes from New South Wales, grows about 3m/10ft high and wide, and is happiest in a warm temperate climate, well-drained soil and dappled shade. Unfortunately Geebungs are not at all easy to propagate, either from seed or cuttings, so plants are seldom offered for sale.

PETREA

(pet-**ree**-ə)

Purple Wreath, Sandpaper Vine, Queen's Wreath, Bluebird Vine

VERBENACEAE

Undoubtedly one of the world's showiest climbers, *Petrea volubilis* is really only at its best in subtropical or tropical areas. Still, if you have a sun-drenched wall sheltered from cold winds, and can't remember a frost, it is worth trying.

Enrich the planting site with organic matter, provide a trellis and water regularly. The rough-leaved, twining stems will soon take off and in summer they're completely hidden by drooping racemes of purple flowers. These fall quickly, but the lavender calyces persist for weeks.

Petrea volubilis. Purple Wreath

Petunia hybrida 'Apple Blossom'. Petunia

Petunia hybrida 'Burgundy'. Petunia

Petunia hybrida 'Shades of Blue'. Petunia

Petunia hybrida 'Blue Frenzy'. Petunia

PETUNIA
(pə-**tyoo**-nee-ə)
Petunia, Sunweed
SOLANACEAE

Visiting your average suburban nursery, it might seem that today's entire range of annual flowers consists of *Petunias*. But as public taste dictates commercial production, there must be enormous demand for these cheerful blooms. They're available in an ever-increasing range of size and colour – albeit at some sacrifice of the fragrance we remember from *Petunias* on a summer's afternoon!

The Grandiflora strains have blooms up to 17cm/7in across; Multifloras have more, but smaller, flowers (5cm/2in across); the Pendulas, such as the 'Cascade' strains, are trailing types useful for hanging baskets; the Nana Compactas have small but prolific blooms on more compact plants.

Colours range from red, pink, blue-violet, purple, white and creamy yellow to bi-colours with darker veining, central 'stars' or picotee edges.

The hotter the summer, the better *Petunias* produce; and the earlier you plant, the better display you'll have.

Sow seed under glass in early spring or even late winter. Do not cover, but maintain a temperature of 21ºC/70ºF. Seeds will sprout within two weeks. Alternatively, you'll find a wide choice of seedlings at your local nursery.

Petunia hybrida 'Bobby Dazzler'. Petunia

Set the plants out in full sun in light, well-drained, sandy soil with plenty of compost and a touch of lime. Water regularly, but do not feed too heavily or the plants will bolt to leaf at the expense of flowers. When you do feed, use a fertiliser rich in phosphate, low in nitrogen. Watch out for snails and use snailbait regularly. Pinch the tips back to encourage bushiness, and deadhead regularly. When the *Petunias* have become straggly and exhausted, cut them back, fertilise and they'll be on their way to a second flowering. You can keep this up well into autumn!

PHACELIA
(fə-**see**-lee-ə)
California Bluebell, Scorpion Weed
HYDROPHYLLACEAE

The California Bluebell (*Phacelia campanularia*) is not a suitable annual for humid coastal areas, for it grows wild in California's Mojave Desert and is used to dry, hot days with a sharp temperature drop in the evening.

A delightful plant for rock garden or low edgings, *Phacelia* grows to around 23cm/9in. It does not transplant, so seed should be sown *in situ* in early spring. Just broadcast in

Phacelia campanularia. California Bluebell

Phaius tankervilleae. Nun's Hood Orchid

Phalaenopsis amabilis. Moth Orchid

Phebalium whitei. Goldmyrtle

sandy soil, rake lightly to cover and water sparingly. Germination is swift, as is growth, and flowering should begin in just 6–7 weeks. Thin seedlings to about 15cm/6in. Do not cultivate or fertilise, and water with a light hand. Blooming should continue right through the summer months. Not for cutting.

PHAIUS
(**fae**-y∂s)
Nun's Hood Orchid
ORCHIDACEAE

Phaius is a giant among terrestrial orchids, found in tropical Africa, Australia and Southeast Asia. *P. tankervilleae* is the typical species seen. It can be raised happily in a bush-house with minimum winter tempera-ture of 15ºC/60ºF and prefers a compost of rough, fibrous soil well mixed with sphag-num moss, charcoal and crushed tile. The container must be well-drained, and semi-shade is preferred year round.

The showy flowers appear in spring on stems that can be at least 1m/3ft high and each bloom is often 12cm/5in across, in shades of white, brown to dark red, and purple. Repot as soon as new growth begins but before flowering.

Phaseolus coccineus. Scarlet Runner Bean

PHALAENOPSIS
(fal-ae-**nop**-s∂s)
Moth Orchid
ORCHIDACEAE

Phalaenopsis blooms, generally white or delicate pink, hang from long, arching stems. They're not so difficult to grow if you can arrange a constant winter temperature of around 15ºC/59ºF, though well-established plants will tolerate 10ºC/50ºF at night provided both soil and air moisture are low. Good ventilation is important but draughts must be avoided.

Grow *Phalaenopsis* in a coarse compost with plenty of treefern chunks into which the plants can run their worm-like roots, and give plenty of water and maximum humidity through the warm weather.

P. amabilis, from Southeast Asia and Queensland, is rather sparse in growth, with only two or three large leathery leaves. The absence of food-storing pseudobulbs means they need weak doses of liquid fertiliser every 2 weeks. Semi-shade suits them in summer, bright light in winter. Flowering can occur any time except midsummer.

PHASEOLUS
(faz-ee-**oh**-l∂s)
Scarlet Runner Bean
FABACEAE

If speed of growth is any indication, *Phaseolus coccineus* must be the bean that Jack planted! Best suited to cool-temperate areas, this super-fast-growing annual creeper can be germinated indoors in late winter and planted out, after frosts have gone, into rich, well-drained soil. Watered and fed regularly, it will quickly cover a fair-sized trellis, decking itself from late spring and well into summer with clusters of decorative bright-red flowers. These are followed by good quality beans, which should be picked and eaten when young, small and tender.

PHEBALIUM
(fee-**bae**-lee-∂m)
Goldmyrtle
RUTACEAE

A showy relative of the Citrus and Correa, *Phebalium whitei* is native to well-drained, sandy areas of the Queensland bush. It may be raised from seed sown in late spring or struck from soft-tip cuttings set out later with humidity. Slow to reach maturity (at only 50cm/20in high), these dainty shrubs burst into a mass of 5-petalled golden spring flowers in warm to subtropical climates. They look best in dappled shade, and benefit from mulch to keep the roots cool and a light shaping after bloom to keep them compact. *Phebalium* is hardy down to −2ºC/28ºF.

PHILADELPHUS
(fil-∂-**del**-f∂s)
Mock Orange, Syringa
SAXIFRAGACEAE

The overpowering orange-blossom fragrance of *Philadelphus* should be reason enough for its presence in any summer garden plan. But when you add masses of gold-centred, snowy flowers on tall, arching canes, the effect is irresistible. They are easy shrubs to grow, and

Philadelphus coronarius. Mock Orange

Philadelphus 'Buckley's Quill'. Double Mock Orange

Philodendron bipinnatifidum. Tree
Philodendron

PHILODENDRON
(fil-oh-**den**-drən)
Philodendron

ARACEAE

Favourite house plants all over the world,
Philodendrons are increasingly popular in
frost-free gardens too. While they are chiefly
grown for their glossy, often weirdly shaped
leaves, Philodendrons *do* flower. The blooms
are more curious than showy, being simply a
fleshy, creamy-white, boat-shaped spathe
around a central spadix on which open the
countless tiny, true flowers. Blooms are rarely
seen indoors but are reliably produced on
mature plants grown in warm-climate
gardens, especially illustrated *P. bipinnatifidum* (syn *P. selloum*).

All *Philodendrons* like a rich but light,
open and well-drained soil. Keep them moist
when night temperatures are always above
13ºC/55ºF but a little on the dry side during
colder weather. Outdoors, grow them in full
or dappled shade and increase from cuttings
rooted in summer in sandy, moist soil.

Philadelphus mexicanus. Mexican Mock
Orange

Philadelphus microphyllus. Small-leaf Mock
Orange

will flourish in almost any soil – even turning on a good display where the pH is alkaline. Depending on the height of individual
species, they can be used in open borders, as
wall shrubs, or along pathways, where the
tall, arching canes will bring heads of bloom
close to the passer-by.

Individual plants should be thinned out
after bloom, cutting away the oldest wood
altogether. New plants strike from 7.5cm/3in
soft-tip cuttings or 15cm/6in pieces of semi-
hardwood in summer and autumn. They
must be kept warm and humid until new
roots are established.

Most species are deciduous, though
P. mexicanus (for one) stays evergreen in

warmer climates. Leaves vary from
5–9cm/2–3½in long according to variety,
except in more compact *P. microphyllus*,
where they rarely pass 2cm/1in. Flowers
appear terminally, sometimes singly, sometimes in large clusters. They are snowy-
white, and 4-petalled except in the cultivar
'Virginal', which generally presents a
number of double blooms. Species
P. coulteri, sometimes called the Rose
Syringa, has petals stained with purple-red.
This effect is more commonly seen in its
hybrid, 'Belle Etoile'.

Flowering well after most other spring
shrubs have finished, most species are
drought and frost hardy.

PHLOMIS
(**floh**-məs)
Jerusalem Sage

LAMIACEAE

These shrubby, old-fashioned perennials
deserve greater popularity, for they do
particularly well under adverse conditions,
including poor soil, salt-laden coastal winds
and prolonged drought. Though not spectacular, they are nevertheless pleasing plants,
with circular whorls of bright yellow flowers
appearing at intervals along tall stems. They
can be cut, and make a useful addition to

Phlomis fruticosa. Jerusalem Sage

Phlox drummondii. Annual Phlox

Phlox paniculata. Perennial Phlox

mixed arrangements. The leaves are generally wrinkled and dull grey-green in colour. *Phlomis* have few needs, but staking keeps them tidy in windy places. Pruning back by about half in autumn results in a neater plant.

PHLOX
(floks)

Phlox, Pride of Texas, Perennial Phlox, Wild Sweet William

POLEMONIACEAE

Popular *Phlox* seem to have acquired few common names, which is odd since they come from Texas, where folks are rarely at a loss for words!

Annual *P. drummondii* is the most widely grown species, yet many gardeners seem to have trouble with them – probably due to over watering. They come from dry country, and like a light, sandy soil with good drainage, enriched with compost and fertiliser. Grow them anywhere with sun at least part of the day. Both seed and seedlings are widely available, with choice of dwarf bedding strains or taller-growing types. 'Sternenzauber' has star-shaped blooms in a good colour range. Water around plants, not on them.

Where winters are frosty, *P. paniculata* are widely grown perennials. In a rich soil that is both moisture-retentive and fast-draining, they spread rapidly into large clumps. Dress with a mulch of well-rotted manure in early spring and thin out the weaker-growing stems. Older clumps are divided in autumn and the woody inner sections discarded before replanting. Alternatively, cut back in autumn and sever plantlets for planting.

Phlox drummondii 'Sternenzauber'. Annual Phlox

Phlox subulata. Moss Phlox

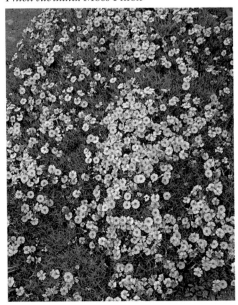

Phlox maculata 'Miss Lingard'. Meadow Phlox

Phormium tenax. New Zealand Flax

PHORMIUM
(**for**-mee-ðm)
New Zealand Flax, Flax Lily
LILIACEAE

Useful accents for the modern garden, the two species of New Zealand Flax are virtually indestructible plants, thriving in wet or dry, hot or cold conditions, even exposed to salt spray. Both evergreen, they form a fan-shaped clump of tough leaves – *Phormium tenax* grows up to 3m/10ft tall and as wide, while the smaller *P. colensoi* rarely exceeds 2m/6ft. Leaf colours vary from green to bronze or red-purple, and can be either plain or variegated.

The flower spikes appear in summer and branch heavily towards the top into panicles of dull red or sometimes yellow bloom. These are pleasant enough, but the plant is really grown for the dramatic effect of the stiff, vertical leaves. Hardy to at least –5ºC/23ºF.

PHOTINIA
(foh-**tin**-ee-ð)
Japanese Photinia, Chinese Hawthorn
ROSACEAE

A popular hedging plant, especially in cooler areas, the Japanese Photinia (*Photinia glabra*) is most often seen in its cultivar, 'Rubens', which has brilliant red new foliage; cultivars of *P. fraseri* include 'Robusta', which has larger leaves of a somewhat bronzier red, and 'Red Robin', again with bright red new leaves. In all types, the colourful spring foliage is followed by large flat panicles of tiny, acrid-smelling white flowers. These are followed by

Photinia glabra. Japanese Photinia

blue-black berries; and finally, in frosty areas, brilliant autumn colouring, for *Photinia* is semi-deciduous, losing a proportion of leaves each year.

Foliage is shiny and toothed and the plants may be increased from seed or semi-hardwood tip-cuttings taken with a heel during the colder months. *Photinias* are customarily pruned regularly to keep them dense and covered with bright red new growth. Hardy down to –10ºC/14ºF.

Phragmipedium schroederae. Long-tailed Slipper Orchid

PHRAGMIPEDIUM
(frag-mð-**pee**-dee-ðm)
Long-tailed Slipper Orchid
ORCHIDACEAE

This a small genus of orchids which resemble the Slipper Orchids, Paphiopedilum (which see), but the 2 main petals are twisted and elongated, to a length of up to 30cm/12in, and flowers may be borne two or three to a stem instead of singly.

Phragmipediums enjoy a winter minimum temperature of 10ºC/50ºF, though they'll tolerate anything above freezing, and prefer constant humidity. But with all that, I have found them easy to grow around the house and most eye-catching, with their striped brickish-pink flowers a great contrast to the green foliage of other plants.

Grow in a moist, peaty mixture with plenty of charcoal and sand. Mist often in warm weather and place in bright light but never direct sun.

PHUOPSIS
(foo-**op**-sðs)
(SYN Crucianella)
Crosswort
RUBIACEAE

Phuopsis stylosa (the only member of its genus) is a mat-forming perennial herb from the Mediterranean area. Valued for its generous summer and autumn bloom in the rockery, it produces globose heads of tiny flowers much in the style of Sweet Alice (see Lobularia). These are musk pink in colour and sometimes exude a rather musky smell in hot weather. They like a poor, sandy soil, full sun or part shade, and are propagated from autumn divisions. Leaves are arranged in a cross-like pattern.

Phuopsis stylosa. Crosswort

PHYGELIUS
(fai-**jee**-lee-ðs)
Cape Fuchsia, Cape Figwort
SCROPHULARIACEAE

Not related to the Fuchsia in spite of its most popular name, versatile South African *Phygelius* is grown both as a herbaceous perennial and as a shrub – the latter in warmer climates.

Plant out in spring (preferably in a sunny position) in light, well-drained soil. Space at

Phygelius aequalis. Cape Fuchsia

60cm/2ft to allow room for rapid, weedy growth. When well fed and watered, the sparsely branched flowering stems will begin to rise in late spring and bloom throughout summer and autumn.

Phygelius grows fast to around 1.2m/4ft, but needs no staking in sheltered positions. Seed may be sown in spring, germinating in a few days, but the plants are most easily multiplied from divisions taken in the same season.

PHYLA
(**fai**-lə)
(SYN Lippia)
Carpet Grass, Mat Grass, Capeweed, Turkey Tangle, Daisy Grass, Frogfruit
VERBENACEAE

Somewhat resembling a prostrate Lantana, this dainty groundcover is popular in many lands. Grown so widely and for such a long time, nobody is quite sure where it originated, but it is seen all around the subtropical world and even recognised as frost hardy, though it becomes very unattractive in winter.

Best in loose, sandy soil, it appreciates moisture in the growing season. It should be sprinkled lightly with fertiliser in early spring to help rejuvenate growth. *Phyla nodiflora* spreads rapidly, blooms from spring to autumn, and takes mowing and regular foot traffic. Step carefully, though, if you'd avoid bee stings. Our honey-making friends adore it!

Phylica plumosa. Flannel Bush

PHYLICA
(**fai**-lik-ə)
Flannel Bush, Featherhead
RHAMNACEAE

Not a member of the Protea family (though from its appearance you might think so), the dainty Featherhead (*Phylica plumosa*) is in fact related to Ceanothus and Pomaderris. It is a small, erect shrub, rarely passing 1.2m/4ft in height and, as in many of the South African flora, it is not the flowers that catch the eye but the colourful bracts surrounding them. The true flowers are inside these in a composite mass, and individually are about the size of a pin's head.

Flowering, which can begin in late autumn, continues right through the cold months and although the tiny flowers don't last, the bracts are extremely long-lived. *Phylicas* are evergreen, have downy new

Phyla nodiflora. Daisy Grass

Phymosia umbellata. Desert Mallow

growth, narrow heath-like leaves and thrive close to the sea. They must have fairly high humidity and well-drained, acid soil. They can be propagated from seed or from autumn cuttings of half-ripened shoots.

Phylicas cut well, and if enough are picked, no further pruning is needed. Not particularly hardy, they may withstand the odd light frost.

PHYMOSIA
(fai-**moh**-see-ə)
Desert Mallow
MALVACEAE

A small genus of the mallow family, Malvaceae, from Mexico and the Caribbean, the eight species of *Phymosia* grow very decoratively in light, well-drained soil and a warm temperate climate. Often seen in California, *P. umbellata* rather resembles a hibiscus bush, both in and out of flower.

The dark leaves are shallowly palmate with 3, 5 or 7 lobes. Blooms appear in small clusters, the deep rose-red flowers emerging from mealy green calyces. Grow this evergreen shrub from cuttings taken in summer and rooted in a warm, humid place.

Physoplexis comosa. Devil's Claw

Physocarpus monogynus. Mountain Ninebark

PHYSOCARPUS
(**fai**-soh-kah-p∂s)
Ninebark
ROSACEAE

This mildly fragrant member of the rose family is rarely seen away from its native Rocky Mountains, but is easy to grow in a sheltered position in average soil with good drainage. Raise it from seed, or strike 10–15cm/ 4–6in hardwood cuttings in winter. These can be taken when the shrub is tidied up by removing about a third of the arching canes. This is preferable to shortening the branches, which interferes with the graceful habit.

Physocarpus monogynus is deciduous, with foliage turning a good colour in autumn. It blooms in spring, doing better in full sun. The 3–5 lobed leaves resemble those of a currant; the flower heads remind one of Spiraea. Water well in drought.

PHYSOPLEXIS
(fai-soh-**pleck**-sis)
(SYN Phyteuma)
Devil's Claw, Horned Rampion
CAMPANULACEAE

How could one possibly guess that this devil-ishly handsome alpine plant belonged to the Campanula family? When it is not in bloom, perhaps the foliage might suggest it – but the umbellate flower clusters are like a mass of purple and pink claws! *Physoplexis comosa* is in fact known as Devil's Claw in many areas.

It is a dwarf-growing (15cm/6in) plant from the European Alps that likes deep, alka-line soil with perfect drainage. It is usually propagated from spring divisions and grown in rock gardens. Wherever you put it, though, slugs will be sure to get there quickly – so be generous with the snailbait!

Physostegia virginiana. Obedient Plant

PHYSOSTEGIA
(fai-soh-**stee**-j∂)
(SYN Dracocephalum)
Obedient Plant, Gallipoli Heath, False Dragonhead
LABIATEAE

Physostegia's giant heath flowers bloom vividly in late summer and autumn. They are good for cutting, but more showy left in the open garden where self-seeding will help them spread rapidly into a dense mass.

Plant in late autumn in any acid soil, with either full or half sun. The latter seems to produce brighter flower colours. Keep constantly moist in the growing season, and push them along with a generous sprinkling of pulverised cow manure in spring. Well-grown plants can reach above 1m/3ft, but a somewhat lower stature is more usual.

Physostegias are propagated from divisions or 8cm/3in cuttings of young growth struck in sharp sand. Seed is easy, too; it should be sown outdoors any time in spring and summer. Cut the plants back hard after bloom in late autumn. The popular name Obedient Plant is apt, for flower stems can be bent any which way and will stay where they're put.

PIERIS
(**peer**-∂s)
Pearl Flower, Lily of the Valley Shrub
ERICACEAE

A relatively small genus of Azalea relatives from the colder parts of Asia and North America, *Pieris* are hardy down to –6ºC/23ºF. They prefer a mildly acid soil

that is both well-drained and rich with leaf-mould, but are fairly slow-growing. A humid atmosphere keeps the evergreen foliage fresh and colourful.

In the case of *P. formosa* var. *forrestii* (syn *P. forrestii*), the leaves change from scarlet in early spring, through cream, to a deep lustrous green in midsummer. Along the way they are joined by panicles of faintly fragrant cream flowers like Lilies of the Valley, which hang from the tips of every stem for many weeks in spring. This shrub grows to 4m/13ft.

P. japonica is more compact, with leaves margined creamy-white in its strain *varie-gata*; flowers are tipped a delicate pink in CV 'Christmas Cheer'.

Pieris species may be propagated from seed collected in autumn for spring sowing, or from 10cm/4in semi-hardwood cuttings in summer.

Pieris japonica. Lily of the Valley Shrub

Pieris formosa var. *forestii* 'Wakehurst'. Pearl Flower

Pilea involucrata 'Moon Valley'. Panamiga, Friendship Plant

PILEA

(**pai**-lee-ə)
Friendship Plant, Aluminium Plant, Artillery Plant, Panamiga, Richweed
URTICACEAE

The dim, humid floors of tropical jungles are the natural home of *Pileas*, but they'll take on a groundcover role in shady parts of any frost-free garden. Elsewhere, they're not averse to life indoors and quickly settle in as house plants.

Illustrated *P. involucrata* 'Moon Valley' has rough, deeply quilted, hairy leaves of apple green flushed pink and veined in red or brown. Tight little clusters of fluffy pink flowers appear mostly in spring and summer, but also at odd times throughout the year. Other species are grown primarily for their foliage, which can be strikingly marked, but they also bloom unobtrusively.

All species are evergreen and like a moist but well-drained soil, semi-shaded conditions and generous water and fertiliser from spring to later summer. Pinch the growing tips to keep plants bushy.

Pimelea ferruginea 'Bon Petite'. Pink Riceflower

Pimelea spectabilis. Snowy Riceflower

PIMELEA

(pai-**mee**-lee-ə)
Riceflower
THYMELAEACEAE

Related to European and Asian Daphnes, the lightly fragrant Riceflowers (*Pimelea* species) are an important shrubby part of the Australasian flora. There are upwards of 100 species of them scattered across Australia from west to east and over to New Zealand – the majority hardy down to –5°C/23°F. *Pimeleas* are easy to strike from semi-hardwood cuttings taken while the plant is in active growth, and many species develop into naturally compact, rounded, bun-shaped plants, typically 60cm/2ft or so tall and much wider.

Set them out when young, for they will not transplant later. Use them by the coast, or in open, windy places, in the front of shrub borders or in the light, dappled shade cast by tall, open trees – a position which seems to suit the two illustrated species admirably. All they need for success is a light, porous soil and plenty of leafmould – they will then flower profusely in spring and summer. They are notably short-lived.

Pinguicula grandiflora. Butterwort, Bog Violet

PINGUICULA

(pin-**gwik**-yoo-lə)
Butterwort, Bog Violet
LENTIBULARIACEAE

The curious *Pinguicula* species are carnivorous in warm weather only. They bear an extraordinary resemblance both to primroses and to Streptocarpus in their charming mauve flowers. But the function of their foliage is quite different. The leaves are covered with a sticky secretion and are able to roll their edges inward to hold a trapped insect while it is being digested.

Grow them in a bright but shaded place in a shallow 13cm/5in pot, using four parts peat, two parts compost and one part sand, and stand the pot in shallow water.

P. grandiflora is native to European mountains, and can be propagated from seed or leaf cuttings. They die back to a small bud in winter, can be moved easily then.

PITCAIRNIA

(pit-**ke**ə r-nee-ə)
Pitcairnia
BROMELIACEAE

Not, as you might imagine, found on the island where HMS *Bounty* met its match, the *Pitcairnias* are a large genus of terrestrial Bromeliads from South America's Andes. Only a few species are cultivated, with shown *P. flammea* being the most popular. *Pitcairnias* are grown for their tall spikes of almost stalkless flowers. These are usually red and yellow and quite zygomorphic in structure (see Glossary). Most species develop rosettes of stiff, spiny, sword-shaped leaves.

As *Pitcairnias* are from cooler climates than other Bromeliads, they can be grown in the open garden even in frost-prone areas. Mulch heavily, and grow in dappled shade where summers are hot.

Pittosporum phillyraeoides. Willow Pittosporum

Pittosporum tobira. Japanese Mockorange

Pittosporum undulatum. Australian Daphne

Platycodon grandiflorus. Chinese Bellflower

PITTOSPORUM
(pit-**tos**-por-ə m, pit-toh-**spor**-ə m)
Mockorange, Native Daphne, Pittosporum
PITTOSPORACEAE

To pronounce on which of the many *Pittosporum* species might be the most attractive would be rather like repeating the infamous Judgment of Paris. Whichever way you choose, you're bound to engender jealousy somewhere, for national feelings tend to run high in such matters. Let me say merely that *Pittosporums* are a genus of about 200 handsome evergreens with flowers as fragrant as orange blossom.

Most are trees, but there are some shrubs among them; all are to be found in an area centring on Australia, but with outlying species in east Africa, Japan, Southeast Asia, New Zealand and Hawaii.

New Zealand's big entry in the contest is blonde: *P. eugenioides* 'Variegatum', a striking tree with cream-margined, grey-green leaves, greenish-yellow flowers and a height of 13m/40ft. It is known locally as Silver Tarata.

Japan throws into the ring the universally popular *P. tobira* or Mockorange, a 7m/23ft

Pitcairnia flammea. Pitcairnia

stiff, shrubby tree with fragrant cream blossom and bright yellow seed capsules.

Australia has two main contenders: the Willow Pittosporum (*P. phillyraeoides*), a slender, weeping tree of 10m/33ft with yellow flowers in axillary clusters; its companion, *P. undulatum*, the Victorian Box or Native Daphne, grows taller, has pointed leaves of a distinctive pale green and creamy-white blossom in 8cm/3in terminal bunches. In Australia, its leaves are invariably disfigured by a gall-forming native insect and it is quite a surprise to find them elsewhere in pristine condition.

Across the seas in Taiwan is a rank outsider, the small (3m/10ft) *P. daphniphylloides*, which bears masses of tiny, fragrant, golden flowers at the ends of branchlets.

Hawaii loves the Ho'awa (*P. hosmeri*), a small tree with wonderfully wrinkled leaves and fragrant cream flowers.

I'll leave it to someone else to make the judgment between them, and in a cowardly fashion just suggest that though they are all beautiful, they are best kept away from paths. Their sticky fruits get on everyone's feet and into everyone's carpets.

PLATYCODON
(plat-ee-koh-də n)
Balloon Flower, Chinese Bellflower
CAMPANULACEAE

Balloon-like buds swell and pop open into big blue star flowers all summer when you've established the charming *Platycodon*. It mixes perfectly with other summer perennials in the open border in all but the hottest districts, where part shade is best. Plant out in autumn or spring at 40cm/16in spacings, then do not disturb after growth begins – for it would rather die than be transplanted.

While *P. grandiflorus* can be propagated from divisions of the white, fleshy roots, they are best grown from seed, which can be sown outdoors and will germinate in about two weeks at a temperature of about 21ºC/70ºF. Seed should not be covered, and the young plants should be pricked out with great care, as they are very brittle. Plants grow slowly to around 60cm/2ft at most, and there are dwarf forms to about 20cm/8in. The Japanese have raised singles and doubles in shades of pink, white and mauve.

PLECTRANTHUS
(plek-**tran**-thə s)
Cockspur Flower, Candle Plant
LAMIACEAE

Frequently mistaken for Coleus or Salvia, *Plectranthus* are a variable genus of plants within the same mint family – some shrubby, some trailing perennials. All grow well in frost-free areas, and can be increased by cuttings, which root easily. They are native to

Plectranthus ecklonii. Cockspur Flower

Africa, Asia and Australasia – the African species being most commonly grown.

P. ecklonii, the Cockspur Flower, is a semi-evergreen shrub for filtered sun. It can reach a height of 1.5m/5ft and produces upright spikes of purple blossom in autumn. P. oertendahlii, the Natal or Prostrate Coleus, is popular as a ground-cover in semi-shade. Its velvety, brightly coloured leaves are backed in purple, and spikes of delicate mauve-white flowers appear in late summer. It's a good choice for hanging baskets, either alone or as a contrast to other plants.

Pleione Versailles. Indian Crocus

PLEIONE
(plee-**oh**-nee)
Pleione
ORCHIDACEAE

Dainty Asiatic orchids, *Pleiones* produce miniature cattleya-type flowers from a single, flattened pseudobulb the size of a fingernail. In spring they should be crowded into shallow containers filled with a mixture of peaty compost, sphagnum, grit and char-coal and kept in a cool, shady spot. Water sparingly at first, gradually increasing the amount as the weather warms, and keep consistently moist through summer.

Flower spikes bearing one or two 10cm/4in blooms appear in summer and the plants can then be brought indoors for short periods. After bloom, a new pseudobulb begins to develop and the old one dies off. Towards the end of autumn, the leaves yellow and fall, and the plants can be stored in a cool, dry spot until they are reset the following spring into fresh soil. Species are similar, with slight variations in flower colour, and more than 30 hybrids, including *Pleione* Versailles, have been registered.

PLEIOSPILOS
(plee-**os**-pil-əs)
Living Stone
AIZOACEAE

There are several closely related genera of South African succulents whose fleshy, ground-hugging leaves look just like so many stones lying on the earth – which protects them from hungry grazing animals. The best known is Lithops (which see), but perhaps the most perfect illusion is that of the various species of *Pleiospilos*, which really do simulate a heap of pebbles – until the yellow, white or pink daisy-like flowers appear to give the game away.

The Living Stones are easy to grow: just treat them as you would cacti, and mulch their pots or beds with suitable stones. This is not just for decoration: the stone mulch helps keep the crowns of the plants dry in case of unseasonable rain or careless water-ing, both of which can rot them.

PLUMBAGO
(plum-**bae**-goh)
Leadwort
PLUMBAGINACEAE

Only one factor prevents more of us from growing lovely evergreen *Plumbago* – and that's an acute lack of space. For it suckers

Plumbago auriculata. Leadwort

Pleiospilos kingiae. Living Stone

heavily, and quickly becomes untidy unless cut right back in late winter. Flowers are only produced on new growth, so heavy pruning not only controls size but improves blooming as well. You can use *Plumbago* as an informal hedge or to disguise ugly walls and fences, for it will climb a little way.

Once established (and it is easy to start from soft-tip cuttings taken during the warmer months and struck in moist, sandy soil) it is hardy down to –3ºC/27ºF and remarkably drought resistant. One of those plants with a curious sticky feel about it, *P. auriculata* produces lavish clusters of sky-blue, phlox-type flowers all through the warm weather; CV 'Royal Cape' has deeper blue flowers; those of var. *alba* are pure white.

The smaller and less vigorous *P. indica* has blooms of orange-red; *P. zeylanica's* are a light, rosy red. Good drainage is essential for all of them.

Plumeria rubra var. *acutifolia.* Frangipani

PLUMERIA
(ploo-**meer**-ee-∂)
Frangipani, Graveyard Tree, Temple Flower
APOCYNACEAE

Often found planted about Asian temples and burial grounds, *Plumeria* has been honoured by the Buddhists for centuries as a symbol of immortality, and in Sri Lanka it is sometimes known as the Tree of Life, due to its remarkable ability to continue flowering even when not in the ground, as any gardener who has ever forgotten to plant a large cutting can testify.

Though seen throughout the warm climates of the world, it seems all *Plumerias* were originally natives of Central America, carried to the East by Spanish traders. There is a great deal of confusion about their

Plumeria obtusa 'Singapore White'. Plumeria

nomenclature, but modern study suggests that the myriad colour varieties are all hybrids among several recognised species. These species are: *P. acuminata* – cream and yellow flowers, pale pointed leaves; *P. alba* – small white and yellow flowers, paddle-shaped leaves; *P. bahamensis* – white flowers, narrow, dark leaves: *P. obtusa* – large, rounded white flowers, dark evergreen leaves with rounded tips; and *P. rubra* – red flowers, shorter rounded leaves.

In really tropical areas, they grow into quite large trees up to 13m/40ft in height, with trunks as thick as barrels. *Plumerias* grow readily from cuttings of any size, taken in winter and thoroughly dried out before planting. They can also be raised from seed. In tropical climates, the richly fragrant flowers appear in clusters directly from bare, blunt ends of the branches, and continue to open all year. In more temperate zones, the new foliage appears first and flowering does not begin until late spring.

Plumeria rubra 'Irma Bryan'. Red Frangipani

Podalyria calyptrata. Sweetpea Bush

PODALYRIA

(pod-ə-**lir**-ee-ə)

Sweetpea Bush, Keurtjie

FABACEAE

Not particularly common away from South Africa, the spring-blooming Sweetpea Bush or *Podalyria calyptrata* is a most useful shrub in exposed positions. Always decorative, *Podalyria* is evergreen – or to be more accurate, evergrey, for its leaves are covered in white, silvery hairs which shine in the sunlight. lt is a slow-growing bush of open, rounded shape to 3m/10ft, made more compact by annual pruning. The pea-flowers, which are very fragrant, are usually a soft mauve-pink, though there are other colour variations, and they appear for months during winter and early spring.

Podranea ricasoliana. Pink Trumpet Vine

Polemonium caeruleum. Jacob's Ladder

Grow *Podalyria* from seed, which must be soaked for hours in hot water before sowing, or from soft-tip cuttings taken in warm weather and stuck in a moist, sandy mix. A gravelly, well-drained soil is best, with heavy regular water over the winter months but much less in summer. Tip-prune young plants to keep compact, and reduce flowered shoots by half on older specimens. Hardy to −3ºC/27ºF.

PODRANEA

(pod-**rah**-nee-ə)

(SYN Pandorea, Tecoma)

Pink Trumpet Vine, Port St John Creeper, Zimbabwe Creeper

BIGNONIACEAE

A showy, evergreen climber from southern Africa, the Pink Trumpet Vine or *Podranea ricasoliana* bears masses of rosy-mauve trumpet flowers over many weeks in summer. They are produced in large, loose panicles at the ends of the twining stems, forming a sheet of colour.

Podranea needs the support of a strong pergola or fence and is inclined to be rampant. Grow in full sun except in the hottest areas, where light dappled shade is appreciated. Water and feed regularly in the growing season; prune back hard in early spring to control size. *Podranea* is easily propagated from summer cuttings.

The name *Podranea* is an anagram of the related Pandorea.

POLEMONIUM

(pol-e-**moh**-nee-əm)

Jacob's Ladder, Charity, Greek Valerian

POLEMONIACEAE

Several of the 25-odd species of *Polemonium* are in cultivation, including Jacob's Ladder, *P. caeruleum, P. carneum, P. pulcherrimum* and the cultivar *P.* 'Lambrook Mauve'. Charming woodland plants and fully hardy, they grow 45cm–1m/18in–3ft tall, are ideal for the shaded garden or for naturalising in damp leafy soil.

Plant out when dormant, in cold weather, at spacings of 30cm/12in. They need to be kept moist and should be fed regularly with complete fertiliser, as the masses of fibrous roots quickly exhaust the soil. Stems which have borne the panicles of mauve, pink or purple cup-like flowers during spring and summer should be cut right back in autumn. Foliage of all species is somewhat fern-like, and collapses fast in dry weather.

POLIANTHES

(pol-ee-an-theez)

Tuberose

AGAVACEAE

Fragrant *Polianthes tuberosa* needs a warm, sheltered, sunny position. Soil should be fertile, very well drained, lime-free, and dug and enriched annually. Plant tubers shallowly in damp earth in spring, but do not water until leaves appear. Thereafter, they must be kept moist until the foliage yellows in autumn.

Flowering occurs in late summer or early autumn, but tubers bloom only once, so clumps should be lifted in late autumn, the offsets separated and stored, and the flowered tubers discarded; the smallest offsets will take two years to flower.

Polianthes tuberosa. Tuberose

Polygala myrtifolia. Milkwort

Pomaderris lanigera. Woolly Pomaderris

POLYGALA

(pol-**lig**-ə-lə)
Milkwort, Bluecaps
POLYGALACEAE

A tidy, evergreen shrub, usually less than 2.5m/8ft tall, *Polygala myrtifolia* is well branched and densely foliaged above but somewhat bare and leggy below. Its rich purple-pink flowers are generously produced from about the end of winter right through summer, with a few being present for most of autumn, too. However, it should be planted with care, as the intense colour seems to clash with many other flowers. Best use it as a background or fence planting, or as a temporary filler behind slower plants.

Not too fussy about soil, *Polygala* does best in light, well-drained earth in sun or dappled shade. It is known to be hardy down to –5°C/23°F.

POLYGONATUM

(po-li-gon-**ah**-təm)
Solomon's Seal
LILIACEAE

A charming and graceful flower for woodland areas or cool shady places, the old-fashioned Solomon's Seal is grown from long tuberous bulbs. Planted out in autumn, these send up a leaf spike in spring and flower only a few weeks later, usually towards the end of spring or early in summer. The flower stems are long and arching with small clusters of green-tipped white bells hanging at intervals. The leaves stand out like pairs of green wings.

Polygonatums thrive in average soil so long as it is kept moist but with the excess draining away freely. A herbaceous perennial, it is not a plant for areas with mild, frost-free winters, for it needs sub-zero temperatures to initiate annual dormancy.

POMADERRIS

(**pom**-ə-de-ris)
Tainui, Native Hazel, Pomaderris
RHAMNACEAE

Native to Australia, the decorative *Pomaderris lanigera* is also popular in California, where it seems to grow better than in its natural range. It is a fast-growing, slender, evergreen shrub with all parts except the trunk covered in greyish down. The 10cm/4in leaves, often with a wrinkled surface, are dark and handsome. The tiny white or yellow flowers that appear during spring have no petals, but consist of stamens borne in woolly masses to 20cm/8in in diameter. They persist for months.

Pomaderris can be struck from well-ripened cuttings, and does best in sandy or gravelly soil, kept moist. In a wind-sheltered spot it will grow to 3m/10ft. It is hardy to –5°C/23°F.

PONCIRUS

(pon-**seer**-əs)
(SYN Aegle, Limonia)
Golden Apple, Trifoliate Orange
RUTACEAE

When a favourite Citrus tree suddenly sprouts spiny shoots below the graft line, and those shoots develop 3-lobed leaves, you have unwittingly acquired a plant of *Poncirus trifoliata,* the close relative used as sturdy stock for grafting all Citrus species.

But *Poncirus* is also a handsome 4.5m/15ft tree in its own right, and is frequently grown as such in countries such as England, which is a little cold for Citrus survival. It is less fussy about soil than the true Citrus, so long as drainage is good, and is usually propagated from semi-hardwood cuttings. Deciduous, its very fragrant 5cm/2in snowy flowers appear before the foliage. Branches are stiffly right-angled.

Polygonatum multiflorum. Solomon's Seal

Poncirus trifoliata. Trifoliate Orange

PONTEDERIA
(pon-tə-**dee**-ree-ə)
Pickerel Weed, Wampee
PONTEDERIACEAE

Pontederia cordata, Pickerel Weed, is a beautiful aquatic plant surely deserving a kinder common name. It is easy to grow, and invaluable for the margins of garden ponds, where it produces handsome arrow-shaped glossy leaves, held above the water on 60cm/2ft stems. During the latter part of summer and into autumn, tall spikes of vivid blue flowers appear among them.

    Pontederias should be planted out in spring with no more than 15cm/6in of water above their roots. They look best clustered in the shallows at the edges of the pond. Pickerel Weed hails from the eastern parts of North America, is completely hardy and, in areas with frosty winters, is not in the least invasive.

Pontederia cordata. Pickerel Weed, Wampee

Porphyrocoma pohliana. Redhead, Fiesta Jewels

PORPHYROCOMA
(por-fai-roh-**koh**-mə)
Fiesta Jewels, Redhead
ACANTHACEAE

Another member of the Acanthus family pressed into service as a house plant is *Porphyrocoma pohliana* (or Fiesta Jewels, as the nurserymen would have it). It's a neat little plant with glossy, very dark green leaves, attractively marked in silver or cream, depending on type. The warm-weather flowers crown the tops of the stems and bear a striking family resemblance to Justicia and Pachystachys (which see). However, in *Porphyrocoma* the flowers are red-violet, and the persistent bracts, so characteristic of the family, are a darker red-purple.

Portea petropolitana var. *extensa.* Portea

PORTEA
(**por**-tee-ə)
Portea
BROMELIACEAE

A really large-growing species of Bromeliad, *Portea* does best in a bright, sunny position in a conservatory, by a large window, or in a bright position outdoors with shade during the hottest part of the summer day.

    It should be planted in a fibrous, chunky mix and kept moist at all times to produce its spectacular rosette of leaves, which are up to 1m/3ft across. Keep the leaf-well topped up and this splendid plant will produce heavy horizontal spikes of green and pink flowers in late summer. *Portea petropolitana* must be kept above freezing point in winter and prefers a temperature of at least 10ºC/50ºF. Propagate by detaching suckers.

PORTULACA
(por-tyoo-**lak**-kə)
Rose Moss, Eleven O'clock, Purslane, Wax Pink, Sun Plant, Pigface
PORTULACACEAE

Vivid waxy blooms in wildly clashing colours appear on these dainty succulents from late spring to autumn. Anywhere it is hot and sunny, in sandy or gravel soil, they flower

Portulaca grandiflora. Rose Moss, Sun Plant

and flourish to excess – in fact, poor soil seems to generate more generous bloom! They are useful in the rock garden, on steep banks, or in terrace planters where the sunshine is hot, forming a dense mat just 30cm/12in high at most. Without sun, they choose not to wake up and shine till mid-morning. Sow where they are to grow, covering the seed lightly. Water sparingly and seedlings should appear in 10–14 days. Thin out if too crowded and they'll bloom in 6 weeks from seed. There are several popular mixtures, some with double blooms, available as seed or seedlings. Go easy on the water, for these are natives of dry places.

Potentilla 'Monsieur Rouillard'. Double Cinquefoil

Posoqueria latifolia. Needle-flower

POSOQUERIA

(po-zo-**kweer**-ee-∂)
Needle-flower, Brazilian Oak
RUBIACEAE

Rivalling the perfume of the Frangipani in gardens of warm climates is the exotic Needle-flower, *Posoqueria latifolia*, whose white blossoms open throughout the spring season.

It reaches small tree size (7m/23ft) only in hot climates, but is decorative any place you find it, with brilliantly glossy 20cm/8in ever-green leaves putting on a show at all times.

The flowers are really extraordinary: 15cm/6in long tubes tipped with pointed buds that spring open as dainty white reflexed flowers, sometimes with projecting anthers. These appear in densely crowded clusters at branch ends and continue to open for months. Occasional yellow plum-sized fruits are edible, if rarely appetising.

Posoqueria is normally propagated from cuttings and grows rapidly in the deep, rich soil it likes. It is hardy down to about –3ºC/27ºF. The name *Posoqueria* is an approximation of its native name in the Guianas.

POTENTILLA

(poh-ten-**til**-l∂)
Cinquefoil, Five-finger, Hardhack, Tormentil
ROSACEAE

Members of the rose family resembling large strawberry plants, the colourful Cinquefoils (*Potentilla* spp.) include everything from annuals to deciduous shrubs. In the perennial garden a number of species are grown, ranging from 5cm/2in mat-forming alpines to the 45cm/18in *P.* 'M. Rouillard', while *P. fruticosa*, the Finger Bush, is a small shrub to around 1m/3ft in height.

All have the tell-tale 5-lobed leaves, and flowers with petals and sepals also in multiples of five. The blooms can be single or double, in pink, scarlet, maroon, white or yellow. *Potentillas* can be divided in autumn or raised from seed. Water lightly except in dry weather, and feed generously in spring.

Potentilla fruticosa. Finger Bush

Potentilla 'William Rollison'. Hybrid Cinquefoil

Pratia pedunculata. Blue Stars

PRATIA
(**prei**-tee-ə)
Blue Stars
LOBELIACEAE

This useful genus of dainty rock-garden plants in the Lobelia family is spread right across the Pacific, with most species native to either Australia or New Zealand.

Most charming is the tiny *Pratia pedunculata* or Blue Stars, which is completely prostrate, forming a dense mat over the moist, rich soil it prefers. Propagate by division in early spring, and keep moist at all times until it makes growth. The toothed foliage resembles that of popular Lobelia erinus (which see), and the mauve-blue blowers are starry, 5-petalled, and less than 1cm/^{1}/$_2$ in in diameter. They open in profusion throughout spring and summer.

Primula obconica cultivar. Poison Primrose

Primula, Polyanthus Group. Polyanthus

PRIMULA
(**prim**-yoo-lə)
Primrose, Polyanthus, Cowslip, Oxlip
PRIMULACEAE

There are more than 400 species of *Primula* found throughout the northern hemisphere and in outlying areas below the equator. They are all, in nature, perennial, but as they cannot stand extremes of temperature, particularly summer heat, many of the popular species will always be grown as annuals.

Primulas vary widely in style, colour and profusion of bloom, but almost all of them are instantly recognisable for what they are – exotic relatives of the humble European Primrose and Cowslip. Their height ranges

up to 1m/3ft, their foliage can be with or without stems, and is borne in a simple rosette from 15–60cm/6–24in across. Individual leaves may be simple, lobed or toothed; often with a deeply veined, cushiony surface. The flowers appear in spring, generally in the form of a loose umbel borne at the top of a straight stem, but they may also appear in whorls at intervals along the stem, or in globose heads. They will always, in the wild species, be single, with a tubular corolla flaring into 5 overlapping lobes, notched at their tips and with an eye in a contrasting colour.

Primulas grow to perfection in cooler, moist climates. Soil should be well enriched with old manure and compost, well-drained

Primula denticulata var. *alba.* Drumstick Primrose

Primula × *kewensis.* Hybrid Primula

Primula malacoides. Fairy Primrose

and acid. Here, with regular water and occasional feeds of soluble fertiliser, they should do well, beginning to bloom in late winter and continuing until spring starts to turn into summer. If the weather turns too warm, mulch around the plants with compost to help keep the delicate root systems cool.

In cold climates, *Primulas* can be divided and replanted immediately after flowering, at spacings relative to the width of their leaf-rosettes, or increased from seed. However, with the exception of the common *P. mala-coides*, this is a long and difficult process, and most gardeners opt to buy established plants, often in bloom.

But for those who have the time and patience to try, *Primula* seed should be sown as soon as possible after it ripens (which means late spring) for bloom the following year. Prepare boxes of fine seed-raising mix

containing sand, sieved compost and milled peat. Sow seed on the surface, spray with a fine mist of water and press flat; do not cover. Top the moistened seed boxes with sheets of glass, or place in plastic bags. Keep in a warm, shaded place at a constant temperature of 21ºC/70ºF, until germination occurs – this may be as long as 40 days.

The seedlings are minute and summer will be almost over before they are large enough to prick out into individual 8cm/3in pots of rich compost. Still your work is not yet done! You'll need to pot them up into larger containers in early autumn for planting out the following spring. Most *Primulas* grow especially well by water or in boggy ground.

Primula 'Argus'. Auricula Primula

Primula japonica. Candelabra Primrose

Primula pulverulenta. Candelabra Primrose

Proboscidea fragrans. Unicorn Plant

PROBOSCIDEA

(prob-oss-**id**-ee-∂)
(SYN Martynia)
Unicorn Plant, Devil's Claw
MARTYNIACEAE

Annual species of *Proboscidea* are native to the United States, and commonly grown there in the south, where the pods are used in mixed pickles. They are not the most beautiful plants in the world – nor is their odour many people's idea of what a perfume ought to be.

But the flowers are quite lovely, rather like those of the Cape Primrose, Streptocarpus (which see). Those of *P. fragrans* are a rich red-purple, gold-throated and fragrant. Blooms of related *P. louisianica* may be cream, violet or light rose. Both species flower over a long period in summer and then produce beak-like seed pods that may be up to 30cm/12in long. Germination takes 18–25 days and the rather slow plants can take most of the growing season to reach their ultimate height of 60cm/ 2ft. Grow in rich, well-drained soil in sun.

Prosopis glandulosa. Western Honey Mesquite

Proiphys amboinensis. Cardwell Lily

PROIPHYS

(**pro**-i-f∂s)
(SYN Eurycles)
Brisbane Lily, Cardwell Lily
AMARYLLIDACEAE

Difficult to grow away from their natural habitat of subtropical Australia and nearby Indonesia, the three species of *Proiphys* are really limited to the tropical weather cycle of dry winters, wet summers. During the former, they are dormant, producing heart-shaped leaves in late spring and bursting into lush white bloom in midsummer, just in time for the southern hemisphere Christmas. Not frost hardy, they need a rich but well-drained soil in which they colonise freely from seed or offsets of the large bulbs. Water is necessary from spring until after the last bloom has faded. They are fragrant, by the way, as if scent were needed!

PROSOPIS

(proh-**soh**-pis)
Honey Mesquite, Algaroba Bean, Algarrobo
MIMOSACEAE

Twenty-odd species of *Prosopis* are found in hot, dry areas of Asia, Africa and the Americas. They are not directly represented in Australia, however, where they are declared noxious weeds. Elsewhere they make a splendid shade tree in desert areas, sending taproots down to 20m/65ft in their endless quest for water.

P. glandulosa var. *torreyana* (from Mexico and Argentina) is propagated from firm young shoots, struck in damp sand. Planted out in sandy soil, they develop a multiple-trunked habit. The bipinnate bright green foliage is deciduous; the stems extremely spiny; the flowers petalless, and crowded into cylindrical spikes, most attractive to bees. They open bright yellow, fading to brown.

PROSTANTHERA

(pros-**tan**-thur-∂)
Mint Bush
LAMIACEAE

Short-lived but splashy-flowering shrubs, Australia's aromatic Mint Bushes (*Prostanthera* spp.) bloom briefly but with incredible profusion, mostly in shades of mauve, and harmonise perfectly with Prunus, Cornus and other treasures of the spring garden.

Grow them in a sheltered position anywhere the soil is gravelly, well drained and rich in leafmould. They can be propagated from firm tip-cuttings taken in summer or autumn and struck in moist, gritty sand. Longer-lived plants can be produced by grafting *Prostanthera* scions onto stock from the Australian Westringia, which is more resistant to root rot. All species can be kept compact by a light trim of new season's growth after blooming is done. *P. ovalifolia* is the most common species, but there are about 50 others.

Prostanthera ovalifolia var. *latifolia.* Purple Mint Bush

Protea cynaroides. King Protea

PROTEA
(**proh**-tee-∂)
Sugarbush, Honeyflower, Protea
PROTEACEAE

Of the many remarkable personalities in Greek mythology, none had a more extraordinary appearance than Proteus. He had the power of assuming any shape, and it was this gift of unlimited shape-changing which suggested the name *Protea* to 18th-century botanists, classifying a newly discovered and highly variable group of South African plants. They believed them unique, though we now know there are close relatives in South America and Australia. The true *Protea* genus, however, will always be associated with South Africa.

There are about 100 species, mostly from the mountainous Cape Province, and they are not too difficult to grow once their needs are clearly understood. Sandy soil is the first rule (preferably acid, though some species will make do with an alkaline pH); perfect drainage the second (they grow well on hillsides or in terraced beds); full sun the third. They are slow growers and relatively short lived, but the beauty of the often gigantic blooms makes every effort seem worthwhile. Flower size is not necessarily related to shrub size, by the way. The startling

Proteas last well when cut, and they retain shape after fading, so are often saved for dried arrangements. Flower size is not necessarily related to shrub size, by the way. The startling

Protea magnifica. Woolly-bearded Protea

King Protea (*P. cynaroides*) produces 25cm/ 10in blooms on a 1m/3ft bush and must be staked in case of overbalancing.

Plants can be raised from autumn or spring sown seed, but germination is erratic and the resultant seedlings not necessarily true to type. *Proteas*, as a generalization, bear concave, silky leaves clasping tough, woody stems. The blooms consist of a number of tubular flowers surrounded by several rows of coloured bracts. All attract honey-eating birds.

Prunella grandiflora 'Loveliness'. Self-heal, Heal-all

PRUNELLA
(proo-**nel**-l∂)
Self-heal, Heal-all
LAMIACEAE

Prunellas are rather untidy perennials in the mint family, thriving in dampish soil. They can easily become a nuisance due to their rampant self-seeding. Pulling out excess plants is easier said than done, though, for those roots have a grip of iron.

Illustrated *P. grandiflora* has the most attractive blooms, somewhat tubular, and whorled on a long spike. Their peak display is summer in cool temperate climates, and they enjoy sun or dappled shade. They like alkaline, well-drained soil, and are planted from spring divisions. Dead-head regularly to avoid excess seedlings.

PRUNUS
(**proon**-∂s)
Flowering Peaches, Plums, Cherries, Apricots and Almonds
ROSACEAE

Roses by many other names might be the simplest way to describe the hundreds of *Prunus* species in a single sentence. For they *are* members of the rose family and they *do* all bear flowers with a passing resemblance to roses.

For horticultural purposes, one has to make an artificial division of this large genus – over 200 species and thousands of cultivars – mainly from the northern hemisphere. That division is between the species grown for the delight of the appetite, and those grown purely for eye appeal. The popular edible species, which include peaches, plums, cherries, apricots and almonds, are to one degree or another bushy trees, rarely above 7m/23ft; they need a deal of pruning or shaping to produce a satisfactory fruit crop.

Prunus mume. Japanese Flowering Apricot

Prunus glandulosa. Dwarf Flowering Almond-Cherry

All are deciduous, with attractive, single rose-type flowers in early spring, either pale pink or white. These generally appear on small, spur-like branchlets designed to take the weight of the fruit. All fruiting species can be grown from their seeds or stones, but are generally propagated by bud grafting, to be certain of variety and quality.

But here we are mainly concerned with the ornamental varieties, which bloom far more profusely than their commercial cousins but fail to produce any useful fruit.

By far the most popular group of ornamentals are the Japanese Flowering Cherries, mostly hybrids of *P. serrulata* with a number of other oriental species, and now known as the Sato-zakura Group. These have both single and double flowers, in a wide range of colours from pure white to deep red, sometimes with variegations. Often the individual flowers are borne on long, hanging stems. In their home country of Japan, their cultivation is a way of life, and springtime cherryblossom viewing is an annual event to which everyone looks forward. 'Okumiyaku' (syn 'Shimidsu sakura'), 'Sekiyama' (syn 'Kanzan') and 'Shirotae' (syn 'Mount Fuji') belong to this group.

Another popular group are the Weeping or Rosebud Cherries, *P. subhirtella* and its cultivars, which include 'Pendula' and 'Pendula Rosea', whose delightful miniature blossoms may appear in autumn as well as spring. They are great favourites, together with the Taiwan Cherry, *P. campanulata*, whose delicate trumpet-shaped red blossom is among the earliest to open in spring.

Prunus campanulata. Taiwan Cherry

Prunus, Sato-zakura Group, 'Ukon'. Japanese Cherry

Prunus persica cultivar. Flowering Peach

Prunus subhirtella 'Pendula'. Higan Cherry, Rosebud Cherry

Less often seen away from its native China and Japan is *P. mume*, the Japanese Flowering Apricot. This is usually the first to bloom, often in midwinter, and has almost as many attractive cultivars as the cherry. The flowers are generally flat and open, with a spectacular display of stamens, and may be in any colour from white to red.

Where space is limited, the Chinese Bush Cherry, *P. glandulosa*, may be the answer. A dainty, suckering shrub, generally less than 1m/3ft tall, it produces many erect stems, packed from top to bottom with single or double white or pink flowers.

In Western gardens, the spring display is provided more by a range of hybrid flowering peaches, cultivars of *P. dulcis* (the Flowering Almond), *P. persica* (the Peach), and many other minor species. These include ornamental varieties of the Wild Cherry, *P. avium*, which may grow to 23m/75ft; *P. blireiana*, the Purple-leafed Plum, with double pink flowers; and the Cherry Plum, *P. cerasifera*, and its cultivars, including 'Pissardii' and 'Thundercloud'. Finally, there are several less common evergreen species, grown as much for their foliage as for their generally white blossom. These include *P. ilicifolia, P. lusitanica* and *P. laurocerasus*, usually grown as hedges.

Prunus, Sato-zakura Group, 'Shirotae'. Japanese Flowering Cherry

Prunus, Sato-zakura Group, 'Okumiyaku'. Japanese Flowering Cherry

PSEUDERANTHEMUM

(syoo-dur-**an**-thə-mum)
(SYN Eranthemum)
Golden Net Bush, Eldorado

ACANTHACEAE

Rarely seen outside the true tropics, *Pseuderanthemums* don't take to cold or even cool weather, becoming decidedly unhappy when temperatures drop below 10°C/50°F. Of 60-odd species, only a few, including *P. reticulatum*, the Golden Net Bush from the Pacific island nation of Vanuatu, are grown

Pseuderanthemum reticulatum. Golden Net Bush

Psoralea pinnata. Blue Pea

Psylliostachys suworowii. Russian Statice

for their flowers. It has golden stems and bright yellow leaves with a network of green lines that could be mistaken for the symptoms of a nutrient deficiency, although in partly shaded positions it tends to settle for a greener tone. Net Bushes are grown from warm-weather cuttings, are generally erect and bushy, and where the climate is warm enough, bloom is continuous. This consists of dainty, carmine-spotted white flowers, borne in panicles both at leaf axils and at branch tips. They are pretty enough, but in tropical gardens flower yield is reduced when they are trimmed regularly to a compact shape. Rich, well-drained soil is necessary, with regular water and fertiliser. Closely planted specimens make a good, dense hedge to something less than 2m/6ft.

PSORALEA

(sor-**ae**-lee-ə)
Blue Butterfly Bush, Blue Pea
FABACEAE

Psoraleas are fast-growing, shrubby members of the pea family with heath-like leaves and blue, mauve, purple or white flowers. There are representative species on almost every continent. Generally they do well in a light, sandy soil.

Psoraleas are mild-climate plants and can tolerate only the lightest frosts. They can be grown from seed, which ripens in summer and autumn, or from spring cuttings of half-ripened shoots, which should be struck in a sandy mixture with warmth and humidity.

Popular *P. pinnata* flowers quite profusely for much of spring, and should be pruned

back hard after bloom to prevent its adopting a leggy, tree-like shape. Alternatively, it can be left to develop naturally and used as a background plant to tall perennials or small shrubs which would hide its bare trunk and lower branches. Flowers are only about 1.5cm/½in across and are attractively shaded mauve and white.

PSYCHOTRIA

(sai-**kot**-ree-ə)
Wild Coffee
RUBIACEAE

Related to Bouvardia, Gardenia, Ixora, Luculia and other beautiful warm-climate shrubs, the *Psychotrias* have been relegated to the status of also-rans. They have many good features: glossy evergreen foliage, a long display of dense terminal clusters of pink, white or yellow flowers (small, it's true, but very fragrant), and a colourful crop of berries to follow. But that's just not enough when it comes to the fierce competition for space in the warm-climate garden, for many other plants outshine these unspectacular shrubs. So most of them remain local favourites in their home territories, which could be South or Central America, Africa, the Caribbean or even Fiji. They can be grown from the seed of dried berries or from cuttings struck under heat.

Illustrated *P. capensis* (Wild Coffee), from Africa, is occasionally seen in other areas with similar climates. It grows into a naturally rounded, compact bush no more than 1m/3ft tall. The bright yellow flower heads appear throughout spring.

PSYLLIOSTACHYS

(sil-lee-oh-**stak**-əs)
Pink Pokers, Russian Statice
PLUMBAGINACEAE

Psylliostachys suworowii used to be classed in the genus *Limonium*, which includes the Statice of flower shops, but now has been given a genus of its own. An annual from Turkestan, it grows about knee-high, and bears densely crowded spikes of lilac or pink flowers in summer.

The spikes don't stand up so much as wave about, and they are apt to look rather floppy and unkempt in the garden, and the foliage is unspectacular. Accordingly, the plant is mostly grown for cutting, for which it is excellent, the flowers lasting well in water. Even better, treat them as everlastings – cut them as they reach perfection and hang them up to dry in a warm but airy place. They hold their colour and shape perfectly.

Psychotria capensis. Wild Coffee

Pterocephalus perennis. Featherhead

PTEROCEPHALUS

(ter-oh-**kef**-∂-l∂s)
(SYN Scabiosa)
Mountain Scabious, Featherhead
DIPSACACEAE

Small perennial relatives of annual Scabious (see Scabiosa), there are 20 or so species of *Pterocephalus*, mostly native to mountain areas of Europe and Asia. *P. perennis* from Greece is probably the species after which the entire genus was named, because its seed head appears to be covered in feathers, and the generic name means Featherhead.

It is a charming plant for rock gardens of temperate climates, spreading into a flat cushion over rock surfaces, where its toothed, elliptical foliage looks attractive all year. In summer, the 4cm/2in flower heads appear; they are tinted a pale mauve-pink and are almost stemless.

Pterospermum acerifolium. Bayur

Pterostylis nutans. Nodding Greenhood

PTEROSPERMUM

(ter-oh-**spur**-m∂m)
Bayur Tree
STERCULIACEAE

The Bayur (*Pterospermum acerifolium*) is among the world's most spectacular tropical trees. Native to India and Indonesia (yet flowering just as well in a warm temperate climate) it grows to 35m/115ft in the wild, but, mercifully, much smaller in the garden.

Its attractive deciduous leaves are the size and shape of a rather wilted dinner plate, and in summer the flower buds develop both at leaf axils and in small terminal clusters. They are like large cigars, and you're most unlikely to see one opening, for that happens at night. The morning after, the cigar is seen to have split into five richly cream, reflexed petals, and in the centre a 15cm/6in fountain of white, fragrant stamens is revealed. The flowers are very long-lasting, on the tree or off, and they will open indoors if you enjoy watching that sort of thing.

PTEROSTYLIS

(ter-oh-**stai**-l∂s)
Greenhood, Parrot's Beak Orchid
ORCHIDACEAE

Most beloved of wild terrestrial orchids in their native Australasian homelands (Australia, New Zealand and New Caledonia), there are at least 120 species of the dainty waxen Greenhood orchids to be found. They grow from succulent underground tubers, sending up a rosette of waxen, oblong leaves. These rosettes are often to be found in large colonies in damp, leaf-rich soil on the shaded side of fallen rotted trees.

The Nodding Greenhood, *Pterostylis nutans*, is one of the most attractive species; each tuber sends up a slender, leafed flower stem in autumn or winter in coastal areas (later inland). Not happy in cultivated gardens, Greenhoods can be raised in shallow pots of leafy bush sand or in a shady, sheltered spot in the garden.

PTILOTUS

(tai-**loh**-t∂s)
Mulla Mulla, Woolly Bears
AMARANTHACEAE

An uncommon genus of perennials even to native-born Australians, *Ptilotus* includes about 100 species that thrive in almost desert areas in the north and west of the continent. They make a marvellous display in sunny gardens with perfect drainage, when their loose mounds of softly hairy grey-green foliage suddenly burst into a haze of woolly pink or green flower heads in spring. These are deliciously fragrant and borne on long red stems that cut well for decoration. The flowers are arranged in globular heads or in spikes according to species and are apparently without petals.

Ptilotus exaltatus. Woolly Bears, Pink Mulla Mulla

Try them in a sandy soil enriched with plenty of decayed manure, and water well from late winter right up to blooming. They need little for the rest of the year. *Ptilotus* can be propagated from short pieces of fleshy root inserted in a sandy mix, or from seed, but germination is rather unreliable.

Illustrated *P. exaltatus* will grow to 60cm/2ft in favourable conditions. *P. spathulatus* bears similar but greenish flower spikes at the tips of trailing stems.

Pulmonaria officinalis. Lungwort

PULMONARIA
(pul-mon-e∂r-ee-∂)
Lungwort, Spotted Dog
BORAGINACEAE

If this charming genus of perennials had a more pleasant popular name, perhaps we'd remember to grow them more often. For *Pulmonaria officinalis* is perfect for fully shaded areas of the garden bed or rockery, growing to just 30cm/12in or less. It develops attractively white-spotted foliage and 2cm/1in pink bell-shaped flowers that fade to blue as they age.

Plant them in any peat-enriched soil in autumn or early spring, at spacings of 30cm/12in to allow for their naturally spreading habit. They are normally propagated from root division, because plants raised from spring-sown seed are said to be inferior. A spring mulch of dampened peat will help to conserve moisture, and they must not be allowed to dry out.

P. rubra has plain green foliage, and brick-red blooms; *P. angustifolia* has deep blue flowers; *P. saccharata* has violet, red-violet or white flowers; there are a number of cultivars, some with bicolour blooms. Most species flower over several weeks in late winter or spring.

PULSATILLA
(pul-s∂-til-l∂)
(SYN Anemone)
Pasque Flower
RANUNCULACEAE

There has been considerable confusion about the nomenclature of these delicate-looking perennials. (In reality, they are as tough as old boots and native to cold, mountainous areas of the northern hemisphere, where they grow in spreading drifts to a height of 15–60cm/6–24in.)

Originally included with the Anemones, *Pulsatillas* come from alpine meadows of North America, Europe and western Asia. They enjoy humus-rich, well-drained soil in open sun and are generally grown in raised areas of the rock garden. All species have feathery foliage that dies back in winter, and frequently the first flowers appear in spring, before the leaves are fully developed. Flowering often continues into early summer. Blooms of illustrated *P. vulgaris* are single and commonly a rich purple, sometimes white or mauve. As in other *Pulsatillas*, petal fall is followed by rapid enlargement of the flower's sexual parts into a puffball of reddish filaments which persists for months.

Pulsatilla vulgaris. Pasque Flower

PUNICA
(pyoo-nik-∂)
Pomegranate
PUNICACEAE

With the smaller scale of modern gardens, every plant has to earn its place. So the larger growing *Punica* varieties are rarely seen now, outside the Middle East. We have found

Punica granatum var. *nana*. Dwarf Pomegranate

more fragrant flowers and much more tasty fruits to take the place of the once-popular Pomegranate!

Contrariwise, the Dwarf Pomegranate, *Punica granatum* var. *nana*, is more widely seen every day. Its harvest may be of little use but it has other advantages. Rarely more than 1m/3ft high or wide, it produces dainty miniatures of the larger Pomegranate flowers and fruits throughout the warmer weather.

Grow it in a fully sunny spot in coarse, gravelly soil enriched with a proportion of well-rotted manure or compost. During prolonged droughts, an occasional deep soaking should keep it going, otherwise rainfall will meet its water needs. Light pruning at the end of each winter will preserve the plant's neat, compact shape. *Punica* will resist heat and drought to a great degree, yet it is also hardy down to around –8°C/17°F.

Punica granatum 'Flore Pleno'. Double Pomegranate

Puya berteroniana. Chilean Lily

Pyrostegia venusta. Flame Vine

PUYA

(**poo**-yə)
Chilean Lily, Puya
BROMELIACEAE

Around 200 species of *Puya* have been identified, all of them from the towering Andes of South America. They are Bromeliads (Pineapple relatives), but unlike most of that large family, they are strictly terrestrial. Generally, *Puyas* are found in arid places and gravelly soil, and need little water apart from usual mountain precipitation.

Illustrated *P. berteroniana* is surely one of the most spectacular, growing 2m/6ft in height. The blue-green, arching leaves have spiky margins and are spine-tipped. The pyramidal inflorescence contrasts three-petalled blooms of the most vivid blue-green with glowing orange anthers. In colder climates, it can be raised in a cool greenhouse.

Pyrus pashia. Himalayan Pear

PYROSTEGIA

(pai-roh-**stee**-jə)
**Flame Vine, Bignonia, Golden Showers,
Orange-flowered Stephanotis**
BIGNONIACEAE

One of the plant world's most dazzling extroverts, exuberant *Pyrostegia venusta* has earned a string of common names, Flame Vine perhaps being the most appropriate. In the tropics it bursts into a flaming sheet of colour at the first approach of winter and stays that way for months.

But gardeners away from the tropics need not feel left out, for *Pyrostegia* will tolerate the odd very light frost if planted against a sun-drenched, wind-sheltered wall. Of course, at the limit of its range, the display is shorter and may be put off until spring. Any soil seems to suit so long as it is well-drained, and the plant grows fast if watered year round. It is an ideal cover for walls, pergolas and fences.

PYRUS

(**pai**-rəs)
Pear
ROSACEAE

We all believe blind Freddie could tell the difference between an apple and a pear – and we would probably all be wrong. For until quite recent times many trees we now know as Quince, Medlar and Crabapple were classed, with many others, as Pears, or botanically as *Pyrus* species.

Pear fruits, for instance, are not necessarily 'pear-shaped'. Sometimes they are round,

Pyrus communis. Pear Blossom

sometimes flattened like a tomato. Their flowers are similar to apple blossom, which is to say they are like white, single roses, and they are as showy in the garden as any ornamental blossom tree. For example *P. salicifolia*, the lovely Willow-leaf Pear from Asia Minor, with its light, flat heads of snowy blossom, would make a splendid feature for an all-white garden.

The Indian Pear, *P. pashia*, has toothed, dark leaves and is quite colourful in bloom, with pink buds and white blossom. The European Wild Pear, *P. communis*, is the ancestor of all the pears we grow for the table. It has varieties with fruits of many colours, and the single flowers may be white or pink, generally with a rather acrid perfume.

Quisqualis indica. Rangoon Creeper

Ramonda myconi. Balkan Primrose

Ranunculus acris. Meadow Buttercup

QUISQUALIS
(kwis-**kwah**-ləs)
Rangoon Creeper
COMBRETACEAE

A showy shrub that will climb if given support, the Rangoon Creeper, *Quisqualis indica*, can also be grown as a sprawling, large-scale groundcover or pruned as a dense, mounded shrub.

A tender tropical, it will take to life in cooler frost-free gardens if given a warm, sunny spot. It needs extra-rich but well-drained soil, regularly fertilised during spring and summer. Generous warm-weather watering should give way to drier conditions in winter, and the plant is pruned in early spring by removing some of the oldest shoots entirely. Clusters of red buds open to white flowers, maturing through pink to red, beginning to appear in summer, and building to a peak display between summer and autumn. Flowers are pleasantly scented.

RAMONDA
(rae-**mon**-də)
Balkan Primrose, Pyrenean Primrose
GESNERIACEAE

For cooler climates than other Gesneriads, *Ramondas* are native to southern European mountain ranges and are known as Balkan Primrose or Pyrenean Primrose. They can be grown in shallow pots of loam, sand and leafmould mixed with small limestone chunks to simulate their natural growing conditions, or raised outdoors in rockery crevices or gaps in dry stone walls. Keep them moist (though never sodden) particularly in hot weather, and grow where they get some sun but not during the hottest part of the day.

Ramondas quite resemble their African Violet relatives and are about the same size. The flowers are generally lavender-violet, but occasionally pink or white. They appear two to six on short stems in late spring. *R. myconi* is propagated from leaf cuttings or divisions in the same way as African Violets (Saintpaulia, which see). Once again, however, it does not like hot conditions, is best grown indoors in warm climates.

RANUNCULUS
(ran-**unk**-yoo-ləs)
Buttercup, Crowsfoot, Gold Knots, Persian Buttercup, Turban Buttercup
RANUNCULACEAE

The common Buttercup is only one of 250 *Ranunculus* species, largely native to the northern hemisphere but with some alpine species south of the equator. Persian Buttercups (*R. asiaticus*) are among the most popular of annual bedding plants, though classed as tuberous perennials.

They are commonly started in autumn from small claw-shaped corms, which may be planted direct or (because their growing season is long) in a shallow seedling flat for later setting out. They can also be started from seed sown under glass in winter (maintaining a temperature of 21ºC/70ºF until leaves appear) for early bloom the following winter. Whether you raise your own plants or take the easy way out with corms, they should be set out in a sunny position in moist soil enriched with compost and fertiliser. They do best in cool districts, either close to the coast or in the hills. It is believed they are the Bible's 'Lilies of the Field' which outshone King Solomon.

Many other species are popular subjects in the perennial garden. The Double Buttercup, *R. acris* 'Flore Pleno', can make a great display in a waterside position. It is propagated from root divisions.

Ranunculus asiaticus. Persian Buttercup

Raoulia grandiflora. Mat Daisy

Rehmannia elata. Chinese Foxglove

RAOULIA
(rou-**oo**-lee-ə)
Scabweed, Mat Daisy, Vegetable Sheep
ASTERACEAE

Though many species of *Raoulia* are called by botanists, few are chosen for the home garden. Yet they are the most charming of alpine mat-forming plants, found generally on gravelly soil near New Zealand glaciers, and suitable for similar garden conditions with perfect drainage. Their climatic range is between cold and cool temperate; their needs, continual moisture.

Raoulias can be raised from seed, or from divisions in early summer. All varieties spread outward to form a mat, leaving the centre to die out.

R. australis bears yellowish flowers, *R. grandiflora* white. Neither grows more than a few centimetres high.

Rebutia senilis. Crown Cactus

REBUTIA
(rə-**byoo**-tee-ə)
Crown Cactus
CACTACEAE

Rebutias are undemanding dwarf cacti that reward the grower with a generous display of fairly long-lasting spring flowers right around the plant, usually at ground level.

R. senilis blooms in red-orange but other species have white, yellow, pink, red or bicoloured flowers, which are commonly 5cm/2in across.

Rebutias are easy to grow in acid, gravelly compost in full sun. During the warmer months they should be kept moist and humid, but as winter nears, reduce the watering. In frosty climates, withhold winter water altogether, or the spring flowers will disappoint.

REHMANNIA
(rae-**man**-nee-ə)
Chinese Foxglove, Beverly Bells
SCROPHULARIACEAE

Related to such popular annuals as the Foxglove, Snapdragon and Linaria, handsome *Rehmannias* are a small Chinese genus of perennials suited to a wide range of climates. In warm-winter areas they spread rapidly to form large clumps of striking evergreen foliage, the leaves deeply toothed. In colder districts, the plant becomes completely deciduous and dies back. In both places deep, rich soil and plenty of water are needed to produce the 45cm/18in nodding stems of gorgeous, golden-throated flowers. These may be pink, purple or creamy-yellow according to species. They appear summer long and are splendid for cutting.

The most popular species, *R. elata*, flowers well for several years, then should be replaced from cuttings or seedlings; the latter will not bloom until the second year. Seeds are sown under glass in winter, germinating in around 3 weeks. *Rehmannia* is effective grown in the shade of deciduous trees.

Reinwardtia indica. Yellow Flax

REINWARDTIA
(rain-**wort**-ee-ə)
(SYN Linum)
Yellow Flax
LINACEAE

Coarse, untidy plants that light up the cold weather with brilliant golden flowers, *Reinwardtias* are grown from winter division or from soft-tip cuttings taken in spring. A light, well-drained soil is best, and *Reinwardtias* should be attempted in warm-winter districts only, for they are not in the

Renanthera storiei. Sealing-wax Orchid

least hardy. They look well in semi-shade, but the flowers, which appear for about 6 weeks in early winter, show up best in full sun, provided ample water can be laid on.

Mature plants grow leggy and should be pinched out regularly to force branching. This will also result in more flowers. Encourage the formation of a dense clump by chopping the whole plant back to half height in late winter, after the last blooms have faded. Yellow Flax is evergreen, though sparsely foliaged, producing many erect or arching 1m/3ft stems from a suckering rootstock. Its leaves are simple and rather soft. If grown in a pot, it can be hidden among other shrubs when not in bloom.

RENANTHERA

(ren-**an**-thur-∂)
Kidney Orchid, Sealing-wax Orchid
ORCHIDACEAE

This small genus of orchids from tropical Asia (found naturally from Vietnam to Malaysia) is limited to about 15 species, few of which are seen in cultivation outside the heated glasshouse. The most popular is *Renanthera storiei*, sometimes called the Sealing-wax Orchid because of the colour of its vivid red blooms. These are the typical open shape of many Asian orchid species, up to 7.5cm/3in in diameter, and appear in panicles of 100 and more blooms. Each panicle grows from the nodes of a tough, epiphytic plant that may climb to 3.5m/10ft high.

Renantheras are grown from cuttings of leafy stem complete with aerial roots. These are potted up in spring, kept moist, and will grow through the tropical summer with light, regular applications of fertiliser. In the right tropical conditions the plants bloom continually, but peak in spring. *Renantheras* will survive temperatures as low as 10ºC/50ºF/. They enjoy full sun in winter, light dappled shade on hot summer days.

RESEDA

(**ress**-∂-d∂)
Mignonette
RESEDACEAE

Quaint, old-world Mignonette, or *Reseda odorata* as it is properly known, is scarcely spectacular. When not in bloom it could easily be passed over as a weed. But ah! when

Reseda odorata. Mignonette

its tiny, greenish flowers open, who could overlook the fragrance?

Mignonette is best planted in drifts, either close to a door or window or in a large container on a frequently used terrace. It needs fertile soil rich in humus, and lime is definitely called for. As it does not transplant well, it should be sown in lightly raked soil in autumn or spring (winter, too, in mild climates) and kept moist for the germination period of 14 days. Thin seedlings to 25cm/10in spacings. Mignonette grows fast to a maximum height of 45cm/18in, and the insignificant but richly perfumed flowers appear for a few weeks in late spring or early summer; bees adore them. Dead-head regularly for prolonged bloom.

RETAMA

(r∂-**tah**-m∂)
(SYN Genista, Lygos, Spartium)
White Weeping Broom, Mt Etna Broom
FABACEAE

So far as the leaves of this small genus of broom plants is concerned, it's here today, gone tomorrow! They fall almost immediately they are produced. In any case, they are not important. We love *Retama* for the white pea-flowers, borne profusely along the silvery stems in spring. They have a sweet, almost cloying fragrance.

Retama monosperma is a short-trunked plant with weeping, slender stems, found all about the Mediterranean. Able to withstand heat, it also thrives down to –3ºC/27ºF, and seems to do well anywhere.

Retama monosperma. White Weeping Broom

Rhaphiolepis delacourii 'Springtime'. Indian Hawthorn

Rheum palmatum 'Atrosanguineum'. Ornamental Rhubarb

Retama is propagated almost exclusively from seed. Just collect it in autumn, store it in a cool, dry place and sow it in pots of sandy mix the following spring after a 24-hour soak in warm water. Set the seedlings out in well-drained, gravelly soil, water lightly and just watch the action! Prune all over lightly after bloom.

RHAPHIOLEPIS
(raff-ee-oh-**lee**-pis)
(SYN Raphiolepis)
Indian Hawthorn, Yeddo Hawthorn
ROSACEAE

Most useful and attractive of shrubs, *Rhaphiolepis* can be relied on for spring display in climates from cold to warm temperate. Hardy down to –9ºC/15ºF, they also thrive close to the sea in sandy soil and are a problem only in dry, desert areas, where they need semi-shade.

Rhaphiolepis indica. Indian Hawthorn

Although *Rhaphiolepis* grow readily from seed, they normally save you the trouble by producing seedlings freely. However, these may not be true to type and a more reliable method is to take cuttings of half-ripened tips during autumn and winter.

All species of *Rhaphiolepis* do best in a rich, well-drained soil and need lots of water through spring and summer. Sweet-scented *R. indica* has slightly toothed leaves and sprays of delicate pink bloom followed by black berries. More commonly seen Yeddo Hawthorn (*R. umbellata*) has leathery, simple leaves, and red-centred white flowers in packed clusters. Both have reddish new foliage. Hybrid *R. delacourii* has several cultivars, including compact 'Springtime', with pink flowers and bronze-pink new foliage.

RHEUM
(ree-∂m)
Ornamental Rhubarb, Giant Rhubarb
POLYGONACEAE

One of the world's great waterside plants, perennial *Rheum palmatum* is closely related to the edible Rhubarb, and makes a stunning display in moist, deep soil. *Rheums* should be planted at least 1m/3ft apart during winter, in a position with as much sun as possible; water heavily, and feed with liquid fertiliser at least monthly.

The showy heart-shaped leaves grow rapidly; deeply lobed and reddish-purple when young, they change to green at maturity, and are far larger than those of the culinary variety. In rich soil, tall, bracted flowering stems may tower as high as 2.5m/8ft with

sufficient feeding, each topped with loosely-branched panicles of red bead-like flowers during summer.

Rheum is propagated from division in the colder months, and should be cut back hard in late autumn. It is hardy, and can survive severe frosts.

RHIPSALIDOPSIS
(rip-sal-i-**dop**-s∂s)
Easter Cactus
CACTACEAE

Here we are playing word games again! At one time these jungle beauties were called Schlumbergera, but the taxonomists have been at work and now we all have to change

Rhipsalidopsis gaertneri. Easter Cactus

Rhipsalidopsis rosea. Pink Star Cactus

Rhodanthe manglesii. Swan River Everlasting

the labels to read *Rhipsalidopsis*. Two species are commonly grown, both with colour variations, and they prefer semi-shade with plenty of humidity. I grow mine in hanging pots on my terrace and use a peaty compost with plenty of leafmould and sand to improve the drainage.

Like related Epiphyllums (which see), these leafy-looking plants consist not of leaves at all, but of flattened stems, from which flowers appear at Easter in the northern hemisphere and in spring in the southern. They need indoor warmth in cold months, for stem segments tend to drop when the temperature goes below 5°C/41°F.

The two principal species are *R. gaertneri*, the Easter Cactus, and *R. rosea*, Pink Star Cactus. The former has 5cm/2in scarlet flowers like many-pointed stars, while the latter produces vivid musk-pink hose-in-hose blooms.

RHODANTHE
(roh-**dan**-thee)
(SYN Acroclinium, Helipterum)
Paper Daisy, Rose Sunray, Everlasting, Strawflower
ASTERACEAE

Often sold under their earlier names, these Australian annuals and perennials all enjoy the same sandy soil and dislike humidity.

The showy Paper Daisy, *Rhodanthe chlorocephala* subsp. *rosea* (sometimes listed as *Acroclinium roseum* or *Helipterum roseum*) is grown worldwide for its ease of cultivation and for its many uses, both in the garden and in dried flower arrangements. The 2.5cm/1in blooms, in shades of white, pink, and red, have a papery texture; the petals close on dull days.

The Swan River Everlasting, *Rhodanthe manglesii* (syn *Helipterum manglesii*) is a shorter, finer plant. Its 30cm/12in stems are

thin and wiry, with small, stem-clasping leaves. The 5cm/2in daisy flowers appear in spring and continue right through until summer. They have several rows of incurved petals, generally opening a deep pink but fading to white and beige tones.

Sow seed of either species direct in sandy, lightly raked soil in earliest spring and water lightly. Germination is fast and the plants may begin to bloom when still quite small. Dead-head regularly to stimulate branching and flower display.

For indoor use, cut stems before blooms are fully open, hang heads-downward in bunches in a dry shady place. When stems are dry, arrange lavishly without water.

Rhodanthe chlorocephala subsp. *rosea*. Paper Daisy

RHODIOLA
(roh-dee-**oh**-lə)
Rose-root
CRASSULACEAE

The generic name *Rhodiola* and the specific one *rosea* are derived from the Greek and Latin for a rose, so one expects that the flowers of this succulent perennial will be pink. Yet they are yellow, in pleasing contrast to the grey-green leaves which develop attractive purple tints if the plant is kept a bit on the dry side. The rosy connection is from the rootstock, which when dried smells like a rose and used to be used in perfumery and pot-pourri. The plant dies back to the roots in winter, and it needs no special care, flourishing in any temperate climate, fertile but perfectly drained soil, and a sunny spot. it grows about 25cm (10in) tall and flowers in early summer. You may still find it offered under its old name *Sedum rosea*.

RHODOCHITON
(roh-doh-**kai**-tən)
Purple Bells
SCROPHULARIACEAE

I have seen this dainty, free-flowering climber from Mexico in glass-houses of cool climates, though I am assured it can be grown outdoors in any range from cool to really tropical. It is evergreen, with sparsely-toothed foliage reminding one of related Asarina (which see).

There is only one species, *Rhodochiton atrosanguineus*, and it grows fast from seed sown in early spring under glass. Seedlings are set out when the weather is continuously warm and will twine around any available

Rhodiola rosea. Rose-root

Rhododendron augustinii. Blue Rhododendron

support. Individual blooms (on slender, thread-like stalks) are purple and resemble others of the Antirrhinum family. They are, however, protected by a showy pink calyx.

RHODODENDRON
(roh-doh-**den**-drən)
Tree Rose, Rhododendron
Ericaceae

Assuming such a visit to be possible, a garden fancier from the mid-19th century would be amazed on visiting a modern *Rhododendron* nursery. Almost every plant he saw would be quite unfamiliar. There would be new flower forms, new colours, new habits of growth, new fragrances. Many of the plants might be unrecognisable to him as *Rhododendrons* at all, so great has the change been in this beautiful genus of plants. Not much over a century ago, gardeners of Europe and North America were limited to

Rhododendron 'Fragrantissimum'

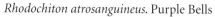
Rhodochiton atrosanguineus. Purple Bells

Rhododendron ponticum. Common Rhododendron

Rhododendron 'Simbu Sunset'. Vireya Rhododendron

Rhododendron lochiae. Queensland Tree Rose

Rhododendron 'Pink Cherub'. Rhododendron

Rhododendron 'President Roosevelt'. Rhododendron

only a few species from mountain areas of their own countries. Perhaps 15 were known in all, as opposed to the 500 and more grown today. And that is only *species* – modern *hybrids* would number several thousand at least.

The *Rhododendron* is a perfect example of supply and demand as applied to horticulture. The later 19th century saw the rise of the great private estate, as newly rich captains of industry vied with the aristocracy in creating their private pleasure domes surrounded by park-like gardens. They engaged designers and landscaping teams who in turn sought out more spectacular

plants to furnish their demesnes. There was such big money to be made that many larger nurseries commissioned plant hunters to explore and bring back new species from all over the globe. One of the great success stories of that era was the *Rhododendron*, whose species were discovered by the hundred in China, Tibet and Assam.

Today, among all flowering shrub genera, majestic *Rhododendrons* surely reign supreme for the sheer size, brilliance and profusion of their flowers. Most types produce great trusses of bloom in a colour range no other plant genus can rival. Even out of bloom they are attractive, densely clothed with dark, evergreen leaves.

But there's a catch. *Rhododendrons* won't grow just anywhere. Most are native to, and do best in, places where winters are cool to cold, springs cool and moist, summers warm and humid. They grow perfectly in many parts of Britain and Ireland, in the western United States, in New Zealand and in the mountain tablelands of eastern Australia. *Rhododendrons* do best protected from hot afternoon sun and strong winds – especially hot *drying* winds. They stay fresh in the rising humidity below tall trees. Generally speaking, the cooler the climate, the more sun is tolerated, especially in winter. Full shade all day results in disappointing flowers, but in warm areas such as the east coasts of Australia and South Africa and the coast of southern California, shade is beneficial, even necessary, during much of the summer. There, light year-round shade may be the only way of growing these desirable shrubs.

Wherever planted, soil should be water-retentive, yet porous enough to allow excess water to drain freely. A light, sandy loam enriched with well-rotted compost or leaf-mould is suitable. *Rhododendrons* detest lime and must have an acid soil with a pH of between 5 and 6. Keep the plants consistently moist year-round – but never sodden – and mulch annually with compost or old manure to conserve water and feed the surface roots. *Rhododendrons* hybridise easily, so do not come true from seed. Propagate them vegetatively from spring layers lifted in autumn or from 12cm/5in semi-hardwood cuttings. These should be taken from early summer to mid-autumn and struck in a gritty mix with warmth and humidity.

Because of their mountain origins, many *Rhododendrons* are perfectly hardy and will withstand temperatures below freezing. Others, from more tropical regions, can stand only the odd light frost.

The Vireyas or tropical Rhododendrons originate in misty mountain areas of Malaysia, Indonesia and New Guinea, with one species, *R. lochiae*, found in northeastern Australia. Warm temperate climates suit them; they tolerate humidity but not frost, and can bloom most of the year. Colours include red, orange, yellow , white and pink; some are fragrant.

Your local nurseryman will advise on the best species for your area. The name *Rhododendron*, most appropriately, means Tree Rose.

Rhododohypoxis 'Appleblossom'. Rose Grass

Rhodohypoxis baurii. Rose Grass

RHODOHYPOXIS
(roh-doh-hai-**pok**-sis)
Rose Grass
AMARYLLIDACEAE

A dainty, dwarf member of the Amaryllis family, *Rhodohypoxis* or Rose Grass makes a beautiful sight when in bloom. Small, tuberous-rooted perennials from the mountains of South Africa, they are dormant in winter and have proved hardy in England. However, they must be kept as dry as possible during cold weather or they will rot. Where winters are wet, the tubers can be stored until spring or the plants grown in pots, sheltered from rain. Plant tubers in early spring into very well-drained acid soil in full sun. The silky-haired leaves will soon appear, growing into grass-like tufts 10cm/4in tall. Masses of star-shaped, rose-red flowers appear during spring and summer, and potted specimens can be brought indoors in bloom. The flowers open singly on wiry stems and are pale pink in bud. There are named cultivars in white and shades of pink, red and purple.

RHODOLEIA
(roh-doh-**lee**-∂)
Silk Rose, Champara, Hong Kong Rose
HAMAMELIDACEAE

Not really common anywhere, even in its native southern China, the Silk Rose, *Rhodoleia championii*, was first discovered only in 1849. But it has been distributed to all continents by garden connoisseurs and is worth seeking out as a medium-sized specimen tree for sheltered gardens. Given the protection of other, larger trees, it will reach 8m/26ft and flower heavily when quite young.

A leggy, sparsely branched plant, it resembles some of the larger Rhododendrons in habit, but is not related to them at all. The dark, leathery, oblong

Rhodoleia championii. Silk Rose

leaves are perfectly smooth above, greyish beneath, and crowd at the end of branchlets. New foliage buds appear in whorls about a central leading shoot on each branch. The spring flowers (midwinter in frost-free areas) appear in heads of 5 to 10 from leaf axils near branch tips: wide, hanging bells of purest carmine about 4cm/2in across. Each blossom is actually a group of 5 flowers, surrounded by a common row of petals.

Rhodoleia enjoys humidity, part sun, and deep, acid soil. It is increased from ripened cuttings.

Ribes speciosum. California Fuchsia

RIBES
(**rai**-bees)
Flowering Currant, Fuchsia Gooseberry
SAXIFRAGACEAE

Though they are not the fruiting currants of the kitchen garden, these *Ribes* species certainly look good enough to eat. They are, of course, members of the same genus, which includes some 150 species in all, mostly native to the Americas, but with some from other parts of the northern hemisphere. The

Ribes sanguineum. Red-flowering Currant

Ricinocarpos pinifolius. Wedding Bush

illustrated species are favourite shrubs for cooler-climate gardens, producing masses of spicily fragrant blooms, usually on spiny stems. These appear for quite a few weeks towards the end of winter and into spring. Where autumns are frosty, most species will colour well.

Ribes can be grown from hardwood cuttings taken as soon as the leaves fall. Cuttings should be 30cm/12in long, and potted so that only the tips appear above the soil. Where winters are frigid, bury the cuttings outdoors until spring, then pot up. *Ribes* are deciduous, have lobed leaves, and grow best in well-drained soil with an annual spring top dressing. Well-grown plants can reach 3m/10ft. *R. speciosum* and *R. aureum* defoliate unless watering is continued in summer. *R. sanguineum* prefers a cool, moist climate and is hardy down to −10°C/14°F.

Richea scoparia. Broom Heath

RICHEA

(**reesh**-ee-∂)
Kerosene Bush, Broom Heath
EPACRIDACEAE

Though these remarkable plants are characteristically Tasmanian, there are two less well-known species in mainland Australia. They are rather straggly shrubs with pointed leaves that clasp the stems, and long spikes of flowers which look much their best in bud, as when the flowers open the petals fall off. Most famous is the giant 'Pandani' of Tasmania, *Richea pandanifolia*, with leaves up to 1.2m/4ft long crowded at the top of a pole-like trunk. But the other species are lower shrubs, the best known being *R. scoparia*, which gets its common name Kerosene Bush from the strong odour of the flowers, whose petals may be white, pink or orange. It grows in abundance all over Tasmania's mountains, but is tricky in gardens, liking a cool but not frosty climate, regular moisture, perfect drainage, and unpolluted air. The genus name honours French botanist Claude Riche, who became separated from his ship-mates on the Western Australian coast in 1797 and presumably perished.

Robinia pseudoacacia. Black Locust

RICINOCARPOS

(rai-**see**-noh-kah-p∂s)
Wedding Bush
EUPHORBIACEAE

Charming shrubs represented on both sides of the Australian continent, the small genus *Ricinocarpos* is ideal for the compact garden. Two eastern Australian species are commonly grown: the pink-flowered *R. bowmanii* and the white-flowered *R. pinifolius* or Wedding Bush. Both have soft needle-leaves and masses of fragrant, starry flowers in spring. They develop into rounded bushes about 1m/3ft high and wide, and seem to prefer an open, sunny situation.

For reasons still not clear, *Ricinocarpus* can be hard to establish in gardens, but some success has been had sowing seed directly where it is to grow, into very well-drained, sandy, acid soil. Neither species is hardy to severe frost.

ROBINIA

(roh-**bin**-ee-n∂)
Locust, Black Locust, Rose Acacia
FABACEAE

As American as apple pie, all 20 species of the genus *Robinia* occur naturally within the mainland of the USA. They are generally spiny members of the pea family and, like so many of their relatives, bear fragrant flowers and dangling pods. The pods led to the popular name Black Locust, as early colonists found they resembled those of the related Locust Tree of southern Europe (*Ceratonia siliqua*).

The commonly seen and frequently naturalised species is *R. pseudoacacia*, from central North America. It is a tall tree, growing to 25m/80ft, with a picturesque gnarled trunk and branches. Its deciduous leaves are a handsome light green. For

Robinia ambigua 'Bella-rosea'. Rose Acacia

Romneya coulteri var. *trichocalyx*. Matilija Poppy

garden usage, many attractive cultivars have been developed from it, differing mainly in form, the presence or absence of spines, and the colour of the foliage.

All *Robinias* bear their flowers in spring in long, pendulous racemes. Those of *R. pseudoacacia* are a creamy-white colour, but several less commonly seen species produce flowers in various shades of pink. These have been crossed with *R. pseudoacacia* to produce rose-flowered cultivars such as the illustrated *R. ambigua* 'Bella-rosea'.

Propagate species from seed or suckers; the fancy varieties must be grafted.

RODGERSIA
(rod-**jer**-see-ə)
SAXIFRAGACEAE

These handsome perennials, their wild origins ranging from Nepal to Japan, never seem to have acquired an English name, gardeners being content to use the Latin one which honours Admiral John Rodgers, USN (1812–82), who commanded the scientific expedition to the Japanese islands during which *Rodgersia podophylla* was discovered. Along with *R. pinnata*, this is still the most familiar species. All are plants for the damp soil by the side of a pond, which they will beautify from spring to autumn with really splendid leaves; the sprays of small white or pink flowers on their 1.2m/4ft stems are a beautiful midsummer bonus. Cool temperate climates and acid soil are preferred.

ROMNEYA
(**rom**-nee-ə)
Matilija Poppy, Tree Poppy, Fried-egg Flower
PAPAVERACEAE

'A miracle of loveliness' is one botanical writer's description of the gorgeous Matilija Poppy, *Romneya coulteri*; 'Fried-egg Flower' is another less elegant but quite understandable name for this stunning hardy perennial from southern California, which appears to thrive on neglect in dry, loose, gravelly soil.

Rodgersia aesculifolia. Rodgersia

Grown from autumn divisions, its grey-green, deeply divided foliage will begin to emerge in winter and gradually build up to stems 2m/6ft and more in height. An occasional deep watering and a mulch of organic material will help it along, particularly at flowering time, which lasts for weeks in spring.

Romneya normally has 5 or even 6 petals, each seeming to be made from snow-white, wrinkled crepe. The central boss of golden stamens exudes a rich, delicious perfume. Each individual flower may reach 23cm/9in in diameter. Pick them by all means – they last for days! Cut the whole plant back hard in late autumn.

ROMULEA
(rom-**yoo**-lee-ə)
Wire Grass, Satin Flower
IRIDACEAE

Wire grass is not a compliment – Australian gardeners have given the name to *Romulea rosea* out of frustration at the strength of its wiry leaves, almost lawnmower-proof when it comes up unbidden in lawns, as it often does. The flowers, little pink stars, aren't much consolation, they feel – and indeed the genus has much better things to offer, like the lilac and gold *R. bulbocodium* and the

Romulea bulbocodium. Satin Flower

Rosa 'Nancy Hayward'. Gigantea Rose

startling red and black *R. sabulosa.* These are the size of small crocuses, and indeed the genus might be called South Africa's answer to the crocus, most of the 50 species coming from that country. They suffer from two faults in gardeners' eyes – the flowers only open out in bright sunshine and the plants are tender to frost – so they have never achieved the crocuses' popularity. A pity, I think.

RONDELETIA
(ron-dә-**lee**-shә)
Rondeletia
RUBIACEAE

These generally fragrant flowering shrubs hail from the Caribbean, where they give a continuous display. However, as none of them is hardy, their flowering period grows shorter the further away they are from the tropics. In cool temperate areas they are raised under glass with winter heat, but they can be grown outdoors anywhere temperatures never drop below freezing. In such climates, the clusters of tiny, fragrant flowers appear briefly in early spring, with a few here and there throughout summer.

Rondeletias do best in a soil that is barely acid and well drained, and need uniform moisture through the warmer months. Most often seen *R. amoena* and *R. odorata* can be raised from 10cm/4in cuttings taken in spring and struck indoors under warm, humid conditions. *R. strigosa*, which has a suckering habit, is best raised from divisions. All are evergreen and improve with an annual pruning.

Rondeletia strigosa. Hairy Rondeletia
Rondeletia amoena. Rondeletia

ROSA
(**roh**-zә)
Rose
ROSACEAE

Roses of one sort or another have been cultivated for at least 5000 years, making them the best-loved flower in history. The Chinese, we know from books, grew them around 3000 BC. Several millennia later, the Greeks had a word for them, *Rhodos*, and gave that name to the Mediterranean island of Rhodes, where they grew to perfection. Greek poets Sappho and Anacreon hailed the rose as the queen of flowers.

Later still, the Romans prized these flowers for their fragrance, enjoying them at banquets, as both a delicacy and a dedication to Venus, their goddess of love. Cleopatra spent 60 pounds' weight of gold to buy rose petals for the famous banquet where she seduced Mark Antony. They carpeted the decks of her galley 20 inches thick beneath a golden net.

Roman historian Pliny describes 12 varieties of rose that were cultivated in Rome. Some are still grown, but now take second place to the beauties raised by modern hybridists. New rose species introduced from Persia and India, and from China and North America, brought with them yellow, pink, bronze and cerise colourings, and the continuous blooming habit we now take so much for granted. The ancients knew roses only as red or white, and could look forward to their blooming only at the height of summer.

Roses are now grown all around the world, though wild species occur only north of the equator, and mainly in the temperate zone of all continents, although some have adapted to life almost on the edge of the tropics. Such a one is the Burmese *Rosa gigantea*, a parent of 'Nancy Hayward'; this is one of a limited number of roses suited to really warm climates.

Generally speaking, roses are at their best in areas with mildly alkaline soil of clay texture, though many patient growers have succeeded in raising prize-winning blooms in acid soil and have even adapted sand to a suitable tilth.

Over 250 wild species have been identified, and almost all of them have been used by hybridists to produce the rainbow of blooms available today. An entire book could be written on cultural directions for varying climates, and your local nurseryman is your best adviser.

In warm temperate climates, roses are planted in midwinter and normally pruned at the same time, except for winter flowering types. Where winters are harder, they are planted in autumn, given a heavy mulch over the roots and pruned when signs of new growth appear in spring.

Roses enjoy full sun, especially in the morning, and do best in a bed of their own, well away from marauding tree roots and without competition from other plants. They need regular feeding, and can exhaust the soil so completely that they leave it in a condition called 'rose sick'. A new rose should never be planted where one has been grown before without complete replacement of the soil over an area 1m/3ft square and as deep as the root system. Regular watering is essential, and a deep surface mulch around the root areas will help produce top-quality blooms.

While most rose plants bought today are of the Large-flowered (Hybrid Tea) or the Cluster-flowered (Floribunda) types, some of

Rosa 'Golden Showers'. Climbing Rose

Rosa 'Iceberg'. Cluster-flowered Rose

Rosa 'Eva'. Hybrid Musk Rose

Rosa 'Harison's Yellow'. Shrub Rose

Rosa laevigata. Cherokee Rose

Rosa 'Broadway'. Large-flowered Rose

Rosa banksiae lutea. Lady Bank's Rose

the original species are coming back into fashion. They do not flower as continuously as the modern hybrids, but have a beauty and fragrance all their own. In recent years, Miniature (Fairy) roses have established their popularity, with blooms that are perfect tiny replicas of their larger relatives; they can be grown in pots or window-boxes, and many have good continuity of bloom.

Roses are no more prone to attack by pests and diseases than any other group of plants, but their blooms are normally so perfect that any sign of damage stands out.

Aphids are the most obvious of pests, though probably the least serious. They crowd new growth of foliage and flower buds, sucking tasty juices and often leaving distortion in their wake. Blast them away with the hose or check with any spray formulated for sucking pests.

Grasshoppers of various kinds chew at foliage, and flower buds may be holed by caterpillars of several kinds. A systemic insecticide is more effective here. Prune away damaged foliage or buds.

A variety of fungus diseases may become apparent, particularly in humid weather. Most serious is powdery mildew, deposited as a thin white coating on new foliage, causing it to distort. Spraying with a recommended fungicide will usually wipe it out, but the damaged leaves should be pruned away and burned.

Black spot is a fungus clearly described by its popular name. Mature leaves become spotted with black or dark brown blotches which soon increase in size. Leaves finally turn yellow and drop. All diseased foliage must be cut and burned, and the affected plant sprayed with a reliable fungicide. It is difficult to cure completely, but in the long run the plant does not seem to be unduly damaged provided regular hygiene is practised.

Finally, a fungus known as dieback may enter the plant's sap system through pruning cuts. All dead wood should be cut away with sterilised secateurs, and large cuts sealed with a bitumen pruning compound.

Roses are such good value that hardly anyone bothers to propagate their own. However, they can be raised from cuttings taken in midsummer. An elderly cousin of mine has been doing this for years and has a fine collection of roses as a result.

ROSCOEA
(ross-koh-ee-∂)
Mountain Ginger
ZINGIBERACEAE

Nature's gift to cool-climate gardeners everywhere, the magnificent *Roscoeas* are high-altitude members of the ginger family from China and the Himalayas. Unlike other genera of this mostly tropical family, *Roscoeas* can tolerate several degrees of frost.

R. humeana, from China, produces showy violet-purple flowers, in appearance somewhere between an iris and an orchid. *R. cautleoides* has yellow to orange blooms; other species flower darker purple or in a butterscotch shade.

Roscoeas need rich, well-watered and well-drained soil, but in cooler gardens they prefer drier conditions in winter. At the limit of their range, stems can be cut down in late autumn and the roots protected with a thick mulch.

Roscoea cautleoides. Mountain Ginger

Rosmarinus officinalis. Rosemary

Rossioglossum grande. Clown Orchid, Tiger Orchid

ROSMARINUS

(roz-ma-**ree**-n∂s)

Rosemary

LAMIACEAE

A tough, picturesque shrub that puts up with a great deal of heat and poor soil, Rosemary is also frost hardy to around –5ºC/23ºF. The glossy aromatic leaves, much used in cooking, are unaffected by the salt-laden winds that sweep seaside gardens.

Pale lavender flower spikes appear in winter, spring and autumn, and bring bees from far and wide. Rosemary (*Rosmarinus officinalis*) tends to woodiness and should be pruned regularly – an all-over trim after bloom is better than occasional hard pruning. The plant produces erect, leafy branches up to 2m/6ft tall and somewhat wider. It makes a splendid hedge, and there's a prostrate cultivar which is a useful wall plant.

Roscoea humeana. Mountain Ginger

ROSSIOGLOSSUM

(**ross**-ee-oh-**gloss**-∂m)

Tiger Orchid

ORCHIDACEAE

Many orchid fanciers still prefer to give *Rossioglossum grande* its old name *Odontoglossum grande*, and indeed it does look very like an Odontoglossum and is grown in the same way – that is, in a well-warmed greenhouse. (It comes from Guatemala.) But the botanists appear to be right: its stubborn refusal to interbreed with any Odontoglossum species proves it is not one of their tribe. This is frustrating to orchid breeders, as it is a splendid large flower in a unique combination of chestnut and gold, and hybrids from it could be dazzling. But it seems this is not to be. It flowers in autumn, and deserves every care.

ROTHMANNIA

(roth-**man**-nee-∂)

Tree Gardenia

RUBIACEAE

Known for many years as Gardenia globosa, and still sometimes sold under that name, *Rothmannia globosa* (together with several other Gardenias) has been switched to a new generic name but is, for all that, no less fragrant or desirable a specimen for the home garden.

The *Rothmannias* are small, lightweight trees with almost black branches and shining Gardenia-type leaves to 15cm/6in long. Like true Gardenias, they enjoy acid soil, plenty of water and regular feeding with an acid-based fertiliser or manure. The spring blooms are quite different from those of the Gardenias, being bell-shaped. In the popular *R. globosa*

Rothmannia globosa. Tree Gardenia

they are creamy-white, borne in clusters at branch ends and leaf axils. Each bloom is broadly tubular, about 5cm/2in long, with round-pointed petals folded outward to reveal a series of pink lines decorating the open throat. The tree is often partly deciduous at flowering time and blooms are followed by woody, dark brown seed capsules 2cm/³⁄₄in wide. *R. globosa* is not hardy at all.

RUBUS

(**roo**-b∂s)

Bramble, Flowering Raspberry

ROSACEAE

For those addicted to the Raspberry, that most delectable of fruits, the illustrated variety will come as a great disappointment. Yes, *Rubus odoratus* is one of those most illogical of plants, a fruit that doesn't bear. It's not much chop as a bramble either, preferring to remain in the shape of a compact bush. But flower it does in profusion – producing masses of musk-pink blooms like single roses.

Rubus odoratus × 'Tridel'. Flowering Raspberry

Rudbeckia hirta 'Irish Eyes'. Cone Flower

Propagate this *Rubus* from division of the root system any time during winter dormancy, setting out the divisions in well-drained ordinary soil. It grows generally to 1.2m/4ft high, but spreads much wider. The flowers open in late spring in a cool temperate climate.

RUDBECKIA
(rud-**beck**-ee-ə)
Gloriosa Daisy, Cone Flower, Marmalade Daisy, Black-eyed Susan
ASTERACEAE

Spectacular *Rudbeckias* or Gloriosa Daisies give your annual display more bounce to the ounce of seed than any other flower. Not fussy, with full sun and plenty of water they produce enormous, single daisy flowers up to 18cm/7in across, and in razzle-dazzle combinations of yellow, orange and mahogany. The raised, cone-shaped eyes are usually purple, black or brown, but in one popular cultivar, they are a pure emerald green. Naturally, it is sold as 'Green Eyes' or 'Irish Eyes'.

Actually biennial, the many hybrids of *R. hirta* flower easily from seed in a single season and are then disposed of to make room for other plants. But as they self-seed readily, they'll accept your kind invitation to

Rudbeckia hirta. Gloriosa Daisy

come again. Sow seed outdoors in spring or summer for bloom the following year, or sow in winter indoors over heat for late summer and autumn bloom. Germination takes 5–10 days, and the young plants are set out at 30–60cm/1–2ft spacings in early spring. Depending on type, they'll grow 45– 90cm/18–36in tall. Any soil suits if well drained; sun or part shade please them equally.

RUELLIA
(roo-**el**-lee-ə)
Christmas Pride
ACANTHACEAE

Best where winter temperatures remain above 10ºC/50ºF, *Ruellias* will tolerate lower temperatures if grown in a sheltered spot.

Ruellia macrantha. Christmas Pride

They are so lovely that they are often kept as winter-flowering greenhouse plants in the northern hemisphere. In milder areas, they are grown from spring cuttings, continually pinched to ensure bushy growth. Give them semi-shade through the hottest weather, plenty of water and a periodic application of liquid fertiliser to hurry growth along.

R. macrantha (one of about 150 species) needs as much winter sun as it can get to force flower production. Blooms are about 6cm/2½ in across, quilted in texture, and coloured a delicious violet-pink. Prune them back by all means, but the best display will come from newly struck autumn cuttings. A fibrous, well-drained soil is preferred, and under ideal conditions plants will grow to 2m/6ft – half that where summers are cool.

Rumex vesicarius. Rosy Dock

RUMEX

(**roo**-meks)
Rosy Dock, Monk's Rhubarb
POLYGONACEAE

Though the perennial *Rumex vesicarius* grows widely in outback Australia and makes a great show in country gardens, it is not native, but has somehow become naturalised from Egypt and western Asia. Recommended for hot, dry areas, it grows as easily from seed as its rampant relative the Roving Dock, which is a terrible pest.

Sprinkle seeds in lightly cultivated soil, cover and water. It'll be up and about in no time, spreading and sending up hollow stems with striking heart-shaped 10cm/4in leaves. These have a mealy surface, and each stem is topped in warm weather with racemes of tiny unremarkable flowers that develop into the flat rosy-red seed pods which are really the plant's chief attraction.

Russelia equisetiformis. Fountain Flower

Ruscus hypoglossum. Butcher's Broom

RUSCUS

(**rus**-kus)
Butcher's Broom, Boxholly
LILIACEAE

These quaint plants are often listed as shrubs, but in fact belong to the lily family, like Asparagus. *Ruscus* doesn't have any real leaves, but for reasons which are clear only to a professor of botany, it substitutes things called *cladodes*, which are a sort of flattened, leaf-shaped stems that bear tiny green and purple flowers right in their middles. And if plants of both sexes are present, these are followed by shiny red berries!

Ruscus species grow anywhere from cold to warm temperate climates, and look better in shade. They are propagated from ripe seed or divisions, but remember, divisions of a male plant will always be male and never bear berries. About 60cm/2ft is an average height.

RUSSELIA

(rus-**sell**-ee-ə)
Coral Blow, Fountain Flower
SCROPHULARIACEAE

Another Central American beauty, and wouldn't you know it from the lush, warm-weather growth and profusion of scarlet flowers like firecrackers at a Mexican fiesta! *Russelia* is a true horticultural celebration, turning from a tangled mess of leafless, cold-weather growth to a glowing fountain of coral-scarlet. Bloom begins in late spring, reaches a peak of profusion in summer, and slowly fades away as the weather turns cool in autumn.

Russelia likes a moderately rich, well-drained soil and is not hard to grow from cuttings. It grows fast, spreads rapidly into a stand of arching, sucker-like stems on which the foliage has been modified to tiny scales. The Coral Blow is a good seaside plant, or effective spilling over a bank or wall. Best results are stimulated by a light pruning of the spent flower heads in winter, at which time some old stems can be taken right back to the base. Hardy to −2ºC/28ºF, illustrated *R. equisetiformis* grows 60–100cm/2–3ft tall.

RUTA

(**roo**-tə)
Rue, Herb of Grace
RUTACEAE

A fine, medium-sized addition to any perennial border, *Ruta* is also grown in the herb garden, for small amounts of its finely chopped leaves add a tangy, bitter flavour to salads. For cooking, fresh sprigs are snipped and dried.

Ruta is native to southern Europe. Easily grown from seed sown outdoors in early spring in lightly cultivated soil, it can also be propagated from 10cm/4in cuttings of lateral shoots in late summer. *Ruta* forms a dense mat of blueish, finely divided foliage from which many-branched stems of golden, buttercup-type flowers emerge in the warmer months. Rue should be cut back to old wood in early spring to keep the 1m/3ft bushes compact.

Ruta graveolens. Rue, Herb of Grace

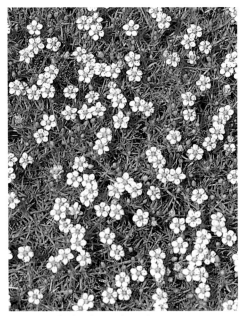

Sagina subulata 'Aurea'. Irish Moss

SAGINA

(s∂-**gee**-n∂)

Pearlwort, Irish Moss

CARYOPHYLLACEAE

Easily confused with the Mat Daisy, Raoulia (which see), these charming perennials are members of the carnation family, and native to the northern hemisphere. Some species are found right into the Arctic, others as far south as the Mediterranean, so there is a species suitable for most climates.

Saginas like a light soil with good drainage, and though small, add a decorative finishing touch to many garden areas. Grow them, for instance, between paving stones, or on shaded rock shelves. Propagate from winter division, keep lightly moist and look forward to the tiny spring flowers, scattered indeed like pearls on a carpet of green velvet.

Sagittaria latifolia. American Arrowhead

SAGITTARIA

(saj-i-te∂r-ee-∂)

Water Archer, Swamp Potato, Arrowhead

ALISMATACEAE

The European Arrowhead or Water Archer, *Sagittaria sagittifolia*, grows quite happily in my small pond, raising its arrow-shaped leaves and early-summer spikes of white flowers above the shallow water. I like it very much, and the double-flowered version, 'Flore-Pleno', is even more attractive. It has never tried to take over, but I hear that in Western Australia the South American *S. montevidensis* spreads so enthusiastically that it is an outlawed weed, despite its pretty purple-blotched flowers. Both species grow from tuberous roots which are edible, those of the north American *S. latifolia*, the Swamp Potato, being traditionally relished by Native Americans. Climates from warm temperate to quite cold are suitable.

SAINTPAULIA

(saent-**por**-lee-∂)

African Violet

GESNERIACEAE

First cultivated just over 100 years ago by Baron von Saint-Paul, African Violets are now popular indoor plants worldwide, and there are thousands of modern hybrids in shades of red, pink, mauve, lilac, purple and white. Some are bicoloured and ruffled, and types with big, fully double flowers are not uncommon. Others have simple, small flowers of remarkable delicacy.

All, I'm sure, are a great deal tougher than the experts tell us. I've read all about them being watered from below with warm water, sheltered from full sun and draughts. But one year, a friend looked after my house while I was vacationing, and when I returned, the 'violets' were flowering as never before. He'd been soaking them in a sink full of cold water, leaves and all – then standing them in a sunny window to dry out!

I also know an elderly lady who lives by the seafront. She grows her African Violets on an open verandah table, where they get wind and salt air for much of the year. She also hoses them when they dry out from the sun. They are magnificent. So if you think I avoid giving any definite advice about these delightful plants, you're right.

I find them easy to propagate from leaf cuttings which I cut off cleanly and stick among a layer of pebbles on top of a moist sand/peat mixture. This is so the leaves themselves don't touch the moist compost and rot. I also grow several varieties massed together about old, semi-rotted pieces of wood in simulation of their natural homes in tropical east Africa.

Saintpaulia 'Fancy Pants'. African Violet

Saintpaulia 'Red Rhapsodie'. African Violet

Salpiglossis sinuata. Painted Tongue

Salvia farinacea. Mealy-cup Sage

SALPIGLOSSIS
(sal-pee-**gloss**-əs)
Painted Tongue
SOLANACEAE

My award for the most improved annual must go to the spectacular Painted Tongue, *Salpiglossis sinuata*. Originally a tall, rangy plant from Chile, its growth habits and fantastic colour range have changed beyond measure in recent years. The new hybrids are lower, more heavily branched and wind resistant than the oldtimers, and bloom profusely throughout the summer in a veritable rainbow of colours. Their open, 8cm/3in flowers have deeply notched petals of yellow, purple, crimson, scarlet, orange, lavender and white, usually with gold or green throats and exquisite marbling in contrasting tones. There are strains particularly suited to pot culture, and others that grow to 90cm/3ft and are ideal for the back of a mixed annual display.

Sow the fine seed direct outdoors in spring or, for faster growth and longer display, sow under glass in winter, with the seed barely covered against light. Prick out into larger boxes, harden off the plants in fresh air, and plant mid-spring. Bloom can be expected in 12 weeks from seed. *Salpiglossis* are prone to aphis attack and root rot, like the related Petunias.

SALVIA
(sal-vee-ə)
Sage, Scarlet Sage, Gentian Sage, Clary, Ramona
LAMIACEAE

Blue, purple, red, white and pink are included in the colour range of *Salvia*, an enormously varied genus in the mint family, with which most of them share highly aromatic spear-shaped foliage. There are annual, perennial and shrubby species, and they are scattered in nature all over the warmer parts of the world. All have tubular, lipped flowers, produced along a spike that rises above the foliage. The individual blooms can be fairly big, as in *S. splendens*, *S. viridis* (syn *S. horminum*) and *S. gesneriiflora*, or tiny but densely packed as in *S. leucantha* and *S. farinacea*.

All the perennial *Salvias* make superb bedding subjects when densely planted, and are often used by paths where their foliage, bruised in passing, will exude a spicy fragrance. Two of the most popular and representative types are *S. farinacea*, a herbaceous perennial, which is cut back to ground level in autumn, and *S. gesneriiflora*, from Colombia, a shrubby perennial which develops quite a woody base.

Shrubby *S. leucantha*, the Mexican Bush Sage, grows to around 1m/3ft tall but usually

Salvia leucantha. Mexican Bush Sage

somewhat wider. Velvety purple flowers cover the top of the plant for many weeks from the end of summer. It is drought resistant and should be cut back hard in winter.

Salvias used for annual bedding display include *S. viridis*, a true annual growing to 45cm/18in and branching heavily to give a splendid mass of ornamental 5cm/2in bracts. These may be white, purple, blue, pink or red. The Bonfire Salvia or Scarlet Sage, *S. splendens*, often grown as an annual, is available in many fine strains, compact and tall-growing.

Salvia splendens. Bonfire Salvia

Salvia viridis 'Rose Queen'. Annual Clary

Sambucus nigra. European Elder

Salvias do best in sun but tolerate part shade. Well-drained soil enriched with rotted manure gives the best results. The herbaceous types are increased from warm-weather divisions, while the shrubby types can be propagated from 8cm/3in spring cuttings. All species can easily be raised from seed, though it is not viable for a long period. Taller *Salvias* need support in exposed spots: a criss-cross of twiggy sticks will do.

SAMBUCUS

(sam-**byoo**-cəs)
Elder

CAPRIFOLIACEAE

The European Elder, *Sambucus nigra*, is a tall deciduous shrub common in hedgerows and waste places in Europe and perhaps more familiar at the table than in the garden – both the cloyingly fragrant flowers and the black berries can be fermented into wine, elder flower wine being 'the poor man's riesling', that from the berries 'the poor man's port' . It is a pleasant shrub, very easy to grow in cool temperate climates, and there are several cultivars with decorative foliage, notably 'Laciniata' with its much-slashed leaves. It is eclipsed, however, by *S. racemosa* 'Plumosa Aurea', one of the very handsomest golden-leafed shrubs. It is usually cut to the ground in winter to encourage the best display of leaves, the flowers being rated unimportant.

SANDERSONIA

(san-dur-**soh**-nee-ə)
Christmas Bells, Chinese Lantern Lily

LILIACEAE

Named for a long-forgotten secretary of the Natal Horticultural Society, this beautiful climbing lily is to a South African Christmas what Blandfordia is in Australia (see Blandfordia). In warm temperate areas,

Sandersonia aurantiaca. Christmas Bells

Sandersonias can be grown in the open garden, but north of the equator they're mostly seen as glasshouse plants, blooming around July.

In earliest spring, enrich well-drained soil with leafmould; bury the tubers 5cm/2in deep and water very lightly. Step up the soakings as the shoots appear, and tie the growing stems lightly to a support until flowering is over. Propagate from offsets taken early in spring.

Sansevieria parva. Dwarf Snake Plant, Mother-in-law's Tongue

SANSEVIERIA
(san-sev-ee-e∂r-ee-∂)
Mother-in-law's Tongue, Lucky Plant, Bowstring Hemp, Devil's Tongue
AGAVACEAE

Along with Aspidistra, *Sansevieria trifasciata* is usually seen only in city offices. There, covered in dust and starved for light and water, it is always among the last of the indoor plants to die. Perhaps if more people knew that this remarkably tough plant responds to good growing conditions with stems of delightful flowers, the plant would be seen more in brighter interiors and warm-climate gardens. Honestly, give Mother-in-law's Tongue rich, well-drained but moist soil and the brightest filtered light and, come summer, you'll be rewarded with sprays of faintly fragrant, pale greenish-white blooms, rather like Tuberoses.

SANTOLINA
(san-toh-**lee**-n∂)
Lavender Cotton
ASTERACEAE

Delicate foliage like feather dusters has brought *Santolina chamaecyparissus* a special place in the mixed border or rockery. It is usually clipped back into a neat mound in early spring, but decorative foliage is only half the story. Left alone, *Santolina* will produce masses of button-sized blooms, like little yellow pompons, over several weeks in summer.

Santolinas of any species (there are 18), while tough and tolerant of neglect, are not frost hardy, being native to mild, coastal parts of the Mediterranean. But as gardeners have discovered, they will grow in any place where there is sun and water. Grow them from seed, cuttings or layers, and tip-prune often to retain a compact, rounded bush around 60cm/2ft tall. Try them in a light, sandy soil, with occasional but regular water. Dead-head continually.

Santolina chamaecyparissus. Lavender Cotton

SANVITALIA
(san-vi-**tah**-lee-∂)
Creeping Zinnia
ASTERACEAE

One species only of this interesting daisy flower is grown for annual display. It is the Creeping Zinnia, *Sanvitalia procumbens*, a prostrate, trailing plant that grows wild in Mexico and tries to act the same way in any sunny position with open, well-drained soil and regular water. It makes a splendid edging plant (if you keep it under control), a fine subject for hanging baskets, and is a rock garden sensation as it opens sheets of 2.5cm/1in black-centred, yellow daisy flowers from early summer right through to winter. There are compact, dwarf, double and semi-double cultivars.

Sanvitalia does not take to transplanta-tion; seed should be sown uncovered in its final position in lightly raked soil, as light is essential to germination. This can be done in autumn, and if the birds leave them alone, they sprout in 10–15 days. Thin the seedlings out to 15cm/6in spacings. In cold areas, sow indoors in winter.

Saponaria ocymoides. Rock Soapwort, Tumbling Ted

SAPONARIA
(sap-on-e∂r-ee-∂)
Soapwort, Bouncing Bet
CARYOPHYLLACEAE

Cottage garden favourites for at least four centuries, the European Soapworts or *Saponarias* are grown easily from seed, cuttings or division of the rootstock in spring. All species grow best in well-drained acid soil; lime is complete anathema to them. *S. officinalis*, the Common Soapwort, has been around longest, and its leaves really can be lathered up with water to remove grease from your hands. Late summer flowers may be pink, white or red.

Dwarf *S. ocymoides*, the Rock Soapwort, is a prostrate perennial that blooms so profuselythat its foliage is often hidden. There are red and white varieties as well as the illustrated pink type.

Sanvitalia procumbens. Creeping Zinnia

Saraca thaipingensis. Sorrowless Tree

SARACA

(sə-**rah**-kə)

Asoka, Sorrowless Tree

CAESALPINIACEAE

Precisely why the lovely *Saraca* should be known as the Sorrowless Tree I have been unable to discover, although it may be something to do with the cheerful display it puts on at many times of the year.

They are among the most spectacular flowering trees for subtropical gardens – particularly at the beginning and end of the tropical dry season. The flowers open a pale orange, then turn red within a couple of days, presenting a razzle-dazzle of gold and purple stamens.Though a large tree in its native jungles of Southeast Asia, *S. indica* remains a manageable 7m/23ft in cultivation. It enjoys a humid atmosphere and rich soil, and is grown in Florida, Hawaii, the Philippines and northern Australia.

In India, *Saraca* is called Asoka, and Buddha is said to have been born under one. *S. declinata* is very similar but with longer leaf stems. *S. thaipingensis* has yellow blossom.

SARCOCHILUS

(sah-koh-**kai**-ləs)

Orange-blossom Orchid, Ravine Orchid

ORCHIDACEAE

Most beloved of Australia's native orchids, *Sarcochilus* of the moist coastal valleys are now widely cultivated in many temperate parts of the world. They spread by means of white, worm-like aerial roots and are fairly easy to establish on old sections of tree trunk or in shallow pots of treefern chunks, or fibre and charcoal. *Sarcochilus* love moisture and should be sprayed regularly and kept damp and shaded the entire year. The evergreen species produce clusters of shiny, sickle-shaped leaves and arching stems of strongly perfumed 2.5cm/1in flowers.

Sarcochilus fitzgeraldii. Ravine Orchid

S. falcatus, Orange-blossom Orchid, produces 3–10 gold-lipped white flowers per stem, any time from midwinter in the tropics to late spring in cooler climates.

S. fitzgeraldii bears crimson-centred white (rarely pink) flowers in spring.

SARITAEA

(sa-ri-**tee**-ə)

(SYN Arrabidaea, Bignonia)

Purple Wonder

BIGNONIACEAE

Life for a garden writer must have been so simple before the wholesale name-changing of the Bignonia family. Think of any beautiful climber in those days, and it was almost certain to be a Bignonia of some sort. Now it might be called anything from Anemopaegma to Tecomanthe – both names hard to pronounce, even harder to remember.

Sarracenia excellens. Pitcher Plant

Saritaea magnifica. Purple Wonder

The one-time B. magnifica is a case in point, first becoming Arrabidaea and most recently *Saritaea magnifica*. Not surprisingly, people prefer its popular name, Purple Wonder! From tropical Colombia, this showy vining shrub climbs by means of tendrils, producing panicles of rosy-purple flowers throughout the warmer months. *Saritaea* makes a good fence cover.

SARRACENIA

(sa-rə-**see**-nee-ə)

Pitcher Plant, Sidesaddle Flower

SARRACENIACEAE

Possibly the plants that gave John Wyndham the inspiration for his novel *Day of the Triffids*, but *Sarracenias*, though truly carnivorous, threaten only insects. Like most other meat-eating plants, they are native to constantly wet, peaty soil and are usually grown in pots where those conditions can be simulated. However, in naturally boggy

Saxifraga caespitosa. Saxifrage

garden spots, partly shaded during the heat of summer, they can be grown outdoors. They are also hardy except in the coldest of climates.

There are many different species and hybrids, all with upright, lidded funnels which can be dramatically veined and spotted. Nodding flowers appear on tall stems in summer, in *S. excellens* a vibrant blood red, in *S. flava* a greenish yellow.

SAXIFRAGA

(**saks**-i-**frae**-gə)
London Pride, Saxifrage, Roving Sailor, Strawberry Geranium, Rockfoil
SAXIFRAGACEAE

Completely hardy, or nearly so, the 300-odd species of *Saxifraga* are all low-growing annuals or perennials. Some are creeping groundcovers with attractively variegated leaves and loose panicles of starry flowers. Others form dense little mounds of foliage, completely hidden in spring or summer by simple 5-petalled blooms. These can be anything from white through yellow to pink, red, mauve and purple, depending on type. *Saxifragas* are mostly native to rocky, well-drained, rather exposed sites, and mound-forming species such as *S. caespitosa* and *S.* 'Ruth McConnell' are perfect subjects for rockery pockets or pots.

Creeping *S. stolonifera* (Roving Sailor or Strawberry Geranium) is a completely different sort of plant, producing rosettes of long-stemmed, furry leaves veined with silver-grey and with rosy-pink reverses. It sends out fine red runners from which new plants develop, much as the common strawberry does, and makes an attractive groundcover in sun or dappled shade.

Saxifraga 'Ruth McConnell'. Saxifrage

Especially effective in the right angles formed by garden steps, *S. stolonifera* looks great in hanging baskets, too; the numerous runners form curtains of foliage, and in late spring the plant is topped with a fine cloud of dainty white and pink raggedy flowers.

Keep *Saxifragas* moist during the warmer months, but dryish in winter.

Saxifraga stolonifera. Strawberry Geranium

Scabiosa atropurpurea. Sweet Scabious

SCABIOSA

(skae-bee-**oh**-zə)
Sweet Scabious, Pincushion Flower, Egyptian Rose, Perennial Pincushion
DIPSACACEAE

Wise women of the Middle Ages had a herb to cure every ailment, and with the prevalence of painful scabies, the Pincushion Flower must have been very popular. It was even named for the disease it was said to cure. Today, the various species of *Scabiosa* are simply handsome flowers, much admired for their long warm-weather displays.

Annual *S. atropurpurea* is the most exciting species, producing masses of 5–8cm/ 2–3in blooms in pink, cherry red, salmon, scarlet, white, crimson, mauve and purple-black. Each bloom is a cluster of flowerets, with pollen-tipped filaments projecting beyond the petal surface, giving the appearance of a cushion stuck with pins. They bloom from midsummer right into winter if flowers are cut or dead-headed. They like a rich, well-drained soil which *must* be alkaline, so lime is indicated in acid areas. Annual Scabious can be sown outdoors after frost, but will bloom earlier if sown indoors in late winter. Germination should take 10–15 days and blooming should begin in 14 weeks. Set them out in full sun at least 25cm/10in part.

Scabiosa caucasica. Perennial Pincushion

Scaevola aemula. Fan Flower

Perennial *S. caucasica* produces larger, though less vibrant flowers, in shades of mauve or pale blue, throughout the summer. Like the annual species, it needs alkaline soil and a fully sunny spot to thrive. It can be propagated from basal cuttings in spring, but seed sown outdoors in autumn will yield flowers the following year. The honey-scented blooms last when cut.

SCADOXUS

(skad-**ok**-səs)

Paintbrush Lily, Fireball Lily, Blood Flower

AMARYLLIDACEAE

These spectacular bulbous plants from southern Africa used to be classed with the blood lilies (Haemanthus) and are still sometimes known by that name in catalogues. The chief point of difference to the botanist is

that while the blood lilies produce only two leaves per bulb, members of the genus *Scadoxus* bear eight or more in handsome bunches. More important to the gardener, they flower in spring and grow through the summer – which makes them much easier to grow than the blood lilies, which flower in the autumn and sulk if they don't get a bone-dry summer dormancy. There are two species of consequence: *S. puniceus* (syn *Haemanthus natalensis*) the Paintbrush Lily, whose orange flowers are cupped in maroon bracts; and *S. multiflorus*, the Fireball Lily. This is rather variable, but at its best earns both scientific and common names by its great umbels of blazing red, starry flowers. Both grow about 50cm/20in tall and prefer rich soil and frost-free climates. In colder ones they make splendid house plants.

SCAEVOLA

(skae-vol-ə)

Fan Flower

GOODENIACEAE

A spreading, sprawling sort of plant used in mass bedding or as groundcover, the dainty Fan Flower (*Scaevola aemula*) is native to Australia. The genus was named for the Roman hero Mucius Scaevola, who proved his courage by burning off a hand. The quaint, lopsided flowers do in fact resemble a hand as much as they do a fan, consisting of five mauve petals arranged in a semicircle around a white and yellow throat.

S. aemula can be grown from seed but is more usually propagated from cuttings of basal shoots struck under glass. Planted out when rooted at a spacing of 45cm/18in, they spread rapidly into a dense mat no more than 30cm/12in tall. Flowers appear profusely from the red stems through spring and summer, after which the plants can be sheared back to promote spring growth.

Scadoxus multiflorus subsp. *katherinae.* Blood Flower

Scadoxus puniceus. Paintbrush Lily, Natal Blood Lily

Schefflera actinophylla. Octopus Tree, Queensland Umbrella Tree

SCHEFFLERA
(shef-ler-ə)
(SYN Brassaia)
Octopus Tree, Umbrella Tree
ARALIACEAE

One of the world's top ten indoor plants, Queensland's Octopus Tree, *Schefflera actinophylla* (syn *Brassaia actinophylla*) gives no hint of its full potential until you've seen it growing unrestrained in a subtropical garden.

The handsome, umbrella-shaped, compound leaves are still there, but are 1m/3ft in diameter and borne all over a many-branched tree that can reach up to 13m/40ft in height. Throughout spring and summer a series of curved and twisting flower stems looking exactly like the tentacles of a red octopus appear. These appear to be covered on one side with round, sucker shapes, which close inspection reveals to be the heads of small red flowers.

New plants can easily be raised from seed or, if you're in more of a hurry, they can be raised from quite large cuttings or air layers. The Octopus Tree enjoys warmth and plenty of water, and its normal habit is to form a single trunk with almost vertical branches appearing from quite low down. If you prefer a more bushy plant, just keep cutting it back.

Other species include: New Zealand's *S. digitata*, which has thin, toothed leaflets and green flowers; Java's *S. polybotrya*, which grows to around 5m/16ft, with warty branches and 20cm/8in pointed leaflets in groups of 5–7. Its greenish Aralia-type flowers are borne in red-stemmed racemes in the cooler months, and soon followed by peppercorn-sized fruits.

Schizanthus wisetonensis. Poor Man's Orchid

Schisandra sphaerandra. Magnolia Vine

SCHISANDRA
(ski-**zan**-drə)
Magnolia Vine
SCHISANDRACEAE

As this uncommon flowering climber was once classed in the Magnolia family, its popular name is presumably a hang-over; but the resemblance is certainly hard to pick! There are about 25 *Schisandra* species, found both in North America and in the eastern provinces of China.

Illustrated *S. sphaerandra* is fairly typical. Deciduous, twining around any strong support, it is frost hardy in the English climate when espaliered against a wall. Like all of the genus it is dioecious, needing plants of both sexes to produce the showy coral-red berries. Propagate from short cuttings of half-ripe wood taken in summer. Deep, rich soil is best, with moisture in the active season.

SCHIZANTHUS
(ski-**zan**-thəs, shi-**zan**-thəs)
Poor Man's Orchid, Butterfly Flower
SOLANACEAE

It's hard to believe these delicate plants are related to Petunias. They have pale, ferny leaves and exquisite, orchid-like blooms in brilliant combinations of violet, purple, pink, crimson, white and scarlet, all beautifully marked in gold.

Schizanthus are from Chile, and do not like heat. Southern hemisphere growers often raise them indoors for winter and spring colour – but in cooler northern climes they make a spectacular summer bedding plant, lasting on well into the autumn.

With care, they can be raised any time. Just sow the seed on fine, moist soil. Do not cover, but instead drape the entire flat with black plastic until the seedlings emerge. In mild areas, set seedlings 30cm/12in apart in lightly shaded, well-drained soil, rich in compost. Pinch back to encourage branching and bloom.

For indoor, winter use, sow in autumn, prick out young seedlings into individual small pots and gradually pot up through several sizes of container. Pinch back each time to encourage sturdy growth, and always keep plants moist.

SCHIZOSTYLIS
(skit-zoh-**stai**-lis)
Kaffir Lily, Crimson Flag, River Lily
IRIDACEAE

Uncommon away from its native Africa, the graceful River Lily grows naturally by flood-prone river banks, and would seem to have

Schizostylis coccinea 'Viscountess Byng'. River Lily

Schlumbergera 'White Christmas'. Crab Cactus

Schoenia cassiniana. Beauty Flower

great possibilities in damp, well-drained positions of warm temperate gardens. There is just one species, grown from division of iris-like rhizomes in earliest spring, or from seed, which takes years to reach the flowering stage. *Schizostylis coccinea* is moderately hardy, but needs overhead protection in frost-prone areas. Otherwise it prefers full sun except in the hottest zones. Leaves resemble those of Gladiolus, are usually evergreen. The pink or red flowers appear in spikes, opening in succession, with each bloom lasting about four days.

SCHLUMBERGERA

(shlum-**burg**-ur-ə)
Thanksgiving Cactus, Crab Cactus, Christmas Cactus, Winter Cactus, Zygo
CACTACEAE

Still widely known and sold as Zygocactus, these most popular of the world's epiphytic cacti are correctly called *Schlumbergera*. Perhaps you prefer to use their common names – but that can be even more confusing, for they change from place to place.

Schlumbergera × *buckleyi*. Christmas Cactus

But labels aside, we can all agree they bear remarkably beautiful flowers considering the small amount of care and attention they demand. Grow them in hanging pots of peaty, well-drained compost so the vivid flowers can be appreciated from below. They appear in autumn in cold-winter areas (it is called Thanksgiving Cactus in the United States) and during winter in milder areas where, among other names, they are called Crab Cactus.

Schlumbergeras should be kept in an area unlit at night, for they must have 12 hours of darkness to trigger flower production. Many colour varieties are grown, ranging from cerise and pale pink to orange, purple, crimson and white, often with contrasting edges. Unlike the related Rhipsalidopsis, which bears open, daisy-like flowers, *Schlumbergera* blossoms are curiously flattened and curve up at an angle from the hanging stems. Should winter night temperatures drop below 10°C/50°F, the developing flower buds will drop, along with many of the stem joints.

SCHOENIA

(shur-nee-ə)
Beauty Flower
ASTERACEAE

Another pretty annual from Australia, the Beauty Flower, *Schoenia cassiniana* (syn *Helichrysum cassinianum*), is from dry outback areas of South and Western Australia and the Northern Territory. It is compact and easy to grow, blooming in early spring even in the cold, frosty conditions experienced in arid areas.

For best results, the soil should be well enriched with compost and old manure and raked to a smooth tilth. Sow seed direct in autumn, scarcely covering it, and do not cultivate after the young seedlings have appeared. *Schoenia* has rough-textured, elongated leaves and bears profuse heads of papery 5cm/2in daisy flowers in a long-lasting display. These are sparsely petalled, and vary from deep rose to white. Thinning of plants is not required.

SCHOTIA

(shot-ee-ə)
Parrot Tree, Tree Fuchsia, Weeping Boer-bean
CAESALPINIACEAE

While travelling in northern Australia, I encountered a tree so attractive to parrots they call it the Parrot Tree. Botanically, it is *Schotia brachypetala*, a small, slow-growing plant from subtropical Africa. In spring, parrots flock to the bright red flowers to gorge upon the intoxicating nectar. Their noisy binge lasts from dawn to dusk, by which time the hapless birds are literally flat on their backs.

Schotia brachypetala. Parrot Tree, Weeping Boer-bean

S. *brachypetala* can grow 13m/40ft. It is easily propagated from the large, bean-like seeds, which should be soaked for 24 hours in warm water, but seedlings must be transplanted with care. *Schotia* is hardy to occasional frosts, but grows faster in a hot climate. Any soil will do.

SCILLA
(sil-lə)
Squill, Jacinth, Peruvian Lily, Wild Hyacinth
LILIACEAE

Time was when popular English and Spanish Bluebells were classed as Scillas. Then they were Endymion, now they've been reclassified as Hyacinthoides (which see). So what is left in the *Scilla* genus? Still about 90 species of flowering bulbs, found variously in the Mediterranean area, Asia Minor, and southern Africa.

Scilla mischtschenkoana. Persian Lily

Scilla peruviana. Cuban Lily, Peruviana Scilla

The most widely seen is *Scilla peruviana*, often known as Cuban Lily; but both names are misleading: it too is from the Mediterranean, and it grows from a large, onion-like bulb. The leaves almost hide a cone-shaped purple-blue inflorescence that may reach 45cm/18in in height. The African *S. natalensis* grows twice as high, with pale blue blooms. Iran's *S. mischtschenkoana* (syn *S. tubergeniana*) is a dwarf rock plant. All are easy to grow and best left undisturbed.

SCUTELLARIA
(skyoo-tel-leər-ee-ə)
Skullcap, Helmet Flower
LAMIACEAE

Quite a large genus within the mint family, Lamiaceae, the *Scutellarias* include around 300 species of perennial herbs and annuals, almost all of them low-growing. Mostly, they're from North America and Europe, but

Scutellaria indica. Helmet Flower

several, including S. *indica,* grow naturally in the Far East. This is a creeping plant, rarely more than 15cm/6in high and easy to grow in any well-drained position.

Scutellarias like full sun except in hot areas, for they are cool temperate plants. Grow from seed or spring divisions, cut right back after the summer blooming, and mulch with milled animal manure in early spring.

SEDUM
(see-dəm)
Stonecrop, Rose Root, Live-forever
CRASSULACEAE

Though *Sedum* is one of the most popular succulent genera, many of them are also frost hardy, a curious paradox which is due to two factors: they are found naturally in cold-winter areas of the northern hemisphere; and when really cold weather kills the succulent foliage, their tough roots are able to survive beneath the snow, to sprout again the following season.

The majority of *Sedums* are low-growing rockery or mat plants, often clinging naturally to almost vertical rock surfaces, as does the showy dwarf perennial *S. sexangulare.*

Sedum aizoön. Live-forever

Sedum sexangulare. Stonecrop

Sedum spectabile 'Brilliant'. Iceplant

Sedum anglicum. English Stonecrop

Selenicereus pteranthus. Queen of the Night

The English Stonecrop, *S. anglicum*, has white or pink flowers held about 10cm/4in above the mat-forming plant.

But other species are generally larger and grow best in a well-prepared soil in full sun. The texture scarcely matters, so long as it is well drained, but there is some evidence that a gravelly mixture suits them best. Spectacular *S. aizoön* spreads rapidly from tuberous roots to send up heads of starry golden flowers on 30cm/12in stems in summer. The more commonly seen *S. spectabile* grows in the same fashion but is much taller. Its foliage is greyish-green and the blooms are borne in large, flat heads in various shades of pink and carmine.

All these *Sedum* species can be propagated by cold-weather divisions, or from small stem cuttings struck outdoors in warm weather. They all self-sow readily, but the named types

do not come true from seed. Water with a light hand – leave the flowered stems over winter and snap them off at ground level in spring to promote new growth.

SELENICEREUS
(se-len-ə-**see**-ree-əs)
Queen of the Night
CACTACEAE

Beautiful and fragrant flowers that open in the dead of night are the principal charm of fascinating *Selenicereus*. Grow them as you would a prize Philodendron – in a large pot with a rough-textured branch or pole for climbing support – or let them snake up a sunny wall or into the branches of an open tree. Just be sure to put them where you won't miss the unbelievable flower display – it's for one night only, the blooms being dead by dawn.

On the illustrated *S. pteranthus*, the aptly named Queen of the Night, each of the tantalisingly fragrant flowers can be 30cm/12in across, with rows of pure white petals surrounded by a ring of reddish sepals. Grow *Selenicereus* in well-drained soil with plenty of leafmould. Water lightly in cold weather, and as often as you can in spring and summer. Increase by stem cuttings dried off for a few days.

SEMPERVIVUM
(sem-per-**vai**-vəm)
Hen and Chickens, Roof Houseleek, Old Man and Woman, Houseleek
CRASSULACEAE

Dainty, sun-loving succulents from the Mediterranean area, *Sempervivums* are remarkably resistant to harsh conditions and a great success in rockeries and dry walls. Or grow them on banks or windy terraces, or in shallow dish gardens filled with stones and just enough compost to root in.

They are really easy to propagate. Just pull away a small leaf-rosette and stick it on some soil. So long as it stays right-way-up it will form roots and begin to multiply, the baby new leaf-rosettes appearing from underneath the leaves of the old. That's where the name Hen and Chickens comes from.

The neat, often colourful leaf-rosettes are the chief attraction of most *Sempervivums*, but species such as *S. arachnoideum*, the Cobweb Houseleek, produce relatively large and brightly coloured flowers on stems held well above the foliage. Mature rosettes of shown *S. tectorum* bloom in midsummer. The dainty, rose-purple flowers appear in

Sempervivum tectorum. Roof Houseleek, Hen and chickens

clusters at the tops of reddish stems, after which the parent plant dies and is replaced by newly formed young rosettes.

Regular water but perfect drainage is the rule with all *Sempervivums*. Try planting a collection of several different varieties in a terracotta 'strawberry pot' or a wide planter.

SENECIO
(sə-**ness**-ee-oh)
Groundsel, Cineraria, Dusty Miller, Cape Ivy, Mexican Flame Vine
ASTERACEAE

The enormous variety of daisy-flowered plants called *Senecio* make up one of the largest of plant genera. They are found on every continent, though the best species originate from Africa and both Americas.

Of the shrubby types, the most popular and useful include Mexico's enormous *S. grandifolius*, which has dark 50cm/20in leaves and trusses of bright yellow daisy flowers in cold weather; the California

Senecio grandifolius. Big-leaf Groundsel

Geranium, *S. petasitis*, has handsome lobed foliage and sparsely petalled flowers in great panicles. All grow from cuttings and need annual pruning to keep compact.

The annuals are grown from late-summer sown seed and, whether potted up or planted out, need consistent moisture and regular feeding.

The genus also includes climbers, the most spectacular of which is *S. confusus*, the Mexican Flame Vine. It grows to 3m/10ft and produces its bright orange blooms all through the warm weather. Fast-growing Cape Ivy (*S. macroglossus*) is good for quick cover. Its light yellow flowers appear singly over many months.

Senecio confusus. Mexican Flame Vine

Senna artemisioides. Silver Cassia

SENNA
(**sen**-nə)
Cassia, Buttercup Bush
CAESALPINIACEAE

The cassias are a vast tribe, including herbaceous plants, shrubs and trees – too vast, it seems, as most of the shrubby species and some of the trees have now been decanted into a genus of their own, the ancient name *Senna* being revived for them. Their clustered, brilliant yellow flowers make shrubby Sennas conspicuous adornments of tropical and subtropical gardens, easily recognised by their long seed pods and pinnate leaves (sometimes bipinnate) which fold up at night. Two that feature in warm temperate gardens also are the Silver Cassia, *S. artemisioides*, which comes from inland Australia; and the South American *S. pendula*, the Buttercup Bush or Autumn Cassia. The Silver Cassia is a most beautiful plant, a rose-bush-sized shrub with ferny silver leaves among which the golden flowers nestle in summer. The fast-growing but short-lived *S. pendula* (syn. *Cassia bicapsularis*, *C. candolleana*) is a tall shrub or small tree with faintly aromatic green leaves, a bit weedy perhaps, but covering itself with clear yellow, scented flowers for many weeks from the end of summer. It is a splendid conservatory plant in cool climates. All the Sennas benefit from pruning after flowering, to keep them compact.

Senna pendula. Buttercup Bush

Sidalcea malviflora 'Mrs T. Alderson'. Checkerbloom

Serissa foetida 'Flore Pleno'. Stinking Serissa

SERISSA

(se-**ris**-sə)

Japanese Boxthorn, Stinking Serissa

RUBIACEAE

Some authorities say there are three species of *Serissa*, others that there is just one; but *S. foetida*, a native of Southeast Asia, is the only one ever encountered in gardens. It is an evergreen shrub about 1m/3ft tall and wide, slender-stemmed but bushy, with small neat leaves. These are indeed foetid if you crush them, but there is no need to do that, and the plant is a very pretty sight in winter, when it covers itself in little mauve buds opening to white flowers. It comes in several versions: the wild single-flowered one, one with double flowers, and one with variegated leaves. Subtropical to warm temperate climates suit it best, and it doesn't mind a bit of shade. In cool climates it makes a very attractive greenhouse pot plant.

SERRURIA

(se-**roo**-ree-ə)

Blushing Bride

PROTEACEAE

I first met *Serruria florida* at my local flower shop and found its palest pink flowers (or rather flower heads) perfectly charming – and very long-lasting in the vase too. About 8cm/3in across, they have an air of delicacy about them which is unusual in the protea tribe, and when I was able to grow the rather straggly, waist-high shrub itself, that same daintiness was revealed in its foliage. Like all the family, it likes a mild temperate climate, sunshine and perfect drainage. In the wild (in South Africa) it varies in colour from ivory to quite deep shades of pink, and these colours are now available to gardeners and florists also. The flowering season is quite long, from spring to early summer, after which it can be given a light trim.

Serruria florida 'Sugar 'n' Spice'

SIDALCEA

(sai-**dal**-see-ə)

Callirhöe, Checkerbloom, Prairie Mallow

MALVACEAE

Obviously related to Hollyhocks, which they greatly resemble, showy *Sidalceas* are altogether smaller plants, growing as low as 70cm/27in, though the illustrated Checkerbloom (*S. malviflora*) will usually reach 1m/3ft.

Unlike Hollyhocks, *Sidalcea* species branch into many flower spikes instead of just one spire-like stem. They prefer full sun, need well-drained, moist soil and simple staking with bamboo canes for, like their lookalike cousins, they are easily blown over. Plant them in autumn or early spring at 35cm/14in spacings, or divide established clumps in the latter season, replanting only the healthy outer growth.

Silene coeli-rosa. Rose of Heaven, Viscaria

Sinningia 'Emperor William' (top) and
Sinningia 'Switzerland'. Gloxinias

Sinningia cardinalis. Cardinal Flower

Bloom lasts for weeks towards the end of summer, and if flowered stems are cut to 30cm/12in immediately after bloom, a second flush from lateral shoots can be expected in autumn. They are generally left alone by insect pests, but like Hollyhocks, they often develop rust on the foliage, especially in humid climates. This is easily treated with a suitable fungicide applied at the first sign of infection.

SILENE
(sai-**lee**-nee)
Campion, Catchfly
CARYOPHYLLACEAE

Related to Carnations, *Silenes* are a large genus of hardy annuals and perennials, mostly from temperate parts of the northern hemisphere. They are frequently used in rock gardens, rocky banks or low borders where they grow easily in light, well-drained, gravelly or gritty soil.

Most commonly seen *S. uniflora* (syn *S. vulgaris* subsp. *maritima*), the Sea

Silene uniflora. Sea Campion

Silene armeria. Catchfly

Campion, spreads its blue-grey leaves over an area of about 30cm/12in square from woody rootstocks, and then produces loose clusters of many-petalled white flowers with an inflated, balloon-like calyx. There are also double white and pink hybrids which can be grown as annuals or perennials.

S. compacta, from the Balkans and Asia Minor, is a short-lived perennial to 120cm/4ft tall. Its late spring flowers, less than 2.5cm/1in across, appear singly over a long period.

SINNINGIA
(sin-**in**-jee-ə)
Gloxinia, Cardinal Flower
GESNERIACEAE

Hybridised from a small-flowered plant from the Brazilian forests, today's Gloxinia blooms are so huge and velvety that they can only survive in a warm, bright room, sheltered from rain, wind and pests.

Nevertheless, they are more popular than ever, and millions of tubers are started

each spring in pots of peaty humus mixed with sharp sand. Once planted, they are watered deeply then kept just moist until leaf growth appears.

Gloxinias (*Sinningia speciosa* hybrids) have open, trumpet-shaped flowers in shades of scarlet, crimson, purple, blue, pink and white, usually with contrasting throats. After bloom, water is reduced and the tubers stored in their pots in a cool, dry spot over winter.

Other species commonly seen include: the Cardinal Flower, *Sinningia cardinalis* (syn *Rechsteineria cardinalis*), with velvety toothed leaves and scarlet 5cm/2in tubular flowers in large whorls or clusters during summer; and the Brazilian Edelweiss, *S. canescens* (syn *R. leucotricha*), which has silvery-hairy leaves and summer flowers in soft coral or orange.

Sisyrinchium idahoense. Blue-eyed Grass

Sisyrinchium striatum. Satin-flower

SISYRINCHIUM
(sis-ee-**rin**-kee-ᵊm)
(SYN Hydastylus, Olsynium)
Satin-flower, Blue-eyed Grass
IRIDACEAE

Related to Libertia (which see), 100 or so *Sisyrinchium* species are widely grown in many parts of the world. They are iris relatives, though many have neither bulb nor rhizome. All have narrow, grass-like leaves, and send up slender spikes of blue, yellow or white flowers on wiry stems. Most are reasonably hardy, but not where the ground freezes hard. *Sisyrinchiums* self-seed easily, or can be propagated from seed or by division of clumps in spring.

S. californicum, Golden-eyed Grass, can grow to 60cm/24in. *S. striatum*, the Satin-flower, bears summer spikes of pale yellow flowers with purplish stripes. *S. idahoense* (syn *S. bellum*) produces amethyst flowers, centred yellow. All prefer a moist, cool location, with peaty soil.

SKIMMIA
(**skim**-mee-ᵊ)
Skimmi
RUTACEAE

Just a handful of species from cooler parts of Asia, the *Skimmias* are related to Citrus and to the fragrant Murraya or Mockorange, which they replace in gardens of cooler climates.

S. *japonica* is most commonly seen in town gardens and in parks, for it is remarkably resistant to polluted city air. Clusters of tiny, but extremely fragrant, creamy flowers join the shining evergreen foliage in early spring, and if you've the right planting combination (you need at least one male plant to every 4 or 5 female plants), you'll get a crop of bright red berries in late summer. These last well into autumn.

A well-drained acid soil is best, with generous moisture in dry weather. As the bushes remain compact and tidy and never exceed 120cm/4ft, little pruning is needed. Cuttings can be taken in summer.

Skimmia japonica. Skimmia

Smilacina racemosa. False Spikenard

SMILACINA
(smai-lᵊ-**see**-nᵊ)
**Solomon's Plumes, False Spikenard,
Treacle Berry, False Solomon's Seal**
LILIACEAE

Handsome rhizomatous perennials from North America and Asia, the *Smilacinas* look better in shaded positions, deeply rooted in moist, rich loam. Some 30 species have been identified, but several are all you're likely to see in a lifetime of gardening.

Illustrated *S. racemosa*, the False Spikenard, grows to around 1m/3ft in height in a suitable position. Before flowers appear in late spring, the entire plant could be mistaken for Solomon's Seal (see Polygonatum).

Propagation is by division and replanting of the rhizome in spring, but clumps do better if left undisturbed for years. A light application of compost in autumn produces bigger flower panicles. *Smilacinas* are frost hardy.

SMITHIANTHA
(smith-ee-**an**-thᵊ)
Temple Bells
GESNERIACEAE

Grown from small rhizomes like Achimenes (which see), *Smithianthas* are virtually always potted up for eventual indoor display. They are grown in a water-retentive (but never soggy) peat-based soil and kept consistently moist and well fed from late spring until the flowering period in late summer.

Smithianthas form pyramids of large, velvety leaves with a purple sheen. The flowers are long, hanging bells in shades of scarlet, orange, yellow, pink and cream, often with spotted throats. They appear in tall, branched spikes up to 60cm/2ft in height. *Smithianthas* like humid warmth, with a winter minimum temperature of 15ºC/59ºF.

SOBRALIA
(sob-**rae**-lee-ə)
Bamboo Orchid
ORCHIDACEAE

Sobralias, or Bamboo Orchids, can be raised anywhere, if you can give them a winter temperature of 13°C/55°F, full sun and fresh air. They grow fast from a clump of large, fleshy roots potted up in a porous mixture of broken pots and brick rubble, charcoal or old grass sods, mixed with sand and sphagnum moss. Give them plenty of water through the warm weather and they'll send up tall, reed-like stems to about 1m/3ft.

The showy Cattleya-like blooms appear at the ends of these, and while each only lasts a few days, many are produced in quick succession, so that a well-grown plant with a number of stems can be in bloom for weeks. *Sobralias* rest during winter and should then be kept dryish.

Sobralia macrantha. Bamboo Orchid

Smithiantha hybrid. Temple Bells

Solandra maxima. Cup of Gold

SOLANDRA
(soh-**lan**-drə)
Cup of Gold, Honolulu Lily
SOLANACEAE

A sprawling, extremely rampant vine which needs solid support and acres of room, the Cup of Gold (*Solandra maxima*) grows rapidly from cuttings in damp soil. It is particularly good near the sea, where it resists salt spray and can be used to form a dense barrier to sea winds. In other frost-free locations it quickly covers fences or eyesores of virtually any size.

The enormous 23cm/9in flowers grow right through the warm weather and have a strong smell, rather unpleasant to some.

But be warned! This is not a plant for small gardens, or for people who do not enjoy regular pruning. It is not hardy at all, though it is often grown in heated green-houses where winters are cold.

Solanum rantonnetii 'Gymea'. Blue Potato Bush

SOLANUM
(sol-**ah**-nəm)
Potato Bush, Potato Vine, Flor de Volcan, Costa Rica Nightshade
SOLANACEAE

Another enormous and most variable genus of plants, the *Solanums* are found all over the world, though mostly in warmer climates. They include climbers, annuals and a tree or two, as well as many food plants such as the eggplant (aubergine) and potato. Most, however, are grown purely for the beauty of their floral display, though it must be confessed, fragrance is something of a rarity among them.

S. rantonnetii, the Blue Potato Bush, is most variable, seen sometimes as a medium-sized shrub barely 2m/6ft tall, sometimes as a vine or even a sprawling groundcover. It is from South America, is not frost hardy and is best grown from soft-tip cuttings struck in warm weather. Heavy pruning is needed to keep it shapely – but just look at the end result! These yellow-centred, purple flowers, though only small, are produced generously from late spring well into summer.

The fast-growing Potato Vine, *S. jasminoides*, bears generous clusters of starry pale mauve-blue flowers throughout the warm weather; cultivar 'Album' has white flowers.

The Paradise Flower, *S. wendlandii*, is a prickly, shrubby climber for tropical and warm temperate gardens. It's inclined to be rather rampant, but heavy pruning at

Solanum jasminoides 'Album'. White Potato Vine

Solidago canadensis. Goldenrod

Solanum wendlandii. Paradise Flower

SOLDANELLA
(sol-də-**nel**-lə)
PRIMULACEAE

There doesn't appear to be an English name, but no matter – *Soldanella* is pretty enough. It means a little *solidus*, a medieval Italian coin, and refers to the almost circular leaves of these diminutive perennials, which do indeed come from the mountains of Italy and other parts of southern Europe. The leaves are unimportant – the charm of the plant resides in the flowers, little hanging bells with their edges deeply slashed and fringed. They are almost always in some delightful shade of blue or mauve and appear in spring, often among the melting snow. In gardens, a cool climate, cool, moist but perfectly drained soil and sunshine are called for – the rock garden is the place to show them off.

Soldanella montana. Mountain Snowbell

SOLIDAGO
(sol-li-**dah**-goh)
Goldenrod
ASTERACEAE

Among the brightest features of North American woodlands in late summer, the handsome, rough-foliaged Goldenrods are easily grown almost anywhere, though they may prove to be relatively short-lived in areas with warm winters. There are over 100 species, varying in height from 30–200cm/1–6ft depending on type, but *Solidago canadensis* is the most commonly seen.

Goldenrods should be planted in colder weather in enriched garden soil and supported with light staking as they grow. Propagation is from divisions of older clumps, but once established, the plants are quick to spread and may become invasive. Surprisingly, since they bloom in densely branched plumes of tiny golden florets, they are members of the daisy family, but only close examination with a magnifying glass makes the relationship clear. There are dwarf species for small gardens.

SOLIDASTER
(sol-id-**ass**-tur)
(SYN Asterago)
Solidaster
ASTERACEAE

A bigeneric hybrid between two North American perennials (see Aster and Solidago), this curious plant was the result of a horticultural experiment at Lyon, France, in 1909. Usually grown in the mixed or herbaceous border, it makes a useful addition to autumn flower arrangements. Because hybrids are sterile, it is propagated

winter's end should keep it to its allotted space. The clusters of lilac-blue flowers are pretty and appear continuously so long as the weather is warm to hot. They are followed by bunches of glossy bright red berries that can persist on the plant for months. However, when these do finally drop, they tend to germinate – so be sure to grow this plant only where volunteer seedlings can be easily rooted out.

Australia contributes about 120 species to the world's stock of *Solanums*, of which the Spiny Nightshade, *S. brownii*, is one of the best. It is a useful boundary or screening plant, being lightly spined and densely foliaged. It grows about 3m/10ft tall, with a similar spread. The leaves are long, narrow and a dusty-green colour, and the small flowers provide a pretty display for much of the spring. Like all the Australian *Solanums*, *S. brownii* prefers a dryish, well-drained soil; it does best in full sun, but it will tolerate light shade for part of the day.

only by division, so that every one of these plants in the world is genetically part of the original cross.

Solidaster grows fast in any average garden soil with regular water, and blooms at much the same time as its parent: that is to say, late summer to autumn. Full sun is best, though the tiny daisy flowers fade to cream in open positions.

SOLLYA
(sol-lee-yə)
Bluebell Creeper, Austral Bluebell
PITTOSPORACEAE

Sold as a climber, the lightweight Austral Bluebell needs a great deal of training to be anything of the sort. It is better described as a sort of loose shrub, growing 60–90cm/ 2–3ft in height. Where it does look good is spilling down a retaining wall from an elevated bed.

Sollya can be grown from semi-hardwood cuttings struck in late summer. It does best in well-drained but moist soil. It is not frost hardy, nor does it like drought-prone positions. Set it in dappled shade and it will romp away in any climate from cool temperate to tropical. The 5-petalled bluebell flowers hang on long stems, generally beneath the foliage.

Sollya heterophylla. Bluebell Creeper

Solidaster luteus. Solidaster

Sonerila margaritacea. Frosted Sonerila

SONERILA
(son-ə-rill-ə)
Frosted Sonerila
MELASTOMATACEAE

Away from their natural homes in steamy Southeast Asia, Sonerilas really need warm, humid, glasshouse conditions. They are chiefly grown for their beautifully patterned leaves – the dainty flowers being something of a bonus.

S. margaritacea is the most popular, a dwarf grower with reddish stems and leaves exquisitely marked with silvery-green between the dark olive veinings of the upper surface. The reverses are palest pink, shaded green, with purple-red veins. Against such remarkable foliage, the 3-petalled flowers may seem a little tame, but take a closer look. They have a delicate beauty of their own and are borne in many-flowered clusters in late summer.

SOPHORA
(sof-or-ə)
Kowhai, Pagoda Tree, Mescal Bean
FABACEAE

Scattered all about the Pacific is a genus of the pea family named Sophora, an old Arabian name for a tree of similar appearance. They are fairly typical pea members, with golden flowers; they are generally frost hardy and have a capacity for display rivalling the European Laburnums.

Most popular is the Japanese Pagoda Tree (S. japonica), a widely used species for street planting. It is a tall grower, to 27m/90ft in height, but is often kept pruned to a more reasonable size. The tiny pea-flowers are cream and appear in dense, terminal panicles, frosting the entire tree in late summer. There is a charming cultivar, 'Pendula', with stiffly weeping branches. This is most effective when grafted on a high, standard stock.

Sophora secundiflora. Mescal Bean

Sophora tetraptera. Kowhai

In both New Zealand and Chile (similar climatic zones of the southern hemisphere) you'll find the Kowhai, S. tetraptera. This is a much smaller tree, rarely above 5m/16ft, evergreen when young but semi-deciduous when mature. It has compound leaves borne sparsely on zig-zag branchlets, with most of the leaflets dropping in spring, just before the flowers open. These are 8cm/3in golden pea blossoms that droop in clusters of 4–8 flowers each, from small spurs.

The Mescal Bean, S. secundiflora, from the southwestern United States, is a slower-growing evergreen shrub or small tree. Its violet-blue flowers are sweetly fragrant and produced any time from late winter to mid-spring.

All species can be increased from seed or cuttings and they do best in a mild, temperate climate.

Sophrolaeliocattleya 'Deep Enamel'. Rocket Burst SLC

SOPHROLAELIOCATTLEYA
(**sof**-roh-lae-lee-oh-**kat**-lae-ə)
SLC Orchid
ORCHIDACEAE

The backbreaking name above has been given to the beautiful trigeneric hybrid orchids which include in their parentage the three genera, Sophronitis, Laelia and Cattleya.

Being the result of such involved crosses, the plants are bursting with hybrid vigour, and can be tougher than any of the three original genera. Still, it must be conceded, they need the same hothouse cultural treatment. Flowers of many SLC species are characterised by a finer texture and richer, deeper colourings. The illustrated S. ' Deep Enamel' is perhaps typical. We found it at the Chelsea Flower Show.

SOPHRONITIS
(sof-rə-**nai**-təs)
Sophrinitis
ORCHIDACEAE

There are about a half dozen species in this genus of orchids from Brazil, but by far the most important is *Sophronitis coccinea*. Resembling a small, almost miniature Cattleya both in growth and flower, its chief attraction is its gorgeous colour – in the best forms, as vividly red as Chinese lacquer. It is perfectly willing to pass it on to its hybrids with its relatives, the Laelias, Brassavolas and the Cattleyas themselves, and indeed the

Sophronitis coccinea. Sophronitis

hybrids are more often seen than the pure-bred species, which has the reputation of being difficult to grow. (I strongly suspect that the plant in the picture has some *Laelia* blood.) It isn't really; it is grown in exactly the same way as a Cattleya, the difference being that it should not be allowed to dry out completely in winter. It can flower at any time from autumn to spring.

SPARAXIS
(spah-**rak**-səs)
Velvet Flower, Harlequin Flower
IRIDACEAE

Naturalising like Freesias and Ixias, the vivid *Sparaxis tricolor* is deservedly popular in warm-climate gardens, though its garish colours are a little much for subdued tastes. The flowers, generally in rust, red, orange or pink, all have a brilliant yellow centre, made even more striking by being outlined and also sectored with sharp black lines. The white form, 'Alba', has the same yellow centre but the black markings are far less prominent.

Sparaxis tricolor. Harlequin Flower

Sparaxis tricolor 'Alba'. Harlequin Flower

Sparaxis flowers are borne in an irregular group on wiry, twisted stems and open only on bright, sunny days, closing at sunset. The plants enjoy fairly heavy soil and full sun except where winters are mild and dry. There, dappled shade is preferred. Plant where they can be left undisturbed and they will soon multiply into a dense clump.

SPARRMANNIA
(spah-**man**-nee-ə)
African Hemp, Wild Hollyhock, Indoor Linden
TILIACEAE

Named for Dr Anders Sparrman, who accompanied James Cook on his second voyage, *Sparrmannia africana* is commonly seen in the northern hemisphere as an indoor plant. It is not frost hardy, and in the open garden of a warm temperate climate will grow to 3m/10ft in height.

Sparrmannia africana. African Hemp

Spartium junceum. Spanish Broom

The hairy leaves can be heart-shaped or heavily lobed, and trusses of 4-petalled white flowers are produced in winter and spring. These have spectacular bosses of gold and crimson stamens which open flat when touched. Propagate from cuttings, then plant in well-drained, leaf-rich soil. Keep up the moisture level and prune hard every third year to control the size.

SPARTIUM

(**spah**-tee- əm)
Spanish Broom, Broom
FABACEAE

The longtime favourite Spanish Broom stands out anywhere, with masses of fragrant canary-yellow pea-flowers blooming throughout the late spring and early summer. I remember it in the south of France, rolled out along the highways like a golden carpet, welcoming the well-heeled to the Côte d'Azur. But in fact, it's an easy plant to grow anywhere the sun is mildly warm. Don't worry about the type of soil: it seems to be happy even in poor, stony stuff, or fast-draining coastal sand. If it has a preference, it is for a little lime to sweeten its growth along. *Spartium junceum* is almost leafless, a mass of hollow, straw-like green twigs springing from a crowded base. And if you want it to do anything but sprawl, you must prune heavily after blooming, right into the old wood. That way you get a bush 3m/10ft tall and about as wide. You can use it as a hedge or deep groundcover, even for seaside planting. In windy places, though, give it some shelter, for it is inclined to be shallow-rooted and may topple.

Both drought and cold resistant (hardy down to −10ºC/14ºF), it's a gardener's delight, easily increased from cuttings or from seed after a 24-hour soaking. Flowers appear in long terminal sprays, are spicily fragrant and make good arrangements. Keep moist in winter, dryish in summer.

SPATHICARPA

(spath-i-**kah**-pə)
Arrowleaf
ARACEAE

Somewhat resembling a small Spathiphyllum, the *Spathicarpa* belongs to the same botanical family, but has leaves shaped exactly like the blade of an arrow. Also, unlike related Aroids, there is no separate spadix; the flowers and seeds are attached directly to the spathe.

Species *S. sagittifolia* grows from a rhizome, and is a plant strictly for the tropical garden or a heated, humid glasshouse.

Spathicarpa sagittifolia. Arrowleaf

Propagation is by division of the rhizome in spring, repotting at the same time; remove just a little of the old soil before placing the plant in a larger pot and packing with new compost. Water sparingly until roots have entered the new mix.

SPATHIPHYLLUM

(spath-ə-fil-əm)
Peace Lily, White Sails, Spathe Flower, White Anthurium
ARACEAE

Frequently mistaken for Anthuriums (which see), *Spathiphyllum* is in fact a much less delicate genus, capable of surviving great extremes of temperature but not, of course, frost. Always greenish or pure white in colouring, the Arum-style flowers appear at almost any time in tropical gardens and last for weeks on the plant. In cooler areas, flowers are more likely in summer, though odd ones still appear at other times.

Indoors, *Spathiphyllums* flourish in a well-drained, peaty mix and should be repotted each spring. Raise them in a warm, sheltered spot and give plenty of water in the warmer months. They survive in the most unlikely places around the house where the level of light is low.

Outdoors, grow them in full shade, sheltered from cold or strong winds. The shining, spear-shaped leaves rise directly from the roots and stay fresh and glossy all year with an occasional sponging.

S. clevelandii or the Peace Lily can reach 90cm/3ft in height, while *S. wallisii* rarely exceeds 30cm/12in.

Spathiphyllum 'Mauna Loa'. Peace Lily

Spathiphyllum wallisii. White Sails

Spiraea japonica 'Anthony Waterer'. Red May

Spathodea campanulata. African Tulip Tree

SPATHODEA

(spa-**thoh**-dee-ə)
**African Tulip Tree, Tulip Tree,
Flame of the Forest**
BIGNONIACEAE

A native of Uganda, *Spathodea campanulata* is now seen right around the warm belt of the world, though it is, in fact, hardy down to −2ºC/28ºF. Still, a frost can cut it to the ground when young.

Easy to propagate from seed, *Spathodea* grows to 17m/55ft in the wild. The flowers are a vivid orange-scarlet lined with yellow and may be 10cm/4in across. They appear in large racemes at the ends of branches and open a few at a time, the whole display lasting months.

S. campanulata goes by many popular names, but my own favourite, from Malagasy, is Baton du Sorcier – the sorcerer's wand, after the old-fashioned magician's wand which used to miraculously produce flags from its innards. In *Spathodea*, the buds, shaped like a finger or small stick, split from end to end, so that the showy, flag-like petals can unfurl.

S. campanulata is seen in southern USA, the Caribbean, eastern Australia and Hong Kong. A less spectacular species is *S. nilotica*, growing only to about 7m/23ft. Its vaguely similar flowers are a soft apricot colour.

SPATHOGLOTTIS

(spath-oh-**glot**-təs)
Tongue Orchid
ORCHIDACEAE

Popular terrestrial orchids in the tropical garden, the 40-odd species of *Spathoglottis* are native to the Southeast Asian area, from India to the Philippines and down to Australia. They bloom continuously through summer in a wide range of colours, mostly rosy-pink, yellow, white and purple.

Grow them from corm-like pseudobulbs in a compost rich with fibrous loam, chopped sphagnum, sand and finely crushed tile. Repotting or replanting is carried out when fresh growth appears in spring. Give them plenty of water as the leaves and flower buds push up. Semi-shade is preferred in a hot climate. Some are deciduous.

SPIRAEA

(spai-**ree**-ə)
**Spirea, Maybush, Garland Flower,
Bridal Wreath**
ROSACEAE

The popular Maybushes or Garland Flowers take their former popular name from their month of blooming in the northern hemisphere, to which they are native. A thicket of erect, often arching stems, they are not particularly eye-catching or elegant for most of the year, but come into their own in springtime, when they are almost smothered under the weight of long, arching sprays of bloom – pink, white or crimson.

All species are hardy down to at least −5ºC/23ºF and, like other members of the rose family, do best in a cold-winter climate. They flourish in sun or part shade, in acid or even slightly alkaline soil, so long as it is rich and well drained. Early-blooming species should be pruned immediately after flowering by cutting out about a third of the oldest growth at the base. Later-blooming species can be pruned any time in winter.

S. japonica 'Anthony Waterer' is a natural hybrid and native to Japan; the tiny cerise blooms are borne in flat heads. *S. betulifolia*

Spathoglottis plicata. Tongue Orchid

Spiraea betulifolia. Birch-leaf Spiraea

Spiraea cantoniensis 'Flore Pleno'. Double Spiraea

forms a thick bush to 1m/3ft at most; its tiny white flowers are grouped together in dense clusters that cover the plant in spring. It is one of the hardiest species, safe in temperatures as low as −26°C/−15°F. *S. cantoniensis* or Reeves' Spiraea grows only 1.5m/5ft high but spreads widely. The flowers are produced in hemispherical bunches clustered closely together all along the ends of the branches.

SPREKELIA
(spr∂-**kee**-lee-∂)
**Jacobean Lily, Aztec Lily, Gold Lily,
Maltese Cross, Jacob's Lily**
AMARYLLIDACEAE

Most often seen in formal flower arrangements, the Jacobean Lily is regal in both colour and shape, somewhat resembling a heraldic *fleur de lys*. Surprisingly, in view of some of its common names, it is from Mexico, not Europe.

Where winter temperatures are never more than a few degrees below freezing, *Sprekelias* can be grown outdoors. The bulbs are planted in spring 15cm/6in deep in rich, well-drained soil that is partly shaded during the hottest part of the day. Where severe winters are the norm, grow in pots, sheltered from the worst extremes of the weather. Wherever grown, they should be kept moist throughout the warmer months but dried off during their winter dormancy. The unusually shaped flowers of *S. formosissima* appear in midsummer.

Sprekelia formosissima. Aztec Lily, Jacobean Lily

Stachys byzantina. Lambs' Ears

Stachys macrantha. Woundwort

Stachys officinalis. Wood Betony

Stachyurus praecox. Stachyurus

Stanhopea tigrina. Tiger Orchid

STACHYS

(stak-iss)

(SYN Betonica)

Betony, Woundwort, Lambs' Ears, Lambs' Tongues

LAMIACEAE

Commonly used as border edging or groundcover in light shade, the many attractively foliaged species of *Stachys* are related to mint, sage and other aromatic plants.

Most commonly planted is the lovely *S. byzantina* (formerly listed as *S. lanata*), grown more for its woolly grey leaves than its spikes of tiny purple flowers. Other species, though, with less distinctive foliage, rely on their flowers for their popularity. Two such are *S. officinalis* and *S. macrantha*: the former

produces tiny pink blooms in dense heads atop stems of glossy foliage; the latter, spikes of rather large, rosy-purple flowers.

All species are planted in colder weather, generally from division of older plants.

STACHYURUS

(stak-ee-**yoo**-rəs)

Stachyurus

STACHYURACEAE

Not cultivated long enough to have attracted any sort of popular name, *Stachyurus* are found naturally in Asia, but seem at home in any sort of temperate climate, being hardy to around –18ºC/0ºF in sheltered places.

Most commonly seen *S. praecox* is attractive at any time of the year. Variable in size, it can be anything from 60–300cm/2–10ft, its branches asymmetrical and weeping, sparsely clothed with simple, medium-sized, deciduous leaves. In cool climates, these take on fiery autumn tints. In the same season,

long chains of unopened yellow and brown blossoms appear, looking like sections of a beaded curtain. From late winter on, these gradually elongate and open, peaking just as the spring foliage appears.

Soil should be rich and well drained, with a generous summer water supply. Grow from seed, or from tip-cuttings taken in late summer and struck with mist and heat.

STANHOPEA

(stan-**hoh**-pee-ə)

Tiger Orchid, Leopard Orchid

ORCHIDACEAE

Native to the jungles of tropical America, *Stanhopeas* grow high up in the trees, nourished by rotting leaves that accumulate in branch crotches. Their unusual flowers are produced in an unusual way, for the spike grows straight down, not up, so that the blooms appear below the plant.

Thus, in the garden, they must be grown in wire or other baskets that aren't solid. Line the basket with coconut fibre or sphagnum moss and fill with a compost of bark chips, treefern chunks, charcoal and leafmould,

Stellaria flaccida. Starwort

Stenocarpus sinuatus. Wheel of Fire

among which the root mass is placed. The basket is then soaked and hung in a warm, bright place. I've found *Stanhopeas* are quite happy in a shade house with winter night temperatures above freezing.

Stanhopeas flower mostly in summer, their curious blossoms reminding one of squid moving slowly under water. Shown *S. tigrina* has a powerful, chocolaty perfume, but its generously produced flowers are fairly short lived. Keep them moist all year round.

STELLARIA
(stel-e∂r-ee-∂)
Starwort, Stitchwort, Chickweed
CARYOPHYLLACEAE

Dainty *Stellarias* are represented in most gardens by the common Chickweed, which bird-lovers serve as salad to their pet canaries. But there are some larger-growing species we do not recommend in garden beds because they seed outrageously and become quite invasive for such slender, light-weight plants.

There are *Stellaria* species found in temperate areas of most continents, but Australian *S. flaccida* is among the most useful. It can be grown from cuttings, seed or divisions and makes a splendid low-maintenance groundcover away from foot traffic, which would pulp it. Spray lightly, and keep moist at all times.

STEMMADENIA
(stem-m∂-**dee**-nee-∂)
Lecheso
APOCYNACEAE

In its native Central America, the sap of *Stemmadenia galleotteana* is said to be poiso-nous, but that does not reduce its popularity

Stemmadenia galleotteana. Lecheso

in tropical gardens. Somewhat pyramidal in shape when young, this evergreen tree then develops a spreading habit, though it never grows very large: a big specimen is no more than 7m/23ft tall. It is related to the Frangipani, and can easily be mistaken for one at a distance.

The glossy, pointed, oval leaves appear in pairs – each leaf about 13cm/5in in length. The crepe-like flowers look rather like those of an Oleander, and appear any time during the warmer months. Sweetly fragrant, they are 8cm/3in wide, pure white with a yellow throat; the 5 broad, overlapping petals have a pleated effect around the edges. These are followed by paired 1cm/½in orange-red fruits. Related *S. glabra* is similar, but with larger leaves and pale yellow flowers.

STENOCARPUS
(sten-oh-**kah**-p∂s)
Firewheel Tree, Wheel of Fire
PROTEACEAE

Australian in origin, the gorgeous Queensland Firewheel Tree seems more appreciated in California, where they have planted some stunning avenues of them. *Stenocarpus sinuatus* (meaning narrow fruit with wavy foliage) can reach 30m/100ft in its native forests but barely half that in cultiva-tion. It needs protection from frosts when young (coping better when well established), and grows slowly to a splendid vertical shape, reminiscent of a Lombardy Poplar.

The dark, glossy, evergreen leaves with sinuate edges may reach 25cm/10in in length, and the flowers appear in long-stalked clusters right out of the trunk or larger branches. At first green, they develop a unique wheel shape before turning a glowing red. Finally, each series of flowers (the spokes of a wheel) splits open to reveal the golden stamens, and the whole flower takes on the appearance of a medieval crown. The warmer the climate, the more heavily the flowers are borne, generally around early autumn.

Stenocarpus is a member of the family Proteaceae, which includes a large number of Australian trees, among them Buckinghamia, Macadamia and Alloxylon, all of which are illustrated in this book.

STEPHANOTIS
(stef-∂-**noh**-t∂s)
Madagascar Chaplet Flower, Floradora, Malagasy Jasmine, Waxflower
ASCLEPIADACEAE

Stephanotis flowers are as sweetly scented as those of Stapelia (which see) are evil-smelling – and yet they are closely related.

Stephanotis floribunda. Floradora

In frost-free climates, grow the quite splendid Madagascar Chaplet Flower against a sunny wall or over an arbor or pergola. Elsewhere, it will thrive in a warm sunroom or heated conservatory, in a large pot of well-drained soil enriched with rotted organic matter. It is a twining plant, twisting around its supports and producing its flower clusters from the leaf axils – snowy-white tubular bells with flaring petals. Long-lasting and deliciously perfumed, they appear over a long period in summer.

Stephanotis are propagated from spring cuttings struck with heat.

Sternbergia lutea. Yellow Starflower

STERNBERGIA
(stern-**berg**-ee-∂)
**Autumn Crocus, Winter Daffodil,
Lily of the Field, Yellow Starflower**
AMARYLLIDACEAE

The dainty Autumn Crocus, *Sternbergia lutea*, is related to giant Hippeastrums and shines with a golden light in early autumn.

Bulbs are planted or potted up in spring, in rich but very well-drained soil with some lime added. Plant them about 2.5cm/1in below soil level, water well once or twice to establish the roots but then give less. Like many other autumn-flowering bulbs,

Stewartia pseudocamellia. False Camellia

Sternbergias like to be baked in summer, with just occasional moisture. As the days cool, and early autumn rains begin, both leaves and cup-shaped yellow blooms will appear.

STEWARTIA
(styoo-**wah**-tee-∂)
Japanese Stewartia, False Camellia
THEACEAE

Like the Gordonia (which see), the genus *Stewartia* is represented in both eastern Asia and North America.

The American *S. ovata* or Mountain Camellia is a 5m/16ft camellia-like shrub with deciduous 13cm/5in leaves and white flowers. The Japanese species, *S. pseudo-camellia* (Japanese Stewartia or False Camellia) can grow into a small tree. It has 8cm/3in pointed deciduous leaves that turn purple in autumn. Flowers appear in late summer, each more than 5cm/2in across; pure white with a boss of orange stamens, they are exactly like small, single camellias except that the petals are furry on their reverses. A temperate climate suits both species.

STOKESIA
(stohk-see-∂)
Stokes' Aster, Blue Thistle, Cornflower Aster
ASTERACEAE

Much admired as a relatively uncommon perennial in English gardens, the beautiful blue *Stokesia laevis* grows like a weed in southern hemisphere climates – quickly spreading by underground stems into a dense clump. Plant them in the mixed border, or in large tubs on your terrace – and please, *do* pick the lovely 10cm/4in daisy flowers! They last well in water and the picking forces dormant buds into bloom, prolonging the display for months.

Stokesia laevis. Stokes' Aster

Streptocalyx sp. Streptocalyx

Stokesia is propagated by divisions of the root mass set out in early spring, or from seed, sown under glass in the cold months. You'll get blooms in the first year if you start them early enough, though they may not come true to colour. Mauve-blue is the common variety, but *Stokesias* also come in white, yellow, pink and purple. Sun or light shade suits them, with light watering; the soil must be well drained. Dead-head often.

STRELITZIA
(stre-**lit**-zee-∂)
Bird of Paradise, Crane Flower
MUSACEAE

Splendid in formal arrangements and wonderful feature plants for the open garden, *Strelitzias* are grown in frost-free areas world-wide. (They will survive lows of −8ºC/17ºF, but the flowers and foliage will be damaged.)

Strelitzia reginae. Bird of Paradise

They are amazingly drought resistant, yet do equally well in moist, tropical gardens. The gaudy orange and blue flowers are so remark-ably formed they remind one of a milliner's fantasy and really do look like some exotic bird, as the common names suggest.

Most often seen *S. reginae* has broad leaves at the ends of long stems. Its daintier cousin *S. juncea* makes do with pointed, rush-like stems, and seems to me an altogether neater plant. The less colourful *S. nicolai* is a tree-sized relative. It bears 45cm/18in purple and white flowers among banana-like leaves. In mild climates, all species begin blooming in early winter; they wait till spring in cooler areas.

Strelitzia nicolai. Crane Flower

STREPTOCALYX
(strep-toh-**kae**-liks)
Streptocalyx
BROMELIACEAE

About 14 species of epiphytic Bromeliads from various parts of South America, the *Streptocalyx* genus is not often seen in hobby collections.

In nature, they grow high up in trees in hot, humid jungles, and if you can arrange similar glasshouse conditions you may find them worth growing. They have a distinct resemblance to the related Pineapple (see Ananas), with spiny leaves growing in a dense rosette and flowers appearing from a crowded panicle. The individual blooms, about 3cm/1in wide, and in shades of purple, white and blue, open one at a time. Keep moist, but drier in winter.

Streptocarpus rexii. Cape Primrose

Strobilanthes anisophyllus. Goldfussia

Streptocarpus hybrid. Cape Primrose

STREPTOCARPUS

(strep-to-**kah**-p∂s)
Cape Primrose
GESNERIACEAE

The popular house plants known as Cape Primroses are mostly large-flowered hybrids of the South African *Streptocarpus rexii.* They can be grown outdoors anywhere winters are frost-free or nearly so. In nature, they occur in moist, well-drained, leaf-rich soil in the dappled shade of open forests, and similar conditions in the garden suit them admirably.

Flowering occurs in summer and autumn, with several stems rising from the rosette of leaves. Each stem produces a number of flared, trumpet-shaped flowers in shades of blue, mauve, pink and white, all with striped throats. Blooming is prolonged by frequent feeding with dilute liquid fertiliser throughout the warm months, coupled with the prompt removal of faded flower stems.

STREPTOSOLEN

(strep-toh-**soh**-lən)
Marmalade Bush, Browallia
SOLANACEAE

Useful in the frost-free garden, yellow and orange flowered *Steptosolen* is a shrub that may turn climber or even groundcover. The sole plant in its genus, it was at one time included in Browallia, and some still refer to it by that name. It has many minor variations in colour and habit but, as a rule, arching shoots emerge from the base and need regular tip pruning when young to help the plant develop a shape. It is an ideal subject for a large hanging basket or shrub border and should be grown in light, fibrous, well-drained soil, kept moist.

Flowering begins in spring, with clusters of the brightly coloured flowers so profuse they weigh down the new growth. Easy to grow from semi-hardwood cuttings struck in either autumn or winter with bottom heat, *Streptosolen jamesonii* is not frost hardy.

Streptosolen jamesonii. Marmalade Bush

STROBILANTHES

(stroh-bil-**anth**-eez)
Goldfussia, Mexican Petunia
ACANTHACEAE

Strobilanthes, from warmer parts of Asia, remain attractive only with a minimum winter temperature no lower than 13ºC/55ºF, for the leaves discolour and drop if it gets too cold. Thus, away from the tropics, they are mostly grown as house or greenhouse plants and are raised fresh each year from heeled cuttings struck in early spring over bottom heat. Even where plants can be successfully over-wintered, they should be pruned back in spring to encourage new, bushy growth or they become weedy and unattractive.

Goldfussia, *S. anisophyllus,* is a small, shrubby perennial, usually less than 1m/3ft tall. Its leaves are a glossy purplish-red, almost black – the perfect foil for clusters of light mauve-blue flowers that dot the plant during warmer months. Grow *Strobilanthes* in very well-drained soil enriched with rotted manure. Keep well watered and fed during the growing season, but only just moist in winter at the cooler end of its range.

STROMANTHE

(stroh-**man**-thee)
Red Rain
MARANTACEAE

Stromanthes need humid warmth and semi-shade, and look best with a minimum winter temperature of around 10ºC/50ºF. The Brazilian species *S. sanguinea* is most commonly seen. It grows to about 1m/3ft away from the tropics, and produces stiff,

Stromanthe sanguinea. Red Rain

branching stems of handsome spear-shaped leaves. These are glossy olive-green with lighter ribs above, a rich purple beneath.

In late spring, the taller branches develop many-stemmed flower heads, but the tiny white flowers are quite overwhelmed by a mass of vivid scarlet bracts. Individual flowers are short-lived, but the head blooms over many weeks.

STRONGYLODON
(stron-gil-**oh**-dən)
Jade Vine
FABACEAE

Although native to the Philippines, the magnificent Jade Vine can be grown in warm areas outside the tropics. But of course, the further from the equator, the more difficult it becomes. For the determined gardener with

Strophanthus preussii. Spider Tresses

Strongylodon macrobotrys. Jade Vine

a sunny pergola, arbor or trellis, sheltered from cold winds, there can be few greater rewards than *Strongylodon macrobotrys* in full bloom.

In good, rich, well-drained soil, kept moist, the Jade Vine develops into a thick-stemmed, woody, twining creeper, densely clothed with glossy dark green leaves. Flowers appear in summer – long, hanging racemes of superb, sickle-shaped pea-blossoms. Their colour is unique in the plant world – a soft jade green.

STROPHANTHUS
(stroh-**fan**-thəs)
Spider Tresses
APOCYNACEAE

Like so many members of the Dogbane family (Allamanda, Mandevilla, Nerium, Plumeria), the eyecatching *Strophanthus* species are rarely seen outside warm-climate gardens. They grow best in sandy soil that has been enriched with peat, need plenty of summer water and full sun, and are definitely not hardy.

Illustrated *S. preussii* is naturally a scrambler growing to about 3m/10ft, but more often seen draped over a tree stump or wall. It is evergreen, with simple shining leaves that sprout from reddish stems. The 5-petalled flowers appear from late spring into summer. They are basically cream, but shaded to orange and marked with purple streaks. The petals develop thread-like extensions up to 30cm/12in long.

Strophanthus are propagated from cuttings struck under glass in moist sand. Several species are cultivated commercially for their seeds, a valuable source of cardiac drugs.

STYLIDIUM
(stai-**lid**-ee-əm)
Trigger Plant
STYLIDIACEAE

There are about 150 species of Trigger Plant, of which most are exclusive to Australia and nearby islands. They would make an eye-catching display in an open, sun-drenched rock garden where you could watch the startling method of pollination. When an insect is attracted to the bright pink flowers of *S. graminifolium* and lands on one of them, the flower's column snaps shut, and the insect is covered with pollen in its struggle to become free. The pollen will later be transferred to another flower. Other species bloom in yellow or white.

Stylidiums are raised from seed, sown in a moist sand/peat mix, and will grow to 60cm/2ft according to species. Hot or warm temperate climates suit them best.

Stylidium graminifolium. Trigger Plant
TONY RODD

STYPHELIA
(stai-**feel**-yə)
Fivecorners
EPACRIDACEAE

A genus of 12 colourful species within the family Epacridaceae or Australian native heaths, the *Styphelias* will rarely be found outside their native land. Difficult to propagate, they can be raised from fresh seed, with a deal of patience. Germination is slow and erratic, viability of cuttings not much

Styphelia triflora. Pink Fivecorners

better. All species of *Styphelia* prefer damp, well-drained, acid soil with filtered sunlight.

Illustrated Pink Fivecorners (*S. triflora*) is a sparsely foliaged shrub to about 1m/3ft. It is typical of the genus, other types varying mostly in colour. The curious popular name is due to the shape created by 5 sharply reflexed petals. These roll back to reveal 5 stamens protruding from a bearded interior.

STYRAX
(**stai**-raks)
Snowbell, Storax
STYRACACEAE

Through all continents of the northern hemisphere you'll find species of the delightful *Styrax* – there are about 120 of them. These have been valued for ages as the source of a resin called benzoin, used in the preparation of toiletries and medicinal products, including the universal Friar's Balsam.

Styrax species vary in height from 1m/3ft shrubs to slender 10m/33ft trees. All are deciduous, and all bear clusters of delicate, fragrant hanging bell-flowers in summer. These vary from snowy-white to cream according to species.

Styrax officinalis. Storax

Most *Styrax* can be propagated only by seed, layers or grafting on to lookalike Halesia (which see). They prefer acid soils, regular water, and most of them are not frost hardy. All species do best with midday shade in warm temperate climates.

SUTHERLANDIA
(suth-ə-**lan**-dee-ə)
Cancer Bush
FABACEAE

For a plant that has been around in gardens since 1683, *Sutherlandia frutescens* doesn't seem to have garnered much attention. I can't understand why: in its late-winter to summer flowering season it can hardly be overlooked. It is a small shrub from South Africa, reminding one a little of New Zealand's Kowhai, but with scarlet flowers followed by bladder-like pink pods that are almost as decorative. Easily grown in most soils, it likes a damp winter and tolerates moderate frosts. Propagation is hardly necessary, as it usually self-seeds freely.

The genus was named in honour of the Scottish botanist, gardener and author James Sutherland, to commemorate the publication of his magnum opus, a Latin description of the plants under his care in the Edinburgh Botanic Garden, now known as the Royal Botanic Gardens, Edinburgh.

Sutherlandia frutescens. Balloon Pea, Duck Plant
TONY RODD

Swainsona galegifolia. Darling Pea

SWAINSONA
(swaen-**soh**-nə)
Swainson Pea, Darling Pea, Swan Flower, Winter Sweet Pea, Sturt Desert Pea
FABACEAE

A shrubby, fast-growing perennial from outback New South Wales and Queensland, the Darling Pea, *Swainsona galegifolia*, makes a colourful show in the dryish garden, provided the soil is well drained. Like many another Australian plant, its seeds need scorching before sowing to ensure germination, and there is a danger it won't come true to colour anyway.

Flowering begins in early spring and continues for several weeks. The illustrated cerise-red is common, but the plant may also flower in mauve, blue, pink, yellow or orange-red. Safer by far to grow it from cuttings of hardened wood struck in sand. Occasional water is needed through the warmer months, and the flexible flowering stems can be cut back hard in late winter. The Darling Pea is a spreading sort of plant, rarely more than 1m/3ft tall. It makes an excellent groundcover for dry, sunny banks.

The Sturt Desert Pea, *S. formosa* (formerly *Clianthus formosus*) is native to the dry outback of Australia. It can be grown in desert areas or containers of perfectly drained gravelly mix. Nick the seed coats before sowing and plant in early summer. It hates humidity, dislikes coastal climates and is sometimes grafted onto small plants of related *Colutea arborescens,* which has a stronger root system. A prostrate plant, it is dazzling in its native environment.

Swainsona formosa. Sturt Desert Pea

Symphyandra wanneri. Ring Bellflower

SYMPHYANDRA
(sim-fee-an-drə)
Ring Bellflower
CAMPANULACEAE

It comes as no real surprise that the colourful *Symphyandra wanneri* is related to the Campanulas. Notice the romantic colour of the flowers and the lightly toothed foliage. But close inspection will make you more aware of the differences: the foliage is hairy, the bell-flowers longer than you would expect. A taxonomist would go further, noting the unusual structure of the flower's anthers.

All *Symphyandra* species are from the European alps or mountains in the Caucasus. They need well-drained soil and do best in a part-shaded position in a cool temperate climate. Grow them from divisions. Keep them moist and wait for summer blooms.

Symphytum 'Rubrum'. Red Comfrey

SYMPHYTUM
(sim-fit-əm)
Comfrey, Boneset
BORAGINACEAE

Once upon a time *Symphytum* was believed to heal wounds of all kinds. The popular name Boneset has lingered into the present century, though all uses of the plant have faded out of mind. Today, 35-odd *Symphytum* species are grown in the wild garden, but they are too invasive to mix with precious border flowers. *S.* 'Rubrum', however, is one of a number of attractive and garden-friendly cultivars.

Each perennial Comfrey plant grows roughly 40cm/16in wide and tall, and develops tuberous roots. Most prefer moist, rich soil and can be propagated from seed, root cuttings or division. Their summer blossoms are in shades of blue, yellow, purple or crimson, and the plants should be cut back hard when blooms have faded.

SYNCARPIA
(sin-karp-ee-ə)
Turpentine, Peebeen
MYRTACEAE

Possibly the finest and most useful tree of Australia's east coast is *Syncarpia glomulifera*, the Turpentine. Often mistaken for a Eucalypt (to which it is related), the Turpentine sends up a towering trunk as high as 25m/80ft. It is particularly sought after and cut for the valuable, straight-grained, heavy pink timber.

Syncarpia glomulifera. Turpentine

The Turpentine's deeply ridged bark is thick and fibrous, the dark, 9cm/3½in leaves tough and wavy, with silvery-grey reverses. Like Eucalyptus blossom, the creamy-white flowers are a mass of stamens and appear each spring. The big difference is that they appear generally seven at a time, fused together on long stalks. When the stamens fall, there remains a multiple-celled seed capsule, rather like the head of a medieval war mace. These give the tree its name *Syncarpia*, meaning 'seeds together'.

There is just one other tree in the genus, the larger-leafed Peebeen or *S. hillii*, found only on Queensland's Fraser Island. *Syncarpia* is grown widely in the southern United States and Hawaii, as both a shade and timber tree. It is hardy to around –7ºC/19ºF.

SYRINGA
(si-rin-gə)
Lilac
OLEACEAE

The 20-odd sweetly scented species of *Syringa* would have to be springtime's favourite shrub group in their native northern hemisphere. Found naturally only in Europe and northeastern Asia, they are perhaps even more popular in America's winter-frigid midwestern states, where they are among the few shrubs that can be relied on to produce a mass of springtime blossom year after year.

The reason is simple. Lilacs thrive on cold. Unless they go cold-dormant, they may not bloom at all the following spring. The

Syringa persica. Persian Lilac

Syringa vulgaris 'Maréchal Foch'. Lilac

Syringa persica 'Alba'. White Lilac

Syringa vulgaris 'Katherine Havermeyer'. Lilac

Syzygium jambos. Rose Apple

SYZYGIUM
(si-**zij**-ee-∂m)
Lilly Pilly, Rose Apple, Jumbool, Malay Apple, Brush Cherry
MYRTACEAE

only alternative (and not a good one at that) is to plant them in semi-shade and force them into dormancy by gradually drying them right out. But really, you'd be better off choosing a plant more suited to your climate!

Lilacs take up a lot of room and in small gardens they are often grafted onto related Privet roots which do not sucker. They can be increased from seed but will take up to 10 years to bloom and may not come true to type. The gardener in more of a hurry will either graft onto Privet stock or propagate from early summer tip-cuttings struck in sandy soil. In mature specimens, excessive suckering should be controlled by pruning

most away, *below* soil level. Spent flower-heads should be dead-headed to prevent seed formation, and a few older shoots can be removed each year.

Lilacs are deciduous, mostly bearing simple, medium-sized oval leaves. An exception is *S. persica*, the Persian Lilac, which often produces 3-lobed leaves. All species yield dense panicles of 4-petalled flowers from the ends of branches. These may be any shade of purple, mauve, white, pink, red-violet or primrose yellow.

A leaf-rich, friable loam grows the best Lilacs, but over-acid soil must be sweetened with a ration of lime. A pH of 6 to 6.5 is ideal.

A taxonomist's nightmare and a great nuisance to gardeners, these lovely trees have changed names as often as Elizabeth Taylor: Jambosa, Phyllocladyx, Eugenia, Stenocalyx and now – Syzygium!

The latest division has most species of Eugenia from Africa, Asia and Australia reclassified as *Syzygium* for reasons involving the seeds. But they are still often labelled Eugenia. There are around 500 species, all with evergreen foliage and often brilliantly coloured new leaves. The flowers are mostly creamy-white, a mass of stamens, and very attractive to bees. In all principally grown species, these are followed by vividly coloured fruits, often pink, and delicately sweet.

Syzygium malaccense. Malay Apple

Tabebuia chrysotricha. Golden Trumpet Tree

Tabebuia riparia. Whitewood

Syzygiums enjoy humidity and are not very hardy, at least when young. *S. jambos*, the Rose Apple or Jambu, is the golden fruit of immortality in Buddhist legends. *S. malaccense*, the lovely Malay Apple, has purple-pink flowers.

There are several dwarf cultivars of *S. australe* which grow well in tubs or pots. They include 'Aussie Compact', 'Bush Christmas' and 'Minipilly'; flowers are white and fluffy.

TABEBUIA
(tab-ae-**boo**-yə)
Trumpet Tree, Poui, Roblé Blanco
BIGNONIACEAE

Among the most beautiful of flowering trees and shrubs for the warmer climate are the *Tabebuias*, all from tropical America and known worldwide under a host of popular

names. There are at least 100 species, all bearing the same spectacular trumpet flowers as the popular climbing Bignonias to which they are related.

All are easily propagated from seed, cuttings or air layers, and they grow fast in deep, rich soil of a tropical climate, flowering while quite young.

All species are showy; some are quite spectacular. Among the best are: *T. rosea*, known variously as the Rosy Trumpet Tree, Pink Poui, Roblé Blanco and White Cedar – take your pick! It is a tall grower, to 20m/65ft, bearing handsome, darkish, pinnate leaves and rosy trumpet flowers in profusion at many times of the year.

Shrubby *T. riparia* or Whitewood hails from Jamaica, and only reaches its maximum height of 6m/20ft in true tropical climates. Its 7cm/3in flowers are pure white with a rich yellow throat.

T. chrysotricha, the Golden Trumpet Tree from Central America, is just 5m/16ft tall and deciduous. Its vivid yellow blossom opens irregularly over a long period, beginning in winter.

The botanical classification *Tabebuia* is an original Indian name for these plants.

TABERNAEMONTANA
(tab-ur-nee-mon-**tah**-nə)
Nero's Crown, Ceylon Moonbeam, Wax Flower, Mock Gardenia, Eve's Apple, Crepe Jasmine, Pinwheel Flower, Fleur d'Amour
APOCYNACEAE

The poet Gray's line 'Full many a Flower is born to blush unseen, and waste its sweetness on the desert air' may sound a little fulsome for modern tastes, but it certainly describes the predicament of lovely *Tabernaemontana*. There are some 100 species, all with fragrant, white, gardenia-scented blooms. They are shrubs or trees, from 1m/3ft upwards in height; all need a semi-tropical or warmer climate, a sheltered, sunny spot and a soil mixture of sand, loam and peat to flourish.

Tabebuia rosea. Pink Poui, Roblé Blanco

Tabernaemontana divaricata 'Flore Pleno'. Fleur d'Amour

Tagetes patula cultivar. French Marigold

Tabernaemontana pandacaqui. Banana Bush
TONY RODD

Eve's Apple or *T. divaricata* (syn *T. coronaria*) is from India, has spirally twisted, white, crepy flowers and pointed, glossy, evergreen leaves. The hanging, half-round fruit has a pronounced depression along one side. This suggests a partly eaten apple and is the origin of this species' popular names. Unlike many tropicals, water is appreciated all year.

Tacca chantrieri. Bat Flower

Tagetes 'Naughty Marietta'. French Marigold

TACCA
(tak-ka)
Bat Flower, Devil Flower, Devil's Tongue, South Sea Arrowroot, Cat's Whiskers, Jew's Beard

TACCACEAE

Striking rather than beautiful, the sinister, whiskered blossoms of *Tacca chantrieri* open on 30cm/12in stalks among heavily veined leaves. They are not quite black, but such a deep purplish-brown it is easy to see how they earned the name of Devil or Bat Flower.

From tropical Southeast Asia and Africa, *Taccas* need the protection of a glasshouse or sheltered courtyard away from the subtropics.

Propagate by division of the rhizome in spring and pot in a mixture of sand, loam and peatmoss. Give water in the warm weather, let dry out almost totally in winter. Repot when growth starts in spring. A winter minimum of 13°C/55°F is needed.

TAGETES
(tag-∂-tees)
African Marigold, Aztec Marigold, Signet Marigold, Irish Lace

ASTERACEAE

If the scent of Marigolds is not to everyone's taste, we can agree on the colours – bold, brassy and wonderfully showy.

The African type (*Tagetes erecta*) grows to 1m/3ft, with cushiony double blooms up to 13cm/5in across, mostly in shades of orange and yellow. Lately, though, some insipid cream or white hybrids have appeared, and the trend has been towards shorter plants with larger flowers. Many good mixtures are available, as well as individual colour strains and dwarf varieties which grow less than 30cm/12in and are useful for edging and planter work.

The French Marigolds (*T. patula*) come in a wider variety. They have similar pungent, fern-like foliage and are rarely more than 30cm/1ft in height. Flowers can be single or double, ruffled or picoteed, and

Tagetes erecta cultivars. African Marigold

Tanacetum cinerariifolium. Dalmatian Pyrethrum

Tagetes tenuifolia 'Golden Gem'. Signet Marigold

Tamarix parviflora. Flowering Cypress

Tanacetum coccineum 'Brenda'. Painted Daisy

Tamarix parviflora, from southeast Europe, has almost invisible, scale-like, deciduous leaves on long. arching stems. Prune back after flowering.

in shades of brown, mahogany and red (along with the usual orange and yellow), many of them beautifully patterned. A compact strain grows only to 15cm/6in and makes wonderful edgings. Finally, there are tiny Signet Marigolds (*T. tenuifolia*). On these the foliage is very fine and sweetly scented, while single 2.5cm/1in blooms are borne in unbelievable profusion.

All Marigolds are easy to grow from seed sown outdoors any time in warm areas; else-where, sow seed indoors in late winter. All species take about 14 weeks to reach flower-ing size, and should be planted in average, well-drained soil in full sun.

TAMARIX
(tam-ə-riks)
Tamarisk, Flowering Cypress, Salt Cedar
TAMARICACEAE

Hard to believe any plant as graceful as a Tamarisk could be so incredibly tough! The feathery branchlets of minute, spicily fragrant pink blossom move in the slightest breeze, yet the same trees thrive in howling coastal gales and salt-laden soil.

They are best grown from 2cm/³⁄₄in thick cuttings set in their final position and watered well. These do not transplant, due to very long taproots, but rooted cuttings bolt into growth and soon make a good-sized bush. Eventually, they can reach 10m/30ft.

TANACETUM
(tan-ə-**see**-təm)
Pyrethrum, Fly-spray Plant, Tansy
ASTERACEAE

This is one of the genera that has been split off the unwieldy old genus *Chrysanthemum*. Its showiest member is *Tanacetum coccineum*, the Florist's Pyrethrum, a herba-ceous perennial originally from the cooler parts of the Middle East and cultivated in many varieties, their single or double flowers coming in every shade from white through pink and crimson. They appear in early summer and again in autumn, on long stems that make them first-rate cut flowers. Give them a temperate climate, sun and very rich

Tanacetum parthenium. Feverfew

Tecoma garrocha. Orange Trumpet Bush

Tecoma smithii. Yellow Bells

soil. The Dalmatian Pyrethrum, *T. cinerari-ifolium,* is a rather unimposing, short-lived perennial with greyish leaves and long-stalked white daisies in summer, its chief claim to fame being the aromatic substances it contains – deadly to a whole range of insects but not to people. Pyrethrum-based insecticides are much used both in house-hold fly-sprays and in the gardens of those of us who prefer not to use hazardous chemical insecticides. Also known as 'Pyrethrum' is the humble Feverfew, *T. parthenium,* a little short-lived perennial that decks itself with white daisies over a long summer season and is a favourite in cottage gardens; it comes in double and gold-leafed varieties as well.

TAPEINOCHILOS
(tap-ae-noh-**kai**-l∂s)
Indonesian Ginger
Zingiberaceae

Spectacular in the subtropical garden, there are about 15 species of *Tapeinochilos* found in Indonesia and northern Australia. Best known is the Moluccan *T. ananassae,* named for the resemblance of its showy inflores-cence to a pineapple. Like all of the group, it dotes on well-drained, moist soil, packed with leafmould.

Grown from divisions of the root mass, the branching, cane-like stems shoot up to 2m/6ft and more during summer. The flower spike rises direct from the roots, each yellow bloom almost hidden in a thorny, bright red bract. If not cut for decoration, these should be pruned back to ground level when flowers are done.

TECOMA
(te-**koh**-m∂)
Yellow Bells, Yellow Elder, Trumpet Bush, Tecomaxochitl
Bignoniaceae

Clustered bells of vivid orange-scarlet set off to perfection by a background of crepy green foliage – that identifies the brilliant *Tecoma garrocha,* a useful small evergreen shrub for frost-free gardens. Its leaves are composed of deeply veined, pointed and sharply toothed leaflets, and from midsummer (and often on through autumn) every branch is tipped with a large panicle of 3cm/1in bell-flowers. These have a 5cm/2in yellow-orange tubes flaring into deeper orange petals.

Related *T. smithii* flowers in a rich yellow (often tinged orange), and its tubular buds may be quite red. It is thought to be a natural hybrid.

Tapeinochilos ananassae. Indonesian Ginger

Yellow-blooming *T. stans* grows to 5m/16ft and catches every eye with its display all through summer and autumn.

Tecomas do best in a warm, sunny spot, but once established will stand the odd light frost. Well-drained, sandy loam with added organic matter is the ideal soil. They can be increased by soft-tip or semi-hardwood cuttings taken during the warmer months. Light pruning of the flowered shoots right after bloom helps keep *Tecomas* shapely.

Tecoma stans. Yellow Elder

Tecomaria capensis. Cape Honeysuckle

Tecophilaea cyanocrocus. Chilean Blue
Crocus   GEOFF BRYANT

TECOMANTHE
(tek-oh-**man**-thee)
Pink Trumpet Vine
BIGNONIACEAE

Tecomanthes, the highly decorative Trumpet
Vines, are native to Australia and New
Guinea. *T. dendrophila*, the New Guinea
species, is suited only to subtropical climates,
where it bears umbels of deep-rose bells on
old wood.

Related *T. hillii* is from Queensland, but
will grow up to 35⁰ from the equator in a
sheltered position. Both like deep, well-
drained soil and plenty of moisture.
Propagate from seed or soft-tip cuttings and
let climb into trees.

Tecomanthe hillii. Pink Trumpet Vine

TECOMARIA
(tek-oh-me ∂ r-ee-∂)
Cape Honeysuckle
BIGNONIACEAE

Technically classed as a shrubby climber, the
brassily blooming Cape Honeysuckle,
Tecomaria capensis, can swing either way. It
will climb up to 3m/10ft, but if a shrub is
preferred it must be pruned hard annually to
control its long, trailing growth. Then, it is
particularly useful in coastal areas, although
it will tolerate inland drought as well as
moist, salt air and is hardy down to
–2⁰C/28⁰F.

The flowers, which appear in terminal
sprays, are tubular and either scarlet or
orange; there is also a yellow cultivar, 'Lutea'.
Blooming begins in late summer and
continues until autumn turns chilly. Grow
from layers or semi-hardwood cuttings
taken any time.

Tecomaria capensis 'Lutea'. Cape
Honeysuckle

TECOPHILAEA
(tek-oh-fil-**lae**-y∂)
Blue Crocus
LILIACEAE

It is a sad testimony to the greed of gardeners
that the rare and remarkable *Tecophilaea
cyanocrocus* should now be in danger of
extinction in its native home, the mountain
meadows of Chile. The fatal attraction is the
extraordinary colour of the flowers, which
look like wide-open crocuses and grow from
crocus-like corms in spring. In the best
forms they are the most dazzlingly pure deep
blue – and they are fragrant too, a very rare
attribute among blue flowers. It is not a
difficult plant to grow, given the sort of mild
temperate climate where such plants as *Iris
unguicularis* and nerines flourish or an
unheated greenhouse in colder places. Give
it sunshine and fertile soil. It sets seed quite
freely in cultivation, so there should be no
need for further plundering of the wild
populations.

TELEKIA
(te-l∂-**kee**-∂)
(SYN Buphthalmum)
Telekia
ASTERACEAE

This small genus of two daisy species ranges
from central Europe to the Caucasus. Just
occasionally they are found in Western
gardens, where their resistance to cold is a
great attraction. Generous moisture, shelter
from strong winds and part shade suit
them best.

Telekia speciosa. Telekia

If you have the chance, propagate them from seed or division in autumn, and with any luck they'll be blooming in the first summer. *T. speciosa* has greyish, serrated foliage, orange-yellow daisy flowers 9cm/3½in across and grows to 2m/6ft.

TELOPEA
(tel-**oh**-pee-ə)
Waratah
PROTEACEAE

There are only four species of this Australian Protea genus; none is widely grown in their homeland and they're rarely seen abroad. It's not that they aren't worthwhile (for they bear striking blooms), but they do have a reputation for being difficult.

Waratahs really only do well in damp, sandy loam covered by a thick mulch of coarse organic matter such as fallen leaves,

Telopea oreades. Gippsland Waratah

Telopea 'Shady Lady'. Hybrid Waratah

Telopea speciosissima (white form). White Waratah

twigs and bark. And if you can provide a cool root-run by placing a few large, flat stones around the trunk, so much the better. In nature, they are understorey shrubs in open forests, and while they accept full sun, bright dappled shade probably suits them better.

Floral emblem of the Australian state of New South Wales is the gorgeous *Telopea speciosissima*. Its bright red, 15cm/6in spring flowers can be seen at a great distance, and that is the meaning of both its botanical and Aboriginal names: 'seen from afar'. The cone-like red inflorescence consists of many curved florets surrounded by common bracts. There is also a rare white form.

Related species *T. mongaensis*, *T. oreades* (the Gippsland Waratah) and *T. truncata* (the Tasmanian Waratah) are sometimes grown by enthusiasts. Several fine new hybrids are said to be the easiest of all to grow.

Waratahs are normally raised from spring cuttings or (the species) from seed, sown in winter in individual pots of gritty

soil and planted out when large enough. They are hardy down to at least –8ºC/17ºF and can be kept compact by regular tip pruning and cutting of flowers.

TEMPLETONIA
(tem-pel-**toh**-nee-ə)
Cockies' Tongues, Coralbush
FABACEAE

This showy, dry-climate shrub from Australia's western deserts is grown also in the American southwest and many other drought-prone areas of the temperate world. *Templetonia retusa* is a sparse-growing shrub which can reach 2m/6ft in height and much more in diameter. It likes gravelly, alkaline soil that includes some leaf litter. Propagated from scarified seed or hardwood cuttings, it looks better for a light, overall trim. The sparse foliage may drop in extremely dry weather. Dull coral pea-flowers appear in early spring.

Templetonia retusa. Cockies' Tongues

Tetradenia riparia. Nutmeg Bush

TETRADENIA

(tet-rə-**deen**-ee-ə)

(SYN Iboza, Moschosma)

Nutmeg Bush, Misty Plume Bush, Ginger Bush

LAMIACEAE

Softly flowered, spicily scented, and fast-growing, the tender South African *Tetradenia riparia* is one of nine species in a decorative genus of the mint family. It is of particular value in a mild coastal climate, where the entire bush bursts into bloom in midwinter, and the display lasts well.

The shrubs are almost completely deciduous, with toothed, velvety leaves developing as bloom fades. The tiny silvery-pink flowers are sprinkled with purple anthers and appear in long terminal panicles.

Hard pruning is necessary to maintain shape, and up to three-quarters of the previous season's growth should be removed after bloom.

Cuttings taken in early spring and struck in sandy, well-drained soil will flower the following winter.

Tetratheca ciliata. Black-eyed Susan

Tetrapanax papyrifer. Ricepaper Plant

TETRAPANAX

(tet-rə-**pan**-aks)

Ricepaper Plant, Chinese Paper Plant

ARALIACEAE

One of the larger members of the Aralia family, the Chinese Ricepaper Plant, *Tetrapanax papyrifer*, can grow to well over 3m/10ft tall. Its huge, deeply lobed, felted leaves may be 60cm/2ft across and provide useful shelter from summer sun for smaller plants. Whitish when young, they turn a rusty colour with age. The fluffy greenish-white flowers are pleasant enough, appearing from late summer onwards in great 1m/3ft panicles.

Tetrapanax is far too big for pots but is popular in courtyard plantings; it's useful in seaside gardens, where it resists salt-laden winds, growing well in the sandy soil found there. It needs lots of water year-round.

TETRATHECA

(tet-rə-**thee**-kə)

Black-eyed Susan

TREMANDRACEAE

Masses of showy pink, mauve or purple-pink bell-flowers on fine red stems typify charming *Tetrathecas*, though most species also have rare white forms. The flowers' black centres have earned them the common name Black-eyed Susan.

All *Tetrathecas* are low, understorey Australian shrubs bringing long-lasting splashes of spring colour to areas with light, sandy soil. They enjoy sun or part shade and

Teucrium fruticans. Germander

thrive only in well-drained places totally free of lime or animal manure (though they do appreciate a leafmould or compost mulch). *T. ciliata* (pink flowers), *T. pilosa* (mauve-pink) and *T. ericifolia* (deep pink) are the most commonly seen species.

TEUCRIUM

(**tyoo**-kree-əm)

Germander, Wood Sage, Cat Thyme

LAMIACEAE

Useful shrubs for the grey-foliage garden, hardy *Teucriums* come in over 300 species. Aromatic *T. fruticans* is the most commonly seen type, growing to 2.5m/8ft, and spreading as wide. It is often trimmed as a neat, low hedge or used in sheltered seaside gardens. Hardy down to –2ºC/28ºF, it can be grown in a wide range of climates, where its all-grey habit contrasts effectively with delicate blue-mauve flowers that have one greatly enlarged petal.

A member of the mint family, Germander thrives in any moderately rich, well-drained soil. Propagate it from cuttings taken with a heel in spring or summer. Trim spent flowers away to promote new growth.

THALIA

(**thah**-lee-ə)

Water Canna

MARANTACEAE

These large, herbaceous perennial plants are the tallest-growing flowering aquatics available. All seven species come from the Americas – mostly from the tropics – and several of them can grow 3.5m/11ft or taller when the climate is to their liking.

Thalia dealbata. Water Canna   *TONY RODD*

Thalia dealbata is the common species, a
native of Florida and Texas, and it is frost
hardy if planted in a container 60cm/2ft below
the water surface. Tall stems of canna-like
leaves shoot up in spring. These have a white,
powdery look and are topped in summer by
panicles of 3-petalled violet flowers.

Thalictrum aquilegiifolium. King-of-the-
Meadow

Thermopsis lanceolata. False Lupin

THALICTRUM

(tha-**lik**-tr∂m)
**Meadow Rue, King-of-the-Meadow,
Lady Rue**

RANUNCULACEAE

Several species of *Thalictrum* are grown as
much for their delicate foliage as for their
relatively short-lived flower display. Closely
related to the Ranunculus and Anemone,
they sprout from fibrous or tuberous roots
and send up tall stems topped with great
clusters of small, fluffy flowers, pinkish-
mauve in the illustrated *T. aquilegiifolium.*
The much-divided leaves are blue-green and
have somewhat the appearance of maidenhair fern or of Columbine foliage.

Thalictrums are generally planted from
divisions of the root mass in early spring, but
take time to re-establish. Single species are
better propagated from seed, which will
germinate in less than a month. They look
best in light shade and really thrive in a rich,
moist soil that drains well. Staking may be
needed, for the flower heads can be top-
heavy. Cut back hard in autumn.

THERMOPSIS

(thur-**mop**-sis)
False Lupin

FABACEAE

Extraordinarily like the North American
Lupins (*Lupinus* spp.), *Thermopsis lanceolata*
is a frost hardy, herbaceous perennial from
Siberia, and used for a long-lasting display of
brilliant golden-yellow. The pea-type flowers
appear at intervals all along the flower stems

from late spring, persisting into the first
weeks of summer.

While it can be planted from spring
division, *Thermopsis* may take years to
re-establish after root damage. Better try it
from seed, which germinates in about 3
weeks. Seedlings should be pricked out
before the heavy taproots become too
established, and transplanted to their final
positions at 45cm/18in spacings in autumn.

Thermopsis leaves are grey-green and
divided into three sharply pointed leaflets.
Cut the flower stems back after blooming for
a second flush. Deep, well-drained soil in full
sun is needed for the best effect.

THEVETIA

(th∂-**vee**-sh∂)
Yellow Oleander, Be-still Tree, Lucky Nut

APOCYNACEAE

Like related Oleanders (which they resemble
in habit though not in colour), the dangerously beautiful *Thevetias* are poisonous in
every part, from their milky sap to their
gorgeous, golden trumpets.

The most commonly seen is *T. peruviana*,
sometimes called the Be-still Tree, because of
the constant air movement of its spidery,
short-stemmed leaves. It grows to 10m/33ft
in height, bears lightly fragrant 5cm/2in
golden trumpet flowers, followed by angular
red fruits which ripen black. Its variety
aurantiaca has salmon-orange flowers.

Closely related *T. thevetioides* (shown)
bears much larger, more open flowers of a
clearer yellow, but rarely exceeds 4.5m/14ft
in height. Forms with orange flowers are also
known. All are increased from seed or
cuttings and enjoy well-watered, sandy soil.
Mature plants tolerate a few degrees of frost.

Thevetia thevetioides. Be-still Tree

Thomasia macrocarpa. Woolly Thomasia

THOMASIA
(tom-**ass**-ee-ə)
Woolly Thomasia
STERCULIACEAE

A decorative genus of 28 shrub species from Western Australia, the *Thomasias* are useful subjects in mild areas, so long as the humidity is not high. They enjoy sandy soil with some peat, and since the flowers hang downward, should be planted in a raised bed where you can look up at them. Most species are propagated from cuttings, but seed is a possibility for those with experience.

T. macrocarpa is most widely in cultivation, having felt-textured, deeply divided leaves and lilac-pink flowers up to 2cm/1in wide. These are petalless, but the calyx lobes have adapted to take their place. Dappled shade, please, in hot areas.

THRYPTOMENE
(**thrip**-toh-meen)
Heath Myrtle, Thryptomene
MYRTACEAE

The Heath Myrtles are a pan-Australian genus of small, slender shrubs which rather resemble miniature versions of their relatives the tea trees (Leptospermum). Most grow 1m/3ft tall and wide or a little less, with tiny but sharply aromatic leaves; the effect is airy and graceful. In late winter or spring they completely cover themselves with small pink or white flowers. They need no pruning, but if you want to make them bushier, the best way to do it is to cut long branches of flowers for the house. They make excellent cut flowers, lasting for two weeks in water and setting off larger flowers very beautifully. Well-drained soils and temperate, not too frosty, climates suit them best.

Thunbergia grandiflora. Sky Flower

THUNBERGIA
(thun-**bur**-jə)
Black-eyed Susan, Sky Flower, Blue Trumpet Vine, Clock Vine, Glory Vine
ACANTHACEAE

A genus of gaily flowered plants from warm climates, *Thunbergias* come in many forms – perennials, shrubs and climbers – with the latter most commonly seen.

Thunbergias are evergreen, and though young plants may die back where winter temperatures drop one or two degrees below freezing, they usually sprout again in spring. The species shown here are all vigorous climbers for a warm, sunny position away from cold winds. Soil should be well drained, contain rotted organic matter and be kept consistently moist throughout the warmer months.

Thryptomene saxicola. Thryptomene

Thunbergia alata. Black-eyed Susan

T. alata, Black-eyed Susan, can be grown as an annual, for it looks and flowers best when young. Its black-throated orange flowers are produced singly all over the lightweight plant from late spring right through summer.

T. mysorensis from India needs at least a subtropical climate or glasshouse to survive. Given that, it will produce great hanging racemes of yellow, red and brown flowers all summer.

T. grandiflora takes cooler conditions. Its yellow-throated, blueish blooms, trumpet-shaped with flared lobes, appear in clusters from spring to early summer.

Thunbergia mysorensis. Mysore Clock Vine

Thunia alba. Bamboo Orchid, Orchid of Burma

THUNIA

(**thoo**-nee-yə)

Christmas Orchid, Bamboo Orchid, Orchid of Burma

ORCHIDACEAE

Few orchids feature handsome foliage, but *Thunia alba* (syn *T. marshalliana*) is one that does. It looks rather like a small grey-leafed ginger lily in growth, and when the clusters of white and pale gold flowers appear in midsummer it is a most attractive sight. In my garden it always flowers for Christmas Day – but only if I remember to repot it in a very rich mix of equal parts orchid compost, sphagnum moss and old manure as soon as new growth appears in spring (it dies down for the winter) and to water it lavishly. Even better, stand the pot in a deep saucer of water; in its native Burma it grows in swamps and bogs, a rare place to find an orchid. In frosty climates it is grown in the same way but in a greenhouse. Don't give it too much shade. In the northern hemisphere it flowers in July.

Thymus 'Porlock'. Hybrid Thyme

Thymus serpyllum cultivar. Creeping Thyme

THYMUS

(**tai**-məs)

Thyme, Mother-of-thyme

LAMIACEAE

'I know a bank whereon the wild thyme blows', wrote Shakespeare. It's the sort of situation I can only dream of – lying about on a groundcover of *Thymus vulgaris* is altogether too much!

These days we grow the original species (only one of a hundred) for the kitchen but prefer its lemon-scented hybrid *T. citriodorus* in the flower garden. It likes a dryish, well-drained position (a bank is ideal) and is relatively hardy except in a severe winter. Water lightly in drought; propagate from cuttings any time in warm weather.

In summer, Thyme becomes a mat of tiny, pale-lilac flowers, and bees come from all directions.

THYSANOTUS

(thai-san-**oh**-təs)

Fringe Lily, Fringed Violet

LILIACEAE

Among the world's most beautiful members of the lily family, slender *Thysanotus* must hold a high place. Though not often met with in cultivation, there are some 20 species, all save one uniquely from Australia – and that one outsider spreads as far as South China and the Philippines.

They are rhizomatous perennials with grass-like foliage and forked panicles of exquisite violet blooms with six petals, three of which are delicately fringed. All species are propagated from offsets; they like damp, well-drained loam. In nature, they occur in open forest areas.

Tiarella cordifolia. Foam Flower

TIARELLA

(tee-ah-**rell**-ə)

Foam Flower, False Mitrewort

SAXIFRAGACEAE

Named for its tiny tiara-shaped seed capsules, the incredibly delicate Foam Flower needs full shade or at least dappled light to prevent complete desiccation in hot weather. Even so, you should not try to grow it unless you live in a cold or cool temperate climate.

Grow *Tiarella* from seed, or division of the creeping rootstock in spring or autumn. Plant in leaf-rich, well-drained garden soil that is constantly moist, but not soggy. A woodland garden or shaded rockery is ideal. The sharply toothed, grape-like leaves are hairy, and colour to red-bronze in autumn. Dainty flowers appear on 30cm/12in stems in spring.

Thysanotus tuberosus. Fringe Lily

Tibouchina 'Alstonville'. Glory Bush

TIBOUCHINA

(tib-oo-**shee**-nə)

Brazilian Spiderflower, Princess Flower, Glory Bush, Quaresma, Lasiandra

MELASTOMATACEAE

Gaudy South American shrubs for acid soil that is rich and well drained, the Lasiandras (as they are commonly called) produce extraordinary colour effects at many times of the year. New growth is shaded with bronze and red, quickly turning to a rich velvet green. The plants are basically evergreen, but odd leaves may turn scarlet or yellow in cold weather. The magnificent flowers most commonly appear through summer and autumn, though some species bloom in spring. While they are generally a rich, glowing purple, pink or white species are also known.

There are 150 or more species in the wild, though cultivars of only three or four of these are widely grown. *T. granulosa*, one of the most popular species, can grow into a small tree 10m/33ft tall, but is usually kept pruned to a smaller size. Flowers are a rich, almost iridescent violet-purple and produced in incredible profusion for many weeks in early autumn. Its cultivar 'Rosea' is similar except the flowers are soft pink and less profuse.

T. macrantha grows only to 3m/10ft at most. Its flowers are a deep royal purple and, though not as generously produced, can be 10cm/4in across. Flowering will begin in autumn and a well-grown specimen may still be in bloom at winter's end.

Tibouchinas can be grown from fresh seed or soft-tip cuttings taken any time during the warmer months. The plants grow best in full sun, but in very hot areas dappled shade is acceptable. Keep moist all through spring and summer, and pinch out the growing tips regularly to promote bushiness. Even so, plants are inclined to be leggy and the brittle branches are soon broken by strong winds. Some species will take the odd light frost, but they're best planted under eaves or large trees where winters are frosty.

TIGRIDIA

(tai-**grid**-ee-ə)

Tiger Flower, Shell Flower, One-day Lily, Jockey's Cap Lily

IRIDACEAE

Garish and gaudy, these dazzling members of the iris family are most effective in a mass. Flowering begins in early summer, and although individual blooms last only a day, each stem produces many buds, which open in succession over a number of weeks. The flowers, anything from 8–13cm/3–5in across, always feature a central bowl, heavily spotted, surrounded by three broad petals in pink, red, orange, yellow or purple.

Plant *Tigridias* anytime from midwinter to early spring into rich, well-drained soil in full sun. They should be watered regularly throughout late spring and summer, but gradually reduce water as autumn becomes cooler, for the corms prefer dryness during their winter dormancy.

Tibouchina granulosa 'Kathleen'. Pink Glory Bush

Tibouchina 'Noelene'. Lasiandra

TILLANDSIA

(til-**land**-zee-ə)

Tillandsia, Spanish Moss, Ball Moss

BROMELIACEAE

Most numerous and widespread genus of the Bromeliad family, *Tillandsias* can be found from the southern United States right down to South America. They can be fingernail-size or up to 4m/13ft in height, and come from warm, humid forests, the most hostile of deserts and all the more pleasant places in between.

Tigridia pavonia. Jockey's Cap Lily

Tillandsia lindenii. Pink Quill

Tillandsia crispa. Air Plant

Tillandsias gain water and nutrients through their leaves. They can be attached directly to trees, fences, or walls in cultivation, or grown in shallow pots of bark chips, treefern fibre, leafmould and sand.

Shown *T. crispa* likes moist shade year-round. It grows in tropical highland forests and can stand a little frost. The flower stems branch freely, and bracts in shades of orange and yellow outshine and outlast the simple flowers.

Popular *T. lindenii* is grown for its big spearhead-shaped rosy-pink bracts atop a 30cm/12in stem. From each, purplish blooms appear, one or two at a time for about 10 weeks.

Tithonia diversifolia. Tree Marigold

TITHONIA
(tai-**thoh**-nee-ə)
Mexican Sunflower, Tree Marigold
ASTERACEAE

If South Africa could name a daisy after dawn goddess Aurora, it was a sure bet some taxonomist would remember her mythical boyfriend Tithonus! So we have *Tithonia*, a small genus of annuals, perennials and shrubs notable for their big, bright daisy-like flowers.

T. rotundifolia, called the Mexican Sunflower, produces its garish orange-scarlet blooms from summer to midwinter in warm-climate gardens. In frost-free areas, sow seed outdoors where plants are to grow in early spring. Elsewhere, sow indoors in winter and plant out in full sun when chills are gone. The plants are inclined to sprawl and are extremely drought resistant.

Tithonia rotundifolia. Mexican Sunflower

Torenia fournieri. Blue Wings

Cousin *T. diversifolia*, the Tree Marigold, is a clump-forming shrub whose cane-like stems can reach 4m/13ft in a year. The brilliant 10cm/4in flowers appear in winter. Cut to ground after bloom, and pinch out tips.

TORENIA
(tor-**ee**-nee-ə)
Wishbone Flower, Blue Wings
SCROPHULARIACEAE

One of the earliest refugees from Vietnam, *Torenia fournieri*, the cool and succulent Wishbone Flower, has been welcomed with open arms. For it is that rare plant, an annual that turns on a stunning display even in shade. Really tropical in its needs – water, rich soil, humidity – it can be grown in the full sun of cooler climates and is happy in glasshouses everywhere. The foliage and growth habits are like those of Impatiens (which see), but the blooms are like Snapdragons in two shades of blue, and are borne in great abundance. There is also a pure white variety, *alba*.

Sow seed indoors, under glass, in midwinter and do not move the plants outside until night temperatures remain above 15°C/59°F. *Torenias* can be grown in pots for indoor use.

TOWNSENDIA
(touns-**en**-dee-ə)
Stemless Daisy, Easter Daisy
ASTERACEAE

Among the lowest-growing of the daisy family, *Townsendias* even make the ubiquitous English lawn species look like a giant. They tower a full 2.5cm/1in above ground

Townsendia exscapa. Stemless Daisy

Trachymene coerulea. Blue Lace Flower, Rottnest Daisy

Tradescantia, Andersoniana Group. Widow's Tears

level, though their open daisy flowers are about the same diameter. All 20 species are from the western United States, all love the well-drained gritty conditions of the scree garden, but need water in dry periods.

They are grown from spring-sown seed, or by summer division of the roots. These divisions sprout rosettes of 7.5cm/3in oblanceolate leaves (widest at their outer ends). Stalkless flowers, borne singly, may be faintly mauve instead of the white we show.

TRACHELOSPERMUM
(trak-el-oh-**spur**-məm)
Star Jasmine, Confederate Jasmine
APOCYNACEAE

One of the most useful evergreen twiners, the Chinese Star Jasmine (*Trachelospermum jasminoides*) can be used as a vine, a groundcover or even as a low shrub. Planted where the roots are shaded from direct sun, it will take a while to establish and then find its way to the light, either outwards or (with strong support) upwards.

The shiny, dark green leaves are evergreen, and the masses of lacy flowers – white and fragrant – are produced profusely in spring and summer. As a groundcover, it can be pinched or clipped back at any time. As a climber it needs regular trimming to prevent legginess. Hardy to around -6ºC/20ºF.

TRACHYMENE
(**trak**-ee-meen)
Blue Lace Flower
APIACEAE

Trachymene coerulea, formerly known as *Didiscus coerulea,* is one of those flowers you see more often in the vase than in the garden. A summer-flowering annual from Western Australia, it is easily grown in sun and well-drained, preferably rather sandy, soil, but it has two faults as a garden plant – its rather straggly, leggy habit and its short season (only about 3 weeks or so). You can prolong the season by making successive sowings from spring to midsummer, but that doesn't help your display beds much; so it is usually grown in the cutting garden. As a cut flower it is a real charmer, the lacy heads of flowers being borne on long stems and lasting very well. They are an unusual shade of powder blue which goes very nicely in mixed bunches.

Trachelospermum jasminoides. Star Jasmine

TRADESCANTIA
(trad-əs-**kant**-ee-ə)
Spiderwort, Inch Plant, Speedy Jenny, Wandering Jew, Creeping Jesus
COMMELINACEAE

If popular names are any indication of *real* popularity, *Tradescantias* must be near the top of the list. Many are numbered among favourite house plants or are used for groundcover in shaded gardens. They often have attractively variegated leaves and spread widely and rapidly by creeping stems which root at intervals. The Spiderwort, *T. blossfeldiana,* is one of the best of these, bearing clusters of tiny mauvish flowers in the leaf axils.

But the North American *T. virginiana* (Widow's Tears) is quite different – a showy herbaceous perennial with flowers up to

8cm/3in wide, in a range of shades from blue through mauve to purple, red, soft pink and brilliant white. It is best planted out in colder weather and will rapidly spread into a dense clump, sending up 60cm/2ft stems furnished at intervals with pointed strap-like leaves. The flowers appear in small terminal umbels in spring and early summer, each flower lasting only a day.

If the stems are cut back hard, they should bloom again in autumn. *T. virginiana* puts on its best show in moist soil with shade for part of each day. Cuttings strike easily in spring and seed germinates readily. The dense clumps should be divided every three or four years.

Tragopogon porrifolius. Salsify

TRAGOPOGON

(trag-oh-**poh**-gǝn)
Salsify, John-go-to-bed-at-noon, Vegetable Oyster Plant, Goatsbeard
ASTERACEAE

In old cottage gardens of Europe, the vegetables grew among the flowers in just the way that companion planting fans tell us they should. Many members of the onion family added their starburst-shaped flower heads to the display, as did the humble Salsify or Oyster Plant. This is a favourite root vegetable in Europe, though relatively unknown in the southern hemisphere. Salsify needs a cool root-run, a sunny position in mildly acid, well-drained soil with constant moisture. *Tragopogon porrifolius* produces open daisy flowers of rosy mauve on hollow stems. Grow it from seed.

TREVESIA

(tre-**vee**-see-ǝ)
Snowflake Aralia, Tropical Snowflake
ARALIACEAE

Away from the tropics, the only *Trevesia* usually seen is the Snowflake Aralia, *T. palmata*. It is grown for indoor use, valued for its big, glossy, irregularly shaped leaves that do resemble a giant green snowflake! But in frost-free areas *Trevesias* can be grown outdoors, and *T. sundaica* is a popular choice for tropical foliage effect. A large shrub or small tree, 6–8m/20–25ft tall, it has big, glossy, deeply lobed leaves and prickly branches. Fortunately, the leaves are interesting and attractive year-round, for the summer flowers must be among the most unremarkable produced by any plant – thick-stemmed clusters of tiny greenish blooms.

Trevesia palmata. Tropical Snowflake

TRICHOSTEMA

(trai-koh-**stem**-mǝ)
Blue Curls, Romero, Vinegar Weed
LAMIACEAE

One of southern California's most attractive wildflowers, *Trichostema lanatum* can be grown in any dryish climate. It is raised from seed, grows 1m/3ft in height in well-drained sandy loam, and needs little water, especially in summer.

The foliage is very like that of Rosemary, though hairy on the underside; but the mauve flowers are borne in 15cm/6in spikes of up to 20, and their buds are covered with striking woolly hairs shaded from pink to crimson or purple. *Trichostemas* have a spicy, sage-like fragrance, and are important bee plants.

Tricyrtis hirta. Toad Lily

TRICYRTIS

(trai-**sur**-tis)
Toad Lily
LILIACEAE

Native solely to mountainous parts of Asia, from the Himalayas to Japan, the strange Toad Lilies resemble orchids more than they do members of the lily family.

All 9 or 10 species grow from a creeping rhizome, preferring sandy, leaf-rich loam that's perpetually moist. They can be grown from seed or division of the rootstock, but need a sheltered position in cooler climates, for they are only half-hardy. The purple-marked white blooms of *Tricyrtis hirta* are produced in late summer and autumn on erect 1m/3ft stems, and make good cut flowers. Grow in dappled shade.

Trichostema lanatum. Blue Curls

Trifolium incarnatum. Italian Clover, Crimson Clover

Trillium grandiflorum. Wake Robin

Trillium erectum. Stinking Benjamin, Squaw Root

TRIFOLIUM
(trai-**foh**-lee-∂m)
Italian Clover, Clover, Shamrock, Trefoil
Fabaceae

Maybe it's the Irish blood in me, but I'll never know why so many gardeners make a fuss about clover coming up in their lawns. If I had my way, I'd plant it everywhere – for clover is the Irishman's Shamrock, and every plant another chance of finding a lucky four-lobed leaf!

At any rate, the choice is wide. There are around 1300 species of clover blooming away in shades of white, pink, red and purple. And would you believe they belong to the pea family? Well they do. And they'll grow from seed in any well-drained ordinary soil. No fancy compost is needed – but the clovers themselves make good green manure later. Sow *Trifolium* species in spring, and dig in the following mid-spring.

Triplochlamys multiflora. Shooting Stars

TRILLIUM
(tril-lee-∂m)
Wake Robin, Birth-root, Trinity Lily, Stinking Benjamin, Lamb's Quarters, Wood Lily, Squaw Root, Brown Beth
Trilliaceae

There can't be many other plants that have collected so many common names – but there are even fewer with all parts of the plant arranged in threes! Three leaves to a stem, 3 petals, 3 sepals, style divided into 3, and 6 stamens!

Trilliums are mostly native to North America, with a few in Japan or the Himalayas. They grow from seed, or divisions of the rhizome, and enjoy deep, leaf-rich, well-drained soil – preferably in the dappled shade of open woodland. Keep moist and semi-shaded at all times, and plant out when dormant. Unpleasant-smelling *T. erectum* has deep purplish petals; *T. grandiflorum* white fading to pink. Both reach 30cm/12in high.

TRIPLOCHLAMYS
(**trip**-loh-klam-is)
(syn Pavonia)
Shooting Stars
Malvaceae

There are only half a dozen species in this showy shrub genus, but what a splash they make in warm-climate gardens! Brazil is their homeland, so that really does mean subtropical conditions at least, with moisture available all year.

Shooting Stars like leaf-rich, well-drained soil, and can be grown from seed or cuttings where the temperature and humidity are high. Growth is fast, and the leaves are simply spear-shaped and slightly toothed. In *T. multiflora* the flowers appear in terminal corymbs, each bloom shaped like a comet, many-petalled and crimson in colour.

TRISTANIA
(tris-**tae**-nee-∂)
Dwarf Water Gum
Myrtaceae

Tristania always was only a small genus from the Australian region, but now it is even smaller, for recent revisions have created *Lophostemon* and *Tristaniopsis* from within its ranks. Still, we are left with the Dwarf Water Gum, *T. neriifolia*, and a handsome shrub it is too!

An upright sort of plant, it produces erect branches from a short trunk and may reach 3m/10ft in time, with a spread of about half that. The flowers appear in clusters at every branch tip during the summer; each one is relatively small, but enough are produced for a very worthwhile display – especially in a partly shaded area of the garden. Grow in leaf-rich, well-watered and drained soil in part or full shade.

Tristania neriifolia. Dwarf Water Gum

Tristaniopsis laurina. Kanooka

Tristellateia australasiae. Spray of Gold

Tritonia crocata. Flame Freesia

TRISTANIOPSIS

(tris-tan-ee-**op**-sis)
Water Gum, Kanooka
MYRTACEAE

Until recently included in the genus
Tristania, this attractive medium-sized tree
(15m/50ft at most) now has a new handle –
Tristaniopsis laurina. It still retains the
common name of Water Gum, which it
shares with the previous entry, for both of
these related plants are found in constantly
moist soil along stream banks. They thrive in
full, dappled or part shade, though they will
adapt to full sun in well-watered gardens.

T. *laurina,* though evergreen, turns a
reddish colour where winters are frosty, and
is hardy to –7°C/19°F. Flowering occurs in
the warmer months, with clusters of tiny
yellow blooms forming at branch tips in a
pretty rather than spectacular display. A
small, decorative street tree.

TRISTELLATEIA

(tris-tel-l∂-**tee**-∂)
Spray of Gold, Galphimia Vine, Bagnit
MALPIGHIACEAE

Originally from Indonesia, Malagasy and
north Queensland, the climbing *Tristellateias*
are now found in gardens all over the warm-
climate world. The name *Tristellateia* is an
allusion to the star-shaped seeds that follow
every fertilised flower. The vines are evergreen, not too rampant in the subtropical
climate they need and love. Leaves are simple
and shiny, and the showy yellow blossoms
appear in panicles of 12 to 16.

Tristellateia australasiae is propagated
from seed or cuttings, and must be grown in
deep, rich soil, with strong support in easy
reach. The plant climbs by twining, or can be
tied to the support. Treat to plenty of water,
especially in the hot season, when blooms are
at their peak.

TRITELEIA

(trai-t∂-**lee**-∂)
(SYN Calliprora, Brodiaea, Seubertia)
**Ithuriel's Spear, Wild Hyacinth, Grass Nut,
Pretty Face, Triplet Lily**
AMARYLLIDACEAE

Triteleias have been fought over by botanists
for the greater part of this century, the entire
genus being split and recombined several
times under various names. At the moment
about 14 species seem to have settled down
as *Triteleia,* at least for the time being!

Illustrated T. *laxa* 'Königin Fabiola' is a
popular bedding variety for any climate
short of tropical. It is grown from seed or
offsets in a heavy soil where summers are
dry, and blooms in spring and summer. It is
native to Oregon.

Triteleia laxa 'Königin Fabiola'. Wild
Hyacinth

TRITONIA

(trai-**toh**-nee-∂)
Blazing Star, Flame Freesia, Montbretia
IRIDACEAE

Another triumph from the vast South
African flora, *Tritonias* are related to Freesias
and Ixias and, like them, produce a small
clump of iris-like leaves. Flowers, too, are
similar: a cluster of flared trumpets on thin,
wiry stems up to 45cm/18in tall, usually in
brilliant shades of orange, red or pink, with a
pure white variety becoming increasingly
popular. But best of all, *Tritonias* don't
bloom until late spring or even early summer
in cooler climates, and that's well after most
other spring bulbs and flowers have finished.

Illustrated T. *crocata* is the most dazzling
of the 50-odd species. Its corms are best
planted in autumn in moderately rich but
well-drained soil, exposed to full sun. (They
can be set out any time up to early summer,
but then may not flower until the following
spring.) *Tritonias* do not have the fragrance
of Freesias but last well when cut for the vase.

TROLLIUS

(**trol**-lee-∂s)
Globeflower
RANUNCULACEAE

Obviously related to the common Buttercups,
brilliant *Trollius* species share the same
needs – deep, moist soil and a preference for
waterside positions. They are propagated by
division in autumn or early spring, and may
be raised from seed sown under glass in cold
weather. But be warned, it is in no hurry to
germinate. Once it does, though, growth
proceeds quickly to the maximum height
of 70cm/27in.

Trollius europaeus. Globeflower

Tropaeolum majus 'Flore Pleno'. Double Nasturtium

Trollius chinensis. Chinese Globeflower

Tropaeolum speciosum. Flameflower

Tropaeolum majus. Nasturtium

Tropaeolum polyphyllum. Canary Bird Creeper

Set the plants out at 40cm/16in spacings, water and feed regularly and you can expect a long sequence of bloom, beginning in spring and continuing well into summer. Preferred varieties have double or semi-double yellow blooms, those of *T. ledebourii* flowering in orange shades. Foliage is deeply divided and most elegant and the plants are completely hardy.

TROPAEOLUM
(trop-ae-**ohl**-ǝm)
Nasturtium, Indian Cress, Bitter Indian, Canary Bird Creeper, Flameflower
TROPAEOLACEAE

Colourful Nasturtiums (*Tropaeolum majus*) make splendid cut flowers and are good to eat, too. But compact modern varieties are a far cry from those of old, where the foliage almost hid the flowers. They are now bushy, and great for baskets, window boxes, containers or dry, sunny spots. The 'Alaska' strain has white marbled leaves, 'Red Roulette' has brilliant semi-double blooms, 'Jewel Mixed' is a rainbow of colours, and 'Golden Gleam' is fragrant.

T. polyphyllum, the Canary Bird Creeper, is a less common yellow species with trumpet-shaped blooms all summer and decoratively lobed leaves. Herbaceous, it sends up new growth to 3m/10ft each spring and can be grown as an annual in very cold areas.

The deciduous Flameflower, *T. speciosum*, produces fresh new leaves each spring and great hanging clusters of scarlet flowers from late spring to early summer. It needs plenty of water and prefers dappled or part shade. Sow seeds of all types direct into well-drained but not over-rich soil.

Tulbaghia simmleri. Sweet Garlic

TULBAGHIA
(tool-**bah**-gee-ə)
**Pink Agapanthus, Sweet Garlic,
Society Garlic**
AMARYLLIDACEAE

Tulbaghias would make an ideal cut flower except for one thing – they smell distressingly like very strong garlic, especially when picked. Oddly, though, and as if to appease flower arrangers, one species, *T. simmleri* (syn *T. fragrans*), has a light, delicate scent, more reminiscent of a subtle perfume than a Russian meal.

Flowers are produced in spherical clusters atop 40cm/16in leafless stems. The first flush occurs in midwinter and another can be expected in late summer.

Dainty in habit and with flowers of a delightful lilac colour, *Tulbaghias* prefer rich soil, kept moist, and filtered sun. They look best in a mass and should be left undisturbed for years.

Tulipa 'Queen of Night'. Single Late Tulip

Tulipa 'Apeldoorn'. Darwin Hybrid Tulip

Tulipa 'Red Riding Hood'. Greigii Group Tulip

Tulipa 'Angélique'. Double Late Tulip

TULIPA
(tyoo-**lip**-ə)
Tulip, Turban Lily
LILIACEAE

Admired all over the world, Tulips can only be grown successfully where winters are suitably cold. Elsewhere, they can be raised in pots – though with some difficulty, and only for one season, since without a cold winter the bulbs will not flower again.

Today, Tulips come in a huge range of colours and there are striped and speckled varieties, fringed and feathered types, strains with one or many flowers to a stem. They are always best planted close together in clumps or beds of a single colour. They need full sun from late autumn to early spring and a well-drained soil, heavily limed. Plant the bulbs 15cm/6in deep and keep lightly moist. After bloom, allow foliage to die back fully before

lifting and storing the bulbs in a cool, airy, dark place.

Of those shown, the so-called Parrot Tulips have very big flowers with cut or fringed petals on long (but weak) stems. The Darwin Tulips such as 'Kleurenpracht' are the most common types, valued for long-stemmed, goblet-shaped flowers. Some hybrids, such as 'Burgundy Lace', have fringed petals. Cultivars and hybrids of *Tulipa greigii* produce big blooms in a dazzling array of colours and patterns. Leaves are usually streaked reddish-brown.

T. fosteriana was one of the parents of most modern Darwin hybrids, and the species is noted for its big, brilliantly coloured flowers, often with a satiny sheen. Some Tulips, such as *T. tarda*, produce small clusters of flowers on each stem. They are good rock garden plants, growing only 15cm/6in tall and flowering freely in late spring.

Tulipa 'Flaming Parrot'. Parrot Group Tulip

TURNERA
(**tur**-nur-ə)
Sage Rose, Marilopez, Yellow Alder, West India Holly
TURNERACEAE

The only one in cultivation of almost 100 *Turnera* species, *T. ulmifolia* grows naturally in Mexico, around the Caribbean and in parts of South America – but it is seen in warm-climate gardens all over the world. A much-branched, shrubby plant, it might easily be mistaken for a yellow Hibiscus when in bloom, but in fact belongs to quite a different family, named rather incestuously after itself.

Strictly for the frost-free climate, *T. ulmifolia* is propagated from seed or cuttings, and grown on in light, well-drained sandy soil. It

Turnera ulmifolia. Sage Rose

needs high humidity, but even then looks better with midday shade from the full sun. The simple leaves are toothed and rather pleated, like an Elm leaf, hence the plant's specific name, *ulmifolia*. Though popular in tropical gardens, the *Turnera* has been described as 'weedy and short-lived'.

Other *Turnera* species have been identified in Malagasy, Mauritius and South Africa, but they are only in local cultivation.

TUTCHERIA
(tut-**cheer**-ee-ə)
Tutcheria
THEACEAE

A small genus with eight species, the *Tutcherias* are found in many parts of Southeast Asia and were at one time classed as Camellias.

T. spectabilis is a small evergreen tree with shining, short-stemmed, alternate leaves of leathery texture. These have a distinctly V-shaped section and hang loosely from the branches. The flowers, which appear at terminal leaf-axils, are cream-coloured and marked radially in rich butterscotch yellow.

Tutcheria spectabilis. Tutcheria

They are 8cm/3in wide and open from a pair of woolly sepals in midsummer (right at Christmas in the southern hemisphere). The seed capsules are quite large, up to 8cm/3in in diameter.

Related *T. virgata* has been used in Camellia hybridisation; it is grown in deep, compost-rich acid soil.

TWEEDIA
(**twee**-dee-ə)
(SYN Oxypetalum)
Baby Blue
ASCLEPIADACEAE

An unusual, twining subshrub, *Tweedia caerulea* can be grown as an annual where winters are cooler than 10°C/50°F. Its chief charm is its 2.5cm/1in starry flowers, which open from pink buds to pale blue with a turquoise centre. Over the following days, the flowers change first to a blue-purple and finally to mauve-pink, with all colours being displayed at once when in full bloom.

Raise *Tweedia* from spring cuttings struck in moist sand and planted into rich, well-drained soil in full sun (or dappled shade where summers are hot). As an annual, it grows to around 1m/3ft (somewhat larger as a shrub) in warm, frost-free gardens.

Tweedia caerulea. Baby Blue

Tulipa 'Cantata'. Fosteriana Group Tulip

Ulex europaeus. Gorse, Furze

ULEX
(**yoo**-leks)
Gorse, Furze, Whin
FABACEAE

An attractive flowering shrub for city gardens in cold climates, Gorse quickly spreads into impenetrable, viciously spined thickets in warmer areas. It is a hated pest in farmers' fields of New Zealand and a proclaimed noxious weed in parts of Australia. But in northern Europe and the cooler parts of North America it is a compact shrub to 2m/6ft that makes a marvellous security hedge.

Small, bright yellow, fragrant flowers cover the plant in spring, except in warm climates, where bloom is virtually continuous. *Ulex europaeus* flowers best in poor soil, for in good conditions it bolts to leaf – or rather to spine, for true leaves are found only in young plants.

Uroskinnera spectabilis. Uroskinnera

Uncarina grandidieri. Catechou

UNCARINA
(un-kah-**ree**-nə)
Catechou, Uncarina
PEDALIACEAE

To paraphrase Oscar Wilde, 'Why is it that whenever some new plant appears, it is said to have been seen at some time or another in Madagascar?' Why indeed? That exotic island does seem to be home to a disproportionate number of remarkable plants – among them the showy *Uncarinas*.

These are soft-foliaged, red-stemmed evergreen shrubs from dry parts of the island, and seem to have no thirst at all. *U. grandidieri* is rare in its native land, but grown elsewhere for the gorgeous, golden-yellow flowers, all of 10cm/4in across. It likes light, well-drained soil. Propagate from seed, if you can get it!

UROSKINNERA
(yoo-roh-**skin**-nur-ə)
Uroskinnera
SCROPHULARIACEAE

Fairly scarce plants from the Central American tropics, *Uroskinneras* are some-times seen in heated glasshouse collections and sold by specialist seedsmen. There are two species only, one of which, *Uroskinnera spectabilis*, is grown for its remarkably showy flowers, in which the relationship can be seen to other favourite plants such as Digitalis, Mimulus and Rehmannia (all of which see).

It is generally raised from seed or cuttings, struck with heat under glass. A well-drained, light, sandy soil is ideal, but remember to

water often and keep up the humidity. Growth is slow, the plant reaching perhaps 40cm/16in over a full season. The leaves are crenate, and the rosy-mauve trumpet blooms appear in the terminal axils.

URSINIA
(ur-**sin**-ee-ə)
Dill-leaf, Little Sunshine
ASTERACEAE

Native to South Africa, annual *Ursinias* are related to Arctotis but have fine, almost cobwebby foliage. They are low-growing plants, ideal for bedding and easy to raise from seed, but seem to be disappearing from seedsmen's catalogues, possibly because they close their flowers on cloudy days.

U. anethoides (the Dill-leaf) produces masses of orange-yellow daisy flowers from late spring to autumn. They have a purplish central disc. Lower-growing *U. pulchra* (Little Sunshine) opens sheets of orange and yellow flowers, the individual blooms often marked with a purplish zone, for a shorter period.

Sow seeds indoors in late winter. Germination is swift, and young plants should be set out at 15cm/6in intervals in well-drained, rather poor soil. Once established, rain usually meets their water needs as they do not care for consistently moist soil.

Ursinia anethoides. Dill-leaf

UVULARIA
(yoo-vyoo-le ə r-ee-ə)
Bellwort, Merrybells, Cowbells
LILIACEAE

Related to the curious Toad Lilies (see Tricyrtis), the three species of *Uvularia* are slender, rhizomatous perennials from eastern North America. They are grown from division of the rootstock in cool temperate climates,

Uvularia grandiflora. Merrybells

Vanda Rothschildiana. Vanda Orchid

Vanda 'Luya Donna'. Vanda Orchid

and prefer a position in dappled shade, where you must provide light, well-drained soil that has a deal of organic material in it.

U. grandiflora is most spectacular, sending up flowering stems to 25cm/10in in spring. The stems are almost leafless at this time, but throw slender branchlets from which one or two pendulous golden blooms are suspended. Strictly for the enthusiastic grower of woodsy plants.

VALERIANA

(val-eer-ee-ah-nə)
Valerian, St George's Herb
VALERIANACEAE

Valeriana officinalis, a perennial from Europe, is a plant with a very long history of use in medicine – so potent were its 'virtues' held to be in the old days that it was given the name All-heal. Some of its uses, notably the sedative effect of its root extract, are supported by modern medicine. This effect was held in such respect that it inspired the proprietary name Valium for a synthetic drug with similar properties. Gardeners, though, have usually held Valerian's ornamental qualities in disdain. They shouldn't; as the picture (taken in Paris a few years ago) shows, it is actually very pretty in midsummer when the airy sprays of tiny flowers appear on their 1m/3ft stems, and the much-divided foliage is attractive too. Not a feature plant, perhaps; but a very effective foil to bolder flowers, both in the herbaceous border and in the vase. It is of the easiest culture in temperate climates.

VANDA

(van-də)
Vanda, Lei Orchid
ORCHIDACEAE

Vanda orchids have become almost a Hawaiian trademark, though they come from Southeast Asia. By nature epiphytic (tree-dwelling) and monopodial (they keep growing from a single stem that gets longer every year), they produce overlapping rows of strap-shaped leaves, and the flowers appear from the leaf axils. These are magnificent flat, open blooms, up to 15cm/6in

Valeriana officinalis. Common Valerian, All-heal

across, which generally include some shade of purple in their colouring.

Anywhere temperatures remain above 12ºC/53ºF, *Vandas* thrive outdoors. They will tolerate night temperatures as low as 5ºC/41ºF, but flowering will be nowhere near as good. If not grown directly on open trees, *Vandas* are usually raised in heavy pots of coarse, leaf-rich compost. They need full sun, plenty of water and high humidity. Mine flower satisfactorily in an open courtyard near a sun-facing wall. Most species bloom in winter.

Vanda 'Blue Moon'. Lei Orchid

Vandopsis cultivar. Vandopsis

VANDOPSIS

(van-**dop**-s∂s)
Vandopsis
ORCHIDACEAE

It is not your imagination if many botanical names seem to end with *-opsis*. Taxonomists have found this Greek root meaning 'resemblance' useful when they have nothing more interesting to say about a plant than that it 'looks like' another plant! In the case of the lovely Southeast Asian orchids *Vandopsis*, they look like Vandas, but there are certain differences in flower structure that rule them out of that genus.

Most *Vandopsis* species in fact have major similarities to Arachnis (which see), and their cultivation is identical. As cut flowers, they are a big export from Singapore, and are seen in florists worldwide.

VANILLA

(v∂-**nil**-l∂)
Vanilla Orchid
ORCHIDACEAE

The laugh was on me, the day I was asked to a wedding in Tahiti, and got all dressed up … for it was merely the day local children set out to 'marry the Vanilla'. No longer a major export from the islands, its culture remains a useful cottage industry. The fragrant spice is obtained by grinding prepared seed pods of the *Vanilla* orchid – and as a preparatory stage it is necessary to pollinate with a fine brush – hence, 'marrying the Vanilla'.

Vanilla planifolia. Vanilla Orchid

There are some 100 species of *Vanilla*, found in the tropics of both hemispheres. They are usually planted at the base of a tree or climbing post to which they attach themselves with worm-like aerial roots. They have flat, leathery leaves, and need a night temperature of 18ºC/65ºF to flower well. The blooms are usually plain colours; and, in the case of *V. planifolia*, that colour is green!

VELTHEIMIA

(felt-**hai**-mee-∂)
Veldt Lily, Forest Lily
LILIACEAE

An attractive bulbous plant from South Africa, *Veltheimia viridifolia* produces towering spikes of green-tipped rosy bells from midwinter to early spring. Bulbs of the Veldt Lily are planted in late summer into well-drained, leaf-rich soil in full or dappled shade. They must be kept moist during the cooler months but can stand drier conditions in summer, although the occasional deep

Veltheimia bracteata. Veldt Lily

soaking in hot dry spells is greatly appreciated. They will tolerate temperatures a few degrees below freezing, but only if planted with overhead shelter so frost is prevented from settling on them.

In very cold climates, Veldt Lilies can be grown in pots brought into a warm, bright room or greenhouse during the winter. Increase from offsets, or from seed sown in autumn or winter in pots of gritty soil, kept just moist.

VERBASCUM

(vur-**bas**-k∂m)
Mullein, Lambs' Tails, Velvet Plant
SCROPHULARIACEAE

Tall, stately perennials or low, spreading groundcovers, *Verbascums* bloom in any temperate climate in shades of yellow, orange, biscuit, mauve and pink, often with contrasting centres.

The plants can be very short-lived, and die off after blooming in their second year. The only way to be sure of a perennial display is to take root cuttings or sow new plants each year until they have begun to self-seed readily. Indoor sowing should take place in a temperature range of 24–30ºC/75–86ºF, when germination will be apparent within 3 weeks.

Tall border species prefer full sun and grow in any ordinary soil that is reasonably drained, and produce branched spikes of open 2.5cm/1in blooms. They are planted out in cold weather and need staking where they are exposed to wind.

Verbascum hybrid. Mullein

Verbena rigida. Vervain

Verbena hybrida 'Gael Red'. Rose Vervain

Dwarf alpine species such as illustrated *V. dumulosum* also need well-drained soil, but are planted in spring. Dead-heading of all types ensures continuous bloom through-out the summer and autumn.

VERBENA

(vur-**bee**-nə)

Rose Vervain, Purple-top, Vervain, Verbena

VERBENACEAE

What would we do for flowers without the Americas? Compiling this book, I couldn't help noticing how many of the flowers we take for granted grow wild on those great continents. Now here's yet another group, the *Verbenas* – almost 200 species, found from Canada to Chile. Mostly they are perennial, but a few of the more decorative types are often raised as annuals, because they are not particularly showy out of bloom.

The Purple-top (*V. bonariensis*) is from South America, but has become naturalised as a roadside flower all over the world. It is a rough-textured, weedy sort of plant that lights up in summer with heads of lilac-purple flowers which are useful for picking, and last well in the vase.

The paler-coloured Vervain (*V. rigida*), with fern-like foliage, is from Argentina and has naturalised all over the southern United States, in both its mauve and white varieties. Like the Purple-top, it flowers easily the first year from seed.

But the commonly grown strain is *V. hybrida*, sometimes called Rose Vervain. A favourite bedding plant in all temperate areas, it is the result of crossing scarlet-flowered *V. peruviana* with other wild species, and is available in a wide range of colours including white, pink, scarlet, ruby, mauve and purple – often with a contrasting white or fluorescent red eye. Like other *Verbenas*, it has a pleasant, spicy fragrance.

Seed of all types can be sown under glass in midwinter. Germination is chancy, and may take up to a month with a constant temperature of 18–21°C/65–70°F. Plants should be pricked out to wider spacing when large enough to handle, and hardened off outdoors before setting in their final position in mid-spring. If that sounds like a lot of bother, you can always buy seedlings. Either way, plant them 30cm/12in apart in full sun and a rich but light soil. Do not overfeed or over-water, for *Verbenas* are always best in warm, dry spots. Cut back right after bloom and, where growing seasons are long, a second flush can usually be had. Many hybrids are available and all produce good displays.

Verbena tenuisecta. Moss Verbena

Verbascum dumulosum. Dwarf Mullein

Vernonia anthelmintica. Ironweed

VERNONIA

(vur-**non**-ee-ə)

Ironweed

ASTERACEAE

Bet you can't think of *one* species of *Vernonia*, yet this seemingly obscure genus is one of the largest in all botany – some 600 species are found all over the Americas and in many parts of Africa. They include annuals, perennials, shrubs and even small trees, all with dainty daisy-type flowers in shades of blue, purple, red or white. The blooms resemble those of a Cornflower, with the stamens more noticeable than the ray petals themselves.

    Vernonias are often relegated to the status of weeds, but in the right subtropical climate many are most elegant. They like a rich, light soil, and are propagated from seed or division.

Veronica gentianoides. Gentian Speedwell

Veronica spicata cultivar. Spike Speedwell

VERONICA

(vur-**on**-ik-ə)

Speedwell, Brooklime

SCROPHULARIACEAE

A large genus of annuals and perennials from the temperate northern hemisphere, *Veronicas* are all hardy or nearly so. Low species are suitable for use in rockeries, dry walls or as groundcover, while the tall types are usually grown in flower borders. All species bear attractive blooms, often at the blue end of the spectrum and usually in a tall spike.

Veronica longifolia. Beach Speedwell

Dwarf alpine species such as *V. prostrata* spread rapidly to form dense mats of tufty foliage and are virtually evergreen provided the dead flower heads are trimmed back at summer's end. Flowers appear in upright spikes that rise to 20cm/8in – a little cylinder of usually pale blue blooms, but soft-pink in *V. p.* 'Rosea'.

    The taller, herbaceous species are planted at 30cm/12in spacings towards the back of the border and should be cut back hard in autumn and divided every 3 or 4 years. They like damp, well-drained soil, and the size of their flower spikes is in direct relation to the richness of the soil. *V. spicata* 'Nana' is a dwarf (15cm/6in) version of a normally 60cm/2ft plant, with long, soft spikes of purple-blue flowers.

    Veronicas of all types can be raised from seed, germinating in about 2 weeks at a temperature of 21ºC/70ºF. Alternatively, soft-tip cuttings can be rooted in pots of very sandy soil kept warm and humid. As well as the usual blue, flowers can be pink or white.

VERTICORDIA

(vur-ti-**kor**-dee-ə)

Featherflower, Morrison, Juniper Myrtle

MYRTACEAE

Not often seen outside their native Western Australia, *Verticordias* are a genus of 50-odd shrubs that should be at home in any place where the humidity is low and the soil is sandy and leaf-rich. Perfect drainage and full sun seem essential, and you might try growing them in raised beds. Still, at present, it must be confessed that they are shrubs for the connoisseur, and the skilled one at that! Though seed fertility is low, semi-hardwood cuttings can be struck in a warm place with misting.

Vestia foetida. Vestia

The *Verticordias'* profusion of spring bloom has made them popular in Australia's cut flower industry, so it is not surprising to find that the name *Verticordia* is from the Latin, and means 'to turn a heart'.

V. chrysantha grows erectly to around 60cm/2ft and bears brilliant yellow flowers. *V. grandis* may reach 1m/3ft in height, topping its branches with clusters of fiery red blossom. *V. plumosa* is a small, open shrub to 50cm/20in. Its pink flowers appear singly or in groups towards the ends of branches.

Verticordia grandis. Scarlet Featherflower

Verticordia chrysantha. Yellow Morrison

VESTIA
(**ves**-tee-ə)
Vestia
<small>SOLANACEAE</small>

There is only one species, *Vestia foetida* (syn. *V. lycioides*), a native of Chile but named in honour of an Austrian professor of botany, L.C. de Vest. It is an upright, evergreen shrub of rather rank growth but with neat leaves rather like those of a box, and I should think it would take to clipping almost as well as that much-used plant does. Handling it releases the rather unpleasant aroma of the foliage. The flowers appear in late spring and are pale greenish-yellow bells, not colourful but of a modest charm reminiscent of the Australian Correas. Warm temperate climates are indicated, though it survives light frosts; soil should be fertile and well drained, the position sunny.

VIBURNUM
(vai-**bur**-nəm)
Viburnum, Snowball Tree, Arrowwood, Guelder Rose, Hobblebush, Cranberry Bush, Laurustinus
<small>CAPRIFOLIACEAE</small>

Dare one class a single genus of shrubs as the most beautiful and varied of all? It could only be said of the *Viburnums* – 120 species and many more named varieties, short or tall, some with brilliant autumn foliage and colourful fruits that birds adore. Some, including *V. tinus, V. burkwoodii* (both shown), *V. carlcephalum* and *V. carlesii* have a honeysuckle-like fragrance.

Viburnum plicatum cultivar. Viburnum

Viburnum tinus. Laurustinus

Viburnums are almost equally divided between deciduous and evergreen, but the division can become blurred in some climates. Of the evergreens, *V. burkwoodii* usually reaches 2m/6ft and bears 9cm/3½ in wide globular clusters of flowers that open pinkish but soon fade to white. The Laurustinus, *V. tinus,* grows to 3m/10ft; its tiny pinkish spring flowers are clustered together in heads.

In most species, at least *some* autumn colouring can be expected, even if it is only in the fruits. But where autumns are frosty, gardeners can expect an extravagant display of scarlet and gold from the deciduous

Viburnum burkwoodii. Burkwood Viburnum

Viburnum macrocephalum. Chinese Snowball

species. First among these is the gorgeous Guelder Rose, *V. opulus.* Its spring display consists of flat heads of hydrangea-like white blossom, and in the preferred variety *V. o.* 'Sterile', these are formed into great 8cm/3in spheres that have suggested the common name Snowball Tree. It grows to around 5m/16ft. *V. plicatum* var. *tomentosum* may reach 3m/10ft, with a much wider spread. It has sterile, relatively large, open, single blooms, in white flushed pink, surrounding the tiny, insignificant, fertile flowers.

All species demand a moderately rich, well-drained soil and plenty of moisture

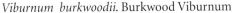

Vicia faba. Broad Bean

throughout spring and summer. They are mostly hardy; of those shown, *V. tinus* is the least so, being able to tolerate temperatures only as low as -18°C/0°F. *Viburnums* are not difficult to propagate, as all but a few sterile hybrids bear seed and these often germinate naturally. Otherwise, it is quite easy to strike cuttings of half-ripened shoots (most easily with gentle bottom heat) or to set layers. Spent flower heads should be removed regularly and an annual light pruning is wise if the plants are to be kept compact. Spider-mite and mildew are common pests.

VICIA

(**vis**-ee-ə)
Broad Bean, Horse Bean, Windsor Bean
FABACEAE

One of the most widely grown flowers in the world, this rather plain pea relative may not instantly be recognisable except to those who prefer home-raised vegetables. *Vicia faba* is simply the Broad Bean plant.

Vicia is grown from seed in any neutral soil, though the richer it is, the better the results. With regular moisture they'll shoot up 60–120cm/2–4ft. The leaves are typically pinnate, the pea-flowers mildly fragrant, and the beans or seeds borne in shining green pods to 20cm/8in long. After harvesting, cut the plants down and turn stalks and roots into the soil as green manure.

Vigna caracalla. Snail Creeper

VIGNA

(**vin**-yə)
(SYN Phaseolus)
Snail Creeper, Corkscrew Flower
FABACEAE

Among the most decorative of vines, the curious Snail Creeper is rarely seen away from country gardens, for the nectar-rich flowers do tend to bring ants.

Vigna caracalla is invariably grown from seed, sown direct in well-drained soil after scarifying. The plants grow best if given

Vinca major 'Variegata'. Periwinkle

Viola hederacea. Australian Native Violet

reasonable support, such as wire mesh or a trellis, and can reach 6m/20ft, though usually less. The leaves are trifoliate, the fragrant flowers lavender and yellowish-cream, twisted into a snail-like spiral. Cut the entire plant back to ground level if it has been damaged by a severe frost.

VINCA
(**vin**-k∂)
Periwinkle, Cutfinger
APOCYNACEAE

Vincas or Periwinkles are the universal groundcover in temperate climates – useful for shade, semi-shade, flat areas, steep embankments or almost anywhere else. They are easily increased by divisions planted out in deep soil. These then send out a mass of suckering shoots which take root wherever they rest on the ground, so that the spreading process starts all over again.

There are single and double flowered varieties in shades of purple, blue and white. The marbled-leaf type shown, *V. major* 'Variegata', is particularly effective. Keep *Vincas* moist at all times.

Viola odorata. Violet

VIOLA
(vee-**oh**-l∂, vai-**oh**-l∂)
Violet, Viola, Pansy, Johnny Jump-up, Heartsease, Ladies' Delight
VIOLACEAE

There seems a great difference of opinion among garden folk as to the position Violets prefer, but judging from my own experience, I'd say that the poet who placed them 'in a green and shaded bed' was on the right track, but probably meant 'a green and *partially* shaded bed' – at least in a temperate climate.

Violets spread rapidly, even invasively, from runners and self-sown seed. There, of course, I am speaking of the perennial spring-flowering *Viola odorata*, the Sweet Violet, in its many forms and colours, such as the magnificent 'Princess of Wales' and 'Coeur d'Alsace'. Both are extremely sweetly scented, bloom early and are ideal plants for rockery nooks or groundcover, loving moist, leaf-rich soil.

Other perennial species, such as the Australian Native Violets, *V. hederacea* and *V. sieberi*, bloom profusely where there is scarcely a ray of sunlight from one month to the next. The former is widely used as a groundcover by modern landscape designers and seems to bloom all year except, stubbornly, when other violets are in bloom. Unfortunately, neither species is perfumed.

Some of the most popular annual species, though, grow well in full sun and

Viola × *wittrockiana*. Pansy

ordinary garden soil, at least where summers are not too hot. These include *V. tricolor*, the European Wild Pansy or Johnny Jump-up. This has small, narrow pansy flowers of the type we know today, looking like hungry little faces. They are black-purple in the cultivar 'Bowles' Black', and appear over a very long season, from spring right through summer. A subspecies has yellow flowers.

Viola wittrockiana 'Space Crystals'. Pansy

V. × *wittrockiana* is the garden Pansy we commonly see. It was the result of hybridisation between *V. cornuta*, *V. tricolor* and others, and now we have the scent of one, the patterned petals of the other, with flattened blooms in an enormous range of colours and up to 13cm/5in in diameter. Those classed as Pansies are normally strongly patterned, while the Violas are usually in solid colours.

Viola tricolor. Wild Pansy, Johnny-jump-up

For late winter display, sow seed in late summer or autumn. For spring, sow in mid-winter. Germination takes 10–20 days. In mild climates, summer-planted Pansies and Violas will bloom in late winter, and will need replacement during spring. 'Space Crystals' is a popular Viola strain, and 'Iris Molly', a greenish-orange shade. 'Roggli Giants' and 'Superb Giants' are the best of the Pansy strains, with rich velvety colours.

Violets, on the other hand, can be propagated by severing young plantlets found at the ends of runners; by division of the clumps; or from seed, which will bloom the first year if sown early enough. They can also be sown in summer for bloom the following season. By their very name, Violets would be expected to have purple flowers, but there are many attractive species blooming in pink, white, biscuit, pale blue and yellow.

VIRGILIA

(vur-**jil**-ee-∂)
Virgilia, Keurboom

FABACEAE

Here is a charming small tree from South Africa guaranteed to grow faster than anything else in the warm-climate landscape. *Virgilia capensis* must be among the most important trees for a new garden, for it may grow 3m/10ft in a year. Though its useful life

Virgilia oroboides. Keurboom, Virgilia

may be only a decade, it helps fill in spaces until the main planting is established, and can be eye-catching in almost any season.

Virgilia grows to 10m/30ft and has small, grey-green compound leaves. From late spring onwards, these make a splendid contrast to the profuse display of mauve-pink blossom. This is made up of thousands of fingernail-sized pea-flowers, many of which are followed by brown pods.

Virgilia prefers light, open soil but it is inclined to be shallow-rooted and can do with staking in exposed positions, at least until it is well established. Keep up the water during summer and the flower display may continue into autumn.

Vitex agnus-castus. Chaste Tree

Vriesea carinata. Painted Feather

VITEX
(**vai**-teks, **vee**-teks)
Chaste Tree
VERBENACEAE

The best-known species is *Vitex agnus-castus*, a tall deciduous shrub from the Mediterranean region, where it grows on moist creek banks, often in the company of Oleanders. It would look very fine with them in the garden also. It matches them in size, and its long sprays of purple-blue flowers would make a most effective contrast to the Oleanders' round pink or red ones. It flowers in late summer, and can be pruned quite hard in winter to keep it more compact – its natural habit is somewhat rangy. The leaves are aromatic and were believed by medieval doctors to have the ability to quench erotic desire when eaten, hence the name Chaste Tree. Warm temperate climates are preferred, though it will survive quite heavy frost in winter, and a sunny position is best.

VRIESEA
(**vree**-see-∂)
Vriesea. Flaming Sword
BROMELIACEAE

Popular house plants since the middle of last century, *Vrieseas* are native to the forests and jungles of Central and South America. They are predominantly epiphytes, revelling in bright, dappled shade and humid but not close conditions. Some species, however, such as illustrated *V. splendens*, grow close to

or on the ground, thriving in the constantly moist, warm, deep shade.

Vrieseas require the same culture as other Bromeliads, but are perhaps a little tougher and more able to cope with the generally hostile conditions plants find indoors. Where the climate is frost-free, they can be grown outdoors as well, affixed to trees, walls or fences. Where that isn't possible, grow them in pots of leafy, open compost mixed with chunks of treefern or bark and a little sand. Water regularly and keep the leaf rosettes filled always. They can flower at any time of the year, according to species. Shown *V. carinata* flowers in winter, while *V. splendens* and its 'Belgian Hybrid' bloom in summer.

Vriesea 'Belgian Hybrid'. Vriesea

Vriesea splendens 'Meyer's Favourite'. Flaming Sword

Wahlenbergia gloriosa. Royal Bluebell

WAHLENBERGIA

(wah-len-**bur**-gee-∂)
Royal Bluebell, Austral Bluebell
CAMPANULACEAE

As recently as 1982, the lovely *Wahlenbergia gloriosa* or Royal Bluebell was proclaimed the floral emblem of the Australian Capital Territory – thus joining a number of outstanding flowers as state symbols.

It is only one of perhaps 150 species of these colourful Campanula relatives, found mostly in Australia, South Africa and New Zealand. They are distinguished from true Campanulas by a different structure of the seed capsule. The Australian species grow fast from seed, and are choice plants for rockeries.

W. gloriosa prefers a cool, mountain climate, and produces its dark blue blooms on wiry stems all summer.

WARSZEWICZIA

(vor-se-**vitch**-∂)
Wild Poinsettia, Chaconia
RUBIACEAE

I really do hope this gorgeously blooming plant is not a tree, though it was so described in a book I read recently. I've been recommending it to tropically situated friends for years, but I have never seen it more than scrambling shrub size. It produces shining,

Watsonia borbonica. Bugle Lily, Watsonia

evergreen leaves and arching terminal flower clusters. In our picture, the orange rosettes are groups of flowers, while the scarlet 'leaves' are enlarged calyx lobes, and appear one to a flower.

Apart from its craving for tropical heat, it has two other disadvantages for the average garden. One, it is supposed to need 150cm/60in of rain a year (which is nonsense); and two, it is not frost hardy. Seed germinates, uncovered and under glass, in 10 days.

WATSONIA

(wot-**soh**-nee-∂)
Watsonia, Suurknol, Bugle Lily
IRIDACEAE

Originally unique to South Africa and certain offshore islands, 70-odd *Watsonia* species are now naturalised in New Zealand, Australia and, I suspect, in many other lands. If one

Warszewiczia coccinea. Wild Poinsettia

were so inclined, one could start a cut-flower business with the acres of free-for-all blooms in bushland surrounding Sydney, especially in the vicinity of creeks and streams.

Spring and summer blooming cormous plants, they greatly resemble the closely related Gladiolus, but multiply from seed at an alarming rate. *Watsonias* like full sun, or part shade in hot districts, and are planted at different times of the year according to species.

Tubular-flowered *W. aletroides* resembles an Aloe (which see) more than it does the other *Watsonias*, blooms in early spring, and reaches 60cm/2ft or more in height. White *W. borbonica* subsp. *ardernei* reaches 1m/3ft or more, and is often sold in a mixture with mauve *W. rosea* and salmon *W. beatricis*. Many other colour varieties exist. All enjoy a loamy soil, and bloom in 3 years from seed.

Watsonia aletroides. Orange Bugle Lily

Watsonia borbonica subsp. *ardernei*. White Bugle Lily

Weigela 'Bristol Ruby'. Red Weigela

Weigela 'Eva Rathke'. Weigela

WEDELIA

(wed-**el**-ee-ə, ved-**el**-ee-ə)
Trailing Daisy, Wedelia, Creeping Daisy
ASTERACEAE

Though native to southern Florida and part of Mexico, the rampageous *Wedelia* is only seen at its best in a truly tropical climate, where heat and humidity combine to help it produce great sheets of foliage starred with golden daisy flowers. Recent visitors to Hawaii may have admired its blanketing of the ghastly new carparks by the Royal Hawaiian Hotel.

In fact, it grows over quite a climatic range, though frost may cut it back temporarily. Grow from rooted cuttings in any soil, and cut back hard if it begins to grow too thickly. Best in full sun with plenty of water, particularly in sheltered seaside gardens.

WEIGELA

(**wai**-jel-ə)
(SYN Diervilla)
Fairy Trumpets, Weigela
CAPRIFOLIACEAE

Masses of red, white or pink trumpet flowers bring leggy *Weigelas* to life for one short burst in late spring, after which they are often cut right back to avoid untidiness. The coarse, deciduous foliage burns badly in summer sun, so *Weigelas* are best planted in part shade. The leaves fall early without a colour display, and the shrubs are bare for a long time in cold weather. In severe winter climates, they are often killed or badly set back, and may be of limited use.

But in spite of all the above bad news, the *good* news is that they make a gorgeous flower display (though without much fragrance), and the arching stems cut well for large arrangements. Grow *Weigelas* in rich, well-drained soil and keep up the water during their growth season. Propagate from winter cuttings of year-old hardwood. *W. florida* is the preferred species – its hybrids include 'Abel Carrière' (rose-pink); 'Bristol Ruby' (crimson); 'Candida' (white); 'Eva Rathke' (crimson), and 'Boskoop Glory' (rose-pink).

Wedelia trilobata. Creeping Daisy

Weigela florida. Fairy Trumpets

Weldenia candida. Mountain Spiderwort

Westringia grandifolia. Coast Rosemary

Wigandia caracasana. Stinging Shrub

WELDENIA

(wel-**den**-ee-∂)
Mountain Spiderwort
COMMELINACEAE

Though it is native to tropical Guatemala, the exquisite *Weldenia candida* is found at such high altitudes we can easily grow it in a cool alpine house.

Related to common spiderworts such as Tradescantia, it grows naturally in 30cm/12in deep sphagnum moss, and these conditions should be reproduced closely. Just insert a small piece of root cutting in a pot of damp sand and sphagnum mix and set the pot on a layer of gravel and ash. Keep moist until a rosette of leaves develops. This will be centred in spring with snowy-white three-petalled flowers. Bright sunlight is needed to keep them open.

WERCKLEA

(**wurk**-lee-∂)
Costa Rican Mallow
MALVACEAE

Found naturally in Central America, the several species of *Wercklea* are Hibiscus relatives the size of small trees. They adapt well to frost-free temperate gardens, but they turn deciduous in cold weather.

W. insignis forms a neat 8m/26ft rounded tree with plate-sized leaves to 40cm/16in in diameter. In a warm-winter climate it will produce 12.5cm/5in rosy-lilac blooms with a yellow eye.

The slightly smaller Costa Rican Mallow, *W. lutea*, bears toothed, heart-shaped leaves that are distinctly furry, and bright yellow flowers with reddish stems and calyces. Both grow easily from seed.

WESTRINGIA

(west-**rin**-jee-∂)
Coast Rosemary
LAMIACEAE

Though some species of *Westringia* have their uses in gardens of Australian native plants, their reputation has become tarnished for me at the hands of get-rich-quick builders. Lookalikes for the European Rosemary (see Rosmarinus), their problem is that they grow too quickly, too well. Set a planting of them around some newly built houses; in six months you have a garden (albeit a colourless one). But when the builder has moved on, suddenly the short-lived bushes die away and half-dead branches appear everywhere. The solution is to confine them to the well-drained coastal garden, then prune lightly and often to keep them dense and compact. *W. grandifolia* is the showiest species.

Wercklea lutea. Costa Rican Mallow

WIGANDIA

(wig-**an**-dee-∂)
Stinging Shrub
HYDROPHYLLACEAE

A very small genus from mountainous areas of South America, the handful of *Wigandia* species are used for pseudo-tropical plantings in temperate gardens because of their very large leaves. Grown from seed or cuttings at a temperature of 13°C/55°F, they can be treated as annuals at the back of the mixed border. But as they are actually shrubs, they can also be grown to their full height of 3m/10ft and pruned back again and again.

The hairy, doubly toothed leaves can be irritating to some people, so best scrub your hands after handling them. The violet flowers resemble giant Forget-me-nots.

WISTERIA

(wis-**tear**-ee-∂)
(SYN Wistaria)
Chinese Kidney Bean, Wisteria
FABACEAE

These wonderful twining climbers were named for an American, Professor Caspar Wistar, which makes the currently accepted spelling of their botanical name rather a

Wisteria floribunda 'Alba'. Japanese Wisteria

Wisteria floribunda 'Violacea Plena'. Double Wisteria

Wisteria brachybotrys 'Shiro Kapitan'. Silken Wisteria

puzzle. They are a small genus found naturally in the Far East and North America, but they make up for the lack of numbers with the sheer beauty of their display. All look similar – but if you're onto a good design, why change?

Most versatile plants, they can be trained as vines, fences, standard shrubs – even as pot plants. All species are completely deciduous, dropping their pinnate leaves early, and generally not developing new foliage until after flowering. This is a very sudden event,

beginning in my climate on the very first day of spring every year – I could set a clock by it! All species can be grown from seed, but this is very slow. The alternatives are cuttings or grafts. I have had best results from root-cuttings, which generally grow at a great rate in the loamy, acid soil *Wisterias* need. And don't let up on the water during the actual flowering period. Water and sun are the two great needs.

Chinese *W. sinensis* is the common type, with fragrant pale mauve pea-flowers in

25cm/10in panicles. Its branches may reach 30m/100ft in length. Japanese *W. floribunda* is a smaller-growing plant with many colour varieties, some with inflorescences up to 1.3m/4ft in length. These may be single or double. Also from China is *W. venusta*, the Silken Wisteria. This has short, white flower clusters, often completely double.
W. frutescens and *W. macrostachya* are North American species, blooming in lilac shades. Both are rarely seen elsewhere.

Wisteria floribunda 'Macrobotrys'. Japanese Wisteria

Wisteria sinensis. Chinese Wisteria

Wyethia elata. Mules' Ears

WYETHIA

(wai-**eth**-ee-ə)
Mules' Ears
ASTERACEAE

Not often grown away from their native western United States, species of the small genus *Wyethia* are worth seeking out for their showy 12.5cm/5in daisy flowers. *Wyethias* grow from a thick, frost-hardy rootstock, something like that of a Dandelion. This produces handsome, shiny leaves up to 60cm/2ft in length, which form a dense clump; in summer, stout, leafy stems appear, topped with one or more blooms, of which the first to flower is always the largest. *Wyethia elata* grows in moist, deep soil, and is propagated by division, or from slow-to-germinate seed. Foliage dies back in cold weather.

XANTHORRHOEA

(zan-thor-**ree**-ə)
Grass Tree, Blackboy
XANTHORRHOEACEAE

Perhaps the most widely noticed summer features in the bushland of Australia are the Grass Trees or Blackboys (*Xanthorrhoea species*). Completely endemic to the southern continent, they have now been grown in other countries as accent plants.

They need dry, sandy soil and are easy to grow from seed, but slow to develop – all of 5 years for a recognisable clump of grassy foliage, and 10 years before a flower spike may shoot up (to 5m/16ft in height). These

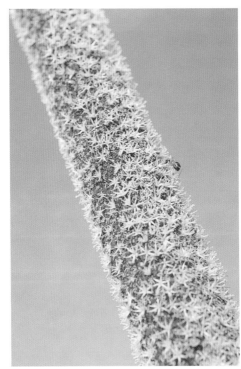

Xanthorrhoea australis. Grass Tree

look like black-tipped spears until they burst into masses of tiny, honey-scented cream flowers. The sometimes-branching trunks may take a lifetime to develop. Full sun is best, and of course, regular water speeds up development.

XANTHOSTEMON

(zan-**thos**-tə-mon)
Golden Penda
MYRTACEAE

The generic name means 'golden stamens', and indeed the long stamens are the distinctive feature of the flowers of *Xanthostemon chrysanthus*, an evergreen tree from the rainforests of Queensland. Somewhat rare in the wild and not common in gardens, it grows about 15m/50ft in height but much less in width, with an open framework of branches and largish glossy leaves, among which the

Xanthostemon chrysanthus. Golden Penda

Xeranthemum annuum. Immortelle

clusters of flowers appear in winter, decking the tree with splashes of gold for a few weeks. It likes a tropical or subtropical climate and deep, rich soil.

XERANTHEMUM

(zeer-**an**-thə-məm)
Immortelle, Paper Flower
ASTERACEAE

So closely do the papery blooms of *Xeranthemum annuum* resemble many Australian native daisies, I was surprised to find they are endemic to southern Europe and Asia Minor. A wonderful sight in any light soil with lime, they send up slender 60–90cm/2–3ft stems and make useful cut flowers. The blooms are typical daisy-form, with a crisp papery texture. Colours range through shades of pink, crimson, purple and white.

Xeranthemums must be sown where they are to grow, generally in the earliest frost-free days of spring. They'll germinate in 10–15 days and should be thinned to about 25cm/10in spacings. Hang flowers upside-down to dry for use in arrangements.

XERONEMA

(zee-**ron**-ə-mə)
Poor Knights Lily
LILIACEAE

Two species of the lovely *Xeronema* are known to horticulture. The first was discovered in New Caledonia in 1878 and named *X. moorei*, the second was discovered only in 1924, on Poor Knights Islands off New Zealand, and named *X. callistemon*.

Both are rhizomatous perennials with a strong resemblance to Iris when not in bloom. During early summer, plump buds

Xeronema callistemon. Poor Knights Lily

appear and burst into the most extraordinary inflorescence – a one-sided bottlebrush of almost petalless blooms. Both species grow from seed or division and should be raised in leaf-rich, sandy soil. They should be ideal in protected coastal gardens.

YUCCA
(**yuk**-kə)
Adam's Needle, Spanish Bayonet, Candle to the Lord, Spanish Dagger
AGAVACEAE

North American *Yuccas* adapt splendidly to garden conditions as eye-catching feature plants. They are in fact desert-dwellers, and valuable accents in low-maintenance gardens of many modern buildings.

Propagation is simply by means of detaching offsets from old stems. These root in pots of sandy loam over spring, and are soon ready to be set out in the open garden.

Yucca gloriosa. Spanish Dagger

Zantedeschia aethiopica. Lily of the Nile, Arum Lily

If mature plants are available, whole heads of foliage may be severed below the leaf-mass and will root in weeks in gravelly soil. The great panicles of bell-flowers appear any time in warm weather – but the razor-sharp leaves are best kept away from paths. Spanish Dagger, *Y. gloriosa*, is the common type.

ZANTEDESCHIA
(zan-tee-**desh**-ee-ə)
Arum Lily, Lily of the Nile, Calla, Calla Lily
ARACEAE

What's in a name? Fortunately, this family of bulbs can be remembered by their form and scent alone – for the name changes have been bewildering. First they were Arums, then Callas, then Richardias and now, would you believe, *Zantedeschia*?

The white Arum Lily, *Z. aethiopica*, is a bog lover, revels in water and mud, and flowers continually. Its hybrid 'Green Goddess' has striking, white-tipped green spathes. The Golden Calla, *Z. elliottiana*, has silver-spotted leaves, a yellow spathe and a spadix that develops into a spike of bright berries. Dwarf *Z. rehmannii* or Pink Calla and its multicoloured hybrids grow less than 30cm/1ft high. *Zantedeschias* are hardy to −12ºC/10ºF, but die down in winter.

Zantedeschia rehmannii. Pink Calla

Zauschneria californica subsp. *cana.* California Fuchsia

Zephyranthes candida. West Wind Flower

Zenobia pulverulenta. Zenobia

ZAUSCHNERIA

(zoush-**neer**-ee-ə)

California Fuchsia

ONAGRACEAE

I can never understand why *Zauschneria californica* is not more often seen in Australian gardens – coming from California (as its name suggests), it flourishes in our long dry summers and mild winters, and is a most distinctive and attractive plant. It is a bushy perennial or soft-wooded shrub, about 30cm/12in or so high but spreading much wider; closely spaced it makes a good groundcover. The grey or silver leaves are the perfect foil for the vivid scarlet of the flowers, which though not large, are borne in profusion for many weeks from summer till autumn. There are no fads about soil so long as drainage is perfect and the position sunny. If need be, the plant can be cut back quite hard in early spring to keep it bushy.

ZENOBIA

(zen-**oh**-bee-ə)

Zenobia

ERICACEAE

Zenobia was the beautiful warrior queen of Palmyra who for a while managed to hold off the all-conquering Romans, and I have no idea how her name was attached to a shrub from the southeastern part of the USA; nevertheless, *Zenobia pulverulenta* does her proud. It is an elegantly open-growing evergreen about 1.5m/5ft tall, attractive in foliage and enchanting in summer when the ends of the stems are crowded with little white bells scented of aniseed. Mild but cool temperate climates suit it best, and it must have an acid-free soil, preferably rich in humus. Though it can take quite severe pruning, trimming off the spent flowers is usually all it needs. In cold districts it will lose most of its foliage in winter.

ZEPHYRANTHES

(zef-ə-**ran**-thəs)

Storm Lily, Rain Lily, West Wind Flower, Autumn Crocus

AMARYLLIDACEAE

The last bulb genus in this book but by no means the least. Easy-to-grow flowers for late summer and early autumn, the Storm Lilies appear like magic after warm late-summer rains. In a mild climate, they can be made to bloom any time of the year by watering copiously after keeping them dryish for about three months. Useful in pots, rockeries or as border edgings, *Zephyranthes* can be planted any time – even moved for effect when in full flower.

Zephyranthes citrina. Yellow Rain Lily

Zephyranthes grandiflora. Pink Storm Lily

The white-flowered *Z. candida*, in particular, multiplies at an astounding rate from bulb offsets and seed. There are many coloured species and hybrids with, perhaps, pink-flowered *Z. rosea* being the easiest to obtain. *Z. citrinus*, the Golden Storm Lily, produces clear yellow flowers. All are hardy to cold but not frigid winters.

ZIERIA
(zee-**ear**-ee-∂)
Stinkwood, Sandfly Bush
RUTACEAE

Related to the daintier Boronias, all 20 species of *Zieria* are larger, woodier plants, native to eastern Australia. They grow easily from cuttings, and romp in shaded areas. The crystalline-textured leaves of *Z. veronicea* are highly aromatic. The 1cm/ ½in flowers vary from white to deep pink, with the darker shades being more highly valued. Any soil seems to suit, so long as drainage is above suspicion.

Z. veronicea is found naturally in Tasmania, Victoria and South Australia, yet it is rarely seen even in specialist nurseries of Australian plants. Growth rarely passes 50cm/20in in height, but a regular, light pruning after bloom will help keep the plant dense and compact.

Zingiber zerumbet. Wild Ginger

ZINGIBER
(zin-**jib**-∂)
Ginger
ZINGIBERACEAE

'Who gave thee that jolly red nose? Sinnamint and Ginger, Nutmeg and Cloves …' Poet Thomas Ravenscroft wrote that rollicking rhyme in an age when merchant adventurers made millions from shiploads of aromatic condiments needed to disguise the gamey flavour of pickled meat – ginger is prepared from the plump rhizomes of a whole family of gorgeous flowering plants.

The genus *Zingiber* provides the best quality root, with over 50 species found around the Indonesian area. All are strictly tropical and produce their flowers on separate stems from the leaves. *Z. zerumbet* unveils a dense spike of overlapping green bracts. As these ripen to rosy red, the white, star-shaped flowers appear from among them, fragrant and marked in orange-yellow. Deep moist soil is important – away from the tropics they must be grown in a heated glasshouse.

Zieria cytisoides. Sandfly Bush

Zinnia elegans 'Peter Pan Gold'. Zinnia

ZINNIA
(zin-ee-∂)
Zinnia, Youth and Age, Little Star
ASTERACEAE

The first *Zinnia* to attract Western eyes grew in the gardens of the last Aztec emperor Montezuma, though doubtless it was less spectacular than the dazzling hybrids of today.

There are several species in cultivation, the smallest being *Z. haageana* (syn *Z. angustifolia*) or Little Star. This grows to 20cm/8in and is used as an edging plant. Foliage is narrow, and the orange-yellow flowers are borne in great profusion. The popular and varied *Z. elegans* has been hybridised to produce a great number of showy strains with single, pompon-shaped or quilled blooms. The hybrid 'Envy' flowers in a range of greens from lime to emerald.

Zinnia elegans, Cactus-flowered Group. Hybrid Zinnia

Zinnia elegans. Youth and Age

Zinnia elegans, Thumbelina Series. Dwarf Zinnia

Zinnia haageana. Mexican Zinnia

'Thumbelina' is a dwarf with tiny blooms and may only reach 15cm/6in. Most spectacular (particularly for container work) are the 'Peter Pan' strains – giant 15cm/6in flowers on plants as low as 15cm/6in in height!

All Zinnias are best sown direct in early spring, as double strains sometimes revert to single when transplanted. Space 15–30cm/6–12in apart in enriched, well-drained soil in sun. Water around plants, not on them, and don't overdo it.

ZYGOPETALUM
(zai-goh-**pet**-ə-ləm)
Zygopetalum
ORCHIDACEAE

Inevitably the final plant in any flower book, *Zygopetalum* is always worth waiting for – a magnificently perfumed orchid that's easy to grow. They have crested green and brown blotched petals and an enlarged lip veined in mauve or rosy-pink over white. Both illustrated species flower in winter or spring and need plenty of light and humidity year-round. However, the plants should never be sprayed with water or the flowers will spot horribly.

Grow *Zygopetalums* in pots of coarse compost incorporating brick rubble, sphagnum and fir chips. Keep well watered in summer, just moist during the cooler months. Where summers are mild, *Zygopetalums* need a minimum of shading and can take full sun in winter. In hotter climates, deeper shade in summer will be necessary. Keep warmer than 5°C/41°F.

Zygopetalum mackaii. Zygopetalum

BOTANICAL RELATIVES

Many popular botanical families include a number of close relatives that do well in the same garden conditions. Immediately following is a list of the principal families, together with the names of all members of those families included in the book. Also, we show a small colour illustration of a typical member of each family.

ACANTHACEAE

The Acanthus family: mostly tropical herbs and shrubs with spikes of two-lipped flowers, often among colourful bracts. Leaves opposite.

Acanthus
Aphelandra
Asystasia
Barleria
Crossandra
Dicliptera
Eranthemum
Graptophyllum
Hypoëstes
Justicia
Mackaya   Porphyrocoma
Megaskepasma   Pseuderanthemum
Odontonema   Ruellia
Pachystachys   Strobilanthes
Peristrophe   Thunbergia

Aphelandra

AGAVACEAE

The Agave family: perennials, shrubs or small trees with fibrous, sword-like leaves in dense rosettes. Tall panicles of lily-like blooms, mostly white or yellow.

Agave
Beaucarnea
Beschorneria
Cordyline
Doryanthes
Polianthes
Sansevieria
Yucca

Yucca

AIZOACEAE

The Ice Plant family: showy perennials with flat or cylindrical succulent leaves and masses of brilliant daisy-like flowers. Formerly Mesembryanthemums.

Aptenia
Carpobrotus
Carruanthus
Cephalophyllum
Delosperma
Dorotheanthus
Drosanthemum
Faucaria
Frithia
Glottiphyllum   Carpobrotus
Lampranthus   Mesembryanthemum
Lithops   Pleiospilos

AMARANTHACEAE

The Amaranth family: annual and perennial herbs, mostly with brightly coloured foliage. Tiny flowers massed in spikes or panicles.

Amaranthus
Celosia
Gomphrena
Ptilotus

Amaranthus

AMARYLLIDACEAE

The Amaryllis family: mostly bulbous plants with strap-like leaves and lily-like flowers in umbels. Ovary *below* the flower except in the onion tribe (*Agapanthus, Allium, Ipheion*).

Agapanthus
Allium
Amaryllis
Brunsvigia
Calostemma
Chlidanthus
Clivia
Crinum
Cyrtanthus
Eucharis
Galanthus
Habranthus
Haemanthus
Hippeastrum   Nerine
Hymenocallis   Pancratium
Ipheion   Proiphys
Ixiolirion   Scadoxus
Leucojum   Sprekelia
Lycoris   Sternbergia
Narcissus   Zephyranthes

Chlidanthus

APOCYNACEAE

The Dogbane family: mostly tropical plants with milky sap. Leaves opposite. Flowers tubular, with 5 petals (lobes). Usually highly fragrant.

Acokanthera
Adenium
Allamanda
Amsonia
Beaumontia
Carissa
Catharanthus
Cerbera
Chonemorpha
Kopsia
Mandevilla   Strophanthus
Nerium   Tabernaemontana
Pachypodium   Thevetia
Plumeria   Trachelospermum
Stemmadenia   Vinca

Cerbera

ARACEAE

The Aroid family: largely tropical plants with fleshy stems and variable leaf shape. Tiny blooms in a densely flowered spike or spadix, enclosed in a brightly coloured spathe.

Alocasia
Amorphophallus
Anthurium
Arisaema
Arum
Dracunculus
Lysichiton
Monstera
Orontium
Philodendron   Zantedeschia
Spathicarpa
Spathiphyllum   Zantedeschia

ARALIACEAE

The Ginseng family: perennial herbs or shrubs from temperate or tropical regions. Leaves palmately divided. Small flowers massed in compound umbels.

Fatsia
Schefflera
Tetrapanax
Trevesia

Fatsia

ASCLEPIADACEAE

The Milkweed family: herbs, shrubs or vines, often without leaves. Mostly from the subtropics. Flowers single or in umbels, 5 petals, 5 stamens joined to form an intricate corona.

Araujia
Asclepias
Calotropis
Ceropegia
Dregea
Hoya
Orbea
Stapelia
Stephanotis
Tweedia

Stephanotis

ASTERACEAE

The Daisy family: over 20,000 species. Composite, densely clustered heads of tiny, tubular flowers, surrounded by petal-like ray florets to make a typical daisy shape. Mostly herbs and shrubs.

Achillea
Ageratum
Ammobium
Anacyclus
Anaphalis
Anthemis
Arctotheca   Chrysanthemum

Arctotis
Argyranthemum
Aster
Asteriscus
Bellis
Brachycome
Brachyglottis
Bracteantha
Calendula
Callistephus
Calomeria
Catananche
Celmisia
Cenia
Centaurea
Chamaemelum
Chrysanthemoides
Chrysanthemum
Chrysocephalum
Chrysocoma
Chrysogonum
Cirsium
Coreopsis
Cosmos
Craspedia
Cynara
Dahlia
Dimorphotheca
Doronicum
Dymondia
Echinacea
Echinops
Emilia
Erigeron
Eriocephalus
Eupatorium
Euryops
Felicia
Gaillardia
Gazania
Gerbera
Helenium

Helianthus
Helichrysum
Heliopsis
Heterospermum
Hieracium
Inula
Layia
Leontopodium
Leptinella
Leucanthemum
Liatris
Ligularia
Lonas
Montanoa
Olearia
Onopordum
Osteospermum
Othonna
Ozothamnus
Pericallis
Raoulia
Rhodanthe
Rudbeckia
Santolina
Sanvitalia
Schoenia
Senecio
Solidago
X Solidaster
Stokesia
Tagetes
Tanacetum
Telekia
Tithonia
Townsendia
Tragopogon
Ursinia
Vernonia
Wedelia
Xeranthemum
Zinnia

BIGNONIACEAE

The Bignonia family: showy tropical and subtropical climbers and trees. Flowers are often tumpet-shaped, 2-lipped with a 5-toothed calyx and 4 stamens.

Anemopaegma
Campsis
Catalpa
Clytostoma
Cybistax
Distictis
Eccremocarpus
Incarvillea
Jacaranda
Kigelia
Macfadyena
Pandorea
Paulownia
Podranea
Pyrostegia
Saritaea

Spathodea
Tabebuia
Tecoma
Tecomanthe
Tecomaria

Podranea

BORAGINACEAE

The Borage family: mostly temperate-growing herbs with rough-textured leaves, flowers arranged in a cyme. These have a 5-lobed corolla, 5-lobed calyx and 5 stamens. Most flowers are blue or purple.

Alkanna
Anchusa
Borago
Brunnera
Cordia
Cynoglossum
Echium
Heliotropium
Lindelofia
Lithodora
Myosotidium
Myosotis
Omphalodes
Onosma

Pulmonaria
Symphytum

Myosotidium

BRASSICACEAE

The Mustard family: all herbs, mostly pungent. The flowers (usually small) have 4 petals and 4 sepals arranged as a cross. Formerly Cruciferae, they include many tasty vegetables.

Aethionema
Alyssum
Arabis
Aubrieta
Aurinia
Brassica
Crambe
Draba
Erysimum
Hesperis
Iberis
Ionopsidium
Isatis
Lobularia
Lunaria

Malcolmia
Matthiola
Nasturtium

Aubrieta

BROMELIACEAE

The Pineapple family: tropical herbs, mostly epiphytic, bearing often spiny leaves in a dense rosette. The 3-petalled flowers often appear among showy, long-lasting bracts on a branching panicle.

Aechmea
Ananas
Billbergia
Cryptanthus
Dyckia
Guzmania
Hohenbergia
Neoregelia
Ochagavia
Pitcairnia
Portea
Puya
Streptocalyx
Tillandsia

Vriesia

Tillandsia

CACTACEAE

The Cactus family: mostly spiny, succulent herbs and shrubs, often branched and with ribbed stems. Usually without leaves. Bisexual flowers, often stalkless and brilliantly coloured.

Aporocactus
Astrophytum
Cereus
Chamaecereus
Cleistocactus
Echinocactus
Echinocereus
Echinopsis
Epiphyllum
Ferocactus
Gymnocalycium
Hatiora
Heliocereus
Hylocereus
Mammillaria
Nopalxochia
Opuntia
Pereskia

Rebutia
Rhipsalidopsis
Rhipsalis
Schlumbergera
Selenicereus

Rhipsalidopsis

CAESALPINIACEAE

A division of the bean family once named Leguminosae, including most species with irregularly shaped flowers (not pea-shaped) and with prominent clusters of 10 or fewer stamens.

Amherstia
Bauhinia
Brownea
Caesalpinia
Cassia
Cercis
Colvillea
Delonix
Lysiphyllum
Parkinsonia
Peltophorum
Saraca
Schotia
Senna

Cassia

CAMPANULACEAE

The Bellflower family: mostly perennial herbs of temperate regions, often with milky sap. Leaves simple and alternate. Flowers bell-shaped, mostly blue, borne singly or in panicles.

Adenophora
Apetahia
Campanula
Codonopsis
Edraianthus
Jasione
Monopsis
Phyteuma
Platycodon
Symphyandra
Wahlenbergia

Campanula

CAPRIFOLIACEAE

The Honeysuckle family: shrubs or climbers, mostly from the temperate northern hemisphere. Flowers tubular, often fragrant, borne in flat-topped cymes or clusters, bisexual.

Abelia
Dipelta
Kolkwitzia
Leycesteria
Lonicera
Sambucus
Viburnum
Weigela

Weigela

CARYOPHYLLACEAE

The Pink family: herbs with stems swollen at nodes. Flowers borne singly or in terminal cymes. Petals 4–5, often fringed. Often fragrant.

Agrostemma
Arenaria
Cerastium
Dianthus
Gypsophila
Lychnis
Petrorhagia
Sagina
Saponaria
Silene
Stellaria

Agrostemma

COMMELINACEAE

The Spiderwort family or Wandering Jews: warm-climate succulent plants with jointed stems, alternate leaves with sheathing bases, delicate 3-petalled flowers.

Cochliostema
Dichorisandra
Tradescantia
Weldenia

Tradescantia

CONVOLVULACEAE

The Morning Glories: twining plants, mostly of the subtropics. Leaves alternate, flowers funnelform, brightly coloured with petals unfurling like an umbrella, opening at dawn in some members.

Argyreia
Convolvulus
Ipomoea
Merremia

Convolvulus

CRASSULACEAE

The Stonecrop family: a large group of mostly perennial succulent herbs from temperate climes. Small flowers in panicles of 4–30, usually brightly coloured.

Aeonium
Bryophyllum
Cotyledon
Crassula
Dudleya
Echeveria
Graptopetalum
Kalanchoë
Rhodiola
Sedum
Sempervivum

Crassula

DIPSACACEAE

The Teasel family: a small group of annual and perennial herbs. Leaves opposite or whorled. Inflorescence bisexual, with small flowers in a dense head surrounded by a cup-shaped involucre.

Cephalaria
Dipsacus
Knautia
Pterocephalus
Scabiosa

Scabiosa

ERICACEAE

The Heath family: possibly the most popular family of flowering shrubs, from the northern hemisphere. Leaves simple, alternate. Flowers bisexual, borne singly or in terminal inflorescence, 5–7 petalled, mostly urn-shaped to cup-shaped.

Agapetes
Andromeda
Arbutus
Arctostaphylos
Azalea
Calluna
Cavendishia
Daboecia
Enkianthus
Erica
Gaultheria
Kalmia
× Ledendron
Ledum
Leucothoë

Menziesia
Pieris
Rhododendron
Zenobia

Azalea

EUPHORBIACEAE

The Spurge family: a very large and variable group of shrubs and herbs, often with poisonous white sap, often cactus-like. Flowers insignificant but often subtended by colourful bracts.

Acalypha
Euphorbia
Jatropha
Pedilanthus
Ricinocarpos
Ricinus

Euphorbia

FABACEAE

The Pea or Pulse family: a vast group of plants of every type, featuring butterfly-shaped blooms with a large prominent petal or standard and the two lower petals united to form a keel. A pod follows in which the seeds are attached alternately to either side. Leaves often pinnate.

Anthyllis
Astragalus
Baptisia
Barklya
Bolusanthus
Brachysema
Butea
Calpurnia
Caragana
Castanospermum
Chorizema
Clianthus
Clitoria
Colutea
Coronilla
Crotalaria
Cytisus
Dipogon
Erythrina
Eutaxia
Galega
Genista
Gliricidia
Gompholobium
Hardenbergia
Hovea
Indigofera
Inocarpus
Kennedia
Laburnum
Lathyrus
Lotus
Lupinus
Medicago
Millettia

Mucuna
Notospartium
Ononis
Parochetus
Phaseolus
Podalyria
Psoralea
Retama
Robinia
Sophora
Spartium
Strongylodon
Sutherlandia
Swainsona
Templetonia
Thermopsis
Trifolium
Ulex
Vicia
Vigna
Virgilia
Wisteria

Brachysema

GESNERIACEAE

The Gesneriad family: a popular group of mostly tropical plants growing from rhizomes, tubers or stolons. Corolla with a 4–5 lobed tube. Grown as indoor plants.

Achimenes
Aeschynanthus
Boea
Chirita
Codonanthe

Columnea
Episcia
Gesneria
Haberlea
Kohleria

Mitraria
Nematanthus
Ramonda
Saintpaulia
Sinningia
Smithiantha
Streptocarpus

Saintpaulia

HAEMODORACEAE

The Bloodwort family: mostly native to the southern hemisphere, these plants of bulbous appearance have fibrous roots. Leaves linear, flowers often densely hairy and long-lasting, partially splitting to 6 lobes.

Anigozanthos
Conostylis
Macropidia

Conostylis

HAMAMELIDACEAE

The Witch-hazel family: mostly deciduous Asiatic shrubs and trees. Bisexual blooms with 4–5 strap-like sepals, petals 0–5. Fruit a woody 2-beaked capsule.

Fothergilla
Hamamelis
Loropetalum
Rhodoleia

Hamamelis

IRIDACEAE

The Iris family: rhizomatous or bulbous perennial herbs with sword-like leaves. Flowers with 6 perianth segments, usually enclosed in papery, spathe-like bracts.

Anomatheca	
Aristea	
Babiana	
Belamcanda	
Chasmanthe	
Crocosmia	
Crocus	
Dierama	
Dietes	
Freesia	
Gladiolus	
Hermodactylus	
Homeria	Romulea
Iris	Schizostylis
Ixia	Sisyrinchium
Libertia	Sparaxis
Moraea	Tigridia
Neomarica	Tritonia
Patersonia	Watsonia

Iris

LAMIACEAE

The Mint family: usually aromatic herbs and shrubs with square-sectioned stems, 4-ranked leaves. Flowers in cymes in the axils of leaves are 4–6 lobed, 2-lipped.

Ajuga
Dracocephalum
Glechoma
Lamium
Lavandula
Leonotis
Moluccella
Monarda
Monardella
Nepeta
Origanum
Orthosiphon

Phlomis

Phlomis	Scutellaria
Physostegia	Stachys
Plectranthus	Tetradenia
Prostanthera	Teucrium
Prunella	Thymus
Rosmarinus	Trichostema
Salvia	Westringia

LILIACEAE

The Lily family: decorative plants, often growing from bulbs, corms or rhizomes. Flowers bisexual, showy, often perfumed; corolla of 6 distinct segments; 6 stamens. Nowadays often split up into smaller, more homogeneous families.

Aloë
Anthericum
Arthropodium
Asphodeline
Asphodelus
Aspidistra
Astelia
Blandfordia
Bulbine

Convallaria

Bulbinella	Leucocoryne
Calochortus	Lilium
Camassia	Littonia
Cardiocrinum	Maianthemum
Chionodoxa	Muscari
Colchicum	Notholirion
Convallaria	Onixotis
Dianella	Ophiopogon
Endymion	Ornithogalum
Eremurus	Paradisea
Erythronium	Phormium
Eucomis	Polygonatum
Fritillaria	Ruscus
Galtonia	Sandersonia
Gloriosa	Scilla
Hemerocallis	Smilacina
Hosta	Tecophilaea
Hyacinthoides	Thysanotus
Hyacinthus	Tricyrtis
Kniphofia	Tulipa
Lachenalia	Uvularia
Lapageria	Veltheimia
Ledebouria	Xeronema

LOGANIACEAE

The Logania family: mostly warm-climate shrubs with simple, opposite leaves. Tubular flowers often in dense panicles or cymes. Several are poisonous.

Buddleja
Desfontainea
Fagraea
Gelsemium

Gelsemium

MAGNOLIACEAE

The Magnolia family: evergreen or deciduous trees or shrubs. Leaves alternate, simple. Flowers large and showy, 3 sepals, 6 or more petals, many stamens spirally arranged. Fruit like a pine cone.

Liriodendron
Magnolia
Michelia

Magnolia

MALVACEAE

The Mallow family: perennials and shrubs with usually palmate leaves. Flowers with regular 5-lobed calyx, 5 petals, stamens united into a single column.

Abelmoschus
Abutilon
Alcea
Althaea
Alyogyne
Anisodontea
Gossypium
Hibiscus
Hoheria
Lagunaria
Lavatera

Hibiscus

Malope	Sidalcea
Malva	Thespesia
Malvaviscus	Triplochlamys
Phymosia	Wercklea

MELASTOMATACEAE

The Melastoma family: mostly tropical herbs or shrubs. Leaves mostly opposite or hairy; flowers bisexual, regular, usually with 5 petals, 5 stamens.

Heterocentron
Medinilla
Melastoma
Oxyspora
Sonerila
Tibouchina

Tibouchina

MIMOSACEAE

The Mimosa family: one of the Legume families. Leaves frequently bipinnate, flowers in dense spikes or globular heads mostly petalless or apparently so, but with showy stamens.

Acacia
Albizia
Calliandra
Mimosa
Prosopis

Acacia

MYRTACEAE

The Myrtle family: largely from the tropics and Australia. The showy flowers often consist of massed stamens, as in Callistemon, the petals small. Fruit a woody capsule or a fleshy berry.

Actinodium
Agonis
Angophora
Astartea
Backhousia
Baeckea
Beaufortia
Callistemon
Calothamnus
Calytrix
Chamaelaucium
Choricarpia
Darwinia
Eucalyptus
Feijoa
Homoranthus
Hypocalymma
Kunzea
Leptospermum
Lophostemon
Melaleuca

Metrosideros
Micromyrtus
Myrtus
Syncarpia
Syzygium
Thryptomene
Tristania
Tristaniopsis
Verticordia
Xanthostemon

Syzygium

OLEACEAE

The Olive family: temperate to tropical trees, shrubs and climbers with simple, opposite leaves (pinnate only in Jasminum). Flowers regular, bisexual or unisexual. Calyx and corolla commonly 4-lobed.

Chionanthus
Forsythia
Jasminum
Ligustrum
Osmanthus
Syringa

Jasminum

ONAGRACEAE

The Evening Primrose family: annuals, perennials and shrubs of various habit. Flowers mostly with 4 sepals, 4 petals, 8 stamens, very showy. Most are from the Americas.

Clarkia
Epilobium
Fuchsia
Oenothera
Zauschneria

Fuchsia

ORCHIDACEAE

The Orchid family: the most numerous and variable family. Epiphytic and terrestrial. Often with thickened rhizomes or pseudo-bulbs. Showy flowers with 3 sepals, 3 petals, one petal modified into a prominent lip. Stamens and style united into a column.

Angraecum
Ansellia
Arachnis
Arpophyllum
Ascocentrum
Bifrenaria
Bletilla
Brassavola
Brassia
× *Brassocattleya*
× *Brassolaeliocattleya*
Calanthe
Cattleya
Chysis
Coelogyne
Cymbidium
Cypripedium
Dactylorhiza
Dendrobium
Disa
Doritis
Epidendrum
Erythrorchis
Euanthe
Gongora
Laelia
× *Laeliocattleya*
Ludisia
Lycaste
Masdevallia
Maxillaria
Miltoniopsis

Odontoglossum
Oncidium
Orchis
Paphiopedilum
Phaius
Phalaenopsis
Phragmipedium
Pleione
Pterostylis
Renanthera
Rossioglossum
Sarcochilus
Sobralia
× *Sophrolaeliocattleya*
Sophronitis
Spathoglottis
Stanhopea
Thunia
Vanda
Vandopsis
Vanilla
Zygopetalum

Cymbidium

PAPAVERACEAE

The Poppy family: herbs and shrubs distributed worldwide. Leaves often pinnately lobed. Flowers solitary and showy with 2–3 sepals falling early. Petals 4–12, deciduous; many stamens.

Argemone
Dendromecon
Eschscholzia
Glaucium
Hunnemannia
Hylomecon
Macleaya
Meconopsis
Papaver
Romneya

Papaver

PITTOSPORACEAE

The Pittosporum family: evergreen trees or shrubs with simple leaves; 5-petalled, fragrant flowers in panicles. Seeds sticky.

Bursaria
Hymenosporum
Pittosporum
Sollya

Pittosporum

PLUMBAGINACEAE

The Leadwort family: shrubs and herbs with alternate leaves. Small 5-petalled flowers with tubular calyces. Lime-loving.

Armeria
Ceratostigma
Limonium
Plumbago
Psylliostachys

Plumbago

POLEMONIACEAE

The Phlox family: annual or perennial herbs. Small, bisexual flowers in axillary or terminal cymose clusters.

Cantua
Cobaea
Gilia
Leptosiphon
Phlox
Polemonium

Phlox

POLYGONACEAE

The Knotweed family: shrubs, herbs and vines with jointed stems. Leaves simple, with papery basal sheath. Petalless flowers with 2–6 calyx lobes.

Antigonon
Eriogonum
Persicaria
Rheum
Rumex

Antigonon

PONTEDERIACEAE

The Pickerel-weed family: aquatic plants, mostly tropical, with succulent leaf stalks, showy but short-lived flower spikes.

Eichhornia
Pontederia

Eichornia

PRIMULACEAE

The Primrose family: annual or perennial herbs mostly from the northern hemisphere. Leaves mostly whorled. Flowers bisexual, corolla 5-lobed, often borne in whorls up tall stems.

Anagallis
Androsace
Cyclamen
Dodecatheon
Lysimachia
Primula
Soldanella

Primula

PROTEACEAE

The Protea family: found almost exclusively in the southern hemisphere. Trees and shrubs mostly from Australia and South Africa. Leaves alternate, often lobed. Flowers in clusters, or showy, bracted heads.

Alloxylon
Banksia
Buckinghamia
Conospermum
Dryandra
Embothrium
Grevillea
Hakea
Isopogon
Lambertia   *Persoonia*
Leucadendron   *Petrophile*
Leucospermum   *Protea*
Lomatia   *Serruria*
Macadamia   *Stenocarpus*
Orothamnus   *Telopea*

Banksia

RANUNCULACEAE

The Buttercup family: herbs from temperate and cold areas of all continents. Leaves alternate, divided. Flowers bisexual, 2 to many petals, often very shiny.

Aconitum
Adonis
Anemone
Aquilegia
Caltha
Clematis
Consolida
Delphinium

Anemone

Eranthis   *Pulsatilla*
Helleborus   *Ranunculus*
Hepatica   *Thalictrum*
Nigella   *Trollius*

RHAMNACEAE

The Buckthorn family: trees, shrubs or climbers, most from warmer parts of the world. Leaves alternate or opposite. Flowers small but often densely clustered, 5 sepals, petals missing or very small.

Ceanothus
Colletia
Phylica
Pomaderris

Phylica

ROSACEAE

The Rose family: trees, shrubs or herbs; leaves alternate, often compound. Flowers regular, 4–5 or more petals and sepals. Fruit is a berry, pome or drupe.

Acaena
Alchemilla
Amelanchier
Aruncus
Chaenomeles
Cotoneaster
Crataegus
Cydonia
Exochorda
Filipendula   *Photinia*
Fragaria   *Physocarpus*
Geum   *Potentilla*
Gillenia   *Prunus*
Kerria   *Pyrus*
Malus   *Rhaphiolepis*
Neillia   *Rosa*
Neviusia   *Rubus*
Osteomeles   *Spiraea*

Rosa

RUBIACEAE

The Madder family: chiefly tropical and subtropical herbs, shrubs, trees and vines. Leaves simple, opposite. Flowers in cymes; corolla usually 4–5 lobed, more rarely 6–9 lobed.

Alberta
Asperula
Bouvardia
Burchellia
Coffea
Crucianella
Gardenia
Hamelia
Ixora   *Psychotria*
Luculia   *Rondeletia*
Manettia   *Rothmannia*
Mussaenda   *Serissa*
Pentas   *Warszewiczia*
Posoqueria

Pentas

RUTACEAE

The Rue family: mainly evergreen shrubs and trees with alternate glossy leaves. Flowers mostly unisexual with 3–5 each of sepals and petals. Fruit a capsule or leathery-skinned berry, as in Citrus.

Adenandra
Boronia
Calodendrum
Choisya
Citrus
Coleonema
Correa
Crowea
Dictamnus
Eriostemon
Geleznowia
Murraya   *Ruta*
Phebalium   *Skimmia*
Poncirus   *Zieria*

Choisya

SAXIFRAGACEAE

The Saxifrage family: herbs or shrubs with alternate leaves. Blooms in many-flowered clusters or panicles, usually with 4–5 petals. Includes some useful fruits, such as currants.

Astilbe
Bergenia
Carpenteria
Deutzia
Francoa
Heuchera
Hydrangea
Philadelphus
Ribes
Rodgersia
Saxifraga
Tiarella

Philadelphus

SCROPHULARIACEAE

The Figwort family: mostly annual or perennial cool-climate plants with soft, puffy flowers that are typically irregular, often 2-lipped.

Angelonia
Antirrhinum
Asarina
Calceolaria
Collinsia
Cymbalaria
Diascia
Digitalis
Hebe
Isoplexis
Jovellana
Linaria
Maurandya
Mazus   *Rehmannia*
Mimulus   *Rhodochiton*
Nemesia   *Russelia*
Otacanthus   *Torenia*
Parahebe   *Uroskinnera*
Penstemon   *Verbascum*
Phygelius   *Veronica*

Calceolaria

SOLANACEAE

The Nightshade family: herbs, shrubs, trees and vines, mostly from South and Central America. Stems often prickly, leaves alternate. Flowers bisexual with 5-lobed calyx and 5-lobed corolla. Many species are poisonous.

Atropa
Browallia
Brugmansia
Brunfelsia
Cestrum
Iochroma
Nicotiana
Nierembergia
Petunia
Salpiglossis
Schizanthus
Solandra
Solanum
Streptosolen

Solanum

Vestia

THEACEAE

The Tea family: trees and large shrubs with simple, leathery leaves. Axillary bisexual flowers petalled in multiples of 5. Many stamens. The Camellia is typical.

Camellia
Gordonia
Stewartia
Tutcheria

Camellia

THYMELAEACEAE

The Daphne family: mostly small trees or shrubs with simple leaves and fragrant petalless flowers with 4–5 lobed calyx.

Dais
Daphne
Edgeworthia
Pimelea

Daphne

VERBENACEAE

The Verbena family: mostly tropical or subtropical herbs, shrubs and vines with opposite leaves. Flowers often small and irregular, in showy clusters.

Aloysia
Callicarpa
Caryopteris
Clerodendrum
Congea
Duranta
Faradaya
Gmelina
Holmskioldia
Lantana
Petrea

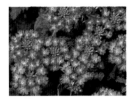
Verbena

Phyla
Verbena
Vitex

ZINGIBERACEAE

The Ginger family: generally tropical rhizomatous herbs, often with cane-like stems of alternate leaves. Showy flowers in spikes or panicles, often very fragrant.

Alpinia
Costus
Curcuma
Etlingera
Globba
Hedychium
Kaempferia
Roscoea
Tapeinochilos
Zingiber

Tapeinochilos

ACKNOWLEDGEMENTS

To the countless people who have so kindly assisted me in preparing the various editions of this book, I thank you. I hope you will forgive me for mentioning but one of your number, Brian Donges. An expert gardener with an astonishing knowledge of the plant kingdom, Brian has tended my garden for more years than I care to remember. Kind and thoughtful, I place great value on his enduring friendship.

In preparation for this book over a number of years, I visited many gardens. Most of the flowers were photographed at:

In the United States
The Brooklyn Botanic Garden and Wave Hill Botanic Garden, New York; The Descanso Gardens, the Huntington Gardens, La Brea Park, Los Angeles State and County Arboretum, the Pacific Coast Botanic Garden, Rancho Santa Ana, the Santa Barbara Botanic Garden, the UCLA Botanic Garden, all in southern California; The Strybing Arboretum, San Francisco; and the Sunset Gardens at Palo Alto.

In France
Bagatelle, the Jardin des Plantes and the Parc des Floralies, Paris; Giverny, L'Hay les Roses, Malmaison, La Source at Orleans, and Villandry.

In Australia
The Botanic Gardens and the Oasis, Brisbane; Mount Tamborine, Rockhampton and Toowoomba, Queensland; The National Botanic Garden, A.C.T.; The Royal Botanic Gardens, Melbourne; in the Dandenong Ranges and at Dromana, Victoria; The Adelaide Botanic Garden, South Australia; The Royal Botanic Gardens, Hobart, Tasmania; The Royal Botanic Gardens and Hyde Park, Sydney; The Stony Range Reserve, Dee Why; Hibiscus Park, Warriewood; Beauchamp Park, Chatswood; the E.G. Waterhouse National Camellia Gardens, Yowie Bay, The Botanic Gardens Annex at Mt Tomah; Lindfield Park and Nooroo, Mt Wilson; Milton Park and Retford Park, Bowral; Paradise Nurseries, Kulnura; also my own garden at Neutral Bay; all in New South Wales.

In the United Kingdom
Beth Chatto's garden, Essex; The Chelsea Flower Show; Exbury House Estate, Great Dixter and Sissinghurst Castle Gardens, Kent; Hidcote, Gloucestershire; the Liverpool International Garden Festival; the Lord Aberconway's garden at Bodnant, Wales; Queen Mary's Garden, Regent's Park, London; The Royal Botanic Garden, Kew; The R.H.S Garden, Wisley, Surrey; Spalding, Lincolnshire; the Saville Garden, Windsor.

In the Federal German Republic
The Berlin-Dahlem Botanic Garden, the Stadtlich Gartenschau Berlin '85 and the Munich Botanischer Sammlung.

In Ireland
Ilnacullin, Garinish, Co. Cork; the Irish National Botanic Garden, Glasnevin; Powerscourt, Co. Wicklow; St. Stephen's Green and Merrion Square, Dublin.

In Asia
The Hong Kong Botanic Garden and the Kadoorie Farm and Botanic Garden at Tai Po; the Shinjuku Go-en, and the Botanic Gardens of Kyoto, Nagoya and Tokyo; the Singapore Botanic Gardens; the Gardens at the University of the Philippines at Makiling.

In Italy
The Villa Taranto, Pallanza; the Orto Botanico at Padua.

In the Pacific
The Jardin Botanique de Tahiti; The Rainmaker Gardens in Pago Pago; the gardens of Rarotonga; Foster Gardens, Kapiolani Park and the University of Hawaii, Honolulu; the Wahiawa Botanic Garden and Waimea Falls Park, Oahu; The Pacific Tropical Botanic Garden, Kauai.

GLOSSARY

Botanists have adopted many specialised words and terms to describe precisely the different parts of a plant, and their appearance, colour, shape and texture.

It is difficult to compile any garden book without using at least a few of these words. As some are not much used in everyday English, and others have a specialised botanical meaning, we include this glossary for the plant lover who is not taxonomically minded.

Most unfamiliar words used in this book (or for that matter, in other garden books) will be found here, together with their meanings.

Achene a small, dry, one-seeded fruit with an undivided outer wall.

Acid said of soil that is deficient in lime – hence, **Acidity**.

Acuminate (of a leaf), tapering (with slightly concave sides) to a point.

Acute (of a leaf), tapering (with straight sides) to a point.

Adventitious occurring away from the usual place – e.g. aerial roots, a flower centred in a leaf.

Aerial root a root appearing above soil level, often from a branch. Used for both support and feeding.

Alate (of a stem or seed), with wing-like projections.

Alkaline said of soil that is rich in lime – hence, **Alkalinity**.

Alternate (of leaves), arranged singly on different sides of the stem, and at different levels.

Angiosperm a plant that has its seeds enclosed in an ovary – as in any flowering plant.

Annual a plant which completes its entire life cycle within a single year, from germination to seeding.

Anther the pollen-bearing tip of a stamen.

Apex (of a leaf or stem), the tip – hence, **Apical**, **Apiculate**.

Appendage an attached secondary part, as in a projecting or hanging bract.

Aquatic a plant which grows naturally in water, sometimes floating, sometimes rooted in mud.

Areole a raised or sunken spot on the stem in Cacti – site of one or more spines or flowers.

Aroid a member of the botanical family Araceae, named for its Arum Lily members.

Articulate (of a stem), jointed or with nodes where it can easily be separated.

Asymmetrical not evenly balanced.

Attenuate (of a stem or leaf), very gradually long-tapering.

Axil the upper angle that a leaf-stem makes with the stem from which it appears. Site of many shoots and flower buds – hence, **Axillary**.

Basal at the bottom – e.g. a basal shoot appears near the trunk base.

Berry a pulpy, generally small, fruit containing one or more seeds, but no true stones.

Bicolor a flower or leaf with two distinct colours borne at the same time.

Biennial a plant which completes its life cycle in a 2-year period – growing the first year, flowering the second.

Bigeneric said of a hybrid between two genera of plants, as opposed to more common hybrids between species or varieties.

Bipinnate (of a leaf), doubly pinnate, the primary leaflets being again divided into secondary leaflets, as in a Jacaranda.

Black spot a fungus disease, principally affecting roses, in which the leaves first become spotted black, later dropping altogether.

Bisexual having organs of both sexes functioning in the same flower.

Bloom (a) a flower; (b) a fine powdery coating on some plants or leaves.

Boss a roundish protuberance on some part of a plant – generally describing a compact mass of central stamens projecting above the plane of the petals.

Bract a modified leaf at the base of a flower, often the most colourful part, as in a Poinsettia or Mussaenda.

Break (in a flower), a spontaneous change in colour or pattern (e.g.,streaking), as the result of a beneficial virus.

Bromeliad a member of the botanical family Bromeliaceae, of which the pineapple is the best known.

Budding grafting by inserting a stem-bud of one plant into the cambium layer of another.

Budworm an imprecise description of the many small caterpillars which invade and destroy flower buds.

Bulb a fleshy growth-bud consisting of overlapping layers of leaf-bases, found underground or just at the surface, and serving as a storage organ – hence, **Bulbous**.

Bulbil a small bulb-like structure usually developing at leaf axils or other unusual places.

Cactus a generally spine-bearing plant, found almost exclusively in the Americas, often with magnificent blooms.

Calcifuge a lime-hating plant.

Calyx the outer covering of a flower bud, usually consisting of united sepals. Often decorative. Plural, **Calyces** or **Calyxes**.

Cambium layer a layer of growing cells beneath the bark or skin of a stem. These develop both inside and out, causing a stem or root to increase in size.

Campanulate (of a flower), shaped like a bell.

Cane (a) the developed, jointed stem of a large grassy plant, e.g. bamboo; (b) the long, arching growth of many plant genera, e.g. raspberries, roses, *Abelias*.

Capsule a dry, divisible fruit composed of two or more sections.

Carpel one of the units comprising a pistil or ovary.

Catkin a scaly-bracted, usually hanging inflorescence.

Chlorophyll the green colouring substance of leaves and plants, necessary for the production of carbohydrates by photosynthesis.

Chlorosis an abnormal yellowing of a plant, most commonly due to a mineral deficiency in the soil.

Cladode a flattened stem having the form and function of a leaf.

Clone any plant propagated by vegetative means, such as division, budding, cuttings, layers. These methods are widely used for plants that do not come true from seed.

Column the structure formed by the union of style and stamens, as in the Orchid family.

Companioning or **Companion planting** a horticultural theory (by no means universally accepted) which proposes that certain plant genera grow better in proximity to certain others, each genus conferring some benefit on the other. For instance, garlic is supposed to protect roses from their natural pests.

Compost a mixture of broken-down organic elements that will stimulate a plant's growth; sometimes, loosely, a potting mix.

Composite like a daisy. That is, a dense grouping of tiny single flowers surrounded by a single row of petals.

Compound (of leaves), a leaf composed of two or more leaflets.

Cone a dense construction of seed-bearing scales on a central axis, often woody and elongated.

Conifer a tree bearing its seed in the form of a cone.

Cordate (of a leaf), heart-shaped.

Corm a solid, swollen part of a stem, usually developing underground – the so-called 'bulb' of a Gladiolus is a good example. Hence, **Cormous**.

Corolla the inner circle or second whorl of petals in a flower.

Corona (in a flower), a crown or circle of appendages – e.g. the outer circle of stamens as in Hymenocallis; an outgrowth of the perianth as in Narcissus.

Corymb a more or less flat-topped inflorescence, the outer flowers opening first.

Cotyledon the first leaf to emerge from a germinated seed.

Creeper a trailing plant that roots at intervals.

Crenate (of a leaf), with shallow, rounded teeth, or scalloped edges.

Crown (a) the corona; (b) the base of a plant where stem and root meet; (c) part of a rhizome with a bud, suitable for propagation.

Cultivar a plant strain, apparently produced only in cultivation, and capable of propagation.

Cutting an amputated section of a plant or tree which will develop new roots and become self-sufficient. These may be taken from stems, branches, sometimes roots or leaves.

Cyme a type of broad, flat-topped inflorescence in which the centre flowers open first.

Dead-head to remove faded flower heads and prevent their seeding. This forces the plant to make new growth, and more blooms.

Deciduous a plant or flower that sheds all its leaves or petals at a particular stage of its growth – generally in autumn (fall).

Defoliate to strip or deprive a plant of its foliage or leaves.

Dehiscence the method of opening of a seed capsule, generally splitting along an existing seam. Hence, **Dehiscent**.

Dentate (of a leaf), toothed.

Dieback a variety of fungal diseases which kill part or all of a plant by causing the tissues to die back from a tip or cut branch.

Digitate (of a leaf), resembling a hand; compound, with all divisions arising from a single point.

Dioecious with unisexual flowers, male and female blossoms borne on separate plants.

Disbudding removing side flowerbuds to concentrate growth in a single flower and enlarge it.

Disc in the family Asteraceae the central area of the flower head, being composed mostly of florets.

Dissected (of a leaf), deeply cut into numerous segments.

Divide to separate a clump of perennial plants into smaller clumps; hence, **Division**.

Divided (of a leaf), separated nearly to the base or the midrib.

Dolomite the mineral calcium magnesium carbonate, $CaMg(CO_3)_2$, a form of lime much used to improve soil without greatly affecting its acidity.

Dormancy the time when a plant makes minimum growth, usually but not invariably in winter. Often when a plant is bare of foliage. Hence, **Dormant**.

Drift a loose term for an informal planting of bulbs.

Drupe a fruit containing 1 (rarely 2) woody-skinned seeds, e.g. a peach.

Dwarf small or low-growing strain of a plant.

Elliptical like a flattened circle with its widest part at the centre.

Endemic native to a particular, restricted area.

Entire (of a leaf), with a continuous, unbroken margin.

Epiphyte a plant growing on another tree or shrub, using roots for support only, and feeding from the chemicals in water and decaying plant or insect tissue, not from its host.

Espalier a shrub, tree or vine trained formally in two dimensions only – generally against a wall or trellis.

Evergreen having foliage that remains green and growing throughout the year.

Exotic in botany, a plant which is foreign to the country in which it grows, as opposed to native.

F1, F2 hybrid respectively, the first and second generation offspring from a given parent plant.

Fall one of the outer petals of Iris and related plants, often drooping.

Family a group of related botanical genera.

Fastigiate with branches or stems erect and more or less parallel.

Fertiliser any material used to enrich the soil and encourage plant growth – by understanding, generally a concentration of chemicals.

Filament a thread-like organ, especially a stamen supporting an anther.

Flat a shallow box of wood or plastic, used for raising seedlings; in common usage, a commercially raised box full of such seedlings.

Floret a very small flower, particularly one component of a composite cluster.

Flower bluntly, the specialised apparatus developed by a plant to enclose the sexual organs, and to attract insects and other pollinators needed for fertilisation.

Friable (of soil), easily crumbled or reduced to a fine texture.

Frost tender describes a fleshy plant which may be destroyed when the unprotected sap freezes.

Fruit the developed ovary of a seed plant, together with its contents, as in a tomato, nut or pod – but not necessarily edible.

Fungicide a chemical preparation for the destruction of any type of fungus.

Fungus a parasitic organism with no chlorophyll, and usually without leaves.

Gall any abnormal vegetable growth or excrescence on plants – a plant's natural reaction to injury caused by various insects, viruses etc.

Generic name a plant's first scientific name, indicating the genus to which it belongs.

Genus a clan or group of closely related species. Plural, **Genera**.

Germinate to begin to grow from a seed or spore. Sometimes, to sprout or put forth shoots.

Gesneriad a member of the botanical family **Gesneriaceae**, which includes African Violets and Gloxinias.

Glabrous smooth, without hairs of any kind.

Gland an organ or appendage which produces various functional secretions.

Glaucous (of foliage), covered with a waxy bloom which is easily rubbed off or marked.

Globose globe-shaped or nearly so.

Glochid a minute barbed spine, often occurring in tufts on Cacti.

Grafting when a bud or shoot is severed from its parent plant and joined to a rooted section of another. Used for rapid multiplication of woody plants.

Greenhouse a structure largely of glass or plastic, built for the protection and cultivation of delicate plants.

***Grex** in plant breeding, hybrid plants of the same (often complex) parentage; of these, the best may be registered and given a cultivar name. The term is used for orchids and rhododendrons. *Group in plant breeding, a set of cultivars with similar characteristics; exact parentage may be uncertain.*

Gymnosperm a plant bearing its seeds naked, not enclosed in an ovary.

Habit in plants, the manner of growth, or tendency constantly to grow in a particular way.

Half-hardy a plant which will resist a moderate degree of frost in a sheltered position.

Halophyte a plant tolerant of salt in the soil or atmosphere.

Hardwood cutting a cutting taken for propagation from a stem which is at least a year old.

Hardy tough or sturdy, but by botanical definition, fully frost resistant.

Heeled cutting a cutting of new wood, still attached to portion of the hardened, previous year's growth.

Herb (a) any non-woody plant; (b) a plant grown for flavouring, perfumery etc.

Herbaceous perennial a non-woody plant which dies back to the roots in winter, sending up new growth in spring.

Herbicide a chemical which will destroy growing plants or weeds.

Humus the rich debris resulting from the rotting of vegetable and other organic matter.

Hybrid the result of cross-fertilisation of different kinds of parent plants.

Incised (of a leaf), deeply and irregularly slashed.

Indigenous native to a particular country or area.

Inflorescence (a) the flowering part of a plant, irrespective of arrangement; (b) the arrangement of blooms in a flower head.

Insecticide a chemical mixture designed to destroy insects. There are both specific and general types.

Irradiate to treat or change by exposure to radiation; used to produce some hybrids.

Invasive said of a plant which grows quickly and spreads to occupy more than its allotted space, usually to the detriment of surrounding plants.

Involucre one or more whorls or close groups of small leaves beneath a flower or inflorescence.

Jointed (of a stem), with nodes, where separation is most likely to take place.

Juvenile (of leaves), the second pair to appear from seedlings, often quite different from leaves of the adult plant.

Keel (a) in a pea-type flower the joined, lowermost petals; (b) a central ridge on the top part of a flower.

Labellum the lip of an orchid, differing strongly from the other petals.

Labiate formed like a lip.

Laciniate (of a leaf), slashed into slender lobes.

Lanceolate (of a leaf), lance-shaped: long and gradually tapering.

Lateral on or at the side – e.g. a side-branch produced from a main stalk or trunk.

Latex a milky sap produced by many plants, such as the Euphorbias.

Lath house a shade house in which light levels are reduced by a canopy of wooden laths. Largely superseded by structures covered with shade cloth.

Layering propagation by pinning a partly cut branch down to the ground until it produces roots.

Leaflet one of the smaller units of a compound leaf.

Leaf axil the acute angle produced at the junction of a leaf with its stem.

Leaf-cutting a method of propagating many tropical plants from portions of their leaves.

Leaf-well the hollow produced by the spiral overlapping arrangement of leaves in (for instance) a Bromeliad.

Legume a plant which produces pea-type seeds attached alternately to both sides of a pod.

Lignotuber a subterranean bulb-like storage chamber of many eucalypts which enables them to regenerate after fire.

Limestone chips fragments of rock consisting principally of calcium carbonate – used as a mulch or dressing around lime-loving plants.

Linear (of a leaf), long and narrow, with sides almost parallel, as in a blade of grass.

Lithophyte a plant which grows on rocks in almost no soil, extracting nourishment principally from the atmosphere, as in many orchids.

Loam a friable topsoil containing sand, clay and silt particles, with the addition of organic matter. Hence, **Loamy**.

Lobe a major segment of an organ, representing a division halfway or less to the middle of that organ.

Marginal in popular botany, a plant grown in over-wet, even soggy conditions around the margins of a pool or watercourse.

Mealy see Glaucous.

Membrane a thin, pliable layer of vegetable tissue, often lining an organ or connecting parts.

Microclimate a purely local combination of climatic conditions.

Mildew several whitish fungi affecting plants exposed to over-humid conditions; downy mildew and powdery mildew are the most common. They distort and disfigure new growth and must be controlled by spraying with fungicide.

Mite any one of a number of small spider relatives that are parasitic on plants and animals. To gardeners, the two-spotted mite (aka red spider-mite) is the worst pest, sucking plant tissues to the point of desiccation and death. Controlled with a special miticide. They are not insects.

Miticide a chemical compound formulated to destroy mites, as opposed to insects.

Monoecious (of flowers), unisexual, both male and female flowers on the one plant.

Monopodial used of a plant in which the main stem continues to grow indefinitely without branching, as in orchid genera such as Vanda.

Monotypic said of a genus which has but a single species.

Moraine a special type of garden reproducing the fast-draining material left behind a glacier: a thick deposit of boulders, gravel and sand. Essential for growing many alpine plants.

Mulch a soil covering to conserve moisture or prevent root damage by heat and frost. May be of organic matter, pebbles, even plastic.

Mutant, mutation a variant, differing genetically and often visibly from its parent or parents and arising spontaneously.

Natural cross a hybrid which has occurred between two distinct but usually related plant species, without human help.

Naturalise the process by which plants are left in casual groups to spread and multiply year after year.

Nectar gland or **Nectary** a nectar-secreting gland, often appearing as a protuberance.

Needle a specialised elongated leaf, as in conifers.

Node the place on a stem where one or more leaves are attached.

Nodule a small, rounded mass or lump, especially on the roots of some plants.

Noxious harmful or injurious to health.

Nut a fruit containing a single seed in a hard shell.

Nutrient deficiency a deficiency of nourishment.

Oblanceolate (of leaves), the opposite of lanceolate – several times longer than broad, but with the widest point more than halfway from the stem.

Oblong (of a leaf), longer than wide, with the sides nearly parallel most of their length.

Obovate (of a leaf), ovate, but with the widest part more than halfway from the stem.

Obtuse blunt, rounded.

Offset a small outside division from a mature clump-forming plant.

Opposite (of leaves), two at each node, on opposite sides of the stem.

Organic composed of live or formerly living tissue.

Osmunda fibre stem fibre from the mature **Osmunda fern**, a component of composts used for orchid growing and seed raising.

Ostiole a minute opening or orifice, as in the fruit of Ficus species.

Oval egg-shaped, an ellipse wider at one end than the other.

Ovary the lower, seed-bearing part of a plant's female organ.

Ovate (of a leaf), oval, with the broadest end at the stem.

Palmate (of a leaf), roughly hand-shaped, with three or more lobes radiating fanwise from a common point.

Panicle a branching cluster of flowers.

Papilionaceous literally, like a butterfly; applied to a flower of the family Papilionaceae.

Peat moss organic material used particularly in composts. Very acid and water retentive.

Pedicel the stalk of an individual flower.

Peduncle the stalk of a flower cluster.

Pendent (of a leaf or stalk) drooping, hanging downwards.

Perennial a plant with a lifecycle spread over a variable number of years. Not necessarily permanent, however, in certain climates.

Pergola a structure formed of horizontal beams or trelliswork, supported on columns or posts, over which climbing plants are trained.

Perianth a collective term for the entire floral envelope consisting of calyx, corolla, petals and sepals.

Petal one decorative segment of a flower's corolla.

Petiole the stalk of a leaf.

Phallic shaped like a male organ.

pH balance the degree of acidity or alkalinity in soil.

pH scale a soil's balance of acidity or otherwise is divided into 14 parts, the number 7 being the centre point and indicating neutrality. Numbers below 7 indicate degrees of acidity; those above, alkalinity.

Phonetic pertaining to speech sounds and their pronunciation.

Phyllode an expanded, leaf-like stalk with no true blade, as in many Acacia species.

Picotee a flower variety in which the petals have an outer margin in a contrasting colour, usually red or white.

Pinch back, pinch out to prune soft leading shoots with the fingernails to encourage branching.

Pinnate (of leaves), like a feather; specifically with leaflets arranged on both sides of a stalk.

Pip (a) a small seed, especially of a fleshy fruit; (b) a rooted growth-bud of certain plants, as in Lily of the Valley.

Pistil the prominent female organ of a flower, generally surrounded by male stamens and projecting beyond them.

Planter a large pot, generally designed to hold an arrangement of growing plants.

Plicate (of a leaf), pleated.

Plume imprecisely, a feather-like inflorescence, as in many grasses.

Pod a dehiscent fruit, usually of the pea family.

Pollen the spores or grains borne by an anther, containing the fertilising male element.

Prick out to transplant seedlings from the boxes in which they were germinated to a large container.

Procumbent used of a plant which trails without rooting at intervals.

Propagate originally, to reproduce a plant by means of cuttings or divisions to ensure it came absolutely true to type. But today the word also refers to reproducing from seed or spores.

Prostrate a general term to indicate lying flat on the ground.

Protead characteristic of a bloom of the family Proteaceae.

Prune to cut, lop or sever excess or undesired twigs, foliage or roots from any plant, generally with the idea of directing growth, reducing size or improving fruit or flower yield.

Pseudobulb the thickened bulbous stem formed by some orchids for the storage of nutriment.

Pubescent covered with fine, downy hairs.

Pyramidal (of a plant), loosely pyramid or cone shaped, tapered from a wide base to a pointed apex.

Pyriform pear-shaped.

Raceme a stalk with flowers along its length, the individual blossoms with short stems – e.g. Delphiniums.

Radical arising from the root or its crown, said of basal leaves.

Ray or **Ray floret** a strap-shaped flower with a tubular base, forming one petal of the corolla of a flower in the daisy family, Asteraceae.

Reed (a) any tall, grass-like plant of the family Poaceae; (b) the stalk of any tall, grassy plant.

Reflexed bent abruptly downward or backward.

Reniform kidney shaped.

Reticulate (of a leaf), having net-like veins or nerves.

Rhizomatous possessing or developing rhizomes.

Rhizome a usually horizontal, swollen stem, on or below the ground surface, that sends up a succession of leaves or stems at intervals.

Rockery, Rock garden loosely, a mound of earth and rocks designed to reproduce the ideal grow-ing conditions for mountain or alpine plants.

Root cuttings a method of propagating Wisterias and other plants from small sections of root.

Root-run the total area beneath which a plant's roots spread.

Rootstock a rooted section of plant used as the base onto which a scion from another plant is grafted.

Rose sick said of soil in which the nutriment has been exhausted by the growing of roses. It must be replaced completely before roses are grown again in the same position.

Rosette an arrangement of leaves radiating from a crown or centre, usually close to the earth.

Runner a trailing stem which takes root at inter-vals.

Rust any of various plant diseases caused by fungus infections, in which leaves or stems become spotted with rust-coloured marks, or turn altogether rusty-brown. Treated with a fungicide and by removal of affected foliage etc.

Sagittate (of leaves), shaped like an arrowhead.

Sap the juice or circulating fluid of a vascular plant.

Saprophyte a parasitic plant, usually lacking chlorophyll, and living on dead, organic matter.

Scale (a) a small vestigial stem-leaf on certain plants; (b) the protective covering of many so-called scale insects which suck vital fluids out of plant tissue. They are variable in form and colour and treated in many different ways; (c) a segment of Lily bulb which may be detached for propagation.

Scape a leafless stem arising from the ground. It may bear one or many flowers.

Scarify to weaken the covering of some hard-cased seeds to hasten germination. Large seeds can be nicked with a knife, smaller seeds rubbed between coarse sandpapers.

Scion the bud or shoot which is grafted onto the stock of another plant.

Scorch variant of scarification. To hasten germination of hard-cased seed by the application of heat.

Scoria a coke-like cellular rock used in crushed form as the growth medium for certain plants, especially Cacti and Bougainvillea.

Scree in horticulture, a raised bed of gravelly growing medium reproducing the natural conditions preferred by many alpine plants.

Secondary next in importance after the main – e.g. a secondary branch or trunk.

Seed a ripened (and usually fertilised) ovule containing the embryonic plant.

Self-seeding the method by which many seed-scattering plants reproduce without human intervention.

Sepal the individual segment of a calyx, an outer petal.

Serrate (of a leaf), saw-toothed, with the teeth pointing away from the stem.

Sessile without a stalk.

Shade house a structure for growth or propagation of shade-loving plants in which the amount of light is reduced by a roof and/or walls of shade cloth.

Shear to prune, usually to produce a relatively smooth plane surface.

Sheath any more or less tubular structure surrounding an organ or part; sometimes the leaf which surrounds the stem of a palm.

Shoot immature combination of leaf and stem.

Shrub a woody plant, usually with multiple trunks, and remaining lower in height than a tree. Not a specific term.

Sideshoot see Lateral.

Simple (of a leaf), having a single blade; the opposite of compound.

Sinuate (of a leaf), wavy-edged.

Slip imprecise term for a stem-cutting.

Softwood unripened, immature tissue of any woody plant. Used for propagation in some species.

Spadix a fleshy spike of minute flowers, characteristic of the family Araceae.

Spathe the sheath or bract which encloses a spadix.

Spathulate (of a leaf), spatula-shaped.

Species the basic or minor unit in plant nomenclature.

Specific name a plant's second name.

Sphagnum the dried parts of a moisture-loving moss, used in pot culture. Very water-retentive.

Spike a series of stalkless flowers on a single stem.

Spine a stiff, sharp-pointed growth from a stem or leaf.

Spire a tall stalk or sprout of a plant.

Spore the reproductive cell of ferns and mosses, differing from a flower's seed.

Spray loosely, a single branching stem or twig with its leaves, fruit or flowers. May be growing or detached.

Stake a strong stick or post pointed at one end; driven into the ground, it is used to support a plant.

Stamen the pollen-bearing or male organ of a flower.

Standard one of the more or less erect petals of a flower.

Stellate star-like or star-shaped.

Stem the main leaf-bearing and flower-bearing axis of a plant.

Sterile (a) non-functional; (b) not bearing flowers or producing fruit.

Stock the parent plant onto which the scion or cutting is grafted.

Stolon a shoot that runs along the ground, taking root at intervals and giving rise to new plants.

Stomata the leaf-pores through which a plant breathes.

Stone a hard-shelled seed of certain fruit – e.g. a peach or plum.

Strain a loose term for a group of plants distinguished from others of the variety to which they belong by some intrinsic quality, such as a more colourful flower.

Strike cause a cutting to take root.

Sturdy tough, resilient, not necessarily hardy.

Style the part of the pistil between the ovary and stigma, often elongated.

Subshrub a very low shrub, usually treated as a perennial, or a woody-based perennial.

Subspecies a major subdivision of a species, ranking above a variety.

Subtend to stand close to and below, as a bract just below a flower.

Subtropical pertaining to a region intermediate between tropical and temperate.

Succulent (of a leaf or plant), juicy, fleshy and often thick.

Sucker an adventitious stem arising from the roots of a woody plant, often from the stock rather than the scion of a grafted plant.

Suffruticose very low and shrubby.

Symbiosis the living together of two plants or other organisms with some advantage to both.

Sympodial having growth of the stem or rhizome periodically terminated, with prolongation of the axis continued from a lateral branch – as with some orchidaceous genera such as Cattleya.

Syncarp a compound fruit, composed of the coalesced fruit of a number of flowers, as in a pineapple or Pandanus.

Systemic said of a poison or other chemical substance which destroys sucking pests by circulating through the sap system.

Tanbark the shredded bark of certain trees used for its acid content as a mulch or fertilizer.

Taproot a main root extending downward from the plant and giving off small lateral roots.

Taxonomy the science of plant classification, hence **Taxonomist**.

Temperate a mild climate, often coastal.

Tendril a twisting, thread-like extension by which a plant clings to a support. It may be part of a leaf or stem.

Terminal (of a shoot), at the tip or end. Hence, **Terminally**.

Ternate in 3s, or divided into 3s, hence a ternate leaf.

Terrestrial plants which grow on the ground, in contrast to tree-dwelling or epiphytic varieties – e.g. orchids, bromeliads.

Tetraploid having 4 rather than the usual 2 sets of chromosomes.

Thorn a sharp, woody, spine-like outgrowth from the wood of a stem.

Thrip a sap-sucking insect, colonies of which rapidly disfigure leaves and flowers. Best controlled with systemic insecticides.

Tip-cutting a cutting of new growth, used for the propagation of carnations and perennial Daisy plants particularly.

Tip-prune pruning of immature growth to force lateral shoots.

Tomentose woolly.

Trapeziform (of a leaf), asymmetrically 4-sided.

Treelet a small tree.

Trellis a frame or structure of latticework.

Trifoliate having 3 leaves.

Trifoliolate (of a leaf), having 3 leaflets to each leaf.

Trigeneric a hybrid crossed from 3 different species.

Tripinnate (of a leaf), bearing leaflets on the leaflets of its leaves.

Triploid having 3 rather than the usual 2 chromosome sets.

Truncate appearing as if cut straight across at the end, as with the leaf of a Liriodendron.

Truss a compound terminal cluster of flowers borne on one stalk.

Tube (a) a hollow organ; (b) the extension of a corolla between the opened petals and the calyx. Hence, **Tubular**.

Tuber a short, thick (but not always subterranean) stem or branch bearing buds or 'eyes' and serving as a storage organ. Hence, **Tuberous**.

Tubercle a small, warty excrescence on a leaf or other plant part.

Tuft (a) a bunch of short hairs, linked or joined at the base; (b) a cluster of short-stemmed flowers growing from a common point.

Tunicate (of a bulb), having concentric layers, as an onion.

Turgid swollen and distended with fluid.

Twig the current season's growth of a woody plant or shoot.

Twiner a plant which climbs by winding around itself or other plants.

Type the common species of a plant, as opposed to its variety or cultivar.

Umbel a group of flowers growing from a common point in a stem, hence, **Umbellate**.

Undulate (of a leaf), having a wavy surface.

Unilateral 1-sided.

Unisexual of 1 sex.

Urceolate (of a flower), urn or pitcher shaped.

Variegated a condition of any plant when the natural green of foliage or stems is broken by other colours.

Varietal name a plant's third scientific name.

Variety (officially Varietas) (a) the subdivision of a species; (b) a recognisably different member of a plant species capable of cultivation.

Vegetation the normal plant cover of any area.

Velutinous velvety.

Vermiculite a lightweight, inorganic substance, used to lighten potting composts and enhance soil moisture.

Verrucose warty.

Vine (a) any climbing plant bearing long trailing, climbing or twining stems; (b) any species of the genus Vitis.

Viscid sticky.

Volubile twining.

Whorl a circle of 3 or more flowers or branches appearing around a stem, branch or trunk at the same level.

Windbreak a specialised planting (generally of trees or shrubs) designed to protect smaller and more delicate plants from prevailing winds.

Wing a thin, dry or membranous extension of an organ.

Woodsy suggestive of or associated with the woods or forest.

Xerophyte a plant adapted to growing in dry regions.

Zygomorphic bilaterally symmetrical, capable of being divided into two equal halves in one plane only, as in many flowers.

INDEX

Page numbers in **bold** type indicate
photographs.

Page numbers in **bold** type indicate photographs.

Page numbers in **bold** type indicate photographs.

Page numbers in **bold** type indicate photographs.

Page numbers in **bold** type indicate photographs.

Page numbers in **bold** type indicate photographs.

Page numbers in **bold** type indicate
photographs.

Page numbers in **bold** type indicate
photographs.

Page numbers in **bold** type indicate photographs.

Page numbers in **bold** type indicate
photographs.

Page numbers in **bold** type indicate photographs.

Page numbers in **bold** type indicate
photographs.